# Lost Decade

# More Praise for Lost Decade

"Getting Asia right is the single most important issue for American foreign policy. This bracing book must be read by anyone who wants to understand or shape policy. Agree or disagree, this is a perspective that must be reckoned with."
—**Dr. Lawrence H. Summers**, former U.S. Treasury Secretary

"An important and well-researched explanation of the flawed assumptions that underpinned US policy for far too long."
—**General H.R. McMaster (ret.)**, former U.S. National Security Advisor

"Three administrations in a row, on a bipartisan basis, have now prioritized Asia in key strategic documents. Yet the day-to-day preferences of the US government have demonstrated that this shift exists on paper only, with few concrete resource or force allocation shifts to speak for over a decade of apparent effort. *Lost Decade* represents an important contribution to help policymakers understand why the long-promised pivot to Asia failed to materialize, and just as important, how America can meet the scale of the challenge in its priority theater."
—**Representative Mike Gallagher**, Congressman, Wisconsin; Chairman of the Select Committee on the Chinese Communist Party

"In *Lost Decade*, Robert Blackwill and Richard Fontaine examine America's decade-plus attempt to focus on Asia. Their account details a critical period in the history of US foreign policy, and it discerns lessons directly applicable to today's policy choices. In calling for a renewed pivot to Asia while maintaining key commitments elsewhere, the authors offer a grand strategic approach to the new world now upon us. All those interested in the great foreign policy issues of our day should read this book."
—**Governor Jon Huntsman**, former U.S. ambassador to China and Russia

"*Lost Decade* raises grand strategic questions about how the United States should deal with China that foreign policy thinkers and practitioners must address. Happily, it provides specific answers that are likely to attract bipartisan support, including a policy 'to-do list.' Even China watchers who disagree with the authors' assumptions and conclusions will find this a valuable read."
—**Dr. Anne-Marie Slaughter**, former Director of Policy Planning, U.S. Department of State

# Lost Decade

*The US Pivot to Asia and the
Rise of Chinese Power*

ROBERT D. BLACKWILL AND
RICHARD FONTAINE

OXFORD
UNIVERSITY PRESS

**A COUNCIL ON FOREIGN RELATIONS BOOK**

# OXFORD
## UNIVERSITY PRESS

Oxford University Press is a department of the University of Oxford. It furthers
the University's objective of excellence in research, scholarship, and education
by publishing worldwide. Oxford is a registered trade mark of Oxford University
Press in the UK and certain other countries.

Published in the United States of America by Oxford University Press
198 Madison Avenue, New York, NY 10016, United States of America.

Library of Congress Cataloging-in-Publication Data
Names: Blackwill, Robert D., author. | Fontaine, Richard, author.
Title: Lost decade : the US pivot to Asia and the rise of Chinese power /
by Robert D. Blackwill, and Richard Fontaine.
Other titles: US pivot to Asia and the rise of Chinese power
Description: New York, NY : Oxford University Press, 2024. |
Includes index.
Identifiers: LCCN 2024001058 (print) | LCCN 2024001059 (ebook) |
ISBN 9780197677940 (hardback) | ISBN 9780197677957 (epub)
Subjects: LCSH: United States—Foreign relations—Asia. |
United States—Foreign relations—21st century. | Asia—Foreign
relations—United States. | China—Foreign relations—21st century.
Classification: LCC DS33.4.U6 .B53 2024 (print) | LCC DS33.4.U6 (ebook) |
DDC 327.7305—dc23/eng/20240208
LC record available at https://lccn.loc.gov/2024001058
LC ebook record available at https://lccn.loc.gov/2024001059

DOI: 10.1093/oso/9780197677940.001.0001

Printed by Sheridan Books, Inc., United States of America

The Council on Foreign Relations (CFR) is an independent, nonpartisan membership organization, think tank, and publisher dedicated to being a resource for its members, government officials, business executives, journalists, educators and students, civic and religious leaders, and other interested citizens in order to help them better understand the world and the foreign policy choices facing the United States and other countries. Founded in 1921, CFR carries out its mission by maintaining a diverse membership, with special programs to promote interest and develop expertise in the next generation of foreign policy leaders; convening meetings at its headquarters in New York and in Washington, DC, and other cities where senior government officials, members of Congress, global leaders, and prominent thinkers come together with CFR members to discuss and debate major international issues; supporting a Studies Program that fosters independent research, enabling CFR scholars to produce articles, reports, and books and hold roundtables that analyze foreign policy issues and make concrete policy recommendations; publishing *Foreign Affairs*, the preeminent journal on international affairs and US foreign policy; sponsoring Independent Task Forces that produce reports with both findings and policy prescriptions on the most important foreign policy topics; and providing up-to-date information and analysis about world events and American foreign policy on its website, www.cfr.org.

The Council on Foreign Relations takes no institutional positions on policy issues and has no affiliation with the US government. All views expressed in its publications and on its website are the sole responsibility of the author or authors.

# Contents

# Acknowledgments

We are indebted to the many people who made this book possible. To begin, we thank former Council on Foreign Relations (CFR) president Richard N. Haass, as well as the current president, Michael Froman, and James M. Lindsay of CFR for their support of this project. We also thank the team at the Center for a New American Security (CNAS) for their support throughout this work.

We are indebted to members of the CFR 2021–2022 study group on the US Pivot to Asia and American Grand Strategy, whose shrewd insights enhanced the shape and substance of this volume.

As the book progressed, we benefited from expert comments on draft chapters by Jeffrey Bader, Ernest Bower, Victor Cha, Elizabeth Economy, Liana Fix, Ryan Hass, Mira Rapp-Hooper, Martin Indyk, Bilahari Kausikan, Charles Kupchan, Mark Lippert, Shivshankar Menon, Joseph Nye, Matthew Pottinger, Will Quinn, Dennis Ross, Danny Russel, Robert Work, Amos Yadlin, and Robert Zoellick, to whom we convey our gratitude. We are especially appreciative of two anonymous reviewers, as well as Michael Green, James M. Lindsay, and Shannon O'Neil, who incisively commented on the entire manuscript. The text was also enriched by interviews on background with current government and former officials engaged in the decision-making around, and the implementation of, the US Pivot to Asia. Our research associates, Benjamin Holtzman, Gibbs McKinley, Shai Cohen, Jemima Baar, John O'Malley, and Reed Kessler, made an indispensable contribution to the book. Emma Swislow and Maura McCarthy provided helpful editing advice and Melody Cook assisted with the book's charts and tables.

None of these contributors bears any responsibility for the final product, which remains ours alone.

We thank our editor, David McBride of Oxford University Press, and his team, as well as our agent, Andrew Wylie, for their support.

Finally, we thank our families for their support and patience, including Karen, Kate, Leah, Joseph, and Andrew Fontaine; and the Blackwill Clan.

# 1

# Introduction

For more than two centuries, the United States was a Europe-first power. In 2011, however, the Obama administration announced a change to America's strategic orientation. Asia would henceforth serve as its priority region, and the United States would refocus its military, diplomatic, and economic emphasis on the Indo-Pacific.[1] This move—the Pivot to Asia—would tap into Asia's dynamism, respond to China's astonishing rise, end Middle East wars, and limit security expenditures in Europe. The notion quickly won support among policymakers in both parties and across subsequent administrations. It coupled sound strategic logic with a keen appreciation of the ways in which the world was changing.

Not all went according to plan, and America's attempted Pivot to Asia sheds great light on the conduct of US foreign policy across a critical decade. This book tells the story of Washington's strategic reorientation and the simultaneous rise of Chinese power and assertiveness. It examines the impulse behind the Pivot, analyzes the challenges it posed for America's global presence and commitments, and investigates where and how it faltered. It looks at responses to the policy from countries in Asia, Europe, and the Middle East, and details China's strategic trajectory. This book then draws on lessons from the decade-long experience to propose a renewed US pivot to Asia today.

Secretary of State Hillary Clinton announced the strategic departure in *Foreign Policy* magazine. After a decade of war in Iraq and Afghanistan, she wrote in October 2011, "the United States stands at a pivot point."[2] The once white-hot wars in Iraq and Afghanistan were winding down, she said, allowing the immense resources deployed there to be rededicated. Americans should resist the siren song of isolation, the "come home" mantra of those wishing to focus on domestic priorities rather than foreign ones. The secretary noted that Europe was replete with allies operating in other theaters, and Russia went wholly unmentioned in the nearly 6,000-word essay.[3] A geographic shift of focus was required.

That shift should, the chief diplomat argued, be to Asia. By virtue of its critical geography, enormous population, economic dynamism, environmental impact, and increasing Chinese power and influence, the Asia-Pacific had emerged as the key driver of global geopolitics and geoeconomics. As a result, the United States would do more, much more, in the Pacific: reallocate and increase military capabilities, deepen existing alliances, strike a region-wide trade deal, establish new partnerships, and step up diplomacy. While "other regions," like Europe, "remain vitally important, of course," the reality was that the United States had overinvested in them—and in the Middle East and Afghanistan above all. "In a time of scarce resources," Clinton continued, "there's no question that we need to invest them wisely where they will yield the biggest returns." That meant Asia. Observing that the administration had paved the way for a pivot over the previous two and a half years, Secretary Clinton concluded, "we are committed to seeing it through as among the most important diplomatic efforts of our time."[4]

Beyond its preoccupation with Europe, the United States has for many decades discerned national interests all over the globe and undertaken diplomatic and military activities virtually everywhere. It fought wars in Asia four times, intervened militarily in Latin America on dozens of occasions, and has long been active in the Middle East. It has traded in every region, sent diplomats to all of them, and sought political influence everywhere.

The Pivot to Asia promised something different—the Indo-Pacific's explicit elevation above other regions of American concern. Yet soon after its announcement, nearly every aspect of this geopolitical and geoeconomic shift was controversial, including its very name. Within months the Obama administration, in response to complaints from allies and partners, tried to jettison the term "Pivot," with its air of reducing commitments in one region to do more in Asia, and despite the suggestions in Clinton's article that it meant just that. "Rebalance" became the administration's more acceptable term of diplomatic art, though its details remained nebulous and the label never stuck. To the present, it is "the Pivot" that is remembered, discussed, measured, and contested in Washington and around the world.

More than a decade after its announcement, a careful examination of the evidence measured by the allocation of military resources, the expenditure of diplomatic time and attention, or successful economic initiatives, indicates that the United States did not, in fact, pivot to Asia. Washington did increase its Asian engagement during those years in some ways. It did not, however, reorient attention and resources from the Middle East, Europe, and the United States to the Indo-Pacific. Military resources in the three theaters remain today broadly similar to where they began. Despite intermittently intensified engagement, diplomatic attention has been highly uneven and dependent on events and personal policymaker interests. In the economic arena, the Trans-Pacific Partnership represented both the Pivot's central initiative and America's greatest strategic failure.

The period from 2011, when the Pivot was announced, to roughly 2021, when the Biden administration started a partial and belated shift of focus to Asia, represents a lost decade. It coincided with a massive expansion of Chinese power and assertiveness, a deepening of America's domestic divisions, and rising doubts in the world about US intentions, staying power, and competence. The Pivot's sound strategic logic foundered on the shoals of execution.

Partly as a result, America's position in Asia today is weaker than when the Pivot was announced. The military balance has deteriorated in China's direction, the US economic agenda has become ever-less ambitious, and America's diplomatic engagement has proved inconsistent. The demand for US presence and engagement in the Indo-Pacific is high, but doubts about America's ability to deliver endure. The Pivot was designed in part to deal with rising Chinese power, but today China's power is greater than ever, with an aggressive foreign policy to match. The Biden administration has spent the past several years hurriedly, but only partially, catching up.

If the 1965 escalation in Vietnam and the 2003 invasion of Iraq represent America's greatest post–World War II failures of commission, Washington's collective failure to respond adequately to the stunning growth of Chinese power across the 2010s stands as perhaps the most consequential US policy *omission* since 1945. The Pivot to Asia should have represented a key feature of America's response. Its story illustrates how the United States did—and, more often, did not—address the arrival of a new superpower competitor, one with illiberal political values, an increasingly revisionist international agenda, and the rising capability to enact it. It shows how America's attempt to maintain global commitments while shifting attention and energy to Asia proved controversial, complicated, and painful. It demonstrates the difficulty in declaring one part of the world more strategically important than all the others. It also shows that a well-resourced, fully implemented Pivot to Asia remains critical to the enduring challenge posed by China.

To be sure, the 2011 Pivot could never encompass *everything* Washington needed to do in the face of China's challenge. As Beijing grew in strength, wealth, and assertiveness, especially during Xi Jinping's tenure, the list of actions necessary for an adequate response was long. A pivot to Asia, however, would represent the necessary centerpiece. Successfully carried out, the United States would be better positioned to compete effectively and deter war.

Yet the reality of the Pivot never matched its rhetoric or intent. Washington created unmet expectations across the Indo-Pacific of significant new regional activism, and it generated similarly unrealized fears of abandonment in Europe and the Middle East. The result was a historic missed opportunity. If the Pivot had been executed as intended, the United States would today still face a major China challenge. But it would be far better prepared to take on that challenge.

The Pivot produced meager results, and the concrete steps to enhance America's position in Asia were far outmatched by China's rapidly growing power. The reasons are clear enough. Policymakers for years underestimated the challenge posed by Beijing and were drawn to crises in other regions. Their approach was predicated in part on an expected peace dividend in Iraq and Afghanistan, wars that continued for years after the Pivot's announcement. Washington slashed its military budget at the very moment it wished to increase defense assets in the Pacific. Approval of a Pacific-wide economic deal ran into rising domestic opposition to trade. Sustained diplomatic engagement required key policymakers to resist the always present attraction of possible breakthroughs in the Middle East and Europe. The steps necessary for a successful shift proved difficult—too difficult, in the event, to get done.

Yet even after a lost decade, the Pivot remains America's proper strategic orientation, and one that should ground US foreign policy. Given Asia's crucial economic and diplomatic importance, and China's abiding threats to international order, the next chapter of global history will be written to a large extent in the Indo-Pacific. Though much time has passed since the initial effort took shape, the United States and China remain closer to the beginning of their long-run rivalry than to the end. A substantial pivot of US focus, time, and resources to Asia would increase the likelihood of American success in this generation's defining competition.

As the history in this book demonstrates, however, success requires balancing a greater focus on Asia with the need for the United States to remain active and to exercise leadership elsewhere. That, events have shown, is no easy task. But the stakes in doing so are high. America today faces its most ominous international challenges in more than half a century, and fashioning a successful and sustainable approach to the world represents a task of paramount importance.

That will be hard but by no means impossible. History suggests that the United States possesses everything necessary to compete effectively with China, deter war, and seize Asia's opportunity—all while meeting its most pressing commitments elsewhere. It has the strength, the wealth, the allies and partners, the values, and, increasingly, the political will necessary for the task. Success, however, requires a significant change.

Critical to the endeavor—but too often missing in Washington's approach—is a strategic concept that aligns American objectives with the policies, resources, and activities necessary to achieve them. That determines how to set priorities and then sustain them. That identifies not only areas in which to do more, but also places where the United States will do less. That balances commitments and crises elsewhere with a focus on Asia as its priority region.

An examination of the lost decade supplies answers to these conundrums. By detailing the Pivot's conceptual origins, its rhetorical adoption, and its implementation challenges, this book details how the United States can successfully pivot to Asia. By identifying the obstacles that hindered a far-reaching shift, and by recognizing Washington's recent success in beginning a partial turn, we can chart its future course.

Today, much is at stake, and time is short. Applying lessons from the recent past to the near future will help make the most of it.

## The Book's Structure

The literature on the Pivot to Asia is extensive.[5] Very few examinations, however, consider the 2011 rebalance in its global context.[6] That context is, of course, what has mattered most—determining how the United States could do more in one region while balancing its presence, resources, activities, and commitments in all the others. This book seeks to conduct such a globally informed examination to inform a successful, latter-day pivot.

Chapter 2 defines US vital national interests and provides a benchmark by which to determine how China, in particular, and Asia, in general, coincide or conflict with them. It articulates five key interests directly relevant to the Pivot to Asia that are implicated in the continued maintenance of liberal international order and that remain threatened by China's policies.

Chapter 3 examines the Pivot's antecedents, detailing the ways in which the Bill Clinton and George W. Bush administrations viewed Asia's relative importance in US foreign policy. It finds that from the mid-1990s, Washington began quiet balancing actions intended to hedge against the eventual rise of a threatening China. While the two administrations focused largely on issues and events in other regions, some of their actions in Asia were consistent with the Pivot's logic and set the stage for the Obama administration's formal announcement.

Chapters 4 through 6 detail the Pivot during the Obama, Trump, and Biden administrations. These chapters demonstrate the improvised nature of the policy's initial announcement, along with the unexpected zeal with which policymakers and political leaders greeted the rhetorical reorientation. They detail the challenges that attended implementation and the ever-present threat of distracting crises outside Asia. The chapters also show how the Trump administration embraced competition with China, making explicit the previously quiet hedging strategy, and how the Biden administration amplified that shift by labeling China as America's top strategic priority, even amid large-scale war in Europe. They also detail how the Biden administration turned the Pivot's fits and starts during the Obama and Trump years into a concrete, sustained effort— though one beset by significant omissions.

Chapters 7 through 10 look at the ways in which Europe, the Middle East, the Indo-Pacific, and China itself responded to the Pivot's announcement and its attempted implementation during the 2010s and beyond. As might be expected, reactions were highly variegated among and sometimes within regions. These chapters also describe the broader power dynamics in each region across the decisive decade. Europe began with a relatively quiescent Russia which, by the early 2020s, had become a destructively aggressive force. The Middle East worried continuously about American withdrawal from the region, even as the United States retained by far the greatest presence of any external power. The Indo-Pacific watched China become both a major security challenge and the most important economic partner of most countries in the region. And China itself grew in strength, economic gravity, and, under Xi Jinping's leadership, assertiveness.

Chapters 11 through 13 dive deeper into the functional issues that comprised the Pivot to Asia and America's broader approach to China. The United States began the decade enmeshed in wars across the greater Middle East, and with a military designed for counterinsurgency and stabilization operations. It ended the period trying to refashion itself for great power conflict with China. Washington also crafted an ambitious economic policy in Asia early on, the crowning achievement of which was to be the Trans-Pacific Partnership. In more recent years, efforts to break down barriers and link economies have given way to a far more defensive approach aimed at limiting the national security risk generated by economic interdependence. Transnational issues, like climate change and global health, have played a key role in the formulation of policies toward Asia as well, even as the hopes of US-China cooperation on them have faded in the face of sustained competition.

Chapter 14 concludes the book by summarizing the key reasons why the Pivot to Asia did not succeed as intended. It makes the case for a new Pivot and offers four principles to guide it. The chapter then provides policy recommendations in a selective "to do list" for policymakers seeking to pivot American grand strategy, at long last, to Asia.

## Historical Context

Pivoting to Asia has never implied first contact with the region. US involvement in the Pacific is, of course, nothing new; America's first encounters with China occurred when the Union consisted of just thirteen fractious states on the eastern seaboard.[7] From the republic's earliest days, it traded with Asia, sailed in the Pacific, and conducted diplomacy with Asians. It would over time possess its own Pacific coastline, gain territories in Asia, fight wars in the region, and, as America's territory and economy grew, define its national interests there in increasingly broad terms. To trace the story of US involvement in Asia is to tell the story of America itself.

Nevertheless, for nearly all of its history, the United States has been a Europe-first power. America's colonial forebears were European, the closest American allies lay across the Atlantic, its primary threats emanated from Europe, and the country's security and prosperity were intimately bound with the destiny of the Continent. The United States fought world wars there, and during the second—even after Japan's attack on Pearl Harbor—Washington adopted a Europe-first approach to the conflict. For more than two hundred years, this core and enduring US preoccupation with Europe was so instinctive, so much part of the national bloodstream, that it was rarely even discussed.

This enduring trait in American foreign policy has shifted dramatically in recent years. Ask policymakers today to declare a region worthy of preeminent US focus, and most would choose Asia. That region possesses the world's largest population, the greatest economic weight, and, critically, is witnessing the dramatic rise of a hostile China. Presidents and policymakers alike increasingly locate America's destiny in Asia, and they look to that region with both excitement and trepidation.

At its announcement, the Pivot captured a sentiment increasingly prevalent in Washington: that America's approach to the world was fundamentally unbalanced. The United States was devoting vast resources, the thinking went, to wars in regions marginal to its vital national interests. It was focused, as a result of history and inertia, on other areas, like Europe, that could manage without intense American engagement. Above all, it was insufficiently dedicated to the Asia-Pacific, the region that would disproportionately shape the future of US security, prosperity, and freedom.[8]

The Pivot to Asia embraced seemingly straightforward strategic logic, but it raised more questions than it answered. If Asia would now come first in US foreign policy, which regions would assume lesser prominence? Would the additional military resources for the Pacific be taken from those devoted to Europe and the Middle East, or would there be more for every region? Would the United States expect allies in other areas to take on more security burdens so that it could focus to a greater degree on the Asia-Pacific? What role would economic agreements play, within and between regions? Was the Pivot animated more by Asia's vast promise or by China's increasing threat? When, in its relations with key partners, should Washington emphasize one more than the other? And at the heart of the matter: What did it mean to pivot to Asia, exactly? What were the Pivot's objectives and the strategies to achieve them, and how would we know if it had succeeded?

Some of these questions are being answered now, with Washington's renewed, incomplete efforts to focus on Asia and China. Others remain unanswered more than a decade after the Pivot's initial announcement. They also represent far more than historical interest. This book's detailed review demonstrates that, across recent presidencies, policymakers have felt an increasing urgency to put Asia first, even as issues and crises in multiple regions demanded their attention.

How they attempted to resolve such dilemmas, and how they allocated diplomatic, military, and economic resources, should inform US foreign policy and grand strategy over the coming decades.

Today China accelerates its bid to dominate Asia, the regional military balance deteriorates, US economic policy in Asia is largely absent, and the American model of liberal democracy is both riven at home and contested abroad. There are new problems, including a violent, revisionist Russia willing to wage brutal war to overturn the European security order, Middle East countries increasingly hedging against the possibility of US disengagement, and Iranian proxies like Hamas launching large-scale terrorist attacks against Israel. And the long-term US-China competition, one that demands a renewed Pivot to Asia, has scarcely begun.

Those and other challenges amount to a daunting global environment for even the most farsighted national security policymakers. As they look forward, they will find lessons in the successes and failures of the recent past. This book attempts to excavate a history of the Pivot to Asia and, in so doing, point the way to America's strategic future.

# 2

# What's at Stake

## The Pivot to Asia and American National Interests

In her October 2011 article and a subsequent speech on the Pivot, Hillary Clinton made clear that the approach drew on an updated calculation of US national interests. She did not claim explicitly, however, that the administration sought a shift in American grand strategy, and President Obama later rejected the notion. In a January 2014 interview, Obama said that he did not need "any new grand strategy, but, rather, the right strategic partners."[1] He added, "I don't really even need George Kennan right now."[2] Actually, he did. The promise of Asia had grown too great for America to neglect.

That reality ran through much of the rhetoric and early positioning of his own administration. What the team did not adequately explain, however—and what has bedeviled policymakers ever since—was how the United States could focus more on Asia while maintaining a responsible level of engagement and leadership in other regions. Henry Kissinger has observed that "[n]o country can act wisely simultaneously in every part of the globe at every moment of time," and hard choices were inevitable.[3] That the Obama administration wished to reap a resource dividend by ending the wars in Iraq and Afghanistan seemed clear enough. Yet top officials simultaneously insisted that, even while pivoting to Asia, they would meet America's broader security commitments in both the Middle East and Europe. To sharpen the dilemma, the administration announced the Pivot at the very moment when the overall resource pie—at least in military terms—was shrinking in the face of severe, congressionally imposed budget caps. A more precise matching of strategic objectives to concrete steps and honest resource trade-offs was in order.

Though it called for stepped-up attention to the region, Obama administration officials often differed on the Pivot's strategic objectives. Subsequent presidents would, in time, draw not on a crisp, Obama-era formulation, but instead on one offered by Japanese prime minister Shinzo Abe. In 2016, Abe articulated the concept of a "Free and Open Indo-Pacific" (FOIP), a phrase that eventually became Washington's regional bumper sticker goal.[4] The Trump administration explicitly embraced the concept, and the Biden administration's Indo-Pacific strategy, released in February 2022, could have been written by Abe himself.[5] "Our vital interests and those of our closest partners," it said, "require a free and open Indo-Pacific, where governments can make their own sovereign choices, consistent with their obligations under international law; and where seas, skies, and other shared domains are lawfully governed."[6] Both the Trump and Biden administrations pursued variations on the Pivot in pursuit of a free and open Indo-Pacific.

The FOIP vision remains attractive but broad—indeed, so broad that it does not, on its own, specifically relate the end goal to the means necessary to attain it. To bring Abe's powerful formulation into distinct policy relevance, and to understand its relationship to the Pivot, it is necessary to first identify America's vital national interests, examine how they relate to the challenges posed by China, and then evaluate the Pivot as a means of improving America's strategic position. In short, why should the United States make Asia its top foreign- and defense-policy priority?

Answering this question requires thinking clearly about national interests and the trade-offs inherent in pursuing them. Andrew Goodpaster, President Eisenhower's national security advisor, once recalled the instructions Army Chief of Staff George Marshall gave America's wartime strategic planners in 1942: to identify the allies' "basic undertakings"—the essential objectives without which the war would not likely be won. As Marshall's maxim put it: when deciding what to do, one is also deciding what not to do, a difficult task for every government at every level.[7]

## Identifying American National Interests

Secretary of State Charles E. Hughes once said:

> Foreign policies are not built upon abstractions. They are the result of practical conceptions of national interest arising from some immediate exigency or standing out vividly in historical perspective. . . . When long maintained, they express the hopes and fears, the aims of security or aggrandizement, which have become dominant in the national consciousness, and thus transcend party divisions and make negligible such opposition as may come from particular groups.[8]

With such guidance in mind, this chapter begins by identifying American vital national interests, determining how they might relate to any pivot to Asia, and then discerning the likely effect of such a move for the extraordinary rise of Chinese power and influence.

Traditional examinations of US vital national interests often look first at those that animated the United States upon its establishment. The founding fathers believed that America should advance these interests principally by providing an example as a shining city on a hill. This was true when the United States was thirteen weak states in a world dominated by predatory European powers, but providing such an example is not enough today. In an increasingly interconnected world, all can see, and many can reach out and touch, America—to harm as well as to help. To protect and advance America's well-being poses a far more expansive challenge now than in the eighteenth century and requires deeper and more sustained engagement beyond America's shores.

Determining how well the Pivot may have advanced America's well-being requires judging it against specifically defined national interests. The international relations theorist Hans Morgenthau is adamant on this point, writing: "The only question which is relevant is . . . the question of what the effect of a certain policy is likely to be upon the national interest, and I am referring to the national interest as the standard of evaluation for foreign policies planned and pursued."[9]

From Washington's farewell address to Biden's national security strategy, the core tenet of US national interests, unsurprisingly, has not changed: to ensure the fundamental security of the homeland and its people. Or, as Alexander Hamilton put it, "Self-preservation is the first duty of a nation."[10] US vital national interests, strictly defined as necessary to safeguard and enhance Americans' survival in a free and secure nation, are the following:

1. To prevent the use and reduce the threat of nuclear, biological, and chemical weapons and catastrophic conventional terrorist attacks or cyberattacks against the United States, its military forces abroad, or its allies;
2. To stop the spread of nuclear weapons, secure nuclear weapons and materials, and reduce further proliferation of intermediate and long-range delivery systems for nuclear weapons;
3. To maintain a global and regional balance of power that promotes peace, stability, and freedom through domestic US robustness, US international power projection and influence, and the strength of US alliance systems;
4. To prevent the emergence of hostile major powers or failed states in the Western Hemisphere; and
5. To ensure the viability and stability of major international systems (trade, financial markets, public health, energy supplies, cyberspace, the environment, freedom of the seas, and outer space).

Instrumentally, these vital interests will be enhanced and protected by augmented global US leadership, improved military and intelligence capabilities, increased international credibility (including a reputation for adherence to clear commitments and evenhandedness in dealing with other states), and strengthened international institutions and rules critical to world order.[11] The debate among American strategists endures about whether a comprehensive list of US vital national interests should include the global defense of democratic values. This book will discuss the role that democratic values should play in US policy toward Asia in Chapters 13 and 14.

As the following enumeration makes clear, these five vital national interests are directly relevant to the Pivot to Asia, to the continued maintenance of a liberal world order, and to Beijing's aggressive external policies. This examination also reveals that, today and for the foreseeable future, only China poses an abiding and proximate threat to all five.

## China's Threat to American Vital Interests

### 1. To prevent the use and reduce the threat of nuclear, biological, and chemical weapons and catastrophic conventional terrorist attacks or cyberattacks against the United States, its military forces abroad, or its allies.

China's burgeoning intercontinental ballistic missile (ICBM) and nuclear capabilities present a threat to the American homeland and its forces abroad.[12] China plans to increase its stockpile of strategic nuclear warheads from an estimated 500 in 2022 to 1,500 by 2035.[13] This rise is accompanied by increased infrastructure-building to produce and separate plutonium. Beijing is reportedly constructing 300 new missile silos in the country's western desert—a tenfold increase over the number operational in 2022—in addition to its arsenal of an estimated 100 road-mobile ICBM launchers.[14] As of October 2023, the PRC possesses an estimated 350 ICBMS, all of which can reach the United States, and China's new D-5C, a silo-based ICBM, can deliver multimegaton warheads.[15] Beijing has also reportedly tested nuclear-capable hypersonic weapons that can evade American warning systems or reduce response times, and it test-launched 135 ballistic missiles in 2021—more than the rest of the world combined.[16] As one analyst observed, "With a significantly expanded nuclear arsenal, China will be freer to coerce or constrain US options in a crisis or use nuclear threats to compel the United States to back down in a conflict."[17]

### 2. To stop the spread of nuclear weapons, secure nuclear weapons and materials, and reduce further proliferation of intermediate and long-range delivery systems for nuclear weapons.

During nuclear negotiations with Tehran, China remained, in the words of Middle East expert Jon Alterman, "happy to be a free rider on global efforts to constrain Iran."[18] Unlike Washington, Beijing does not feel threatened by Tehran and "instead sees Iran as a useful instrument" for its broader geopolitical ambitions with respect to the United States.[19] An analysis by the International Crisis Group concurred, observing that China advocates a diplomatic solution over sanctions because a "pursuit of the diplomatic track delays punitive action and maximizes Beijing's bargaining power with regard to both Iran and the West."[20]

While China has called for the United States to return unconditionally to the Joint Comprehensive Plan of Action (JCPOA)—which it sees primarily as a means to "increase its economic engagement with Iran without the threat of US sanctions"—Beijing continues to permit state-owned enterprises and individuals to violate the Missile Technology Control Regime (MTCR) and "proliferate technology that Iran has used to improve the accuracy, range, and lethality of its ballistic missiles."[21] In February 2020, five Chinese state-owned entities and individuals came under US sanctions for aiding technology transfers and other assistance to Iran in furtherance of its missile program.[22] In 2023, Washington levied additional sanctions on Chinese companies that supply parts for Iranian drones used by Moscow to attack Ukraine.[23]

At the same time, Beijing has undermined sanctions against Tehran by dramatically boosting its economic support for the Islamic Republic. As will be discussed in Chapter 8 on the Middle East, Iran and China finalized an agreement to increase cooperation across multiple domains.[24] China has steadily remained the Islamic Republic's top trading partner, and commerce between the two countries exceeds $20 billion annually.[25] If Iran eventually acquires a nuclear weapon, Beijing, through its economic assistance, will bear substantial responsibility.

Beijing has also looked away as its citizens and corporations violate the MTCR vis-à-vis North Korea, despite China's stated aim of finding a peaceful solution to Pyongyang's nuclear program. A January 2023 Congressional Research Service report indicates that "Chinese financial companies set up paper companies to act as agents for North Korean financial institutions, evading sanctions to finance the North's proliferation of weapons of mass destruction (WMD) and ballistic missile programs."[26]

## 3. To maintain a global and regional balance of power that promotes peace, stability, and freedom through domestic US robustness, US international power projection and influence, and the strength of US alliance systems.

Beijing has mounted an all-out assault on the military, economic, and diplomatic balance of power in Asia, and on America's alliance system in the region.

China's military modernization, made possible by unprecedented increases in defense spending, laid the foundation for this rapid change.[27] Lt. General Robert Ashley, director of the Defense Intelligence Agency (DIA), described the People's Liberation Army's (PLA) transformation "from a defensive, inflexible ground-based force charged with domestic and peripheral security responsibilities to a joint, highly agile, expeditionary, and power-projecting arm of Chinese foreign policy that engages in military diplomacy and operations across the globe."[28] The PLA's modernization includes a new command-and-control structure, upgraded equipment across the navy, air force, and army, expanded and improved training for cadets, and the establishment of the Strategic Support Force to centralize its new combat capabilities. In addition to the buildup of its nuclear arsenal, Beijing now boasts the world's biggest navy, as well as the largest ballistic and cruise missile inventory.[29]

On the economic front, China has pursued two strategies to undermine American power in the Indo-Pacific. First, as will be detailed later in this book, Beijing threatens and coerces America's partners in Asia to adopt policies conducive to Chinese regional dominance. Second, the PRC created and promotes international economic organizations and initiatives that exclude the United States, privilege China's position, and undermine global rules and standards. These include the Regional Comprehensive Economic Partnership (RCEP), the Asian Infrastructure Investment Bank (AIIB), and the Belt and Road Initiative (BRI)—all which further China's strategic objectives and undermine American influence.

China also sought to expand its leadership in international governing institutions and weaken US influence. At the United Nations in particular, Beijing has become more assertive and activist: it mounts an assault on democratic norms, including the rule of law, human rights, transparency, and accountability. China heads four and has nine deputies present across fifteen principal UN agencies, and it uses this newfound leadership to advance its interests at the expense of the United States.[30] Simultaneously, Beijing has established regional and multinational bodies, such as the Shanghai Cooperation Organization, which are largely designed to oppose US foreign and defense policies.

Beijing attempts to undermine the strength of the US alliance system in the Indo-Pacific, without which the United States would find it difficult to compete effectively and to deter war with China. Foreign Minister Wang Yi has observed, "The Indo-Pacific Strategy concocted by the United States is keen on creating various sorts of small cliques by ganging up on others under the banner of 'freedom and openness.'" The strategy, he said, with its emphasis on allies and partners, "aims to contain China and attempts to make Asia-Pacific countries 'pawns' of US hegemony. . . . The people of this region should warn the United States sternly that the outdated Cold War script must not be repeated in Asia."[31]

Beijing consistently urges US allies to rethink their bilateral relations with Washington. When asked in March 2022 to reflect on Japan-US relations, Wang stressed, "Cold War alliances and geopolitical confrontation have long lost people's support. This is the inevitable trend of history. We hope that Japan will go along this trend instead of against it, decline to pull chestnuts out of the fire for others, and avoid pitting itself against its neighbors."[32] Two months later, during a meeting of the Quad group in Japan, a Chinese Foreign Ministry spokesperson added, "We hope that the Japanese side will learn from history, bear in mind regional peace and stability, act with prudence, refrain from acting as a cat's paw, and avoid adopting the ill-conceived beggar-thy-neighbor approach."[33] During a February 2023 meeting of Japanese and Chinese officials, Beijing "expressed its firm position and serious concern over Japan's efforts to advance its military build-up, hype up the 'China threat' in its defense security policy documents, strengthen military and security ties with non-regional forces in neighboring areas, and continue its negative moves on issues concerning China's core and major interests such as Taiwan and the South China Sea."[34]

When Washington and Seoul released a joint statement in May 2021, Chinese Foreign Ministry spokesperson Zhao Lijian warned the two to "refrain from playing with fire," and added, "China always opposes relevant countries in creating small cliques targeting other countries including the 'Quad' and 'Indo-Pacific strategy.'"[35] After the United States and South Korea engaged in joint military exercises in March 2023, the ministry said, "We are gravely concerned over the moves of the US and the ROK [Republic of Korea] in their military exercises. The crux of how the Korean Peninsula situation gets to where it is today is clear. The main reason is that the parties concerned have refused to respond to the denuclearization measures taken by the DPRK [Democratic People's Republic of Korea]."[36] The statement notably left out any criticism of Pyongyang's multiple provocations.

After the AUKUS (Australia/United Kingdom/United States) defense technology-sharing agreement was announced, Zhao Lijian declared, "What the US and Australia push for is wars and destruction."[37] In similar rhetoric used toward Japan and South Korea, he added, "The US and Australia should follow the trend of the times, respect the common aspirations of countries in the region, discard the outdated Cold War zero-sum mentality and narrow-minded geopolitical perception, view China's development in a correct way, and stop interfering in China's internal affairs and making waves in the Asia-Pacific region."[38]

China not only makes rhetorical demands but also puts pressure on American alliances with coercive and aggressive action. Japan, for example, has long laid claim to the Senkaku Islands in the East China Sea (ECS) and, since 1972, official US policy extends its security commitment to the Senkakus.[39] Beijing has moved beyond declarations of sovereignty and, since 2012, has "conducted regular incursions into the islands' territorial waters, and official Chinese aircraft have repeatedly appeared in the airspace above them."[40] The PLA has dispatched coast guard ships to patrol the waters and intimidate Japanese fishing boats.[41] As King's College professor Alessio Patalano observes, "Every successful step Beijing takes in undermining the status quo around the Senkakus through coercion and force is a direct challenge to the credibility of the US-Japanese alliance and, crucially, to the principles informing the maritime rules-based order."[42]

China has placed similar pressure on South Korea. When Seoul agreed to deploy a Terminal High Altitude Area Defense (THAAD missile defense) system in 2017, Beijing retaliated with coercive economic measures and political intimidation.[43] Chinese aircraft entered South Korea's air defense identification zone (ADIZ) at an increasing rate in the latter half of the 2010s and peaked at seventy times in 2021.[44] Chinese bombers repeated this incursion at the end of 2022, in conjunction with Russian combat aircraft.[45]

Australia was victim to Beijing's economic threats throughout the decade, but after the AUKUS agreement—which would provide Australia with a conventionally armed, nuclear-powered submarine capability—was announced, the rhetorical assault escalated.[46] In September 2021, immediately after the AUKUS announcement, the Chinese Foreign Ministry denounced the agreement as "extremely irresponsible."[47] Later that month, Foreign Minister Wang warned that AUKUS "may trigger the risk of nuclear proliferation, induce a new round of arms race, and undermine regional prosperity and stability."[48]

Philippine bases play a key role in US planning for the Indo-Pacific, and Manila too has been on the receiving end of Chinese coercion. As a professor at the US Marine Corps University observed, "For years, China has bullied the Philippines and other neighbors, building islands within their waters, harassing their fishing boats and security personnel, plundering fish from their waters, and blocking their routine military actions. And while the world focused on Russian troops amassing at the Ukraine border, China blatantly violated the Philippines' sovereignty, presumably so it could spy on a US-Philippine military exercise."[49] In 2012, Beijing began construction on three islands within Manila's exclusive economic zone. When the Philippines sued China and won at the Permanent Court of Arbitration in 2016, the PRC dismissed the ruling and continued its activity.[50]

## 4. To prevent the emergence of hostile powers or failed states in the Western Hemisphere.

Beijing has made a successful effort to deepen its strategic involvement with Latin American nations, increasingly at the expense of the United States.

China is now South America's top trading partner and the second largest for Latin America as a whole, after the United States. That is a significant leap for a country that, in 2000, accounted for less than 2 percent of Latin America's exports. Beijing now has free trade agreements with Chile, Costa Rica, Ecuador, and Peru. Twenty-one countries in Latin America and the Caribbean have signed on to the BRI. China has built ports, railroads, and dams, installed 5G networks throughout Latin America, and loaned the region's nations over $100 billion.[51] It also won favor with many Latin American countries after it delivered vaccines and other medical supplies during the COVID-19 pandemic.[52]

Notably, China has made a concerted attempt to engage Latin America and the Caribbean in the security domain. Beijing's 2008 and 2016 policy papers for the region outline Chinese commitments to increase "military exchanges and cooperation," assist the "development of the army in Latin American and Caribbean countries," and "enhance cooperation in military trade and military technology."[53] Between 2002 and 2019, senior PLA leaders conducted 215 visits to their counterparts, with Chile, Cuba, Brazil, and Argentina accounting for over half of these interactions.[54] Since 2012, there have been five China–Latin America high-level defense conferences. The most recent, in 2022, involved leaders from the defense ministries and militaries of twenty-four regional countries.[55] Cuba, described by Beijing as "a good brother, good comrade, and good friend," has hosted Chinese spy facilities since 2019, according to US intelligence officials.[56] In addition, China has significantly expanded its arms exports to the region, with sales to Venezuela and Bolivia valued at $500 million and $150 million, respectively.[57]

Through a combination of economic incentives and diplomatic pressure, Beijing wields substantial influence in Latin America—on some issues more than Washington. Many Latin American nations now support Beijing's positions at the United Nations and other international forums. The region's countries defended the PRC when China was accused of human rights violations and did not support Western sanctions following Russia's invasion of Ukraine.[58] Over the past two decades, the number of Latin American countries that recognized Taiwan's sovereignty shrank from twenty to only seven, and Beijing continues to use loans and investments to reduce that number even further.[59]

## 5. To ensure the viability and stability of major international systems (trade, financial markets, public health, energy supplies, cyberspace, the environment, freedom of the seas, and outer space).

Over the past fifteen years, China has sought to weaken virtually all these major global systems.

Through its repeated violations of international commercial practices, Beijing has disrupted the stability of world markets. It uses hundreds of billions of dollars in government subsidies and intentional overproduction to flood global markets with artificially low-priced Chinese goods and services.[60] It also restricts market access to foreign companies and imposes arbitrary nontariff barriers.[61]

During the COVID-19 pandemic, China delayed the transmission of crucial data for weeks and continues to resist any serious inquiry into the origins of the virus.[62] In addition, China's role in the fentanyl epidemic poses a direct threat to American citizens. The US Drug Enforcement Administration labels Beijing the "main source for all fentanyl-related substances trafficked into the United States," via cartels in Mexico.[63] As Brookings Institution expert Vanda Felbab-Brown argued in congressional testimony, China "sees its . . . counternarcotics enforcement, and more broadly its international law enforcement cooperation, as strategic tools that it can instrumentalize to achieve other objectives."[64] After then-Speaker of the House Nancy Pelosi visited Taiwan in August 2022, Beijing suspended all counternarcotics cooperation with the United States, and collaboration revived only after a Xi-Biden meeting in November 2023.[65]

China has created a sprawling and immensely powerful cyber operations command, which it employs to interfere with other nations and repress its own citizens. It uses cyberattacks and cyberespionage as elements of influence campaigns in the United States, through which it tries to shape public perceptions of China, suppress criticism, and mislead American voters.[66] It has penetrated US infrastructure and critical facilities and continues to steal data on hundreds of millions of Americans.[67] At home, Beijing utilizes its widespread cyber controls to surveil its own citizens and brutally violate their human rights.[68]

China consistently hampers global efforts to slow climate change and mitigate its impact. It emits more greenhouse gases than any other country and constructs new fossil fuel infrastructure across the world as part of its BRI.[69] It also pollutes its air, soil, and waterways, despite the consequences.[70]

China claims sovereignty over the South China Sea and declares the area its "inherent territory," inconsistent with the UN Convention on the Law of the Sea.[71] When, in March 2023, the USS *Milius* entered the waters near the Paracel Islands in the South China Sea, Beijing proclaimed the action as illegal. Its foreign ministry warned, "China will take all necessary measures to safeguard its sovereignty and security and uphold peace and stability in the South China Sea."[72] As maritime expert Isaac Kardon has argued, "Rather than changing the rules, China is changing the international environment in which those rules take effect." Beijing's assertive behavior in the South China Sea challenges established norms in the maritime domain, such as geographical boundaries, the rights of countries to control natural resources within their delineated zones, and international dispute-resolution mechanisms. As the PRC undermines the Law of the Sea, other countries are tempted to follow suit. The net result is an erosion of international laws and norms.[73]

In pursuit of Xi's "eternal dream" for China to become a "space power," Beijing has also made a concerted effort to rapidly expand its private and state industries.[74] The PLA draws an explicit link between space and conflict; its 2020 Science of Military Strategy document describes "the dominance of space [as] inseparable from the outcome of war."[75] The US Defense Intelligence Agency estimates that, between 2019 and 2022, China doubled its satellites in orbit from 250 to 499 and, in the latter year, the PRC launched forty-five defense-related satellites.[76] The United States that year sent thirty.[77] China surpassed its national record in 2023 and launched forty-one satellites on a single rocket.[78] The PRC does not share launch and re-entry data, nor does it adequately invest in rocket designs that avoid large, uncontrolled reentries to Earth. As a result, in May 2020, two villages in the Ivory Coast were hit by fragments of a Chinese Long March 5B rocket. In November 2022, Spanish airspace closed as a 23-ton piece of another Long March 5B began to plummet to Earth at 15,000 miles per hour. Though the rocket fragment landed in the Pacific Ocean, it was an example of China taking, in the words of NASA administrator Bill Nelson, "unnecessary risks."[79]

## The Clash of National Interests and Ambitions

This enumeration vividly demonstrates China's comprehensive policies to undermine each of America's five vital national interests meant to safeguard and enhance Americans' survival and well-being in a free and secure nation and to bolster international order. As US Defense Secretary Lloyd Austin explained in late 2022, "The PRC is the only country with both the will and, increasingly, the power to reshape its region and the international order to suit its authoritarian preferences."[80] By threatening nuclear annihilation, Beijing could deter the United States from acting in a crisis. In attempting to dominate Asia, China could prompt nuclear proliferation across the region, beginning with South Korea or even Japan, as countries seek a last-ditch nuclear-deterrent capability. A China-dominated Asia could fatally fragment the United States' Asian alliance system, as one US ally after another kowtowed to Beijing. The PRC could undermine US ties with Mexico and other countries in Latin American to distract the United States from pursuing its national interests in Asia and elsewhere. A China that dominated Asia would alter global values, rules, and practices to the United States' disadvantage. Steve Tsang, director of the China Institute at London's School of Oriental and African Studies, summed up the Chinese president's ambitions. "Xi Jinping," he said, "is not trying to out-compete America in the existing liberal international order dominated by the US. His long-term goal is to change the world order into a Sino-centric one."[81]

Although China's history is marked by many times in which it possessed regional dominance but eschewed power elsewhere, this era is different. It is a period characterized by Beijing's growing nationalism and ambition, unprecedented involvement in the international system, and a perception that the global economy may have decisive effects on China's internal stability. In this context, Singapore's Lee Kuan Yew emphasized:

> They [the Chinese leadership] have transformed a poor society by an economic miracle to become now the second-largest economy in the world—on track, as Goldman Sachs has predicted, to become the world's largest economy. . . . They have followed the American lead in putting people in space and shooting down satellites with missiles. Theirs is a culture 4,000 years old with 1.3 billion people, many of great talent—a huge and very talented pool to draw from. How could they not aspire to be number 1 in Asia, and in time the world?[82]

Successive US administrations spoke routinely about a strategic partnership with China, pursued an "engage but hedge" strategy vis-à-vis the PRC, and profoundly misread Beijing's strategic intentions. Washington's approach to China continued long after Beijing's international misbehavior accelerated under Xi Jinping, and when hedging should have transformed into much stronger and more decisive action to counter China's threats to American vital national interests.[83] History is filled with such dangerous, even fatal, miscalculations, going back to the Romans, the Greeks, the Egyptians, the Chinese, and earlier.[84]

Washington has now entered the fourth phase of its relationship with China since the end of World War II. In the first, Mao Zedong's 1950 decision to go to war with the United States in Korea produced a long period of antagonistic interaction. Phase two saw Richard Nixon and Henry Kissinger open the relationship to better meet the global Soviet threat and, they hoped, help end the Vietnam War on honorable terms. In the third phase, the United States sought to bring China into the international system, hoping it would eventually become a "responsible stakeholder" in it.[85] Now, in phase four, the United States continues to digest the aggressive elements of Chinese power projection, has embraced strategic competition, and is urgently attempting to respond to the China challenge.

Now at their lowest point in five decades, US-China relations are unlikely to improve markedly in the foreseeable future.[86] While American policymakers interpret Chinese political will and actions largely in terms of the interests articulated above, Beijing naturally sees things differently. Chinese leaders describe their growing ambitions and capabilities as inevitable for a great power reassuming its rightful place in the world. The Pacific should represent, they sometimes suggest, a Chinese sphere of influence like the Western Hemisphere is for the United States. The South China Sea might be likened to Beijing's

Caribbean, and Taiwan to its Cuba—though with even closer historical ties. Beijing inevitably seeks a global order conducive to its autocratic form of government, just as the United States has pursued an international system safe for democracy. China's expanding economic interests, increased defense capabilities to protect those interests, its global presence and influence, and its national ambitions—these are, some observers suggest, not so different from America's trajectory many decades ago.

Almost every international issue now divides Washington and Beijing. They disagree about the most effective political structures for modern societies, the future of Taiwan, freedom of navigation, and the nature of maritime claims in the South China and East China Seas. They contest arms control, how best to curtail the North Korean and Iranian nuclear weapons programs, cyber penetration and other influence operations, and the place and nature of alliances in the current era. They differ on bilateral trade, intellectual property, human rights, 5G networks and advanced technology, and climate change. They dispute the merits of Beijing's BRI, the India-China confrontation in the Himalayas, the proper character of technical standards, and the appropriate roles and missions of international organizations. Where they do theoretically agree—on the dangers of climate change, nuclear proliferation, and global pandemics, for instance—their nominal accord has produced virtually no common action. As Henry Kissinger warned in May 2023, "Both sides have convinced themselves that the other represents a strategic danger. We are on the path to great-power confrontation."[87]

Various administrations, including that of Joe Biden, have maintained hotlines with the PRC for crisis communications, but their efficacy remains questionable. When, for instance, a Chinese spy balloon drifted across the United States, the Biden administration called PRC officials who declined either to answer the phone or respond to requests to talk. The two sides do not need additional mechanisms of communication, but rather relationship-building between senior-most policymakers. This is critical to ensure that counterparts will indeed communicate during a crisis, and in turn requires extensive diplomacy before a crisis looms. The point in such diplomatic engagement is not to foster agreement where it does not exist, but rather to promote understanding, communication, and a degree of additional transparency.

While some of the recommendations made in this book will increase tensions with China, the United States should do all that it can, through diplomacy, to prevent tension and competition from becoming confrontation and crisis—and certainly from becoming conflict. This requires not only stronger, traditional relationships between the national security advisor, secretary of state, and secretary of defense and their counterparts, but also frequent communication between intelligence chiefs and the most senior military officials. It is true that US policymakers are often subjected to ritualized PRC rhetorical declarations, rather than substantive conversations with their Chinese counterparts. But more exchanges between the two governments are better than fewer.

In any case, there is not today, nor will there be in the foreseeable future, some attainable US-China grand bargain. The United States and China have different histories, political cultures, values, perceived national interests, long-term foreign policy goals, and visions of domestic and international order. This is especially true given that both governments currently strive for primacy in the Indo-Pacific. Quality diplomacy on both sides will be required to avoid catastrophe.

## Toward a New Grand Strategy

Because American efforts to integrate China into the liberal international order generated new threats to Washington's leadership in Asia—and produced a consequential challenge to American power globally—the United States today requires a new grand strategy. In that context, Rush Doshi—a China scholar who went on to serve on the Biden National Security Council (NSC) staff—provides a useful definition: "Grand strategy," he writes, is "a state's theory of how it can achieve its strategic objectives that is intentional, coordinated, and implemented across multiple means of statecraft—military, economic, and political. What makes grand strategy 'grand' is not simply the size of the strategic objectives but also the fact that disparate 'means' are coordinated together to achieve it."[88]

Such a strategy—one that deliberately incorporates elements that limit China's capacity to misuse its growing power, even as the United States and its allies continue to interact with the PRC diplomatically and economically—is all the more necessary in light of the long-term strategic rivalry between Washington and Beijing. This grand strategy cannot be built on a bedrock of containment, as was the earlier effort to limit Soviet power, both because of the current realities of globalization and because no Asian nation would join the United States in such a policy.[89] Nor can it entirely jettison the notion of integrating China into the international system, not least because of the intertwined character of the global economy.

Rather, Washington should strive to ensure that Beijing is either unwilling or unable to overturn the regional and global order. That, in turn, requires a renewed Pivot to Asia.

This new US grand strategy directed at the Indo-Pacific—one implicit in the Pivot—would possess several critical elements, all discussed in detail later in this book. It should revitalize the US economy, nurture those disruptive innovations that bestow on the United States asymmetric economic advantages, and train a next-generation workforce. It should create new preferential trading arrangements among Washington's allies and partners to increase their mutual gains, including through instruments that consciously exclude Beijing, and establish a technology-control regime that prevents China from acquiring military and strategic capabilities that would enable it to inflict harm on the United States and its partners. It must build up US allies and partners on China's periphery to project military power effectively and promptly along the Asian rimland and along vital sea lanes, despite Chinese opposition. It should promote democracy, human rights, and universal values. And it should do all this while working with Beijing in ways that promote US national interests and reduce the possibility of major confrontation or even war.

Such objectives seem straightforward and even obvious. They have not, however, been sufficiently achieved over the past two decades. American efforts did not create the conditions for either a secure balance of power in the Indo-Pacific or a stable US-China relationship. Today the balance of power continues to erode and the bilateral relationship remains highly unstable. A renewed, proper Pivot to Asia could help right the balance and set the conditions for a long-term US-China equilibrium.

The remainder of this book examines the Pivot's background, announcement, implementation, and place amid a panoply of enduring American priorities. Multiple administrations have found compelling the imperative to focus on Asia as the priority region. Their success in applying this strategic logic, however, has been wanting. An examination of this history helps point the way toward what a new Pivot to Asia might comprise, and how it could succeed.

# 3

# The Pivots before the Pivot

## The Clinton and Bush Administrations

In any given year, a secretary of state issues thousands of statements, articles, commentaries, and speeches. Most represent texts labored over by dozens of lower-level officials, sanded down as they move through the bureaucracy, and quickly forgotten after publication. Foreign policymakers perennially complain that the media pays insufficient attention to their pronouncements, foreign officials demonstrate too little knowledge of authoritative statements, and the US government itself is not easily galvanized by a grand strategic vision issued from on high.

Far rarer is the official announcement that shifts the very parameters within which foreign policy is made, provokes lasting and searching debate, and is remembered and argued over many years later. One might recall for instance, George Kennan's *Foreign Affairs* article, which in July 1947 proposed the containment of Soviet communism.[1] Or John F. Kennedy's pledge in 1961 to "bear any burden" to "assure the survival and success of liberty,"[2] or a decade later when Richard Nixon, on national television, announced the opening to China.[3] Ronald Reagan, in his famous Westminster address, dedicated America to "foster the infrastructure of democracy,"[4] and George W. Bush, days after 9/11, declared a war on terror that "will not end until every terrorist group of global reach has been found, stopped, and defeated."[5] With such pronouncements were born containment, the Kennedy Doctrine, normalization with Beijing, institutionalized democracy promotion, and the global war on terror.

Secretary Clinton's landmark *Foreign Policy* article enunciated a similarly tectonic shift in US foreign policy. That effect came unexpectedly even to its authors, and administration officials, as detailed later in the book, would complain that far too much was read into an article—and a term, the "Pivot," that merely summarized President Obama's preexisting approach. Nevertheless, a rough Washington consensus quickly gelled that pivoting to Asia, in broad terms, was an important and urgent American task. Whether or not it was meant as a new strategic impulse, it generated one. And for all that was new in the approach, it also reached back to notions that had originated in Bill Clinton's administration and had gathered strength, in ups and downs, ever since.

## Before the Pivot: The Clinton Administration

The successful conclusion of the Cold War was the first condition necessary for any eventual pivot to Asia. Even before his election, then-candidate Bill Clinton observed the new possibilities opened by the Soviet Union's collapse; among them, he said, was the opportunity to strengthen ties with Japan and get tough with China.[6] A Clinton administration, the candidate said, would not look at Tokyo as a predatory trader but a potential partner: "an important bilateral relationship, perhaps our most important one."[7] The approach to Beijing would change, too; at the 1992 Democratic National Convention, which took place just three years after the Tiananmen Square massacre, the party platform linked renewal of China's most-favored-nation trade status to improvements in human rights and other issues.[8] Chai Ling and Li Lu, two leaders of the student protest, spoke at the convention to great applause.

On the campaign trail, Clinton criticized his opponent, President George H.W. Bush, for his Tiananmen response, accusing him of "failing to stand up for our values." Instead, Clinton said, Bush "sent secret emissaries to China signaling that we would do business as usual with those who murdered freedom in Tiananmen Square." Famously labeling PRC leaders the "butchers of Beijing," the candidate stirred alarm in China with his hardline views.[9] America, Clinton pledged, would possess the world's strongest defense, champion democracy, and refuse to coddle tyrants like those who had spilled blood on Beijing's streets.

As is so often the case, campaign pledges clashed with government policy from the new administration's outset. Washington's approach to Japan hardened, while its ties with China grew more pragmatic. Just months after his inauguration, President Clinton complained about the trade deficit with Japan during a meeting with Prime Minister Kiichi Miyazawa. "The world needs a strong Japan," Clinton said, and it required US-Japan cooperation. But "it can only happen," he added, "if we are making real progress on this trade deficit."[10] The new president then extended China's most favored nation trade status for a year, without having obtained significant human rights concessions from Beijing.[11] The administration described the move merely as a stop-gap measure; it attached a raft of conditions to further MFN extension, from the release of political prisoners to protections for Tibet and greater access by Chinese people to foreign radio and television.[12]

The first attempt by the Clinton administration to assemble a coherent approach to the Asia-Pacific region took place in July 1993. In a speech at Waseda University, the president called on Japan and other countries to join the United States in creating "a new Pacific community," one that would rest on a revived US-Japan partnership, increased trade, open economies, and support for democracy.[13] A few months later, at a meeting of the Asia-Pacific Economic Cooperation forum, Clinton expanded on the vision. "We have agreed that the Asia-Pacific region should be a united one, not divided," he said. "We have agreed that our economic policies should be open, not closed."[14]

From the outset, however, the administration's outreach to Asia remained riddled with contradictions and lurching, reflecting internal divisions between democratic enlargers, who sought Pacific partners in a grand effort to increase the number of democracies in the world, and economic nationalists, who favored managed trade, a Japan-like industrial policy, and who saw in Asia—and in some of the same countries coveted as allies by the democratic enlargers— economic rivals to the United States. Economic engagement with China rested in tension with the desire to condition trade on human rights improvements, and suspicion of Japanese trade practices seemed to conflict with the desire to strengthen ties with America's most militarily capable ally in Asia. Clinton's vision of a united Asia would, on its face, make no distinction between democracies and dictatorships, for all of the administration's desire to enlarge the former and shrink the latter.

In February 1994, President Clinton both lifted the trade embargo on Vietnam, a major step toward normalization with that erstwhile Asian enemy, and threatened Japan with aggressive action after the failure of trade talks with Tokyo.[15] Four months later, Clinton—despite his administration's repeated protestations to the contrary—renewed China's MFN status without human rights conditions.[16] In doing so, the president offered reasoning similar to that which he had condemned in his predecessor—namely that US jobs and economic prosperity depended on continued trade with China. Indeed, Clinton flipped his previous arguments on their head; liberalizing trade with China, he now suggested, would itself foster positive change in the country's human rights practices.[17]

## The Nye Report

After two years of policy zigs and zags, the administration in February 1995 published the United States Security Strategy for the East Asia-Pacific Region. Guided by Assistant Secretary of Defense Joseph Nye, the "Nye Report" contained in both policy and personnel a handful of direct precursors of the Obama Pivot a decade and a half later. Joining Nye in its production was Michael Green, who would serve as senior director for Asia on the George W. Bush NSC staff, working both to revitalize regional alliances and hedge against China's uncertain trajectory. Also included in the effort was Kurt Campbell, whom Nye had brought to the Pentagon from Harvard, and who became both the key architect of the 2011 Pivot and its central revitalizer during the Biden administration.[18]

If there was an intellectual grandfather to the Obama Pivot, the Nye Report was it. At a moment when many policymakers saw global integration as an untrammeled good, open economic frameworks as worthier pursuits than power politics, and Cold War–era alliances like the one with Japan—including tens of thousands of forward-deployed American troops buttressing them—as expensive anachronisms, the report offered very different strategic logic. Asian stability and prosperity did not obviate the need for American alliances and a resident force presence, it said; rather it showed that peace and development were possible only with such a US military posture. The Cold War might be over, it added, but "Asia remains an area of uncertainty, tension, and immense concentrations of military power," one that demanded not the diminishment of America's alliance structure there, but rather its amplification. The United States would, as a result, maintain the forward deployment of American troops, endeavor to develop multilateral security initiatives, reinvigorate alliances—with the US-Japan alliance assuming top priority—and would, from such a position of strength, encourage a rising China to define its interests in ways compatible with America's own.[19] The US presence in the region would enable continued stability and prosperity.[20]

As Nye later recalled, "In the early 1990s, there was a widespread belief both within and without government that 'geo-economics' had replaced geo-politics. Many people in both Japan and the United States regarded the bilateral Cold War alliance as obsolete. . . . The early stages of Clinton's Asia policy were guided by economic governmental agencies; little interest was evinced in security issues. . . . I did not share these views."[21] In light of the report, Washington pledged to maintain roughly 100,000 US troops in East Asia, to begin work with Japan on guidelines for its support in a security crisis, to continue the defense commitment to South Korea in the face of a nuclearizing North, and to recognize "America's permanent interest in the security of the Asia-Pacific Region."[22] Nye observed at the time that among the stabilizing effects of the US military presence in Asia was "deterring the rise of hegemonic forces," though he declined to name those possible forces.[23] Despite the Soviet Union's demise, a security architecture previously directed against communist dangers would henceforth serve regional security and stability by guarding against future, unknown threats.

Among these, the report suggested in muted tones, might be the People's Republic of China. Beijing was engaged in a military buildup, the Nye Report observed, and while the country's leaders insisted on its defensive nature, "others in the region cannot be certain of China's intentions." The long-term goals of Beijing's military modernization were unclear, it went on, and "absent a better understanding of China's plans, capabilities and intentions, other Asian nations may feel a need to respond to China's growing military power."[24] Here, amid America's deepening trade and investment relationship with China, and during an express period of US-China engagement, one discerns the hedging strategy that would assume ever-greater importance across the Clinton, Bush, and Obama administrations.

In an accompanying article, Nye articulated the policy alternatives to the Clinton administration's approach to Asia, some of them then-fashionable. America could, for example, withdraw its military presence from Asia and pursue a hemispheric or an Atlantic-only strategy—a sort of "anti-Pivot," to use the Obama-era vernacular. It could recognize the Cold War's end by withdrawing from its Pacific alliances and allowing balance-of-power politics to take the place of American leadership. It could create loose regional security institutions or attempt to forge a NATO-like regional alliance. The Clinton administration, Nye explained, rejected each of the alternatives. Instead, the United States would strengthen its alliances and give them new rationales after their Cold War purposes ebbed. US troops in Asia would stay put, reversing "a halt to the reductions planned in the more euphoric phase of the early post-Cold War period." And Washington would develop regional institutions, like the Asia-Pacific Economic Cooperation (APEC) forum, the Association of Southeast Asian Nations (ASEAN) Regional Forum, and as-yet-uncreated security dialogues.[25]

## Between Engagement and Hedging

The combination of presence and prudence that animated the Nye Report proved useful within months. In 1996, ahead of Taiwan's first popular presidential election, Beijing mounted a major effort at intimidation. The PLA mobilized 100,000 troops on the mainland across from Taiwan, launched missile salvos into waters near the island, and conducted nuclear weapons tests and combined forces exercises. Clinton dispatched two aircraft carrier battle groups to the region in response, including the USS *Nimitz*, which sailed through the Taiwan Strait.[26] The crisis subsided with the election and inauguration of Taiwanese president Lee Teng-hui, but both Washington and Beijing drew lessons from the experience that would alter their approaches to defense in the region.

For Beijing, its inability to stop the US Navy from sailing into waters adjacent to China, just as the PRC attempted a show of strength, was nothing short of a humiliation—one that Chinese leaders resolved not to repeat. As future secretary of defense Ashton Carter, then a mid-level Pentagon official, recalled, "The Chinese defense minister came to the Pentagon and stated ruefully that he had 'lost face' in the encounter. Then secretary of defense Perry replied simply, 'You deserved to.' China's leadership clearly took the lesson to heart: its military investments since then seem designed in part to deter us from providing that kind of protection to our friends in need."[27] Numerous observers have cited the Strait crisis as the genesis of China's investment in anti-access/area denial

(A2/AD) capabilities designed to hold at risk US aircraft and naval vessels that might approach the Chinese rimland in a crisis.[28] The PLA's increased A2/AD capabilities have, in turn, contributed to a shift in the region's military balance of power away from the United States and toward China.

For Washington, the episode underscored the enduring importance of American military presence in Asia. The Pentagon redeployed, for the first time, a Los Angeles–class submarine from Europe to Guam. President Clinton signed a new joint declaration on security with Japan that cast the alliance as the basis for stability and prosperity in Asia, and he pledged to revise three-decade-old bilateral defense guidelines to better deal with regional crises.[29] Speaking to the Japanese Diet in April 1996, Clinton asked the assembled parliamentarians to "Consider what might happen if the United States were to withdraw entirely from this region." It could, he said, "spark a costly arms race that could destabilize northeast Asia. It could hinder our ability to work with you to maintain security in a part of the world that has suffered enough in the 20th century through world war and regional conflicts and that is now in the midst of profound change."[30] At a moment when the US defense budget was falling dramatically, the president argued against seeking a chimerical peace dividend in Asia. America certainly was not pivoting *to* the Pacific in the mid-1990s, but by then—and in contrast to some arguments earlier in the decade—it would not pivot *away* from Asia, either.

The publicly offered rationales for US engagement in Asia remained abstract—maintain security, prevent arms races, and ensure regional stability. The growing US hedging strategy, however, was not lost on Beijing. After the US-Japan joint declaration, Chinese officials denounced the notion that their country represented a military threat to the region and condemned US and allied efforts to enhance their power projection. "If Japan's self-defense forces further build up armaments," a Foreign Ministry spokesman said, "it is bound to cause concern and vigilance among other Asian nations. We urge Japan to move with caution."[31] For all of the administration's talk about economic interdependence, deep engagement with China, and the potentially liberalizing effects of trade and information flows, parts of the US government accelerated an old-fashioned balance of power policy in Asia, one that aimed to maintain the US presence and bolster key alliances in order to hedge against an increasingly powerful and assertive China.

The 1997 Quadrennial Defense Review (QDR) added to this picture, still *sotto voce*. Explicitly pointing out the North Korean threat, the QDR observed, "Between now and 2015, it is reasonable to assume that more than one aspiring regional power will have both the desire and the means to challenge US interests militarily." The report offered no view about which other regional power might offer such a challenge, and it emphasized that the United States "will continue to engage China, seeking to foster cooperation . . . and influence it to make a positive contribution to regional stability and act as a responsible member of the international community." Yet "China's efforts to modernize its forces," it went on, "and improve its power-projection capabilities will not go unnoticed, likely spurring concerns from others in the region." Whether the United States might be included in the countries concerned by growing Chinese power projection capabilities went unmentioned.[32]

On the human rights front, the Clinton administration's hopes for Chinese improvements dimmed as the years went by. Clinton and top foreign policy officials continued to assert that interdependence—trade and information flows above all—would have a liberalizing effect on China. Respect for human rights was not a prerequisite for engagement, Clinton argued; rather, engagement would, as he put it in 1997, "increase the spirit of liberty over time." Yet doubts remained among key administration officials. Secretary of State Madeline Albright the same year reiterated the hope that greater integration would have a transformational effect on Beijing's domestic practices, but noted, "Given the nature of China's government, that progress will be gradual, at best, and is by no means inevitable."[33]

By this point in the administration, the early contradictions in its China policy had been resolved. Trade with China and the promotion of human rights, officials held, lay not in tension but rather were mutually reinforcing. Engagement and integration would foster constructive Chinese foreign policy, even as the country grew stronger on the back of that very engagement. Whether one prioritized business with China, human rights there, or Beijing's international behavior, the right policy response was deep engagement. If engagement had not worked yet, that was because it would take time. And if time failed to reveal a changed China, Washington could fall back on the quiet, but increasingly important, hedging component of its strategy.

Subsequent actions flowed from this broad approach. In November 1997, during Chinese president Jiang Zemin's visit to the United States, he and Clinton agreed on a commitment to control nuclear exports and announced a "constructive strategic partnership" that contained little in the way of specifics but aimed to set a tone of cooperation.[34] Six months later, the administration declined to sponsor an annual UN resolution that condemned China's human rights record, citing recent improvements in Beijing's practices and its decision to sign the International Covenant on Civil and Political Rights, which guarantees freedom of expression, assembly, movement, and religion.[35]

The 1997 Asian financial crisis reaffirmed for administration officials that events in the region—economic events, at the very least—directly affected US national interests. Clinton pledged funds to bail out South Korea, participated in a relief package for Indonesia, and in 1998 won congressional approval for $18 billion in International Monetary Fund (IMF) funding that went disproportionately to Asian countries.[36] The crisis appeared to some officials as also an opportunity—to push long-stalled structural reforms on Japan, to welcome a new democratic government in Jakarta after President Suharto's fall from three-decade rule, and to demonstrate the indispensable nature of American leadership.

May 1998 saw India test nuclear weapons for the first time since 1974, eliciting a reciprocal Pakistani nuclear test and strong condemnation in Washington. Calling the Indian tests a "terrible mistake," Clinton cut off direct aid to New Delhi, canceled loans and loan guarantees, resolved to oppose assistance to India from international financial institutions, and stopped licenses for some US exports to the country.[37] This punitive approach to India would not last. It quickly dawned both on key congressional actors and the executive branch that penalizing India would produce more costs than benefits. The US agricultural and aerospace industries sought relaxation of the sanctions almost immediately, and the punishments were inconsistent with the administration's own quiet efforts to strengthen existing regional partnerships and forge new ones. Clinton first waived some of the sanctions on India just six months after they had been applied.[38]

Strangely, US-India relations emerged warmer from the nuclear test crisis than they entered it. Clinton would go on to value New Delhi's contributions to resolving the 1999 Kargil crisis, which saw fighting between India and Pakistan in Kashmir. The administration established a bilateral dialogue between Deputy Secretary of State Strobe Talbott and Minister of External Affairs Jaswant Singh, focused on securing India's adherence to the Comprehensive Test Ban Treaty (CTBT), which Clinton had signed in 1996. Twelve rounds of talks clarified their strategic positions, but the US demand became difficult to sustain once the Senate itself rejected the CTBT in October 1999.[39] Soon, in the words of Commerce Department official Raymond Vickery, "President Clinton was finished with treating India as anything but a friend."[40] In his final year in office, Clinton would become the first US president in twenty-two years to visit India, a trip credited by his supporters with setting in motion a sustained, bipartisan effort to strengthen bilateral ties with the preeminent South Asian power.[41] In the coming years, India's role in US strategy in Asia—and the pivot toward what would become known as the "Indo-Pacific region," explicitly including India— became central.

Warming ties with Vietnam would play a similar, though less important, role. Veterans of the Vietnam War in Congress, including Senators John McCain and John Kerry, led the politically difficult task of normalizing relations. After diplomatic ties were restored in 1995, the two countries established a bilateral trade agreement in July 2000 to boost the then-small commercial flows.[42] As with India, US industry played an important role, eager for access to the Vietnamese market and to low-cost manufacturing there.[43] The clearing away of bilateral tensions that followed the Vietnam War, the boost in economic relations between the two, and the convergence of strategic interests in Asia would eventually lead, in future administrations, to the once-unthinkable establishment of military ties between the former enemies.

By the close of Bill Clinton's eight years in office, key conditions for an eventual pivot had settled into place. The Soviet threat that once animated key regional alliances had ended, as had the Cold War, but the United States retained its security architecture and a forward-deployed military presence in Asia nevertheless. Washington discerned both security and economic interests in the region and would intervene when necessary to protect both. Nascent moves to establish strong partnerships with India and Vietnam took shape.

Yet overhanging it all was the US hope during the 1990s that China itself would change, and thus the Asia-Pacific along with it. On a 1998 visit to China, Clinton articulated as much. "There may be those here and back in America who wonder whether closer ties and deeper friendship between America and China are good," Clinton said. "Clearly, the answer is yes."[44] Washington retained deep concerns about Chinese human rights abuses, but largely believed that quiet talks, more trade, and deeper Chinese integration would lead to improvements. The accidental NATO bombing of the Chinese embassy in Belgrade, in May 1999, elicited tens of thousands of protesters at the US embassy in Beijing— but also millions of dollars in American compensation to the families of those killed.[45] Six months later, in moves that would still be debated vigorously two decades later, the Clinton administration supported China's bid to join the World Trade Organization (WTO) and, the following year, pressed Congress to enact permanent MFN status for China. In his letter advocating normal trade relations, the president summed up the then-predominant thinking about China's future. "By integrating China more fully into the Pacific and global economies," Clinton wrote, permanent normal trading relations "will strengthen China's stake in peace and stability. Within China, it will help to develop the rule of law; strengthen the role of market forces; and increase the contacts China's citizens have with each other and the outside world."[46]

Commerce, peace, stability, and human rights—all, in this holistic vision, would move forward harmoniously, and involve no trade-offs. A globally integrated, wealthier, and liberalizing China would anchor Asian peace and security. Stability in Asia would, in turn, be good for Americans and for prosperity on both sides of the Pacific. This was the public, and often private, rationale for US-China policy toward the latter half of the 1990s. Years later, many observers would argue that it was Washington's continuation of this engagement, long after its lofty ambitions had failed, that required a pivot to Asia, one that would slow Beijing's steady advances at America's expense.

In any case, engagement with China did not, over the years, lead Beijing to sustained improvements in its human rights record, or to moderate its foreign policy ambitions, or to become (as later officials would hope) a responsible stakeholder in the international order. The policy of engagement was based on a hope, one that went unrealized. Yet engagement with China represents only part of the story of the Clinton administration's Asia policy. As we have seen, officials in it pursued quiet hedging strategies over the years that aimed to maintain US forces in the region, renovate American alliances, and establish new relationships with countries like India and Vietnam, with the aim of balancing power against an increasingly powerful China whose future intentions remained opaque. And soon, a new administration would enter office with very different instincts about the best way to manage relations with Beijing.

## The Bush Administration's "Outside-In" Approach to Asia

Had candidate George W. Bush been asked where the United States should pivot its foreign policy, unsurprisingly as a Texan, he might well have pointed to Latin America rather than Asia. "Should I become president," he said on the campaign trail, "I will look south, not as an afterthought, but as a fundamental commitment to my presidency."[47] He touted his experience as a border-state governor, and pledged to boost hemispheric trade, provide microcredits for businesses in poor Latin American countries, secure debt relief, and pursue a "special relationship" with Mexico.[48] Upon taking office, the new president's first visit was to Mexico, where he met newly inaugurated Vicente Fox; his second was to Canada for the Summit of the Americas. He called on Congress to renew Trade Promotion Authority so that his administration might negotiate a Free Trade Area of the Americas (FTAA), essentially expanding the North American Free Trade Agreement (NAFTA) to encompass thirty-four countries in the hemisphere.[49] He agreed to pursue with Mexico a bilateral agreement on temporary workers and undocumented Mexicans living in the United States.[50] And at the summit of hemispheric leaders, three months after taking office, Bush announced "the century of the Americas."[51]

The momentum behind Bush's focus on the Western Hemisphere would fade quickly, a victim of the 9/11 attacks, domestic politics, and rising preoccupation with other regions. There would be no FTAA, no comprehensive migration agreement with Mexico, and no new special relationship with that country. While Bush did make progress in improving ties with countries like Chile and Colombia, the pivot south never took place.

Although Bush's initial instinct to look south reflected his Texas roots, knowledge of countries south of the US border, and personal experience with Mexico, the same was not true of Asia. The new president had little expertise in Pacific affairs and, beyond some key themes—a strong defense, freer trade, skepticism about China—when in office he largely relied on advisors to fill in the policy blanks.

A document published just weeks before the 2000 election sheds light on these advisors' thinking. A report published by the National Defense University—subsequently known as the "Nye-Armitage Report"—was nominally about the rationale for and methods to upgrade the US-Japan alliance. In fact, however, it went beyond this mandate and offered a vision of Asia that was vitally important to America's future, demanded a strong and increasing US presence, and would remain secure and prosperous only within the framework of robust American alliances.

Some who participated in its production had cut their teeth on then-assistant secretary of defense Nye's 1995 Pentagon report, including Michael Green and Kurt Campbell. Others would go on to senior positions from the outset of the Bush administration: Richard Armitage as deputy secretary of state, Paul Wolfowitz as deputy secretary of defense, James Kelly as assistant secretary of state for East Asia and Pacific affairs, and Torkel Patterson as the NSC senior director for Asia. "Asia," the group believed, "should carry major weight in the calculus of American political, security, economic, and other interests." The region was vital to American prosperity, increasingly democratic, and yet riven by potential instability. While "major war in Europe" would be "inconceivable for at least a generation," they said, "the prospects for conflict in Asia are far from remote" as North Korea loomed and China underwent momentous changes.[52] American alliances—with Japan above all—were critical to manage this quickly changing theater, and events in Asia were unlikely to be confined to the region: "The US-Japan alliance," the authors wrote, "is central to America's global security strategy."[53]

Using the "special relationship" between the United States and Great Britain as a model, the report called for implementation of the 1996 revised US-Japan defense cooperation guidelines, expanded military contacts between the two countries, and the sharing of defense technology, and it encouraged Tokyo to remove its 1992 self-imposed limits on peacekeeping and humanitarian relief operations.[54] The governments should share more intelligence, the authors argued, and explore the possibility of a free trade agreement. Elsewhere in the region, they should support the "revival" of Indonesia and encourage an independent and activist ASEAN.

Michael Green observed later that "the Nye Initiative toward Japan now became, in effect, a core pillar of Bush's Asia policy."[55] In the barest outlines, an eventual pivot is perceptible: Asia, by virtue of its economic and demographic weight, has a strategic importance more significant to the United States than other regions; China's emergence injects critical, potentially dangerous uncertainties; the end of the Cold War and the rise of globalization offer opportunities but also key challenges for US policy in Asia; and the degree to which the United States and its Japanese ally "respond, individually and as alliance partners, will define significantly the security and stability of the Asia-Pacific as well as the possibilities of the new century."[56]

Republican Asian policy had long seen a philosophical split between two broad camps: the first held that a stable and properly functioning US-China relationship was the prerequisite for American success elsewhere in the region. Get those ties right, the thinking went, and American allies and partners would be ready for cooperation and unafraid of being forced into grand strategic choices. The Nixon-Kissinger opening to China and George H.W. Bush's management of relations with Beijing were often offered as chief examples of this "inside-out" principle in action. The second camp, however, held not that good US-China relations produced productive partnerships with other countries, but rather the reverse: strong alliances and partnerships were necessary for stable US-China ties; shore up the former and the latter would flow from them. Here the Reagan administration's approach offered an attractive "outside-in" model.[57]

The George W. Bush team came down decidedly in the partners-first camp. As Green describes it, "Asia strategy flowed from this central premise that China's rise would best be shaped through a mix of engagement and shoring up a favorable strategic equilibrium centered on the maritime democracies."[58] That would include the region's five US treaty allies—Japan, South Korea, Thailand, the Philippines, and Australia—but also, potentially, India. And the strategic reverberations of increased cooperation with them would have not only regional consequences but global ones. As one of this book's authors observed in September 2001, in a speech given as US ambassador to India, Washington would "intensify collaboration with India on the whole range of issues that currently confront the international community writ large. In short, President Bush has a global approach to US-Indian relations."[59]

As a candidate, Bush criticized the Clinton approach to China as inconsistent: "One year," he charged, "it is said to be run by 'the butchers of Beijing.' A few years later, the same administration pronounces it a 'strategic partner.'" Bush's view would be clear and consistent, he said: "China is a competitor, not a strategic partner."[60] The new president's approach, however, was shaken early when a US surveillance plane collided with a Chinese jet fighter off the coast of Hainan Island in April 2001.[61] With the American crew held in Chinese detention, the administration sent a carefully worded letter of sympathy and condolence that won their release.[62] It demonstrated the effectiveness of diplomacy with Beijing, even—or especially—in the face of crisis.

In its early months, the Bush administration seemed poised to seek a balance of power in Asia aimed at precluding the emergence of any hostile hegemon. As the 2001 Quadrennial Defense Review, released just after 9/11 but largely prepared before then, put it: "Maintaining a stable balance in Asia will be a complex task. The possibility exists that a military competitor with a formidable resource base will emerge in the region."[63] The administration's approach would strengthen US allies and Washington's ties with them; encourage China's emergence as a constructive actor, including through increased trade and Chinese WTO membership; maintain diplomatic channels with Beijing to manage crises; and forge new partnerships with countries like India and Indonesia.

## 9/11 and the Galvanizing Force of Global Terrorism

The September 11 attacks upended Bush's foreign policy plans. It elevated counterterrorism as its number one priority and focused it on areas that posed the greatest threat of violent extremism—especially the Middle East and South Asia, but also Southeast Asia. Geopolitical competition receded as the imperative to join forces against a radical terrorist threat rose, and the administration would soon include in its ambitions the invasion and occupation of Iraq. As Bush put it in his January 2002 State of the Union address, "In this moment of opportunity, a common danger is erasing old rivalries. America is working with Russia and China and India, in ways we never have before, to achieve peace and prosperity."[64] In October, when he met with Chinese president Jiang Zemin for the first time, Bush welcomed Beijing's offer of help on intelligence and counterterrorism finance, observing that the Chinese had "no hesitation, no doubt that they would stand with the United States and our people during this terrible time."[65]

Terrorism would remain the focus of Bush's efforts for the duration of his administration but, as early as 2002, his team sought to adapt Asia policy for the new reality—and to retain the balance-of-power approach with which they had entered office. In a speech before the Japanese Diet in February 2002, Bush thanked Tokyo for its partnership on counterterrorism and aid to Afghanistan, but quickly moved on: "The success of this region," he said, "is essential to the entire world, and I'm convinced the 21st century will be the Pacific century."[66] The notion of a "century of the Americas" had disappeared entirely, and it would not return during the Bush years. In its place was a recognition of Asia's importance, in words that preview Hillary Clinton's Pivot article (itself titled "America's Pacific Century") a decade later: "America," Bush said, "is a Pacific nation, drawn by trade and values and history to be a part of Asia's future. We stand more committed than ever to a forward presence in this region."[67]

Bush's 2002 National Security Strategy, a document remembered mostly for the doctrine of preventive action against gathering terrorist threats, set out a vision of Asia as well. The events of 9/11 had elicited counterterrorism cooperation from key allies and friends, the strategy observed, including Australia, Japan, South Korea, Thailand, the Philippines, Singapore, and New Zealand. In the future, the administration would look to Japan "to continue forging a leading role in regional and global affairs"—picking up once again on the Nye-Armitage report—and would employ the relationship with Australia to that end as well. Notably, the strategy reiterated the hope, expressed earlier in Bush's State of the Union address, that the common threat of terrorism would reduce interstate friction. "We are attentive to the possible renewal of old patterns of great power competition," the document said. "Recent developments have encouraged our hope that a truly global consensus about basic principles is slowly taking shape."[68]

No consensus of the kind actually took shape. There would be no geopolitical convergence between Beijing and Washington during the Bush years, and the two governments would only grow more distant in outlook in the era to come. As Clinton had, the Bush team was bent on engaging China but, to an ever-greater degree, simultaneously hedging both by strengthening ties with other countries in the region and helping them grow in power. The administration struck free trade pacts with Singapore and Australia, designated the Philippines and Thailand as major non-NATO allies (a status that entitles designated countries to defense trade and security cooperation benefits), launched a formal new strategic partnership with India, formed a quadrilateral task force of Australia, Japan, India, and the United States to coordinate relief efforts following the 2004 Indian Ocean tsunami—the genesis of the Quadrilateral Security Dialogue (subsequently known as the "Quad")—supported Vietnamese admission into the WTO, and called on China, in a major speech by Deputy Secretary of State Robert Zoellick, to become a "responsible stakeholder" in the international system. As Michael Green would later reflect, "Nye's original 'engage and balance' approach to Asia had taken deeper root in US strategy."[69] Even as the war in Iraq dominated the Bush administration's focus, its array of activities in the Indo-Pacific region generated what one scholar has labeled the "Pivot before the Pivot."[70]

## Transforming the US-India Relationship and Seeking New Partners

The transformation of the US-India relationship represented a centerpiece of the Bush approach, and it became instrumental to future administrations' balancing efforts. When Bush took office, more than a hundred individual economic sanctions against India were in force, virtually no defense cooperation was taking place, Washington complained vigorously about every Indian missile test, and decades of diplomatic distrust plagued the bilateral relationship. Within a year, nearly all the sanctions were gone, defense discussions blossomed, India tested its missiles without US comment, and an intense and constructive diplomatic dialogue had begun. By June 2005, the administration had struck a landmark ten-year defense cooperation agreement with India that aimed to expand high-tech cooperation, boost missile defense, plan joint military exercises, increase bilateral commerce, and, critically, share civilian nuclear technology.[71]

Civil nuclear cooperation, given India's status as a de facto nuclear weapons state and non-signatory of the Non-Proliferation Treaty (NPT), would upend decades of US policy restricting such collaboration to NPT members. It required changes to domestic US and Indian law, as well as to multilateral export control regimes, and it required Washington to make an exception for India that it would not (and indeed, to this date has not) made for any other country. After a long and winding process, the US-India Civil Nuclear Agreement took effect. More was at stake than energy cooperation. Bilateral trade galloped ahead, from $20 billion in 2000 to $142 billion in 2018, and US foreign direct investment more than doubled.[72] The civil nuclear agreement carried broad strategic implications as well. As the *New York Times* put it, the move removed "a decades-long source of antagonism between the two countries," and produced "a significant gain in India's international status: from that of pariah, since it first tested a nuclear weapon in 1974 and refused to sign the Nuclear Nonproliferation Treaty, to something close to acceptance as a nuclear-armed nation."[73]

As the Bush administration wore on, it built on its attempted, unnamed pivot with a combination of moves. Singapore and the United States signed a strategic framework agreement in 2005 that enabled the two militaries to better cooperate, including in naval exercises.[74] In 2006, it agreed to realign the alliance with Japan, including to relocate US bases in order to reduce their domestic political friction, with a multi-billion-dollar contribution from Tokyo.[75] A month later the United States conducted the largest military exercise in the Pacific since the Vietnam War, which included some 22,000 American troops.[76] In 2007, the first quadrilateral military exercise took place among the United States, India, Japan, and Australia.[77] On the economic front, the administration granted Vietnam permanent normal trading relations status, signed a free-trade agreement (FTA) with South Korea, pursued (unsuccessful) FTA negotiations with Malaysia and Thailand, proposed a free trade area of the Pacific, and joined talks on the Trans-Pacific Partnership agreement, a trade pact then consisting of New Zealand, Singapore, Chile, and Brunei.

The administration also enhanced the US presence in Asia, strengthened alliances and partnerships, deepened economic connections, and helped friendly nations become more powerful. It built on the Clinton-era policy of engaging China and encouraging its peaceful evolution while hedging against a downturn in relations with it, largely by balancing its growing power. By the end of the Bush administration, US ties with China, Japan, Taiwan, and India were all relatively good, even if in its waning days a global financial crisis would help convince China's leaders—including newly named vice president Xi Jinping—that the West had entered a period of decline and China one of ascendance.[78]

## No Bush Pivot to Asia

What the Bush administration did not do, however, is pivot to Asia. It did not devote more time, energy, resources, and attention to that region by diminishing devotion to others. The hundreds of billions of dollars expended by the United States in Iraq and Afghanistan made the increase in military and other resources devoted to Asia pale in comparison. As late as July 2007, Bush would cancel a planned US-ASEAN summit—one set to mark thirty years of US relations with ASEAN—in order to focus on the imminent release of a "report card" to Congress on the surge in Iraq.[79] Secretary of State Condoleezza Rice skipped the annual ASEAN Regional Forum in 2007, for the second time in three years. The post–9/11 wars—in Iraq, in Afghanistan, and against terrorism more generally—consumed a very large proportion of defense resources, diplomatic engagement, policymaker time, and domestic political capital. The US military focused on counterinsurgency tactics rather than countering China's growing A2/AD capabilities, the largest US embassy in the world was in Baghdad, and the vast majority of security assistance went to countries in the broader Middle East.

The presidential candidate seeking to replace Bush made this seeming imbalance a key foreign policy theme during the 2008 election. "Over the last eight years," Senator Barack Obama said during a debate, "this administration, along with Senator McCain, have been solely focused on Iraq. That has been their priority. That has been where all our resources have gone. . . . In the meantime, we've got challenges, for example, with China. . . . The conspicuousness of their presence is only matched by our absence, because we've been focused on Iraq."[80] Soon Obama would gain the presidency, and with it his own chance to end the wars, redeploy US resources, lift America's strategic gaze from a region of long and grinding fights, and pivot to Asia. That shift would, in the event, prove easier said than done.

# 4

# Rhetoric Meets Reality

## Obama's Pivot to Asia

As a candidate for president, Barack Obama offered a foreign policy vision in stark contrast to that of the departing George W. Bush. Railing against a "foreign policy based on a flawed ideology," Obama pledged to end the wars Bush had started in Iraq and Afghanistan, to repair American standing in the world, to negotiate with the leaders of Iran and North Korea, and to focus on the transnational issues that he believed had been woefully ignored.[1] Asia featured prominently in his concept of America's role in the world.

Referring to himself after inauguration as "America's first Pacific president," Obama pointed to his childhood in Indonesia and Hawaii as formative experiences.[2] "The Pacific rim has helped shape my view of the world," he told a Japanese audience during his first year in office.[3] Whether he was, in fact, the first "Pacific president" is debatable—George H.W. Bush, for instance, served in the Pacific during World War II and led the US Liaison Office in China during the Nixon administration, and earlier presidents had their own Asia experiences—but Obama early on emphasized the region's importance. "Increasingly the center of gravity in this world is shifting to Asia," he observed on the presidential campaign trail, adding later, "It's time to strengthen our partnerships with Japan, South Korea, Australia and the world's largest democracy—India—to create a stable and prosperous Asia."[4]

Candidate Obama's instincts coincided with and were shaped by those who assumed key administration roles after Inauguration Day. A mid-2008 strategy authored by, among others, Anne-Marie Slaughter, Antony Blinken, Kurt Campbell, and James Steinberg, called for a "renewed US commitment to comprehensive engagement in [Asia] as a first-order priority of a national security strategy, not only as a peripheral interest to be subordinated to other regions or policy problems that compete for policy makers' interest and attention."[5] The same year, Campbell—who would serve as Obama's creative assistant secretary of state for East Asia and Pacific Affairs—argued that "America's strategic preoccupation in Iraq and Afghanistan is undermining its ability to adapt to major power shifts in the Asia-Pacific" and declared that it was time to "reassert America's strategic presence in the region."[6]

During the presidential transition, Obama challenged his advisors to examine the country's global priorities and determine where America was "overweighted" and "underweighted."[7] It appeared obvious to the president-elect that the United States was overweighted in Iraq, and he had already pledged to withdraw all American troops from the country. Others concurred. Jeffrey Bader, a campaign advisor who was Obama's first NSC senior director for Asia, recalled that Obama aimed to prioritize the Indo-Pacific even before he took office.[8] Secretary Clinton, Campbell remembered, said privately that "we are overinvested in the wars and machinations of the Middle East," and that it was time to reorient toward Asia.[9] The team decided to focus on early, visible signs of engagement in Asia. For a start, soon-to-be Secretary of State Hillary Clinton would make her initial official trip to Asia, making her the first to do so since Dean Rusk in 1961.[10]

## An Asia-First Foreign Policy

The new president instinctively wished to forge an Asia-first foreign policy, and his incoming team explored ways to engage more in Asia. Bader observed that "the general perception in Asia in 2009 was that the United States was distracted by the war in Iraq and global war on terrorism."[11] James Steinberg, who took a leading role on Asia policy during the presidential transition before serving as deputy secretary of state, recalled that "the frame for the Bush administration was dominated by counterterrorism," including in Asia, and he observed that, if the Nixon Doctrine aimed to avoid land wars in Asia, the Obama Doctrine was about avoiding land wars in the Middle East.[12] Danny Russel, who handled Asia on the NSC in Obama's first term and succeeded Campbell at the State Department in the second, observed that "there had been a phenomenal diversion of American resources . . . most importantly USG [US Government] mindshare—the time and attention of the US leadership—away from the Asia-Pacific region and lost in the sands of the Middle East."[13] Mark Lippert, a close aide to Obama in the Senate who became the NSC's chief of staff, put it bluntly: "Obama's fundamental strategic impulse," he recalled, "in the context of finite resources, was to right-size in the Middle East, hedge in Europe, and put strong focus on Asia, where he believed that the future of US strategic interests would increasingly lie."[14]

There were solid geopolitical and economic grounds for focusing more on the Pacific, and the political resonance was palpable as well: Obama had spent his campaign railing against a Bush approach that he labeled overly focused on Middle East threats, too militarized, insufficiently aimed at multilateral solutions to transnational challenges, and lacking in diplomatic engagement. Yet events intruded soon after Inauguration Day. Campbell recalls that the greater Middle

East animated the administration's first two years, with high-level officials attending meetings on Afghanistan nearly every day.[15] And before Clinton's 2011 article and subsequent speeches by Obama and others, there was little public articulation of a grand strategic shift to the Asia-Pacific. What the administration wished to accomplish in Asia—engage China, deal with North Korea's nuclear program, re-evaluate free trade agreements, strengthen the US-Japan alliance, engage more in Southeast Asia's political architecture, and forge cooperation on transnational issues—was clear enough. But there was as yet no public inkling of a geographic pivot from other regions toward the one most central to America's future. Indeed, as scholar and Bush administration official Victor Cha pointed out, "The priorities for the administration's early approach to Asia were not laid out in any formal document," even if there remained a strategic impulse behind them.[16]

If there was a unifying theme to the administration's early Asia approach, it was to build positive relations with China while strengthening ties with regional allies and potential new partners. Clinton, speaking ahead of her initial trip to the region, deemed it "essential . . . that we have a positive, cooperative relationship" with China. Some, she added, "believe that China on the rise is, by definition, an adversary. To the contrary, we believe that the United States and China can benefit from and contribute to each other's successes."[17] In the aftermath of the global financial crisis, the administration moved to coordinate economic responses with Beijing, including through the Group of 20 (G20).[18] While the administration strove to improve bilateral ties, it would simultaneously use "smart power" to "work with historic allies and emerging nations to find regional and global solutions to common global problems."[19] The notion of pivoting to Asia remained publicly unrealized; when asked why she was traveling to Asia first, Clinton noted its obvious importance—and then quickly hastened to mention that she was preparing for a NATO summit in Europe, would soon travel to Cairo, was working toward a Summit of the Americas, and would be addressing challenges in Africa.[20]

Nevertheless, the impulse to put Asia first remained real, particularly in diplomatic terms. Japanese prime minister Taro Aso became the first head of state hosted by Obama at the White House, and Indian prime minister Manmohan Singh was accorded the first state dinner of the new administration. Together with Chinese president Hu Jintao, Obama launched a bilateral "Strategic and Economic Dialogue," a mechanism unlike those in place with any other country, aimed at upgrading relations and smoothing difficulties.[21] The administration acceded to the Treaty of Amity and Cooperation with ASEAN, named the first-ever US ambassador to the Southeast Asian bloc, and announced the Lower Mekong Initiative to provide aid across the region (and, subtly, to compete with Chinese influence there).[22] Obama made a nine-day swing through Asia in November 2009, visiting Japan, Singapore, China, and South Korea.

Despite the flurry of activity, little was linear in the administration's approach to Asia—or to the region itself. The Democratic Party won elections in Japan in 2009, ending the Liberal Democratic Party's long rule, and Prime Minister Yukio Hatoyama signaled a new independence from Washington. He quickly sparked a diplomatic spat over the US Marines' Futenma air base in Okinawa, and endorsed the concept of an "East Asia Community" that would bring together the largest Asian countries—and exclude the United States.[23] The president did not initially share his predecessor's desire to cut trade deals in Asia, even in a region seeking to lower barriers after the global financial crisis, and he initiated a review of the previously negotiated US-Korea Free Trade Agreement (KORUS). China was on the verge of passing Japan as the world's second largest economy, and Obama's early efforts to build positive bilateral ties raised regional fears about the prospect of a Washington-Beijing "G2"-style condominium. Those fears were overblown. In six hours of meetings in Beijing during Obama's first year, President Hu gave little in the face of requests on Iran sanctions, Chinese currency valuation, and human rights.[24] Obama even publicly reiterated his predecessors' hope for China's long-run transformation: "When you start seeing economic freedom," he observed, "then political freedom starts . . . gearing up."[25]

## Rising Chinese Power

The Asian military balance was shifting, too. The Pentagon's 2010 Quadrennial Defense Review observed that the United States "welcomes a strong, prosperous, and successful China that plays a greater global role," but went on to fret about Beijing's military development and decision-making processes, and noted that its defense modernization programs raised "a number of legitimate questions regarding its long-term intentions."[26] The need for US forces to deter and defeat aggression in A2/AD environments—the first public inkling of what would become the "counter A2/AD" focus of American force planning—made an appearance, as did the goal of deepening strategic relationships with countries like Vietnam and Indonesia. For all the positive talk about the potential of constructive US-China relations, Obama's first QDR evinced hedging approaches as well.[27]

Similar threads ran through the administration's first national security strategy, released in 2010. Washington would, the document said, "deepen and update" its alliances with Japan, South Korea, Australia, the Philippines, and Thailand. It would play a stronger role in ASEAN, the APEC forum, and the East Asia summit. In addition to participating in this so-called regional architecture, in which diplomacy takes place, the administration pursued the nascent Trans-Pacific Partnership (TPP) trade agreement. In echoes of the Bush administration's "responsible stakeholder" notion, the Obama strategy welcomed "a China that takes on a responsible leadership role" to advance global priorities like economic recovery, countering climate change, and nonproliferation. Here, too, however, doubts about China's trajectory were present, if barely perceptible. "We will monitor China's military modernization program," the document said, "and prepare accordingly to ensure that US interests and allies, regionally and globally, are not negatively affected. More broadly, we will encourage China to make choices that contribute to peace, security, and prosperity as its influence rises."[28]

Trendlines in Chinese behavior clarified matters. Amid its flurry of Asian diplomacy, the Obama administration in July 2010 offered to facilitate talks over competing claims to islands in the South China Sea, an entreaty abruptly rejected by Beijing. Its leaders insisted that territorial claims there related to Chinese "core interests," were intrinsic to their sovereignty, and remained consistent with the UN Convention on the Law of the Sea.[29] They also complained about US arms sales to Taiwan. By mid-year, Washington and Beijing had effectively suspended regular talks between the two militaries, and China postponed an invitation for a visit by Secretary of Defense Robert Gates.[30] Obama publicly and privately pressed China to raise the value of its currency immediately, a move Beijing resisted but acceded to over time.[31] Observers in China increasingly spoke of American decline and disarray after the global financial crisis and inconclusive Middle East wars. Jeffrey Bader, the NSC senior director for Asia, observed that "by the middle of 2010 many China-watchers inside and outside the US government were beginning to write about what they saw as a more assertive China . . . the emergence of a somewhat different China from the one the United States had been dealing with for several decades."[32]

By the next year, China had become the world's second-largest economy. It was actively developing ports in Pakistan, Bangladesh, Sri Lanka, and Myanmar, making expansive maritime claims, improving its power-projection capabilities, supplying generous economic assistance to Southeast Asia and beyond, and showing little inclination to return the reassurance Washington had previously put on offer. The demand for greater American engagement in Asia was palpable among regional leaders, who were increasingly forging intra-regional security ties as a hedge against both China's rise and an American absence.[33] A change was also taking place among the American public: for the first time, polls showed that Americans saw Asia as more important than Europe.[34]

As the relative importance of Asia rose and as the region became more contested, the perception grew that the United States had been—and remained—distracted with other issues in other places. On the eve of the Pivot announcement, President Obama moved to withdraw the last US troops from Iraq, some seven years after the invasion. They would indeed leave—with dire costs that required an American return—by the end of 2011. Since taking office, Obama had nearly tripled the number of troops in Afghanistan to over 100,000, even as some two-thirds of Americans now said that war was not worth fighting.[35] In April 2011, the Congressional Budget Office estimated the costs of Iraq operations to that point at $752 billion, while Afghanistan war costs crested in 2011, at over $107 billion for the year.[36] To many observers both within and outside the administration, America had little to show for such titanic expenditures of national resources. Washington was seemingly trapped in an endless cycle: It was devoting maximum time, energy, and resources to regions with low return on investment, while the Pacific's vast dynamism went relatively untapped, and China was on the move. That, top officials believed, had to change. America had to pivot.

## Birth of the Pivot

Secretary of State Clinton's 2011 Pivot article put international attention on the administration's approach, but most Obama administration officials describe its strategic logic as the product of previous planning rather than the impetus for it. The internal strategy, they recall, was to do more in Asia by winding down the wars in Iraq and Afghanistan while holding resources stable in Europe. The administration pursued the approach even as the implementation of it remained a work in progress. By detailing administration efforts up to that point, the article described an approach that took shape even before Inauguration Day.

Other administration officials remember more improvisation.[37] Obama clearly wished to draw down in Iraq and Afghanistan and do more in Asia, but what else the Pivot might mean for the various regions remained opaque. The weighing up of specific costs and benefits, the consideration of risks and alternatives, and the calculation of resource trade-offs all remained incomplete. The *Foreign Policy* article, some administration officials recall, was not intended to announce a new strategic departure, and as a result was not backed by a rigorous planning process. The authors of a congressionally mandated assessment later found that the Pivot was "not built on an interagency process marrying strategy and resources—ways and means—to objectives."[38]

Many US strategic pronouncements are issued and quickly forgotten, as events change and new personalities come to drive new priorities. The Pivot to Asia was different. It became a defining, enduring feature of US foreign policy—a dominant theme of the Obama administration's global efforts and one that was continued, in different ways and under different labels, by the presidents to come. As a result, Clinton's article would be seen, in coming months and years as—for lack of a better term—*pivotal*, and illustrative of the decisive break the Obama administration wished to make in US grand strategy.

It was not seen that way at the time, even by those involved in its production. The article, multiple administration officials recall, was intended to describe their ongoing strategic approach, rather than announce a dramatic departure in US policy.[39] Campbell, the article's principal author, noted "the rarest of occurrences"—when "a government lays out a policy innovation and the new approach begins to attract enormous attention and serious questions."[40]

It certainly attracted both. Campbell recalled readers performing "a textual analysis like a biblical tract about what this meant."[41] And while the article may have described an overall strategy, the administration lacked key implementation details. Backed by insufficient policy planning and without a sustained diplomatic campaign to prepare American allies, questions immediately arose after the article's publication. The administration had to improvise answers. Yet the concept caught on, the name stuck, and senior officials filled in blanks over the coming months. Interested observers, foreign and American alike, relied mostly on speeches to discern the goals, proposed steps, required resources, and geographic implications of the Pivot to Asia.

## What's in a Name? The "Rebalance"

A good deal of consternation attended its very terminology. "Pivot," as Campbell would later recall, became "suddenly and indelibly affixed to US policy."[42] Former National Security Advisor Tom Donilon and others at the NSC worried that the name suggested a diminishment of commitment in other regions—a pivot *to* Asia by pivoting away *from* the Middle East and Europe—which would be received poorly by friends outside the Pacific. "The term 'pivot,'" Russel added, "created considerable misunderstanding of the policy" by connoting "weathervane-like fickleness."[43] These officials preferred the term "rebalance," believing that it elided any connotation of geographic abandonment. Campbell subsequently explained that the label implied not a pivot from one region of the world to another, but rather a pivot of *strategies*, and at other times he likened the approach to basketball—a pivot to keep moving down the court toward some goal.[44] Still, as he later acknowledged, "an unintended consequence of using the term 'Pivot' was that our allies thought we were turning away from them."[45]

It is by no means obvious that the issue was merely rhetorical or that a rebranding would have settled matters. One *rebalances* something that is unbalanced, after all, and if the strategy required more focus and resources in Asia, the implication remained that other regions would receive less. Over the coming years, some administration officials—including Donilon as national security advisor, Secretary of Defense Leon Panetta, and Secretary of State John Kerry— would consistently refer to the administration's "rebalance" to Asia. Campbell,

Asia hands inside and outside the administration, and President Obama himself would stick with "pivot."

In fact, the questions raised by the Pivot announcement were rooted not just in its name but also in its strategic logic, and they would not disappear if one word or another had been chosen to describe it. The Pivot was the public declaration by the United States that a region was now preeminent in its foreign policy, and for the first time that region was the Asia-Pacific. The natural corollary to such an announcement was to wonder what such an ordering of American priorities meant for a country that simultaneously defined its interests in global terms, had security commitments with scores of others, enjoyed strong economic relationships in every region, and retained a presence on every continent. At its core, no name for the new approach could relieve the inherent trade-offs any government faces in allocating its time and resources across issues and regions.

The Pivot's rhetorical packaging was not the only area that demanded more specifics. Clearly the administration wished to do more in Asia, and for straightforward reasons. The world's economic and demographic weight was moving to Asia, China was quickly emerging as a regional if not global competitor, and yet—as contrasted with, for example, the number of America's treaty allies in Europe, its trade integration in North America, or its military activities in the Middle East—Asia was underrepresented in US foreign policy activities. If American officials had participated in too few Asian diplomatic gatherings, made too few trips to the region, allocated insufficient military resources there, not pursued enough trade and investment agreements, and proposed a paucity of regional initiatives, the logic went, now was the time to step up.

## Controversy and Challenges

This "do more" mantra would turn out to be the least controversial attribute of the Pivot, and the one that would garner the most support from leaders in both parties, policymakers in future administrations, and outside observers. Though it had not previously been articulated as such, the notion of putting Asia first immediately acquired a commonsensical status. As Henry Kissinger observed:

In the immediate postwar period . . . the focal point of foreign policy was Europe: the restoration of Europe, the protection of Europe. . . . Europe remains important, but it is now safe from military attack. But in Asia, we have seen the emergence of a number of major countries of a scope much greater than [that of] the European national states: India, Japan recovering, and China. A rebalancing of American policy was inevitable.[46]

Richard Haass, president emeritus of the Council on Foreign Relations, described the new approach as "the best idea of [Obama's] presidency," and added that "America's strategic 'pivot' to Asia thus needs to be substantial and lasting."[47] Joseph Nye wrote that "the United States wasted the first decade of this century mired in wars in Iraq and Afghanistan. . . . The Obama administration's pivot towards Asia signals recognition of the region's great potential."[48]

Opposition to the Pivot among American experts came from several directions. Some Bush administration officials were miffed by the suggestion that the United States had to "return" to a region in which they had engaged deeply.[49] Others worried that the policy would be insufficiently resourced amid domestic priorities and budget sequestration, or that the United States might abandon the imperative to remain engaged in Europe, the Middle East, and Asia simultaneously. As the foreign policy expert Robert Kagan wrote, "Let's by all means give Asia the attention it deserves. But the world won't afford us the luxury of downgrading the importance of the other two regions. That's what it means to be a global superpower."[50] Still others feared that the Pivot, with its emphasis on beefing up military power in Asia, would provoke China. Zbigniew Brzezinski, national security advisor to Jimmy Carter, for instance, observed that the "so-called 'strategic pivot' " would be understood by Beijing "to mean that the United States is beginning to fashion a coalition against China, something which at this stage at least is premature and runs the risk of becoming a self-fulfilling prophecy."[51] Events would demonstrate that Beijing required no such prompting in order to adopt a more assertive foreign policy.

After the Pivot article's publication, administration officials endeavored to answer some of the questions it engendered. Obama embarked on an eight-day Pacific tour in November 2011, attending ASEAN meetings and becoming the first US president to participate in the East Asia Summit. "As we end today's wars," Obama told the Australian parliament, "I have directed my national security team to make our presence and mission in the Asia Pacific a top priority."[52] Strong language from the president, but even then Asia stood as "a" top priority and not "the" priority—a reflection of continuing administration debate over core principles of the "Pivot" or "Rebalance."

Cognizant that the recently passed Budget Control Act would soon impose draconian "sequestration" caps on military spending, Obama pledged that "reductions in US defense spending will not—I repeat, will not—come at the expense of the Asia-Pacific." The president announced a larger American military presence in Australia and the expansion of military activities with countries like the Philippines. Within weeks, the Pentagon would declare the deployment of littoral combat ships to Singapore and the stationing of Marines in Darwin, Australia.[53] By the end of the year, the administration welcomed Japan's newfound interest in the TPP trade agreement, won congressional approval of the KORUS, sent the secretary of state to Myanmar (making her the highest-ranking US official to visit since the 1960s), confirmed that the disputed Senkaku Islands were covered under the US-Japan alliance, and held consultations with regional governments after the death of North Korean leader Kim Jong-Il. The new policy direction—do more in Asia—seemed clear: "As President," Obama explained, "I have, therefore, made a deliberate and strategic decision—as a Pacific nation, the United States will play a larger and long-term role in shaping this region and its future."[54]

## The Rest of the World

If the impulse to become more diplomatically, economically, and militarily active in Asia was relatively straightforward, what the Pivot meant for other regions was not. As administration official Derek Chollet recalled, "The parts of the world where 'events elsewhere' took place wondered how this strategic shift would affect them." Europeans especially, he added, "fretted that more American time and attention in Asia meant less for them."[55] Campbell recalled, "Once the word pivot became affixed to US Asia strategy, there were immediate questions about what the word meant for the durability of US commitments in the Middle East and the future of transatlantic ties."[56] Bush administration official Thomas Christensen worried, "A deeper strategic problem for US diplomacy raised by the pivot is that it makes the United States appear unsteady and unable to handle two problems at once."[57] Clinton, for her part, insisted in her memoir that "America had the reach and resolve to pivot *to* Asia without pivoting *away* from other obligations and opportunities."[58]

The question of what precisely the Pivot meant for other regions would never be fully resolved. Officials made clear from the policy's inception that the shift was predicated, at a minimum, on the end of wars in the greater Middle East. In October 2012, Obama argued, "part of the reason that we were able to pivot to the Asia-Pacific region after having ended the war in Iraq and transitioning out of Afghanistan, is precisely because this is going to be a massive growth area in the future."[59] "Our desire to pivot," he added the next month, "was a response to a decade in which we understandably, as a country, had been focused on issues of terrorism, the situation in Iraq and Afghanistan. And as a consequence, I think we had not had the same kind of presence in a region that is growing faster, developing faster than any place in the world."[60] Campbell noted that the Pivot was "an argument against the overall orientation of the previous foreign policy strategy, which focused inordinately on the seemingly endless war on terror."[61]

That a successful pivot would require the diminishment of US military activity in the greater Middle East was clear as well as logical. From the beginning, Obama framed greater engagement in Asia as a peace dividend possible only with an end to wars in Iraq and Afghanistan, and Steinberg observed that "if there's anything that's a tradeoff," it may be in "force posture."[62] It appeared obvious that Washington would benefit from redirecting to Asia some of the tremendous, ongoing expenditures associated with the wars, along with the diplomatic exertions necessary to continue those fights. In Europe, the implications were more opaque. The Continent relied on an enduring US military presence for its defense, and NATO was vividly dependent on the United States for the 2011 military intervention in Libya. The Syrian civil war began to generate refugee flows that would destabilize European politics, and Russia appeared increasingly revisionist, though it would not seize Crimea until 2014. What the Pivot might mean for a Europe still dependent on the United States was unclear, and officials on the Continent resorted to speculation and reading between the lines.

In the face of such concerns, the administration routinely insisted that the United States *was* actively pivoting or rebalancing to Asia but *not* pivoting or rebalancing away from any other region. In March 2013, for instance, Tom Donilon, now national security advisor, addressed the Asia Society on broad US policy:

> In the coming years, a higher proportion of our military assets will be in the Pacific. Sixty percent of our naval fleet will be based in the Pacific by 2020. Our Air Force is also shifting its weight to the Pacific over the next five years. . . . The Pentagon is working to prioritize the Pacific Command for our most modern capabilities—including submarines, Fifth-Generation Fighters such as F-22 and F-35s, and reconnaissance platforms.

By obvious implication, a diminished proportion of military assets would be available for deployment to other regions. In the same address, however, Donilon hastened to reassure: "Here's what rebalancing does *not* mean. It doesn't mean diminishing ties to important partners in any other region."[63] State Department officials tried to reassure their transatlantic colleagues that the United States meant not to pivot to Asia *from* Europe, but rather to pivot to Asia *with* Europe. This was, unsurprisingly, a hard sell with NATO allies increasingly worried about their own region.

One way out of the conundrum, at least with respect to military resources, might have been to generate more for all regions; a proportional increase in Asia need not mean a decrease elsewhere if the overall pie was growing. In fact, however, spending was on the decline. The Budget Control Act, passed in

2011, imposed draconian caps on defense expenditures. In the coming years, US defense expenditures would amount to $500 billion less than previously anticipated.[64] Defense spending stood at 4.6 percent of GDP in 2010, 4.2 percent in 2012, 3.4 percent in 2014, and 3.2 percent in 2016.[65] In military terms, the pie was shrinking—no matter which region got the largest slice.

Still, had savings from the wars ending in Iraq and Afghanistan been large enough, the redeployment of those military resources to Asia may have squared the rhetorical and practical circle. Despite Obama's pledge to remove all troops from Afghanistan by the end of his second term, however, he left office with a force of nearly 10,000 still in the country, accompanied by many thousands of contractors.[66] US troops returned to Iraq in order to fight the Islamic State (or ISIS). The administration also conducted episodic military activities in Libya, Yemen, and Somalia. To be sure, the American military commitment in the Middle East was far less than at the height of the George W. Bush surge in Iraq, and resources expended in Afghanistan declined significantly from their heights during the Obama surge. Yet the peace dividend was much smaller than originally anticipated.

The difficulties in rededicating focus from other places and issues to the Asia-Pacific went beyond the bean-counting of military resources. Economic assistance faced similar challenges. In 2014, for instance, the administration's budget requested $93.7 million in aid for East Asia to support a "strategic rebalance." Not only was this figure dramatically lower than assistance budgeted for the Middle East ($1.2 billion) or South Asia ($1.18 billion, mostly for Afghanistan and Pakistan), but it also was lower than US aid for every other region in the world. The nation of Liberia, for instance, was set to receive more economic assistance that year than all of East Asia and the Pacific combined.[67]

Further stretching resources was the fact that only twenty-four hours remained in a day, and the time of senior policymakers was at a premium. How they allocated their time turned not only on the administration's stated strategic priorities, but also on their personal projects and preferences. John Kerry, during his confirmation hearing for secretary of state, said that he wanted to "take on the word 'pivot,'" which he said "implies that we are turning away from somewhere else. I want to emphasize we are not turning away from anywhere else. Whatever we do in China should not, or in the Far East . . . should not come and, I hope, will not come at the expense of relationships in Europe or in the Mideast or elsewhere. It can't."[68] Indeed, in contrast to Clinton's focus on diplomacy in the Pacific, Kerry would dedicate his first year at the State Department to the pursuit of an Israeli-Palestinian final-status peace agreement. In the years following, he and other senior State officials would focus on securing a nuclear deal with Iran and an agreement with Russia to manage the Syrian civil war.

## From Diplomacy to Defense

While the cross-regional implications of the Pivot remained unresolved, its approach within Asia itself marked a further elaboration of strategic logic first articulated in the 1995 East Asia Strategy Review. The Nye Report had made the case for strengthened Asian alliances, especially but not limited to Japan, and for new multilateral security initiatives. It argued for the stabilizing effect of forward-deployed US troops and against a retrenchment or peace dividend in Asia. Washington should, the report said, engage with China from a position of strength and encourage Beijing to evolve in constructive ways, and America's strengthened regional presence and relationships would hedge against a possible downturn in Chinese behavior.

Now, sixteen years after the Nye Report was published, the Obama administration doubled down on the engage-but-balance approach to Asia. Where the Clinton administration had resolved to retain the American military presence in Asia, the Obama team would seek to augment it. Where the Nye Report made the alliance with Japan the centerpiece of US engagement in Asia, the administration would now deepen that relationship and others besides. And it would add an ambitious trade component, which would itself signal US commitment and presence in a region that placed significant value on economic engagement. As a result, after the Pivot's announcement the administration wished to give greater meaning to the strategy across the defense, diplomatic, and economic domains.

Precision on its ultimate objectives, however, remained elusive. In 2014, the Center for Strategic and International Studies reviewed three years of official statements about the Pivot to Asia, attempting to discern its key goals. While common themes emerged, the precise contours were all over the map. In her 2011 article, Clinton described six lines of activity as fundamental to the Pivot. In November that year, Obama highlighted three critical components. A year later, Donilon emphasized five "distinct lines of effort" and, in April 2013, a White House fact sheet on the rebalance listed six objectives. By late 2013, National Security Advisor Susan Rice described the administration's policy as seeking progress in four key areas, and the State Department released its own fact sheet with seven objectives for the rebalance to Asia. In each case, not only the number of goals but also their character shifted, and all this in the first three years after the policy's announcement.[69]

The administration continued to emphasize its Asian diplomacy and defense cooperation, and it aimed more at Southeast Asia, an intra-theater shift of geographic focus from Northeast Asia that some would describe as "the Pivot within the Pivot."[70] Obama became the first US president to visit Myanmar in 2012, taking advantage of a limited political thaw there, and the administration agreed with ASEAN to support the drafting of a regional code of conduct for the

South China Sea.[71] It sealed a US-Vietnam Comprehensive Partnership in 2013 and increased cooperation in a range of areas as well.[72] The 2014 QDR pledged to "maintain a robust footprint" in Northeast Asia while "enhancing our presence in Oceania and Southeast Asia," and emphasized deepening security ties with non-treaty allies, flagging Singapore, Malaysia, and Vietnam for special attention.[73] In 2014, Obama became the first US president in decades to visit Malaysia and later agreed on a new 10-year defense agreement—the Enhanced Defense Cooperation Agreement (EDCA)—with Manila.[74] The same year, the administration launched the US-ASEAN Defense Forum and, in 2016, Obama hosted foreign ministers and heads of state from all ten ASEAN countries for two days of discussions.[75] The administration then rescinded the ban on the sale of lethal military equipment to Vietnam, which had been in place since the 1970s.[76] This intensification of US engagement with Southeast Asia during the Obama years was one of the administration's most important, least-noticed accomplishments.

Building on the Bush administration's ties with India also became increasingly important. Early in his first term, Obama endorsed India's permanent membership on the UN Security Council and reformed export controls to give India better access to US technology. The administration went on to establish the US-India Defense Technology and Trade Initiative, aiming to boost co-production and development, and in 2016 it made India a "major defense partner" and concluded an agreement on defense logistics. Obama and Prime Minister Narendra Modi appeared to enjoy productive personal ties as well.

As crises erupted in other regions, the administration endeavored to demonstrate the continuing importance of Asia in its foreign policy. In November 2015, for example, just after horrific terrorist attacks took place in Paris, and amid ongoing military operations against the Islamic State, Obama left a multilateral summit meeting in Turkey to visit the Philippines and Malaysia—a signal, his aides said, of the priority the administration placed on Asia despite crises in Europe and the Middle East.[77] It was, and remains today, a difficult balance. The price of focusing time and attention on Asia, it appears, is the absence of significant crises in other regions.

Despite military activities elsewhere, the Pentagon issued new strategic guidance in 2012, emphasizing, "while the US military will continue to contribute to security globally, *we will of necessity rebalance toward the Asia-Pacific region*" [emphasis in original]. It pledged to expand security ties with new regional partners, invest in the relationship with India, defend against North Korean provocations, and maintain a regional balance of military power.[78] The resources necessary to carry out such a plan, the document suggested obliquely, would come from other regions. "Most European countries are now producers of security rather than consumers of it," it explained. "Combined with the drawdown in Iraq and Afghanistan, this has created a strategic opportunity to rebalance the US military investment in Europe."[79] The same year, Secretary of Defense Leon Panetta announced that by 2020 the US Navy would move from a 50/50 percent split of its forces between the Pacific and the Atlantic to a 60/40 split between the oceans. The Department would later pledge to base 60 percent of the Air Force in the Pacific as well.[80]

In time, the defense pivot would become more complicated than such a straightforward accounting suggests. More naval vessels would be stationed in the Pacific, but the overall size of the US fleet shrank during the intervening years. Unlike in the Middle East and Europe, the Asia theater was never the beneficiary of Overseas Contingency Operations (OCO) funding—the billions of dollars in "emergency" spending that funded both the counter-ISIS campaign and the European Deterrence Initiative (EDI), an effort to support rotational force deployments, infrastructure investments, and new capabilities in Europe after Russia's seizure of Crimea. From 2014 through 2021, nearly $30 billion was allocated to EDI through OCO funding, while no such emergency funding went to the Asia-Pacific. When, in 2020, Congress established an analogous Pacific Deterrence Initiative, it allocated no dedicated funding.[81]

In the meantime—and with greater consequence than its effort to shift US military resources—the Obama administration encouraged its Asian defense partners to do more themselves. In 2015, for example, it welcomed the decision by Shinzo Abe's government to reinterpret Article 9 of the Japanese constitution, allowing the country to engage in "collective self-defense"—joint military action with other countries, even if the home islands were themselves not attacked.[82] It also urged Tokyo to beef up its ballistic missile defenses and purchase F-35 aircraft, won access for US naval ships to Cam Ranh Bay in Vietnam, agreed to deploy THAAD missile defenses to South Korea, donated naval vessels to the Philippines, and restored defense cooperation with New Zealand.[83]

## The Trade Stumbling Block

While the Pivot yielded more activity in Asia on the diplomatic and defense fronts, the trade agenda started with huge ambition but ended in failure. The administration was almost entirely quiescent on the trade front in its first term, only winning approval of the US-Korea Free Trade Agreement (KORUS). The lack of an affirmative economic agenda taxed the American effort to signal leadership and engagement in Asia, where trade relations have outsized importance relative to other regions. All of this seemed to turn positive when the administration expressed interest in the TPP agreement, and more still when Japan indicated a willingness to negotiate its entry into the pact.

Suddenly available was not simply another bilateral trade deal but a pan-regional one that included some of the world's biggest economies. Administration officials, and many observers outside government, concluded that US entry into TPP—an agreement which, not incidentally, excluded China—would provide not only economic benefits but strategic ones as well. American membership would signal regional leadership, demonstrate staying power, and further bind key Asian economies to the United States and each other. At a moment when China's economic gravity was quickly making it the top trade partner of numerous Asian nations, TPP would provide greater market access to countries wishing to diversify their portfolio of commercial relations.

As the negotiations progressed, administration officials pointed to the agreement as critical to the Pivot to Asia. National Security Advisor Donilon described it as "an absolute statement of US strategic commitment to be in the Asia-Pacific for the long haul."[84] Secretary of Defense Ash Carter famously said that passing TPP was as important to him as an aircraft carrier.[85] But time was running out on the administration's clock. Having waited until late in the second term to complete the negotiations—the agreement was signed in February 2016—Obama was forced to press for congressional approval in his final year, never a period of great presidential sway.

He tried. In his last State of the Union address, Obama called on Congress to approve TPP, saying, "You want to show our strength in this new century? Approve this agreement."[86] In May 2016, the president observed that "the Asia-Pacific region will continue its economic integration, with or without the United States. We can lead that process, or we can sit on the sidelines and watch prosperity pass us by."[87] And in September, during a visit to Laos, he said, "Failure to move ahead with TPP wouldn't just have economic consequences. It would call into question America's leadership in this vital region."[88]

And so it would. By the end of his eight-year term, Obama lacked the political muscle to push TPP through Congress, and the politics of trade were growing more difficult. The agreement became embroiled in the 2016 presidential race, and, during the campaign to succeed Obama, the final four candidates in both parties all opposed the TPP agreement. It went unapproved by the United States, and, in January 2017, newly elected President Donald Trump would formally withdraw the United States from the pact.[89]

With the demise of TPP, the United States had virtually nothing to show for the Pivot's economic pillar. KORUS was merely a renegotiation of the deal already reached under the Bush administration in 2007, and, despite agreement to work toward comprehensive bilateral investment treaties with China and India, neither came to fruition. Administration officials touting the TPP's strategic value were correct, but the flip side was also true: the searing retreat of the United States from economic leadership in Asia—especially while China was gaining—had geopolitical reverberations. The defeat raised questions about American staying power and political commitment to Asia, precisely the areas in which the administration was trying to reassure the region.

## Sharpening US-China Competition

In the years following the Pivot's announcement, the administration's approach to China hardened, with officials placing less emphasis on the potential for cooperation and complaining more about Chinese behavior. The administration had started out by speaking of the need for "strategic reassurance" with Beijing and respect for one another's "core interests."[90] Regional worries caused the administration to drop most of the suggestive rhetoric for the remainder of Obama's first term, and it instead emphasized the need for closer alliances and partnerships in Asia. Whereas China went wholly unmentioned in the seventy-nine pages of the Bush administration's 2001 QDR, Obama's 2012 defense strategic guidance referred to the "friction" that might be caused by China's growing military power, noted that Beijing was pursuing asymmetric means to counter US power-projection capabilities, and pledged to ensure US military freedom of action in contested areas.[91] By 2013, Obama was publicly demanding that Beijing cease cyberattacks on the United States and end its billions of dollars in intellectual property theft.[92] The administration also opposed, unsuccessfully, the creation of the China-led Asian Infrastructure Investment Bank (AIIB).

Its disposition toward China depended, however, not only on events but also on personnel. John Kerry, in his confirmation hearings for secretary of state, expressed skepticism about the Pivot and opposed an overly militarized approach to Asia.[93] Susan Rice, who replaced Tom Donilon as national security advisor, spoke publicly in November 2013 of operationalizing China's proposal for a "new model of major power relations."[94] This formulation raised fresh regional anxieties about a framework in which only "major powers" like Washington and Beijing would steer events.[95] This appeared to not at all be what the administration had in mind, and the gap between rising skepticism toward Beijing and the rhetorical characterizations soon narrowed. Vice President Biden, a month after Rice, emphasized that "this new model of major country cooperation" had "to be based on trust," and at the following year's Shangri-la Dialogue in Singapore, Secretary of Defense Chuck Hagel endorsed a "new model of relations"— jettisoning the reference to "major powers." Hagel made more news by charging that "China has undertaken destabilizing, unilateral actions asserting its claims in the South China Sea."[96]

In the administration's last years, the rhetorical zigs and zags of its early second term subsided, and its public pronouncements increasingly mirrored the underlying engage-but-balance approach. By 2015, speeches and documents featured increasing references to US-China competition rather than cooperation. Obama's second national security strategy observed, "While there will be competition, we reject the inevitability of confrontation. At the same time, we will manage competition from a position of strength while insisting that China uphold international rules and norms on issues ranging from maritime security to trade and human rights."[97] Here the administration foreshadowed its successor, which would make competition with China the explicit centerpiece of US policy.

Events were pushing policymakers in precisely this direction. In September 2015, Obama won at least a theoretical concession on cybertheft, his number one priority with China, when Xi pledged that Beijing would not steal intellectual property for commercial gain, a commitment he did not fulfill.[98] And another problem was lurking: Xi denied privately and publicly that China was militarizing artificial islands it had established in the South China Sea, when in fact it was doing precisely that.[99] Throughout the year, Obama publicly demanded that China halt its construction on disputed land in the South China Sea and cease its military activities in the region. Beijing would not do so.[100]

The slide in US-China ties grew vivid during Obama's final trip to Asia, four months before his departure from the White House. Arriving in Hangzhou for the G20 summit, the American president met with President Xi, and the differences were stark. Obama emphasized human rights while China's leader stressed its opposition to interference in its internal affairs. Obama threatened "consequences" if China violated maritime law in the South China Sea while Xi said that Beijing would "unswervingly safeguard" its claims there.[101] The long-hoped-for cooperation with China seemed more distant than ever, and the areas of disagreement and competition more numerous.

## The Consensus

By the conclusion of the Obama administration, the notion of an American pivot to Asia had become commonplace inside government. The declaration of a geographic rebalance had utility within the US government as a signal of policy priority. As Michael Green notes, after the announcement of a pivot, "Captains and majors coming back from multiple deployments to Afghanistan and Iraq began applying to study Chinese, Korean, and Japanese instead of Urdu and Arabic."[102] Intelligence officials seeking to make the case for greater attention to Asia, despite security crises in the Middle East, Afghanistan, and Europe, found greater support after the president declared the Pacific to be America's strategic priority.[103] The Pentagon announced that, for the first time, a four-star general would command the Army in the Pacific and, as scholar David Shambaugh concluded, "Since the Obama administration's pivot initiative, INDOPACOM (as US Pacific Command would become known during the Trump administration) has become *the favored* regional command in resources, equipment, training, exercises, defense partnerships, and deployments."[104] The administration put TPP negotiations ahead of those for a Trans-Atlantic Trade and Investment Partnership (TTIP) agreement, and for a time the focus on Asia-Pacific matters received a bureaucratic boost it would have otherwise lacked.

Yet the Pivot never outgrew its early improvisation. Without a careful planning process, a rigorous weighing of costs and benefits, an analysis of alternative scenarios, or prior consultations with allies, the strategy remained rhetorically confusing and even contradictory. Although on paper the United States was pivoting, or rebalancing, to Asia, it had not previously left the region. While Washington would increase at the margin the share of defense and other resources devoted to the Pacific, it would not diminish its commitment to other regions. The United States planned to reap dividends from the end to wars in Iraq and Afghanistan, but they raged on—and combat began in new Middle East theaters. Asia would remain preeminent in foreign policy even as Russia emerged as a direct threat to its European neighbors—and to American elections. The strategy would endure despite sequestration cuts to defense spending, the administration insisted, while at least one Pentagon official claimed it could not.[105] The Pivot's economic centerpiece, one with strategic-level positive effects, would be an ambitious trade agreement sweeping up 40 percent of global GDP, though the administration left congressional approval to the very end of a two-term presidency—too late, it turned out, to see it through.

And yet the Pivot's obvious strategic appeal endured. At its most foundational, US policy has long aimed to ensure that the Asia-Pacific region does not fall under the domination of a hostile hegemon. The Pivot was in part a method intended to ensure that it would not. For that reason, and against all odds, much of its rhetorical essence would be retained by the incoming administration. As the Trump team took office, it would employ balancing to compete with China rather than encourage cooperation. It would explicitly prioritize the China challenge and the Asian theater in its national security planning. And President Trump would—episodically and inconsistently—apply his own merciless logic to reducing commitments in Europe and the Middle East.

# 5

# Turning on China

## The Pivot during the Trump Administration

In winning election in 2016, Donald Trump became the first US president to enter office without prior public service. His lack of policy experience did not, however, prevent him from holding deep-rooted views about America's place in the world and the role of Asia in US foreign policy. During the campaign, Trump often expressed disappointment with the way foreigners treated Americans, and derided previous presidents' tolerance for the abuse. The United States, he said, had "become a dumping ground" for immigrants wreaking violence.[1] Allies were free-riding, underinvesting in their own defense while growing rich under American protection. Fruitless foreign wars had sapped US resources and consumed the lives of servicemen and women, while—above all—a legacy of terribly negotiated trade deals had positioned key countries to steal American jobs and wealth. Much of his pitch to voters relied on a pledge to right these wrongs.

### Trade Enters Center Stage

Trade, and Asia's role in it, featured prominently in Trump's campaign promises. For all of Washington's focus on other elements of Chinese behavior, from militarizing the South China Sea, to Uyghur repression in Xinjiang, to the theft of intellectual property, Trump zeroed in on the trade deficit. His rhetoric about Japan was rooted more in the 1980s than the early twenty-first century, by which time worries about Japanese economic competition had faded as Japan sank to the world's number three economy and became a source of allied solidarity rather than a threat to American jobs. But before his election, Trump rarely framed events in Asia in terms other than trade and its purported ravaging of the US economy.

"We're going to bring jobs back from Japan, we're going to bring jobs from China," he said in a 2015 presidential debate.[2] In a subsequent debate, he added that the TPP agreement was a "horrible deal." It was, he said, "a deal that was designed for China to come in, as they always do, through the back door and totally take advantage of everyone" and observed that China was "the number-one abuser of this country."[3] He asserted that the United States was "losing now over $500 billion in terms of imbalance with China, $75 billion a year imbalance with Japan," adding that India, too, took advantage of the United States.[4] In yet another debate, Trump accused China of "ripping us on trade. They're devaluing their currency and they're killing our companies."[5] He observed that "we've lost anywhere between four and seven million jobs because of China," and asked, "Who the hell has to lose $505 billion dollars a year?"[6]

Trump's hyper-focus on trade, his belief that trade deficits represent money taken by foreign countries from the United States, and his identification of China as the greatest offender endured throughout the campaign and his presidency. As a candidate and in the early years of his term, trade policy played an over-whelming role in Trump's approach to Asia. At various times he accused China, Japan, India, and Vietnam of stealing American jobs and wealth, labeled Beijing and Tokyo as currency manipulators, and floated the idea of imposing significant tariffs to right the situation.[7] As one analyst put it during the president's first year, where Obama had sought a rebalance to Asia, Trump was rebalancing toward trade.[8]

Yet economic relations did not comprise all of Trump's early views on Asia. He also rejected the idea of greater US engagement in Asia, and there was thus no mention of any US pivot to the Pacific. He asserted during the campaign that China had "tremendous control" over North Korea, and that he would "let China solve that problem" of Pyongyang's nuclear program.[9] He observed that because of the growing national debt, the United States could "no longer defend" Japan and South Korea, that America should not serve as the world's policeman, and he indicated a willingness to withdraw US forces from both countries unless their governments paid more in host nation support.[10] Beijing's militarization of the South China Sea illustrated the fact that China was "totally disregarding our country," a situation made far worse because "we have made China a rich country because of our bad trade deals."[11]

The contrast with the previous administration's rhetoric on Asia could hardly have been starker. Where Obama and his senior officials often described the re-gion in rhapsodic terms—as the most promising, dynamic part of the world, and the one in which America's destiny would be written—Trump saw a far darker picture. Key Indo-Pacific countries were ripping off the United States, bolstered by bad trade deals and the deployment of US troops to countries unwilling to pay their fair share. They disrespected the United States and had taken advantage of weak American presidents unwilling to pursue an agenda that put America first. Trump would. Asia would represent a key arena in which his policies would play out.

During the transition, Trump began fulfilling some campaign pledges, mod-ified a few of his approaches, and took unprecedented diplomatic steps. He announced in November 2016 that he would withdraw the US from TPP upon

taking office and instead pursue "fair bilateral trade deals that bring jobs and industry back."[12] In a stroke, the indispensable economic pillar of Obama's Pivot
to Asia was eliminated. Prime Minister Shinzo Abe became the first international leader to meet the president-elect, and he began a relationship that would
reduce Trump's previous animosity toward Japan.[13] Trump held a phone call
with Taiwanese President Tsai Ing-wen—no president or president-elect had
spoken directly with a Taiwanese leader since the 1979 normalization of ties with
China—foreshadowing an irreverence for diplomatic norms that would be on
vivid display in summits with North Korea.[14] He went on to say that he did not
feel "bound by a one-China policy unless we make a deal with China having to
do with other things, including trade."[15]

## The Rise of Personal Diplomacy

As Abe demonstrated during his Trump Tower meeting, personal relationships
would become unusually important in the new administration. Rather than
relying on mid-level diplomacy, the administration "elevated the importance of
leader-to-leader diplomacy."[16] Partly as a result, Trump spent more time in the
Indo-Pacific region during his first three years in office than Obama did in his
first four, making a total of five trips to Asia as president.[17] As he did so, Trump
focused on high-profile official visits to China, Japan, and India, as well as bilateral nuclear diplomacy with North Korean leader Kim Jong Un. Where Obama
put an emphasis on multilateral diplomacy, attending almost all the APEC,
ASEAN, and EAS summits, Trump missed six of the eight multilateral meetings
in the region over his first three years.[18]

The impact of Trump's personal diplomacy was profound, and frequently
led to reversals of his positions. After taking office, Trump spoke with Indian
leader Narendra Modi; instead of repeating his criticism of Indian trade
practices, he labeled the country a "true friend and partner" and invited Modi
to Washington.[19] During Modi's subsequent visit in June, Trump declared his
intention to continue America's alignment with India, even while decrying
the bilateral trade deficit.[20] After speaking to acting South Korean president
Hwang Kyo-ahn, gone were the campaign-era threats to withdraw American
forces from the peninsula. The United States, Trump now said, had an "ironclad" commitment to defend South Korea, and he agreed to strengthen the two
countries' capabilities against the North.[21] Trump told Abe in a call that he was
"dispatching Mad Dog [Secretary of Defense James Mattis] to Japan quickly," on
what was widely branded a "reassurance trip." Trump emphasized to Abe that
"this is very meaningful," and then agreed to play golf with the prime minister at
Mar-a-Lago.[22]

Indeed, some of the administration's early diplomacy seemed an effort to reassure Asian countries that Trump's campaign-era rhetoric was only that, through statements that were undoubtedly written by officials. In another encounter with Abe, the president said publicly that the United States was "committed to the security of Japan and all areas under its administrative control and to further strengthening our very crucial alliance."[23] On the phone with Xi Jinping, Trump told the Chinese president that he would not upend preexisting US policy on Taiwan and would honor the One-China policy.[24] And in March 2017, Secretary of State Rex Tillerson visited Japan, South Korea, and China.

Despite elements of continuity with its predecessor, the new administration's approach to Asia also featured major departures. The secretary of state declared during his trip that "the policy of strategic patience" with North Korea had ended, and suggested the possibility of preemptive military action against its nuclear program.[25] In Beijing, Tillerson publicly adopted Chinese catchphrases, including the need for "mutual respect" and "win-win" cooperation, words that were widely interpreted to mean US deference toward China's "core interests" like Taiwan, Hong Kong, Tibet, and the South China Sea.[26] Tillerson even took advantage of public portions of his trip to call for cuts to the State Department budget.[27]

A focus on specific issues and bilateral relationships—especially trade and North Korea—animated the administration's early months more than a concentration on any particular region. Ahead of Tillerson's trip, acting Assistant Secretary of State for East Asia and Pacific Affairs Susan Thornton addressed the previous administration's elevation of the Indo-Pacific among its global priorities. "On the issue of pivot, rebalance, et cetera," she said, "that was a word that was used to describe the Asia policy in the last administration. I think you can probably expect that this administration will have its own formulation . . . we haven't seen in detail what the formulation will be or if there even will be a formulation."[28] Before the administration published its national security strategy in late 2017, it gave little indication of Asia's preeminence in its foreign policy.

Instead, personal interactions continued to significantly shape the president's approach to Asia. Following their first meeting, Trump and Xi agreed on a 100-day plan to avoid a trade war—a move that would prove wholly unsuccessful.[29] After speaking with Australian prime minister Malcolm Turnbull, the president declared, "We get along great. We have a fantastic relationship. I love Australia," setting aside previous friction over a deal to resettle in the United States refugees held by Canberra.[30] Together with Vietnamese prime minister Nguyen Xuan Phuc, Trump declined to repeat his previous criticism of the bilateral trade deficit and instead announced some $8 billion in commercial deals and the transfer to Vietnam of a US Coast Guard cutter.[31]

## Fire and Fury

Trump did, however, quickly elevate North Korea in his pantheon of threats. In just his third month in office, the president said that the United States was prepared to act alone if China did not bring Pyongyang to heel.[32] An administration official said that the "clock is very, very quickly running out" and that all options remained on the table for dealing with North Korea. Thornton described North Korea's weapons program as "an urgent and global threat."[33] Trump talked North Korea and trade with Xi at a Mar-a-Lago meeting, punctuating the session with a US missile strike against Syria. The administration then reportedly dispatched an aircraft carrier to the Sea of Japan, a move described by Trump's national security advisor, H. R. McMaster, as designed to "give a full range of options to remove" the North Korean threat.[34] Trump upped the rhetorical ante by telling a Fox Business news interviewer, "We are sending an armada, very powerful. We have submarines, very powerful, far more powerful than an aircraft carrier, that I can tell you."[35] It soon emerged that the carrier had not deployed north after all, but rather sailed south for joint exercises with the Australian Navy.[36] But the sense of crisis over North Korea was just beginning.

In July, after Pyongyang tested a missile that could reach Alaska, Trump called on China to "put a heavy move on North Korea and end this nonsense" and at the G20 summit thanked Xi for his efforts, adding that it was "an honor to have you as a friend."[37] Never a model of consistency, however, Trump within weeks was accusing China of doing "nothing" to help on North Korea, even as his State Department cited Beijing's "unprecedented steps" to increase pressure on the regime.[38] In Manila for the ASEAN summit, and then on a Southeast Asia swing, Tillerson consistently raised North Korea and urged governments to cut funding streams to the North.[39] After the *Washington Post* reported that Pyongyang had successfully miniaturized a nuclear warhead for mating to a ballistic missile, and as a North Korean spokesman said that Pyongyang was considering a plan to attack Guam, Trump publicly warned Pyongyang—in perhaps the harshest terms since the Korean War—to stop its threats. If it did not, the president said, the country would be "met with fire and fury and frankly power, the likes of which this world has never seen before."[40]

Previous administrations had wrestled with the problem of North Korea's nuclear program for decades, and Obama reportedly told Trump during the transition that Pyongyang would loom as the new president's top foreign policy challenge.[41] Never before, however, had events seemed to build toward crisis like they were now. Pyongyang was testing new ballistic missiles with longer ranges than ever before, perfecting warhead production, and issuing dramatic public threats of attack. Some senior officials in the administration believed that, unlike other nuclear weapons states, North Korea was undeterrable.[42] Trump himself seemed galled that previous presidents had not taken decisive action to eliminate the festering threat and appeared resolved to do so once and for all. He declared that if North Korea "does anything in terms of even thinking about attack[ing]," then "things will happen to them like they never thought possible."[43] The US military, he said, was "locked and loaded."[44]

The crisis continued when North Korea launched a nuclear-capable missile over Japan in August 2017, a move Abe called an "unprecedented and grave threat" to his country. The missile traveled more than the distance necessary to hit Guam, and Pyongyang reiterated its threats to strike the US territory. Even before the missile overflight, Tokyo had deployed Patriot missile defense systems and an Aegis destroyer along a possible missile flight path.[45] When Pyongyang tested a hydrogen bomb in September, Trump threatened to stop trading with any country doing business with North Korea and announced that he would approve the sale of new military equipment to Japan and South Korea.[46] The same month, in his first speech before the UN General Assembly, Trump promised to "totally destroy North Korea" if it threatened America or its allies. "Rocket man," he said of Kim Jong Un, "is on a suicide mission for himself."[47]

Other presidents struggled to manage the North Korea problem, but none had their Asia agendas as consumed by it as Trump did during his first year in office. While trade remained on the agenda with nearly every country, North Korea quickly became the top non-trade issue. Countries in the region, including those who sought closer ties with the United States to balance growing Chinese power, privately fretted about the degree to which US-China relations had become focused on the hope that Beijing would resolve the North Korea crisis.[48] Trump praised Xi during a visit to Beijing and even declared, "I don't blame China" for its trade deficit with the United States.[49]

The two central pillars of the administration's Asia policy—trade and North Korea—even converged in several ways. Trump signed an executive order targeting individuals and companies in third countries doing business with the North, and he heaped praise on China when its banks dialed back its dealings with Pyongyang.[50] On his first trip to Asia as president, Trump emphasized both of his priorities during a five-country swing. In Tokyo, he carped on the trade deficit and observed that Japan could shoot North Korean missiles "out of the sky" by buying more military equipment from the United States.[51] Speaking before the South Korean legislature, the president mentioned trade only briefly but insisted that "the world cannot tolerate the menace of a rogue regime that threatens with nuclear devastation . . . the longer we wait the greater the danger grows and the fewer the options become."[52] At the APEC summit in Vietnam, Trump pivoted back to trade, declaring trade imbalances unacceptable, accusing countries of stripping jobs, factories, and industries from the United States, and offering bilateral trade agreements with countries wishing to engage in "fair and reciprocal trade."[53]

## Rejecting Globalization

In contrast to his recent predecessors, Trump portrayed Americans not as beneficiaries of globalization, but rather as the victims of it. The administration's constant complaints about trade deficits, its withdrawal from the TPP, enthusiasm for tariffs, criticism of other trade agreements (Trump replaced NAFTA with a new agreement and renegotiated KORUS), and casting of economic interactions as zero-sum affairs together handed China an opportunity to seize the mantle of globalization. In January 2017, Xi Jinping delivered a speech at the World Economic Forum in Davos, declaring, "We should commit ourselves to growing an open global economy. No one will emerge as the winner in a trade war."[54] Ten months later, at the APEC summit, Xi called for fostering "an open economy that benefits all. Openness brings progress, while self-seclusion leaves one behind." In contrast to the Trump administration's attacks on the World Trade Organization (WTO) and withdrawal from the TPP, Xi added, "We should support the multilateral trading regime and practice open regionalism to make developing members benefit more from international trade and investment."[55]

Words would prove easier than actions. For all of Trump's protectionist instincts, and in an era when skepticism about trade agreements had risen in both political parties, the American economy nevertheless remained far more open than China's. Even as the administration withdrew from various pacts, undermined the WTO's dispute-resolution mechanism, and imposed a variety of tariffs, its moves together paled in comparison to enduring Chinese practices. Beijing, throughout the Trump administration, continued to subsidize state-owned enterprises, force foreign firms to transfer technology, steal intellectual property, limit the renminbi's convertibility, and enforce investment rules that favored local companies over foreign ones.[56] US absence from the two pan-regional trade agreements—the TPP and the RCEP, which included China—undermined America's attempt to expand its regional presence and balance China's growing economic weight. Yet while Trump emphasized the "America first" character of his international economic policy, Beijing never successfully overcame the perception that, for all its purported embrace of enlightened globalism, the actual approach was resolutely "China first."

## Competing with China

Trade and North Korea did not on their own consume the entirety of Asia policy. Before long, the administration began to take steps that resembled its predecessors' hedging strategies. In Vietnam, Trump announced a three-year agreement on bilateral defense cooperation and reaffirmed a plan for an aircraft carrier visit to Cam Ranh Bay the next year.[57] The president put aside Washington's concerns about Thailand's military coup and human rights abuses in the Philippines to meet with the leaders of both countries, and he revived the US-Japan-India-Australia Quadrilateral Security Dialogue that had lain fallow since 2010.[58] The administration began referring to the region as the "Indo-Pacific," picking up on Japanese terminology, and suggested that India should play an integral role not only in its immediate neighborhood but also in East Asia. In a major conceptual shift, it identified the goal of US policy as the promotion of a "free and open Indo-Pacific," a formulation that would endure, with varying definitions, through Trump's term and into the Biden administration.

At the end of its first year in office, the Trump administration issued a National Security Strategy (NSS) which would, together with the soon-to-follow National Defense Strategy (NDS), alter how Washington conceptualized and talked about foreign policy. Hedging against China had increased since the middle of the Clinton administration, but the new strategy put the problem in stark terms. China and Russia, it said, "challenge American power, influence, and interests, attempting to erode American security and prosperity. They are determined to make economies less free and less fair, to grow their militaries, and to control information and data to repress their societies and expand their influence." While US policy for decades was rooted in the belief that China's integration into the international order would have a liberalizing effect, the document said, "China expanded its power at the expense of the sovereignty of others." Beijing was spreading features of its authoritarian system, building the world's most capable military after America's, and growing its nuclear arsenal. "China and Russia," it said, "want to shape a world antithetical to US values and interests. China seeks to displace the United States in the Indo-Pacific region, expand the reaches of its state-driven economic model, and reorder the region in its favor."[59] Henceforth relations with China would be characterized not by engagement but competition—competition for influence, for allies and partners, and for leadership.

Nadia Schadlow, a deputy national security advisor for strategy and the NSS's lead drafter, observed that the Obama-style Pivot to Asia did not appear in the document. Nevertheless, she noted, "there was definitely a sense that we're going to reduce a military presence in the Middle East," and that a greater focus on the Indo-Pacific would be required in light of the China threat.[60] The Obama effort to pivot to Asia, Schadlow added, was not premised on the recognition of a revisionist China or the need to treat China as an adversarial competitor.[61] The Pivot, she said, was during the Trump administration "superseded by a strategy premised on competing with a major revisionist power."[62]

The NDS, issued a month later, doubled down on the shift of emphasis toward competition. It said that "China is leveraging military modernization, influence operations, and predatory economics to coerce neighboring countries to reorder the Indo-Pacific region to their advantage." The stakes, it said, went well beyond Asia: "it will continue to pursue a military modernization program that seeks Indo-Pacific regional hegemony in the near-term and displacement of the United States to achieve global preeminence in the future."[63] America's military advantage in the Indo-Pacific was eroding in China's direction, and the need to re-establish its military edge must take precedence. As a result, great power competition, and competition with China in particular, assumed center stage in the administration's list of national security priorities—a greater priority than counterterrorism, stabilization operations in the Middle East, or even North Korea.

McMaster circulated to the cabinet a third strategy, the "US Strategic Framework for the Indo-Pacific," in early 2018 after briefing it to the president. Matthew Pottinger, who led Asia policy at the NSC and went on to serve as deputy national security advisor, observed that the document— declassified at the administration's end—remains "the most important guide for what we actually did."[64] The strategy aims to maintain "diplomatic, economic, and military preeminence in the fastest-growing region of the world" just as China's rising power and influence "challenge the U.S. ability to achieve its national interests in the Indo-Pacific region."[65] In listing multiple lines of effort aimed at this and other objectives, Pottinger recalls, the document nowhere uses the term "Pivot." Nevertheless, he added, "I was very much sympathetic with the Hillary Clinton/Kurt Campbell period of the first term of Obama. . . . I viewed our strategy as an attempt to pick up where they left off in 2012."[66]

As a result, one may discern a de facto prioritization of the Indo-Pacific in the Trump administration's regional priorities. It never specifically embraced or rejected the Pivot, either in rhetorical or policy terms, but the upshot of its articulated strategy was to put rhetorical emphasis on China as its preeminent challenge and Asia as the priority theater. "If you read the assumptions, the end states we're seeking, and then the objectives and actions," Pottinger observed, "you can see that it was very much about trying to shift resources and focus and intellectual energy to the first island chain. It also had the newer idea of stitching together the Indo-Pacific into a broader theater."[67]

Such crisply articulated formulations had, however, only an inconsistent claim on the administration's policymaking. It is not clear, for instance, that Trump ever read the NSS, though he delivered a speech emphasizing some of its elements.[68] John Bolton, after succeeding McMaster as national security adviser, said that the NSS was "written and filed away . . . and consulted by no one."[69] Nevertheless, the twin documents had an impact in other parts of the administration that far outweighed most others issued over the years. The NDS shaped Pentagon thinking and budgeting until the final days of the Trump administration, even as personnel changed. The strategies clarified within government the country's national security priorities, even amid crises like North Korea and under a president prone to rapid shifts in attention and activities. It also freed policymakers and experts publicly to abandon, at last, the hope of engagement with China and to adopt the reality of acute competition. Instead of engage-but-hedge, America would now primarily balance. The balancing strategy that had for more than two decades been secondary to engagement with China now became the major thrust of US efforts.

## The End of Engagement

Remarkably, the strategies were largely well-received, even by those who opposed the Trump administration and many of its policies. Kurt Campbell, who was at the center of the Obama Pivot (who would return to government as President Biden's Indo-Pacific coordinator) wrote with Ely Ratner (who himself would go on to serve as Biden's assistant secretary of defense for Asia), "The Trump administration's first National Security Strategy took a step in the right direction by interrogating past assumptions in US strategy." The combination of diplomatic and commercial engagement, regional balancing, and efforts to integrate China into the liberal international order, they said, had largely failed. Now necessary was "acknowledging just how much our policy has fallen short of our aspirations."[70] Thomas Wright, who became a key drafter of the Biden administration's 2022 NSS, argued that though Trump's NSS suffered from "contradictions and shortcomings," the document was ultimately a "valuable and thoughtful contribution to the discourse."[71]

Not all observers agreed with the diagnoses, and some believed the administration was far too confrontational and discouraging about the possibilities of cooperation with Beijing. Robert Zoellick, who served as president of the World Bank and deputy secretary of state in the George W. Bush administration, criticized the NSS premise that "cooperation with China failed," as well as its emphasis on "constant confrontation," warning that "those who assume that China has not acted constructively within the US-guided system—who assume that China is only a disrupter—are misleading themselves."[72] In addition, Trump would routinely make statements and take actions at odds with his own stated strategies for the remainder of his term. For all these caveats, however, the elevation of Beijing and the embrace of a fundamentally competitive relationship with China represented the crossing of a Rubicon.

While the two public strategies broke a taboo against declaring the long-enduring engagement policy a failure, they also reflected existing trends, including the increased power and ambition of China under Xi Jinping, the growing prominence of America's balancing efforts in Asia, and the retreat of other threats—terrorism most prominently—that previously took top priority in national security thinking. Though they did not represent an explicit rhetorical Trump pivot, akin to the Obama aspiration to rebalance US attention, energy, and resources from other regions to Asia, senior officials did offer strong echoes.

In June 2019, the Pentagon issued the Indo-Pacific Strategy Report, the first publicly issued US strategy document on Asia since the 1995 Nye report. In it, Acting Secretary of Defense Patrick Shanahan declared the Indo-Pacific "the Department of Defense's priority theater" and labeled it "the single most consequential region for America's future," invoking largely the same reasoning—demography, economics, geopolitical contestation, and America's Pacific orientation—that had animated the Obama administration. The strategy contained elements that would have been familiar in the Nye balancing approach twenty-five years prior, including sustaining US presence in the region, deepening alliances with Japan and other nations, and remaining militarily prepared for a spectrum of future security challenges in Asia.[73]

Similarly, Secretary of State Mike Pompeo wrote in November 2019 that US engagement in the Indo-Pacific region was "a top priority" for the administration and that "the US government has taken many steps to meet President Trump's prioritization of the Indo-Pacific." He went on to tout a 25 percent increase in assistance to the region compared to the last three years of the Obama administration, "representing a dedicated shift of resources to the Indo-Pacific."[74] Fleshing out the administration's concept for a "free and open Indo-Pacific," Pompeo observed that "free" meant the ability of nations to protect their sovereignty against coercion, while "open" meant both "access to seas and airways" and "fair, reciprocal trade."[75] While the Obama administration might have favored a less cramped view of trade agreements and included democracy and values in the mix, the Trump administration's FOIP notion rhymed considerably with the vision of Asia outlined in its predecessor's Pivot approach.

Beyond the rhetorical framing, the administration would make concrete efforts to prioritize the Indo-Pacific above other regions—by attempting to redeploy troops from the Middle East and Africa to Asia, for instance, and by increasing military and other financial assistance to Asia but not to other regions—that echoed Obama's attempted Pivot. In the implementation, however, it would also run into formidable obstacles like those that bedeviled its predecessor.

## Changes in North Korea and Trade Policy

Before that, however, came a dramatic shift in one of the two pillars of Trump's early approach to Asia. In March 2018, the president agreed to meet Kim Jong Un in person, after the North Korean leader pledged to stop testing nuclear weapons and move toward denuclearization.[76] Tillerson, who the day before had said, "in terms of direct talks with the United States . . . we're a long way from negotiations," would quickly be replaced as secretary by Mike Pompeo.[77] As CIA director, Pompeo had played a key role in North Korean diplomacy, secretly visiting Pyongyang for talks with Kim.[78] On a return trip in May 2018, now as secretary of state, he won the release of three American prisoners held in the North.[79] His engagements had the effect of preparing the way for an unprecedented meeting between the American and North Korean leaders.

The Trump-Kim summit was on, off, and then back on again before it took place in Singapore in June 2018.[80] A more dizzying change in US policy was hard to envision. The president who, just months before, was threatening to rain down fire and fury on North Korea was now embracing its leader. The two issued a vague joint statement, and Trump agreed to suspend American joint military exercises with South Korea, one of Pyongyang's long-standing demands. Kim made no specific commitments to disarm, and he clearly reveled in the attention given to him by the American president and the global media.[81] But the nuclear and missile tests that had provoked so palpable a sense of crisis would not resume during the Trump presidency. Despite more dramatic summit meetings in Hanoi and in the Korean demilitarized zone, and irrespective of futile efforts by US diplomats to win progress on denuclearization, North Korea would not again assume such a central place in the administration's foreign policy efforts.

Things were changing on the trade prong of the administration's approach to Asia as well. Trump's fixation on trade deficits had not dimmed—far from it—but the administration's gaze shifted.[82] It won minor changes to KORUS and declared victory with Seoul.[83] Trump threatened Japan with a 25 percent tariff on imported automobiles unless Tokyo agreed to bilateral trade talks, which it would do in short order.[84] The two sides would go on to ink an agriculture-focused trade agreement in October 2019 that provided for limited tariff reductions and quota expansions to improve market access. By the fall of 2018, Trump's trade wrath fell more squarely on China. He announced tariffs on $250 billion worth of Chinese-made goods and declared the trade imbalance unacceptable.[85] "I am a Tariff Man," he wrote. "When people or countries come in to raid the great wealth of our Nation, I want them to pay for the privilege of doing so."[86]

## China, China, China

The national strategies issued by the Trump administration had lumped together the challenges posed by China and Russia as the return of a generalized "great power competition." China, however, was quickly overtaking Russia as the administration's priority. Given the relatively paltry economic relationship with Russia, Trump focused his trade energies—and his tariffs and negotiations—on Beijing. Trump's seemingly warm relationship with Vladimir Putin, though it clashed directly with his administration's increasingly hardline policy toward Moscow, helped turn Russia policy into a domestic political football. China was different, as attitudes toward Beijing hardened in both political parties. In his first day on the job as acting secretary of defense, Patrick Shanahan gathered civilian leaders to emphasize the Department's focus. It was, he said, "China, China, China."[87]

Bilateral tensions increased across the board. Washington and Beijing imposed retaliatory tariffs on each other's goods in multiple rounds, while Chinese human rights abuses, efforts at technology dominance, and regional assertiveness made headlines. In December 2018, Canada arrested the chief financial officer of Huawei, a Chinese telecommunications conglomerate, at US request.[88] The Department of Justice subsequently indicted the company on a variety of charges, including sanctions evasion.[89] By 2019, 60 percent of Americans had an unfavorable opinion of China, up from 47 percent just a year earlier.[90] Before the end of the year, the US Commerce Department put 28 Chinese companies on the "Entity List," barring Americans from doing business with them, over their alleged involvement in human rights abuses against Uyghur Muslims in Xinjiang.[91]

Yet consistency remained rare in the administration's approach to Asia. There appeared during the Trump era two parallel tracks, which only sometimes proceeded in synchronization. The president, focused largely on trade issues, personal relationships, the need for allies to pay more for their defense, and North Korea, took the lion's share of attention at home and abroad. In many ways, Trump pivoted *away* from any constructive, multilateral relationship with Asia. Several senior officials were, simultaneously, attempting to strengthen America's military presence in the Indo-Pacific, resist the expansion of Chinese economic and diplomatic influence, strengthen relationships with key allies and partners, and, ultimately, to raise the priority assumed by Asia in the administration's foreign policy. They were, in other words, deepening and strengthening the balancing activities—now called "competition"—inherited from their predecessors, and adding to them.

Congress reinforced those efforts. It passed the BUILD Act in October 2018, establishing a new Development Finance Corporation to make loans and investments in poor and low-income countries. Beijing's Belt and Road Initiative was the primary driver behind the legislation, which aimed to leverage private sector funds to compete with Chinese economic influence.[92] The bill, which Trump promptly signed into law, signaled shifting priorities. The president entered office proposing to abolish the Overseas Private Investment Corporation (OPIC), and numerous members of Congress remained deeply skeptical of foreign aid. Rep. Ted Yoho, a Republican from Florida, told the *New York Times*, "My whole impetus in running for Congress in the first place was to get rid of foreign aid. It was my thing." Yet both he and Trump supported the BUILD Act, which would build on OPIC, rather than replace it, and would increase overall development assistance. "I've changed, and I think he's changed," Yoho said, "and it is all about China."[93] Democratic Senator Chris Coons, who had pushed a more generic form of the idea for three years prior to passage, noted, "We rebranded to focus it on China." Speaking about the initiative, Bob Corker, chairman of the Senate Foreign Relations Committee, added, "So much of our foreign policy now is focused on trying to check China, especially their nefarious activities."[94]

Congress also played a key role in maintaining overall foreign affairs spending, including on diplomacy and foreign aid, in Asia and elsewhere. Trump's fiscal year 2018 budget request sought $40.5 billion in foreign affairs spending, a cut of over 30 percent from the previous year, proposed to end development assistance as an aid category, and recommended halving support for health programs in South and Central Asia. Congress rejected the request in its entirety, instead appropriating $55.9 billion for FY18, 38 percent more than requested.[95] The next year, Congress answered Trump's proposed $42.2 billion in the FY19 foreign affairs budget, a 24 percent cut from the previous year's allocation, by appropriating $56.1 billion in foreign affairs spending.[96] Trump finally proposed a $44.7 billion foreign affairs budget for FY21, a cut of 22 percent from the previous year's enacted level, excluding emergency funds. This was again rejected in favor of an overall budget of $62.7 billion, including $5.3 billion in emergency funds.[97]

In December 2018, the Asia Reassurance Initiative Act (ARIA) became law, which authorized spending on regional partnerships in a variety of areas.[98] The bill, which received bipartisan support in both houses, specified that its funding aimed to "counter the strategic influence of the People's Republic of China."[99] A year later, Congress would appropriate $2.5 billion to fulfill the legislation's goals, a move that co-sponsor Senator Cory Gardner said was aimed to "ensure the United States remains the preeminent Pacific power for generations to come."[100] Two years later, the new Pacific Deterrence Initiative aimed to improve US military posture in the Indo-Pacific and enhance regional partnerships to counter China.[101]

Yet even as senior administration officials and Congress worked to solidify ties with key countries across the Indo-Pacific, the parallel presidential track often pointed in a different direction. ARIA supported US participation in the APEC forum, for instance, but Trump declined to attend the APEC leaders' meeting in 2018 and missed the East Asia Summit meetings in 2018 and 2019.[102] In June 2019, the Pentagon issued an Indo-Pacific Strategy Report that touted the strengthening of Asian alliances, including with Japan. The alliances were, the report said, "indispensable to peace and security in the region and our investments in them will continue to pay dividends for the United States and the world."[103] That month, Trump openly questioned the same alliance. "If Japan is attacked," he said, "we will fight World War III. We will go in and we will protect them and we will fight with our lives and with our treasure. We will fight at all costs, right? But if we're attacked, Japan doesn't have to help us at all. They can watch it on a Sony television, the attack." Trump also demanded enormous increases in Japan and South Korea's host-nation support payments, reportedly requesting in late 2019 that Seoul pay five times the existing level, or about $5 billion annually.[104] Trump similarly asked Japan to quadruple annual payments for US forces stationed in the islands to around $8 billion.[105] Both countries refused, later agreeing to incremental increases during the Biden administration.[106]

In the meantime, Trump's personal leader-level diplomacy continued, with mixed results. After the Commerce Department banned US companies from selling to Huawei in May 2019, Trump spoke by phone to Xi the next month and announced that he would allow it—only to reverse the policy again later.[107] The president threatened new tariffs on $300 billion in Chinese imports, but after meeting with Xi at the G20 summit, said that he would not impose them.[108] After failing to reach agreement in Hanoi, Trump asked Kim Jong Un to meet at the Korean demilitarized zone and there invited him to visit the White House. The two agreed to restart negotiations, talks that would again fail to bear fruit.[109] During a visit to Washington by Prime Minister Modi, Trump publicly offered to mediate between India and Pakistan over Kashmir. He observed that American mediation, a long-standing ask of Islamabad and opposed by New Delhi, was a request of Modi's.[110] It was not, and Modi later rejected the offer.[111]

The administration had some notable diplomatic successes, including the Quad's revival. In 2019, Trump and Prime Minister Lee Hsien Loong extended by fifteen years an agreement allowing US forces to use Singaporean air and naval bases.[112] India and the United States agreed on the purchase of new American military equipment, including helicopters, as well as energy purchases.[113] The president never made human rights a major priority, but his administration took an increasingly hard line in response to Chinese practices in particular. In October 2019 it sanctioned a group of Chinese technology companies connected to human rights abuses in Xinjiang, including Hikvison and Dahua Technology, global leaders in video surveillance.[114]

In January 2020, Trump and Chinese vice premier Liu He agreed on the elusive first phase of a bilateral trade agreement. The pact cut some US tariffs on Chinese goods in exchange for Chinese pledges to purchase more American farm, energy, and manufactured goods, and barred forced technology transfer. Beijing committed to buying $77.7 billion in additional American manufactured products over the 2017 level, with a $32.9 billion increase to come in 2020 and $44.8 billion in 2021. Even with the new agreement, however, US tariffs remained on some $370 billion in Chinese goods.[115] The Chinese commitments would ultimately go unfulfilled, and the tariffs would remain in place through the end of the Trump administration and into the next one.[116]

## COVID-19 Infects US-China Relations

Some observers blamed the emergence of COVID-19 for China's failure to meet its purchase commitments.[117] Whatever its effect on Chinese trade practices, by early 2020 the global pandemic affected the Trump administration's Asia policy, along with nearly everything else. By March, the president publicly and routinely blamed China for the pandemic, calling it the "Wuhan virus" and emphasizing its origins in China. Robert O'Brien, who succeeded Bolton as national security advisor, charged that the "outbreak in Wuhan was covered up."[118] Beijing tried to reverse the accusations, ludicrously asserting that the US military had somehow brought COVID to Wuhan.[119] Trump went on to announce American withdrawal from the World Health Organization, which he said mishandled the pandemic, and said, "The world is now suffering as a result of the malfeasance of the Chinese government."[120] In June, Trump labeled the pandemic the "kung flu" and began using the term at public rallies.[121] Gone were the hopes of getting a transformative trade deal with Beijing, and in its place the administration took a series of steps aimed at responding to Chinese behavior. "We were unshackled," Pottinger remembers.[122]

By mid-2020, in a world reeling from pandemic, recession, and uncertainty—and amid a vigorous US presidential campaign—relations with China were deteriorating rapidly. In a May 2020 Rose Garden address, the president previewed a series of actions that would be taken against China: (1) reviewing disclosures by PRC companies listed in United States securities markets;

(2) eliminating policy exemptions that gave Hong Kong different and special treatment; (3) revising the State Department travel advisory for Hong Kong; (4) sanctioning officials involved in eroding Hong Kong's autonomy; and (5) restricting high-risk PLA researchers from entering the United States and threatening US intellectual property.[123]

In July, Trump rescinded Hong Kong's preferential economic status after Beijing abridged internationally agreed commitments to the territory's political autonomy. Congress passed, and Trump signed, a law that imposed sanctions on Chinese officials who violated the fundamental rights of Hong Kong citizens. In announcing the steps, Trump added that "we hold China fully responsible for concealing the [coronavirus] and unleashing it upon the world."[124] The president went on to use emergency powers to ban TikTok, a popular Chinese social media platform, from operating in the United States. His executive order noted the possibility that ByteDance, the company that owned TikTok, could pass users' personal data on to Chinese authorities. "This data collection," the order read, "threatens to allow the Chinese Communist Party access to Americans' personal and proprietary information—potentially allowing China to track the locations of Federal employees and contractors, build dossiers of personal information for blackmail, and conduct corporate espionage."[125] A US judge blocked the ban on TikTok, which never went into effect, but the gloves were off in the administration's overall approach to China.[126]

In a parting blow, Secretary of State Pompeo said the administration had determined that China committed "genocide and crimes against humanity" in abusing Uyghur Muslims in Xinjiang.[127] He declared that the "morally repugnant, wholesale policies, practices, and abuses are designed systematically to discriminate against and surveil ethnic [Uighurs] as a unique demographic and ethnic group, restrict their freedom to travel, emigrate, and attend schools, and deny other basic human rights of assembly, speech, and worship."[128] Antony Blinken, Biden's nominee to replace Pompeo at State, would agree with the genocide label during his confirmation hearing.[129]

## The Problem of the Pivot

Even when the administration attempted to reorient resources toward the Indo-Pacific, it ran into some of the same practical challenges that had bedeviled its predecessor. After the trio of strategy documents had been issued, Pottinger recalls struggling in 2018 to deprioritize other objectives and issues in order to enhance Asian engagement.[130] One solution was to rebalance diplomatic resources within the region itself, by demoting the importance of mid-level diplomacy, ending broad dialogues with Beijing, to thereby "deprioritize China in order to have a strategy for the broader region that could hem in China."[131] Another was to shift bureaucratic resources. At the administration's outset, for example, the NSC Asia directorate comprised just five officials, while the Middle East directorate boasted nineteen—with another twenty working in the counter-terrorism directorate, disproportionately on the Middle East. By the end of the administration, the NSC Indo-Pacific directorate had become the White House's largest.[132]

Shifting military resources would prove far more difficult. Asked about the administration's plans to draw down troops in Afghanistan, Africa, and else-where in 2019, Secretary of Defense Mark Esper highlighted the importance of China as the Pentagon's number one priority. In 2019, he said, "I should like to go down to a lower number . . . because I want to either bring those troops home, so they can refit and retrain for other missions or/and be redeployed to the Indo-Pacific to face off our greatest challenge in terms of the great power competition that's vis-a-vis China."[133] The Pentagon's plans included abandoning a recently built, $110 million drone base in Niger and ending assistance to French forces battling militants in Mali, Niger, and Burkina Faso.[134]

The proposed redeployment generated backlash abroad and at home. France's Minister of Defense visited Washington to warn that cuts to US military as-sistance would decimate joint counterterrorism efforts in West Africa.[135] She said that US support was "critical to our operations and its reduction would se-verely limit our effectiveness against terrorists," in a joint news conference with Esper.[136] Rep. Mac Thornberry, the ranking Republican on the House Armed Services Committee, urged the secretary to "carefully consider the adverse implications of reducing our force posture in Africa," and cautioned that "the threat of violent extremism and terrorism persists" in the region overseen by US Africa Command.[137] By the end of January 2020, Esper announced that the United States would not remove all of its forces from Africa, and instead would carry out a global troop review aimed at freeing up more resources to address challenges from China's military.[138]

Trump's proposal to withdraw 9,500 US troops from Germany, down to a total of 25,000, faced an even greater backlash. Robert O'Brien, the president's na-tional security advisor, stated that "the main reason" for the reduction was the imperative to deploy US forces in a more forward and expeditionary manner in order "to counter China and Russia."[139] Pentagon officials further explained that the plan was "part of the Pentagon's broader effort to redistribute US forces across the world to better compete with new threats from Russia and China."[140] The president himself, however, described things differently. "We're protecting Germany and they're delinquent," he said. "Until they pay, we're removing our soldiers, a number of our soldiers." Germany, he added "takes, and then on top of it they treat us very badly on trade."[141]

A bipartisan outcry in Congress helped stall the effort. Senator Mitt Romney condemned the plan as a "grave error," stating that "is a slap in the face at a friend and ally when we should instead be drawing closer in our mutual commitment to deter Russian and Chinese aggression."[142] He and senators on both sides of the aisle introduced legislation to prevent the withdrawal of troops from Germany.[143] In the end, the administration never implemented the plan, and it was formally withdrawn under the Biden administration.[144] The damage to the US-German alliance remained, however, and with no benefit to Indo-Pacific force posture.

The Trump administration did succeed in a drawdown, one which garnered largely bipartisan support. The president had campaigned on a promise to bring US troops home from the Middle East and end the "forever wars," a sentiment which, by November 2019, had become a common refrain from presidential candidates in both parties. Despite increasing the number of troops in Afghanistan at the beginning of his term, Trump reduced the total number of US forces there from just over 7,000 in November 2016 to 4,000 in November 2020.[145] By January 15, 2021, that number was down to 2,500, with the residual soon to be withdrawn by the incoming Biden administration.[146] Whatever the specific merits of an Afghanistan drawdown, however, it did not appear to translate into new US capability in the Indo-Pacific.

There should have been more military resources available for all regions during the Trump administration, as the shackles of sequestration were loosened and then eliminated. Congress began legislating around the spending caps beginning with the 2018 defense budget, and the limits expired in 2021.[147] Yet from a force deployment perspective, at least, the changes were relatively modest. Total US troops deployed in the Middle East (excluding Afghanistan and Turkey) stood at slightly more than 42,000 in 2016 and rose to nearly 46,000 in 2020. In the Indo-Pacific, the total went from 77,355 in 2016 to 87,550 in 2020. The number of total American troops in Europe rose by around 8,000 over the same time span.[148] The vaunted increase in the percentage of the US Navy based in the Indo-Pacific (from 50 percent to 60 percent), a goal dating back to the Obama administration, took effect. Even then, however, America's military presence in the region was a mere handful of ships greater than what it was previously.[149] The administration aspired to a larger navy but did not build one; emphasis instead went into making Asia the last region to see its naval presence shrink.[150]

As Trump prepared to depart office, it also became clear how little his administration had to show for its efforts to transform trade with Asia. The president conducted an almost exclusively defensive policy—renegotiating existing deals (as with South Korea), achieving modest sectoral agreements (as with Japan), putting sanctions in place (as with Chinese individuals and entities), and imposing tariffs (on Chinese goods and the production of steel and aluminum elsewhere). Beijing never fulfilled its purchase agreements, and the flurry of trade activity did not transform either the US economy nor win major new market access in the Indo-Pacific.

By withdrawing from the TPP, however, and by demanding trade concessions (and vastly increased host-nation support) to offset America's regional security commitments, the administration undermined its aim of balancing Chinese economic weight.[151] The remaining eleven TPP signatories formed the Comprehensive and Progressive Agreement for Trans-Pacific Partnership (CPTPP), which entered into force in March 2018 without the United States. Though its goals largely remained largely the same as the TPP, the most significant change was to suspend intellectual property provisions pushed by the United States.[152] The other pan-Asian trade agreement, the Regional Comprehensive Economic Partnership (RCEP), came into force in 2020. The United States again stood apart from RCEP's fifteen member states, including China, and with more than two billion people covered by the agreement.[153]

The Trump administration did not enter office pledging to pivot to Asia, and several of its moves—the withdrawal from the TPP, trade disputes with allies, fights over host-nation support, and the overwhelming early focus on North Korea—detracted from the effort to balance Chinese power. No later than the middle of the president's term, however, the rough outlines of an attempted pivot were visible.

The administration reframed relations with China as fundamentally rooted in competition rather than cooperation, and explicitly sought closer relations with Indo-Pacific nations to balance growing Chinese power. It abandoned previous efforts to shape Chinese behavior and instead aimed to constrain it. It modestly increased the defense budget and, to a lesser extent, the military presence in Asia. It attempted to redeploy forces from other regions to the Indo-Pacific but largely failed to do so. It described the China challenge as global in scope, but implicitly suggested that Asia was the priority theater in which US-China rivalry would play out. And unlike many other elements of Obama foreign policy, President Trump never condemned or openly rejected his predecessor's Pivot. Instead, he—or, more accurately, his senior officials—focused on the long-term threat to international order posed by China's growing power and assertiveness, sounded the alarm publicly about it, shifted to an explicit focus on competition, and attempted to enlist in that competition a number of countries across the Indo-Pacific, where Beijing's will and weight were felt the most.

Remarkably, and possibly to its own surprise, the Biden administration would maintain and build upon much of the Trump administration's approach.

# 6

# Gaining Ground

## Biden Policy toward Asia and China

During the presidential campaign and in the early days of his new term, Joe Biden consistently highlighted his differences with Donald Trump. This was as true of his foreign policy approach as anything else. Where Trump pledged an inward-facing, America-first approach to the world, Biden stressed the importance of US engagement and leadership. While Trump consistently denigrated allies, Biden insisted that America's alliance network comprised a core national strength. As Trump withdrew from a clutch of international agreements and institutions—the Paris Agreement, the Iran nuclear deal, the WHO, and more—Biden pledged the multilateral approach pursued by all of Trump's predecessors since the end of World War II. The administration's early mantra—"America is back!"—captured the back-to-the-future quality of the new president's inclination.

Yet for all its departures, the new administration's diagnosis of Asia—and of China in particular—bore striking similarities to that of its predecessor. While nearly every one of Biden's senior advisors served in the Obama administration (as Biden did himself), their policies from the outset were far closer to those they directly inherited. The world had changed since 2016, and national security views shifted along with it. On both sides of the aisle in Washington, Xi Jinping's China appeared more capable and aggressive than ever before, the United States appeared to be falling behind in multiple areas, and domestic politics had turned against trade and unfettered globalization. The incoming Biden administration would reflect these sentiments.

This became clear even before Election Day. During the campaign, Biden pledged opposition to the TPP, despite his own role during the Obama administration in stressing its merits. He spoke out against human rights abuses in Xinjiang, charging Beijing with interning Uyghurs in "concentration camps." Candidate Biden called for increased US naval power in Asia so that "the Chinese understand that they're not going to go any further" and promised to reshore the production of medical and other supplies "so we will never again be at the mercy of China." Rather than opposing Trump's imposition of stiff tariffs on a huge range of Chinese goods, Biden expressed support for using them to combat Beijing's economic transgressions. "We're not looking for a war" with China, the soon-to-be president stressed, but he simultaneously made clear that "we are a Pacific power and we are not going to back away."[1]

Trump's refusal to concede after the lost 2020 election truncated the incoming team's transition period, and global shock at the January 6 assault on the US Capitol added to a sense that Biden was taking over a deeply divided, even dysfunctional, political system. The new administration quickly set about to stress President Biden's ability to unite Democrats and Republicans in common cause, to work with US allies and partners, to restore America's reputation for reliability, especially in Asia, and to take a tough stand against China.

## Continuity on China Policy

The administration's early signals showed vivid differences between its approach to dealing with China and that of its most recent Democratic predecessor. In his Senate confirmation hearing, secretary of state nominee Antony Blinken said that China posed "the most significant challenge of any nation-state."[2] The team invited, for the first time, Taiwan's de facto ambassador to attend Biden's inauguration, drawing predictable objections from Beijing.[3] During the administration's first month in office, John Kerry, who had been appointed a special envoy for climate, accused China of "insufficient" effort to combat climate change, and Blinken stressed that the United States would not soften its stance on other issues in order to strike environmental agreements with Beijing. "Strategic competition with China," White House Press Secretary Jen Psaki said during the administration's first month in office, "is a defining feature of the 21st century. China is engaged in conduct that hurts American workers, blunts our technological edge, and threatens our alliances and our influence in international organizations."[4]

The hard edge surprised multiple observers. Administration officials would later privately describe their own shock at their onboarding briefings. Out of office for at least the four years of Trump's term, it was clear on their return that China had made advances across multiple fronts—military, intelligence, economic, and diplomatic—and that America's position was much weaker, especially in the Indo-Pacific, than some incoming officials had appreciated.[5] They were no longer dealing, they quickly concluded, with Obama's China—or Obama's America, for that matter. Their previous hopes for a fundamentally cooperative relationship with Beijing had been supplanted by the reality of US-China competition, if not hostility. While they might disagree with particular policies and approaches, they deemed the Trump administration's overall take on China largely correct.

Biden's foreign policy appointments both reflected the new realization and reinforced the shift. Kurt Campbell took up a newly established role as the White

House's senior coordinator for Indo-Pacific affairs. With Jake Sullivan, Biden's new national security advisor, Campbell had written a widely noticed article declaring that "the era of engagement with China has come to a unceremonious close."[6] Working for Campbell as NSC director for China was Rush Doshi, author of a book arguing that "since the end of the Cold War, China has pursued a grand strategy to displace American order first at the regional and now at the global level."[7] At the Pentagon, Ely Ratner took up the role of assistant secretary of defense for Indo-Pacific affairs; he had, three years prior, coauthored an article with Campbell concluding that previous US policies "have failed to change China in the ways we intended or hoped."[8]

Campbell and Ratner's 2019 article summarized much of the strategic logic that would inform the Biden administration's approach to Asia. "Washington has been largely focused elsewhere," in recent years, they wrote, especially but not exclusively the Middle East. Despite the previous effort to pivot to Asia, they wrote, "at the end of Obama's time in office, budgets and personnel remained focused on other regions," a "strategic distraction" that "has given China the opportunity to press its advantages." Dealing with China, the two said, now required "doing away with the hopeful thinking that has long characterized the United States' approach to China." Rather than endeavoring to transform China, a better approach would build up America's own sources of power and strengthen US alliances and partnerships.[9]

Consistent with such logic, Biden held his first call as president with Japanese prime minister Yoshihide Suga in January 2021.[10] Suga also become the first foreign leader to visit the White House.[11] The new president quickly met with the leaders of South Korea and Australia as well, and the administration moved to resolve the bitter, Trump-era disputes with Seoul and Tokyo over host-nation support payments for the stationing of US troops. In his first foreign policy address, in February, Biden flagged "the growing ambitions of China to rival the United States" and promised to "confront China's economic abuses; counter its aggressive, coercive action; to push back on China's attack on human rights, intellectual property, and global governance." While this competition need not preclude cooperation in areas of shared interest, he added, America would "compete from a position of strength" by building back better at home, enhancing American power projection into Asia, working with allies, renewing the US role in international institutions, and reclaiming lost credibility and moral authority.[12]

## Competing While Cooperating?

From the outset, the administration's approach to China drew general bipartisan support but also revealed strategic contradictions. China was the clear priority of US foreign policy, given that it was, as Biden's first strategy document put it, "the only competitor potentially capable of combining its economic, diplomatic, military, and technological power to mount a sustained challenge to a stable and open international system."[13] In light of this reality, the administration hoped to compete with China across a raft of issues while preserving the ability to cooperate in areas like climate change, global health, and nonproliferation.[14] Tensions in some areas of the relationship need not preclude, administration officials insisted, the possibility of collaboration in others. Beijing, however, roundly rejected the lack of linkage, and the competitive nature of the US-China relationship would soon crowd out almost entirely the chances for cooperation, even in areas where the two countries theoretically shared vital national interests.

It was also widely recognized among Biden's Asia policy officials that economic leadership remained a *sine qua non* for US engagement in the region, and America's failure to join the TPP had struck a fatal blow to the Pivot to Asia. Yet the new president had, like Trump, rejected a return to the trade agreement and proposed no similarly ambitious deal to replace it. The new administration even embraced the steep tariffs its predecessor had imposed on hundreds of billions of dollars in Chinese imports. And while the incoming team was broadly cognizant of what it hoped to avoid—an Indo-Pacific dominated by China, a further deterioration of the regional military balance, technology standards and economic rules established by Beijing, international organizations shaped by China, and an increase in autocracy at the expense of democratic rule—what it sought to positively achieve remained publicly obscure. What kind of long-term relationship with China was consistent with US national interests and pluralist values? The strategic objectives of America's China policy, and how US engagement in the Indo-Pacific might help attain those goals, would remain at best a work in progress.[15]

The role of diplomacy posed another dilemma. With allies and partners, the administration's path was straightforward: embrace them, harmonize approaches to China, establish new initiatives, strengthen their defenses and security cooperation with the United States, and generate enhanced diplomatic frameworks with them. In March, for instance, Biden held the first-ever (virtual) leader-level meeting of the Quad, alongside his Japanese, Australian, and Indian counterparts. The four committed to a "free, open, secure and prosperous Indo-Pacific region."[16] In April, Biden met in person with Japan's Suga, pledging to "take on the challenges from China . . . and ensure the future of a free and open Indo-Pacific," and called Narendra Modi to pledge assistance as COVID-19 ravaged India.[17] The administration successfully inserted language related to China and Taiwan in multiple diplomatic communiques, including those of the G7, the US-EU summit, and the NATO leaders meeting.[18] And in May, South Korean president Moon Jae-in became the second foreign leader to meet Biden in person—making the first two presidential meetings with Asian leaders, an un-precedented diplomatic signal.[19]

Generating productive diplomacy with China proved far more difficult. Biden's early call with Xi reflected only the recitation of mutual grievances, and a meeting in Alaska that drew Blinken and Sullivan together with top Chinese diplomats Yang Jiechi and Wang Yi produced a fiery public exchange.[20] In full view of television cameras, Blinken opened the Alaska talks by citing his "deep concerns with actions by China, including in Xinjiang, Hong Kong, Taiwan, cyberattacks on the United States and economic coercion toward our allies." Sullivan noted China's "economic and military coercion [and] assaults on basic values." Yang, seemingly caught off guard by the criticism, angrily called on the United States to "change its own image," charged that "many people within the United States actually have little confidence in the democracy of the United States," complained about sanctions (some imposed by the administration just prior to the meeting), and declared that "there is no way to strangle China."[21] Administration officials would, in coming months, express hope that diplomacy with Beijing could minimize misunderstandings and establish "guardrails" around the competitive bilateral relationship. Those goals would remain distant, not least because of few meetings between senior and mostly unbending figures from the two sides.[22] In part due to the COVID pandemic and Beijing's lockdowns, no Biden cabinet member visited China in the first two years of the administration.

Its emphasis on an indefinite, tense competition with China, a desire to work more closely with allies and partners to manage it, and the ambition to boost American strength and global presence led the Biden administration to attempt a new—and this time more effective—pivot to Asia. While it would never explicitly embrace the "pivot" or "rebalance" rhetoric, the Biden team's early moves were clear. Senior officials hoped to stabilize actual or would-be hotspots elsewhere in ways that would free up national security resources and policymaker attention for Asia.

## Competing Priorities

Biden officials entered office hoping to establish a "stable, predictable" relationship with Russia that would minimize Moscow's disruptive international activities.[23] They offered to talk "anywhere, anytime" with North Korea, drawing Pyongyang into a diplomatic process that would forestall provocative missile and weapons tests, while avoiding Trump-style military threats and summit diplomacy.[24] The administration hoped to return to the JCPOA—and even to make it "longer and stronger"[25]—thus buying several years' time against Tehran's acute nuclear threat. And the president intended to withdraw all US forces from Afghanistan, with his administration explicitly arguing (among other reasons offered) that doing so would permit a greater focus on the Indo-Pacific.[26]

The first two years of the Biden administration would not proceed according to these hopes. North Korea refused talks and began firing missiles and threatening new nuclear tests.[27] Iran declined to return to the JCPOA, continually adding new conditions for its re-entry, and enriched uranium to ever-higher levels. Biden would withdraw chaotically from Afghanistan but leave behind a country in turmoil, a Taliban conquest which returned the country to a highly repressive form of Islamism, an enduring need for a US military "over the horizon" capability to deal with terrorist threats, and a serious blow to America's international credibility and reputation for competence.[28] Most consequentially, Russia would invade Ukraine, launching the first major state-on-state land war in Europe since 1945 and shaking the very foundations of global politics and security.

By the Biden administration's midway point, Campbell argued that though "the process started slowly and was contested," the Pivot was "taking root and being locked down."[29] There was, indeed, a flurry of activity to highlight, and significant momentum. But the desire to pivot still posed, to a greater degree than ever before, a fundamental question: Could the United States address its number one challenge, China, by focusing more on its priority region, the Indo-Pacific, and yet simultaneously employ the necessary attention and resources in other areas where vital national interests persisted?

## Renewing the Pivot

First, however, the administration would take early steps to clearly identify China as its top priority and the Indo-Pacific as the region deserving of its greatest attention. The White House's early strategic guidance offered a raft of actions and proposals for change at home and abroad. "Taken together," the document said, "this agenda will strengthen our enduring advantages, and allow us to prevail in strategic competition with China or any other nation."[30] Lloyd Austin, after taking up his position as secretary of defense, would routinely label China the Defense Department's "pacing challenge" and the Indo-Pacific as its "priority theater."[31] Later in the year, Secretary of State Blinken would say that "what happens in the Indo-Pacific will, more than any other region, shape the trajectory of the world in the 21st century."[32] Within the White House, the Indo-Pacific directorate, led by Kurt Campbell, was the NSC's largest, most active, and most influential.[33]

This early focus on the region invited observers to wonder whether a renewed Pivot to Asia was in the offing. In April, one journalist opined that while "Obama talked about a 'pivot to Asia,'" Biden was "actually doing it." The president had so far, for instance, resisted the urge of every president to pursue a Middle East peace agreement, and even took a month to call Israeli prime minister Benjamin Netanyahu.[34] He early on made a firm commitment to the full withdrawal of American forces from Afghanistan. He retained and added to Trump-era restraints on China and sought new initiatives with partners across Asia.

The administration seemed to have little hesitation in applying sanctions, restrictions, and tariffs against China. In June, Biden barred US investment in nearly sixty Chinese companies active in defense and surveillance activities.[35] The White House then announced a new "supply chain trade strike force," headed by the US trade representative, to impose tariffs or other measures on trade violators, including China.[36] In December, Biden signed the Uyghur Forced Labor Prevention Act, which required potential importers to demonstrate that goods produced in Xinjiang did not employ forced labor.[37]

The new team simultaneously sought to enlist allies and partners in budding coalitions. This effort went well beyond the Indo-Pacific. On Biden's maiden visit to Europe in June 2021, G7 leaders criticized Chinese human rights abuses, and the European Union agreed to work with Washington toward a "free and open Indo-Pacific."[38] NATO leaders then, for the first time, declared China a security challenge. At American behest, the alliance stated that Beijing's goals and "assertive behavior present systemic challenges to the rules-based international order and to areas relevant to alliance security."[39]

## Democracy versus Autocracy

Consistent with such rhetoric, Biden framed US-China competition as part of a grand ideological contest of democracy against autocracy. At his first press conference, the president predicted that future generations would write "on the issue of who succeeded: autocracy or democracy." China had, he said, "an overall goal to become the leading country in the world. . . . That's not going to happen on my watch."[40] The framing would become vivid at the end of Biden's first year, when he hosted a virtual "Summit for Democracy."[41] The gathering of one hundred leaders was an effort to forge common action in defense of democratic political systems, to fight corruption, and to promote human rights. It also enlarged the stakes in the US-China competition. The issue, the president suggested, was not merely superpower rivalry, but the very survival of the democratic way of life in a world where dictatorship was on the march.

China, unsurprisingly, reacted sharply and negatively to Biden's efforts to place bilateral competition into an ideological framework. Viewing it as little more than the attempt to forge an anti-China narrative, Beijing launched a propaganda assault that criticized American democracy and insisted that China was itself democratic.[42] Chinese leaders would increasingly echo those themes in the coming months, including in the February 2022 joint manifesto issued by Xi and Vladimir Putin. "There is no one-size-fits-all template to guide countries in establishing democracy," the two autocrats wrote in their declaration, and "a nation can choose such forms and methods of implementing democracy that would best suit its particular state. . . . It is only up to the people of the country to decide whether their State is a democratic one."[43]

While European allies generally favored the emphasis on democratic solidarity, Indo-Pacific partners were markedly less enthusiastic. Just three of ten ASEAN members made the Summit for Democracy invitation list, and partners like Singapore and Vietnam were left out.[44] Officials in democratic allies like Japan and Australia privately fretted that, if the contest with China were framed too tightly as a showdown between democracy and autocracy, key potential members would be absent from the necessary coalition. These governments favored as broad a front as possible in dealing with China; the nature of its members' political system was much less important to them.

Whether and how the administration would work with friendly autocrats, even in the shared enterprise of balancing Chinese power in Asia, remained an open question throughout the Biden term. The White House sought, with some success, to resolve the dilemma in its February 2022 Indo-Pacific Strategy document, which emphasized openness and rule of law rather than expressing a wholesale preference for democratic regimes.[45] Later that year, the national security strategy also distinguished between revisionist autocracies, like Russia and China, whose designs the United States would oppose, and those "countries that do not embrace democratic institutions but nevertheless depend upon and support a rules-based international system." America could work with those.[46]

## An Attempted Military Pivot

While diplomacy and rhetorical moves comprised the highlights of the administration's early Asia policy, it took military steps as well. In May, the Department of Defense noted that in the new fiscal year it would invest $66 billion in the Indo-Pacific region, including $5.1 billion for the Pacific Deterrence Initiative (PDI). The department said the resourcing demonstrated that it was "prioritizing China as the number one pacing challenge."[47] Two months later, on a visit to Manila, Secretary of Defense Lloyd Austin secured the reactivation of the Visiting Forces Agreement, the pact under which US troops rotate through the Philippines—and which President Rodrigo Duterte in February 2020 had vowed to terminate.[48] In August, the United States conducted the largest military exercises in the western Pacific since the Cold War.[49]

Yet the most consequential military move during Biden's first year in office came not in East Asia but in Afghanistan. Over months, the president and senior officials offered several reasons for withdrawing the last American forces from the country. Among them was that leaving Afghanistan would free senior policymakers to focus more on the Indo-Pacific and would permit the United States to redeploy military resources tied up there.[50] Previewing the withdrawal, Blinken said, "We have other very important items on our agenda, including the relationship with China. . . . And that's where we have to focus our energy and resources."[51] The Pivot-style logic seemed straightforward: do more in Asia by doing less in Afghanistan. As Biden put it, "We also need to focus on shoring up America's core strengths to meet the strategic competition with China and other nations that is really going to determine—determine our future."[52]

The reasoning resonated with some China experts. Stanford University's Oriana Skylar Mastro, for instance, wrote that "it was just dumb luck that Mr. Xi and his predecessors, thanks in part to the war in Afghanistan, could build national power, undermine international norms" and do more without the United States "thwarting their plans."[53] The end of the war in Afghanistan, she added, "could bring these good times . . . to an abrupt end."[54] The Brookings Institution's Ryan Hass argued that America's standing in Asia would not be damaged by its withdrawal from Afghanistan; in fact, its turn to East Asia as a result would "open up new opportunities" for the United States and its partners in the region.[55] Ashley Townshend, an Australian security analyst at the Washington-based Carnegie Endowment, tweeted: "Withdrawing from Afg [sic] doesn't mean US more/less likely to back away from other commitments. In fact, US may be in better position to focus elsewhere."[56]

Not everyone was convinced. Michael Green, for instance, observed that "there is one argument for a complete withdrawal from Afghanistan that is just plain wrong: the idea that retreat will somehow enhance US strategic competition with China. It won't. On the contrary, it will complicate that problem. In fact, maintaining a modest US presence in Afghanistan would advance, rather than hinder, competition with China. It is bad geostrategy to pull out completely."[57] Asian nations were bound to wonder about US staying power and whether a Taliban-controlled Afghanistan would eventually compel a US re-engagement, once again distracting Washington from the Indo-Pacific.

The disastrous withdrawal from Afghanistan shook many American allies, including some of the very ones the administration had hoped to reassure. Australian prime minister Scott Morrison called the situation "very distressing."[58]

Defense Minister Peter Dutton called it "disappointing and tragic."[59] Rep. Kang Min-kuk, the floor spokesman for South Korea's conservative main opposition People Power Party, argued that "[u]nless its partner has strong defense capabilities and strong will for self-reliance, the U.S. could leave the partner to pursue its own national interests. The Moon Jae-in government and the military should do their best to strengthen the Republic of Korea-U.S. alliance and maintain a strong military, using the Afghan situation as a turning point."[60] In Taiwan, President Tsai Ing-wen responded to the chaotic drawdown in Afghanistan by saying the island would be forced to boost its own defense. "It is not an option for us to do nothing ourselves and rely only on the protection of others," she said.[61]

Nevertheless, the administration after the withdrawal voiced strong intentions to pivot to Asia. In his first speech to the UN General Assembly, Biden observed that, following war in Afghanistan, "the United States turns our focus to the priorities and the regions of the world, like the Indo-Pacific, that are most consequential today and tomorrow," although even then the priority was "like" the Indo-Pacific, not "the" Indo-Pacific.[62] Almost exactly a decade prior, in strikingly similar terms, the Obama administration had pledged greater investment in Asia as the wars in Afghanistan and Iraq reached their ends.[63] Events had not unfolded as intended. Now, perhaps, and at long last, the Pivot was at hand.

New initiatives continued, including the surprise decision to form AUKUS, the Australia–United Kingdom–United States defense technology-sharing agreement. The keystone to the new arrangement was Washington's pledge to help Australia acquire nuclear-powered submarines, which would make Australia one of just seven countries to possess such a naval capability.[64] The United States had shared nuclear propulsion technology just once, with the United Kingdom in the 1950s, and the move was seen as potentially transformative: Effectively doubling the allied fleet of nuclear submarines acting in the Pacific would strengthen the American side of the military balance. That the effort was directed against China barely needed mentioning.

AUKUS promised to enhance Australian military capability in the Indo-Pacific and anchor Britain's post-Brexit presence there. But the agreement also illustrated the fallout that attends difficult trade-offs between issues and regions. Acquiring submarines under the AUKUS framework meant that Canberra would terminate its preexisting, $90 billion contract signed with the French company Naval Group.[65] The cancellation amounted to a huge loss for France's shipbuilding industry, one that came as a shock to Paris, and amid a closely-fought French presidential election. "The US and the UK have stabbed [France] in the back in Australia," wrote France's recently departed ambassador to Washington.[66] Paris recalled its existing envoys to both the United States and Australia and denounced the agreement. Josep Borrell, the European Union's top foreign policy official, noted that he learned of AUKUS on the very day he

presented the European Union's own Indo-Pacific strategy. "The lack of communications and confrontations between the close partners," he said, has "created
real difficulties."[67] Observing that Biden at the UN General Assembly convened
Quad leaders—a meeting that by definition excluded Europeans—two reporters
added acidly, "When Biden . . . declared 'America is back,' European leaders
didn't think he meant back to the arrogant exceptionalism that has often defined
Washington's approach to the EU and toward NATO."[68]

## Diplomacy and (Little) Trade Policy

If communication with allies required finesse, diplomacy with China—especially
after declaring an era of open competition with it—was harder still. A series of
leader calls and quiet meetings between American and Chinese senior officials
produced little more than a formal exchange of denunciatory talking points.
The US side continually spoke of the desire to identify areas of cooperation
with Beijing, particularly on transnational issues, but virtually no such collaboration materialized. Instead, the administration turned to a different objective: establishing "guardrails" that would bound the competition and prevent it
from spiraling into confrontation or even conflict. In September, Biden spoke
with Xi by phone, telling the Chinese leader that the United States wished to
"responsibly manage the competition."[69] Yet throughout the first two years of
Biden's term, identifying the boundaries of US-China competition would remain
as elusive as forging cooperation.

While the diplomatic element of the administration's approach remained difficult, the trade pillar of its Asia policy was wholly absent. Biden, like Trump,
evinced no desire to explore an American return even to a modified TPP agreement, and the administration dismissed more modest ideas like a regional agreement to govern digital trade. Opposition to trade liberalization was rooted in US
domestic politics, but the tension was palpable between this approach and the
administration's express desire to compete vigorously with China.

China illustrated the point vividly by applying to join the CPTPP the day after
AUKUS was announced.[70] The move sounded an alarm in Washington and regional capitals. It was by no means lost on the administration's Asia policy hands
that their lack of an affirmative trade policy handicapped the effort to signal regional engagement, presence, and influence. Beijing was already a member of
RCEP, the other pan-regional trade agreement (to which the United States was
also not party); now it wanted to join the largely made-in-America TPP. Outside
experts called on Biden to overcome domestic political skepticism and rejoin
the agreement. Economist Jeffrey Schott, for instance, wrote: "It would be unthinkable for Washington to sit on the sidelines and watch China take the lead

in the Asia-Pacific region."[71] Unfortunately, it was all too thinkable. Biden would show no more appetite for the TPP after China's application than before, and his advisors had to go looking for other options that might signal economic engagement without launching a new trade agreement.

By the end of Biden's first year in office, the administration's focus on China and its effort to pivot to Asia were clear. China had been the overriding focus of the Interim National Security Guidance and a central theme in US diplomacy at the G7, European Union, NATO, and Quad summits. Officials had forged AUKUS, even as it led to new tensions with France. With the major exception of trade policy, each of the instruments of national security were increasingly aimed at dealing with the China challenge, primarily in the Indo-Pacific. Indeed, the focus on China and Asia had grown so tight that some observers worried that the outer edge of an unbalanced foreign policy was discernable.[72] The United States remained, after all, a global power with interests in multiple regions and challenges with a spectrum of actors. Russian leader Vladimir Putin would soon remind the world of this daunting strategic reality.

## Russia and China Align

In early 2022, Vladimir Putin, attending the Winter Olympics in Beijing, met with his Chinese counterpart. The two leaders pledged friendship, solidarity, and cooperation with "no limits" in pursuit of a world order very different from the past. In an expansive joint manifesto, they laid out their vision. China and Russia would forge an "international relations of a new type," multipolar and no longer dominated by the United States. There would be no further NATO enlargement, no color revolutions, no globe-spanning US missile defense system, and no American nuclear weapons deployed abroad. Actors "representing but the minority on the international scale"—that is, the United States and its allies—might continue to interfere in other states and "incite contradictions, differences and confrontation," but Beijing and Moscow together would resist them. In the world order to come, no one would pressure China or Russia on human rights or interfere in their internal affairs. Democracy itself would be redefined and subject to no universal standard. Russia would join with China to oppose both "any forms of independence for Taiwan" and the formation of alliances opposed to Beijing in Asia.[73]

The manifesto seemed to validate precisely the danger that Biden and his team had warned against. Here was China, combining the will to overturn international order with an increasing capability to do so, now joined in the effort by aggressive Russia as an aggrieved junior partner. Two large, nuclear-armed great powers were each closer to one another than either was to the United States.

They had specified desired revisions to the Western-forged international order, changes that would harm US vital national interests and democratic values. Russia was the declining power, however, in the joint effort, and China the rising one. As a result, it seemed only logical to focus the lion's share of US attention on the Indo-Pacific, its home region. If ever there were another wake-up call that demanded a pivot to Asia, this was no doubt it.

Instead, it led to a diplomatic pivot to Europe. On February 24, 2022, Russian armies swarmed into Ukraine, attempting to overthrow the Kyiv government and forcibly seize Ukraine. The international response to Moscow's brazen aggression was immediate and dramatic. The world's largest economies, save China and India, imposed sweeping export controls and severe sanctions on Russia, including against its central bank. Germany killed the $11 billion Nordstream 2 gas pipeline, announced a one-time increase in defense spending of €100 billion, and committed to spend 2 percent of GDP on defense annually.[74] The European Union for the first time financed arms transfers to Ukraine, and the United States began providing huge quantities of weapons to the Ukrainian military.[75] Finland and Sweden aligned with the West and against Moscow, and within months would seek NATO membership for the first time.[76]

The Indo-Pacific response was similarly remarkable. Governments in the region saw issues at stake larger than land war between two European powers. As Kurt Campbell observed, "Every country in Asia, in the Indo-Pacific, wants to ensure that Ukraine is a cautionary tale, that no one contemplates again, or in another theatre, some sort of operation that would be so destabilizing and so destructive."[77] South Korea, Japan, Australia, New Zealand, and Singapore all joined the sanctions against Russia and provided assistance to the Ukrainian resistance.[78]

Japan, seeing in Russia's invasion the possible antecedents—and responses—to a Chinese attack on Taiwan, took unprecedented steps on both sanctions and equipment to Ukraine's military. The about-face was especially remarkable after a decade of the Liberal Democratic Party accommodating Moscow in an attempt to negotiate the return of Japan's Northern Territories.[79] "We want to demonstrate what happens when a country invades another country," a Japanese official told the Washington Post. Prime Minister Fumio Kishida warned that "Ukraine today may be East Asia tomorrow" and announced that "Japan needs to implement a fundamental upgrade of its defense capabilities."[80] By the end of the year Japan would set out a new strategic course, with a major increase in defense spending and the acquisition of long-range strike capabilities. Even the Philippines, which condemned the Russian invasion, made news when President Rodrigo Duterte (somewhat oddly) offered his country's facilities to US forces if the war in Europe somehow drew in the United States.[81]

The Russian invasion demonstrated the practical difficulty of focusing US foreign policy exclusively, or even largely, on Asia when threats to world order intervened elsewhere. As early as late 2021, the administration's top foreign policy officials were increasingly consumed by the looming crisis in Europe. The White House and State Department engaged in vigorous diplomacy with Moscow, attempting to head off an attack on Ukraine, and with major European capitals to prepare for that effort's failure. The Treasury Department fashioned sanctions at a level never before imposed on such a large economy and endeavored to win foreign government support for them. The Defense Department and intelligence community devoted vast resources to monitor Russian movements and communications, worked with Ukraine, devised a system for generating and transferring military equipment to Kyiv, and reassured skittish NATO allies on the eastern periphery. Within weeks, the United States would increase its military presence in Europe by some 20,000 troops.[82]

Early into the conflict, administration officials rejected the notion that dealing with Russia in Europe and focusing on China in Asia posed difficult trade-offs. On the contrary, National Security Advisor Jake Sullivan said, the two efforts were "mutually reinforcing." "There's a certain level of integration and symbiosis in the strategy we are pursuing in Europe and the strategy we're pursuing in the Indo-Pacific," Sullivan added. "And President Biden's unique capacity to actually stitch those two together is going to be a hallmark of his foreign policy presidency."[83]

That assessment would prove overly dismissive of the inherent trade-offs, but there was an element of strategic logic in Sullivan's observations. How the war in Ukraine turned out would matter a great deal to the geopolitical situation in Asia, as the diplomatic activism by multiple countries in the region suggested. At stake in the resistance to Russia's invasion was a cardinal principle of post–World War II international order: a prohibition against changing borders by force. The outcome of the war would either undermine or reinforce the norm against territorial conquest, certainly in Europe, but in Asia as well. The Indo-Pacific had major stakes in the European fight.

Nevertheless, the administration's focus on Russia and Ukraine, which was soon followed by the transfer of tens of billions of dollars in military and economic assistance, was blatant. That such efforts would detract from a vigorous approach to China and Asia seemed just as clear. As a result, senior officials soon began distinguishing between China, which they described as America's most consequential strategic challenger, and Russia, which was the "acute threat."[84] This distinction suggested a temporal asymmetry that could help square matters. Washington would focus its attention and resources primarily on Russia and Europe now, while retaining a sustained focus on China and Asia over the long run. Such claims, however, begged the question: When would the long run begin?

For a few, all the focus on Ukraine amounted to a titanic distraction from the China challenge that threatened to derail the long-awaited Pivot to Asia just when it was finally moving forward.[85] Elbridge Colby, a defense expert who served as the primary drafter of Trump's National Defense Strategy, wrote, "Preventing China from establishing . . . hegemony over Asia must therefore be the priority of US foreign policy—even in the face of what is happening in Europe. The simple fact is that Asia is more important than Europe, and China is a much greater threat than Russia."[86] Senator Josh Hawley struck a similar tone, writing, "there is still time to deny China's hegemonic ambitions, starting in Asia. But—and here is the key point—doing so will require us to do *less* in other theaters." The United States, he argued, should refrain from sending forces to Europe to reassure allies, end its support for Ukraine's NATO bid, and reduce the American military footprint in Europe.[87]

Some policymakers and experts drew different lessons. Days before the start of the war, Matthew Kroenig, an expert at the Atlantic Council, warned that moderating a response to Russia "to focus on the greater threat posed by China . . . would be a mistake."[88] Though acknowledging China as the superior long-term threat, former CIA director and defense secretary Robert Gates argued that "[w]e cannot pretend any longer that a national security focus primarily on China will protect our political, economic and security interests."[89] "The United States can't simply return to its previous business of focusing predominantly on China," Andrea Kendall-Taylor, an expert at the Center for a New American Security, told a congressional hearing.[90] US lawmakers also expressed support for a more permanent US troop presence in central and eastern Europe. Rep. Mike Rogers of Alabama, a Republican on the House Armed Services Committee, said that establishing permanent American basing in the Baltics, as well as Romania and Poland, "would send a great message to our NATO allies."[91]

## Biden's Indo-Pacific Strategy

In part to demonstrate the enduring importance of Asia even amid crisis in Europe, in February 2022 the administration released its Indo-Pacific Strategy. Its rhetorical packaging, by now commonplace in official statements, embraced language of the sort originally invoked to justify the Pivot. "The United States," the strategy said, "is an Indo-Pacific power. The region, stretching from our Pacific coastline to the Indian Ocean, is home to more than half of the world's people, nearly two-thirds of the world's economy, and seven of the world's largest militaries. . . . In the years ahead, as the region drives as much as two-thirds of global economic growth, its influence will only grow—as will its importance to the United States."[92]

The basic logic of the Biden Pivot was consistent with the framing a decade prior—but the approach to China had changed significantly. If in 2011 the Pivot was necessary to create conditions in which the United States could forge a co-operative relationship with China, it would now help America and its partners resist the Chinese menace. "The PRC is combining," the document said, "its economic, diplomatic, military, and technological might as it pursues a sphere of influence in the Indo-Pacific and seeks to become the world's most influential power." Pledging to open new embassies and consulates, especially in Southeast Asia and the Pacific Islands, to expand the regional US Coast Guard presence, and to launch an Indo-Pacific Economic Framework, the document placed regional priority on Asia. "The PRC's coercion and aggression spans the globe," it acknowledged, "but it is most acute in the Indo-Pacific."[93]

Illustrating the point, in April 2022 the Solomon Islands surprised many by announcing a new security agreement with China.[94] A leaked draft of the agreement suggested that the islands would allow Chinese naval vessels to make logistics stops there—the precursor, some worried, to a permanent basing arrangement.[95] Within days of the new announcement, Campbell, the NSC Indo-Pacific coordinator, joined Assistant Secretary of State for Asia Daniel Kritenbrink on a delegation to the Solomons, adding Fiji and Papua New Guinea to the itinerary for good measure.[96] There they pledged greater American engagement and assistance. Two months later the United States would join Australia, New Zealand, Britain, and Japan in launching a "Partners in the Blue Pacific" initiative to coordinate Pacific Islands assistance—and provide alternatives to China's own.[97] In July, the administration announced that it would establish new embassies in Kiribati and Tonga, triple aid to the Pacific Islands, and name an envoy to the Pacific Islands Forum.[98] Despite the flurry of activity, however, the Solomons a month later turned away a US Coast Guard cutter and announced a temporary moratorium on visits of foreign naval vessels.[99]

The administration persisted. Biden in September hosted a first-ever summit with Pacific Island leaders, attempting to demonstrate greater American engagement in this now clearly contested region.[100] The initial refusal of the Marshall Islands and the Solomon Islands to sign a joint statement made headlines even in Washington.[101] The two did eventually join the declaration, after language on Taiwan was reportedly dropped from the text.[102] The summit-level diplomacy, behind-the-scenes jockeying, and media coverage were remarkable given the tiny size of the countries. To a degree, such moves were reminiscent of Cold War rivalry, in which the United States and Soviet Union found themselves in fierce competition over the alignment of countries like Angola, Laos, and Nicaragua.

Policymakers saw Southeast Asia, along with the Pacific Islands, as the Indo-Pacific's most contested regions. In May, Biden hosted ASEAN leaders for their first-ever summit in Washington. The president announced $150 million in US investment across Southeast Asia, a not-so-subtle gesture of competition with China's own spending in the region. Observers were quick to point out, however, that the previous fall, Beijing had announced ten times that amount—$1.5 billion—for Southeast Asia (though even then it appeared doubtful that much of the commitment would be delivered).[103] The same week that ASEAN leaders landed in Washington, Congress finalized a bill to provide some $40 billion in assistance to Ukraine.[104] As Campbell observed, "Several administrations in succession in the United States have tried . . . to launch more fundamental efforts, policies, frameworks in Asia, East Asia, Indo-Pacific, and found themselves stymied or misdirected or directed toward other pursuits."[105] For all of the strategic logic connecting events in Europe with outcomes in Asia, and all the efforts to "walk and chew gum at the same time," in a favored administration phrase, the resource trade-offs would endure.[106]

## Indo-Pacific Diplomacy

Diplomatic bandwidth remained finite as well. In a quantitative study conducted by the University of Sydney's US Studies Centre, researchers examined the diplomatic activities of the president, secretary of state, and defense secretary across the first eighteen months of the Obama, Trump, and Biden presidencies.[107] In an overall measure of diplomatic interactions (e.g., meetings, in-person or remote, and phone calls with counterparts), Biden, Blinken, and Austin's 233 engagements with the Indo-Pacific exceeded the Trump administration's 228 engagements and Obama's 114 engagements.[108] The Biden administration also exceeded its predecessors in attending regional summits. Its diplomatic engagement with Asia, however, was dwarfed by that with Europe. While the three officials made twenty-two visits to Indo-Pacific countries in the first eighteen months, they made over seventy trips to Europe. Biden traveled regularly to Europe, including on his first trip as president, but his first Asia visit came at the administration's sixteen-month mark. He hosted eleven meetings with European leaders in Washington and only seven with Indo-Pacific leaders.[109] Such figures are limited indicators; they do not reflect the qualitative measures of diplomacy, and the COVID-19 pandemic imposed uneven strictures on diplomatic engagements, while Russia's invasion generated a great deal of crisis diplomacy.[110] Nevertheless, for an administration that explicitly framed its top strategic competitor as China and the Indo-Pacific as its priority region, the amount of senior-level diplomatic engagement with Europe remains striking. As one analyst observed, "Perhaps it was never truly possible for the world's greatest superpower, with binding strategic alliances spanning the globe, to be able to have a laser-like focus on one region of the world. In that case, a true 'pivot' to Asia was never really possible."[111]

Nevertheless, Biden traveled to Asia in May 2022 for the first time as president. Visiting Japan and South Korea, the president announced the long-awaited Indo-Pacific Economic Framework (IPEF), the administration's alternative to rejoining the TPP. The framework included twelve initial partners, representing some 40 percent of global GDP. Fiji joined days later, and the initiative was publicly welcomed by regional governments hungry for any form of US economic engagement.[112] But what the region really sought—increased trade through greater market access—remained decidedly off Washington's table.

While in Tokyo, Biden made major news by saying that he would use force to defend Taiwan against Chinese aggression.[113] The comments overshadowed the IPEF launch and commitments by Japan to boost its defense budget and capabilities, and they represented the latest salvo in a months-long era of heightened tension over Taiwan. Presidential aides hastened to insist that the policy of strategic ambiguity remained unchanged, and Secretary of State Blinken gave a major speech on China three days later that reiterated the traditional position of strategic ambiguity.[114] In fact, however, Biden's remarks appeared to represent a classic "Washington gaffe," in which a politician inadvertently says what he really believes. Biden had twice before made similar comments as president and would shortly do so again.

By June, with Asia-focused diplomacy increasing even as Washington delivered tremendous levels of assistance to Ukraine, Washington and Canberra announced what two Australian analysts described as "the most significant enhancements to bilateral force-posture initiatives in a generation."[115] These included increased rotations of US air, land, and sea forces, upgrading facilities to enable Australia to serve as a forward operating hub for high-end warfighting, and the deployment of nuclear-capable bombers to Australian airfields.[116] Secretary of Defense Lloyd Austin traveled to Singapore to address the Shangri-La Dialogue, the annual gathering of Asian security policymakers. "The Indo-Pacific," he said, "is our priority theater of operations. Today, the Indo-Pacific is at the heart of American grand strategy. . . . No region will do more to set the trajectory of the 21st century than this one."[117] Austin noted that more US military—some 300,000 troops—were stationed in the Indo-Pacific than in any other region, and that the administration planned more than $6 billion in funding for the Pacific Deterrence Initiative.[118] A particularly exuberant, DOD-written news article summarized Austin's remarks, adding, "American strategists no longer talk about the 'US pivot to Asia.' That has happened."[119]

Members of Congress remained unconvinced. While promoting legislation that would increase spending in the Indo-Pacific, Rep. Ami Bera said, "Going back to the Obama administration, we've been trying to do this pivot to the

Indo-Pacific. We're getting there, but we're getting there awfully slowly."[120] Kurt Campbell acknowledged that the gap between rhetoric and funding was "a valid criticism." "Over time," he added, "one of the hardest things in government is to make choices among existing . . . priorities and regions. And that's difficult."[121]

A variety of comparisons illustrate the gap. In Biden's FY23 foreign assistance request, for instance, the Indo-Pacific—home to more than half of the world's population—was to receive a mere 7.7 percent of the overall funding (see Figure 6.1).[122] A 2023 Senate Foreign Relations Committee staff report recommended that the United States should "seek additional resources and allocate a larger portion of foreign assistance to the Indo-Pacific," invest more in the State Department's Indo-Pacific operations, and incentivize other US agencies to "increase their grants, loans, and other financing activities in the Indo-Pacific."[123]

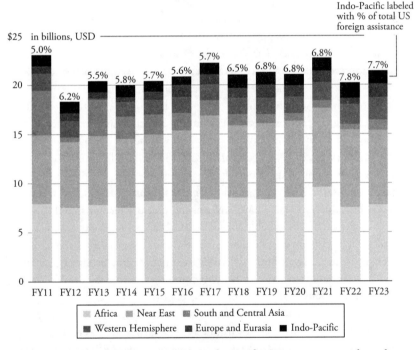

**Figure 6.1.** US foreign assistance to the Indo-Pacific region as compared to other regions.

Source: US Senate, Committee on Foreign Relations, *Strategic Alignment: The Imperative of Resourcing the Indo-Pacific Strategy*, February 2023, 32, https://www.foreign.senate.gov/imo/media/doc/resourcing_the_ips_-_sfrc_democratic_staff_report_2023.pdf. This graph was created by the Congressional Research Service using annual Department of State, Foreign Operations and Related Programs, and Congressional Budget Justifications, FY2013-FY2023. FY2022 estimate compiled by CRS from the FY2022 653(a) report. The amount for FY2023 is based on the requested amount for that year.

Funding for the State Department's Overseas Programs and Public Diplomacy in the Indo-Pacific also lagged behind Washington's stated priority.[124] In the administration's FY23 request, Department of State Overseas Programs and Public Diplomacy funding for the Indo-Pacific represented just 19.6 percent of total funds—hardly a dramatic increase from the 16.3 percent of funds dedicated to the region in 2014.[125] Funding for the Voice of America (VOA) in the Indo-Pacific also showed little increase compared with other regions. VOA funding for the East Asia and Pacific Division increased by just over $10 million from 2013 to 2022, while funding for Africa over the same period increased by more than $20 million.[126]

## Speaker Pelosi Goes to Taiwan

The congressional role in US policy went well beyond the power of the purse. In August, Speaker of the House Nancy Pelosi visited Taiwan, becoming the first speaker to do so since Newt Gingrich twenty-five years before. The trip occurred weeks before China's 20th Party Congress, at which Xi Jinping expected to win an unprecedented third term as leader. Perhaps partly as a result, Beijing reacted sharply, suspending bilateral cooperation in areas where it still existed, and launching large-scale military exercises that rehearsed a multi-day blockade of Taiwan.[127] During the exercises, five Chinese ballistic missiles landed within Japan's claimed exclusive economic zone, drawing deep concern in Tokyo.[128] Chinese military forces began regularly crossing the middle line of the Taiwan Strait and vastly ramped up cyber-attacks against the island.[129] The upshot, as two analysts observed, was that "tensions in the Taiwan Strait reached levels not seen in nearly thirty years."[130] ASEAN warned that the tensions could lead to "open conflicts and unpredictable consequences," calling for maximum restraint, and India—in its first-ever statement of the kind on Taiwan—accused China of "militarism in the Taiwan Strait."[131] After the visit, Beijing established a "new normal" in its military incursions, sending fighter jets across the Strait's median line on an almost daily basis and conducting lengthy live-fire drills.[132]

The heightened tensions continued. In September, Biden said publicly for a fourth time that the United States would defend Taiwan if it were attacked by China, including—and unlike in Ukraine—that he would be willing to employ US forces.[133] Beijing reacted predictably poorly, charging that the president was encouraging Taiwanese independence and departing from America's traditional One-China policy. Once again, the administration hastened to insist that the president had made no change to the policy of strategic ambiguity, but his express commitment to defend the island, not the feeble walk-backs by other officials, endured.

Countries across the region began contemplating what role they might play if war erupted over Taiwan. Japan announced its greatest military buildup since World War II and aimed to boost its counterattack capability, further eroding the pacifist policy it held since 1945.[134] Japanese prime minister Kishida pledged to double defense spending to 2 percent of GDP by 2027, and the country's concurrently released national security documents highlighted China as the "the greatest strategic challenge ever to securing the peace and stability of Japan"—noting that China had not ruled out the use of force to assert control over Taiwan.[135] Australian officials privately told American interlocutors that remaining wholly out of a US-China clash over Taiwan was unthinkable, and an October poll showed that nearly half of Australians favored sending troops to defend Taiwan in a contingency.[136] Amid reports that China's military activity near the island had unsettled senior Filipino officials, the Philippines and the United States committed to doubling the number of troops engaged in a joint exercise.[137] They subsequently reached a deal giving US troops access to four bases across the Southeast Asian country.[138]

## Competing with China Domestically

In the United States, domestic political opinion continued to harden against China. Amid disagreement about nearly every aspect of domestic policy during the Biden years, Republicans and Democrats found accord on actions they deemed necessary for effective competition with China. In late 2021, Biden pitched a $1 trillion infrastructure bill, which would rebuild roads, provide broadband access, upgrade bridges, and more, as a way to boost America against China.[139] In his 2022 State of the Union address, Biden pointed to China as reason to pass the Bipartisan Innovation Act, which aimed to invest in emerging technologies and domestic manufacturing. "We used to invest 2 percent of our G.D.P. in research and development," the president stressed. "We don't now. China is."[140] Blinken, delivering his major China address in May 2022, called for "a modern industrial strategy" that would make the American economy more competitive and supply chains more resilient.[141] A poll taken in June showed that 82 percent of Americans had an unfavorable view of China, a rise of more than thirty points over five years.[142]

Similar concerns drove the CHIPS and Science Act, a mammoth industrial policy bill signed into law during August. The act provided $280 billion over a decade to spur domestic semiconductor production, increase technology research and development, and boost STEM education.[143] A central goal of the legislation was, as the White House put it, to "counter China."[144] In calling for its passage, Senate Majority Leader Chuck Schumer, who drafted the initial text with Senator Todd Young, described it as "a legislative package to outcompete China and create new American jobs." If America did not better compete, he added, "our rivals—chief among them the Chinese Communist Party—would likely beat us to the punch and reshape the world in their authoritarian image. Frightening. A frightening prospect."[145] Secretary of Defense Lloyd Austin expressed support for the legislation, observing, "China, the US military's pacing challenge, has already spent $150 billion updating its semiconductor industry. The investments made through the CHIPS Act are critical to our national security."[146] H. R. McMaster, Trump's national security advisor, expressed similar support, saying, "It is vital that Congress act now to counter Chinese economic aggression, compete, and secure competitive advantages necessary to preserve peace and promote prosperity."[147] For the first time in many decades, the overriding argument behind federal spending on domestic, non-defense industrial production focused on the need to compete with a would-be aggressor. Failure to do so, the proponents cautioned, could yield international leadership to Beijing, and even endanger the peace Americans enjoy. At its signing, Young said, "Today, America goes on offense against the Chinese Communist Party. We have a national security imperative to ensure we don't fall behind China in technological innovation. . . . The Chinese Communist Party actively lobbied against this legislation because they know that this bill is bad for China and good for the United States."[148]

Having worked to boost America's ability to make semiconductors at home, the administration quickly pivoted to restrain China's ability to produce its own. Previous restrictions had sought to keep US-produced chips from the Chinese security services. The new strictures, however, went far further, by stopping the export of the most high-end chips to China's advanced supercomputing facilities no matter their purpose, bad or benign.[149] The controls aimed not only to stop the PRC's use of American chips, US tools, and any foreign chips made with US tools, but also to frustrate Beijing's ability to find alternatives. And though the administration announced the measures unilaterally, it began persuading key source countries like Japan and the Netherlands to follow suit. As the *Washington Post* put it, "The aim is not only to make it harder for China to *buy* chips but also to make it harder for China to *build* chips—thereby stymying both its work in AI today and its hopes of harboring an entirely domestic microchip industry tomorrow."[150]

Here, and with little fanfare, US policy toward China crossed a Rubicon. For years, Beijing had accused the United States of containing China and trying to prevent its rise, and American officials always rejected the charge. Barack Obama declared, over a decade before, that "we welcome China's rise."[151] In its 2020 China strategy, the Trump administration assured that "[w]e do not seek to contain China's development," and envisioned a situation in which "both of our nations, businesses, and individuals can enjoy security and prosperity."[152] Secretary of State Antony Blinken, in May, echoed the theme: "We don't seek to block China," he said, "from its role as a major power, nor to stop China—or any other country, for that matter—from growing their economy or advancing the interests of their people."[153]

This no doubt remained the administration's rhetorical aim. The effect of their policies was another matter. The rationale for the ban was, at one level, entirely straightforward: Beijing uses such chips and equipment to build weapons that target American forces and surveillance devices that repress its citizens. It explicitly aimed to use such imports to develop its own, indigenous ability to produce chips even without US technology. Yet the same semiconductors that power missiles and surveillance tools can be used for a range of civilian applications. And while the new export controls were limited to high-end capabilities, the Commerce Department made clear that restrictions would not be relaxed, even as high-end chips become commodity ones over time.[154] Given the importance of advanced semiconductors to a modern economy, the effect will be to constrain Chinese technological development and economic growth.

The new steps flowed from a policy first outlined by National Security Advisor Jake Sullivan in September, one that aimed to keep China as far behind as possible in its development of key technologies.[155] In announcing the new measures, administration officials hinted at similar controls to come on quantum computing, artificial intelligence, large-scale data sets, biotechnology, and clean energy technology—the very areas that represent the new commanding heights of a modern economy. Overstating matters a bit, columnist Edward Luce reflected, "Imagine that a superpower declared a war on a great power and nobody noticed. Joe Biden this month launched a full-blown economic war on China—all but committing the US to stop its rise—and for the most part, Americans did not react."[156] In a sign of the times, not only were there no prominent American political voices opposing the sweeping measures, but within weeks Japan and the Netherlands, key chipmaking powers, agreed in principle to join the US effort.[157]

## National Security and Defense Strategies

In the fall of its second year, the Biden administration issued its NSS and NDS, both of which had been delayed after Russia's invasion of Ukraine. Nowhere in either document did the terms "pivot" or "rebalance" appear. Yet echoes of the by-now decade-old ambition remained. The strategies focused on China as America's top national security priority and, less explicitly, the Indo-Pacific as the priority region. China, the NSS said, "is the only competitor with both the intent to reshape the international order and, increasingly, the economic, diplomatic, military, and technological power to do it."[158] For the defense strategy, "the most comprehensive and serious challenge to US national security is the PRC's coercive and increasingly aggressive endeavor to refashion the Indo-Pacific region and the international system to suit its interests and authoritarian preferences."[159] While Russia posed "acute threats," the Defense Department would prepare to prevail in conflict by "prioritizing the PRC challenge in the Indo-Pacific region, then the Russia challenge in Europe."[160] The NSS observed that competition with China was increasingly global, but "most pronounced in the Indo-Pacific."[161] As the *New York Times* described it, "What leaps from the pages of Mr. Biden's strategy, which was drafted by the National Security Council with input from around the administration, is a relentless focus on China"—even nine months into the war in Ukraine.[162]

National security strategies rarely introduce new ideas and policies, but rather impose an intellectual superstructure on the many national security–related activities an administration is already conducting. The Biden NSS proposed to deal with China via a combination of investing in domestic and international strength, working with allies and partners, and bilateral competition.[163] This articulation, by that point in the administration, was not novel. More interesting was the set of reactions to the national strategy. Hardly a Washington voice rose to contest the focus on China, the real though less-explicit prioritization of Asia, or the general tone of hawkishness. In one of the document's few vivid criticisms, Nadia Schadlow, who drafted the Trump NSS, charged Biden's version with holding out unrealistic hopes of cooperation with Beijing in light of its focus on competition.[164]

The administration tried to reorient its military deployments and posture consistent with these stated regional priorities. For the first time in thirty years, the US Navy in 2022 had not a single carrier strike group present in the Middle East; at multiple points throughout the year, two of the eleven US strike groups were present in the Indo-Pacific.[165] Facilities upgrades supported B-52 operations from northern Australia, making Australia, in the words of security expert Ashley Townshend, "one of the only places in the Indo-Pacific that can operate as a forward operating location for [U.S. Stratcom] Bomber Task Force (BTF) missions and strategic operations (w Hawaii, Guam, Diego Garcia)."[166] Townshend argued that the upgrades would improve the strategic bomber operations crucial for "conventional and nuclear deterrence, high-end conflict, and reassuring allies and partners."[167] The US Army also moved equipment and vehicles from the CENTCOM area of responsibility to the Pacific.[168]

At the same time, some experts and GOP lawmakers pushed back against the Air Force decision to replace F-15 fighter squadrons permanently stationed in Japan with rotational forces. The Pentagon said the decision was aimed at modernizing squadrons in the region, but the lawmakers said that it sent "the wrong signal" to China and US allies in the Indo-Pacific region.[169] Even if the decision proves advantageous, as experts at the Center for a New American Security argued it would, serious trade-offs were involved. The opportunity costs of supporting rotational forces alone are significant, since the bill for increased logistical support of rotational forces would take priority over other DOD costs.[170] Two analysts observed mid-year that, "[t]aken together, these efforts have only nudged US posture in the direction of rebalance objectives."[171]

Yet things appeared to be moving, albeit slowly. The administration requested $6.1 billion for the Pacific Deterrence Initiative, an unprecedented amount that was boosted to $11.5 billion by Congress, which authorized an additional $1 billion for INDOPACOM's unfunded priorities.[172] The defense authorization bill for fiscal year 2023 included numerous other provisions for the Indo-Pacific, including establishing a Joint Force Headquarters in the Indo-Pacific and the Taiwan Enhanced Resilience Act, which aimed to bolster Taiwan's defense capabilities.[173] Ratner, the assistant secretary of defense overseeing Asia, suggested more moves were in the offing: "2023," he said, "is likely to stand as the most transformative year of US force posture in the region in a generation."[174]

As Washington engaged in these efforts, it grew ever clearer that the measure of effectiveness would not simply be the amount of military resources deployed in Asia versus other regions—whether, for instance, 60 percent of a shrinking navy was based in the Indo-Pacific rather than elsewhere. Nor were comparisons with past levels of resource expenditures particularly meaningful. A military pivot—which was, from its very inception, aimed to balance power in Asia—would have to occur while Chinese power continued to rise. In 2022, Beijing possessed the world's largest navy, which was disproportionately focused on the Pacific in contrast to America's globally dispersed presence. Beijing had the biggest air force in Asia, was completing its third aircraft carrier, and had developed hypersonic and other advanced weapons. It was engaged in a major expansion of its nuclear arsenal and had acquired counter-space capabilities to threaten US and allied satellites. Beijing was expanding a naval installation in Cambodia and had reached a security agreement with the Solomon Islands.[175] It was against this backdrop that the Biden administration attempted to do more in Asia.

Coming out of the US midterm elections and the Chinese Communist Party congress, however, China suddenly looked anything but almighty. Severe COVID lockdowns prompted widespread protests across major cities at levels not seen since the 1989 Tiananmen Square demonstrations. Unable to contain the popular anger online or in the streets, the government caved, reopened cities, and watched as the pandemic spread wildly through the population.[176] At the same time, America, for all its divisions and political dysfunctions, conducted a drama-free election in which voters sent the most extreme voices home. Biden, anticipated to take a major political hit after Republican gains in both houses, watched as Democrats did far better than expected. Perhaps Americans, given their proclivity to detect existential foreign threats and worry about internal decline, had grown too pessimistic about the China challenge and America's Asian opportunity.

## An Asia Policy for a Global Power

Yet by the midpoint of Biden's term, North Korea was back to testing missiles—indeed, more than ever before—and US officials were girding for a seventh nuclear test. Iran was continuing to enrich uranium and began to provide weapons to Russia for its war in Ukraine. The flickers of a new ISIS threat arose in Syria, with US special forces conducting increasing numbers of raids. Turkey was blocking the accession of Sweden and Finland to NATO and threatening military action in Syria against the same Kurdish forces that were keeping ISIS at bay. And the United States during 2022 provided more assistance to Ukraine than it had to any country in a single year since South Vietnam during the Vietnam War.

In early 2023, Beijing made its presence felt by floating a spy balloon across the continental United States, spurring a week's worth of wall-to-wall media coverage.[177] The vaunted Ukrainian counteroffensive stalled mid-year and the war against Russia reached a battlefield stalemate. And in October 2023, Hamas launched a large-scale terrorist attack against Israel, eliciting a war that resulted in massive civilian casualties and displacement in the Gaza Strip, concerns about Israeli security, and the prospects of wider conflict in the Middle East. A month later, Biden met with Xi at the APEC summit in San Francisco, their first meeting in over a year. The two leaders agreed to restart some cooperation that had been suspended after the Pelosi visit and to resume military to military communications. The summit, which had been aimed at reducing tensions, succeeded in projecting a less frosty tone, though Xi reportedly said during the meeting that Beijing would reunify Taiwan with China, and that only the timing remained undecided.[178]

The multiplying international crises forced real resource tradeoffs on the administration. At the end of 2023, Biden submitted to Congress a supplemental appropriations request totaling over $100 billion; the proposal included $61 billion for Ukraine and to replenish US military stocks, $14 billion in Israel-related aid, $11 billion for border security and migrant issues, $9 billion for humanitarian assistance—and a total of $2 billion for security assistance to the Indo-Pacific.[179]

How to allocate finite national security time, attention, and resources across multiple issues in multiple regions is the perennial challenge of a global power like the United States. Kurt Campbell observed during the Biden administration that balancing responsibilities across regions "is the hardest [challenge] when you're going up against a dominant country in Asia—when we are a global power."[180] This is the stuff of grand strategy, and the prevailing approach in 2023 offered several abstract answers to the problem. Washington would work with allies, augmenting its own power with their resources. It would take advantage of time, dealing with acute threats like Russia now while also handling longer-term challenges like China. It would shore up its own strength by growing a more innovative and resilient economy, increasing the military budget, and dampening its political divisions.

All to the good as objectives. And yet the question remained: In a world of multiple challenges, inevitable crises, and an unprecedented competitor like China, how should—indeed, how could—America do everything, everywhere all at once?

# 7

# Please Stay

## Europe and the Pivot

The Obama administration's announcement of a pivot to Asia left America's European partners predictably uneasy. They worried that the United States was embarked on a historically mistaken policy that would leave Europe vulnerable, and wondered what the approach meant for US commitments—and what it implied of US demands. Charles de Gaulle may have summed up the traditional European reaction to major American initiatives when he said, "You may be sure that the Americans will commit all the stupidities they can think of, plus some that are beyond imagination."[1] Yet there was virtually no consultation with the transatlantic allies before the initiative was unveiled—and as Europe was mentioned in only eight sentences of Secretary Clinton's 4,000-word Pivot speech in November 2011, the Pivot emerged as a source of early angst to Washington's most intimate international collaborators.[2]

This was nothing new. European leaders in preceding decades had first learned from television and the front pages about John F. Kennedy's 1962 Cuban Missile Crisis, Lyndon Johnson's 1965 escalation in Vietnam, Richard Nixon's 1971 unilateral cancellation of the international convertibility of the US dollar to gold, Nixon's 1971 Opening to China, Henry Kissinger's 1973–1974 diplomacy during the Yom Kippur war, Ronald Reagan's 1983 Strategic Defense Initiative, Bill Clinton's 1994 abrupt troop withdrawal from Somalia, and George W. Bush's 2001 War on Terror. Europeans often expect allied consultations to consist of a back-and-forth with Washington in advance of a policy decision, in which European views are considered and can sway the outcome. Americans, even in administrations most dedicated to close transatlantic ties, tend to view allied consultations as informing European capitals that a decision has just been made—and will be imminently announced. Historically, protected by two large oceans and friendly neighbors, America's sometimes chaotic, sometimes combative, sometimes brutal interagency process tends to formulate US foreign policy largely without foreigners.

In the spring of 2013, two years after the Pivot's announcement, significant percentages of European respondents said the United States took the interest of their country into account "not too much" or "not at all" when making international policy decisions. In Germany, 48 percent fell into the two categories; in Italy, 53 percent; in Britain, 57 percent; in Poland, 61 percent; in France, 65 percent; in Greece, 79 percent; and in Spain, a whopping 80 percent.[3] Such sentiments were widespread during the Obama presidency, but European publics were even more critical of the Bush and Trump administrations. Indeed, by 2018, during the Trump presidency, many of the numbers had spiked—Italy rose to 70 percent, Britain to 72 percent, Germany to 80 percent, France to 81 percent, and Spain to 90 percent. Only in Poland and Greece did the numbers fall, to 56 percent and 70 percent, respectively.[4]

While European governments may have grown accustomed to Washington's ways, the Pivot announcement generated more questions than usual. At issue was not only the announced policy, but also the strategic impulse that underlay it. As Daniel Fried, a senior Europe policy official in both the Bush and Obama administrations, recalled, "The Obama team initially treated Europe as passé and sometimes a drag. The Europeans understood this and reacted with dismay, expressing frustration that the US seemed to dismiss what Europe could contribute to a common Asian policy. Obama himself had scant regard for Europe, several senior European leaders from both East and West told me."[5]

Although most European governments kept any consternation private, a few brave souls broke with convention. Ine Eriksen Søreide, then Norway's defense minister, stressed that "[t]he debate on NATO and on this relationship, seen from Europe, tends to be about fear of US abandonment. These fears have been accentuated by the US intention to re-balance to the Asia/Pacific."[6] Malcolm Rifkind, chair of the UK Parliament's Intelligence and Security Committee (and a former foreign secretary), wondered if, "[h]aving relied upon the United States for security and economic growth since the latter half of the 20th century, the nations of the EU will soon find that they are no longer the focal point of American attention."[7] Central European Policy Institute president Tomas Valasek captured the essence of Europe's reaction, saying, "America's focus on Asia puts NATO in uncharted waters.... The US pivot now further widens the gap between America's defense priorities and European capabilities.... Never before in NATO's history were America's allies of so little use for the kinds of scenarios that most occupy America's defense analysts."[8]

Behind such concerns lay a crucial reality. As the second decade of the twenty-first century began, and despite the economic miracle that rebuilt Europe from the ashes of Hitler's war, the Continent's flourishing democracies, the European Union's progress toward integration, the Soviet Union's demise, and Europe's advanced military capabilities—despite all that, America's NATO allies profoundly worried that a serious US geographic reorientation would fundamentally jeopardize their stability, prosperity, and peace.

## Europe's Enduring Military Strength

At first glance, European doubts about US abandonment in favor of Asia seem to defy rational explanation. After all, Europe had major advantages in almost every category over Russia, the only conceivable military threat to its vital national interests. Europe's total population of 600 million, for example, easily surpassed Russia's by a 4 to 1 margin.[9] European defense spending more than quadrupled that of Russia.[10] Compared to Russia's 1,364,000 men and women under arms, European NATO allies possessed some two million (see Figure 7.1).[11] The European Union's combined GDP far exceeded Russia's, by a 10 to 1 margin, and its total trade dwarfed Russia's by 15 to 1.[12] Since the end of the Cold War, Russia's GDP had never amounted to more than 15 percent of Europe's.[13] Moscow did hold a massive advantage over Europe in nuclear weapons, but in 2011 the British and French nuclear arsenal—some 440 strategic nuclear weapons—could destroy Russia as a modern society.[14] Capability matters in judging a threat, as does intent. And Vladimir Putin, for all his efforts to re-establish a sphere of influence among non-NATO post-Soviet states, had never made significant and genuine threats against NATO territory.

Why, then, did Europe fret that it could not contend with Russia in the absence of a dominating US military presence on the Continent? The most basic explanation can be found in the two catastrophic wars of the twentieth century, conflicts

| | Europe | Russia | Ratio |
|---|---|---|---|
| Population | 594,889,767 | 142,960,908 | |
| Defense Spending | $289.41 billion | $66.51 billion | |
| Troops | 2,004,680 | 1,364,000 | |
| GDP | $13.14 trillion | $1.3 trillion | |
| Trade | $10.6 trillion | $711.12 billion | |
| Deployed Nuclear Weapons | 440 | 2,430 | |

Figure 7.1. Europe and Russia Data.
All data are from 2011. Currency values are in constant 2015 US dollars, unless otherwise noted.

that shattered Europe. These calamities, which killed 50 million Europeans, ended only after the United States crossed the Atlantic and entered the wars. By issuing a NATO treaty commitment in April 1949, the United States helped ensure that sixty years of peace on the Continent would follow. Any suggestion that Washington might loosen that sacred guarantee reminded Europe of its inability to manage its own affairs, and of its propensity over five centuries to bring death and destruction upon itself.

Then there was the Russian bear, even if it had been geographically, demographically, militarily, and diplomatically weakened by the Soviet collapse. Although the allies topped Russia in all the categories listed above, except nuclear weapons, a central question hovered over the European reaction to the Pivot: *Could* it fight without key US-enabling functions, like airlift, surveillance and reconnaissance, and munitions, if it had to?[15] *Would* NATO fight without US forces as its spine? While no one—not in the Obama administration nor outside it—seriously posited Washington's abandonment of Europe, the Pivot announcement nevertheless raised European questions about America's long-term intentions.

The Continent's concern also reflected the fact that, over the decades, most of its national armies had hollowed out due to inadequate and inefficient defense spending.[16] When Europeans had to choose between guns and butter, they mostly chose butter. In addition, polls showed that most young Europeans did not have the stomach to risk death in combat.[17] In the spring of 2015, for example, a majority in Germany, Italy, and France, and a near-majority in Spain, said that their country should not use military force to defend a NATO ally in a military conflict with Russia. While the poll drew some criticism for failing to remind respondents that, under Article V of the North Atlantic Treaty, NATO members are obliged to come to one another's defense, it nevertheless indicated a softness in European publics' willingness to fight.[18] If Bismarck was right that wars are won through "blood and iron," the idea that European armies would provide enough of both, and would bring combined arms formations briskly to the battlefield to confront a Russian invasion, seemed to many altogether fanciful.[19]

How, then, could European countries resist the Kremlin's coercive intervention in their domestic politics, which accelerated during the 2010s? How could they avoid Russian cyber interference in their national infrastructure and government institutions? How could deterrence be maintained with a reduced US security role in Europe? And how could a potentially revanchist Russia be persuaded indefinitely that the risks of attacking NATO territory outweighed the advantages, without the American eagle on the front lines?

The announcement that the United States was pivoting to Asia brought these European nightmares into persistent and prolonged daylight. The Obama administration tried to reassure the allies; it argued that thousands of US troops would remain on the Continent, that the American commitment to the defense of Europe was as strong as ever, and that US nuclear deterrence would be unaffected by a US Pivot to Asia.[20] In time, it would speak not of pivoting *from* Europe to Asia, but rather pivoting *with* Europe to Asia. Leaders on the Continent remained unconvinced.

## America's Military Presence in Europe

As the years passed, however, the allies were largely relieved. No significant pivot from Europe occurred. Secretary Clinton often visited Asia while in office, and Obama's first-term team increased its diplomacy in the Indo-Pacific, but the momentum was not sustained.[21] Instead, US transatlantic diplomacy proceeded full bore, with no consequential diminishment in favor of Indo-Pacific objectives. During the 2010s, the United States pushed to enlarge NATO eastward toward the Russian border and led the effort to enhance NATO's permanent force posture in Poland.[22] This NATO expansion, with its wider geographic commitment to Europe, coincided with a roughly sustained level of US forces on the Continent. Washington not only pressed the allies to spend more on their own defense, but also managed the alliance effort in Afghanistan and backstopped NATO's intervention in Libya, including when European countries ran short of ammunition and other equipment.[23] The United States also collaborated with Europeans on the Iran nuclear agreement and consulted with Europe in responding to the Arab Spring.[24] It led the effort to crush the Islamic State caliphate, which posed a greater threat to Europe than to the United States.[25] All this amounted to a great deal of activism in the European neighborhood for a country purportedly shifting its focus to Asia.

There was, in fact, no US military pivot from Europe. Although Washington withdrew over 200,000 troops in the decades *before* the Pivot was announced, the United States decreased its overall troop presence on the Continent by only 8,000 from 2011 to 2020, and in the same time period deployed troops to three additional European countries: Norway, Poland, and Romania.[26] Each successive deployment brought US troops further east on the Continent (Figure 7.2). Although there was a small decrease in the overall troop presence in Europe, those forces generally did not transfer to the Indo-Pacific; instead, they were mainly sent to aid crisis management in the Middle East. Nor was there any reduction in US air power in Europe; rather, the number of squadrons deployed to the region increased from eleven in 2014 to thirteen in 2020.[27]

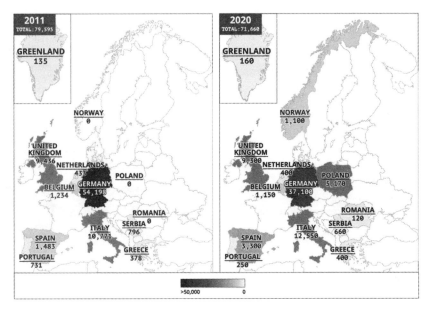

**Figure 7.2.**  US troop deployment changes from 2011 to 2020.

Source: All data are from the International Institute for Strategic Studies (IISS) *Military Balance*. The data from the *Military Balance* represent a snapshot of deployments in early November of each year. ©2012, The International Institute for Strategic Studies, originally published in *The Military Balance* 2012 (reproduced with permission); ©2021, The International Institute for Strategic Studies, originally published in *The Military Balance* 2021 (reproduced with permission).

## US Diplomacy in Europe

There was also no diplomatic pivot from Europe, though many Europeans suspected otherwise. From 2009 to 2020, US presidents visited Europe fifty-eight times and Indo-Pacific countries forty times (see Figures 7.3 and 7.4). During the same period, secretaries of state traveled to European nations on 304 occasions, more than double the 138 visits they made to Indo-Pacific nations. Secretary Clinton traveled to European countries seventy-eight times and those of the Indo-Pacific forty-nine times. Secretary Kerry's European visits amounted to nearly four times the number of stops he made in Asia. Under President Trump, Secretary Tillerson visited Europe nineteen times and the Indo-Pacific sixteen times. Pompeo's travel took him to European nations forty-seven times and to the Indo-Pacific twenty-nine times. The various secretaries of defense across the Obama and Trump administrations visited Europe seventeen more times than the Indo-Pacific.[28]

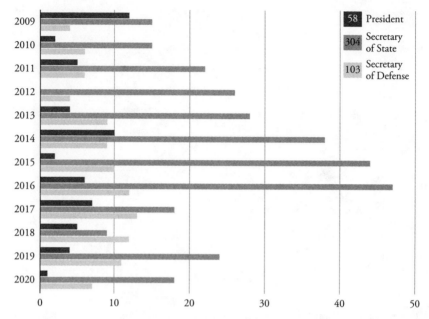

**Figure 7.3.** US president, secretary of state, and secretary of defense visits to European countries, 2009–2020.

Source: Department of Defense, Historical Office, *Secretary of Defense Travels*, accessed: July 22, 2022, https://history.defense.gov/DOD-History/Secretary-of-Defense-Travels/; Department of State, Office of the Historian, *Travels Abroad of the Secretary of State*, accessed: July 22, 2022, https://history.state.gov/departmenthistory/travels/secretary; Department of State, Office of the Historian, *Travels Abroad of the President*, accessed July 22, 2022, https://history.state.gov/departmenthistory/travels/president.

In short, the diplomatic commitment and activity that Washington brought to transatlantic relations did not fall victim to America's announced Pivot to Asia. Multiple problems arose over the decade, ranging from policy disagreements to French desires for "strategic autonomy" and, above all, to President Trump's threats to abandon NATO and charge European members for protection. The Pivot to Asia was not one of those causes. Through the decade after its announcement, Europe remained the top destination of high-ranking US officials.

## Sustained Transatlantic Economic Ties

There was also no US economic pivot from Europe. The dollar reigned supreme across the Atlantic, and the US goods trade deficit with Europe rose by 83.5 percent between 2011 and 2020.[29] Americans were not only buying more European products but were doing so at an accelerated pace. In addition,

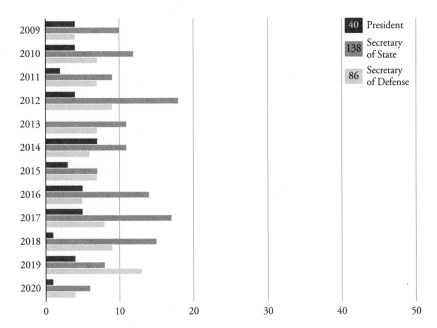

**Figure 7.4.**  US president, secretary of state, and secretary of defense visits to countries in the Indo-Pacific, 2009–2020.

Source: Department of Defense, Historical Office, *Secretary of Defense Travels*, accessed July 22, 2022, https://history.defense.gov/DOD-History/Secretary-of-Defense-Travels/; Department of State, Office of the Historian, *Travels Abroad of the Secretary of State*, accessed July 22, 2022, https://history.state.gov/departmenthistory/travels/secretary; Department of State, Office of the Historian, *Travels Abroad of the President*, accessed July 22, 2022, https://history.state.gov/departmenthistory/travels/president.

US foreign direct investment (FDI) in Europe increased substantially over the decade, reaching $3.66 trillion in 2020. European FDI into the United States witnessed an even greater increase of 91 percent, reaching nearly $3 trillion the same year.[30]

In 2013, the European Union and United States began to negotiate the Transatlantic Trade and Investment Partnership. Senators Max Baucus and Orrin Hatch, the Finance Committee's top Democrat and Republican, issued a statement virtually impossible to imagine today. "A comprehensive U.S.-EU FTA," they said, "negotiated and implemented with the highest standards, would have a multiplier effect and would be certain to generate much needed economic growth on both sides of the Atlantic. There is no doubt that a U.S.-EU FTA is an enticing opportunity."[31]

All told, from 2011 through 2020, there was no military, diplomatic, or economic pivot from Europe to Asia. The Obama administration's new activities in Asia did not come as a result of a reduced commitment to Europe. The same was true of the Trump administration, even with its weakened relationship with the Continent.

## The Shock of Russia's War

It would take Russia's invasion of Ukraine, not a US pivot to Asia, to pulverize every truism that Europeans held dear about security on the Continent.[32] In February 2022, European governments and publics went to bed in one world and awoke in another. It is no exaggeration to observe that the outbreak of major state-on-state land war in Europe produced a change in outlook and policy akin to 9/11's effect on the United States.

What were neglected national security priorities—defense spending, energy diversification, sanctions—took shape almost overnight. The costs and risks Europe was now prepared to absorb in order to punish Russia and support Ukraine shifted dramatically. As former Swedish prime minister Carl Bildt wrote, "The unravelling and eventual elimination of a European state would threaten all Europeans' security, not to mention undermining global stability and opening a Pandora's box of other issues."[33] A mid-April 2022 poll, conducted by the European Union, found overwhelmingly high numbers in support for the imposition of punitive sanctions on Moscow, the provision of lethal and humanitarian aid to Kyiv, and greater European cooperation, especially on defense matters.[34] The result would shape the ways in which Europeans saw their national interests both across the Continent and in Asia. It would also put Europe temporarily at the top of the Biden administration's priority list, even as it had begun to execute an oft-postponed Pivot to Asia a decade after its initial announcement.

All this took place just after Europeans had begun trying an Asian pivot of their own. In 2020, Germany published an Asia strategy that identified the region as "a priority of German foreign policy" because the "region is becoming the key to shaping the international order in the twenty-first century."[35] Two months later, the Netherlands formulated its own Indo-Pacific strategy.[36] In March 2021, British prime minister Boris Johnson (and thesaurus-wielding officials hunting a synonym for "pivot" and "rebalance") announced a post-Brexit "tilt" to Asia.[37] The next month the European Union issued its first strategy for cooperation in the Indo-Pacific, observing, "today, the Indo-Pacific is the focus of the world's attention."[38] France issued an Asia strategy that echoed Secretary Clinton's Pivot article from a decade prior: the Indo-Pacific region, it said, is the global economy's center of gravity, home to important maritime trade routes, at the forefront of globalization, and of critical demographic weight. As a result, the French said, "the Indo-Pacific region is a priority for French diplomacy and is an essential partner."[39]

Amid war in Europe, however, the Continent looked to its immediate periphery first. European leaders agreed to strengthen NATO, expand the alliance to Sweden and Finland, and increase the alliance's Rapid Reaction Force from 40,000 to 300,000.[40] They agreed to move NATO military forces eastward on a permanent basis and to substantially boost allied defense spending.[41] The leaders decided to supply Kyiv with modern weapons, including, in early 2023, main battle tanks.[42] They embraced a coordinated sanctions regime against Moscow and dramatically reduced their dependence on Russian energy.[43] Governments offered support for Ukrainian refugees, they made funds available for Kyiv's weapons programs, and the European Union opened accession negotiations with Ukraine in December 2023.[44] In sum, Europe agreed to rupture the West's relations with Russia on behalf of Ukraine and the Continent's future.

The war in Ukraine fortified the European view that deep and continued US transatlantic leadership remained indispensable to the future of the Continent, and that nothing less would do. German chancellor Angela Merkel's 2017 declaration—after contentious meetings with President Trump—that "Europeans truly have to take our fate into our own hands" seemed outdated already.[45] French president Emmanuel Macron's insistence on European "strategic autonomy" appeared quaint during a crisis in which the United States deployed additional troops to Europe, provided more military assistance to Ukraine than did any other country, and led the effort to exact economic punishment on Russia for its aggression.

While some experts on Asia may have hoped that the invasion, and the poor performance of the Russian army in Ukraine, might together have led Europe to desire less American involvement in its defense, the opposite occurred. In the absence of Washington's dominating leadership, Europe would have failed the Ukraine test. Former German foreign minister Joschka Fischer observed, "Without US military power, Europe probably would have done little to nothing in response to Putin's war. US military protection will remain indispensable for a long time to come."[46] British defense secretary Ben Wallace called the deployment of additional US troops to Europe "a continued commitment to reassuring allies that as you move from tripwire to more pointed defense, that there will be a more permanent presence of US forces in Europe."[47] Despite the possibilities inherent in a pivot, rebalance, or even tilt to Asia, America's core role in Europe remained unchanged.

The Biden administration's decision, at the June 2022 NATO summit, to enhance its military commitment to Europe reinforced Washington's indispensability to the allies. As discussed in Chapter 11 on defense, the United States boosted troop levels in Europe and moved them east on the Continent. It sent F-35 squadrons, F-22 stealth fighters, and naval destroyers to Europe, as well as missile defense systems. The Biden team submitted a substantially increased defense budget to Congress, to which Congress then added billions of dollars more. Some administration officials suggested quietly that some of the 20,000 additional troops deployed to Europe after the Russian invasion might not stay indefinitely, but others pointed out that the additional US weapons systems announced at the Madrid Summit were long-term, requiring thousands of added personnel to operate.

## China in Europe

Beijing, widely criticized in Europe for its support of Russian aggression, may have welcomed America's renewed preoccupation with the Continent and hoped that it would turn minds in Washington away from the Indo-Pacific. Paradoxically, however, the Ukraine war concentrated European minds not only on the *actual* threat from Russia but also the *potential* threat from China. In a stroke, Russia's invasion of Ukraine helped undermine fifteen years of Chinese diplomacy and, months into the war, Europe emerged with a tougher position on China—and one linked more closely to the United States—than it had before shots were fired on Kyiv.

The allies for the first time publicly called out Chinese behavior in June 2022. The Madrid Summit Declaration said, "We face systemic competition from those, including the People's Republic of China, who challenge our interests, security, and values and seek to undermine the rules-based international order."[48] Significantly, the leaders of Australia, Japan, the Republic of Korea, and New Zealand also attended the summit. In another sign of deepening cooperation between NATO and key players in the Indo-Pacific, the Republic of Korea opened a dedicated mission to NATO in November 2022 and Japan pledged to do the same in 2023.[49] In January 2023, NATO secretary-general Jens Stoltenberg visited Japan and South Korea, in an explicit effort to strengthen the organization's partnership with the two Asian nations, and he underscored that "what happens in Asia, the Indo-Pacific, matters for Europe and NATO, and vice versa."[50] The four Indo-Pacific leaders participated again in the 2023 Vilnius NATO Summit, which repeated, "The People's Republic of China's stated ambitions and coercive policies challenge [NATO's] interests, security and values."[51]

The Madrid and Vilnius communiqués came as serious rhetorical setbacks to Beijing. It had worked assiduously to develop a special relationship with the nations of Europe, and to separate them on policy toward China from Big Brother on the Potomac. If Beijing could persuade the Continent that it wished to normalize relations with the United States, that the United States was determined to spur a new Cold War, and that China was a valuable and good-faith economic partner to Europe, Washington would find it near-impossible to build a transatlantic balancing coalition against it.

By 2020, China had signed bilateral commercial deals with fifteen EU countries as part of the BRI, and it developed ports, major roadways, telecommunications networks, and other critical infrastructure in multiple European nations.[52] (Many European countries have since grown disillusioned by the initiative).[53] Beijing also nurtured relationships with leaders like Hungarian prime minister Viktor Orban and then-Czech president Milos Zeman, and it attempted to influence Central and Eastern European media.[54]

While Beijing has employed a variety of tactics to entice European governments to remain neutral in the confrontation between the United States and China, the most persuasive tool in its arsenal continued to be its vast domestic market. In 2020, China-EU trade was valued at $709 billion, making Beijing the bloc's largest trading partner—exceeding the $671 billion in EU commerce with the United States.[55] In both 2021 and 2022, China was the European Union's largest import partner and third largest export destination in terms of goods.[56]

Such figures reveal that, in a time of global economic downturn, China holds a lock on Europe's prosperity. That reality is never far from the minds of Beijing's policymakers, nor of Europe's political leaders. Despite warnings from their American ally, Europeans are reluctant to push back against Beijing as firmly as Washington has. Heather Conley, a former State Department official, aptly noted, "The Europeans have already experienced deep economic trauma because of cutting off Russia. They cannot imagine cutting off China."[57]

Because of its strong economic relationship with China, especially in the manufacturing and automobile sectors, Germany has been particularly unwilling to confront Beijing.[58] As historian Adam Tooze points out, there is a "fundamental difference between Germany and the vast majority of its Western partners in their dealings with China. . . . China is a vital market for many German industrial exporters. For much of the last decade Germany ran a trade surplus with China. So much so that the question arises whether in the process of decoupling from China, Germany is at risk of losing a major driver of its economic growth."[59] Xi Jinping stressed this dependence during a 2017 visit to Berlin, saying, "Developing China-Germany ties is just like driving a car; we should look further to guarantee safety. As long as both sides fulfill energy and hold steady the steering wheel, the China-Germany cooperation car will go fast and stable to the bright future."[60] He did not need to mention the word "Volkswagen."

In 2021, China was Germany's second largest export destination, buying some €104 billion worth of goods—over half of all EU exports to China. A German Economic Institute study found that the first of half of 2022 witnessed record-high German investments in the PRC, and more than a million German jobs depend directly on Chinese demand.[61] Norbert Röttgen, who chairs the Bundestag's foreign policy committee, called the Sino-German economic relationship "a dependency that leaves us helpless."[62]

In November 2022, Chancellor Scholz visited Xi in Beijing, where he evinced Germany's hesitancy to upset China. Experts Fergus Hunter and Daria Impiombato observed, "The chancellor left the strong impression that his priority is boosting Germany's economic relations with China at a time when other European leaders and his own coalition partners in Berlin are pushing the opposite. China may view Scholz's Germany as a weak link in a Western coalition—and could seek to exploit this."[63] In June 2023, Chancellor Scholz and Chinese premier Li Qiang relaunched bilateral consultations that began during Angela Merkel's tenure, after a three-year hiatus. About the same time, two German companies—Volkswagen and BASF—announced billions of dollars of new investment in China.[64]

Key to China's Europe agenda is pressing for the abandonment of Taiwan as an international entity. In 2020, after the Netherlands Trade and Investment Office in Taiwan was renamed the "Netherlands Office Taipei," China threatened to halt medical aid to the Dutch amid the roaring COVID-19 pandemic, and to boycott Dutch goods. When in November that year the European Parliament adopted a report that called for greater ties with Taiwan, Chinese foreign minister Wang Yi responded, "It's vile in nature and has an egregious impact. . . . China strongly condemns and rejects this move." Wang also castigated Czechia, Lithuania, and Slovakia for accepting visits from Taiwanese cabinet ministers.[65] In November 2021, Lithuania agreed that Taiwan could open a "Taiwanese Representative Office" in Vilnius, a change from its previous practice of referring to Taiwan as "Chinese Taipei."[66] Beijing responded to the name change with a host of diplomatic and economic punishments. Beijing recalled its ambassador, downgraded diplomatic relations, banned all imports from Lithuania, and pressured European firms to remove Lithuanian products from their supply chains.[67]

China vehemently and vocally opposes NATO involvement in the Indo-Pacific—precisely what the allies suggested at the Madrid Summit. Foreign Minister Wang urged NATO "not to look for imaginary enemies in the Asia Pacific or artificially create contradictions and divisions. We firmly oppose certain elements clamoring for NATO's involvement in the Asia Pacific, or an Asia Pacific version of NATO on the back of military alliances." The alliance, he added, "should adhere to its original geographical positioning."[68] If NATO's involvement in Indo-Pacific security goes beyond rhetoric and communiqué language, one can expect China to use its coercive economic instruments to try to stop the trend.

## Europe's Hardening Approach

Despite Beijing's best efforts, European perceptions of China, as noted earlier, have grown more critical in recent years. Europe toughened its stance as Beijing violated ever more human rights norms, especially in Xinjiang, abridged its international commitments by extinguishing democracy in Hong Kong, and exported technology that allows autocracies to better repress their populations. Beijing's "wolf warrior" diplomacy and threats, economic and otherwise, against Taiwan and countries like Australia, Canada, and India, have put off many European officials as well.

Public sentiment shifted too. A 2017 Pew survey of nearly a dozen EU countries found that only in France, Germany, and Italy did 50 percent or more of the population have unfavorable views toward China.[69] Five years later, the majority of the population in every nation polled held unfavorable views toward China—and the figure was over two-thirds in Sweden, the Netherlands, Germany, the United Kingdom, and France. In ten of the eleven countries polled in 2022, Beijing's human rights violations were considered the most significant factor contributing to unfavorable reactions among Europeans—more so than China's military power, its economic competitiveness, and even Chinese interference in the polled country's domestic politics.[70]

Beijing's crackdown on the Uyghur population is a crucial case in point, one that has helped define the current EU-Chinese relationship. Through its Global Human Rights Sanction Regime, the EU imposed sanctions on China in March 2021 for the first time since the Tiananmen Square massacre. When Beijing responded with its own sanctions, Brussels suspended ratification of the EU-China Comprehensive Agreement on Investment, which had been called "the most ambitious agreement that China has ever concluded with a third country."[71] Europeans have continued to raise their voices; in March 2023, EU Commission president Ursula von der Leyen castigated Beijing for "becoming more repressive at home and more assertive abroad."[72]

London's relationship with Beijing represents another stark example of the adverse change in Europe's view of China. In 2015, George Osborne, then-Chancellor of the Exchequer, announced and celebrated "a golden decade" in the China-UK relationship.[73] By the summer of 2022, the two contenders for British prime minister, Rishi Sunak and Liz Truss, sought to outcompete each other in hostility toward Beijing. Sunak warned that China "is the biggest-long term threat to Britain and the world's economic and national security,"[74] while Truss promised to crack down on Chinese-owned companies and referred to the Xi government as an "authoritarian regime."[75]

In September 2022, 424 members of the European Parliament voted to condemn China's response to Speaker Nancy Pelosi's visit to Taiwan. The resolution urged "the PRC to immediately stop all actions and intrusions into the Taiwanese ADIZ and the airspace violations above Taiwan's outer islands" and rejected "the PRC's economic coercion against Taiwan and other democracies in its region, as well as against EU Member States." The resolution also called on EU members to "assume a stronger role when it comes to the situation in the Taiwan Strait and the Indo-Pacific," "increase their economic and diplomatic presence throughout the Indo-Pacific region," and "enhance the existing partnership with Taiwan."[76]

EU foreign affairs chief Josep Borrell criticized China's support for Russia's war, and Belgian foreign minister Hadja Lahbib cautioned in October 2022 that Beijing's commercial vessels could transport military equipment.[77] The same month, a European Union report observed that "China has become an even stronger global competitor for the EU, the US and other like-minded partners," posing challenges that could "widen the divergence between China's and our own political choices and positions."[78]

The 2022 NATO strategic concept reflected a watershed in Europe's view of China. For the first time, the allies singled out China in explicating their strategic raison d'être, and they did so in stinging terms. "The People's Republic of China's (PRC) stated ambitions and coercive policies challenge our interests, security and values," the concept said. "The PRC employs a broad range of political, economic and military tools to increase its global footprint and project power, while remaining opaque about its strategy, intentions and military build-up." Beijing, the document added, seeks to "control key technological and industrial sectors, critical infrastructure, and strategic minerals and supply chains" and "uses its economic leverage to create strategic dependencies and enhance its influence." It strives to "subvert the rules-based international order," including in the space, cyber, and maritime domains, and "the deepening strategic partnership between the People's Republic of China and the Russian Federation. . . run[s] counter to our values and interests."[79]

If Beijing's early hopes were that the war in Ukraine would distract the transatlantic allies from a focus on China, then—as previously stressed—the opposite was the case. European attitudes toward China toughened, and more NATO countries discerned an interest in the Indo-Pacific than before the war. After the Madrid Summit, Evan Medeiros, who served as senior director for China in the Obama White House, observed, "Now that European leaders seem to have abandoned their illusions about China, Asian policy makers want to lock in Europe['s] cooperation for the long slog of strategic competition with China."[80] After a December 2023 visit to Beijing, Ursula von der Leyen stressed, "We have been clear since the beginning of the war that how China will position itself vis-à-vis the Russian aggression toward Ukraine, this will define also our relationship."[81]

Yet transatlantic differences persist over China and Asia policy. While the Pentagon identifies China as its top priority, Europe does not agree. As

Stoltenberg stressed at the 2022 Madrid Summit, "China is not our adversary, but we must be clear-eyed about the serious challenges it presents."[82] A poll conducted in 2022 found that just 7 percent of Germans consider China a "major military threat" while 34 percent believe it a "minor" threat. When the same survey asked Americans, the numbers were 64 percent and 26 percent, respectively.[83] Where most US policymakers now reject the notion that China will become a responsible international stakeholder in the foreseeable future, some European officials still hold out hope. Brussels in April 2022 reaffirmed its previous approach toward China, one that famously described the PRC with the triptych of partner, competitor, and rival.[84] German chancellor Scholz said, in May 2023, "Our relations with China are accurately described as being threefold, with China as our partner, competitor and systemic rival—although rivalry and competition have certainly increased on China's part."[85]

Perhaps most starkly, the United States may go to war with China over Taiwan, while Europe will not. President Biden four times has publicly committed to defend Taiwan against attack. On the other hand, Christoph Heusgen, former national security advisor to Chancellor Merkel, observed, "Beijing should not delude itself about the consequences of an invasion [of Taiwan]. Our possible response should be coordinated within the European Union and clearly communicated. This is not about military intervention—there are other options for sanctions."[86] A June 2023 poll conducted by the European Council on Foreign Relations found that 62 percent across the Continent think their country should remain neutral if war broke out between the United States and China over Taiwan.[87]

In short and all told, the European Union is more willing than the United States to maintain China as an economic and diplomatic collaborator—at least for now. The bloc sees Beijing as a partner in its quest to confront global challenges like climate change, global health, nuclear disarmament, COVID-19 economic recovery, and reform of multilateral organizations.[88] Josep Borrell summarized the European perspective, saying, "Certainly, the United States are our most important ally but, in some cases, we will not be in the same position or on the same approach towards China."[89] He added a week later, "The truth is also that a vast majority of Indo-Pacific and European countries do not want to be trapped into an impossible choice. They don't want to have to choose either the US or China. We, like them, don't want a world that is split into two camps."[90] Scholz added to this sentiment, stressing, "The way forward is not through de-coupling, but smart de-risking."[91]

At the same time, Brussels seeks to curb China's coercive influence by leveraging Europe's role as a regulatory superpower.[92] The depth and breadth of Europe's economic relationship with China forces Beijing to bend to some extent to the bloc's market rules and regulations; these internal market norms have spillover effects that frame global regulations. For instance, the EU's 2016

General Data Protection Regulation (GDPR) prompted international businesses, including those in China, to elicit consent for the use of personal data. China's subsequent Personal Information Protection Law, enacted in 2021, is a direct emulation of the GDPR and testament to the EU's influence in the digital space.[93]

Brussels also presses disputes regarding China's industrial policies, unfair market access, and intellectual property theft through international organizations, particularly the WTO. In June 2018, Brussels filed complaints charging China with treatment of intellectual property inconsistent with the Agreement on Trade-Related Aspects of Intellectual Property Rights (TRIPs).[94] In January 2022, Brussels requested dispute consultations to challenge Beijing over its block on Lithuanian imports. The following month, the European Union did the same over China's theft of intellectual property.[95] The EU pushed for such consultations until the WTO's Dispute Settlement Body (DSB) agreed to examine Chinese practices in January 2023.[96] In July, Brussels and Beijing informed the DSB that they had agreed to initiate arbitration procedures, and in September 2023, the European Commission announced it began an investigation into Chinese electric vehicles, which, it alleged, benefit unfairly from state subsidies.[97]

In light of Europe's extensive economic dependence on China, the bloc has announced modest steps to diversify. In May 2021, the EU Commission announced an industrial strategy that aims to decrease Continental reliance on the Chinese market and strengthen European security and autonomy.[98] While China provides 52 percent of the EU's "strategic imports," the bloc hopes to diversify supply chains in sectors such as pharmaceuticals, cloud computing, rare earth mining, semiconductor production, and microchips.[99] Europe also seeks to diminish Beijing's influence in the developing world. In November 2021, the EU announced a plan to invest €300 billion in infrastructure globally to provide "a true alternative" for emerging markets to China's debt-trap financing, and in 2022 the bloc introduced a proposed anti-coercion instrument directed at Beijing.[100] In March 2023, the European Parliament proposed the Net Zero Industry Act, a move aimed at cutting the Continent's dependence on China for green technology.[101]

## Europe Looks to Asia

Europe's Indo-Pacific activism is increasing but, unlike the United States, is mostly restricted to diplomatic and economic activities. The European Union's top priority in Asia is to pursue investment and trade agreements with partners in the region. It has signed trade deals with Australia and New Zealand, and has entered into trade negotiations with India, Malaysia, the Philippines, Thailand, and ASEAN.[102] The EU also engages countries in the region on issues like freedom of the seas, the green energy transition, and digital governance and connectivity.[103] Europe's security hand in the Indo-Pacific is weak. While there are examples of European defense collaboration with Asian partners, these activities are marginal and largely limited to freedom of navigation exercises, counterterrorism, and intelligence sharing. In the Indo-Pacific strategies published by various European governments, none foresees an important security role in Asia.[104]

France, for example, has almost no power projection capability in Asia, despite possessing five permanent military bases, three military commands, combat air deployments, multiple frigates and control ships, and thousands of personnel.[105] For six months starting in August 2021, Germany deployed one frigate to conduct freedom of navigation and military exercises with Australia, Japan, Singapore, and the United States.[106] In October 2021, the European Union and Japan mounted a joint naval exercise, and in August the following year, France and Germany sent air force contingents to Australia's "Pitch Black" multinational air force exercise.[107] German Air Force chief of staff Ingo Gerhartz highlighted the purpose, saying, "We want to demonstrate that we can be in Asia within a day."[108] After deploying a carrier strike group to the Indo-Pacific in 2021, the United Kingdom permanently stationed two warships to the region in 2022.[109] In their first-ever joint exercise, the European Union and the United States conducted a naval drill in the Indo-Pacific in March 2023 and, in May, Paris announced that the *Charles De Gaulle* aircraft carrier would be deployed to the region in 2024.[110] London then declared that its HMS *Queen Elizabeth II* and *Prince of Wales* carriers would do the same by 2025.[111] Such moves were welcomed by American policymakers wishing to signal a unified front in Asia, but ultimately were of mostly symbolic importance. As security experts at the International Institute for Strategic Studies observe, Europe lacks the ability to deploy its military capabilities to the region quickly, and doing so would "significantly weaken conventional deterrence in Europe vis-à-vis other near-peer adversaries such as Russia."[112]

In a 2022 speech introducing Germany's first national security strategy, Defense Minister Christine Lambrecht detailed Europe's constraints:

> Germany and Europe depend on a security architecture whose stability they cannot ensure on their own. . . . [The United States] has now, for good reason, turned its focus towards security in the Pacific region, however. In future [sic], it may thus not be able to guarantee the defense of Europe to the extent that it used to in the past. The consequences are obvious: we Europeans, and before anyone else that means we Germans, must make more efforts towards credibly projecting enough military strength that other powers will not even think about attacking us.[113]

Put simply, Europe possesses neither the resources nor the political will to sustain a substantial military presence in the Indo-Pacific. If America meaningfully pivots to Asia, in military terms it will do so mostly alone.

Europe remains, of course, only a semi-unified political actor. The overlapping trips to Beijing taken by French president Macron and EU president von der Leyen in April 2023 illuminated the cleavages. In a Beijing press conference, the EU chief reminded the PRC that "arming the aggressor [Russia] would be against international law," and in her private conversation with Xi she shared "deep concerns about the deterioration of the human rights situation in China," with a particular focus on Xinjiang.[114] Before his meeting with Xi, however, Macron struck a different tone. "China," he tweeted, "has a major role to play in building peace. This is what I have come to discuss, to move forward on."[115] The French and Chinese leaders then committed themselves to a vaguely worded "global strategic partnership" and praised the arrival of a "multipolar world"—a thinly veiled jab at receding US primacy.[116] Asked about Taiwan, Macron observed, "The worse thing would be to think that we Europeans must become followers on this topic and take our cue from the U.S. agenda and a Chinese overreaction."[117] Europe, after decades of integration, still contains multiples, and not least on policy toward China and Asia.

## Rebalancing Military Resources

The Biden administration, addressing the competitive requirements of the Indo-Pacific and Europe, for a time asserted that Eurasia now comprises one strategic, geographic, and policy area. Thus, officials argued, any pivot from Europe to Asia has been conceptually overtaken by combining the two regions.[118] Such a rhetorical formulation, however, relieves none of the inherent trade-offs between Europe and Asia, and the administration soon abandoned such reasoning. Indeed, some tools need not be zero-sum; it's possible, for instance, for Washington to pursue ambitious economic agreements in both regions simultaneously (even if it now pursues them in neither). Military resources and diplomatic bandwidth represent a far harder case. Objectives and strategies are, after all, about deciding among policy alternatives, and as historian Hal Brands puts it, "Long-term competition occurs in a world of finite resources. . . . The essence of long-term competition, then, is strategic choice. Countries must choose where to focus and where to economize."[119]

Russian armed forces, in the early stages of the Ukraine war, proved unable to defeat a largely volunteer, poorly trained, disorganized, crudely equipped, and idiosyncratically led Ukrainian resistance. As Secretary Blinken put it in June 2023, "The Kremlin often claimed it had the second-strongest military in the world, and many believed it. Today, many see Russia's military as the second-strongest in Ukraine."[120] Estimates in late 2023 placed Russian dead and wounded at 315,000, including a staggering 100,000 casualties from December 2022 to May 2023, and it is likely that the Kremlin will continue to be beset by manpower shortages unless it launches another mobilization wave or uses conscripts.[121] It has also suffered significant destruction of its military equipment and has consumed large quantities of munitions. As the *New York Times* reported in December 2023, for example, "At the start of the war, Russia had 3,500 tanks but has lost 2,200, forcing them to pull 50 year old T-62 tanks from storage."[122]

Over the course of the conflict, Russia's battlefield performance nevertheless improved modestly. As a result, Ukraine's June 2023 counteroffensive made little progress against strong, dug-in defenses. Looking forward, an *Economist* defense reporter noted, "The crucial question for 2024 is which side can rebuild more high-quality forces the quicker."[123] To these ends, Moscow has ramped up defense production and may produce more than 2 million shells in 2024, in addition to those it receives from North Korea, along with hundreds of new and refurbished tanks.[124]

Russia will, however, require years to reconstitute its pre-February 2022 military strength and, as a result, Moscow will pose no serious conventional military threat to NATO territory for the foreseeable future. Long gone are worries about Soviet armored columns breaking through thin NATO defenses and racing westward through the Fulda Gap. Surely Washington should consider these structural and operational weaknesses of the Russian armed forces when deciding on the type and number of American troops and weapons devoted to the future defense of Europe, especially given acute security challenges in the Indo-Pacific.

Policymakers should also take into account NATO's growing strength and unity. Projected defense spending has soared throughout Europe after the Ukraine invasion. Germany, Denmark, Finland, Latvia, Estonia, Lithuania, Belgium, Romania, Italy, Poland, Norway, Sweden, and others all pledged to substantially increase defense spending and to meet or exceed 2 percent of their GDP.[125] The number of NATO countries that met the 2 percent defense spending goal nearly quadrupled from three in 2014 to eleven by the Vilnius Summit in the middle of 2023.[126] The non-US members of NATO boast more active-duty troops than Russia, more battle-ready tanks, more artillery systems, more combat capable aircraft, and more attack helicopters.[127] They also outmatch Russia's naval forces, aircraft carriers, destroyers, frigates, and submarines.[128] The non-US allies continue to suffer shortfalls in areas like strategic lift; intelligence, surveillance, and reconnaissance; munitions; and missile defense—all areas in which US capacity and capability remain necessary. But the overall military balance since Russia's invasion has shifted decisively toward Europe and away from Moscow.

For their part, Europeans made notable strides to advance their own defense, even as they fell short of the most optimistic projections. Despite initial excitement surrounding German chancellor Olaf Scholz's promise to resuscitate Berlin's anemic armed forces, the German Defense Ministry vaguely indicated in early 2023 that only €30 billion of a €100 billion special purpose fund established for weapons purchases had been "earmarked for major purposes."[129] In November 2023, Federal Republic of Germany defense minister Boris Pistorius declared that, "as the most populous and an economically strong country at the heart of Europe, Germany must be the backbone of deterrence and collective defense in Europe," though he still conceded that the turnaround in its military capabilities would take time.[130] In July 2023, France planned to increase its military budget over the next seven years to €413 billion, an increase of about €100 billion over the previous period. It hopes to spend 2 percent of GDP on defense—the target codified by NATO—by 2027. But Paris is playing catch up after a quarter of a century of defense cuts.[131] "We are still making up for this collapse," said Michel Goya, a military historian and former colonel in the French marines.[132]

The inclusion of Sweden and Finland into NATO also provides a significant boost to its military power. Finland has one of the most capable air forces in Europe, and Sweden's Gripen fighter jets are especially equipped to destroy Russian Sukhoi fighters.[133] Sweden and Finland's navies are respectively the fifth and eleventh largest in the world, and their combined naval forces will substantially improve NATO's power projection at sea.[134] In addition, Sweden has 24,000 active troops and 31,800 reservists, and while Finland only has 23,000 active military personnel, it can mobilize up to 900,000 reservists in case of war.[135] Finland's addition to NATO also doubled the size of Russia's border with NATO, which will require Moscow to expend significantly more resources to protect the 830-mile-long boundary.[136] Sweden's militarized Gotland Island could serve as an "unsinkable aircraft carrier" that would threaten the headquarters of Russia's Baltic Sea fleet in Kaliningrad 200 miles away.[137]

In light of the newfound unity and power of NATO's European members and Russia's endemic conventional military weakness, the United States should over time substantially reduce its air and naval forces devoted to European defense. Planners in the Pentagon should decide the details, but as noted above, for a start, such a redeployment should reverse the air and naval enhancements that Biden announced at the 2022 Madrid Summit.

While Washington should begin to pivot military resources from Europe to Asia, it should not reduce its military, diplomatic, or economic support for Ukraine. A Russian victory in Ukraine would jeopardize the security and stability of the entire region, as an emboldened Moscow would present a further risk to other neighbors and require additional Western intervention on the Ukraine model. Ukraine's defeat would set a dangerous precedent that territory could again be taken by force without eliciting decisive countervailing consequences—a lesson that could encourage Beijing to invade Taiwan. As Secretary-General Stoltenberg proclaimed, "President Putin must not win this war, because that will not only be a tragedy for Ukrainians, but also make the world more dangerous. It will send a message to authoritarian leaders all over the world, also in China, that when they use military force, they get what they want."[138]

# 8

# America Is Going Home

## The Middle East and the Pivot

The leaders of the Middle East were no less concerned than their European counterparts when the Pivot was announced, as mentions of the region were virtually absent from administration pronouncements.[1] The few early references argued that crises were "winding down" in the region, and that increased multilateral efforts represented the best way forward in the Middle East.[2] By 2011, even a third of US veterans said the wars in Iraq and Afghanistan were not worth fighting, and expressions of US recommitment to a troubled region were few and far between.[3]

Some observers welcomed the notion of jettisoning US involvement there in favor of the promising Pacific. In mid-2013, for example, Council on Foreign Relations president emeritus Richard Haass wrote, "In contrast to the Middle East, Asia is a locus of great-power competition, where US military presence and action may prove extremely useful in heading off or handling many potential problems. The Obama administration was wise to place a greater emphasis on this part of the world in 2011."[4]

Analysts in the region, unsurprisingly, reacted differently. Haviv Rettig Gur of the *Times of Israel*, for example, warned, "Several Middle Eastern countries have read American behavior—the so-called strategic 'pivot' to Asia, cuts in the defense budget, and the unwillingness to intervene in Syria—as signs of growing American reluctance to shoulder the burden of regional security."[5] The Brookings Doha Center's Greg Gause added, "There's a lot of talk in Saudi Arabia about America abandoning them. The more extreme view is 'The US is going to cut a deal with Iran and sell us out.' The less extreme view is 'It's going to pivot to Asia and cut us out.'"[6]

Administration officials over time attempted to reassure regional partners of American staying power. Speaking in Bahrain in December 2012, Deputy Secretary of State Bill Burns asserted, "For all the logical focus on pivots in other directions, however, the fact remains that the United States cannot afford to neglect what's at stake in the Middle East."[7] At the same session, Senator John McCain captured the theme with his familiar zest, observing, "The idea that the US can pivot away from the Middle East is the height of foolishness."[8]

The administration's broad notion was not to withdraw from the region but rather to reap an immediate peace dividend by quickly ending the war in Iraq and encouraging a broader regional détente—especially between Saudi Arabia and Iran—that would keep the United States from being drawn further into the region's conflicts. The Pivot's architects never attempted to withdraw the Fifth Fleet from Bahrain, downsize US bases in the United Arab Emirates (UAE) and Qatar, remove troops from Kuwait, or end bilateral assistance to Israel and Egypt. They did believe that the United States had squandered enormous blood and treasure in the sands and mountains of the greater Middle East, and they wished to invest American resources in a region that would provide higher returns.

Nevertheless, the impression that the Obama administration—and later the Trump administration—left was quite different from the on-the-ground realities. It soon became an article of faith among key Middle East governments that the United States would not in the future act as the guarantor of regional stability, and that they would be forced to preserve security on their own. That, had it reflected reality, would represent a radical change from America's dominant role in the area since the 1967 Six-Day War. There would have been no United Nations Security Council (UNSC) Resolution 242, the defining document of that conflict which postulated peace between Israel and the Arabs, without the United States. There would have been no rearmament of Israel after that war, no regional empowerment of the Shah's Iran and, in the context of the 1973 Yom Kippur War, no expulsion of Soviet influence in the Middle East. Direct negotiations between Israel and its Arab enemies provided by UNSC Resolution 338 would not have occurred without the United States.

Without the United States, there would have been no Israel-Egypt peace treaty, Israel-Jordan peace treaty, intense negotiation between Israel and Syria, or powerful international champion of Palestinian rights. There would have been no 1991 liberation of Kuwait, but also no 2003 US invasion of Iraq, with its terrible effects on the balance of power in the region, without the United States. There would likely have been no regular flow of oil from the Middle East during these decades without the United States.

Every American president from Lyndon Johnson to Barack Obama affirmed that American vital national interests demanded that the United States seek to shape the Middle East to its and subsequently the globe's advantage. Although the United States erred in its policies from time to time, sometimes very seriously, Middle East governments assumed that American attention to the region was a strategic and tactical given. The general US disaffection with regional wars, frustration at Middle East politics, decreasing dependence on regional oil exports, and the rising attractiveness of Asia as a theater for American engagement threw these convictions into question.

## From Arab Spring to MBS

Even as the Pivot's antecedents were taking shape, American commitment to the Middle East remained sacrosanct. In a September 1993 speech, for instance, Bill Clinton evinced a determined investment in the region. "For more than a quarter of a century," he said, "our Nation has been directly engaged in efforts to resolve the Middle East conflict. We have done so because it reflects our finest values and our deepest interests, our interests in a stable Middle East where Israelis and Arabs can live together in harmony and develop the potential of their region."[9] George W. Bush's view was no different. "I have been convinced," he stressed, "that no region is more fundamental to the security of America or the peace in the world than the Middle East."[10]

Barack Obama articulated a somewhat different rationale for Middle East engagement. Early in his administration, he observed, "It is a vital national security interest of the United States to reduce these [Middle Eastern] conflicts because whether we like it or not, we remain a dominant military superpower, and when conflicts break out, one way or another we get pulled into them. And that ends up costing us significantly in terms of both blood and treasure."[11] Rather than focus on the Middle East because of oil, terrorism, or Israel, the objective was to avoid getting sucked into its quagmires. Partly as a result, as the 2010s rolled along, the United States gave the Middle East reason to believe that America was on its way out of the region, to observe that the United States was often on the short end of competence, and to conclude that Washington was an unreliable partner.

The decade began with Obama's abandonment of Egypt's Hosni Mubarak—America's strategic partner for nearly three decades—in February 2011. US support for the democratic aspirations of Egyptians who long suffered under his regime later gave way to photos of a sick and broken Mubarak in a cage during his trial. While the administration rightly wished to support the pluralist impulses of the Arab Spring, friendly autocrats saw in the Mubarak example a possible future for themselves.

Israeli officials were scathing, with one emphasizing, "Jordan and Saudi Arabia see the reactions in the West, how everyone is abandoning Mubarak, and this will have very serious implications."[12] Former Obama deputy national security advisor Ben Rhodes later recalled, "Saudi leader Mohammed Bin Salman and Emirati leader Mohammed bin Zayed resented the way that Obama had broken with Hosni Mubarak when he faced mass protests in 2011, perhaps seeing it as a harbinger for what would happen if protests of that scale came to their kingdoms."[13] Martin Indyk, a two-time former US ambassador to Israel, makes the point more strongly. "King Abdullah," he said, "was in charge in Saudi Arabia at the time, and he was horrified by Obama pulling the rug out from under Mubarak."[14]

A month later, the United States—with the help of NATO—commenced a military intervention that devastated Libya. What started as a limited operation to prevent a massacre by the forces of Muamar Qaddafi became a months-long effort to topple the dictator. Middle East expert Alan Kuperman described the catastrophic consequences. "Obama's intervention in Libya," he wrote, "was an abject failure, judged even by its own standards."[15] With Mubarak imprisoned in Cairo and Qaddafi killed after NATO aircraft decimated his security detail, few Middle East potentates—none of whom was democratically elected—could feel safe in their beds at night.[16] The implicit, decades-long bargain that, in the name of shared interests, Washington would tolerate widespread repression and horrific human rights abuses, seemed broken.

Matching rhetoric to decisive action might have reassured at least a few friendly leaders in the region. In the context of the Syrian civil war, the Obama administration repeatedly called for the removal of Bashar al-Assad. "The time has come for President Assad to step aside," Obama declared, and in August 2011 a senior White House official confidently asserted that the administration was "certain Assad is on his way out."[17] But as the decade ended, Obama was long gone from office while Assad ruled safely in Damascus. Buttressed by massive Russian and Iranian military intervention, the Syrian dictator had won the civil war, and the United States looked weak, unable to exert its will on the region.

In October 2011, it was more of the same. Just ten days after the original Pivot article was published, Obama confirmed the withdrawal from Iraq of America's remaining 46,000 combat troops by the end of the year.[18] Although this move was conducted in collaboration with the government in Bagdad, it raised questions about whether more US forces from around the region would be going home as well—and what would happen to Iraq after the last Americans left.

Next came the US failure to act in response to Assad's use of chemical weapons on Syrian civilians. In August 2012, President Obama announced that his administration had "been very clear to the Assad regime . . . [and] with every player in the region that [the use of chemical weapons was] a red line for us." Obama went on to warn ominously that "there would be enormous consequences if we start seeing movement on the chemical weapons front or the use of chemical weapons."[19] Assad brazenly crossed that red line just a year later, when the Syrian military released sarin gas on a rebel-controlled part of Damascus, killing nearly 1,500 civilians, including 400 children.[20] Obama did not respond with military force, and his ultimatum disappeared in a cloud of unconvincing White House rhetoric. As former secretary of defense Leon Panetta agonized, Obama's decision not to follow through on the red line, "sent a mixed message, not only to Assad, not only to the Syrians, but [also] to the world."[21]

In July 2015, President Obama signed the Joint Comprehensive Plan of Action (JCPOA), widely known as the Iran nuclear deal. Administration officials

Jake Sullivan and Bill Burns secretly negotiated the framework for an agreement without consulting US regional allies, including Israel.[22] Whatever its intrinsic merits—and many experts were troubled by its contents—the agreement generated consternation among America's closest partners in the Middle East. Israeli prime minister Benjamin Netanyahu referred to the accord as a "historic mistake," one that "threatens Israel and the entire world."[23] America's moderate Arab partners worried that the nuclear agreement was Obama's first step to normalized relations with Iran. As scholar and former CIA analyst Kenneth Pollack testified before Congress, "The Saudis and their Sunni Arab allies fear that the United States intends to use a nuclear deal with Iran as a 'Get Out of the Middle East Free' card. The Gulf states are convinced that this is the Obama administration's intent."[24] A Saudi diplomat referred to the deal as "extremely dangerous," and warned, "Maybe we'll look to other partners like China if America is giving everything to Iran."[25]

Equally troubling to regional partners was Obama's 2016 interview with the *Atlantic*'s Jeffrey Goldberg. The president doubled down on his decision not to enforce his Syria red line, asserted that the Middle East could not be fixed, and argued that it would be a mistake to invest significant US resources in the region.[26] Obama said that Saudi Arabia and Iran would "need to find an effective way to share the neighborhood and institute some sort of cold peace" and observed that, if the United States supported Saudi Arabia in managing Iran, "[it] would mean that we have to start coming in and using our military power to settle scores. And that would be in the interest neither of the United States nor of the Middle East."[27]

The desire to avoid new Middle East wars drove a good deal of Obama's thinking. As Ben Rhodes put it, "The president takes the . . . view . . . that overextension in the Middle East will ultimately harm our economy, harm our ability to look for other opportunities and to deal with other challenges, and, most important, endanger the lives of American service members for reasons that are not in the direct American national-security interest."[28] The contrast between Middle East risks and Asian opportunities seemed obvious to many administration officials.

Throughout the Obama administration, there also was a pervasive sense that Middle Eastern oil was no longer important enough to go to war. As far back as his first presidential campaign, Barack Obama pledged to reduce America's need for Middle Eastern energy. In an October 2008 presidential debate, Obama proclaimed, "our goal should be, in 10 years' time, we are free of dependence on Middle Eastern oil, and we can do it."[29] He was not alone; in 2012, Governor Mitt Romney, running against Obama, offered his own plan for "North American energy independence." "We're not going to have to buy oil from the Middle East, Venezuela, or any other place we don't want to," the Republican candidate said.[30]

US reliance on Middle Eastern oil dropped sharply during the Obama years as American crude production soared. In 2008, the United States produced 7.8 million barrels per day (bpd) of petroleum; by 2016 that number jumped to 14.6 million.[31] In 2021, the US produced 18.8 million bpd, a 241 percent increase since 2008.[32] Similarly, whereas American net imports of crude stood at 11.1 million bpd in 2008, the US became a net *exporter* of petroleum in 2020.[33] In late fall 2023, American oil production increased to over 13 million bpd; by December, the United States was on track to produce more oil than any country in history.[34] While events in the Middle East would continue to affect the global oil price, the American fracking boom and the perception of insulation from price spikes led politicians on both sides of the aisle to diminish the Middle East's geopolitical importance.

During these same years, the Obama team raised concerns about the human rights and governance practices of friendly Arab regimes and at times linked them to specific policies. In 2011, for example, Obama delayed a scheduled $53 million weapons sale to Bahrain due to the country's human rights abuses.[35] Two years later, the president announced a partial freeze on military sales to Egypt until there was "credible progress" toward free elections and a democratically elected civilian government.[36] Cairo was enraged. "You turned your back on the Egyptians," President Sisi thundered, "and they won't forget that."[37] In 2016, the White House halted a $350 million precision-guided weapons sale to Saudi Arabia over the Kingdom's bombing campaigns in Yemen's civil war.[38]

After taking office, Donald Trump amplified the "get out" impulse of his predecessor (if not his support for human rights and democracy). In December 2018, he announced the pullout of all American soldiers from Syria within 30 days, a move that led to the resignation of his own secretary of defense.[39] A few days before the announcement, Trump reportedly told Turkish president Recep Tayyip Erdogan on a phone call that Syria "is all yours. We are done."[40] Although Trump later backtracked and agreed to allow some US troops to remain, in October 2019 he ordered American forces out of portions of northern Syria, where tensions brewed between Turkish and Kurdish forces. This was seen across the Middle East as a clear betrayal of Washington's Kurdish allies in Syria, who had fought alongside US troops against ISIS. As a former minister in the region put it, "This has left a bad taste for all of America's friends and allies in the region, not only among the Kurds. . . . The Russians don't abandon their allies. They fight for them. And so do the Iranians."[41]

In June 2019, Iran shot down an unmanned, $176 million American RQ-4 Global Hawk reconnaissance drone over the Strait of Hormuz.[42] After Trump ordered missile attacks on Iranian radar and missile installations in retaliation, he abruptly called off the strikes while the operation was underway, in an apparent change of heart.[43] Philip Gordon, who would go on to serve as national security advisor to Vice President Kamala Harris, observed, "Trump is in a box of his own making. . . . He has put in place policies—'maximum pressure' on Iran—guaranteed to provoke an aggressive Iranian response, but he's not prepared to respond aggressively in turn, and the Iranians know it."[44]

A similar episode occurred later that year. In September, Iranian missiles and drones attacked an oil field and processing facility in Saudi Arabia, which temporarily disrupted the majority of the Kingdom's oil production.[45] President Trump tweeted that the United States was "locked and loaded" and prepared to retaliate, pending Saudi Arabia's confirmation of the culprit.[46] Even after Riyadh asserted that it had evidence that Tehran was behind the strike, however, Trump chose not to order a military response. Instead, he tweeted that the United States would "substantially increase Sanctions [sic] on the country of Iran."[47] The muted American reaction gave Gulf countries one more powerful reason to question US commitment to their security.[48] For Saudis in particular, the unanswered attacks represented a watershed event, and a prime example that the decades-long "oil for security" bargain with America was broken. The conviction grew that the Kingdom could not rely on the United States alone for protection, even with a vociferously pro-Saudi and anti-Iran leader in the White House.[49]

Trump brought his "America First" message to the Middle East in late 2019, tweeting, "We're getting out [of the Middle East]. Let someone else fight over this long blood-stained sand. The job of our military is not to police the world."[50] Trump also tweeted that he was "slowly and carefully bringing our great soldiers and military home" after calling American military engagement in the Middle East, "the worst decision ever made in the history of our country!"[51] His words radiated to the morning headlines, further suggesting that a dangerous US withdrawal was underway.

The downturn in US relations with friendly Arab regimes continued when, at the November 2019 Democratic presidential debate, Joe Biden reflected the furious American reaction to the horrific murder of journalist Jamal Khashoggi in Ankara, apparently ordered by Saudi Crown Prince Mohammed Bin Salman (MBS). Speaking to the Democratic base and beyond, candidate Biden was passionate. "I would make it very clear," he promised, "we were not going to . . . sell more weapons to them, we were going to . . . make them pay the price and make them . . . the pariah that they are. There's very little social redeeming value . . . in the present government in Saudi Arabia."[52]

Most US politicians and experts across the political spectrum agreed with Biden and demanded a fundamental re-evaluation of the US relationship with the Kingdom. As enormous strains predictably beset relations between Washington and Riyadh, Saudis were astonished that the death of one man, no matter how brutal, could call into question the decades-old partnership between Saudi Arabia and the United States. Other Arab governments, most of whom had dismal human rights records of their own, must have wondered when such a per-ilous Washington sandstorm would hit them.

In his final year, Trump channeled his "Come Home America" spirit in agreeing with the Taliban to withdraw all US troops from Afghanistan within 14 months. As journalists Peter Baker and Susan Glasser detail, "the deal put all the conditions on the Americans, not the Taliban. Trump was so eager to come to terms that he cut the Afghan Government itself out of negotiations altogether, although its troops had been fighting alongside America for two decades."[53] Partner Arab governments again concluded that the United States would abandon its friends if push came to blood.

## Declining US Influence

In sum, US prestige, influence, and credibility steadily declined across the Middle East over the 2010s. In episode after episode, in country after country, Washington vividly displayed for leaders in the region its hesitation to defend their perceived vital national interests, abetted by episodic displays of acute American incompetence. Even though the United States remained the greatest foreign power by far in the Middle East—and during the decade surged troop levels in Afghanistan and deployed over 10,000 troops in Syria and Iraq to de-feat ISIS—it could not shake the region's conviction that America was resolved to substantially reduce its commitment. As Michael Singh, managing director of the Washington Institute for Near East Policy, astutely described, "the United States . . . is undergoing a period of flux in its international priorities, leaving its partners with scant assurance that the places or issues on which Washington focuses today will occupy its attention tomorrow, or that supporting the United States on a particular issue will earn US reciprocity on others."[54] As a conse-quence, some Middle East nations began to turn toward China and Russia in search of a more reliable partnership. A poll conducted by the Washington Institute affirmed this reality (Figure 8.1).

The same data found that respondents in the region put greater importance on good relations with China than on good relations with the United States.[55] This shift in Middle Eastern perceptions of Washington and Beijing has had a major impact on Chinese engagement in the region. Although the United States has far more military bases in the Middle East than does China, for example, Washington lags well behind Beijing in its infrastructure and port investment (Figure 8.2).[56]

Though many of the policies described above had nothing to do with Washington's announced reorientation toward the Indo-Pacific, the Pivot con-cept provided Middle East leaders with a fundamentally revised US strategic

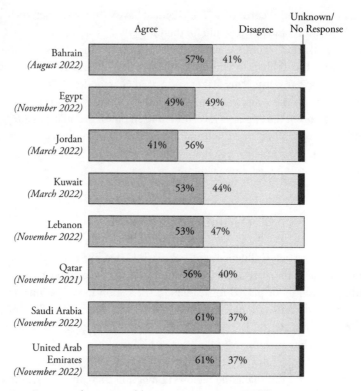

**Figure 8.1.** Response by personal interview surveys in Middle East countries to the following statement: Our country cannot count on the United States these days, so we should look more to Russia or China as partners.

Source: Washington Institute for Near East Policy, "TWI Interactive Polling Platform," Fikra Forum, Washington Institute for Near East Policy, https://www.washingtoninstitute.org/policy-analysis/twi-interactive-polling-platform.

paradigm for America's global priorities and resources, one into which all these Washington actions and statements during the 2010s could be solidly placed and credibly explained. As the impression of US withdrawal became rooted among the nations of the region, they began to accommodate their policies to what they perceived as a new and historic reality—one without persistent US leadership, one without intense American involvement, and one without reliable support from Washington.

Leaders in every country in the Middle East pondered the same strategic issue: In the face of this American disengagement and disinterest, how should they reorient their policies? Each nation answered that question differently, but all looked for opportunities and identified dangers that emerged from the new

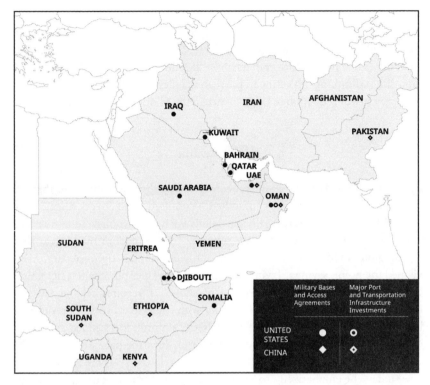

**Figure 8.2.** American and Chinese installations in Afghanistan and Pakistan, the Middle East, and the Horn of Africa. Points on the map do not indicate precise locations of bases or infrastructure.

Source: Data table sourced entirely from the Brookings Institution. Madiha Afzal, Bruce Riedel, and Natan Sachs, *The United States, China, and The "New Non-Aligned" Countries*, Policy Brief, Brookings Institution, February 2023, https://www.brookings.edu/wp-content/uploads/2023/02/FP_20230213_china_regional_strategy.pdf.

balances of power in the region. As regional expert Marc Lynch correctly stressed, "The perception of US decline in the Middle East is less about its capabilities than about its policy choices and its inability to translate capabilities into outcomes.... The more that regional powers publicly doubted US capabilities or intentions, the more independently they acted based on that perception."[57]

Middle Eastern governments, like their counterparts elsewhere, seldom announced publicly all the motivations behind their actions. Moreover, nations in the region often had multiple reasons to undertake new policies, and not only because of their fear of American withdrawal. (Qatar was a notable exception to the broader trend; it doubled down on its partnership with Washington, made huge investments in the United States, allowed expanded US use of Al-Udeid airbase, and aided the American withdrawal from Afghanistan.[58]) Nevertheless, it is safe to say that, at least by the mid-2010s, the perception that the United States was "going home" drove policymaking by virtually every regional leader. As Amos Yadlin, a retired Israeli general, wrote, "America has not left the [Middle East] nor is it leaving. More than its physical military footprint, its reputational footprint is dimming, reflecting in the regional players' behaviors."[59] The net effect was a steady reduction of US influence in the Middle East over the 2010s.

## Saudi Arabia

By the end of the decade, Saudi Arabia was leading the way. Convinced that US policy in the Middle East was "muddled," "confused," and "hypocritical" after the 2018 Khashoggi murder, Riyadh launched its own policy re-evaluation, one that did not assume American support.[60] The Kingdom made clear that Washington could stuff its concerns about Saudi human rights abuses. MBS vivified the point, saying, "Trying to impose your values on others is not going to be effective. It will get you a negative reaction."[61] It repaired relations within the Gulf Cooperation Council (GCC) and with Qatar in an effort to produce a united Gulf front against Iran. At a 2021 GCC summit, MBS ended a 3.5-year embargo of Qatar and announced his intent to "turn the page on all points of difference" and effect "a full return of diplomatic relations." "There is a desperate need today," he emphasized, "to unite our efforts to promote our region and to confront challenges that surround us."[62] Dania Thafer, executive director of the Gulf International Forum, reported that the breakthrough came alongside Saudi expectations that the incoming Biden administration would reduce America's presence in the Gulf, take a harder stance against the Kingdom, and re-engage with Iran.[63]

Saudi Arabia also ramped up its relations with Israel. The two were united by their mutual priority to counter both Iranian influence in the region and the destabilizing threat of proxy groups like Hezbollah, Hamas, and the Houthis.[64] As one Arab official commented, "Israel, unlike the US, isn't going anywhere. Israel actually acts and doesn't talk about it."[65] Jerusalem also was not going to emphasize human rights in its relations with Riyadh. Saudi Arabia guaranteed Israeli shipping free transit through the Red Sea in return for Jerusalem accepting its acquisition of two islands in the Tiran Straits; the agreement made possible a second deal that allowed Israeli commercial aircraft overflight rights over Saudi Arabia.[66] In addition, Riyadh began negotiations to allow Muslims living in Israel to charter direct flights to Saudi Arabia for the annual Hajj pilgrimage.[67] Saudi donations to the Palestinian Authority decreased by 81 percent from 2019 to 2020, and MBS de-emphasized the Palestinian issue in the Saudi media. The Crown Prince called Israel a "potential ally" in April 2022, and in February 2023,

*Haaretz* reported that Jerusalem and Riyadh were in talks to enhance military and intelligence ties.[68] By late 2023, the Biden administration was involved in extensive talks to broker Saudi-Israeli normalization, though Hamas' attack on Israel and Jerusalem's response did, at the very least, put them on pause.[69]

After first taking a hard line against Iran, Saudis then shifted in an attempt to improve ties with Tehran. Foreign Minister Faisal bin Farhan al-Saud stressed, "Our hands are stretched out. We are trying to send the message that going into a new era of cooperation in the region can deliver benefits for all of us."[70] In Yemen, after five rounds of reconciliation talks beginning in April 2021, the Houthis gave in to Iranian prodding and a truce was reached in April 2022. In March 2023, Saudi Arabia and Iran shook the region's geopolitics by announcing—in Beijing—the resumption of diplomatic relations.[71] The Kingdom also began to warm relations with Damascus; in May 2023, Syrian dictator Bashar al-Assad attended an Arab League summit in Jeddah, marking the first time in over a decade that he was invited.[72] As US influence in the region has declined, MBS has shown a newfound willingness to plot a multi-aligned course less dependent than before on Washington's preferences.[73]

With profound doubts that the United States would defend the Kingdom in extremis or prevent Iran from acquiring nuclear weapons, Riyadh aimed to pressure the Biden administration to provide the Kingdom with NATO-like security guarantees, even as it sought to reduce tensions with Tehran. Riyadh also linked normalization of relations with Israel to US security assurances, advanced technology arms sales, and assistance with Riyadh's civilian nuclear development.[74] In March 2023, a Saudi official told the *Wall Street Journal*, "We have to accept reality and figure a way to live with a nuclear Iran. . . . So, we will go from hostile relations to better relations."[75]

That the Saudi-Iran deal was announced in China represented a powerful symbol of the gradual shift in the Middle Eastern strategic situation. States like Turkey, Saudi Arabia, the UAE, and Egypt—all previously dependent on the West—began to diversify their foreign relations and declare greater strategic independence. Several—Saudi Arabia included—wished actively to play the China card with Washington. Having concluded that the United States had lost its long-standing appetite for Middle East engagement, but that it plainly was worried about China, senior officials in multiple capitals warned their American counterparts that Beijing would move into any vacuum of power that attended a US withdrawal.[76] The Saudi-Iran diplomatic agreement reflected not only Riyadh's desire to pursue alignment with multiple great powers, but also to show Washington that Saudi Arabia had alternatives to the United States—including the country that concerned American policymakers the most.

Biden officials were, initially, more concerned with deterrence and stability in the Indo-Pacific than in the Middle East. In a move that reverberated in Riyadh for months, the United States withdrew Patriot missile defense batteries in 2021 from Saudi Arabia in order, American officials said, to focus more on challenges from China and Russia.[77] The withdrawal took place even as Houthi rebels in Yemen continued firing missiles into the Kingdom. Kristian Ulrichsen, a research fellow at Rice University's Baker Institute, observed, "From the Saudi point of view, they now see Obama, Trump and Biden—three successive presidents—taking decisions that signify to some extent an abandonment."[78] Over time, Washington would come full circle, sending Patriot batteries to Saudi Arabia in March 2022.[79] Such a move may have been the right one, but the United States won no points for consistency.

Riyadh accelerated bilateral relations with Beijing, which naturally expressed no concern over the Kingdom's human rights abuses. China and Saudi Arabia signed a "strategic partnership" as early as 2016, tied to "stable long-term energy cooperation."[80] Weapons sales from the PRC to the Kingdom nearly quintupled in 2016–2020 compared to the previous five years, the result of a $60 billion arms deal signed between Beijing and Riyadh in 2017—an agreement reached only after the United States refused to sell the Kingdom armed UAVs.[81] As part of the arrangement, Saudi Arabia hosted China's first drone factory in the Middle East.[82] By 2020, China became Saudi Arabia's top trading partner and, the following year, bilateral trade hit $87 billion, dwarfing that between the Kingdom and the US and EU combined.[83] In 2019, Saudi Arabia joined thirty-six states in signing a letter to the UN Human Rights Council defending Beijing's abuses in Xinjiang and, three years later, even deported several Muslim Uyghurs back to China.[84]

In 2021, Riyadh agreed to become a "dialogue partner" of the Shanghai Cooperation Organization (SCO)—a counterpoint to US-led multilateralism—despite Washington's protestations. In August 2022, a Chinese foreign ministry spokesperson described the two countries as "comprehensive strategic partners," and in December, Xi Jinping visited Riyadh—a trip described by Saudi commentator as "the culmination or crowning of a deep strengthening in relations over the last few years."[85] The two countries signed $50 billion worth of investment agreements during the visit, and Chinese state media claimed that Riyadh purchased $4 billion in arms from Beijing.[86] After the visit, the two countries released a 4,000-word joint statement that detailed plans for the future, including greater cooperation and agreement on a range of political issues, not least of which was Riyadh's support for the One-China policy.[87] In March 2023, Saudi Arabia approved its "partial membership" in the SCO and, at the end of the year, the Kingdom's Future Investment Initiative Institute hosted its first gathering in Asia, in Hong Kong.[88]

To diversify its security and energy partnerships, Riyadh also strengthened ties to Moscow. After the two countries supported different sides in the Syrian civil war, relations worsened. In September 2016, however, as Russia's regional influence grew following Assad's military success, the two countries signed a joint statement pledging cooperation in world oil markets.[89] Three months later, MBS played a key role in facilitating the first deal between Russia and the Organization of Petroleum Exporting Countries (OPEC) in fifteen years, creating OPEC+.[90] The crown prince then visited Moscow in 2017 and signed more than fifteen cooperation agreements on oil, military, and space exploration.[91] Two months later, Riyadh concluded a "military cooperation agreement" with Moscow to launch a "common endeavor to preserve stability and security in the region" and address "shared challenges." Knowing that Russian weapons would carry no constraints regarding their use—unlike those purchased from the United States—Saudi Arabia signed agreements to acquire Su-35 fighters and the S-400 missile defense system.[92]

Perhaps most important for Putin, and in a striking example of the decline of US influence in Riyadh, MBS refused to condemn Russia's attack on Ukraine and declined to take Biden's call after the invasion.[93] The *Economist* observed that "whether Saudi Arabia is playing one party off the other or not, it is becoming child's play to do so. If the adversary of one party can so easily become the other party's friend, America has developed a new strategic weakness, one that will ensure its future unreliability on the world stage."[94]

In October 2022, Saudi Arabia spurned the United States and aided Russian president Vladimir Putin when OPEC+ decided to cut two million barrels of oil a day in order to maintain energy prices—despite personal pleas from top officials in the Biden administration not to reduce production.[95] Riyadh also rebuffed British and French appeals for more oil.[96] Six months later, Saudi Arabia and OPEC+ again announced a surprise cut, this time by more than one million barrels per day.[97] As Adam Taylor at the *Washington Post* described it, "Now, by pushing a production cut at OPEC Plus, Saudi Arabia isn't just indirectly supporting Russia or pushing the world closer toward a recession—it's shaking the very slippery, oil-based foundations of its relationship with the United States."[98] Then, in December 2023, Putin made a rare visit outside Russia for talks with MBS in Riyadh, where the two discussed OPEC+ cooperation and the various crises in the Middle East.[99]

To begin to lessen its dependence on American arms, the Kingdom ordered substantially more weapons from Britain and France. Since the outset of the Yemen civil war in 2014, the value of UK arms sales to Riyadh reached over £23 billion.[100] And four percent of Saudi weapons imports in 2015–2019 were from France, which made Paris the third largest arms exporter to the Kingdom, after the US (73 percent) and UK (13 percent).[101] These purchases, of course, barely made a dent in American arms sales to Saudi Arabia, but it was a start.

## Israel

As American credibility and influence declined throughout the region, Israel, too, drew strategic conclusions. It continued its uncompromising rhetoric toward Iran and opposed US re-entry into the JCPOA. In February 2022, Prime Minister Naftali Bennett vowed "Israel will maintain freedom of action in any situation, with or without an [Iran nuclear] agreement."[102] His successor, Prime Minister Yair Lapid, shared the sentiment, saying, "Israel is not against any agreement. We are against this agreement, because it is a bad one. . . In our eyes, it does not meet the standards set by President Biden himself: preventing Iran from becoming a nuclear state."[103] Mossad chief David Barnea offered the Israeli perspective with some gusto, saying, "We will do anything we need in order to defend ourselves against any threat, and there will be threats. We are committed to dealing with said threats, even if they are nuclear."[104]

Jerusalem boosted its military capabilities, conducting long-range air exercises over the Mediterranean that corresponded in reach and scale to an attack on Iran. It announced that the IDF's F-35 stealth fighters could now fly from Israel to Iran without refueling, acquired a new one-ton bomb that could be carried inside the F-35s without jeopardizing their stealth radar signature, and further ramped up exercises to simulate long-range combat missions.[105] Defense Minister Gantz in May 2022 called the drills "the largest and most extensive exercises we have conducted in years."[106] Although Israel naturally wished to increase its own capability to strike Iran if necessary, Jerusalem's decision-making may have been affected by a larger sense of American inconstancy.

Before the October 2023 war in Gaza, Israel also reinforced the security of key Arab governments. As regional expert David Makovsky argued in March 2022, "Given Arab perceptions that the US is engaged in retrenching in the Mideast, it is Israel being welcomed by key Arab states, expanding its regional profile and at least partly filling that void."[107] In addition, while contacts had occurred for several years, shared concerns about Iran's regional behavior and the JCPOA, a changing of the ruling guard in some countries (MBS, for example, was far more open to quiet cooperation with Israel than previous Saudi leaders), and—at that time—the Palestinian issue's diminishment as a driver of Arab foreign policy together prompted increased security and intelligence collaboration over the decade.[108] Israel's burgeoning engagement with moderate Arab regimes has, of course, been disrupted by Hamas' attack and Jerusalem's furious military response.

Until the Gaza conflict, Jerusalem maintained good relations with Moscow in order to secure Russian acquiescence to Israel's airstrikes on Iranian forces and proxies in Syria. In turn, Israel remained neutral in 2014 as Russia invaded Crimea and was absent for a UN vote to condemn the invasion.[109] When

Moscow banned Western food imports in August 2014, Israel increased its food exports to Russia that year to $374 million.[110] In September 2015, as Russia began its military campaign in Syria, Netanyahu visited Putin to "coordinate military actions" and prevent the two sides from accidently firing on each other.[111] From this meeting to July 2018, Netanyahu met with Putin nine times, more than any other world leader.[112] Israel declined to join US-led sanctions on Russia in 2018, and defense minister Avigdor Liberman explained, "We greatly appreciate our relations with Russia. Even when our close partners put pressure on us, like in the case of sanctions against Russia, we do not join them."[113] When Russia launched its full-scale invasion of Ukraine in February 2022, Israel did not co-sponsor the UN Security Council resolution to condemn Putin's actions.[114]

Despite this recent history, the Israel-Russia bilateral relationship deteriorated precipitously after Hamas' attack. From the outset, the Kremlin refused to describe the assault as terrorism, did not acknowledge Israeli suffering, and instead blamed the war on Western policy mistakes.[115] On October 26, a Hamas delegation visited Moscow for talks on the release of foreign hostages, and on that day a spokesman for the terrorist organization described Russia as "our closest friend."[116] In the aftermath, Israel summoned the Russian ambassador and said the meeting had sent "a message legitimizing terrorism against Israelis."[117] In November 2023, during a UN General Assembly meeting, the Kremlin representative argued that Israel lacked the right to self-defense as "an occupying power."[118] In a sign of worsened relations, Jerusalem ceased informing Moscow before it attacked Iranian-backed militias in Syria.[119]

## Iran

Unsurprisingly, Iran sought to take advantage of the perceived US withdrawal from the Middle East. The new government of President Ebrahim Raisi, elected in the summer of 2021, toughened its approach to nuclear talks. Deputy Foreign Minister Ali Bagheri Kani, the new lead Iranian negotiator, wrote that Iran had two goals in the wake of the revived Vienna talks: the removal of sanctions and "to facilitate the legal rights of the Iranian nation to benefit from peaceful nuclear knowledge."[120] Rather than return to the JCPOA, as Biden administration officials hoped, Iran instead demanded a guarantee that the United States would not once again withdraw from it, a pledge that Washington had no ability to meet.[121] When discussions resumed in 2021, Iran refused to negotiate directly with the United States. All this suggested that Tehran had recalculated the likelihood, should the talks fail, of a US attack on its nuclear facilities—as well as the limited economic benefits that would attend Iranian re-entry.

Tehran substantially increased the Islamic Revolutionary Guard Corps Quds Force (IRGC-QF) throughout this period.[122] Seth Jones, an expert in counterinsurgency and counterterrorism, summarized the Quds Force's expanded reach during the decade. "The IRGC-QF," he said in 2019, "and its leader, [Qasem] Soleimani, took advantage of . . . opportunities to provide money, weapons, and other assistance to partners in the absence of significant balancing by the United States and other countries." While the United States killed Soleimani in January 2020, estimates of Quds Force strength in 2023 ran as high as 195,000.[123]

Iran found common cause with Russia as well. The two signed an agreement on military cooperation, Tehran purchased Russian S-300 surface-to-air missiles, and Iranian officials shared intelligence on Syria and Iraq with Moscow.[124] In July 2022, Putin visited Tehran to expand commercial ties and evade Western sanctions applied after his invasion of Ukraine.[125] During the visit, Ayatollah Ali Khamenei endorsed Putin's war, saying, "In the case of Ukraine, if you had not taken the helm, the other side would have done so and initiated a war. . . . If the road is clear for NATO, they know no boundaries or limits. And if Ukraine had not been stopped, they would have started the same war, with the excuse of Crimea."[126] By August 2022, Russia was employing hundreds of Iranian drones against military and civilian targets in Ukraine, and subsequent reports indicated that Tehran would receive at least 24 Su-35 fighter jets from Moscow.[127] In a February 2023 interview, CIA director Bill Burns warned that the military partnership was "moving at a pretty fast clip in a very dangerous direction right now," and that the mutual exchange of lethal military equipment would have implications for both Ukraine and US partners in the Middle East.[128]

Iran also bolstered relations with China. After the United States imposed full sanctions on Iranian oil exports in 2019, Beijing increased its imports to a record high 900,000 barrels per day by 2021.[129] Tehran also concluded a twenty-five-year agreement with Beijing that promised greater diplomatic, economic, and military cooperation, and pledged $400 billion of Chinese investment in Iran.[130] Tehran went on to purchase arms from Beijing valued at up to $10 billion, sought the PRC's help to modernize the Islamic Republic's submarine and surface fleets, and incorporated Chinese satellite navigation systems into its defense architecture.[131] China steadily remained Iran's top trading partner.[132]

Intensified Chinese-Iranian collaboration, and shared opposition to perceived Western domination, provided a solid foundation for increased trilateral cooperation with Moscow. In September 2022, Iran agreed to join the Shanghai Cooperation Organization, and an Iranian parliament spokesman said, "In the new world order a triangle consisting of three powers—Iran, Russia, and China—has formed." Possessed by more than a degree of wishful thinking, he added, "This new arrangement heralds the end of the inequitable hegemony of the United States and the West."[133]

## Turkey

As visions of the Ottoman Empire danced through Ankara's imagination, Turkey also sought to fill the perceived space left by the United States. Seeking a Syrian ceasefire, Ankara participated in the Astana talks with Iran and Russia in 2017.[134] When Saudi Arabia led other Sunni Arab states in a blockade against Qatar the same year, Turkish and Iranian ministers met to coordinate a response.[135] President Erdogan condemned the 2018 protests in Iran and praised President Hassan Rouhani's leadership, criticized Trump's withdrawal from the JCPOA and the implementation of "maximum pressure" against Tehran, and denounced the American assassination of Soleimani.[136] In that same spirit, in July 2022, Erdogan met with Raisi and Putin in Tehran, signaling, in part, resistance against the West's attempt to isolate Russia and Iran.[137]

Ankara also sought to repair relations with Saudi Arabia and the UAE. Saudi-Turkish relations were strained after July 2013 when Riyadh backed the coup that overthrew Egyptian president Mohamed Morsi, whom Ankara supported.[138] In December 2015, Turkey and Saudi Arabia established a "Strategic Cooperation Council," which increased high-level engagements and signaled a mutual desire to smooth over their differences.[139] While tensions re-emerged in 2017 over the Qatar blockade, in 2022 Turkish foreign minister Mevlut Cavusoglu said that Ankara was taking "concrete steps" to boost engagement with Riyadh.[140] A week later, a Turkish court transferred the Jamal Khashoggi murder trial to Saudi Arabia, at the Kingdom's request, and for the first time since the 2018 murder Erdogan visited Saudi Arabia, hailing a "new era of our relations."[141] MBS then returned the favor, traveling to Ankara.[142] In addition, after a decade of bitter relations and proxy wars, UAE leader Mohammed bin Zayed visited Ankara in November 2021 and, following the visit, announced a $10 billion investment fund in Turkey.[143] Three months later, Erdogan visited the UAE for the first time in nine years, and the two countries signed a dozen bilateral agreements on economic and defense cooperation.[144]

After nearly eight years of bad blood following the coup against Morsi, Ankara also sought to de-escalate tensions with Egypt. In March 2021, Turkey ordered Muslim Brotherhood media channels to cease criticism of Egypt and to rebuild trust between the two publics.[145] A month later, a presidential spokesman said, "Given the realities on the ground I think it's in the interests of both countries and the region to normalize relations with Egypt."[146]

Even ties with Israel were on the mend after a years-long rift over the death of Turkish civilians during an Israeli raid on Gaza-bound aid ships.[147] Israeli president Isaac Herzog flew to Ankara in March 2022 to meet with President Erdogan, making him the most senior Israeli official to visit Turkey since Prime Minister Ehud Olmert some fourteen years earlier.[148] Two months later, Foreign Minister Cavusoglu became the first senior Turkish official to visit Israel in fifteen years.[149] In August, Ankara and Jerusalem normalized relations, exchanging ambassadors for the first time since 2018.[150] But Hamas' October 7 attack derailed the bilateral relationship. Ankara maintains ties with the terrorist organization and, at a pro-Palestine rally in Istanbul in November, Erdogan called Hamas "a liberation group." He branded Israel an "occupier" and described its government as made up of "war criminals" who seek to "eradicate" Palestinians.[151] Jerusalem recalled its diplomats from Turkey and told its citizens to leave the country "as soon as possible."[152]

Over the decade, Turkey intensified its engagement with Russia. In 2016, Moscow and Ankara began to cooperate in Syria after the Kremlin supported a Turkish incursion to attack Kurdish fighters.[153] When Erdogan ignored US warnings and bought Russian S-400 air-defense systems in 2017, Washington removed Turkey from the F-35 fighter program, prompting Ankara to purchase more S-400s and seek Moscow's support to build nuclear power plants.[154] Economic ties between the two countries accelerated as well. Bilateral trade between Turkey and Russia swelled to $26 billion by 2019 and $62 billion in 2022, as Ankara relied significantly on Russian energy. Turkish imports of Russian energy imports grew still more during the Ukraine war.[155] With ties to both Russia and Ukraine, Ankara also successfully mediated an agreement to export grain through the Black Sea.

Ankara deepened its ties with China during the 2010s as well. Erdogan criticized China's treatment of the Uyghurs as "genocide" in 2010, but remained mostly quiet about the issue thereafter.[156] Turkey purchased a $3 billion Chinese missile system, became a Shanghai Cooperation Organization "dialogue partner," joined the Belt and Road Initiative, and received billions of dollars in Chinese loans.[157] Bilateral trade increased, too, as Beijing became Ankara's largest import partner.[158] Altogether, Beijing provided a viable alternative source of support for Ankara's political and economic objectives—without the political complications of Russia or the conditions imposed by West.[159]

Over a decade and a half, America's closest friends in the Middle East have pursued strategies to reduce their dependence on the United States, establish new alignments with external powers, and, more recently, de-escalate key regional tensions. To be clear, not every decision made by regional governments was driven by the perception of US withdrawal or Washington's desire to focus more on Asia. But the enduring US dissatisfaction with its regional role in the

Middle East, the rise of China, and the clear attractions of the Indo-Pacific together shaped regional calculations.

## Going Nowhere

Overall, Middle East nations began hedging. Doubt about America's defense commitment pushed multiple countries to reduce risk in their policies rather than pursue confrontation without the certainty of a US military backstop. Countries in the region established new and stronger ties with each other, thawed relations with some former enemies, and built links to outside powers like Russia and China. Yet these countries were simultaneously "careful not to burn their bridges with us," veteran diplomat Dennis Ross stressed. "They still see us," he added, "as the one they would need to turn to in the crunch."[160] The Biden administration welcomed some of this behavior; the general relaxation of tensions between Saudi Arabia and Iran, and between Riyadh and Doha, made conflict in the region less likely. The prospect of Saudi-Israeli normalization elicited the administration's full-throated support—and behind-the-scenes diplomacy.

Despite the fears of a reduced American role in the Middle East, however, the United States was not, in fact, leaving. While nations maneuvered intra-regionally, fed by the widespread conviction that America was on its way out, the data below demonstrate there was virtually no US military, diplomatic, or economic reorientation away from the Middle East during these years. Washington may have been less active in the region, or less effective than before, but it remained as *present* as ever.

## US Military Footprint

The US military did not pivot from the Middle East over the 2010s, and it did not redirect American forces from the region to Asia during the decade. Indeed, as Figure 8.3 demonstrates, while total US troops deployed to the Middle East declined from 2011 to 2020, the only significant reductions occurred in Iraq and Kuwait. Army, Navy, and Air Force deployments to the Middle East actually *increased* in Bahrain, Qatar, the UAE, Saudi Arabia, Syria, and Jordan.

The years that followed the Pivot's announcement in 2011 actually witnessed a sharp *increase* in ship visits to the Middle East. The last year when the US had fewer than forty ships in the region was 2012; since 2013, an annual average of forty-five ships have deployed to the Middle East (Figure 8.4). The US naval presence increased over the decade as US Central Command (CENTCOM) core power projection almost always included aircraft carrier strike groups. The trend

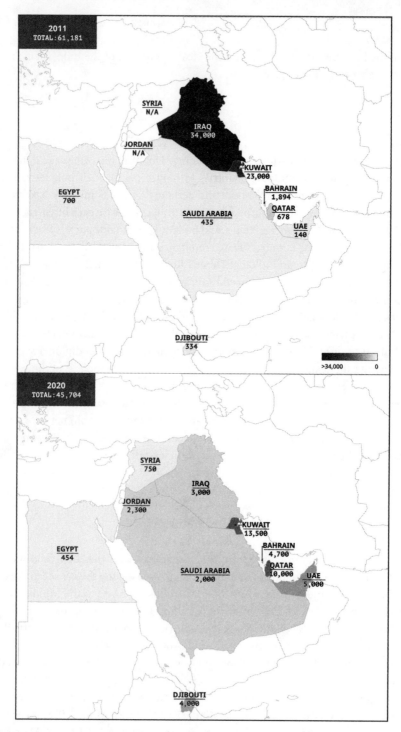

**Figure 8.3.** US permanent base and operational troop deployment changes, 2011–2020.

Source: All data are sourced from the International Institute for Strategic Studies (IISS) *Military Balance*. The data from the *Military Balance* represent a snapshot of deployments in early November of each year. ©2012, The International Institute for Strategic Studies, originally published in *The Military Balance* 2012 (reproduced with permission); ©2021, The International Institute for Strategic Studies, originally published in *The Military Balance* 2021 (reproduced with permission).

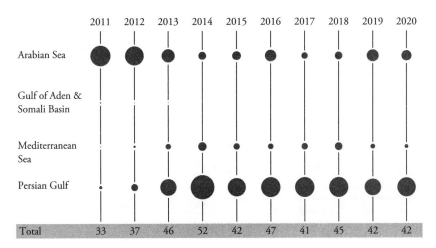

**Figure 8.4.** US ship deployments in the Middle East, 2011–2020.

Source: All data are sourced from the IISS *Military Balance*: International Institute for Strategic Studies, "Chapter Three: North America," Military Balance 112, no. 1 (2012): 39–70, https://doi.org/10.1080/04597222.2012.663212; International Institute for Strategic Studies, "Chapter Three: North America," Military Balance, 121, no. 1 (2021): 30–65, https://doi.org/10.1080/04597222.2021.1868792.

did not change until ten years after the Pivot's announcement, as American aircraft carriers did not operate in the region in 2021 or 2022.[161] They were soon back. After the Hamas attack on Israel, Hezbollah's rocket strikes in the north, and increased Iranian proxy attacks on US facilities in the region, Washington deployed two carrier strike groups to the Middle East in late 2023.[162]

Additionally, there was no reduction of American air power in the Middle East; the number of squadrons deployed to the region increased from fifteen in November 2014 to twenty-two in November 2020.[163]

## Diplomatic Activity

There was also no US diplomatic pivot from the Middle East to Asia. While American presidents visited Middle East countries fifteen times and Indo-Pacific countries forty times over the decade, secretaries of state traveled to Middle East nations a total of 187 times—forty-nine more than to the Indo-Pacific (see Figures 8.5 and 8.6). Much depended on events and personalities. Secretary Clinton traveled to the Middle East on forty-one occasions and to Asia on forty-nine. John Kerry, however, visited Middle East nations a remarkable ninety-seven times, and went to Indo-Pacific countries forty-seven times—less than half

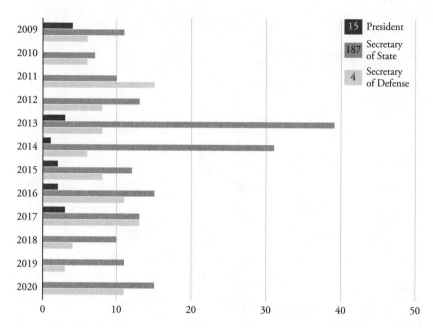

**Figure 8.5.** US president, secretary of state, and secretary of defense visits to Middle East nations, 2009–2020.

Source: Department of Defense, Historical Office, *Secretary of Defense Travels*, accessed July 22, 2022, https://history.defense.gov/DOD-History/Secretary-of-Defense-Travels/; Department of State, Office of the Historian, *Travels Abroad of the Secretary of State*, accessed July 22, 2022, https://history.state.gov/departmenthistory/travels/secretary; Department of State, Office of the Historian, *Travels Abroad of the President*, accessed July 22, 2022, https://history.state.gov/departmenthistory/travels/president.

that number. Under President Trump, Secretary Tillerson visited the Middle East and Indo-Pacific at a similar rate, eighteen and sixteen times, respectively. Mike Pompeo's travel took him to Asia twenty-nine times, while he made thirty-one visits to the Middle East. Between 2009 and 2020, secretaries of defense went to the Middle East on ninety-nine occasions and the Indo-Pacific eighty-six times.

## Economic Engagement

There was no US economic reorientation from the Middle East. From the Pivot's announcement in 2011 until 2020, the US direct investment position in the Middle East more than doubled from $36 billion to nearly $80 billion.[164] In the same period, 84 percent of all US Foreign Military Financing (FMF) went to the Middle East, amounting to $50 billion, of which $44 billion went to Israel and Egypt.[165] Israel has received the most US foreign assistance of any country and, in 2016, Jerusalem and Washington signed a memorandum

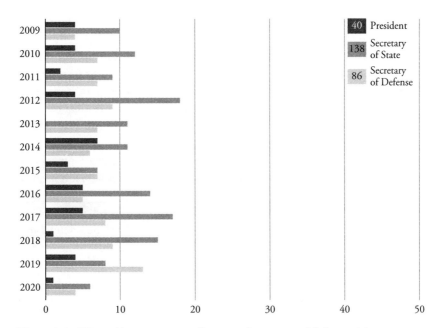

**Figure 8.6.**  US president, secretary of state, and secretary of defense visits to countries in the Indo-Pacific, 2009–2020.

Source: Department of Defense, Historical Office, *Secretary of Defense Travels*, accessed July 22, 2022, https://history.defense.gov/DOD-History/Secretary-of-Defense-Travels/; Department of State, Office of the Historian, *Travels Abroad of the Secretary of State*, accessed July 22, 2022, https://history.state.gov/departmenthistory/travels/secretary; Department of State, Office of the Historian, *Travels Abroad of the President*, accessed July 22, 2022, https://history.state.gov/departmenthistory/travels/president.

of understanding that will provide Israel with $3.3 billion annually from 2019 to 2028, likely securing Jerusalem's place as the top recipient of US aid (other than wartime aid for Ukraine) for years to come.[166] From 2011 to 2020, by contrast, East Asia and the Pacific countries received less than $760 million in total FMF.[167] The Middle East also held priority over the Indo-Pacific in economic and development assistance. From 2011 to 2020, the United States supplied the Middle East with $15.5 billion through the Economic Support and Development Fund. During that same period, the United States contributed $3.7 billion to the East Asia and the Pacific, just over a fifth of the aid sent to the Middle East.[168]

## The Pivot Paradox

Herein lies the supreme irony of the purported American withdrawal from the Middle East. No such withdrawal occurred, and no pivot of resources or attention to Asia took place. Nevertheless, the perception of American commitment to the region, both rhetorical and actual, seriously eroded during the decade. The effect stemmed from a combination of misguided US policies; American war-weariness; increased domestic oil production (and a corresponding sense that free-flowing Middle East oil was no longer an interest worth fighting for); fluctuating policies toward regional autocrats (ranging from an emphasis on human rights under one president to a full-throated embrace of dictators from another); and a general conclusion that Americans had little to show for their titanic investments in blood, treasure, and diplomacy. Together with the obvious rise of other geopolitical priorities, in Asia especially, these developments led many in the region to expect a dramatic shift of US priorities—even if its presence did not yet reflect them.

This sentiment among policymakers and politicians was echoed by public opinion. A 2019 Reagan Foundation opinion poll, for instance, found that 37 percent of respondents believed that the United States should focus its military forces on the Middle East; in 2022 only 11 percent of respondents felt the same way.[169] Conversely, in 2019 only 16 percent of respondents thought the United States should focus its military resources on East Asia; two years later that number rose to 37 percent.[170]

The perception that the United States was withdrawing from the region was just that—a perception. The underlying indicators of troop deployments, basing, regional partnerships, diplomatic activity, foreign aid, and more did not support this conclusion. By the early 2020s, however, the notion of a US departure was commonplace, and helped drive a decline of US influence in the Middle East.

## The Renewed Effort at Regional Commitment

Biden's first policies toward the Middle East did not improve the perception. Because of the war in Yemen, he placed a temporary freeze on US arms sales to the Kingdom and went on to re-examine Emirati weapons purchases approved by Trump near the end of his term. Biden tried to revive the JCPOA despite opposition among key regional partners, declared a formal conclusion to the US combat mission in Iraq, ended the US troop presence in Afghanistan, withdrew Patriot and THAAD missile defense systems from the region, and declined to nominate an ambassador to Saudi Arabia for fifteen months.[171] As one administration advisor put it bluntly, "They are just being extremely purposeful to not get dragged into the Middle East."[172]

The Biden administration did undertake diplomatic activity in the region. Washington appointed special envoys for hotspots, including Yemen, Libya, and the Horn of Africa, worked with Egypt and Qatar to limit Israeli-Hamas hostilities in 2021, and helped reach a truce in Yemen. But such diplomacy did little to reassure American partners that the United States was in the Middle East to stay.

Biden sought to address regional doubts during a visit to Israel and the Gulf in July 2022. In the buildup to it, Jerusalem agreed to join the US-led Middle East Air Defense Alliance, a network aimed at countering the intensifying drone threat posed by Iran and its proxies.[173] The day before his arrival in Jeddah, Biden reiterated the classic US strategic premise regarding the Middle East, one not held by his two immediate predecessors. "The reason I'm going to Saudi Arabia," the president said, is "to promote US interests. . . . We have an opportunity to re-assert what I think we made a mistake of walking away from: our influence in the Middle East."[174]

A day later, at a meeting with Arab leaders, Biden proclaimed, "Let me state clearly that the United States is going to remain an active, engaged partner in the Middle East. . . . We will not walk away and leave a vacuum to be filled by China, Russia, or Iran. And we'll seek to build on this moment with active, prin-cipled American leadership."[175] Foreign policy scholar Walter Russell Mead saw in Biden's words a shift back toward the region. "America's strategic Pivot from the Middle East," Mead wrote, "was a mistake, President Biden acknowledged on his recent swing through the region. Admitting that is a good thing; you can't begin to fix a problem before acknowledging that you have one."[176] Dennis Ross and James Jeffrey, a former ambassador to Iraq, went further, writing, "The trip represents a transformation of Washington's approach to the region. No longer are we talking about a pivot away from it."[177]

Biden administration officials seemed to conclude that the only thing worse than an indefinite US presence in the Middle East was the emergence of a vacuum that could be exploited by adversaries. The change in strategic direction was also aided by the focusing power of spiking oil prices, which reached $109 a barrel in May 2022—just as US inflation hit a four-decade high of 9.1 percent.[178] As journalist Alexander Ward put it:

> Biden had spent the last 18 months mainly ignoring the region. . . . Now Biden and his team have concluded they must ramp up Washington's presence in the Middle East so China and Russia don't fill an America-sized hole, so that Tehran can be kept at bay, so that a ceasefire in Yemen can hold, faster modernizations can happen in Saudi society, and maybe even better relations between officials in Jerusalem and Riyadh.[179]

With renewed focus on the Middle East, Biden sought to turn his declarations into actions. He outlined a five-part "new framework for the Middle East" that included support for economic development, military security, and demo-cratic freedoms to push back on Chinese and Russian influence.[180] In a broad reaffirmation of the Carter Doctrine, he pledged to ensure that Middle East partners "can defend themselves against foreign threats" and promised not to "tolerate efforts by any country to dominate another in the region through military buildups, incursions, and/or threats."[181] He began to normalize relations with the Saudi crown prince and tried, unsuccessfully, to convince the Kingdom to increase its oil supply.[182] He reaffirmed that CENTCOM would preserve the flow of trade through the Bab al-Mandab and the Strait of Hormuz and pledged to help regional partners integrate air and maritime defenses.[183]

Biden also committed the United States to play an "active role" in continued Arab-Israeli normalization, building on the Trump administration's Abraham Accords success.[184] He signed the Jerusalem Declaration, affirming US support for Israel's security and American commitment to "use all elements of its national power to ensure" that Iran does not acquire a nuclear weapon.[185] The administration initiated dialogues with Israel on critical and emerging technologies, such as artificial intelligence, and on safeguarding technology ecosystems. In a nod toward Riyadh's concerns, Biden pledged to "pursue a diplomatic process to achieve a wider settlement in Yemen" that considered Saudi Arabia's security needs.[186] He secured a $3 billion GCC investment in projects that aligned with the US Partnership for Global Infrastructure and Investment.[187] The administration pledged $1 billion toward food security in the region and $100 million to improve Palestinian patient care and promised to supply Saudi Arabia and the UAE with over $5 billion in missile defense capabilities. Biden secured Saudi financing for infrastructure projects (aimed at countering China's Belt and Road Initiative) and cellular technology (that could erode Huawei's global dominance).[188] By 2023, the administration, as indicated above, was making a major push on Saudi-Israeli normalization, even considering providing Riyadh with a civilian nuclear reactor and making a binding security pledge. In October 2023, after Hamas attacked Israel, President Biden promptly visited Tel Aviv and Secretary of State Antony Blinken conducted shuttle diplomacy in the region over the following months.[189] After Houthi rebels targeted commercial ships crossing the Red Sea, the United States in January 2024 attacked more than 30 military sites in Yemen controlled by the Houthis.[190] In all this, the Biden administration sought to show that the United States had not, in fact, pivoted away from the Middle East.

## Weakened Major Conventional Threats to the Region

The regional security picture has changed over the past decade. ISIS capabilities have largely been broken. Iran's conventional capabilities pose a real but not existential threat to US partners in the Middle East, while the threats to Israel posed by Tehran's proxies Hamas and Hezbollah, as the October 2023 attack demonstrated, have increased. Russia's feeble conventional power projection, as demonstrated in the war in Ukraine, has been dramatically exposed, and the United States is no longer dependent on Middle East energy, even as regional shocks can affect global prices. Key US partners possess formidable military assets to defend themselves and are working together more closely than ever. All this presents the United States with new opportunities.

Iran's official defense budget peaked in 2010 at $23.7 billion (in constant 2020 US$) and, in seven of the eleven years since, Tehran allocated less than $20 billion to defense. From 2017 to 2020, its defense budget decreased by a third, to $15.9 billion.[191] The Islamic Republic is estimated to have roughly 300 combat-capable aircraft, including at least fifty that are antiquated, US-made models. The same is true of the Iran's three anti-submarine aircraft, all six of its surveillance planes, and twenty-nine of its transports. A 2023 survey by the International Institute for Strategic Studies estimates that only 60 percent of the American equipment in Iran's possession can be used, and outdated European aircraft make up a significant remainder of the fleet. The Islamic Republic maintains patrol and coastal combatants, amphibious ships, submarines, and other maritime vessels, but many are simply derivatives of older European or Chinese vessels that have been given Persian names.[192]

Instead of employing obsolete conventional forces to advance its national interests, Tehran depends on terrorism, covert action, intimidation, proxies, and new systems like missiles and armed drones. These have proved quite effective. Iranian drone and missile attacks on Saudi Arabia's Abqaiq oil field in 2019 knocked 50 percent of the Kingdom's oil production offline in a stroke.[193] The IRGC-QF has supplied ballistic missiles—as well as technology and know-how—to the Houthis in Yemen, Shiite militants in Iraq, and Hezbollah in Lebanon, and each group has employed them in attacks.[194] The Islamic Republic also supported Hamas and in recent years has provided rocket designs to increase the lethality of its missiles.[195] In recent years, Tehran or its proxies have attacked Saudi Arabia, the UAE, Israel, the previous government in Yemen, rebels in Syria, Iraq's Kurdistan region, and US forces in Iraq.

Absent active conflict with Iran or its proxies, however, US air and naval assets are of little relevance to any of these destabilizing Iranian regional activities. As defense analyst Elbridge Colby has emphasized, "There is at present no regional power that could plausibly establish hegemony over the Gulf States. . . [Iran] comprises less than one-fifth of the region's economic power. Saudi Arabia, Egypt, and Turkey all rival it in strength, and Israel and the United Arab Emirates (UAE) are also significant players."[196] Where the United States has made shows of force—including the stationing of an aircraft carrier strike group in the Persian Gulf and dispatching B-52s to the region—the moves resulted in no discernable deterrent effect on Tehran.[197]

Russia also poses no conventional military danger to friendly governments in the region. As discussed previously, Moscow's incompetent performance in Ukraine makes vividly clear its puny power-projection capabilities. While its intervention on behalf of the Assad regime was decisive in Syria, many in the Middle East now distrust Russian weapons and are uneasy with Moscow's burgeoning relationship with Tehran in the context of the Ukraine war.

In addition, ISIS has been largely shattered, does not hold territory, and currently threatens no government in the Middle East.[198] In the event of an ISIS resurgence, the United States should avoid employing high-end capabilities like fourth- and fifth-generation fighters to deal with the threat; instead, it should use drones, special forces, covert action, aircraft less intrinsic to deterrence in the Indo-Pacific, and increased friendly government capabilities. Only when absolutely necessary should the United States employ its highest-end systems in a counterterror campaign.

If a crisis does arise in the Middle East that demands significant air and naval assets, the United States can quickly deploy them from adjacent regions, as it did after the October 2023 Hamas attack on Israel. The carrier battle group assigned to United States European Command (EUCOM) provides Washington with carrier-strike capabilities in the region. In addition, CENTCOM maintains US forces at the Incirlik air base in Turkey and in Greece.[199] American long-range bombers, such as the B-52, could be temporarily stationed at these bases and give Washington the ability to retaliate if US national interests are seriously threatened. EUCOM also maintains two brigade combat teams in Italy and Germany, naval facilities in southern Europe, and air force bases across the Continent to support American and joint operations in the Middle East.[200]

In the period ahead, Middle Eastern countries should take a greater role in their own security. Saudi Arabia, for example, has the largest friendly air force in the region, with 455 combat-capable aircraft. This includes 368 fighters (231 of which are F-15s), an estimated twelve surveillance planes, seven tankers, and at least sixty-two transports. The UAE Air Force includes nearly eighty F-16s, sixty French fighters, surveillance planes, transports, and more. Kuwait hosts F-18s and European fighters, Qatar has more than sixty fighter aircraft, and Bahrain's fleet includes F-5s and F-16s. And Israel's considerable arsenal comprises 345 combat aircraft, including F-15s, F-16s, and nearly forty F-35s. Governments friendly to Washington also possess naval capabilities, including submarines, frigates, mine warfare ships, landing craft, coastal combatant vessels, and more.

In addition to their present capabilities, US partners in the region plan to modernize their forces. Riyadh intends to increase advanced military production as outlined in Saudi Vision 2030, while the UAE has consolidated defense firms in an effort to bolster its own domestic military production. Kuwait is modernizing its missile defense and land- and air-combat platforms, while Qatar has deployed an early warning radar system and Patriot missile defense systems. Israel maintains a strong defense-industrial base that specializes in armored vehicles, unmanned systems, guided weapons, radars and sensors, and cyber security.[201]

## Performance, Not Presence, Matters Most

Ultimately, the perception of American withdrawal from the Middle East has been driven far more by what the United States did or did not do in the region, and turned little on America's actual resource footprint. The presence or absence of the Fifth Fleet in Bahrain, or the air base at al Udeid, or an aircraft carrier floating offshore, mattered far less to regional friends than their level of confidence in American commitment to their security and the quality of US policies that affected them. An active but less well-resourced United States would be, in the minds of most regional governments, far preferable to a richly endowed United States that wished to avoid being tied down by Middle East obligations. As problematic as US inconstancy proved to its wider credibility in the region, the lesson from it illuminates new possibilities. Washington now has the flexibility to reduce its force posture in the region without jeopardizing its commitments and its vital national interests.

New regional realities also permit a shift of military resources. Diplomatic developments like the Abraham Accords and the reduction of bilateral rivalries have produced fragile momentum toward increased stability.[202] To put it succinctly, it is no longer 1967, and Israel is not surrounded by hostile Arab nations. It is not 1973, and Leonid Brezhnev has not threated to send Soviet airborne troops to Egypt. It is not 1991, and Saddam Hussein has not attempted to swallow Kuwait. It is not 2001, and catastrophic terrorism from the greater Middle East has not struck the American homeland. It is not 2003, and the United States has not invaded Iraq. It is not 2010, and friendly governments are not threatened by internal revolution, nor is it 2014, and ISIS has not conquered much of Iraq and Syria.

At this writing, the international consequences of Hamas' October 2023 attack on Israel continue to unfold. Some assert that the mass-casualty terrorist event produced "a watershed moment" with regional and global ramifications, comparable to those that followed 9/11.[203] The ultimate path of events in the Middle East remains unclear, and many of the more apocalyptic forecasts may or may not fade with time. Nevertheless, support from Arab populations for the Palestinian cause—despite the barbaric attacks on Israeli civilians—demonstrated that the historic dynamics of this issue persist. The attacks themselves showed how determined Hamas remains to the Jewish state's destruction.

As the *Washington Post* observed, "It turns out the 'old' Middle East was impossible to bury."[204] President Biden's unwavering support of Jerusalem, which included military assistance, convinced many Arabs that the United States was complicit in Israel's Gaza operations.[205] "There is tremendous anger in the Arab world, even by those who do not support Hamas," said Nabil Fahmy, a former Egyptian foreign minister. Western powers, he added, "are giving Israel a green light . . . the West will have blood on its hands."[206] Beijing and Moscow saw opportunity in such reactions and sought to fan the flames of grievance against the United States.[207] Hamas' attacks, and Israel's response to them, set back Saudi-Israeli normalization, which animates Iran and Hamas' purposes.[208] Western support for Israel, while it represented the right policy response, nevertheless weakened efforts to lead developing countries in condemnation of Russia's war against Ukraine.[209]

Most relevant to this book, some argued in the attacks' immediate aftermath that the United States would once again become mired in the Middle East, and again unable to focus on Asia. Defense analyst Aaron McLean, for instance, contended, "Hamas' attack on Israel, the potential for that war to escalate into a regional conflict, and the way in which Iran made the initial attack possible, are the latest indications that [America's] ambition [to pare back its military commitments in the Middle East and in Europe] may be too clever by half."[210] In a similar fashion, the *Wall Street Journal* argued, "The upsurge in Middle East violence . . . and the intensive American efforts to prevent the conflict from spreading, could eclipse longer-term U.S. efforts to focus on the Indo-Pacific."[211] Yet the notion that the war in Gaza rendered the US Pivot to Asia strategically unsound is misguided.

In fact, the crisis reaffirmed a central argument of this book. As a global superpower, the United States retains vital national interests in the Middle East, and Washington reacted to the Gaza war with strength and purpose. When confronted with the conflict, the Biden administration in October 2023 surged two aircraft carrier battle groups, attack and support aircraft, guided missile cruisers, destroyers, a Marine expeditionary unit, a nuclear submarine, air defense systems, and combat aircraft from outside the area to the Middle East.[212] The secretary of state commenced regional shuttle diplomacy, the president visited Israel, and Congress appropriated billions of dollars in assistance. None of these moves turned principally on the preexisting US military footprint in the region, and Hamas' attack appears to have had nothing to do with the degree of US presence. Instead, and as this chapter argues, US influence in the Middle East primarily hinges on performance rather than presence. The combination of strong support for Israel, high-level diplomacy, a surge of military resources, and a rapid aid package made a major difference. As Israel deals with Hamas and Gaza stabilizes over time, the United States should continue its shift of selected military resources to Asia, even while continuing intense diplomatic engagement in the Middle East.[213] Only a war with Iran—a potentially cataclysmic event that the United States should seek ardently to deter—would justify a long-term delay in the Pivot to Asia.

Washington must at the same time reassure partners and convince adversaries that the United States is committed to the Middle East now and in the future. As this chapter has argued, that perception has and will continue to turn far more on the quality of US policy than on the amount of military resources resident there. As a result, competence and coherence are key. As the *Economist* accurately observed, "For the past half-century the United States has been the only country willing and able to bring any kind of order to the region."[214] The Gaza war showed once again that the United States is still the external power to which regional leaders turn in crisis. Meeting those turns with effective action matched to clear objectives will remain indispensable to enduring American influence in the Middle East.

# 9

# We Don't Want to Choose

## The Indo-Pacific and the Pivot

Except for US treaty allies, countries across Asia exhibited a schizophrenic response to the announcement that America was pivoting to the Pacific. Worried about a broader US weakening and withdrawal from the world and China's growing, coercive economic and diplomatic influence, they welcomed, sometimes behind closed doors, a renewed American commitment to a favorable Indo-Pacific balance of power. At the same time, they feared that Washington's increased regional activism would inevitably alarm Beijing, and potentially lead to a US-China confrontation that would disrupt decades of peace and prosperity. As a result, most countries of the Indo-Pacific wished to have it both ways, enjoying security benefits from the United States and economic benefits from China.

The Philippine national security advisor summarized the desire, saying in 2022, "We are cognizant of the contest between the two hegemons. We're just trying to look at it from a point of view that will really match our interests. . . . Whatever China is offering us in terms of trade . . . or infrastructure, we'll take it. Whatever the US is offering us in terms of security umbrella has to be taken into consideration also."[1] Indeed, all the nations of Asia at the time of the Pivot announcement, including America's closest partners, aimed to maintain productive relations with both Washington and Beijing. With few exceptions, they sought to increase their trade relations with China while drawing closer to the United States in the security domain. As time passed, however, Beijing's aggressive policies and an awakened America would make it increasingly difficult to avoid bending toward one side or the other.

But while the American private sector made significant regional investments in capital, technology, and training, the US government did not sustain a significant increase in economic aid, trade agreements, military presence, or diplomatic engagement. The announcement of a pivot to Asia heightened regional expectations about what Washington might soon deliver. In time, however, doubts emerged that the United States would—or even could—devote substantially more resources to Asia given the continued wars in Afghanistan and Iraq, the need to deal with Russia's emergent renegade behavior, other US global

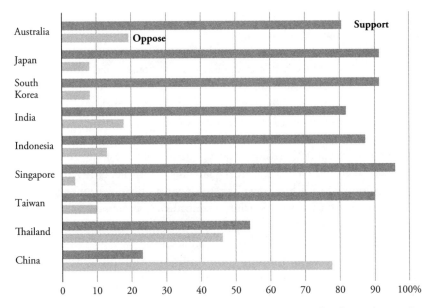

**Figure 9.1.** Support for the US Pivot to Asia among "strategic elites" in Indo-Pacific countries.

Source: All data are from David Berteau, Michael J. Green, and Zack Cooper, *Assessing the Asia-Pacific Rebalance* (Washington, DC: Center for Strategic and International Studies, 2014), 19, https://csis-website-prod.s3.amazonaws.com/s3fs-public/legacy_files/files/publication/150105_Berteau_AssessingAsiaPacificRebal_Web.pdf.

preoccupations and responsibilities, and increased pressure on the US budget and defense spending.

Nevertheless, national security experts from America's Pacific allies, as well as those in India, Singapore, Taiwan, and Indonesia, backed the US Pivot concept, as Figure 9.1 demonstrates.

## Japan

Japan was among the most enthusiastic supporters of the Pivot. Of all the nations of Asia, Japan felt most threatened by China as Beijing grew more powerful. The PRC singled Tokyo out for frequent vitriolic attacks, including for war crimes committed in China during World War II and the purported revival of "Japanese militarism."[2] Tokyo also watched warily as China rapidly modernized and expanded its military capability. Popular sentiment shifted partly as a result. In 2011, 61 percent of Japanese had an unfavorable view of China; by 2020, that number had climbed to 86 percent.[3] By 2022, 88 percent thought that the PRC's military power was a serious problem for their country.[4]

Throughout the 2010s, constitutional limitations and public opposition to assuming a major military role in the Indo-Pacific constrained Tokyo's defense policies and kept it dependent on US security guarantees.[5] Japanese also increasingly questioned the credibility of America's extended nuclear deterrence as Beijing built up its nuclear forces and capabilities.[6] Security elites worried that American wars in Afghanistan and Iraq, Washington's global security concerns, and its domestic political divisions would undermine the US treaty commitment to defend Japan and serve as the final guarantor of regional order. The Pivot, it seemed, promised a way to lock in US presence and participation for a generation.

Japanese foreign minister Koichiro Gemba avidly promoted the Pivot in a meeting with Clinton a few days after her 2011 article was published. "Referring to Secretary Clinton's article 'America's Pacific Century,'" the foreign ministry said, Gemba "felt sympathy with its contents and to create prosperous and stable world [sic] on the basis of democratic values was one of his primary diplomatic goals."[7] The same week, the minister amplified the theme, saying, "As you know, US President Obama stated in Australia, which is a strategic partner for Japan, that the United States was going to review its diplomacy and security priorities and would place the greatest importance on the Asia-Pacific region. This new policy is very encouraging, as Japan-US cooperation in the Asia-Pacific region has been and will remain a pillar of Japan's diplomacy."[8]

Six months later, a spokesperson for Prime Minister Yoshihiko Noda waxed similarly enthusiastic. "From a Japanese government point of view," he said, "US intention [sic] to rebalance defense priorities toward the Asia-Pacific region is welcome. And also, it's not only limited to defense issues. . . . [We] welcome US efforts . . . to advance its diplomatic and economic engagement in the region."[9] In short, Tokyo hoped that a renewed and more potent American pledge to peace and stability in Asia would make Japan safer and more prosperous.

Japan's enthusiasm for the Pivot reflected Tokyo's increasingly tense relations with Beijing and a new departure under Prime Minister Shinzo Abe. As Michael Green, a foremost American expert on Japan and Asia, explained, the Japanese prime minister sought to rebuild his country's defense architecture, enhance its ties with the United States, and forge new regional partnerships with Australia, India, and the Philippines.[10] Abe also pushed for higher defense spending and, in 2013, overcame domestic political opposition to win an increase for the first time in over a decade.[11] Since then, Japan has raised its defense budget every year, inching closer to Abe's goal of 2 percent of GDP.[12]

As early as 2007, during his first term, Abe delivered a historic address to the Indian parliament. In it, he envisioned a new geostrategic construct to link East Asia's economic engine with South Asia's growing industry, via the vital sea lanes that connect the Indian and Pacific Oceans.[13] Abe recognized a rising India's potential to balance increasing Chinese military assertiveness in the region and called for a "Free and Open Indo-Pacific." The term "Indo-Pacific," scarcely used before the speech, evolved into the geographic construct for several nations' regional strategies, despite Beijing's distaste for the phrase.[14] As previously discussed, Abe's "free and open" objective became, in time, the primary pillar of American policy in Asia as well.

Abe's administration published its 2013 Defense White Paper early in his second term, criticizing Beijing's aggression and coercion.[15] In a departure from the tone of previous years, the document charged the PRC with "resort[ing] to tactics viewed as highhanded, including attempts to use force to change the status quo, as it insists on its own unique assertions that are inconsistent with the order of the international law."[16] Abe also led a major change in Japan's policy toward Taiwan. In 2013, Tokyo and Taipei signed a bilateral fishing rights agreement and, two years later, Abe and his government began to describe Taiwan as a "precious friend" and an "important partner."[17]

Articulating sweeping strategic concepts was new for a postwar Japanese government, and in time Washington adopted significant elements of Abe's vision. Green summed up Abe's paramount influence during the 2010s. "Under Abe," he said, "Japan has developed a grand strategy for competing with China without war. . . . And the Trump administration in its first national security strategy in 2017. . . put forward the framework for our strategy that would be competing with China. . . . Japan has been adjusting to the rise of China faster than we have."[18]

Abe moved to reform Japan's security policies, partly in an effort to reinforce the US Pivot.[19] In a 2015 address to a joint session of the US Congress, Abe said, "We support the 'rebalancing' by the US in order to enhance the peace and security of the Asia-Pacific region. And I will state clearly. We will support the US effort first, last, and throughout."[20] Repeating the point later the same day, Abe affirmed, "Our efforts will complement the rebalancing now being pursued by the US. And those efforts, with the US and Japan joining forces, should lead the region, from the Asia-Pacific to the Indian Ocean, to more enduring peace and stability. That's what I hope for."[21]

From 2011 to 2020, Tokyo and Washington maintained a robust arms trade relationship, with the United States supplying almost 95 percent of Japan's defense imports.[22] As the decade closed, Tokyo ordered 105 F-35 Joint Strike Fighter aircraft, at a cost of some $23 billion, and the two countries processed more than $20 billion in active defense trade cases, including missile defense systems, fighter aircraft, UAVs, helicopters, and military electronics.[23]

Despite Abe's preoccupation with the threat from Beijing, however, Japan's economy became progressively more dependent on China throughout the decade.[24] In 2010, China consumed 19 percent of Japanese exports and accounted for 22 percent of Japan's imports.[25] By 2020, China purchased 22 percent of

Japanese exports and supplied 26 percent of Japan's imports, a record high.[26] That same year, China overtook the United States as the top destination for Japanese exports.[27] Though trade has declined recently, China remains Japan's largest trading partner.[28] Shin Kawashima, an expert at the University of Tokyo, made the consequences explicit. "If Japan is completely dependent on China in terms of economic and technology," he said, "Japan will be afraid that China will use this dominant position to impose some economic sanctions on Japan."[29]

In December 2022, influenced by the changing Asian strategic landscape and the shock of Russia's invasion of Ukraine, Japan released a new national security strategy. It declared China an "unprecedented strategic challenge" to international order and aimed to greatly enhance its defense posture.[30] Tokyo pledged to raise military spending from 1 percent to 2 percent of GDP by 2027, which would produce the world's third-largest defense budget.[31] The 2023 defense budget alone witnessed an increase of 26.3 percent over the 2022 budget, to $51.3 billion.[32] Tokyo also aimed to acquire long-range missiles with the capability to strike both mainland Asia and ships in the surrounding seas.[33] Walter Russell Mead concluded that Japan's objective was to "develop a world-class arms industry based on cutting-edge technology, and upgrade its self-defense forces into one of the world's most powerful militaries."[34]

Washington welcomed all these steps. National Security Advisor Jake Sullivan observed that "Japan has taken a bold and historic step to strengthen and defend the free and open Indo-Pacific with the adoption of its new National Security Strategy, National Defense Strategy and Defense Buildup Program. . . . Japan's goal to significantly increase defense investments will also strengthen and modernize the US-Japan Alliance."[35] In January 2023, American and Japanese officials announced that, by 2025, a US Marine Littoral Regiment with advanced intelligence and anti-ship capabilities would be stationed in Okinawa. The two countries deepened their security alliance to include outer space, and Secretary Blinken noted that an attack in that domain could "lead to the invocation of Article 5 of our Japan-US security treaty."[36]

Overall, at the heart of Japan's strategic concept was the challenge of pursuing a more robust security policy and enduring potential confrontation with Beijing while expanding Japan's economic relationship with China. As Tokyo navigated these rocky shoals, virtually all Japanese policymakers were unified: a meaningful American pivot to Asia would help their efforts.

## South Korea

South Korea matched Japan's support for the Pivot, but for a different reason. Although Seoul sought to maintain a calculated balance between Washington and Beijing throughout the 2010s, it hoped that the US reorientation toward the Indo-Pacific would provide additional American resources and political resolve to contain the growing threat from North Korea. In the two years leading up to the Pivot announcement, Pyongyang had conducted a nuclear test, sunk an ROK naval vessel, bombarded one of Seoul's islands with 200 missiles, killed South Korean soldiers, and undertook uranium-enrichment activities.[37] Shortly after Secretary Clinton spoke about a pivot in 2011, the North threatened to bring down "a sea of fire" on Seoul's presidential palace.[38]

Consequently, South Korea was determined to ensure strong relations with the United States. President Lee Myung-bak traveled to Washington on a state visit just two days after the publication of Clinton's article in October 2011. When asked during a joint press conference about US-ROK coordination on Pyongyang's nuclear threat, Lee underscored, "President Obama and I will remain in complete agreement when dealing with North Korea. . . . And when it comes to cooperation between our two governments, we speak with one voice, and we will continue to speak with one voice."[39]

After her 2013 election, President Park Geun-hye chose the United States for her first foreign trip. In a joint press conference with Obama, she explicitly reinforced the Pivot in the context of her own strategy, "We noted together," Park said, "that Northeast Asia needs to move beyond conflict and divisions and open a new era of peace and cooperation, and that there would be synergy between President's [sic] Obama's policy of rebalancing to Asia and my initiative for peace and cooperation in Northeast Asia as we pursue peace and development in the region."[40]

South Korea also worked hard to cultivate strong relations with China. Park, a Mandarin speaker, chose Beijing as her second foreign visit in June 2013. That summit established high-level communication channels between national security counterparts.[41] In the same year, Seoul announced that it would not join a missile defense arrangement in Asia led by the United States.[42] When Xi Jinping visited South Korea in July 2014, the ROK and China formed an "enriched strategic cooperative partnership."[43] As an independent US assessment of the Pivot concluded in 2014, "Seoul wants a rock-solid US commitment with respect to the North Korean threat, but does not want to be explicitly asked to support US strategies vis-à-vis China."[44]

China and South Korea signed a free trade agreement in 2015 that aimed to raise annual bilateral trade to over $300 billion, eliminate 90 percent of tariffs, and lift both countries' GDP.[45] South Korea also joined the AIIB and declined to enter the Trans-Pacific Partnership.[46] The effort to cultivate Beijing as a partner in dealing with the threat from Pyongyang reached a visible apogee in September that year, when Park attended China's World War II Victory Day parade.[47]

South Korean hopes for solidarity with Beijing in dealing with the North fizzled in 2016, when China refused to impose stronger sanctions on North Korea after a new nuclear test. Many in Seoul concluded that, despite all the effort to forge a partnership with Beijing, China did not restrain Pyongyang from provocative behavior. As a result, South Korea recalibrated its foreign policy and agreed to discussions with the United States, leading to the deployment of a THAAD missile defense system in 2017.[48] China reacted sharply and punitively. Beijing restricted South Korean entertainment, from TV shows to video games, banned consumer products, limited tourism to South Korea, closed Lotte stores in China, and halted defense discussions with Seoul.[49]

China and South Korea partially mended relations in October 2017, when Seoul and its new president, Moon Jae-In, agreed with Beijing to "Three No's": no additional THAAD deployments, no participation in US missile defense networks, and no trilateral military alliance with Tokyo and Washington.[50] But the relationship did not resume its 2013–2015 heights—some Korean companies simply exited the Chinese market, and Chinese tourism in South Korea remained below its earlier numbers.[51] Public perception shifted, too. Unfavorable views of China among South Koreans grew from 50 percent in 2013 to 75 percent in 2020.[52] And, most dramatically, while in 2015 only 29 percent of South Koreans had "no confidence" in Xi Jinping to do the "right thing regarding world affairs," by 2022, that number had reached a remarkable 87 percent.[53] Late that year, when China declined to impose new sanctions on North Korea over multiple missile tests, relations deteriorated further.[54]

All the same, South Korea worked hard throughout the decade to protect its economic relationship with China. The PRC was the destination for roughly 25 percent of South Korea's exports, an especially consequential reliance given that foreign trade made up nearly two-thirds of Seoul's economy.[55] From 2011 to 2020, the value of South Korean imports from China grew 116 percent, and South Korean exports to China rose by 120 percent.[56]

While South Korea was protecting its economic ties to China, it also boosted its security relations with the United States. In 2011, Seoul and Washington agreed to a "proactive deterrence" policy that would allow them to respond to Pyongyang's aggressive behavior quickly and decisively.[57] A 2012 joint statement between the two governments described the alliance as "a linchpin of stability, security, and prosperity in the Asia-Pacific region and increasingly around the world."[58] The alliance was soon put to the test. After an uptick in North Korean threatening activity the following year, Washington sent B-52 and B-2 bombers to participate in military exercises with Seoul.[59] B-52 and B-1B bombers flew in again after Pyongyang conducted two nuclear tests in 2016.[60] The United States and South Korea also held "2 + 2" meetings between the foreign and defense ministers to better coordinate on a range of issues, from Asian security to public health to cyber threats.[61] In June 2016, the Korean, Japanese, and American navies conducted missile tracking drills in response to the North's ballistic missile tests a few months earlier.[62] Until President Donald Trump postponed them in 2019, the two air forces also held annual Max Thunder exercises with a range of combat aircraft.

During a joint press conference with Trump in June 2019, President Moon aligned the two nations' foreign policies. "Under the regional cooperation principles of openness, inclusiveness and transparency," Moon said, "we have agreed to put forth harmonious cooperation between Korea's New Southern Policy and the United States' Indo-Pacific Strategy."[63] In that same spirit, South Korea joined talks with the United States, Taiwan, and Japan in 2022 to form the "Chip 4" alliance, aimed at stabilizing and preventing China's domination of the semiconductor supply chain.[64] Washington and Seoul also maintained a strong arms trade during the decade. The United States supplied two-thirds of South Korea's weapons imports from 2011 to 2020, and the ROK bought missiles, F-35A fighters, Global Hawk UAVs, and many other advanced arms.[65] South Korea has remained one of the top purchasers of US military equipment and was the third-largest importer of US weapons in 2020.[66]

Despite the bilateral efforts to promote security cooperation, South Korean policymakers worried about US resolve in the Indo-Pacific, a fear that grew acute during the Trump administration. After the American president tweeted his intention to remove troops from the peninsula, a South Korean lawmaker exclaimed, "If the United States withdraws its troops abruptly, our nuclear umbrella will disappear."[67] Trump's departure from the White House did not eliminate the sense among some South Koreans that, in the absence of a solid American security commitment, Seoul would have to take matters into its own hands. Retired ROK general Chun In-bum, for example, said in 2022, "Either American extended nuclear deterrence is formidable and credible, or South Korea acquires its own nuclear weapons. I have never doubted an American soldier. But I would be foolish to place my nation's security in the hands of an American politician."[68]

The sentiment spread among the public. In May 2022, a survey found that more than 70 percent of South Koreans supported Seoul's development of nuclear weapons.[69] In January 2023, President Yoon Suk-yeol warned, "It's possible that the problem [of Pyongyang's threats] gets worse and our country will introduce tactical nuclear weapons or build them on our own . . . if that's the case, we can have our own nuclear weapons pretty quickly, given our scientific and technological capabilities."[70] Following a February 2023 barrage of missile tests by the North, conservative party leader Chung Jin Suk advocated strengthening Seoul's preemptive "kill-chain" strategy and, if such a response failed to deter Pyongyang, considering the development of indigenous nuclear capabilities.[71]

To quell the nuclear anxieties, President Biden invited President Yoon to the United States in April 2023. There the two released a new "Washington Declaration," pledging to strengthen nuclear consultation. In the document, Seoul reiterated its commitment to nonproliferation and Washington affirmed that its defense of the ROK "is backed by the full range of U.S. capabilities, including nuclear."[72] "The United States' commitment to the ROK and the Korean people," it went on, "is enduring and ironclad, and . . . any nuclear attack by the DPRK against the ROK will be met with a swift, overwhelming and decisive response."[73] The two governments established a Nuclear Consultative Group to enhance strategic planning discussions, and the United States announced that it would periodically deploy a nuclear submarine near South Korea.[74]

Over time, such moves may not prove sufficient to quell South Korean calls for an independent nuclear weapons capability. As Busan-based professor Robert Kelly noted, the Washington Declaration "will blunt the current wave of South Korean nuke-talk. But that debate will likely return, because the declaration does not solve the problem driving it. Namely, the United States may hesitate to fully fight for South Korea in a Korean conflict because North Korea can now range the U.S. mainland with a nuclear weapon."[75] This dilemma will grow acute if a US administration less fully committed to South Korea's defense takes office.

Over these years, South Korea's attempt to balance between the United States and China shifted significantly. The change is best demonstrated in Seoul's first Indo-Pacific strategy, released in December 2022. Across its forty-three pages, China is explicitly mentioned in just two paragraphs: once as a "key partner," and again in the context of a trilateral commission with Japan.[76] The PRC represents, however, the strategy's shadowy presence. "Peace, stability, and freedom of navigation and overflight in the SCS," the document said, "which constitutes strategically important sea lines of communication, must be respected." In this passive tense and without mentioning Beijing, the strategy also "reaffirm[ed] the importance of peace and stability in the Taiwan Strait for the peace and stability of the Korean Peninsula and for the security and prosperity of the Indo-Pacific."[77] It further described the US-ROK alliance "as the linchpin for peace and prosperity" on the peninsula and said that Seoul planned to expand cooperation with the Quad.[78]

South Korea's national security strategy, released six months after the Indo-Pacific document, displayed the same sentiment: while there was no overt mention of China as a threat, the text outlined the importance of strengthened ties with the United States and included a jab at Beijing. "We will make it clear," it said, "that the THAAD deployment is a matter of our security sovereignty."[79] Within two weeks of the strategy's release, South Korea announced it would move forward with the deployment of an additional THAAD battery in 2024.[80]

Absent were previous notions of solidifying firm ties with Beijing in order to jointly manage the threat posed by Pyongyang.

## Australia

Australia joined Japan and South Korea in their spirited affirmation of the Pivot. Announcing the deployment of US Marines to Darwin in November 2011, Australian prime minister Julia Gillard highlighted the importance of bilateral ties as part of the Pivot. "Our alliance," she said, "has been a bedrock of stability in our region. So, building on our alliance through this new initiative is about stability."[81] In March 2013, Australia's soon-to-be prime minister, Kevin Rudd, wrote in *Foreign Affairs*, "The Obama administration's renewed focus on the strategic significance of Asia has been entirely appropriate. . . . The Obama administration's 'rebalance' has served as a necessary corrective, reestablishing strategic fundamentals."[82]

During these same years, however, Canberra simultaneously sought to develop harmonious relations with Beijing. Defense Minister David Johnston affirmed, "We don't subscribe to the concept that you must choose between the US and China. . . . We see that there is a balance between our relationship with China and sustaining our strong alliance with the United States."[83] Australia's 2013 defense white paper outlined Canberra's optimistic outlook on Australia-China relations, saying, "The Government does not approach China as an adversary. Rather, its policy is aimed at encouraging China's peaceful rise and ensuring that strategic competition in the region does not lead to conflict. . . . Australia is committed to developing strong and positive defense relations with China through dialogue and appropriate practical activities."[84] After Prime Minister Gillard's 2013 visit to Beijing, the two countries agreed to hold annual leadership meetings.[85]

Attempting to sustain the balance, in 2015 Australia disregarded the Obama administration's concerns and joined the China-led AIIB.[86] That same year, Canberra extended a ninety-nine-year lease at the Port of Darwin—near the US Marine deployment—to a Chinese firm with links to the PLA, which generated concern in Washington.[87] In addition, Australia and China signed a landmark free-trade agreement that went into effect in 2015.[88]

As the decade wore on, however, problems arose. Canberra staunchly opposed Beijing's aggressive military expansion into the South China Sea. After the UN Convention on Law of the Sea tribunal in 2016 rejected Chinese historic claims in the South China Sea, Australia called the judgment "final and binding," and urged China to "abide by the ruling."[89] In response, China's jingoistic,

English-language *Global Times* harshly warned Australia to "carefully talk and cautiously behave," and called it a "paper cat."[90]

To make bilateral matters worse, reports emerged in 2017 that Beijing had intervened in Australian domestic politics.[91] A 2018 book uncovered significant Chinese donations to Australian politicians and institutions, as well as ties between PRC intelligence agencies and prominent Chinese-Australians.[92] That same year, the Australian Security Intelligence Organization (ASIO) warned about unprecedented levels of foreign espionage. "In the current climate," it said, "we are facing a raft of different countries that are seeking to conduct espionage and foreign interference."[93] Later that year, Canberra passed a new national security law that increased penalties for political interference by foreign governments. Prime Minister Malcolm Turnbull banned Huawei from Australia's 5G networks over security concerns, which caused further tension with Beijing.[94] At points during the latter half of the decade, the PRC also launched massive cyberattacks against both Australia's parliament and its national university.[95]

Things grew far worse when, in 2020, Canberra called for an inquiry into the origins of COVID-19. In a United Nations General Assembly speech, Australian prime minister Scott Morrison urged the world to launch an independent investigation into the causes of the disease.[96] Beijing responded harshly, imposing trade sanctions against Canberra. It slapped 80 percent tariffs on Australian barley—one of the country's most important agricultural exports—and a 200 percent tax on Australian wine. It also restricted imports of Australian beef, cotton, lobsters, lamb, timber, and coal.[97]

China's ambassador to Australia threatened more economic sanctions. "I think in the long term," he said, "if the mood is going from bad to worse, people would think, 'Why should we go to such a country that is not so friendly to China?' The tourists may have second thoughts. . . . Maybe the ordinary people will say, 'Why should we drink Australian wine? Eat Australian beef?'"[98] As Kurt Campbell, President Joe Biden's Asia czar, told the Lowy Institute, "China's preference would have been to break Australia. To drive Australia to its knees."[99]

It did not succeed. Australia held firm in the face of economic coercion, but even as bilateral tensions rose across the decade, mutual trade ballooned.[100] China was Australia's largest trading partner—and the only one that saw sustained increases—throughout the decade. By 2020, China accounted for 41 percent of Australian exports and 29 percent of its imports.[101] That year alone, two-way trade expanded by 17 percent from the previous year, and it reached a then-record high of $252 billion.[102] In the first half of 2023 alone, Australia's exports to China were valued at a record-breaking $103 billion.[103]

Beijing attempted to use its commercial ties to drive Canberra and Washington apart. China promised "a fatal blow" to the country's economy if Australia did not distance itself from the United States.[104] "Given Australia's high dependence on the Chinese economy," the *Global Times* cautioned in 2020, "it would be extremely dangerous for Canberra to become a player in a diplomatic club led by the US."[105] That same year, Beijing advised Chinese tourists and students not to visit or study in Australia, which threatened approximately $16 billion in annual revenue.[106] Chinese investment in Australia dropped 61 percent in 2020 from the previous year and reached its lowest level in six years.[107]

Polls in Australia vivified the dramatic change in ties between the two nations. In 2013, only 35 percent of Australians held an unfavorable view toward China; by 2020, that number had skyrocketed to 81 percent.[108] A 2021 article summed up the turnaround. "Nearly 10 years ago," it read, "Australia thought it was on the cusp of a beautiful friendship with China: It was opening up its economy to Beijing, wanted to teach Mandarin in schools and invited the Chinese president to address parliament. Now, that's all over."[109]

In the years after the announcement of the Pivot—and as its strategic relationship with China declined—Canberra substantially upgraded its bilateral security ties with Washington. The United States increased military assets dedicated to Australia, in a rare example of Washington shifting resources to the Indo-Pacific during this period. In 2013, Canberra emphasized the importance of its alliance with Washington in its national security strategy, asserting, "The Australia-United States Alliance remains our most important security relationship . . . it remains an important anchor for peace and security in our region."[110] In 2014, Australia began to collaborate on American ballistic missile defense systems in north Asia and purchased 72 F-35 aircraft from the United States.[111] The next year, Australia became the second-largest recipient of American arms transfers, behind only Saudi Arabia.[112]

In 2015, following a meeting between President Obama and Prime Minister Turnbull, the two countries signed a defense cooperation agreement that pledged to "enhance military interoperability and intelligence cooperation, as well as build cooperation with regional partners."[113] A year later, the United States and Australia established a joint cyber security dialogue.[114] Australia's 2016 defense white paper called for a greater American role in the Indo-Pacific and explicitly endorsed the Pivot, saying, "Australia will seek to broaden and deepen our alliance with the United States, including by supporting its critical role in underpinning security in our [Indo-Pacific] region through the continued rebalance of United States military forces."[115]

In these years, Canberra and Washington also increased the size and complexity of their biennial Talisman Sabre military exercise.[116] By 2021, Australia and the United States had $27 billion in active defense trade cases, including helicopters, UAVs, tanks, missiles, and combat aircraft.[117] The United States also began construction, just south of Darwin, of facilities that by 2026 will house six nuclear-capable B-52 bombers.[118] In July 2023, Washington and Canberra announced an upgrade to their joint military facilities in Australia and the enhancement of America's rotational presence on northern military bases.[119] Washington agreed to increase American nuclear submarine visits to Australia and cooperate with Canberra on the production of rocket launchers.[120] In stark contrast to previous US-Australian military cooperation in the Middle East and Afghanistan, the allies were now focused squarely on the Indo-Pacific neighborhood. Australia, Defense Minister Richard Marles told reporters, "at this moment has no better friend than America."[121]

Canberra took other steps to strengthen its national security. After withdrawing from the Quad in 2008, Australia rejoined the reconstituted group in 2017.[122] Three years later, Prime Minister Morrison pronounced that Australia would boost its defense budget by 40 percent over ten years. Where its military had previously been active in the mountains of Afghanistan or attempting to stabilize East Timor, these increases were specifically slated for investment in long-range military assets to ensure a "sovereign Indo-Pacific free from coercion and hegemony."[123]

In 2021, Australia, the United Kingdom, and the United States announced AUKUS, the trilateral defense technology arrangement that aimed to help Canberra acquire nuclear-powered (but conventionally armed) submarines.[124] The agreement laid the foundation for cooperation on artificial intelligence, hypersonic missiles, undersea technologies, and autonomous systems.[125] It also pledged the deployment, by 2027, of American and British nuclear-powered attack submarines to Australia's west coast.[126] Not all of Canberra's steps in this period involved security; in 2022 it signed on to the Indo-Pacific Economic Framework and worked with Washington to establish the Partners in the Blue Pacific initiative.[127]

Nobody doubted that China's aggressive behavior drove Canberra's decision-making; by 2022, some 90 percent of Australians believed the PRC's military power to be a serious problem for their country. The following year, over half of Australians believed that China was more of a security threat than it was an economic partner.[128] And a July 2023 poll showed that 87 percent of Australians had an unfavorable opinion of China.[129] In light of the changing regional security picture, and the continuing reassessment of Chinese intentions, Canberra chose to double down on its alliance with the United States. An America pivoting to Asia, it was widely believed, would be unambiguously good for Australia.

With the May 2022 election of Prime Minister Anthony Albanese, however, Australia cautiously pursued more amicable economic and diplomatic ties with China, even as its substantial security concerns persisted. A series of mutual diplomatic concessions followed: Beijing released an Australian journalist who had been detained for over three years and Canberra chose not to revoke the ninety-nine-year lease in Darwin. In a telling sign of Australia's priorities, before he traveled to Beijing, Albanese visited Washington in October 2023. There, President Biden urged caution: "trust, but verify" everything when it comes to Beijing.[130] Albanese's three-day long visit to China in November marked the first by an Australian prime minister since 2016.[131] The leaders exchanged cordial words but the years of high tariffs and poor relations had taken a toll. As the University of Sydney's James Curran opined, "There will always be that nervous glance backward at this part of the relationship's history. . . . It won't be easily erased because what came with it was a whole other set of assumptions and fears."[132] Canberra will want to pursue mutually beneficial economic relations with China, but its security policies are unlikely to diverge from those of Washington.

## India

New Delhi was positive about the Pivot when it was announced, but only behind closed doors. As Sukh Deo Muni, a former Indian ambassador, wrote in August 2012, "India's positive response to the US 'pivot' . . . has not been made public and formal except in the classified bilateral discussions between the two countries. There has been no statement either explicitly endorsing or welcoming the US strategic shift or disapproving it otherwise."[133] India's policy of "strategic autonomy"—as well as its wish not to unduly offend Beijing—prevented any public statement or policy that could be perceived as moving toward an alliance with the United States.

US consistency presented another concern. Despite the transformation of the US-India relationship in preceding years, decades of toxic relations during the Cold War left India instinctively questioning American reliability, resolve, and staying power. "What if," one Delhi-based strategist asked, "India climbed on the US Pivot bandwagon that China condemned, and Washington then did an about face and joined Beijing in a G-2 strategic partnership?"[134] Such worries endured. As External Affairs Minister Subrahmanyam Jaishankar explained in 2022, "For almost 50 years, for various reasons I'm not saying we were at fault, or the US was at fault, but the fact was we regarded the US with suspicion with a lot of wariness. It was a very substantive relationship, but the overall foreign policy assessment of the US was of deep caution if not of deep suspicion."[135]

Nevertheless, after Japan, India was the Asian nation most concerned with the strategic implications of China's rise and the Indo-Pacific balance of power. As Jaishankar put it:

More than 50 per cent of our trade goes towards the East, towards the Pacific Ocean. The line between the Indian Ocean and Pacific Ocean is only on the map, exists on an atlas, but there is no such thing in reality. . . . We should go beyond the historical lines in our thinking, because our interest has increased. Indo-Pacific is a new strategic concept going on in the world.[136]

Within this strategic context, Beijing and New Delhi maintained a history of unresolved territorial disputes on their shared border. Beijing also provoked New Delhi as the largest arms exporter to Pakistan, helping Islamabad acquire nuclear weapons and rejecting the legitimacy of India's nuclear program.[137] At the United Nations, China endorsed Pakistan's claim to Kashmir and made clear that it would block India's permanent membership on the Security Council, an aspiration the United States publicly supported.[138]

As concerns about Beijing rose in New Delhi, its initial hesitancy to publicly embrace the Pivot faded. In February 2013, Nirupama Rao, India's ambassador in Washington, joined an event explicitly focused on "America's Asian Pivot: The View from India." "We welcome the US engagement in the Asia of the Indo-Pacific," Rao said. "The continuance of economic growth and prosperity in both our countries is in many ways linked to the opportunities for growth and prosperity in this region."[139] Around the same time, influential Indian foreign policy strategist C. Raja Mohan described India's quiet support for the Pivot, writing, "The US rebalancing strategy toward Asia announced by the Obama administration has been long overdue. . . . A strong and sustainable US role in Asia is welcome in New Delhi, which knows that the regional powers, including India, are not in a position to balance China on their own."[140]

Although ties between New Delhi and Beijing were tenuous for decades, the two nations made serious efforts to maintain good relations for the first half of the 2010s. Indian prime minister Manmohan Singh hosted Chinese premier Wen Jiabao—and hundreds of Chinese business leaders—in 2010, and Wen proclaimed that "India and China are friends."[141] At a summit of Brazil, Russia, India, the PRC, and South Africa (known collectively as the BRICS group) in China the following year, Singh and Chinese president Hu Jintao agreed to fully restore Indian-Chinese military cooperation.[142] At the 2012 BRICS summit in New Delhi, Hu affirmed that "it is China's unswerving policy to develop Sino-Indian friendship, deepen strategic cooperation and seek common development," and that China desired a "lasting and sincere friendship" with India.[143] That same year, Chinese prime minister Li Keqiang declared that "China-India relations are one of the most important bilateral relationships in the 21st century world. We have tremendous room for expanding cooperation. Building on what we have achieved and looking ahead to the future, we must firmly seize the new opportunities in strategic cooperation between China and India."[144]

The bilateral relationship degenerated after a series of border incidents in the Himalayas. The year 2013 saw a three-week border standoff at Depsang in the disputed Aksai Chin region and, in 2014, PLA troops moved two kilometers inside the Line of Actual Control (LAC)—India's de facto border.[145] In 2017, hundreds of Indian and Chinese soldiers faced off near the LAC in Doklam, near the border with China and Bhutan.[146] The conflict boiled over in 2020, with several violent skirmishes between the Indian and Chinese militaries. In June, troops from the two sides clashed in the Galwan Valley, which led to the deaths of at least twenty Indian soldiers—the first loss of life on the India-China border in fifty years.[147] The Indian public was outraged, and relations between the two great Asian powers nosedived.

Polls in India revealed a startling turnaround in public opinion. In a 2015 survey, 32 percent of Indian respondents held an unfavorable view of China. Four years later, that number rose to 46 percent.[148] In a 2020 poll, 84 percent of Indian respondents said that Xi Jinping had betrayed Prime Minister Narendra Modi and believed that "the distrust of China has never been this high."[149] A 2022 survey found that 43 percent of Indians cited China as their country's "greatest military threat," while only 13 percent named Pakistan.[150]

Even so, economic ties with China continued to grow in importance to New Delhi. Between 2010 and 2020, India's imports from China increased by 50 percent and its exports to China grew by 17 percent.[151] In 2020, the same year of deadly border skirmishes in eastern Ladakh, the PRC was India's largest trading partner and accounted for 14 percent of all of India's imports.[152] New Delhi relied on China for a wide variety of products and was especially dependent on Chinese telecommunications, electronics, and pharmaceuticals.[153]

China's strategic ambitions in the Indo-Pacific caused further tensions. India opposed the China-Pakistan Economic Corridor, which ran through Indian-claimed territory, and objected to Beijing's burgeoning presence in the Indian Ocean.[154] In 2018, former Indian national security advisor Shivshankar Menon voiced fear that China "will bring the People's Liberation Army" to the Hambantota port in Sri Lanka.[155] Two years later, Ashok Malik, a foreign ministry adviser, observed, "China's presence in the Indian Ocean to our east and west is changing our perceptions of maritime security like nothing since the Europeans arrived at the end [of the] 15th century."[156]

While Indian leaders expressed concern over China's increasingly aggressive actions, US-India security cooperation advanced, and the two nations joined in increased military exercises and expanded weapons trade.[157] In 2015, Washington and New Delhi reaffirmed a 10-year defense framework that provided for arms sales, technology transfer, and multilateral operations.[158] In 2017, India joined the re-established Quad and participated in the group's accelerated cooperation.[159] During the decade, New Delhi purchased close to $20 billion worth of American aircraft, missiles, drones, and helicopters, and in 2020 announced an additional $10 billion in defense deals with the United

States under negotiation.[160] New Delhi and Washington also concluded several agreements to counter China's influence in the region and boost cooperation on semiconductors, weapons production, and artificial intelligence.[161] As foreign policy expert Brahma Chellaney said, "The strategic partnership between the United States and India is pivotal to maintaining the balance of power in the vast Indo-Pacific region and counterbalancing China's hegemonic ambitions."[162]

To reflect this growing collaboration, the United States and India announced the US-India Initiative on Critical and Emerging Technologies (iCET) in May 2022, aiming to expand technology cooperation and defense industry collaboration.[163] In January 2023, the first iCET meeting took place, led by the countries' national security advisors, which resulted in an ambitious, multi-pronged plan to deepen ties across six areas, including defense technology, semiconductor supply chains, space, and next-generation telecommunications.[164]

Prime Minister Modi's state visit to Washington in June 2023 saw a range of agreements with President Biden, marking what they called "a new level of trust and mutual understanding."[165] The two countries agreed to jointly produce fighter jet engines in India, and New Delhi's defense ministry announced it would purchase dozens of Predator drones.[166] An American memory chip firm announced that it would invest up to $825 million to build a factory in Gujarat, and an Indian solar energy firm promised a $1.5 billion investment in the United States.[167] As part of improved economic relations, Washington and New Delhi also agreed to end six World Trade Organization disputes, and India promised to cut retaliatory tariffs on certain foods.[168] New Delhi agreed to join the Artemis Accords, a space cooperation arrangement of twenty-six nations, and India committed to a joint mission with NASA in 2024.

After Biden met with Modi during the September 2023 G20 summit in New Delhi, a meeting that Xi Jinping ostentatiously did not attend, the United States and India released a joint statement in which the two leaders "expressed their appreciation for the substantial progress underway to implement the ground breaking achievements of Prime Minister Modi's historic . . . visit to Washington."[169] To build on the summitry, the two countries held their fifth "2 + 2" meeting between foreign and defense ministers in November 2023 where they "reaffirmed their commitment to further deepen the multifaceted defense partnership through wide-ranging dialogues and military exercises of increasing complexity and sophistication, accelerated joint projects initiated under the June 2023 Roadmap for U.S.-India Defense Industrial Cooperation and expanded collaboration in emerging domains, such as space and artificial intelligence."[170] The Modi government further strengthened its tactical ties with Washington when it implicitly took Israel's side immediately after the October 7 Hamas attacks.

With the Pivot, as with so many US policy initiatives, India offered its usual response—listen, study, doubt, verify, and, as the situation sometimes dictated, support. All the same, it is likely that the US-India relationship will grow ever closer in coming years. While no formal alliance is in the offing, New Delhi and Washington are witnessing a convergence of strategic interests, prompted by the desire to ensure an Indo-Pacific balance of power amid the continued rise of China.

## Southeast Asia

Largely because of their flourishing trade with China, ASEAN states were generally muted in their reactions to the Pivot. The bloc's trade deficit with China grew tenfold, from $10 billion in 2010 to $103 billion in 2019.[171] Between 2011 and 2020, ASEAN's total imports from China surged from 13 percent to 23 percent, reflecting Southeast Asia's ever-increasing dependence on Chinese capital goods for their own exports.[172] During this period, trade between ASEAN and the PRC nearly doubled, from $295 billion to $519 billion, and the percentage of Chinese trade relative to the bloc's total rose from 12 percent to 19 percent. The *Wall Street Journal* found that Beijing's total trade with ASEAN countries grew 71 percent from July 2018 to November 2022 alone.[173] Even in the COVID years, trade between Southeast Asia and China rose from $508 billion in 2019 to $722 billion in 2022.[174]

Figure 9.2 vividly displays why no ASEAN nation during the decade went all-out to oppose Beijing's aggressive policies. They were simply too dependent on commerce with China.

With these economic realities ever-present, Indonesia publicly cautioned the United States about the dangers of provoking Beijing. At the ASEAN summit in November 2011—shortly after the Clinton article and the announcement of US Marines to be based in Australia—Indonesian foreign minister Marty Natalegawa warned that the Pivot could lead to a "vicious circle of tension and mistrust."[175] At the same summit, and in response to the Darwin deployment, Singaporean foreign minister Kasiviswanathan Shanmugam stressed that ASEAN countries did not want to get "caught between the competing interests" of Washington and Beijing.[176] Malaysian prime minister Najib Razak echoed those words and emphasized the need to "constructively manage" the US-China dynamic in the region in order to prevent increased tension.[177]

In the early 2010s, only the Philippines voiced clear praise of the Pivot and the deployment in Darwin. A spokesman for President Benigno Aquino said, "if you are asking me in general how I view the increased engagement of the US in Australia and in the region, we view the [US military] presence here . . . as ultimately a stabilizing force, and we welcome that."[178] The Philippine government expressed further support for the Pivot in October 2013, when Foreign Minister

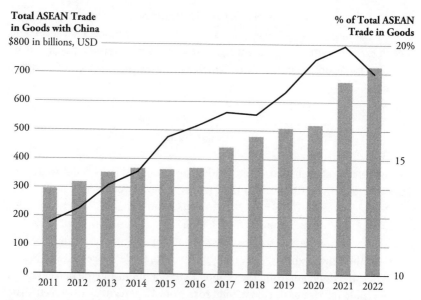

**Figure 9.2.**  Total ASEAN trade in goods with China, 2011–2022.
Source: ASEAN, "Trade in Goods (IMTS), Annually, HS 2-digit up to 8-Digit (AHTN), in US$,"
ASEANStatsDataPortal, ASEAN, https://data.aseanstats.org/trade-annually.

Albert del Rosario spoke positively about the reorientation and characterized the presence of increased US forces in the Philippines as "a minimum credible defense posture through capability building and combined activities."[179]

While the Philippines outwardly supported the Pivot in the beginning of the decade, President Rodrigo Duterte's 2016 election brought an about-face in bilateral relations with Washington and China.[180] Irked by criticism of his brutal drug war—a campaign that earned notoriety for its thousands of extra-judicial killings—and hoping to play off Beijing and Washington, Duterte made his preferences clear by taking his first trip outside of ASEAN to Beijing.[181] He did not mince words. "And in the shifting of political and cultural thing [*sic*]," Duterte said in Beijing's Great Hall of the People, "America has lost it. I mean, I realigned myself in your ideological flow and maybe I will also go to Russia to talk to Putin and tell him that there are three of us against the world: China, Philippines and Russia."[182] In the same speech, Duterte stressed, "I have separated from [the US], so I will be dependent on you for all times."[183]

Duterte's stated realignment was, however, no model of consistency. Though reduced, military exercises between the United States and the Philippines continued throughout the decade.[184] Manila would neither allow the United States to re-establish military bases nor maintain special forces on its southern islands after 2014, but the Enhanced Defense Cooperation Agreement (EDCA) and its basis, the 1999 Visiting Forces Agreement (VFA), permitted the United States to maintain a rotational military presence at five Philippine installations.[185] US special forces in fact returned to Mindanao in 2017 to help the Philippine military fight an ISIS offshoot that had taken the city of Marawi.[186] The Philippines filed to withdraw from the long-standing VFA in 2020, but Duterte then reversed the decision a year later.[187] In addition, from 2016 to 2019 the Philippines received $268 million in foreign military financing from the United States. Throughout his tenure, Duterte also pursued enhanced security relations with Japan—the principal US ally in the region.[188]

Convinced of the threat posed by Beijing in the South China Sea and cognizant of its geographic reality as a front-line state in a Taiwan crisis, Manila returned to defense cooperation with the United States after Ferdinand Marcos Jr.'s election in June 2022 as president.[189] In his first address to the nation's congress in July, Marcos declared, "I will not preside over any process that will abandon even one square inch of territory of the Republic of the Philippines to any foreign power."[190] The following September, amid reports that China's military activity had unsettled senior Philippine officials, Manila and Washington committed to doubling the number of troops engaged in a joint exercise.[191] In November 2022, Philippine officials reportedly wanted to expedite talks to implement projects under the EDCA, and had decided to provide US armed forces with greater access to the country. This included a possible return to Subic Bay, which was once the largest American naval base in Asia.[192] In March 2023, *Bloomberg* provided more details on the expansion: "Philippine President Ferdinand Marcos Jr. said the US will gain expanded access to military sites in northern Philippines close to Taiwan, as well as in Palawan province near South China Sea, paving the way for greater American presence in key locations as tensions with Beijing linger."[193]

Using the same words as Secretary del Rosario nine years prior, a defense department spokesperson highlighted that the endeavors aimed to "build a more credible mutual defense posture."[194] In April 2023, Washington and Manila conducted their largest joint military exercise in thirty years, with nearly 18,000 personnel participating.[195] Days later, President Marcos traveled to Washington, agreeing to a joint statement that illustrated the quickly deepening bilateral ties. The two leaders observed "the historic momentum in U.S.-Philippine relations" and resolved to "continue expanding engagement and cooperation on all issues of common concern."[196] In November 2023, the US began to advise the Philippines on the repair of the *Sierra Madre*. Manila had intentionally grounded the naval vessel more than two decades prior on Second Thomas Shoal in the Spratly Islands, in order to challenge China's territorial claims in the South China Sea.[197] After Chinese and Philippine ships collided in December 2023 as a result of "reckless" PRC maneuvering, the State Department said, "The United States stands with our Philippine allies in the face of these dangerous and unlawful actions. We reaffirm that Article IV of the 1951 U.S.-Philippines Mutual Defense Treaty extends to armed attacks on Philippine armed forces, public vessels, or aircraft—including those of its Coast Guard—anywhere in the South China Sea."[198]

During the 2010s, Malaysia under Najib Razak embraced Beijing. The two countries signed eight memoranda of understanding on economic cooperation and BRI investment, and Kuala Lumpur accepted tens of BRI projects worth over $100 billion, though many were later stalled or stopped entirely.[199] In the security sector, China and Malaysia in 2013 announced a comprehensive strategic partnership focused on intensified military cooperation and, in 2014, the two countries conducted their first-ever defense simulation, which was followed in 2015 by a major exercise.[200] The next year, Malaysia purchased four Chinese naval vessels and signed fourteen agreements with Beijing worth $34.25 billion, ranging from defense to education to agriculture.[201] The ever-closer bilateral relationship stalled, however, when charges of corruption led to Razak's electoral defeat and subsequent arrest in 2018.[202]

Razak's successor, Mahathir bin Mohamad, was initially more skeptical of China. He canceled a major BRI project—the East Coast Rail Link, which would link the coasts of peninsular Malaysia—and likened the Chinese initiative to modern colonialism.[203] In an interview before his election, Mahathir observed, "With the changes in [China's] leadership, we see more ambitious leaders coming in and maybe they like to flex their muscles a bit and that is very worrisome . . . they have managed to increase their influence over many countries in Southeast [and South] Asia." China was, he added, "inclined towards totalitarianism."[204] Because of Kuala Lumpur's trade dependence on Beijing, however, Malaysia still sought cordial relations with China, much like most of ASEAN. Mahathir renegotiated the rail link deal on better terms for Malaysia in April 2019, which steadied the relationship. In the same year, the two countries established a bilateral consultation mechanism and, by 2022, though he was no longer in office, Mahathir supported more cooperation with the PRC. He called on his ASEAN partners to do the same and blamed the West for aggravating Beijing.[205] Ahead of the APEC summit in November 2023, Malaysia's new prime minister, Anwar Ibrahim stated that while his country was not "tilting to China," it was "geographically closer than the US" and that "China is our neighbour, an important country and has matured in terms of its economic vibrancy, and we would benefit immensely as we continue to engage with it."[206]

During these years, China dominated Indonesia's economic portfolio as the country's largest trading partner and a top source of investment.[207] In 2013, the two formed a comprehensive strategic partnership, and Joko Widodo's 2014 election fortified these enhanced relations. He prioritized infrastructure development, and under his leadership Indonesia joined the Asia Investment

Infrastructure Bank and proposed just over $90 billion in BRI projects to Chinese investors.[208] Chinese foreign direct investment in Indonesia increased by an astonishing 600 percent between 2015 and 2020.[209] By 2020, one in five Indonesian goods was exported to China, while over one in four imports was sourced from the PRC.[210] Despite Indonesia's strong economic ties to China, Washington sold over $5 billion in weapons to Jakarta over the decade, and the United States and Indonesia also signed two agreements to enhance defense cooperation. In November 2023, President Widodo visited Washington where the two sides upgraded ties to the "comprehensive strategic partnership" level and pledged to collaborate in climate, energy, digital connectivity, defense, and critical minerals.[211] Despite the warm words between Widodo and Biden, however, Jakarta—like most ASEAN nations—is determined to avoid a stark choice between Washington and Beijing.[212]

In the same period, Thailand's economic dependence on China grew significantly. Between 2011 and 2020, Thailand's exports made up 65 percent of its GDP, on average.[213] The United States and China represented Thailand's top two export markets and maintained similar proportions of Bangkok's export portfolio.[214] However, Thailand's imports from China grew from 13 percent in 2011 to a quarter of the country's total in 2020, while the United States hovered at five to seven percent throughout the period.[215] Chinese tourism to Thailand also expanded in these years; by 2020, a third of all tourists in Thailand were Chinese.[216]

When the West condemned Thailand's 2014 coup, the military junta turned sharply toward China.[217] Less than a year after the upheaval, Beijing and Bangkok signed an agreement to increase military cooperation over five years.[218] In 2015, Thailand purchased submarines from the PRC and then procured tanks in 2016.[219] In September 2019, Bangkok signed a shipbuilding pact with Beijing, followed two months later by an agreement between Thai prime minister Prayut Chan-o-cha and Chinese defense minister Wei Fenghe to intensify defense cooperation even further.[220] As part of this strengthened security collaboration, the two militaries conducted multiple bilateral exercises, as well as trilateral drills with Malaysia.[221] They also entered discussions on the construction of a joint military production facility.[222] In 2022, China upgraded the equipment and weapons included in the annual "Falcon Strike" exercise.[223] The exercise was repeated in 2023, and Beijing and Bangkok agreed to coordinate air defense, air support, and large-scale deployment trainings.[224]

During the 2010s, Singapore and Beijing upgraded their free-trade agreement, and by 2013 the city-state became the largest foreign investor in China, with the PRC its top source of imports.[225] In 2014, China became Singapore's largest export market and principal trading partner.[226] Throughout the decade, Singapore's exports to China totaled half a trillion dollars, while Chinese imports were valued at some $440 billion.[227]

Despite Chinese complaints, these same years witnessed Singapore's growing bilateral defense cooperation with the United States.[228] Following the signing of an EDCA, Prime Minister Lee Hsien Loong and President Trump renewed two memoranda of understanding in 2019 that allowed American forces to use Singapore's naval and air bases, as well as maintain a military presence.[229] Singapore's Ministry of Defense observed, "The renewal of this document underscores the support for US presence in our region which remains vital for regional, peace, stability, and prosperity."[230] From 2011 to 2020, Singapore also purchased radars, missiles, and combat aircraft from the United States worth an estimated $6.5 billion.[231] This was in addition to the $38 billion that private American companies sold to the city-state from 2016 to mid-2022.[232]

Kishore Mahbubani, Singapore's former permanent representative to the United Nations, observed that "Singapore has always worked hard to anchor the US presence in Southeast Asia."[233] At the same time, Singapore's leaders remained adamant that no choice between the United States and China should be forced upon them. Shanmugam, now as law and home affairs minister, emphasized, "we want the tensions to cool down and if we take sides, that is highly disruptive, either for our security or our economy or many other aspects."[234]

While the United States and China were top export destinations for Vietnam's goods, Hanoi became ever more dependent on Chinese imports. They grew from 23.3 percent to 32.2 percent of Vietnam's portfolio and remained the top source of goods throughout the decade.[235] The value of PRC imports grew from $25 billion in 2011 to $84 billion in 2020, a 239 percent increase. Moreover, nearly half of these imports were capital goods, further cementing Vietnam's reliance on China.[236]

As the PRC asserted itself in the disputed South China Sea, Hanoi deepened security ties with the United States. After President Obama lifted the arms embargo in 2016, naval engagement increased and culminated in visits by US warships in Vietnam.[237] As will be discussed in Chapter 11 on defense, an American aircraft carrier anchored in Hanoi in 2018 for the first time since the Vietnam War and returned in 2020.[238] A Foreign Ministry spokesperson said the visit would "continue to promote bilateral relations within the framework of the two countries' comprehensive partnership and contribute to maintaining peace, stability, security, cooperation and development in the region."[239] The following year, Vietnam released a white paper that denounced China's actions in the South China Sea and noted that it was "ready to participate in security and defense cooperation mechanisms . . . including [those] in the Indo-Pacific region."[240] Capitalizing on the opportunity, President Biden visited Vietnam in September 2023 and the two countries upgraded their relationship to a "comprehensive strategic partnership," a status Hanoi had previously reserved only for China, India, Russia, and South Korea.[241]

In contrast with the rest of ASEAN, Cambodia and Laos during the decade were near supplicants of Beijing, largely for geoeconomic reasons. Phnom Penh relied significantly on imports from the PRC throughout the decade, which often doubled the value of the next largest importer.[242] By the end of 2020, China made up 37 percent of Cambodia's imports, at over $7 billion.[243] In 2017, 70 percent of Phnom Penh's FDI came from Beijing, and by 2019, Cambodia owed the PRC some $4.5 billion.[244] During these same years, China held half of Laos's public debt and provided the largest amount of FDI to the country.[245] Vientiane was also a recipient of substantial BRI funds, as well as $7 billion from Chinese private companies.[246] At the beginning of the 2010s, one in twenty of Laos's exports went to China. By 2020, that number rose to one in four, and the PRC became the second-largest source of imports for Vientiane.[247]

Reflecting Beijing's economic sway, in July 2012, Cambodia, as chair of the yearly ASEAN Conference, insisted that the disputed Scarborough Shoal and South China Sea exclusive economic zones go unmentioned in the joint communiqué, which in the end was not published.[248] In 2016, Phnom Penh blocked an ASEAN resolution that criticized Chinese practices in the South China Sea and continued to frame the issue as a quarrel among claimants, not between the bloc and Beijing.[249] In the military arena, China sent hundreds of millions of dollars in military equipment to Cambodia throughout the decade and the two nations conducted joint military activities. Phnom Penh also extended the PLA's maritime reach when it allowed Beijing to build its first overseas naval installation in the Indo-Pacific at its Ream Naval Base on the Gulf of Thailand.[250] Satellite imagery in July 2023 showed the base had nearly been completed.[251]

Exemplifying their strategic collaboration with China, Cambodia and Laos joined the Philippines at the United Nations to defend the PRC's actions in Xinjiang, where Beijing systematically oppressed the Uyghur population.[252] When Beijing's policies in Xinjiang were again scrutinized at the UN in 2020, Phnom Penh and Vientiane were the only two ASEAN members that came to China's defense. Both states then endorsed China's new Hong Kong Security Law that same year.[253]

In total, with Cambodia, Laos, and the Philippines under Duterte as outliers, most Southeast Asian countries simultaneously pursued three goals across the decade—increased trade and investment with China; quiet support for the pivot of US security resources and presence to the Indo-Pacific; and urging Beijing and Washington to show restraint and settle their differences peacefully. As Singapore prime minister Lee put it in 2017, the US-China relationship is "the most important bilateral relationship in the world. . . . I express my hope that the US will be able to maintain a stable and constructive relationship with China. . . . Good US-China relations will benefit the region and the world."[254]

## Elite Observations

As the 2010s progressed, US implementation of the Pivot was rightly questioned across the Indo-Pacific. Some Asian policy elites concluded that the Pivot's incomplete execution signaled weakness in America's ability to sustain focus on and commitment to Asia; they saw Pivot rhetoric as a near panic-level response to China's rising power. Others welcomed the increased diplomatic attention given to the region in the early Obama years, including Washington's 2009 accession to ASEAN's Treaty of Amity and Cooperation (TAC), formal US participation in the East Asia Summit starting in 2011, the appointment of a resident ambassador to the ASEAN Secretariat in Jakarta, the regular attendance of annual summits by senior American officials, and Secretary Clinton's stepped-up regional travel. They observed, however, that US diplomacy throughout the decade remained highly contingent on events and personalities, and that the meetings did not produce increased resources in most areas.

Professor Waheguru Pal Singh Sidhu expressed an emblematic view in November 2012. "This pivot" to Asia, he said, "will be successful only when the US can disentangle itself from the Middle East. Until then, Washington is likely to pirouette between the Middle East and the Asia-Pacific."[255] Similarly, William Choong, an expert at the Institute of Southeast Asian Studies, concluded in 2013 that "Washington has failed to reassure allies and partners that the pivot—coming at a time when the US is plagued by fiscal and economic ills—is sustainable. Even if this were so, the US force alignment is relatively modest."[256] Singaporean Bilahari Kausikan recalled:

> As Permanent Secretary of the Ministry of Foreign Affairs, I told then-Assistant Secretary of State Kurt Campbell a Pivot connotes something inconstant because what "pivots" one way can easily "pivot" another way, whereas what the US ought to convey to friends, partners, and allies is constancy. Moreover, the metaphor created expectations that were impossible for a global power like the US to fulfil as there would inevitably be crises elsewhere—usually in the Middle East—that would require US attention and when attention focused elsewhere even for a short period, there would be an overreaction from Asian countries, particularly in Southeast Asia.[257]

Two years after the Pivot announcement, journalist Stuart Grudgings went further, observing:

> The lack of a US [Marine] presence there [in Darwin] two years after the policy was announced underlines questions about Washington's commitment to the strategic "pivot" to Asia. . . . President Barack Obama's cancellation of a trip this

week to four Asian nations and two regional summits due to the US government shutdown has raised further doubts over a policy aimed at re-invigorating
US military and economic influence in the fast-growing region, while balancing a rising China. While US and Asian diplomats downplayed the impact
of Obama's no-show, the image of a dysfunctional, distracted Washington adds
to perceptions that China has in some ways outflanked the US pivot.[258]

Asian governments wondered if America was up to China's challenge, and
whether the United States, as Beijing asserted, was in historic decline. During the
2010s, Japan, South Korea, Australia, and India applauded the Pivot announcement and concept at its outset, while they sought to maintain good relations
with Beijing. But as the decade evolved, their ties with China deteriorated. They
remained vulnerable to economic coercion, improved their own defenses with
Washington's help, and deepened security cooperation with the United States
and with each other.[259] At the same time, they worried about US competence and
commitments in the Indo-Pacific. Most other Indo-Pacific nations simply tried
to stay out of the line of fire between China and the United States.

By 2020, governments in Asia could observe that, since the 2011 announcement, no significant and sustained diplomatic, military, or economic US pivot to
the Indo-Pacific from the Middle East and Europe had occurred. Figures 9.3, 9.4,
and 9.5 vividly illustrate high-level US diplomatic activity across regions.

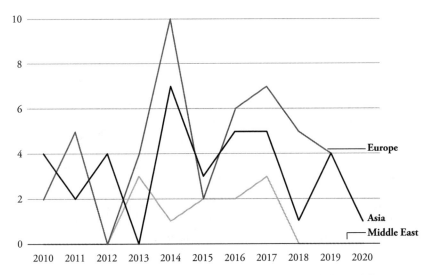

**Figure 9.3.** US presidential visits to nations in Asia, Europe, and the Middle East,
2010–2020.

Source: Department of State, Office of the Historian, *Travels Abroad of the President*, accessed July
22, 2022, https://history.state.gov/departmenthistory/travels/president.

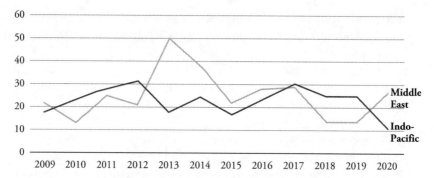

**Figure 9.4.** US president, secretary of state, and secretary of defense visits to countries in the Middle East and Indo-Pacific, 2009–2020.

Source: Department of Defense, Historical Office, *Secretary of Defense Travels*, accessed July 22, 2022, https://history.defense.gov/DOD-History/Secretary-of-Defense-Travels/; Department of State, Office of the Historian, *Travels Abroad of the Secretary of State*, accessed July 22, 2022, https://history.state.gov/departmenthistory/travels/secretary; Department of State, Office of the Historian, *Travels Abroad of the President*, accessed July 22, 2022, https://history.state.gov/departmenthistory/travels/president.

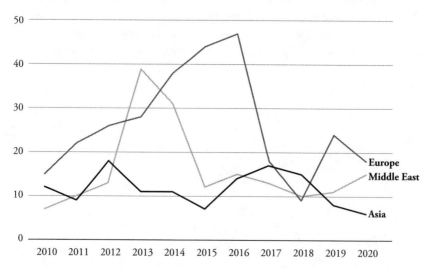

**Figure 9.5.** US secretary of state visits to nations in Europe, the Indo-Pacific, and the Middle East, 2010–2020.

Source: Department of State, Office of the Historian, *Travels Abroad of the Secretary of State*, accessed July 22, 2022, https://history.state.gov/departmenthistory/travels/secretary.

## Stable Levels of Military Resources

As earlier chapters detail, there was no significant reallocation of US military resources to Asia from Europe or the Middle East during the 2010s. The US Pacific Fleet, for instance, in 2016 comprised 140,000 sailors, more than 200 ships, and 1,200 aircraft.[260] In 2022, the Pacific Fleet had approximately the same number of ships and aircraft, but less than 130,000 sailors.[261] The Seventh Fleet, headquartered in Japan and the largest of the US Navy's forward deployed forces, shrunk over the decade following the Pivot's announcement.[262] In 2011, the Seventh Fleet deployed 60–70 ships, between 200 and 300 aircraft, and approximately 40,000 sailors and Marines.[263] In 2022, the Seventh Fleet had 50–70 ships and submarines, 150 aircraft, and just over 27,000 sailors and Marines.[264]

Snapshot comparisons of deployed forces and assets can be problematic, but the absence of a significant military plus-up in Asia is self-evident. And while the numbers do not consider qualitative enhancements in the combat capabilities of US military forces devoted to Asia, there were declines in key areas. Reductions, where they occurred, reflected aircraft that were decommissioned, ships that rotated out of the region—along with their associated aircraft squadrons and detachments—and the gradual drawdown of Marines in Okinawa, Japan.[265] Michael Green provided the reasons behind the reduction: "A $500 billion cut over ten years in the Pentagon meant that even if you are prioritizing the Pacific for the Navy, the Marines, or the Air Force, even if you were creating a 4-star general for the Army in the Pacific writ-large, you were sending the Navy on a trajectory to be the smallest size it had been since 1915."[266]

The same was true of Air Force and Army assets devoted to Asia. According to Department of Defense figures, the number of active-duty Army personnel permanently assigned to countries in the Indo-Pacific decreased from 23,000 in 2011 to 21,000 in 2020.[267] Similarly, the Pacific Air Forces (PACAF) had 29,314 active-duty military personnel in 2011 and 29,952 in 2020; only a 2 percent increase after nearly a decade.[268] More consequentially, between 2011 and 2020, the number of PACAF combat aircraft dropped from 263 to 257, and transport planes from 38 to 30.[269] Additionally, the Air Force began to withdraw two squadrons of F-15 Eagles permanently based in Okinawa and replace them with a rotational deployment of F-22s. Pro-Pivot Republican lawmakers argued that the move would "send the wrong signal, not only to the Chinese Communist Party, but also to our allies and partners in the Indo-Pacific."[270]

## A Deteriorating Regional Balance

Had Chinese military capabilities been standing still over the decade, the relative stagnation in the amount of US forces dedicated to the region might have mattered little. On the contrary, however, and as the next chapter will describe in detail, Beijing made dramatic and sustained advances in military capabilities and capacity throughout the period. As the 2018 National Security Strategy lamented, "For decades the United States has enjoyed uncontested or dominant superiority in every operating domain. We could generally deploy our forces when we wanted, assemble them where we wanted, and operate how we wanted. Today, every domain is contested—air, land, sea, space, and cyberspace."[271] In March 2021, INDOPACOM Commander Admiral Phil Davidson cautioned that China was "on track to overtake the United States as the most powerful military in the Pacific within the decade—potentially as soon as 2026—with the wherewithal sooner than previously expected to establish permanent, regional primacy."[272] During the 2010s, China was bent on catching up and surpassing the United States in regional military power. As the 2020s dawned, Washington belatedly committed to catch up with China. It had a great deal of work to do.

The regional balance did not shift only in military capability that could be used in a conflict. Over the 2010s, the region perceived Chinese actions and relative American inaction as reflecting Beijing's ascendance. After a tense 2012 standoff with China over Scarborough Shoal, for example, Manila asked for assistance from ASEAN and its American ally. Washington refused to intervene directly or confirm whether its Mutual Defense Treaty applied to the Scarborough Shoal.[273] A few months later, the United States helped negotiate an understanding between the Philippines and China to mutually pull back from the disputed land. Manila withdrew its ships, but Beijing did not, which eventually gave the PRC control of the contested feature.[274] Washington's failure to defend the Philippines and moderate China's aggressive behavior damaged its reputation across the Indo-Pacific.[275]

The United States again lost credibility by remaining passive in response to the PRC's militarization of features in the South China Sea. Beginning in 2013, China built more than 3,000 acres of militarized artificial islands—including in the Spratly and Paracel Islands—that caused anxiety in Malaysia, Vietnam, and the Philippines.[276] The United States attempted to counter Chinese actions in the South China Sea through diplomacy, by launching complaints at the United Nations, and by conducting freedom of navigation exercises.[277] It avoided more direct steps, like sanctions or taking a position on rival claims in favor of other countries in the region.

Overall, in the decade after the Pivot announcement the Indo-Pacific military balance tilted toward China, a shift widely acknowledged in the region. A 2016 congressionally-mandated review determined bluntly that "the balance of military power in the region is shifting against the United States."[278] The Philippines' ambassador to China, Jose Santiago Santa Romana, observed in 2018, "Whereas before the South China Sea was dominated by the US 7th Fleet, now the Chinese navy is starting to challenge the dominance. . . . I think we will see a shift in the balance of power."[279] And in its 2020 Defense Strategic Update, Canberra worried that, compared to just four years before, "Australia's strategic environment has deteriorated more rapidly than anticipated."[280]

The failure of the TPP further weakened US leadership in the Indo-Pacific. As Chapter 12 on economic matters details, the TPP was commonly hailed as the economic cornerstone of the Pivot. Clinton herself called it "the gold standard" for trade agreements, before reversing herself and opposing it during her presidential campaign.[281] Then-Vice President Joe Biden called for its completion in multiple Asian capitals and then publicly advocated for congressional approval, before himself coming to oppose the deal on the campaign trail.[282] Donald Trump was consistently contemptuous of the Pivot's economic centerpiece, and immediately withdrew the United States from the TPP once in office.[283]

The failure of the TPP, which had by that point attracted unusual bipartisan opposition, produced a huge blow to the American position. As Timothy Heath of RAND observed, "The withdrawal has exacerbated regional doubts about US international leadership and of its role in Asia. To be clear, concern about Washington's commitment dogged the rebalance since it became clear that a fiscally strapped US, burdened with global woes, would only commit limited resources to the initiative."[284]

As America was otherwise engaged, distracted, or dormant, Beijing was ever more assertive across Asia in the 2010s. As a result, by the end of the decade many US policymakers and experts were gripped by a sense of urgency. China was, many concluded, ably coupling a more aggressive will with greater ability to project power, and the United States had fallen behind in the effort to deal with Beijing's challenge. America had to catch up.

The strategic trend lines were indeed, by the end of the decade, abundantly clear. The Pivot had resulted in new, small-scale military and diplomatic initiatives in the Indo-Pacific, but not a grand reorientation of American strategy and resources. Countries across the Indo-Pacific were more economically dependent on China than when the decade began, Washington's trade policy was less ambitious than before, the PRC had greater relative military power than before, and the United States was beset by domestic divisions. As the Lowy Institute's 2023 Asia Power Index underscored, "China's overall power still lags the United States but is not far behind." "Washington," it said, "is unlikely ever to reestablish a decisive lead."[285] The region, assiduously attuned to such power shifts, sought to navigate the changes.

A decade after Washington declared Asia its priority region, the demand among Asian allies and partners for American engagement there was perhaps never higher. But their confidence in US leadership, competence, and staying power remained fragile or worse. As the 2020s dawned, Washington belatedly took concrete moves to align its actions with its by-then chief national security objective. The United States would increase its capabilities in Asia, strengthen relationships with countries in the region, constrain Chinese power, and make up for lost time.

# 10

## We Will Build in Any Case

### China Rises as the Pivot Stalls

No audience anywhere was likely more absorbed by the Pivot strategy than China. From the start, Obama administration officials made no mention of the challenge of a rising China—and even sought explicitly to reassure Beijing that the United States would benefit from China's flourishing. Nevertheless, throughout the 2010s, China worked successfully, as will be described in detail in this chapter, to fundamentally alter the balance of power in Asia and beyond at the expense of the United States.

Here a profound conundrum arises. Beijing, with its multitude of government organizations and think tanks that study American foreign and defense policies to the tiniest detail, surely realized over the decade that no such US Pivot to Asia from Europe and the Middle East was actually underway. Indeed, as described in detail in earlier chapters, during the 2010s Washington devoted more resources to Europe and the Middle East than it did when the Pivot was announced, and no significant surge of US resources to the Indo-Pacific occurred.

China's aggressive actions during the decade remind one of former defense secretary Harold Brown's comment about the Soviet military buildup. "When we build," he observed, "they build. When we cut, they build."[1] As the United States was not pivoting to Asia, China increased its power and assertiveness, seeing opportunity in the presence of Western weakness. While the counterfactual clearly cannot be run, it appears fairly certain that, Pivot or no Pivot, Beijing would still have ended quantitative American military dominance along China's coast and in the Taiwan Straits, stolen intellectual property, used economic coercion against its neighbors and beyond, and so forth. In short, the Pivot to Asia had likely no material effect on Chinese security policy, but did give Beijing a rhetorical argument to explain its extraordinary defense buildup.

Hillary Clinton, in describing the Pivot in 2011, was no outlier in her initially upbeat treatment of China's role. Successive US presidents, in the fifteen years prior, spoke routinely about a strategic partnership with China, even as they began to take limited hedging steps in the event of rivalry.

At their 1997 summit, for example, Bill Clinton and Jiang Zemin said they were "determined to build toward a constructive strategic partnership between China and the United States through increasing cooperation to meet international challenges and promote peace and development in the world."[2] Welcoming Hu Jintao to the White House in 2006, George W. Bush proclaimed, "The United States welcomes the emergence of a China that is peaceful and prosperous, and that supports international institutions. As stakeholders in the international system, our two nations share many strategic interests. . . . The United States and China will continue to build on our common interests; we will address our differences in a spirit of mutual respect."[3] Similar sentiment endured after the Pivot's announcement. Standing alongside Xi Jinping in 2015, President Barack Obama declared "Our two nations are working together more closely across a broader range of critical issues—and our cooperation is delivering results, for both our nations and the world."[4] He later told the *Atlantic*'s Jeffrey Goldberg, "We have more to fear from a weakened, threatened China than a successful, rising China."[5]

A week after the initial article, *People's Daily* asked rhetorically, "The United States has never left Asia, why will it need to 'return' to Asia? . . . Many Western scholars believe that the reassertion of the leading US role in Asia is directed against China because only China's rise can pose a potential challenge to its hegemony. If the United States adopts this mentality in 'returning' to Asia, it will face a zero-sum game with China."[6] In time, this analysis would prove not far from the mark.

In November 2011, the *Global Times* threatened "any country which chooses to be a pawn in the US chess game," saying that it would "lose the opportunity to benefit from China's economy."[7] PLA Major General Luo Yuan added:

> The United States is making much of its "return to Asia," has been positioning pieces and forces on China's periphery, and the intent is very clear—this is aimed at China, to contain China. The United States has committed a fatal strategic error. It has misjudged its foes, it has placed its strategic focus in the wrong location, and its strategic means are wrong. . . . China has not provoked US interests, so what are you doing running to Asia to encircle China?[8]

The same month, Shen Dingli, a professor of American studies at Fudan University, was equally emphatic. "The United States," he said, "has alienated one billion Chinese. It's not smart public diplomacy."[9] The *Jiefang Daily*, a major Chinese news publication, claimed that the Pivot was designed "to pin down and contain China and counterbalance China's development."[10] Scholar Wu Xinbo piled on in December 2012, writing, "China began to see in the so-called US pivot, or rebalance, toward Asia a shift of focus from economic and diplomatic engagement to one more centered on security issues. Beijing also could not help noticing what seemed to be a strong element of counterbalancing against China's growing power and influence in the region."[11]

Wu was, of course, at least partially right. Even if the administration simultaneously sought to engage Beijing in constructive relations, the Pivot was the first comprehensive conceptual effort to counterbalance Chinese power. The Obama administration pitched the move as an overdue increase in activity across the world's most dynamic region. While it was indeed aimed at benefiting from Asia's promise, the engage-but-hedge strategy, *sotto voce* though it was in the administration's public articulation, was obvious. The implications of this new US strategic orientation were not lost on Chinese policymakers.

## Enduring Chinese Suspicions

Beijing's suspicion of the Pivot would endure. In 2014, China's ambassador in Washington warned, "The problem with this rebalancing is that it's not balanced. There has been too much stress on the military and security aspect, stressing traditional alliances without addressing adequately the real needs and concerns of the regional countries for economic prosperity and sustainable development. . . . There are people in China who really believe that the US policy is to contain China."[12] That same year, Chinese state councilor Dai Bingguo quipped to Secretary Clinton, "Why don't you pivot out of here?"[13] China's 2015 Defense White Paper denounced the Pivot as one of many trends that "have a negative impact on the security and stability along China's periphery."[14] In 2016, China's foreign ministry spokesperson asserted that East Asia had been calm and peaceful before "the Americans came along with the rebalance stuff."[15]

Chinese objections continued during the next administration. In May 2020, near the end of the Trump term, the Carnegie-Tsinghua Center summed up a decade of commentary. "From the Obama administration's 'rebalance of Asia,'" they wrote, "Chinese apprehension that the US has ideological designs on China, that the US does not want to interact peacefully with China strengthened."[16] In characteristically overheated terms, the *Global Times* saw it no differently in 2022. "The Asia-Pacific rebalance," it said, "is crude and short-sighted, out of touch with reality, and ignores the core demands of ordinary Americans and the peace and prosperity of Asia-Pacific countries."[17]

## Chinese Ambitions

Xi Jinping moved decisively during these years to fortify China and extend its power and influence, including in Europe and the Middle East. In his treatise on Chinese grand strategy, Chinese theorist Ye Zicheng explains, "There is a close connection between the rejuvenation of the Chinese nation and China's becoming a world power. If China does not become a world power, the rejuvenation of the Chinese nation will be incomplete. Only when it becomes a world power can we say that the total rejuvenation of the Chinese nation has been achieved."[18] Xi appeared bent on making China the dominant nation in Asia, and a far more significant power in other regions.

In this strategic context, Xi Jinping pursued four core lines of effort. Chinese leaders saw threat in US campaigns to support democracy, the rule of law, and the protection of minorities—all viewed in Beijing as thinly veiled attempts to foment secession or engineer regime change—and sought to guard against them. Second, Beijing pursued economic policies that would produce gains not only in the narrow sense—pertaining to the bilateral terms of trade and return on investment—but in the larger strategic sense. Third, Beijing advanced a variety of policies aimed to pacify its periphery. Fourth, China sought to advance Beijing's status as a central actor in the international system, and pursue a security concept which demands that Indo-Pacific security be managed by Asians alone, led by Beijing.[19]

Simply put, China—Pivot or no Pivot—aims to replace the United States as the most important and influential nation in the Indo-Pacific, and to dominate that region. These strategic objectives encompass the greatest prolonged threat to the peace and prosperity of the United States and its global allies and partners since the end of the Second World War. They collide with US vital national interests and commitments, America's alliance system and the balance of power in Asia, US democratic governance and values, and the principles and practices of the liberal international order.

Beijing, convinced that the United States was in secular decline, during the 2010s moved to project increasing economic and diplomatic influence to boost its own power and influence in Asia, and to undermine the foundations of American standing there.[20] Chinese officials increasingly argued that the US alliance system represented a Cold War artifact and should be dismantled, and that America's Asian allies should loosen their US connections. Failure to do so, they suggested, would inevitably produce a negative PRC reaction. They also argued that US efforts to maintain its presence and power in Asia amounted to a thinly veiled attempt to contain China, and that such moves should be condemned and resisted. Chinese leaders argued that US military power in the region was dangerous and should be reduced—even as the PLA continued to build up capabilities specifically designed to fight the United States. And they contended that the US economic and political model is fundamentally flawed and inferior to the combination of state capitalism and "Chinese democracy."[21]

Thus, while the implementation of the Pivot continued to falter throughout the decade, China moved to undermine the balance of power in Asia and to erode America's global position.

## Military Modernization and Increased Power

China's military transformation began in the aftermath of the 1991 Gulf War. Its defense leadership was shocked by the ease and speed with which the United States combined stealth, precision-guided munitions, integrated battle networks, and information and electronic warfare to defeat the Iraqi military. Like Baghdad's forces, the PLA was at the time focused on fighting a land-based, defensive war. Its equipment was based on decades-old Soviet technology, its navy was incapable of blue water operations, and its air defenses were feeble. China's military had little experience in combined-arms operations, and most of even its newest technology had been acquired abroad. As one analysis assessed, "In the minds of PLA scholars, the Gulf War heralded a profound shift in the character of modern warfare."[22] If the United States could defeat Iraq so easily, Beijing concluded, it could win a war with China.[23]

Beijing's 2010 national defense strategy described a "revolution in military affairs with Chinese characteristics" that shifted focus "from quantity and scale to quality and efficiency, from a manpower-intensive to a technology intensive model." The approach, the strategy said, would "take mechanization as the foundation and informationization as the focus."[24] The PLA developed its own arsenal of precision-guided munitions, including large quantities of land-based ballistic and cruise missiles that could hold US naval assets and regional bases at risk.[25] China's navy went on to become a modern fleet, armed with advanced air defenses and anti-ship cruise missiles, and it fielded nuclear-power ballistic missile submarines. Beijing also made advances in anti-submarine warfare and developed stealth aircraft. It built significant cyberwarfare capabilities and put them to peacetime use by stealing intellectual property, including defense technology and weapons blueprints, and conducted espionage.[26]

Already by 2010, Admiral Robert Willard, then-commander of the US Pacific Command, said, "China's rapid and comprehensive transformation of its armed forces is affecting regional military balances and holds implications beyond the Asia-Pacific region."[27] Beijing's "evolving military capabilities," he added, "appear designed to challenge U.S. freedom of action in the region or exercise aggression or coercion of its neighbors, including U.S. treaty allies and partners."[28] In 2012 the IISS *Military Balance* highlighted "a significant and continuing shift in the distribution of relative military strength away from the West and towards Asia."[29] That was just the beginning.

While US government officials were relatively quiet about the shift in public, it was by no means lost on outside observers. Ashley Tellis, a keen observer of Asian security, wrote in 2012 that China's military modernization could "threaten the U.S. military's ability to operate in proximity to the Asian land mass, thereby holding at risk the larger structure of regional stability that since

World War II has been built on American hegemony."[30] A study the same year by defense analyst Thomas Mahnken observed that, as the regional balance of power shifted against the United States and its allies, the growth of Chinese military power "may allow it to decouple America's allies from the US extended nuclear deterrent, to destroy US and allied fixed bases in the region, and to threaten US power projection forces."[31] This, in turn, "could allow China to coerce US allies and partners in the Asia-Pacific region, hold US forces at arm's length, and control the seas along the Asian periphery."[32] In October 2023, the Pentagon's annual China Military Power report described Beijing's strategy as "a determined pursuit of political, social, and military modernity to expand the PRC's national power, perfect its governance, and revise the international order in support of the PRC's system of governance and national interests."[33] The PRC has, the document added, "increasingly turned to the PLA as an instrument of statecraft to advance its foreign policy objectives."[34]

As Figures 10.1 and 10.2 demonstrate, China has modernized its armed forces through unprecedented increases in military spending.[35] Its defense spending grew more than 800 percent from 1993 to 2018, by which point China's expenditures were roughly equal to that of all other countries in the region combined.[36] Beijing more than doubled its official annual defense budget between 2011 and 2023, while its actual defense spending is believed to be much higher. The IISS *2023 Military Balance* reported a $16 billion increase in China's 2022 defense budget—the largest-ever annual increase in absolute terms, and in 2023, Beijing announced a 7.2 percent boost in its defense budget.[37] China's military spending remains a fraction of America's, the world's largest, but Beijing is able to concentrate its expenditures in Asia, whereas the United States retains a presence and conducts operations globally. And while the United States has well-armed allies in the region, China retains geographic advantages in any Pacific military contingency.

China's navy became the world's largest seagoing force during the 2010s, due to exponentially increased ship production. More than 70 percent of its fleet is now classified as "modern."[38] Over the last decade, it doubled its stock of underway supply ships to boost its ability to project power at sea, successfully introduced its first three aircraft carriers, and fortified major warships with anti-cruise ship missiles.[39] While China's navy is expected to grow to 440 ships by 2030, the US Navy is projected to have only 290 ships by the same year—which may still be a long shot.[40] Beijing made qualitative improvements as well. In early 2023, for example, Beijing began employing a pump-jet propulsion system on a nuclear-powered submarine that would reduce noise and make it harder to detect.[41] By 2022, the PLA Air Force was flying at least 200 fifth-generation J-20 fighters, less than half the US fleet of 180 F-22s and 450 F-35s, but the US Air Force chief of staff predicted that China could overcome US air superiority by

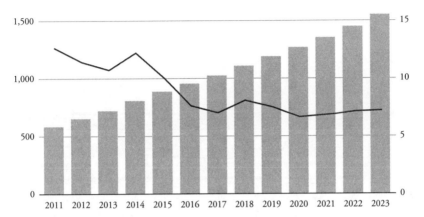

China's Total Annual
Defense Budget

% Growth from
Previous Year

¥2,000   in billions, RMB ⸻⸻⸻⸻⸻⸻⸻⸻⸻ 20%

**Figure 10.1.** China's announced annual defense budget, 2011–2023. The above numbers represent China's announced annual defense budget, not its actual annual defense spending. Additionally, the growth rates presented reflect China's announced growth rate. That is based on the percentage change from the newly announced budget compared to the final spending from the previous year, which will always likely be different from what is budgeted.

Source: Data for the chart are sourced from CSIS China Power Project, Chinese Central Government, National Bureau of Statistics of China, and the World Bank. Original chart can be found at China Power Team, "What Does China Really Spend on Its Military?," China Power, Center for Strategic and International Studies, https://chinapower.csis.org/military-spending/.

2035.[42] As China's air force deployed new UAVs, bombers, and stealth aircraft, its army integrated new equipment, tanks, transportation vehicles, and artillery.[43]

In stark contrast to its long-standing policy of minimal deterrence—which involved the development of a nuclear arsenal just large enough to credibly threaten sufficiently destructive retaliation—China began to expand the numerical size of its nuclear weapons systems, as well as their survivability and diversification.[44] In 2021, the Pentagon and the CSIS Missile Defense Project reported that Beijing planned to increase its land-based nuclear force to 1,000 weapons by 2030, to build 300 intercontinental ballistic missile silos in its western deserts, and to commission more advanced nuclear submarines.[45] The Department of Defense stated that, in 2021, the PRC had "launched approximately 135 ballistic missiles for testing and training, more than the rest of the world combined," and forecast that China would have 1,500 nuclear weapons by 2035.[46] STRATCOM

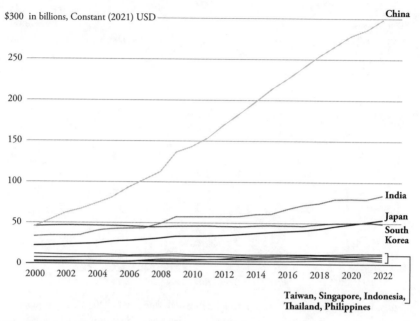

**Figure 10.2.** Eight defense spenders among Indo-Pacific countries compared to China, 2000–2022.

Source: Stockholm International Peace Research Institute, SIPRI Military Expenditure Database, 2023, https://www.sipri.org/databases/milex.

Commander Admiral Charles Richard added, "As I assess our level of deterrence against China, the ship is slowly sinking. . . . It is sinking slowly, but it is sinking, as fundamentally they are putting capability in the field faster than we are."[47]

China aggressively challenged American space superiority in preparation for a potential future conflict and developed the world's second largest space program.[48] China launched its first military satellite in 2000 but within a decade had dozens in space, platforms involved in intelligence, surveillance, and reconnaissance as well as military command, control, and communications. It also fielded counterspace capabilities that could threaten the satellites so vital to US battle networks and military operations.[49] As the Pentagon reported in 2022, the PLA was investing in "counterspace capabilities and related technologies, including kinetic-kill missiles, ground-based lasers, and orbiting space robots, as well as expanding space surveillance capabilities . . . that can contest or deny an adversary's access to and operations in the space domain during a crisis or conflict."[50] Over the decade, Chinese satellites in orbit as well as launches per year doubled, and Beijing perfected anti-satellite missiles.[51] China also invested in the development of directed energy weapons to damage satellites.[52] Beijing routinely trained PLA electronic warfare units to conduct jamming operations that could target the Global Positioning System (GPS) and Satellite Communications (SATCOM).[53] The Director of National Intelligence's 2023 *Annual Threat Assessment* predicted that "by 2030, China probably will achieve world-class status in all but a few space technology areas."[54]

As a result of China's military modernization, it methodically altered the balance of military power in its favor in the waters adjacent to the Chinese mainland—especially in the Taiwan Strait. US Air Force secretary Frank Kendall described this new reality in 2021, cautioning, "We're the dominant military power until you get within about 1,000 miles of China."[55] Harvard professor Graham Allison went further, asserting that the United States would either lose a "limited war" with China over Taiwan or "have to choose between losing and stepping up the escalation ladder to a wider war." Allison made his daunting conclusion exquisitely plain, saying that "the era of US military primacy is over: dead, buried, and gone."[56]

## Taiwan Troubles

After the election of Democratic Progressive Party (DPP) candidate Tsai Ing-wen in 2016, China magnified its economic and diplomatic pressure on Taiwan. It imposed sanctions on Taipei in response to its perceived attempts to advance Taiwanese independence and limited mainland tourism to the island. Beijing suspended export licenses for two-thirds of Taiwan's food producers, imposed visa bans on Taiwanese officials, levied import restrictions on over 100 Taiwanese goods, and restricted exports to Taipei.[57] On the diplomatic front, China sought to end Taiwan's international representation, and stopped Taiwanese participation in multinational organizations. During this period, nine countries ended their recognition of Taiwan as an independent country, and instead established diplomatic ties with Beijing.[58] Each of these nations quickly received economic assistance and political support from China.[59]

Having erased American military dominance in the western Pacific, Beijing has grown more confident in its ability to threaten Taiwan with invasion or blockade. It has conducted countless military exercises over and around the island, and at an ever-increasing rate.[60] In response to Speaker Nancy Pelosi's August 2022 visit to Taipei, Beijing for the first time practiced a full-scale blockade of Taiwan and sent 450 aircraft across the median line of the Taiwan Strait.[61] Daniel Kritenbrink, the State Department's top Asia official, detailed Beijing's objectives. "The goal of this campaign," he said, "is clear: to intimidate and coerce Taiwan and undermine its resilience."[62] Chinese defense minister General Wei Fenghe did not contest that proposition. "China," he pledged, "will resolutely smash any schemes for

Taiwan independence. If anyone dares to split off Taiwan, we will not hesitate to fight, will not flinch from the cost, and will fight to the very end."[63]

Beijing continued its aggressive action toward Taiwan when other international leaders began to travel to Taipei. In November 2022, Beijing dispatched forty-six military aircraft toward Taiwan in response to a visit by UK trade minister Greg Hands.[64] One month later, after a visit by a top member of Japan's Liberal Democratic Party, twenty-nine Chinese warplanes—including eighteen strategic bombers—and three Chinese Navy ships boldly entered the Taiwan Strait in a show of force.[65] In December, shortly after Congress passed a defense spending bill that promised increased military aid to Taipei, Beijing sent a record-breaking seventy-one warplanes and seven warships near Taiwan, forty-seven of which crossed over the median line.[66]

After Taiwanese president Tsai Ing-wen's April 2023 visit to Central America—which included stopovers in Los Angeles and New York and a meeting with US House Speaker Kevin McCarthy—the PLA made another show of force and tested its ability to "seize control of the sea, air and information" through a days-long exercise around the island.[67] Beijing shattered December's 2022 record as ninety-one military aircraft penetrated Taiwan's ADIZ, accompanied by live-fire exercises off the coast of Pingtan.[68] Then, in June 2023, Chinese military aircraft flew closer to the island than ever before when PLA fighters were spotted just over twelve nautical miles away from Taiwanese airspace.[69] In the days after DPP candidate Lai Ching-te was elected president in January 2024, the PLA conducted military patrols around Taiwan with five naval vessels and 24 aircraft—11 of which entered Taiwan's ADIZ.[70] While Chinese incursions have diminished substantially since the aftermath of the Pelosi visit, PRC penetrations of Taiwan airspace remain numerous and consequential.

US intelligence officials report that Xi has instructed his military to be ready to invade Taiwan by 2027.[71] Chinese officials naturally leave the specifics behind closed doors, but interested observers have reached similar conclusions. Chao Chun-shan, an advisor to Taipei's past four presidents on cross-Strait relations, told the *Financial Times*, "Beijing will not wait for Taiwan. Xi has said that the Taiwan question cannot be dragged out without resolution. . . ."[72] Another advisor, Chang Wu-ueh, added that Xi "doesn't regard [reunification] as just a slogan. It's an action plan that must be implemented. It's number one on the agenda."[73] In remarks at Stanford University, Secretary Blinken said that China had made "a fundamental decision that the status quo was no longer acceptable and that Beijing was determined to pursue reunification on a much faster timeline."[74] Cross-strait relations are unlikely to improve after Lai's election. He and his running mate, Hsiao Bi-khim, are reported to be "deeply disliked and mistrusted" by Beijing, and in statements before the election, China labeled Lai a "trouble-maker" and "dangerous separatist."[75]

Such dire forecasts are of special concern since the United States has in re-cent years persistently lost wargames that posited a military confrontation with China over Taiwan.[76] In addition, even when Washington prevails in these simulations, it is at the cost of thousands of lives, hundreds of aircrafts, tens of ships, and multiple aircraft carriers. Such a loss would, in the words of one de-fense analyst, "have potentially disastrous results on the nation's ability to project power abroad."[77] A June 2023 Council on Foreign Relations study concluded, "Given shifts in the military balance of power and China's growing assertive-ness throughout the Indo-Pacific . . . deterrence is dangerously eroding, and the United States and China are drifting toward war. . . . The United States needs to raise the cost of Chinese aggression against Taiwan, with the aim of persuading Xi Jinping that an attack on Taiwan will not succeed and would come at the cost of achieving his modernization objectives."[78]

## Dominating the South China Sea

During the 2010s, China expedited its militarization of islands in the South China Sea, despite Xi Jinping's promise to President Obama not to do so.[79] Vice Admiral Karl Thomas in 2018 sized up the situation, observing, "They've com-pletely militarized those islands. They already have all the bunkers they need, they already have all the fuel storage capacity they need, the ability to house troops, they have the missiles, the radars, the sensors."[80] Beijing ignored the Permanent Court of Arbitration judgment that dismissed its claims of sover-eignty over the South China Sea, built hangars and airstrips across twenty-seven military facilities, each of which was likely fitted with radar and signal intelli-gence capabilities, and developed and tested underwater communication equip-ment that will give submarines and drones the ability to communicate within a range of 11,600 square miles.[81] Beijing also constructed deep-water harbors at many of these outposts, built three airbases in the Spratlys and one in the Paracels, outfitted the bases with combat aircraft and anti-ship cruise missiles and radar systems, and consistently harassed Southeast Asian states' maritime activities.[82] By 2018, Admiral Phil Davidson told the US Senate, "China is now capable of controlling the South China Sea in all scenarios short of war with the United States."[83]

Not only did Beijing dramatically expand its military reach into the South China Sea, but it also constructed Indian Ocean ports in Myanmar along the Bay of Bengal in Kyaukpyu, in Bangladesh at Chittagong, in Malaysia at Malacca, in Pakistan at Gwadar, and on the west coast of Africa. In Sri Lanka, China built and funded a facility, acquired a ninety-nine-year lease, and then used it to dock a surveillance ship.[84] PLA Navy warships and submarines also conducted "antipiracy operations" in the Indian Ocean.[85] Rajeswari Pillai Rajagopalan, an expert at New Delhi's Observer Research Foundation, summarized India's reaction, "Clearly [the Chinese] are coming closer and closer to India and that is extremely worrying given its adversarial, hostile relations with China."[86]

Seeking to bolster its influence in the South Pacific, the PRC became the second largest donor to the region after Australia, and signed an MOU with Fiji on police cooperation that has led to PRC officers embedded in the Fijian police force, extrajudicial deportations, and the transfer of Chinese surveillance technology to Suva.[87] A leaked security pact between the Solomon Islands and China allegedly would permit Beijing to send police and military personnel to the islands to help quell social unrest.[88] Contestation between China and the United States and its allies continued across the Pacific Islands. In response to the Beijing's deal with the Solomon Islands, Australia in November 2023 successfully won the right to veto any security pact Tuvalu might consider with other nations.[89] Together with its efforts in the South China Sea and elsewhere, however, Beijing remains determined to expand the zone of potential Chinese military activities thousands of miles from its shores.

## Employing Economic Coercion

Through its ever-greater economic resources and enormous consumer market, China threatened, coerced, and punished US allies and partners in the Indo-Pacific during the decade when their policies bumped against Beijing's geopolitical objectives. It embargoed rare earth exports to Japan after a fishing boat incident in the Senkakus.[90] Because of a dispute with Manila in the South China Sea, Beijing stopped the import of Philippine bananas, putting some 200,000 jobs at risk.[91] As New Delhi deliberated over whether to employ Huawei for its 5G network, Beijing in the same coercive spirit threatened sanctions on India's businesses in China.[92] When Japan and Australia signed a broad defense pact, Chinese state media stressed that Tokyo and Canberra would pay a price for the transgression.[93] China imposed tariffs when Mongolia hosted the Dalai Lama, prompting Ulaanbaatar to promise that it would no longer extend invitations to the spiritual leader.[94] When Canberra had the temerity to support an independent investigation into the origins of COVID-19, China blocked key Australian agricultural imports.[95]

Beijing applied similar economic coercion across the globe. When Canadian authorities detained the chief financial officer of Huawei, Meng Wanzhou, Beijing limited canola oil imports from Ottawa and arrested two Canadian citizens on trumped-up charges.[96] When Cameroon and China each nominated individuals to lead the UN Food and Agriculture Organization, Beijing canceled $78 million of Cameroon's debt and Yaoundé immediately withdrew its candidate.[97] When Taipei opened a de facto embassy in Vilnius, China not only blocked Lithuanian imports but stopped any goods that had Lithuanian parts.[98] Such PRC import restrictions were often paired with Chinese state media's encouragement for its citizens to boycott goods from targeted countries.

Economic power based on interdependence served, however, as a double-edged sword. It also made China dependent on the world for technology, commodities, energy, food, and market access at a level China has never known. In an effort to dull that sword, Xi Jinping publicly described in May 2020 a "dual circulation" strategy which, as the US-China Commission described it, "aims to diminish China's dependence on exports and critical imports, while encouraging Western companies to remain reliant on supply chains routed through China."[99] Beijing hopes to insulate China's economy from external volatility by boosting domestic consumption, enhancing its manufacturing capabilities to retain China's standing as a powerhouse of exports and critical node in global supply chains.[100]

## International Institutions

China has become more actively involved in multilateral institutions over recent years. Some observers view Beijing's role as a largely positive development, and one that the United States encouraged for decades in pursuit of responsible international behavior. Thomas Christensen, a scholar and former State Department official, posits that "it is only natural for Asian states to have some groupings that do not include the United States, and it is not necessarily a signal of anti-American conspiracy or a great boon for Chinese power when they do."[101] While this may be true of some initiatives, others represent a PRC desire to sharpen the rivalry. The Shanghai Cooperation Organization, for instance, continues to collect aggrieved, anti-Western nations like Iran and Belarus. Likewise, Beijing has used the Belt and Road Initiative to exploit developing countries in need of infrastructure investment to extract raw materials, to seize valuable assets like ports to compensate for defaults, and to buy political influence. It is hard to see how any of this could be viewed positively by the United States.

At the United Nations, China has weakened and vetoed resolutions, and has blocked discussions in the Security Council, in an effort to thwart US policies. Beijing vetoed condemnation of Syrian president Assad's human rights atrocities, vetoed sanctions on the regime after the country's use of chemical weapons, and vetoed a ceasefire in the civil war as well as lifesaving aid to victims of it.[102] China prevented Security Council statements that would have condemned human rights violations committed against Rohingya Muslims in Myanmar, and on the military takeover in the years that followed.[103] Beijing stopped a UNSC call for free and fair elections in Venezuela, impeded the designation of Lashkar-e-Taiba and Jaish-e-Mohammad as terrorist groups, and barred the Security Council from discussing COVID-19 at the beginning of the pandemic.[104] It obstructed any dialogue on the end of democracy in Hong Kong, prohibited any discussion of its Uyghur suppression, and rejected a UNSC statement calling for an end to violence in the Tigray region of Ethiopia.[105] China refused to condemn Putin's invasion of Ukraine and was the only Security Council member to vote in favor of a Russian resolution that absolved Moscow of the war's subsequent humanitarian crisis.[106] In October 2022, US Ambassador to the UN Linda Thomas-Greenfield condemned Beijing and Moscow for their protection of North Korea in the UNSC, saying, "The DPRK has enjoyed blanket protection from two members of this council . . . two permanent members of the Security Council have enabled Kim Jong Un."[107]

Across the United Nations, Chinese nationals held nine deputy positions and led an unprecedented four of fifteen agencies: the Industrial Development Organization, the International Civil Aviation Organization, the International Telecommunications Union (ITU), and the Food and Agriculture Organization, along with numerous auxiliary UN offices.[108] Beijing has used these and other positions to guide international standard-setting in a manner consistent with its autocratic brand of government. At the ITU, for instance, it supported a state-centric vision of the internet that would impose limits on online freedom of speech.[109] On the Human Rights Council (HRC), China sponsored resolutions and amendments to make it easier for countries to disregard human rights mechanisms, empowered states to delegitimize and oversee civil society, and emphasized sovereignty over violations of basic rights.[110] It voted to keep Russia on the HRC after Moscow's invasion of Ukraine and abused Interpol's Red Notice System, a mechanism for locating and extraditing criminal suspects, as part of its forced repatriation campaign of dissidents.[111] By 2019, China became the second largest financial contributor to the United Nations and, as a senior European diplomat put it, "At the UN, China's influence is massive. They really are so powerful there and so much more sophisticated than, say, the Russians, who are only really able to spoil things. . . . They know how to work the system to their advantage."[112]

In addition, China created alternative international organizations to ones that include the United States or reflect Western values and priorities. Beijing sought to integrate both its four BRICS partners and its regional neighbors into economic ventures to rival those of the liberal international system, including a New Development Bank (widely perceived as an alternative to the World Bank and the IMF), the Asian Infrastructure Investment Bank (a rival to the Asian Development Bank), and the Regional Economic Cooperation Partnership (an

Asia-Pacific FTA) that would knit China closer to its neighbors in Asia. In other regions, Beijing initiated the Forum on China-Africa Cooperation, the China-Arab Cooperation Forum, and a variety of similar bodies that privilege China's position and undermine standards of governance established by the World Bank, the Organisation for Economic Co-operation and Development (OECD), and other international institutions.[113]

## The "No Limits" Partnership with Moscow

As the 2020s dawned, China intensified its relationship with Russia, and to-gether they opposed a Western-led international order. In February 2022, Xi and Putin had declared their "no limits" friendship, and all that came along with it, including a slew of new initiatives between the two countries.[114] In December 2022, the *Wall Street Journal* reported that Xi "instructed his government to forge stronger economic ties with Russia" and build "on a trade relationship that has strengthened this year and become a lifeline to Moscow in the face of Western pressure."[115] And despite Beijing's professed neutrality on the war in Ukraine, in an October 2023 summit meeting in Beijing, Xi once again stressed China's un-bending commitment to a close relationship with Russia.[116]

While neither Moscow nor Beijing can decisively secure outcomes for each other's primary concerns—namely Taiwan for China, Ukraine and the European order for Russia, and regime survival for both—the two countries can and do collaborate in these and other dimensions to act against the interests of the United States and the West.[117] In the UN Security Council, the two nations were aligned on almost all votes.[118] China refused to condemn the Russian invasion of Ukraine, supported Moscow's "legitimate security concerns" in Ukraine, and denounced the United States as the "culprit of current tensions surrounding Ukraine."[119] After the invasion, China became the largest importer of Russian oil.[120] Moscow and Beijing have also signed agreements to boost cooperation in the finance, technology, trade, energy, and aerospace sectors and, as bilateral trade increased, China and Russia pursued de-dollarization and used the ren-minbi or ruble in trading practices.[121]

Moscow and Beijing throughout the 2010s increased the frequency and complexity of their joint military drills on sea, air, and land, including China's first dispatch of its navy, air, and ground forces to a single Russian exercise.[122] In the Sea of Japan, East China Sea, and South China Sea, they together sim-ulated "island-seizing" operations.[123] Chinese and Russian bombers landed at each other's airbases after conducting joint exercises over the East China Sea and the Sea of Japan.[124] In December 2022, as the war raged in Ukraine, Russia and China held joint naval exercises to "strengthen naval cooperation between the two nations, enhance their combat capability to jointly counter threats at sea, and to maintain peace and stability in the Asia-Pacific region."[125] Three months later, the two countries conducted naval exercises in the Gulf of Oman in partnership with Iran.[126] The PLA also participated in annual Russian strategic command-staff exercises, while both parties cooperated closely on arms technology, including rocket engines, missile defense systems, and drones.[127] China boosted its purchases of Russian military equipment and was the second largest importer of Russian weapons during 2016–2020, after India. During those years, Beijing spent more than $5 billion on Russian arms—accounting for 18 percent of all Russian weapons exports—including advanced technology, such as S-400 missile defense systems and Su-35 fighters.[128] The two countries amalgamated their navigation satellites, and Moscow helped Beijing construct a missile attack early warning system.[129]

China and Russia have edged closer to a *de facto* alliance over the last decade, the principal purpose of which was to undermine the vital national interests, democratic values, and policies of the United States. Indeed, the resistance to what Beijing and Moscow view as an anachronistic, Western-dominated international order appears to be the main glue that binds the two countries together. Beijing's perception of global order posits the decline of America and its allies, the ineffectiveness of Western-style democracy, the naturally dominant role of China in the Indo-Pacific, and the primacy of the state over the individual rather than the reverse.

## The Middle East

While the United States touted a pivot to Asia, the PRC expanded its role in the Middle East, Africa, and Latin America, where it employed increasing geoeconomic weight to bend nations toward China's international policy preferences and away from those of the United States. Beijing loaned billions of dollars to developing countries in the Global South; as the *New York Times* reported, "More than half the world's poor countries owe more to China than to all Western governments combined."[130] Over the decade, low- and middle-income countries' loans to China tripled to $170 billion and Beijing became the world's largest creditor.[131]

Because of Beijing's engagement in these regions, many countries viewed China more positively than the United States.[132] According to a 2022 Arab Barometer poll, China remains more popular than the United States across the Middle East and North Africa, and similar polls, such as the Afrobarometer, showed the same results in Africa.[133] Although Beijing's involvement in the Middle East, Latin America, and Africa is primarily economic, it has begun to cultivate diplomatic influence and security engagement in those areas, although it cannot decisively influence military outcomes outside its periphery.

China ramped up commercial ties across the Middle East over the past decade, mainly through the BRI and crude oil purchases. From 2016 to 2020, the PRC was the most significant investor in the Middle East.[134] By 2021, the Middle East and North Africa accounted for 38 percent of Beijing's BRI investment, compared to just 8 percent in 2020.[135] Chinese investments in the region grew by 360 percent from 2020 to 2021 alone, reaching over $200 billion.[136] As part of the BRI, Beijing invested in energy, infrastructure, telecommunications, and technology in Saudi Arabia, the UAE, Bahrain, Qatar, Kuwait, Oman, Egypt, Syria, and Iraq.[137] In 2016, Xi Jinping proclaimed, "We must encourage and support China's internet companies to go global . . . so as to achieve the principle of 'wherever our national interests are, [our] informatization will also cover those areas.' "[138] Beijing launched major telecommunications and technology projects through firms like Huawei, across over a dozen Middle Eastern and North African nations as part of its Digital Silk Road (DSR) initiative.[139]

In the energy sector, China became the world's largest importer of crude oil and received nearly half its supply from the Middle East—much of it from Saudi Arabia. In 2020, it purchased almost $25 billion worth of oil from Riyadh.[140] At the end of 2022, Beijing agreed to a $60 billion, twenty-seven-year agreement with Qatar to purchase four million tons of liquified natural gas (LNG) each year.[141] Energy ties between Beijing and the region are bound to deepen as OPEC projects that India and China will need an extra 8.6 million barrels of oil per day by 2045.[142] Beijing has used its energy demand to push for integration of the renminbi. Both Qatar and the UAE host renminbi clearing centers, and Saudi Arabia reportedly considered accepting the currency in exchange for oil.[143]

Recognizing that its energy supply from the Gulf relied on the US security architecture, China also sought to increase its military capabilities in the region.[144] In 2017, the PLA opened its first overseas base in Djibouti, not far from America's own installation, which provides access to the Middle East. In a more permissive era, a Chinese company built a port in Haifa, Israel, which stoked US fears of Beijing's espionage against US Navy vessels often docked there, and it attempted to construct one in the UAE.[145] That project was suspended after American protestations but, in December 2022, US intelligence again detected construction, stoking fears that Abu Dhabi, a longtime US partner, was drifting toward a PRC embrace.[146] These worries intensified when in July 2023, when the Chinese Ministry of Defense announced that the first bilateral military exercise between China and the UAE would take place the following month.[147]

The Pentagon has warned that the PLA will seek to expand its regional reach and designated Oman, Iran, Saudi Arabia, Bahrain, and Yemen as potential future hosts to Chinese bases.[148] In 2020, as the United States applied comprehensive sanctions against Iran, Beijing and Tehran announced an economic and security partnership that would increase Chinese investment in the Iranian economy and provide for discounted oil sales to China. The agreement specified deeper military cooperation between the two, including intelligence sharing, joint military exercises, and collaboration on weapons technology.[149] Between 2019 and 2022, China, Iran, and Russia held three joint naval exercises in the Indian Ocean, and China increased its arms exports to the Middle East.[150] From 2012 to 2016, China's arms sales to Saudi Arabia increased by 290 percent, and its sales to the UAE went up by 77 percent from 2017 to 2021.[151]

In March 2021, as detailed in Chapter 8 on the Middle East, China and Iran inked a twenty-five-year agreement in line with their Comprehensive Strategic Partnership.[152] Beijing has now forged strategic partnerships with twelve Arab countries and has cultivated strategically savvy ties with actors across the political spectrum in the region, from Iran to the Gulf Cooperation Council (GCC) states. To tie regional heavyweights closer, China has sought to intertwine its BRI programs with major regional development plans like Saudi Arabia's Vision 2030, as well as to weave trade, technology, and security together into multisectoral agreements.[153]

As the *New York Times* reported, "Chinese companies are building new cities in Egypt and Saudi Arabia, selling facial recognition technology to Gulf governments and partnering with them on artificial intelligence research. Beijing has also expanded its maritime footprint in the region, an important conduit on its Belt and Road Initiative needed to reach trading partners in Europe."[154] In December 2022, Xi Jinping visited Saudi Arabia to join the inaugural China-Arab States Summit and the China-GCC summit, which was reported to include nearly $30 billion worth of energy and infrastructure deals.[155] Only a few months after disregarding President Biden's appeals for oil, Saudi Crown Prince Mohammed bin Salman warmly greeted Xi and signaled closer Chinese-Saudi ties. Chinese Foreign Ministry spokesperson Mao Ning called the visit a "landmark in the history of Sino-Arab relations," and a "joint strategic decision of both sides to strengthen solidarity and coordination."[156] As discussed in Chapter 8, China's growing influence in the region was made evident in March 2023 when Beijing announced a Saudi-Iran agreement on normalizing diplomatic relations.[157]

Following the October 2023 Hamas attacks on Israel, China sought to take advantage of Arab frustrations, undermine the United States, and bolster its regional relations by criticizing Israel and supporting the Palestinians.[158] In a call to his Egyptian counterpart, Foreign Minister Wang Yi said the PRC "will continue to stand on the side of international morality and support the Palestinian people in restoring their legitimate national rights." China, he added, "supports the Arab and Islamic countries in forming a common position and speaking with a united voice."[159] In October, China's ambassador to the UN blasted a US-proposed resolution calling for a "humanitarian pause" but not a ceasefire. The measure, he alleged, "[set] aside the consensus of the members" and was "seriously out of balance and [confused] right and wrong."[160] In November 2023, Wang met in Beijing with foreign ministers from Egypt, Indonesia, Jordan, the Palestinian Authority, and Saudi Arabia, stressing, "China is a good friend and brother of Arab and Islamic countries. China has always firmly upheld the legitimate rights and interests of Arab and Islamic countries and firmly supported the just cause of the Palestinian people to restore their legitimate national rights and interests."[161]

The increased Chinese activism across the Middle East coincided with the perception, as earlier described, that the United States was departing the region. Leaders and policymakers across the region largely concurred in their basic analysis. The United States, it was widely thought, was on its way out of the Middle East. It was tired of endless wars and had little appetite to remain the security guarantor of last resort. America needed Middle East oil less than at any time in many decades and wished to pivot from the region to Asia. China, on the other hand, was stepping up its Middle East activism and securing pragmatic relationships with governments on new issues. If the United States left behind a vacuum, regional leaders consistently warned, China would most likely fill it.

## Africa

China also broadened and deepened its security, diplomatic, and economic involvement in Africa. US intelligence agencies reported in 2021 that China planned to construct a military facility in Equatorial Guinea, on the country's Atlantic coast.[162] Beijing fostered military bilateral cooperation with many African nations and positioned itself to capture an ever greater market share of weapons sales to the region.[163] It expanded its use of private military and security contractors (PMSCs) to protect its investments, with PMSCs operating in fifteen countries across the continent, and it increased arms sales to seventeen African nations.[164] Its weapons transfers to Sub-Saharan Africa (SSA) eclipsed American arms sales during the decade, as Beijing accounted for 22 percent of Africa's armaments between 2010 and 2021 at $2.04 billion, while Washington made up just 5 percent, at $473 million.[165] The United States has tried to play catch-up on non-defense trade in Africa but is woefully outmatched by China. Washington's two-way trade with Africa is a fourth of Beijing's, which climbed to $254 billion in 2021.[166] In 2023, the PRC hosted in Beijing its third China-Africa Peace and Security Forum with officials from nearly fifty African countries to increase and expand its military cooperation with the continent.[167]

China vastly intensified its economic relations with countries in Africa during the decade. Under the BRI, Chinese companies have developed multibillion-dollar infrastructure projects throughout the continent.[168] The *South China Morning Post* reported in August 2023 that whereas in 2013, "Western firms were running 37 per cent of African infrastructure projects versus 12 per cent for Chinese companies. . . . Now, the tables have turned." By 2022, "Chinese companies accounted for 31 per cent of African infrastructure contracts valued at US$50 million . . . compared with 12 per cent for Western firms."[169] Similarly, American foreign direct investment in the region is only half that of China.[170]

PRC economic assistance generated support from many of the fifty-four African nations in the UN.[171] In 2020, when the UN General Assembly criticized Chinese actions in Hong Kong and human rights violations in Xinjiang, twenty-one African countries defended Beijing in a joint public statement.[172] In August 2022, to gain favor, the PRC announced that it would forgive twenty-three interest-free loans to seventeen African nations and would contribute $10 billion in International Monetary Fund special drawing rights to the continent.[173] Twelve African nations then voted against or abstained from a motion to debate China's human rights abuses in Xinjiang at the UN Human Rights Council in October 2022.[174]

Beijing used its diplomatic punch in Africa to promote Moscow's policies. When the General Assembly voted to denounce the Russian invasion of Ukraine in March 2022, twenty-six African countries—more than half of those represented at the UN—refused to condemn the Russian aggression.[175] When the General Assembly in February 2023 debated a resolution that called for Russia to leave Ukraine, Eritrea and Mali voted in opposition while thirteen other African countries abstained.[176] Seeking to promote authoritarianism in Africa, in February 2022, China opened its first overseas leadership training school in Tanzania, providing lessons on the CCP's successful fusion of political party and government. *Axios* reported that the school's teachers "train African leaders that the ruling party should sit above the government and the courts and that fierce discipline within the party can ensure adherence to party ideology."[177]

The commander of the US Southern European Task Force outlined Beijing's objectives in Africa in 2022, observing, "They are seeking to influence events on the continent in their favor using political influence, disinformation, economic leverage, and malign military activity."[178] As Zhang Hongming, a senior fellow at the Chinese Academy of Social Sciences, explained, "Africa is the cornerstone of Chinese diplomacy . . . the 53 [African] allies not only widen the radius of China's activities on the international stage, but also enhance the strategic depth of China's game with the United States, thus strengthening China's initiative and influence in international affairs."[179]

## Western Hemisphere

PRC activities also surged in Latin America across the 2010s and beyond, with Beijing signing trade pacts, increasing arms sales, constructing military installations—and building allegiances. Stunningly, China overtook the United States as the region's top trade partner as China–Latin America commerce skyrocketed from $12 billion in 2000 to $495 billion in 2022.[180] Experts estimate that trade will grow beyond $700 billion by 2035, and twenty Latin American countries have joined the BRI.[181] With high borrowing costs, sinking commodity prices, and a sluggish global economy, Latin America's bleak economic outlook makes it difficult for regional governments to refuse Chinese investment, even with all the strings attached.[182]

As the United States withdrew or ceased pursuing trade pacts, Beijing signed free-trade agreements with Chile, Costa Rica, Ecuador, and Peru, and began official trade talks with Honduras, Nicaragua, Panama, and Uruguay.[183] It loaned over $137 billion to Latin American governments and is predicted to soon overtake the World Bank and the Inter-American Development Bank as the largest holder of debt in the region.[184] Beijing's COVID-19 "vaccine diplomacy" provided Latin American countries with medical supplies and hundreds of millions of vaccine doses. In addition, China became a voting member of the Caribbean Development Bank and the Inter-American Development Bank and prompted six Latin American nations—Argentina, Brazil, Chile, Ecuador, Peru, and Uruguay—to join the AIIB.[185]

In August 2023 remarks, General Laura Richardson, commander of US Southern Command, spoke on Latin America's growing dependency on China and warned that the region's leaders were "working on a stopwatch not a calendar. And we have to be able to have alternative methods, alternative companies, alternative options for them to be able to select. . . . And that's where we're getting out-competed by the Chinese right now."[186] In the same month, the Central American Parliament—made up of six states from the region—voted to oust Taiwan as a permanent observer and replace it with China.[187]

Beijing sold hundreds of millions of dollars of military equipment to Venezuela, Bolivia, and Ecuador.[188] It also negotiated the construction of a joint military training installation in Cuba and built spy facilities on the island to keep tabs on US military installations.[189] It constructed close to forty ports throughout Central and South America, which a US-China Commission report warned could allow "China to further increase its military presence [in Latin America] in the future."[190] China planned to install Huawei equipment in the 5G networks of at least a dozen Latin American nations and increasingly used satellite ground stations in South America, including those owned by PLA-linked companies.[191] The *Washington Post* reported in November 2023 that the Pentagon "is increasingly concerned that China's growing network of facilities in Latin America. . . for its civilian space and satellite programs has defense capabilities. U.S. officials say the ground stations. . . have the potential to expand Beijing's global military surveillance network in the southern hemisphere and areas close to the United States."[192]

As it did in Africa, Beijing consistently convinced countries in Latin America to vote against or abstain from UN resolutions that criticized China's human rights record.[193] When thirty-nine Western countries condemned Beijing's crackdown on Hong Kong and its human rights abuses in Xinjiang at the UN General Assembly in 2020, only two Latin American nations (Haiti and Honduras) denounced the PRC, while six (Antigua and Barbuda, Cuba, Dominica, Grenada, Nicaragua, and Venezuela) defended China.[194] Six Latin American countries voted against or abstained from a motion to debate Beijing's human rights abuses in Xinjiang at the UN Human Rights Council in October 2022—only Honduras and Paraguay voted for the debate.[195] China also helped persuade five Latin American nations (Bolivia, Cuba, El Salvador, Nicaragua, and Venezuela) not to vote against the Russian invasion of Ukraine.[196]

## The Would-Be Peacemaker

Building on its comprehensive outreach during the 2010s, China launched a global diplomatic campaign. In February 2023, Xi announced a peace plan for Ukraine.[197] While the "plan" was little more than a list of abstract bromides, its diplomatic gumption was hard for many nations in the Global South to resist; American officials reportedly wished to avoid being seen as an obstacle to peace if brokered by the PRC.[198] A month later, as noted in an earlier chapter, Beijing hosted a normalization agreement between Iran and Saudi Arabia.

China's peace moves are attractive to many developing nations. Unlike the United States, Beijing rarely comments on the domestic policies of other countries, so long as they do not conflict with the PRC's geopolitical objectives or sensitivities. The Chinese concept of world order—one fundamentally opposed to the liberal international system—rejects universal values in the name of national sovereignty. As the *Economist* describes it, China is "a superpower that seeks influence without winning affection, power without trust and a global vision without universal human rights."[199]

## Stealing and Spying

In addition to overt military and diplomatic actions, China and its state-sponsored enterprises stole a vast quantity of intellectual property (IP). In 2020, the director of the US National Counterintelligence Security Center put the cost to the United States of Chinese IP theft at $500 billion per year.[200] The threat was magnified at a global level: Lior Div, CEO of Cybereason, a cybersecurity firm that investigated Beijing's IP theft campaign, said in 2022, "In our assessment, we believe that we're talking about trillions, not billions." "The real impact," he concluded, "we're going to see in five years from now, ten years from now, when we think that we have the upper hand on pharmaceutical, energy, and defense technologies. And we're going to look at China and say, how did they bridge the gap so quickly without the engineers and resources?"[201]

In a 2019 report from the CNBC Global CFO Council, almost one-third of North American–based companies surveyed reported Chinese IP theft within the past ten years.[202] In 2019 alone, the FBI investigated over 1,000 cases of IP theft linked to individuals associated with the PRC.[203] The Made in China 2025 plan aims to render China the world's foremost manufacturer in robotics, artificial intelligence, aerospace, and other industrial areas. The plan is, a former US national security official told the *New York Times*, a "road map for theft."[204] By 2021, 80 percent of Department of Justice investigations into economic espionage in 2021 involved China, and in the following year, the FBI opened a counter-intelligence case against China every twelve hours on average.[205]

Beijing acquired confidential IP from American firms in China in a variety of industries, including telecommunications, biotechnology, information technology, energy, manufacturing, aviation, and more—including people.[206] Through the Thousand Talents Plan, Beijing recruited scientists from American labs and stole scientific research and technology.[207] In addition, it used complex licensing requirements to gain access and required US business partners in joint ventures to transfer IP to the Chinese government. Beijing forced American firms in local courts to relinquish their data and employed aggressive antitrust investigators to coerce employees and seize company materials.[208] Under the guise of product security reviews, China also pressured US companies to hand over tech knowledge.[209] Nearly one-fifth of members of the American Chamber of Commerce in Shanghai reported coerced technology transfer to the Chinese government. Chinese companies then used stolen IP, along with government subsidies, to produce and sell products at prices that undercut American businesses.[210] Beijing in 2023 further enhanced state control over commercial data by expanding its legal definition of national security.[211] In response, the US National Counterintelligence and Security Center warned that "the revised law is vague about what constitutes espionage and gives the government greater access to and control over companies' data, potentially turning what would be considered normal business activities into criminal acts."[212]

Beijing also mounted sophisticated cyber penetrations of US infrastructure and critical facilities. It breached the Office of Personnel Management and stole professional and personal details on millions of federal employees, and harvested data on almost half of all Americans in a 2017 cyberattack on Equifax.[213] It infiltrated the networks of American defense contractors and launched cyberattacks against US oil and natural gas pipelines.[214] China stole sensitive data from American nuclear power plants, solar product manufacturers, and steel companies, and targeted major American network service providers and telecommunications firms.[215]

China-based operatives successfully carried off extensive hacking campaigns against major US companies, such as Microsoft and Google, and penetrated US banks and financial institutions, including the Federal Deposit Insurance Corporation (FDIC).[216] China attacked US health systems, obtaining the medical records on millions of Americans, and breached the computer systems of US state governments.[217] As FBI director Christopher Wray stressed, "[China has] a bigger hacking program than that of every other major nation combined. And their biggest target is, of course, the United States."[218] In its 2022 annual report to the Congress, the US-China Economic Security Review Commission concluded, "China's activities in cyberspace are now more stealthy, agile, and dangerous to the United States than they were in the past. Urgent questions remain concerning the United States' readiness for the China cyber challenge, including the adequacy of resourcing for U.S. military cyber forces, the sufficiency of existing protections for U.S. critical infrastructure, and the scope of public-private cybersecurity cooperation."[219] China's pernicious cyber capabilities were on full display in July 2023, when it was discovered that the PRC hacked the emails of US commerce secretary Gina Raimondo and high-ranking State Department officials.[220] The same month, the *New York Times* reported that the Biden administration was "hunting for malicious computer code it believes China has hidden deep inside the networks controlling power grids, communications systems and water supplies that feed military bases in the United States and around the world."[221]

The Chinese spy balloon that in January 2023 spent days drifting across the United States generated global headlines.[222] Before American forces shot it down, the craft surveilled Malmstrom Air Force Base in Montana, home to 150 Minuteman III intercontinental ballistic missiles.[223] Domestic outrage at the provocation led to the eleventh-hour cancellation of Secretary of State Blinken's first visit to China during the Biden administration. Despite the Pentagon's statement that the most recent balloon posed no threat to commercial aviation, civilians, or military assets, and that three Chinese balloons had flown above US territory during the Trump administration, voices in Congress— magnified by the media—clamored over the danger to homeland security and sovereignty.[224]

In October 2023, intelligence principals from the "Five Eyes" countries (Australia, Canada, New Zealand, the United Kingdom, and the United States) gave an unprecedented joint interview in which they warned about China's global espionage campaign. "The People's Republic of China represents the defining threat of this generation, this era," FBI Director Christopher Wray said. "There is no country that represents a broader, more comprehensive threat to our ideas, our innovation, our economic security, and ultimately, our national security."[225] Australian Security Intelligence Organisation Director-General Mike Burgess added, "The scale of the theft is unprecedented in human history."[226]

As the *New York Times* reported in December 2023, China's spy agency, the Ministry of State Security (MSS), "once rife with agents whose main source of information was gossip at embassy dinner parties, is now going toe-to-toe with the Central Intelligence Agency in collection and subterfuge around the world."[227] The MSS employs artificial intelligence to track foreign spies and compile dossiers on persons of interest.[228]

## Political Influence and Interference

In 2021, the director of national intelligence concluded that "Beijing has been intensifying efforts to shape the political environment in the United States to promote its policy preferences, mold public discourse, pressure political figures whom Beijing believes oppose its interests, and muffle criticism of China on such issues as religious freedom and the suppression of democracy in Hong Kong."[229] It spent $280 million to influence American politics, launching a social media campaign process to impact the midterm elections.[230] Beijing created fake Twitter, Facebook, and other social media accounts to shape public opinion on China and censored anti-China content on TikTok and WeChat.[231] It spread pro-Chinese messaging via state-run Chinese newspapers and on radio stations throughout the United States and paid reputable American news sources—such as *USA Today*, *Time*, *Foreign Policy*, *CNN*, and the *Los Angeles Times*—to display pro-China inserts from the CCP-run *Xinhua News Agency* and *China Daily*, and funded research at over 100 leading US universities and think tanks.[232] The PRC established more than one hundred Confucius Institutes—university-based organizations nominally aimed at promoting Chinese language and culture—and sought to influence student populations.[233] Incredibly, China opened secret "police stations" across major cities in the United States to monitor and intimidate the Chinese diaspora.[234] Through these and other activities, Beijing increasingly aimed to convert its economic and diplomatic strength into domestic influence inside the United States—and at a scale that overwhelmed US government efforts to track them.

## Trade Violations

China has persistently violated international commercial practices in recent years. As early as 2010, the US Trade Representative stressed, "China actively seeks to help its domestic producers through myriad additional policies and practices that impede, disadvantage and harm the foreign competition and skew the playing field against imported goods and services and foreign manufacturers and services suppliers."[235] Beijing incentivized overproduction to flood global markets and sink prices for key goods, and it provided domestic enterprises with hundreds of billions in subsidies.[236] It also restricted market access to foreign electronic payment services providers and barred workers from organizing and forming trade unions.[237] China encroached on other countries' maritime rights by employing "the world's largest deep-water fishing fleet, by far, with nearly 3,000 ships" to engage in illegal or unregulated fishing.[238]

It wasn't supposed to be this way. As *New York Times* columnist Thomas Friedman explained, "When China joined the WTO and won immense tariff-free or reduced-tariff access to Western markets, it promised to sign on to a WTO side agreement on government procurements that would have limited China's ability to discriminate against foreign suppliers when making huge government purchases. But China never signed it. Instead, it kept steering its tremendous state buying power to its state-owned industries—and continued subsidizing them as well."[239]

## Transnational Priorities

While much attention justifiably focused on the US withdrawal from (and subsequent re-entry into) the Paris Climate Agreement, China emitted more greenhouse gases than any nation on the planet over the past decade—accounting for approximately 30 percent of global greenhouse gas emissions—and failed to meet its Paris goals.[240] China now stands as the world's largest coal producer and has constructed more coal plants than any other country in recent years.[241] It uses fossil fuels for 85 percent of the country's energy needs and has only increased its reliance on coal and gas in recent years.[242] According to UN data, by the middle of the century 85 percent of the Chinese population will be faced with serious climate hazards.[243] Beijing has boosted its foreign efforts as well, building fossil fuel infrastructure across over a dozen BRI partner states, which has contributed to skyrocketing greenhouse gas emissions.[244]

China has seriously and notoriously damaged global health. Not only did COVID-19 originate in China, but Beijing suppressed reports of the initial outbreak in Wuhan, which significantly stalled international preparation for the pandemic.[245] Chinese doctors and scientists first noticed the mysterious illness in late December 2019. By January 5, three separate government labs had fully sequenced its genome and identified it as a new coronavirus, but Beijing prohibited the labs from publishing their information and instead ordered them to destroy their samples. Not until January 8, when a *Wall Street Journal* article disclosed information on the virus, did the world learn of this new coronavirus. China then delayed for an additional two weeks before it sent the WHO critical data on COVID-19 patients.[246] Since the outbreak of the pandemic, Beijing has restricted any serious inquiry into the origins of the disease.[247]

## Increased Hostility to Democracy and Human Rights

China built an oppressive surveillance state which systemically and brutally violated the human rights of its own people, cracked down on and disappeared government dissenters, prevented freedom of the press and speech, and limited personal expression.[248] As the *Economist* described, "Under Xi Jinping, the Communist Party is building the most ambitious police state in China's history, with the legal powers and surveillance tools to bring order and ideological conformity to every corner of daily life."[249] In both public and private spaces, the PRC deployed 500 million surveillance cameras with servers that can collect 2.5 billion facial recognition photos at any given time. It has used personal phones to trace physical movements and track online activity, including political speech. Beyond the digital domain, Beijing has collected DNA from its citizens and established iris tracking databases. PRC police stressed that the goal of this unprecedented level of surveillance was "controlling and managing the people."[250] In 2023, a revised law called on "the whole of society" to be wary of spies, offering tens of thousands of dollars to those who report espionage activities.[251]

Chinese courts are not independent, and the country's judicial process has relied on forced confessions, often preceded by torture. Authorities have the right to detain the accused for up to six months with no access to counsel or communication with the outside world. A 2022 *New York Times* report summarized the PRC's strategic purpose. "The Chinese government's goal," it said, "is clear: designing a system to maximize what the state can find out about a person's identity, activities and social connections, which could ultimately help the government maintain its authoritarian rule."[252]

China engaged in the largest-scale internment of an ethnic or religious minority since World War II, by detaining up to a million of the Muslim-minority Uyghur population in hundreds of "re-education" camps across Xinjiang.[253] Prisoners reported sterilization, torture, sexual abuse, and forced labor, and some died while in detention.[254] While children of detainees were sent to state-run orphanages, an estimated 16,000 mosques were desecrated or demolished across the province, and Beijing made it illegal to wear veils in public or grow long beards.[255] In 2022, the United Nations found "serious indications of violations of reproductive rights through the coercive and discriminatory enforcement of family planning and birth control policies," and reported that detentions were "marked by patterns of torture or other forms of cruel, inhuman or degrading treatment or punishment." China's treatment of its Uyghur population, the UN concluded, "may constitute international crimes, in particular crimes against humanity."[256]

With the same brutal objectives, China restricted freedoms in and changed the ethnic character of Tibet. It moved hundreds of thousands of Han Chinese to Tibet and appointed a government-backed Panchen Lama—the second-highest-ranking Lama in Tibetan Buddhism—who was rejected by most of the Tibetan people.[257] In a supreme irony, the officially atheist state even declared the authority to discern reincarnations by approving future Dalai Lamas.[258] Beijing has forced one million Tibetan children to attend state-run boarding schools that sever their connection to local language, culture, and religion.[259] Photos of the Dalai Lama and prayer flags are prohibited in homes, and families are subject to random inspections.[260] Beijing cracked down harshly on Tibetan monks for contacting monks in Nepal and reinforced military patrols to prevent Tibetans from fleeing the country.[261]

In violation of international commitments Beijing made during the former British colony's handover, China crushed democracy in Hong Kong. It imposed a "national security" law that cracked down on dissent in Hong Kong and greatly expanded the criteria for crime, including acts of political opposition. It ended free and fair elections, blocked genuine political discourse, and abolished impartial judicial review and the rule of law. Beijing restricted freedom of the press and speech and forced independent newspapers and television networks to close.[262] It also moved to stop public protests and imprisoned peaceful demonstrators who opposed China's oppression. As the US-China Economic Security Review Commission reported in 2022, "Freedoms of speech, expression, assembly, association, and religion in Hong Kong—once among the most progressive in the region—have all but vanished as the territory now ranks near the bottom of global freedom indices."[263] Since Beijing passed the national security law, the government reportedly arrested 248 people and charged 140, including politicians, media moguls, book authors, radio hosts, and ordinary citizens.[264]

## International Pushback and China's Domestic Challenges

Despite the PRC's remarkable centralization of domestic control and increased international power during the decade, China's bright star dimmed as the 2020s began. Beijing's aggressive international behavior boosted America's purposes in the Indo-Pacific. It helped provide a rationale for a US balancing strategy, and spurred others in the region to respond as well. Across Asia, nations increasingly worried about Beijing's determination to dominate Asia.

Globally, once exuberant recipients of Chinese investment began to view Beijing not as a generous benefactor but as an exploitative debt collector.[265] In the choice between recompense for its investment and the preservation of international goodwill, China has strong-armed indebted nations at the cost of its diplomatic image. Scholar and former policymaker Susan Shirk described the effect that Xi has had on his country's international standing. "By exercising its growing economic and military power to coerce other countries," she wrote, "China has harmed its reputation as a responsible power and is triggering a negative international reaction. In short, China's political system itself—both in its collective leadership and personalistic leadership forms—impedes the exercise of self-restraint necessary for a peaceful rise."[266]

China's decades of superb economic performance also began to slump as growth stagnated and then gradually fell.[267] Its economy faltered during the pandemic—with only 2.2 percent growth in 2020—and failed to meet the government's 5.5 percent target in 2022.[268] The National Bureau of Statistics reported that China's economy expanded by only 3 percent in 2022, which, aside from the COVID-depressed 2020 figure, marks the worst year for GDP growth since Mao Zedong's death in 1976.[269] Its debt ratio surged from 150 percent of GDP in the first decade of the twenty-first century to almost 300 percent of its GDP in June 2022, as many Chinese real estate developers struggled to stay afloat. As Logan Wright of the Center for Strategic and International Studies noted, "A credit bubble of historic proportions that drove China's growth over the past decade is currently unwinding, and slowing the economy as a result."[270] From 2012 to 2022, Chinese debt skyrocketed from $37 trillion to $52 trillion.[271] Moreover, in November 2023, a *Financial Times* columnist concluded, "In 2022, China's share of the world economy shrank a bit. This year it will shrink more significantly, to 17 per cent. That two-year drop of 1.4 per cent is the largest since the 1960s."[272]

In addition, China's state-owned enterprises also continued to drag down growth, accounting for 90 percent of China's corporate bonds and more than half of bank loans but just a third of GDP.[273] Beijing has cracked down on the country's most successful tech firms and entrepreneurs, and FDI in Shanghai fell 20 percent between 2021 and 2022.[274] Direct foreign investment began to slow in the first quarter of 2022. In the July–September 2023 period, it fell $11.8 billion, the first contraction since records began in 1998.[275] In the same period, Beijing's middle class suffered, as 4.4 million small businesses were forced to close in 2021, and its banking system strained under the weight of public protests and bank runs.[276] The renminbi dropped to a fourteen-year low in 2022, and its youth unemployment rate surged to more than 20 percent.[277] Although in October 2023 there were indications that the Chinese economy might be recovering more rapidly than anticipated, *Washington Post* columnist Ishaan Tharoor observed, "China's economy is in the midst of a generational slowdown, impacted in part by Xi's draconian pandemic-era restrictions as well as policies aimed at reining in the private sector."[278] The *New York Times* reported in December 2023 that the CCP "made clear that it expected banks, pension funds, insurers and other financial organizations in China to follow Marxist principles and pay obedience to Mr. Xi."[279] In addition, corruption, the stifling tendencies of central planning, poor relations with countries Beijing relies upon for critical technology such as the United States, France, and Germany, and China's faltering economy have also slowed its pace of modernization.[280] In January 2024, reporters at *Bloomberg* concluded, "Years of harrowing losses have left Chinese stocks with a diminished standing in global portfolios, a trend that's likely to accelerate as some of the world's biggest funds distance themselves from the risk-ridden market. An analysis of filings by 14 US pension funds with investments in Chinese stocks show most of them have reduced their holdings since 2020."[281] It is clear that, for the foreseeable future, China will get nowhere near its traditional double-digit growth rates.

China's demographic profile deteriorated in the aftermath of its one-child policy, with its population growth declining 94 percent, working-age population rapidly dwindling, and the median age of its citizens climbing.[282] Even after Beijing announced a three-child policy in 2021, China's fertility rate remained very low at 1.3, and its population was projected to begin dropping in 2025. In 2022, the UN predicted that the Chinese population will decline 43 percent from 1.4 billion today to less than 800 million by 2100.[283] In January 2023, the government released a report stating that, for the first time since the Great Leap Forward, Chinese deaths outnumbered births the previous year. CFR Senior Fellow Sebastian Mallaby in August 2023 asserted, "You have to go back to the plagues and famines of the late medieval period to find a loss of population so severe."[284] This plummeting Chinese population, coupled with an increasing old age-dependency ratio, will further weaken China's economy over the long-term. [285]

In a remarkable show of defiance seen worldwide, Chinese citizens in November 2022 marched the streets to protest harsh COVID lockdowns.[286] Minxin Pei, an expert on China, called the demonstrations "the greatest domestic crisis President Xi Jinping has faced in his decade in power."[287] The *Financial Times* observed, "Even if the unrest can be stamped out as quickly as it flared, it will go down as a remarkable moment in modern Chinese history and evidence that the country's much-vaunted 'social stability' is much more brittle than it seems."[288]

When Beijing eased COVID restrictions in response, infections spread rapidly throughout the country. By the end of January 2023, Chinese authorities confirmed that an estimated 1.2 billion people in China—80 percent of China's population—had contracted COVID-19.[289] Chinese hospitals quickly became overwhelmed by the number of patients and COVID deaths skyrocketed. A health data firm in the United Kingdom estimated that China faced over 5,000 deaths per day in December, with millions of daily infections.[290]

China has recently exhibited challenges in defense as well. The PLA struggles with an outdated command structure and has lacked sufficient joint operations capabilities, while its defense industry remains dependent on the United States and its partners for critical high-tech imports.[291] Beijing has made enormous strides in its military modernization efforts but, as the *Wall Street Journal* reported, "PLA publications say some officers make flawed operational decisions, struggle to lead their troops and sometimes don't understand their own orders. Rank-and-file troops are caught in a top-down system of command, potentially leaving them ill-equipped to improvise in battlefield situations—a situation that has hobbled Russia's military in its invasion of Ukraine."[292] China's armed forces also faced issues of corruption among the top brass and lower-level officials. Xi launched a July 2023 campaign that called for an "early warning mechanism for integrity risks in the military."[293] The crackdown resulted in the removal and replacement of the two generals that commanded the PLA Rocket Corps, and the foreign and defense ministers were relieved shortly afterward.[294] In late 2023, the CCP removed nine generals from the National People's Congress.[295] Former CIA analyst Christopher Johnson observed, "Xi's willingness to take on the embarrassment of such a massive purge shows how determined he is to ensure that his military can carry out his mandate to 'fight and win wars.' "[296] However, "the corruption inside China's Rocket Force and throughout the nation's defense industrial base is so extensive that US officials now believe Xi is less likely to contemplate major military action in the coming years than would otherwise have been the case," according to the American intelligence community in January 2024.[297] Other defense deficiencies remain for China's goal to integrate Taiwan, including insufficient numbers of large amphibious ships, a lack of combat experience for a military that has not seen conflict since the 1979 land war with Vietnam, mediocre capabilities in carrier operations and submarine stealth, and an inadequate supply of skilled recruits for its booming fleet.[298]

In the early 2020s, China's crude "Wolf Warrior" diplomacy offended governments and undermined Beijing's public image.[299] China has recently suffered from historic droughts, major energy shortages, and the most severe heatwave in recorded history, along with hundreds of thousands of demonstrations and riots.[300] The BRI encountered major implementation challenges in more than a third of its projects and caused resentment across the developing world.[301] The economies of its three close partners—Russia, North Korea, and Iran—all seriously weakened. And its support of Russia's invasion of Ukraine alienated most of Europe.[302]

## China's Trajectory

As the decade evolved, more and more Western analysts argued that because of these and other negative factors, Chinese power had peaked. Such assertions led to headlines such as "The Dangers of China's Decline" in *Foreign Policy*, "China's Dangerous Decline" in *Foreign Affairs*, and "China's Decline Became Undeniable This Week. Now What?" in the *New York Times*.[303] Still, it is too soon to conclude definitively that this baleful prognosis will hold true over the decades ahead.[304] After all, the Chinese leadership has overcome enormous problems in the last half-century to reach its current superpower status. And even if China is now in systemic decline, it will continue to represent—as this book's Chapter 2 on national interests enumerates—the only global threat to world order and American peace and prosperity.

In any case, Xi Jinping has fundamentally changed China. As former secretary of defense Robert Gates wrote in *Foreign Affairs*, "Xi's call for 'the great rejuvenation of the Chinese nation' is shorthand for China becoming the dominant world power by 2049, the centenary of the Communists' victory in the Chinese Civil War."[305] Lee Kuan Yew similarly argued, "The size of China's displacement of the world balance is such that the world must find a new balance in 30 to 40 years. It is not possible to pretend that this is just another big player. This is the biggest player in the history of the world."[306] The Chinese president has strengthened the Chinese Communist Party, rid the country of collective leadership, and ensured his lifetime rule. He has installed a massive security surveillance system, suppressed dissent, and overseen crackdowns in Hong Kong, Xinjiang, and Tibet. Unlike his immediate predecessors, Xi has suppressed the private sector while amplifying control of the economy. He has modernized Beijing's military, militarized the South China Sea, and suggested that reunification with Taiwan cannot be postponed indefinitely. Xi has intensified geoeconomic coercion to bully states that challenge Beijing's objectives, supported Russia's invasion of Ukraine, and sought to undermine US national interests in every part of the globe. In short, under Xi, China has grown more repressive at home and more aggressive abroad. At this writing, there are no signs that these trends will abate.

Throughout the 2010s, as China systematically increased its power and influence in Asia and globally, there was comparatively little US strategic response. There was virtually no US pivot from other regions to Asia, and no significant increase in US budgetary resources for the Indo-Pacific, ceding Beijing's leaders plenty of running room. Washington's inadequate reaction fortified their conviction that the United States was in long-term decline, distracted and divided, and not up to the new Great Game. Across Asia, many nations came to similarly bleak conclusions and doubted US commitments, reliability, and staying power. Washington is now embarking on a major, belated—and still partial—effort to bend these curves in the opposite direction.

# 11

# Balancing Military Power in Asia

## Defense Policy and the Pivot

From its inception, the Pivot to Asia sought to rebalance military resources and efforts toward the Indo-Pacific. While economic initiatives need not be zero-sum affairs, and diplomacy can surge and adapt as needed, defense poses starker trade-offs. A military unit in one region is not deployed in another, a war in one part of the world consumes resources that could be used elsewhere, and every country possesses a finite number of ships, aircraft, ground forces, vehicles, and personnel. America's defense budget remains the world's largest but is hardly infinite, and it shrank during the years immediately after the Pivot's announcement. In attempting to rebalance to Asia, some of the most difficult dilemmas arose in the defense sphere.

As first publicly articulated, the Pivot aimed to solve a relatively modest defense problem. In her key article, Secretary Clinton noted the importance of maintaining peace and security in Asia, which was "increasingly crucial to global progress," alongside defending freedom of navigation in the South China Sea, countering North Korean proliferation, and ensuring transparency in the military activities of "the region's key players."[1] This, in turn, would require updating US alliances and ensuring that their defense capabilities and communications infrastructure are "operationally and materially capable of deterring provocation" in the region, an exceedingly ambitious objective. It also meant forging a durable military-to-military dialogue with China and establishing a more geographically distributed, politically sustainable US force posture.[2]

Later that year, Obama observed that a continued American presence in Asia was necessary for a variety of goals: responding to humanitarian crises and disaster relief, maintaining treaty commitments to allies, and countering piracy and violent extremism. In 2013, in remarks elaborating on the Obama administration's effort to rebalance, National Security Advisor Tom Donilon added to the defense rationale. Asian security, he said, was the foundation for the region's economic growth, and both required a stabilizing US military presence.[3] As a result, the president said, though overall defense spending was on the decline, Asia would be protected from cuts.

Behind closed doors at the Pentagon, the problem was viewed more starkly. By 2010, China's increasingly capable A2/AD network threatened America's ability to operate in the western Pacific.[4] Multiple classified wargames indicated that, should war with China break out over Taiwan, the United States would either lose or suffer grievous losses.[5] A growing impression in Asia that America was unable to effectively project power threatened to erode its conventional deterrent against China and undermine US alliances.[6] In order to deter war over Taiwan, and reassure allies, the United States had to re-establish a healthy combat overmatch in Asia.[7]

Doing so would require a vast change in defense policy. When the Pivot was announced, the United States had spent huge sums outside Asia and built a military to conduct highly resourced counterterrorism, counterinsurgency, and stabilization operations throughout the greater Middle East. In the meantime, as noted in the previous chapter, China had made rapid strides in military modernization across the board. American allies were focused on their immediate neighborhood (as with South Korea on the peninsula, for instance), acting together with the United States in areas like Afghanistan (in the case of Australia), or taking only modest steps to increase military capability and capacity (Japan). On top of it all, sequestration was slashing American defense spending. The upshot was the regional military balance shifting against the United States and toward China, as previously discussed in detail.

Worries over the Asian balance of power have a long history in US foreign policy. For at least a century, Washington has aimed to keep the region from falling under the domination of any foreign hegemon. If it did, policymakers generally believed, American national interests would be under direct threat: trade with the region could be interrupted, freedom of navigation constricted, allies and partners coerced, and hostile ideologies proliferated.[8] Given Asia's vast resources, a foreign hegemon could employ them to project global power in ways deeply damaging to the United States.[9] Japan represented the major hegemonic threat in the first half of the twentieth century and the Soviet Union for most of the second. The United States destroyed the former and contained the latter, until its demise in 1991.

By the end of the Cold War, the United States itself enjoyed uncontested primacy in Asia, with the most powerful military, the largest navy, bases across the region, tens of thousands of troops deployed, and five allies bound by treaty to the United States—but, unlike in Europe, not to one another. American military might underwrote a hub-and-spoke alliance system, which guaranteed freedom of the commons, supported an open door to trade, and dampened local rivalries that may have otherwise erupted into conflict. Washington retained its Cold War–era troop presence in Northeast Asia, projected power at will—as during the 1996 Taiwan Strait Crisis, when Bill Clinton sent two aircraft carriers into

Taiwan waters—and hedged against future uncertainties. But it faced no serious challenger.

That dominance would not last, and by the early 2010s, the state of affairs was changing rapidly. The Pivot architects, and their successors, aimed to right the Asian military balance during a time of growing Chinese power, diminishing American defense spending, and, despite efforts to end them, continuing US wars in other regions. This would prove no easy task.

## Eroding Deterrence

For all the drivers of a defense pivot to Asia, the most obvious was China's rapid military modernization, detailed in the previous chapter. A shrinking defense budget forced the Pentagon to prioritize its spending, and the erosion of the US monopoly over key defense technologies—including precision strike weapons— was palpable. Andrew Marshall, the legendary director of the Pentagon's Office of Net Assessment, referred to the ability of other countries to catch up with America's first-mover advantage as a "maturation" of the precision strike regime.[10] In plainer English, defense analyst Barry Watts concluded in 2011, "The story of conventional precision strike from the early 1990s to the present, then, has been largely one of U.S. monopoly and dominance. That happy situation, however, is coming to an end. In the years ahead, U.S. forces will be confronted with long-range [guided missiles] such as those the Chinese are developing as part of a broader A2/AD strategy in the Western Pacific."[11]

For would-be Pivoteers, Asia represented a real conundrum. Despite expectations, there was little peace dividend from drawing down Middle East wars. In 2011, the last American forces withdrew from Iraq, ending the tremendous investment in occupying and stabilizing that country, but they would return just three years later to fight the Islamic State. Also in 2011, the United States joined other NATO countries in a military intervention that toppled Libyan leader Muammar Gaddafi. The temporary surge of US troops in Afghanistan would soon end, but the war there would grind on for another decade. In Obama's last year in office, the president who wished to end Middle East wars and pivot to Asia bombed Iraq, Syria, Pakistan, Afghanistan, Libya, Yemen, and Somalia.[12]

Just as the Obama administration began discussing a rebalance of military resources to Asia, sequestration budget caps became law. On top of this, the Pentagon's 2012 defense strategy abandoned the decades-old "two-war planning construct" under which the US military would be prepared to fight two large-scale land wars simultaneously.[13] With a shrinking overall budget, enduring major commitments in the greater Middle East and Europe, and a rapidly modernizing Chinese military, what was the United States to do in Asia?

## Changes to Military Posture

The Pivot's logic suggested that, whatever the risks elsewhere, Washington would seek to transfer defense personnel and assets from other regions to Asia. Indeed, soon after the Pivot's announcement, the Obama administration took steps to deploy personnel and military assets into new locations across the Indo-Pacific. The 40,000 US troops stationed in Japan, 28,500 in South Korea, and 4,500 based in Guam represented the baseline.[14] The Darwin deployment began with 200 US Marines (at first—the total would grow to 2,500 by 2019) who would conduct exercises and train with the Australian military.[15] Obama also announced increased rotations of US aircraft through northern Australia.[16] Washington transferred a littoral combat ship (LCS) to Singapore from its previous home in San Diego, and over the decade four LCSs would deploy there.[17] The administration endorsed (and then later questioned) the 313-ship navy plan, an objective first announced in 2006, which implied a significant rise from the total of 287 ships in 2012.[18] And it scrapped a plan to reduce the carrier fleet to ten, instead retaining the full complement of eleven aircraft carriers.[19] Such moves appeared to reflect the 2012 Defense Strategic Guidance, in which Obama directed a military "emphasizing the Asia-Pacific and Middle East while still ensuring our

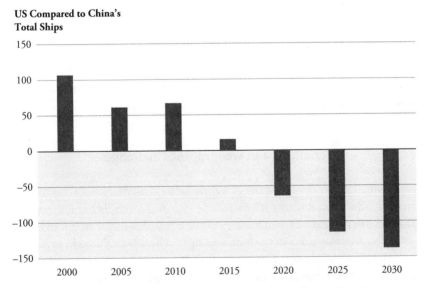

**Figure 11.1.** Difference in number of Chinese and US Navy battle force ships, 2000–2030.

Source: US Library of Congress, Congressional Research Service, *China Naval Modernization: Implications for U.S. Navy Capabilities—Background and Issues for Congress*, by Ronald O'Rourke, RL33153, 2023, 10, https://sgp.fas.org/crs/row/RL33153.pdf.

ability to maintain our defense commitments to Europe"—and while "reduc[ing] our overall capacity."[20] Where cuts were necessary, they would focus on army and marine ground forces, the force structure less relevant (outside the Korean peninsula) than the navy and air force in a possible Asian fight.[21]

In subsequent years there would be more modest moves toward the Indo-Pacific. Following the EDCA, the FY2016 National Defense Authorization Act established the Maritime Security Initiative as a fund to boost the capabilities of key Southeast Asian countries.[22] In 2016, the United States designated India as a Major Defense Partner and liberalized defense technology transfers, after signing a series of "foundational agreements" permitting greater military cooperation.[23] Obama revoked the ban on the sale of lethal arms to Vietnam and then, in 2018, the USS *Carl Vinson* became the first aircraft carrier to visit the country since the end of the Vietnam War. A second carrier visit took place two years later.[24] As mentioned in Chapter 9 on the Indo-Pacific, Manila in 2021 reinstated the bilateral Philippines-United States VFA and green-lit construction at key bases under the EDCA.[25] The next year, the two countries agreed to double the number of troops in joint exercises.[26] In 2023, the United States and the Philippines also announced that they planned "to accelerate the full implementation of the Enhanced Defense Cooperation Agreement," completing projects in five locations and designating four new ones.[27]

In 2021, the United States and Australia announced new force posture initiatives, including plans to turn northern Australia into a forward operating hub for high-end warfighting. The plans included the deployment of nuclear-capable US bombers to Australian airfields and increased rotations of US naval vessels.[28] The two, together with Britain, announced AUKUS.[29] Washington also agreed to deploy a marine littoral regiment to Japan for the first time and to create an Indo-Pacific Partnership for Maritime Domain Awareness.[30]

## Personnel and Geographic Challenges

But moving US forces around the global chessboard, as previously mentioned, proved harder than it seemed. Toward the end of the Trump administration, his team tried—without much success—to draw down US troop levels in Africa and redeploy units to the Indo-Pacific.[31] When Trump sought to punish Germany by withdrawing 7,500 troops from the country, officials justified the move as necessary to bulk up in Asia.[32] The Biden administration canceled the withdrawal after taking office but sought its own changes, including ordering the removal of Patriot and THAAD antimissile batteries from the Middle East (including in Iraq, Kuwait, Jordan, and Saudi Arabia) and the reduction of jet fighter squadrons assigned to the region, in order to transfer them east.[33] A satellite image in late August 2021 showed that multiple batteries were removed from Saudi Arabia.[34] After Russia invaded Ukraine in 2022, however, the administration would increase US troop levels in Europe by 20,000 personnel.[35]

The defense pivot was challenged not only by numbers but by geography. China scholar Oriana Skylar Mastro has pointed out that the United States has two air bases within 1,000 kilometers of the Taiwan Strait, while China has thirty-nine within 800 kilometers of Taipei.[36] US forces are disproportionately concentrated in Northeast Asia, and while Beijing can focus its own forces in the immediate vicinity, American aircraft and naval vessels have multiple roles across several regions. As defense analyst Chris Dougherty observed, "Far from being a deterrent to aggression, American military bases in Asia are a tempting preemptive target."[37] Even as the United States sought to distribute its forces throughout the Asia-Pacific region, acquire new and stronger partners, and win rotational access at geographically important military installations, vulnerability remained a major challenge.

Part of the problem, as defense analyst Stacie Pettyjohn stresses, is also that many posture changes in the region remain aspirational. Announcements dating back to 2012—the AUSMIN agreement, the decision to rotate aircraft through northern Australia, and infrastructure improvements—all lagged behind their announced schedules. If there was an increase in exercises in Australia it was hard to discern beyond the Marines, and the United States failed to deliver on promises to build better infrastructure in "locations that would be needed to support regular rotations of US forces."[38]

A congressionally mandated assessment of the Pivot concluded that "four years into the rebalance," the Defense Department had increased the share of its capabilities dedicated to Asia and deployed its most advanced new systems to the region, including the F-22, Virginia-class fast-attack submarines, the DDG-1000 stealth destroyer, and THAAD systems.[39] But this was not the whole story. China's A2/AD challenge was growing rather than shrinking, and was increasingly able to hold America's forward-deployed and forward-operated forces at risk. Beijing was investing in cyber capabilities, electronic warfare, naval assets, missiles, and reconnaissance systems pursuant to its "plans to push the United States out of the region in a conflict."[40] As a result, the assessment said, at risk were US bases and naval assets, American allies and partners, and "the freedom to use international air and waterways on which the U.S. economy depends." The evaluation was stark: "At the current rate of U.S. capability development," the authors concluded, "the balance of military power in the region is shifting against the United States."[41]

In part as a result, the 2018 National Defense Strategy formalized the department's shifting focus. "Inter-state strategic competition, not terrorism," it said, "is now the primary concern in U.S. national security. . . . It is increasingly clear that China and Russia want to shape a world consistent with their authoritarian model—gaining veto authority over other nations' economic, diplomatic, and security decisions."[42] Suddenly Washington concentrated on—perhaps even obsessed about—great power competition, with the ambition of resisting Chinese and Russian revisionism occupying the top rung of preoccupation.

And while public documents like the 2018 NDS and the Trump administration's national security strategy generally articulated symmetrical concern with both Moscow and Beijing, behind closed doors China was the focus.[43] Building on its predecessors' A2/AD concerns, it observed that for decades the United States "could generally deploy our forces when we wanted, assemble them where we wanted, and operate how we wanted. Today, every domain is contested—air, land, sea, space, and cyberspace."[44]

As noted in earlier chapters, allies quietly observed the same phenomenon, with Japanese and Australian officials fretting behind closed doors that geography and Chinese military modernization were combining to offset traditional US military advantages in Asia. An independent Australian assessment in 2019 concluded, "Chinese counter-intervention systems have undermined America's ability to project power into the Indo-Pacific, raising the risk that China could use limited force to achieve a *fait accompli* victory before America can respond; and challenging US security guarantees in the process." While the Pentagon was increasingly focused on these challenges, the report concluded, "America no longer enjoys military primacy in the Indo-Pacific and its capacity to uphold a favourable balance of power is increasingly uncertain."[45]

## Military Funding for the Pivot

Yet throughout most of the decade following the Pivot's announcement, sequestration cuts to the defense budget combined with a raft of other defense priorities to sharply limit the resources available for Asia. As former PACOM official Eric Sayers put it in 2018, "The scale of resource commitment to the region continues to fall short of the sizable objectives the U.S. government has set for itself."[46] Both CENTCOM and EUCOM were able to circumvent spending cuts by employing overseas contingency operation (OCO) funds—so-called emergency funds necessary to conduct ongoing wars. Pacific Command (later Indo-Pacific Command), on the other hand, never had authority to tap OCO funding.[47] Assistant Secretary of Defense for Acquisition Katrina G. McFarland in March 2014 admitted that, as a result of defense budget cuts, "[r]ight now, the [Asia] pivot is being looked at again, because candidly it can't happen."[48]

Several measures illustrate the challenges in devoting a greater share of US military resources to Asia. FMF, for example, which provides grants and loans for the purchase of US weapons, shows a disjunction between America's stated strategic priorities and the underlying budgeting. In 2016, the administration requested $69 million in FMF for Asia, roughly equivalent to the amount sought for the Western Hemisphere. It requested $4.9 *billion* for the Middle East that same year. By 2019, the amount requested for the Middle East had risen to over $5 billion, while FMF sought for Asia had fallen to $42 million.[49] For FY2021, FMF sought for Asia rose slightly to $86 million—but the request for the Middle East still dwarfed that number at over $5 billion.[50] The FY2023 request amounted to $129 million for Asia, and over $5 billion for the Middle East.[51]

A similar imbalance characterized the amounts spent on International Military Education and Training (IMET). In 2018, the Trump administration requested $26.1 million for Europe and Eurasia, $15.1 million for the Middle East, and $9.8 million for East Asia. As Sayers pointed out, Jordan and Lebanon were scheduled to receive as much IMET as Vietnam, Mongolia, Sri Lanka, Malaysia, and Indonesia combined, despite Washington's emphasis on the Indo-Pacific as America's "priority theater."[52] The FY2023 request showed only a minor rebalance, with under $15 million for Asia, $17.6 million for the Middle East, and $24.9 million for Europe and Eurasia.[53]

Another relevant measure relates to International Security Cooperation Programs, which build partner defense capacity in various regions. The sums devoted to the Indo-Pacific saw a jump from 16 percent of the total in FY2019 to 26 percent the next year, moving to 21 percent in FY2021—a meaningful increase.[54] Congressman Rob Wittman, who compiled these and the following figures, observed, "While encouraging, Washington should be concerned that policymakers have been discussing a pivot to the Indo-Pacific since at least 2011, yet only saw real resource shifts beginning in FY2016 with the establishment of the Maritime Security Initiative and again four years later in FY2020."[55] The Regional Defense Fellowship Program provides training and professional military education for officers from partner nations. From FY2019 to FY2022, INDOPACOM's share of the total has ranged from 11 percent to 15 percent, with no significant increase over the years.[56] Other accounts, including the Pentagon's Overseas Humanitarian, Disasters, and Civic Aid funding, were relatively flat over four years (with INDOPACOM seeing only 17–19 percent of the total funding).[57]

The European Deterrence Initiative (EDI) provided funding for US military presence and readiness in Europe and to build allied capacity.[58] Where EDI provided dedicating funding, however, the Pacific Deterrence Initiative (PDI) did not—instead it aggregated funds spent across the defense budget on Indo-Pacific efforts so they could be tracked over time. PDI was, therefore, a "budget display" rather than new money.[59] Even then, in 2021 the funding level for PDI was just two-thirds the amount dedicated to EDI—and this before Russia's 2022 invasion of Ukraine.[60] By 2022, the Pentagon requested $6.1 billion for the accounts that comprise PDI—a decrease of $1 billion from the total authorized by Congress the previous year.[61] Dustin Walker, who led the development of PDI as a staffer on the Senate Armed Services Committee, observed, "A sizable portion of the initiative funds maintenance of existing facilities, operation of steady-state forces, and execution of legacy posture initiatives. No notable shifts of forces west of the international date line are funded."[62] In light of such facts, FY2023 saw a huge increase in PDI, with the total rising to $11.5 billion.[63] The bulk of additional funding, however, was dedicated to maintaining current capabilities and posture or implementing legacy posture initiatives, rather than building new bases or expanding infrastructure at existing locations.[64]

The effort to insulate the Indo-Pacific from defense budget cuts and reductions in force structure was worthy. So too were the attempts to achieve rotational or other access to new bases and distribute US forces deployed in the region (Figure 11.2). The military diplomacy engaged in by US officials was valuable, as were the tighter defense linkages with new partners like India and Vietnam. But all this did not amount to either a substantial increase in US power projection into

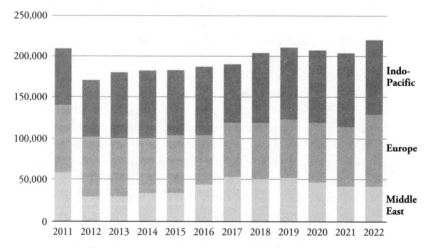

**Figure 11.2.** American troops deployed in Europe, the Middle East, and the Indo-Pacific, 2011–2022.

Source: All data are from the International Institute for Strategic Studies (IISS) *Military Balance*. The data from the *Military Balance* represent a snapshot of deployments in early November of each year. ©2012–2023, The International Institute for Strategic Studies, originally published in *The Military Balance* 2012–2023 (reproduced with permission).

Asia, or a defense pivot to Asia from other regions. Today, the US Pacific Fleet consists of approximately 200 ships (to include five aircraft carrier strike groups) and nearly 1,100 aircraft—but as two defense analysts at the Center for a New American Security concluded in 2022, this has not amounted to "a significant and sustained uptick in the number of American bases or forces in the region to counter China's growing military power."[65]

## Air-Sea Battle

The Pentagon, however, also proposed solutions to the defense problem in Asia that hinged less on a quantitative increase in military resources than a qualitative shift in technology and concepts of operation. Robert Work, who served as deputy secretary of defense under both Obama and Trump, recalled, "The department never really did a pivot to Asia. It did a reorientation towards China. And this started in 2010."[66] The 2010 Quadrennial Defense Review directed the navy and air force to develop a "new joint air-sea battle concept for defeating adversaries across the range of military operations, including adversaries equipped with sophisticated anti-access and area denial capabilities."[67] China had fielded a robust A2/AD network; Air-Sea Battle (ASB) would figure out how to overcome it. That, Work said, was "the start of the department's reorientation towards China, away from the Middle East and towards great power competitors."[68]

The next year the Pentagon established an ASB Office, charged with developing a concept for defeating China's military advantages. Such a move might have appeared straightforward given the new challenge in Asia. The initiative was modeled on AirLand Battle, the 1970s-origin concept that sought to counter a numerically superior Soviet military attack in Europe. But the initiative was controversial from the beginning, including within the Defense Department. A concept that included air and sea appeared to leave out the US Army and possibly the Marine Corps as well. And while defense officials were privately sounding the alarm about Chinese military advances, the administration's most senior officials publicly stressed the need for cooperative relations with Beijing.[69] Overtly preparing for a battle in the air and at sea against America's would-be partner seemed inconsistent with an approach grounded in positive engagement.

Nevertheless, the Pentagon published the concept in 2013, making clear that every military service would have a role to play in it. ASB's concepts of operations remained classified, but its overall solution to the A2/AD challenge was to "develop networked, integrated forces capable of attack-in-depth to disrupt, destroy and defeat adversary forces."[70] While China was nowhere named in the public document, it was clear that the approach would include disrupting PLA command and control, constricting its ability to coordinate attacks on US or friendly forces, destroying its weapons platforms, and defeating weapons after they were launched (e.g., via missile defense) so that the US military could continue operations.[71]

In time, the ASB Office would disappear as a standalone entity. Absorbed into the Joint Staff's J7 directorate in 2015, the concept itself would be renamed as the Joint Concept for Access and Maneuver in the Global Commons and given the awkward acronym JAM-GC.[72] The underlying concept, however, endured. Individual services began adjusting as well. The army emphasized its role in operating land-based missile systems that could hold Chinese assets at risk. The Marine Corps adopted Force Design 2030, a new concept focused on operations in the western Pacific.[73] In time, the department would augment ASB (or JAM-GC) with efforts to acquire new technologies and field new capabilities, including through nontraditional procurement processes.

## Strategic Capabilities Office

To this end, in 2012, Ashton Carter—serving then as the defense undersecretary in charge of acquisition—established a new Strategic Capabilities Office (SCO). SCO's charge was to explore new technologies that might be applied to the A2/AD problem in the western Pacific. Importantly, Carter emphasized the need for speed; he wanted capabilities that could be fielded in five years or less. In an inauspicious start, the SCO's first director, a young physicist and Rhodes Scholar named Will Roper, lacked office space and so set up shop in the Pentagon courtyard. He remained there for nine months, awaiting an office and a computer, and started the effort without staff or even a budget.[74] In time, however, the SCO would convert the SM-6 missile, designed to intercept both aircraft and missiles, into an antiship missile, develop swarming micro-drones, test and demonstrate hypervelocity projectiles fired from cannons, and begin work on an "arsenal plane" to deliver munitions beyond the effective range of anti-aircraft defenses, along with a raft of classified projects.[75]

The next year Carter, by now deputy secretary of defense, briefed Obama and the NSC on China's considerable threats to the US space constellation.[76] Robert Work recalls that the president was shaken by the threats to GPS satellites on which so much military and commercial navigation depends. Prior to the briefing, he remembers, "I was unable to use the words China and competition in the same speech or paper. Our policy was engagement.... After the brief, although there was no official document or memo, we were able to say we and China were in a heated competition in space, and were able to talk about possible war in space."[77]

# Third Offset Strategy and the Defense Innovation Unit Experimental

Work, who in 2014 would assume Carter's position as deputy secretary, ushered in the department's Third Offset Strategy, an approach that hoped to draw on advanced technology to offset some of China's advantages, stemming from geography and technology, in denying access to US forces. The new strategy was part of Secretary Chuck Hagel's Defense Innovation Initiative (DII), an explicit effort to stop and then reverse the erosion of US dominance in key warfighting domains.[78] In announcing the new initiative, Hagel observed, "While we have been engaged in two large land mass wars over the past thirteen years, potential adversaries have been modernizing their militaries, developing and proliferating disruptive capabilities across the spectrum of conflict. This represents a clear and growing challenge to our military power."[79] The first two offset strategies sought to offset the Warsaw Pact's numerical superiority over NATO forces in Europe. The third would offset the rising threats to American deterrence posed by countries that increasingly applied high-end military technology to the task of denying US freedom of action.[80] Just as the United States had combined networked precision strike with stealth and surveillance to transform the security landscape in the 1970s and 1980s, the DII and Third Offset Strategy would absorb breakthrough technologies—artificial intelligence, autonomy, high-speed projectiles, and more—and employ them in new operational concepts.[81]

To absorb such technologies from the commercial sector, the Department in 2015 established the Defense Innovation Unit Experimental (DIUx). Later, the "Experimental" would fall away in favor of a more permanent-sounding "DIU"), a kind of Pentagon embassy to Silicon Valley. Its mission was to identify new commercial products and help rapidly prototype and field them.[82] DOD also made investments in new programs, like tactical boost glide and air breathing hypersonic weapons and new space capabilities. But though the effort was commendable, Pettyjohn points out that the DIU has not been "as innovative or as game changing as one would hope."[83] The DIU transition rate was low until very recently and has since only made progress on marginal points such as personnel management.[84] From 2016 to 2021, DIU helped transition thirty-five prototypes into production or service contracts with DOD and had a transition rate of about 41 percent—up from 30 percent in previous years.[85]

The attempt to arrest the erosion of military technical superiority against China was a worthy objective. But it met limited success and was not the rebalance most often described by senior US officials. As Robert Work recalled:

> The way I interpreted the Pivot to Asia was that senior defense leadership was saying we were moving away from the era of engagement and toward an era

of strategic competition, particularly a long-term strategic competition with China, in the region of most strategic importance to the United States in the 21st century. . . . We were also pivoting away from our programmatic focus on counterterrorism and counterinsurgency over the past ten or fifteen years toward fighting against near peer adversaries with advanced capabilities.[86]

## China Outpaces the United States

For all the effort put into reorienting US focus toward China, the fact was that Beijing remained no static adversary. On the contrary, Chinese military modernization was proceeding faster than any overall increase in US capability. While the Department of Defense initiated a raft of efforts to quickly adopt commercial technology for military use, China was undertaking similar efforts. The PLA hosted DARPA-style competitions and established its own version of DIU, in Shenzhen, to harness advanced commercial technologies.[87] As the Pentagon attempted to integrate artificial intelligence, autonomy, and other technologies into new networks, China embarked on a parallel effort. As defense analyst Paul Scharre observed, "China's vision of 'intelligentized' warfare envisions combat with intelligent weapons, equipment, platforms, decision-making, and logistics enabled by AI, communications networks, big data, cloud computing, and IoT devices."[88]

From its inception and through the decade, senior officials outside the Pentagon did not describe defense enhancement as a matter of technology absorption, new concepts of operations, and investments in new weapons systems. Instead, the more general focus was on the resources—personnel, military assets, basing, foreign military assistance, and more—assigned to the Indo-Pacific region as opposed to others. Here operations and maintenance for Middle East wars and to maintain military readiness together consumed a disproportionately large share of US defense funding. The Department of Defense sacrificed investments in R&D and procurement, just as China was increasing the sums allotted to both.

In the end, then—more than a decade after the 2011 announcement of a US pivot to Asia—little meaningful shift of military resources to the Indo-Pacific had taken place. The United States did establish new basing and porting arrangements, make major investments in new systems and R&D, forge new defense relationships, and more. But the United States in 2022 had more troops stationed in Europe than it did in 2011.[89] By 2017, the number of ships in the navy was lower than 2011—witnessing only a minor increase through 2021.[90] The freeing up of resources from ending Middle East wars never saw fruition in Asia, and nothing moved from Europe. With the exception of submarines, the highest-end systems—like F-35s—tended to deploy to Europe and to be used in the Middle East rather than in the Indo-Pacific. 2021 marked the first year in three decades during which an aircraft carrier did not operate in the Middle East.[91] And while the net deployment of US military resources in Asia was essentially flat for over a decade, China made increases in virtually every area.

## Europe Goes to War

The eruption of Europe's first major state-on-state land war since 1945 affected the defense pivot to Asia, and not in wholly predictable ways. The United States boosted troop levels in Europe and moved them east on the continent in an effort to reassure NATO allies. It sent extra F-35 deployments to Europe but only rotational forces to Asia.[92] In less than a year, Washington provided Ukraine with an astonishing $29.3 billion in military assistance.[93] That assistance strained the US defense industrial base, as the Defense Department quickly ran down supplies of Javelin anti-tank missiles, Stinger anti-aircraft missiles, 155-millimeter ammunition, and other munitions and systems, none of which could be replenished in a matter of months. Despite this titanic effort, Pentagon leaders insisted that American aid to Ukraine would affect neither the focus on Asia nor the provision of weapons to partners in the Pacific.[94]

Indeed, the Biden administration's NDS, issued during the war's height, jettisoned its predecessor's equivalence of Moscow and Beijing in America's pantheon of threats; now China was the central focus. "The most comprehensive and serious challenge to U.S. national security," it said, "is the PRC's coercive and increasingly aggressive endeavor to refashion the Indo-Pacific region and the international system to suit its interests and authoritarian preferences." As a result, the NDS "advances a strategy focused on the PRC and on collaboration with our growing network of Allies and partners on common objectives. It seeks to prevent the PRC's dominance of key regions while protecting the U.S. homeland and reinforcing a stable and open international system."[95] President Biden publicly and repeatedly pledged to use US forces to defend Taiwan in the event of a Chinese attack.[96]

The invasion had ripple effects across Asia. Japanese prime minister Fumio Kishida observed that "Ukraine today could be East Asia tomorrow."[97] Tokyo responded by pledging to double defense spending and to acquire hundreds of long-range missiles.[98] South Korea began a national discussion about acquiring its own nuclear arsenal.[99] Taiwan boosted its defense budget by 14 percent in one year and extended the period of mandatory military service from four months to a year.[100] Asia, like Europe, was responding to the Russian invasion with its own rearmament, and in so doing created new opportunities to join with the United States to increase deterrence.

The regional defense lines became increasingly blurry as well. Britain, which post-Brexit had announced a "Tilt" to the Indo-Pacific, in 2021 joined AUKUS and sent a carrier strike group to the Indo-Pacific.[101] France conducted naval patrols in the South China Sea and issued an Indo-Pacific strategy, pledging to act as a "stabilizing force."[102] In 2022 Japan and Britain signed a Reciprocal Access Agreement that gave access to each other's military installations. NATO issued a new strategic concept after the Russian invasion which said, for the first time, that China's "stated ambitions and coercive policies challenge our interests, security and values."[103] The leaders of Australia, Japan, New Zealand, and South Korea participated in the NATO summit for the first time.[104]

Such reactions to the Ukraine war, and the increasing intertwining of Europe and Asia that preceded it, illustrate the limitation of a strict regional delineation. Indo-Pacific nations saw their future bound up to some degree with the success or failure of Russia in Europe, and European countries increasingly discern their future in Asia. For a global power like the United States, regional priorities demanded an approach subtler than a broad "do more" mantra, even in matters of defense resources. Washington must remain militarily engaged and present in multiple regions, simultaneously and indefinitely, though with varying amounts of resource demands.

The defense pivot has generally been described in quantitative and geographic terms: count the deployments and assets and installations across Asia and compare them to previous years. Yet the central defense problem the Pivot has attempted to solve is rising Chinese military power—which it has made little progress against. As Pettyjohn observed in February 2023, to date the Pivot has not "been real in resources, or certainly in posture."[105] Yet Beijing still seeks the capability to invade Taiwan by 2027 and to possess the world's most powerful military by 2049.[106] A component of the American answer to this problem incorporates military resources and activities in the western Pacific. But the competition—and potential conflict—would also play out in space, in cyberspace, and even in homeland threats. An abiding focus on increasing resources in Asia is, as a result, only a partial answer, and one that has not been met.

# 12

## Pivoting from Offense to Defense

### The Changing Role of Economic Policy

Well before the Pivot's announcement, Asia's economic dynamism spurred vigorous US efforts to access the region's markets, labor forces, and capital. American commerce in Asia began centuries ago, and by 2008 the unique economic potential in the Asia-Pacific was undeniable. The region then accounted for nearly 37 percent of global GDP (in purchasing power parity terms) and made up 40 percent of global economic growth.[1] India and China each saw sustained, double-digit growth as they integrated into global markets and supply chains, and many of the world's most dynamic economies were Asian. As a result, from 1980 to 2010, Asia's share of global exports and imports nearly doubled.[2] The notion of an "Asian century," which by the early 2010s became commonplace, referred mostly to the eastward shift of global economic gravity.[3]

For roughly a decade prior to the Pivot rollout, the United States had welcomed China into the WTO, signed free-trade agreements (FTAs) with Australia, Singapore, and South Korea, inked a trade and investment framework agreement with ASEAN, enacted a bilateral trade agreement with Vietnam, and started FTA talks with Thailand. When the Doha Round of global trade talks stalled, Washington used APEC to secure a framework accord.[4] Asia was growing richer, more populous, and more economically integrated with the rest of a globalizing world. The United States, policymakers widely believed, needed to reap the benefits of engagement with Asia or risk getting left behind.

Rapid Chinese economic growth helped focus American minds. In the two decades after its WTO accession, Chinese exports grew by some 870 percent. While overall global trade increased by 180 percent over that period, China's total trade value surged 810 percent.[5] In 2001, before it joined the WTO, China accounted for approximately 4 percent of global trade. By 2013 it surpassed the United States in total trade volume, and by 2021 it accounted for some 13 percent of total global trade.[6] In the decade from 2001 to 2011, Chinese GDP grew (in constant 2015 US dollars) from $3 trillion to $8.28 trillion (Figure 12.1).[7]

The Pivot's architects naturally wished to harness this economic dynamism for American benefit. That imperative acquired greater urgency given the financial crisis that coursed through the globe in 2008. Hillary Clinton, in her Pivot article, argued that "[o]ur economic recovery at home will depend on exports

**GDP Growth
(Annual %)**

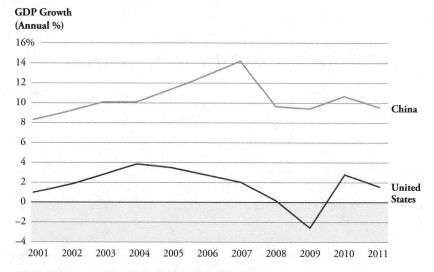

**Figure 12.1.** China's and the United States' GDP growth in annual %, 2001–2011.

All data are sourced from The World Bank, 2011–2011, GDP growth (annual %)—China, United States, https://data.worldbank.org/indicator/NY.GDP.MKTP.KD.ZG?end=2011&locations=CN-US&start=2001.

and the ability of American firms to tap into the vast and growing consumer base of Asia."[8] In November 2011, when President Obama articulated the Pivot before Australian lawmakers, the US unemployment rate stood at 8.6 percent, with some 13.3 million Americans out of work.[9] "As the world's fastest-growing region," Obama said, "and home to more than half the global economy—the Asia-Pacific is critical to achieving my highest priority, and that's creating jobs and opportunity for the American people."[10] Clinton highlighted specific administration initiatives, including the US-Korea Free Trade Agreement and the nascent Trans-Pacific Partnership (TPP).[11] Wendy Cutler, then a senior Asia-focused official with the US Trade Representative, recalled that the White House and State Department focus on the Pivot helped re-energize the administration's economic agenda in Asia.[12]

At this point, most policymakers still subscribed to the notion of a causal link between economic growth and liberal governance, especially in China.[13] Successfully engaging in commerce, it was thought, required the kinds of institutions and practices characteristic of democratic government, and a rising middle class would eventually demand basic rights and liberties. "As we grow our economies," Obama said in Canberra, "we'll also remember the link between growth and good governance—the rule of law, transparent institutions, the equal administration of justice. Because history shows that, over the long run, democracy and economic growth go hand in hand."[14] In pursuing deeper economic engagement as part of the Pivot, then, the United States could simultaneously promote its deepest values.

Even if domestic liberalization did not result from economic engagement, however, there might be other benefits. By expanding the global economy's rules-based architecture, the United States could create incentives for Beijing to modify its economic practices in line with key agreements. Cutler recalls that "there was still the hope, then, that by developing high standard rules and getting more and more countries to sign on . . . China would have no choice but to come into that orbit and agree to the same rules."[15] Trade agreements would also lower taxes on exchange, create dispute-resolution mechanisms, and enable the dynamic US private sector to engage more deeply in Asia.[16] And following the 2008 global financial crisis, Washington and Beijing sought to harmonize their fiscal and monetary policy responses, including through the G20.[17]

Asia's own trade liberalization also drove American economic interest. By the early 2010s, with global trade talks (via the WTO Doha Round) going nowhere, countries in the region increasingly pursued their own deals. In 2000, for example, Asia had just three FTAs in effect; by 2011 the number had exploded to around fifty, with another eighty in progress.[18] China, Korea, Japan, Australia, and New Zealand each struck trade agreements with ASEAN.[19] After ASEAN-EU FTA negotiations were suspended in March 2009, the European Union pursued bilateral negotiations with ASEAN nations, including with Singapore and Malaysia in 2010, Vietnam in June 2012, Thailand in March 2013, the Philippines in December 2015, and Indonesia in July 2016.[20] In November 2011, the year the US Pivot was announced, the idea of the Regional Comprehensive Economic Partnership (RCEP) first appeared at the ASEAN Leaders Summit in Bali.[21] Amid this flurry of activity, however, America was on the outs: with the exception of KORUS, the United States was party to none of these deals. It was time to get in the game, many policymakers thought, or be left behind in a region on the move.

The final driver of the economic pivot revolved around China's increasing economic gravity. In 2001, more than 80 percent of countries had a larger trade volume with the United States than China. By 2018, that figure had fallen to barely 30 percent.[22] In 2023, China stood as the top trade partner of some 120 countries around the world.[23] The shift was especially pronounced in Asia, as highlighted in the Indo-Pacific chapter. Economic power confers leverage, especially against smaller countries, and by 2010 China's economy had grown bigger than any except the United States.[24] Over the years, American policymakers worried ever more about Beijing's ability to weaponize its economic gravity, coercing countries fearful of disrupting ties to the world's second-largest economy.

In more than a decade since the Pivot's announcement, the strategy's economic component changed radically. At the beginning, US policy sought to harness opportunity via a raft of economic agreements with multiple countries, crowned by the pan-regional TPP. Doing so would provide greater access to Asian markets, signal enduring US leadership in the region, and create alternatives to China's ever-increasing economic weight. Yet virtually all of those efforts failed over time, and Washington's offensive agenda—one that aimed to open markets, facilitate trade and investment, and lower barriers to commerce in the Pacific—increasingly yielded to a defensive effort, focused instead on blunting the national security risk that attended China's economic activities. Instead of trade agreements and investment frameworks, the focus of US policy turned to export controls, investment screening, tariffs, domestic industrial policy, and sanctions. This shift to a defensive effort, one aimed at reducing risk from China rather than seizing opportunity in the Indo-Pacific, produced an economic approach to Asia utterly different from the Pivot's original conception.

## From KORUS to the Trans-Pacific Partnership

From the outset, efforts to pivot economically to Asia were affected by US domestic politics. During the 2008 global financial crisis, the politics of trade took a hit, with fewer Americans aspiring to gain from free trade and more fearing its dislocating effects.[25] The trajectory of KORUS proved an early illustration of the difficulties associated with even bilateral pacts. After it was signed, worries spread quickly that Democratic members of Congress might oppose the measure over the treatment of autos and beef.[26] These worries proved valid. Obama denounced KORUS as "badly flawed" on the campaign trail, and insisted on renegotiating after taking office in 2009.[27] Seoul made concessions to the administration on automobiles and agriculture, and the agreement entered into effect three years later.[28]

That, however, was not the end of KORUS's story. Donald Trump denounced the pact during his own presidential campaign, calling it a "job-killing trade deal," and after inauguration said that the United States would either renegotiate or terminate the agreement.[29] A *third* round of talks then began and Seoul made minor concessions once again, this time not only on autos but also on steel exports. Trump and South Korean president Moon Jae-in signed the re-renegotiated agreement in September 2018. Even as a relatively straightforward, bilateral trade deal, KORUS's difficulties would prove a canary in the coal mine for more ambitious efforts.

The TPP became extraordinarily ambitious, though it hardly began that way. At the outset, the TPP was little more than a trade agreement among Brunei,

Chile, New Zealand, and Singapore. The United States joined talks with the group in 2008, and Australia, Peru, and Vietnam subsequently did so as well.[30] By 2011, the membership was broad enough for the secretary of state to envision an expansive accord. "Our hope," Hillary Clinton wrote, "is that a TPP agreement with high standards can serve as a benchmark for future agreements—and grow to serve as a platform for broader regional interaction and eventually a free trade area of the Asia-Pacific."[31] In time the TPP would become the very core of America's Pivot to Asia.

Given American enthusiasm and the ever-greater promise of market access, new countries sought to join the talks. Malaysia, Mexico, and Canada came aboard, and then, in 2013, the great prize: Japan. A US-Japan FTA, though casually discussed over the years, had never been in the offing. Now, however, the TPP offered a version of just that—and included a raft of other markets to boot. On the table was a high-standards, Pacific FTA that represented some 40 percent of global GDP. It included most of America's top trade and geopolitical partners and excluded China.

The importance of the TPP to the Pivot could hardly have been greater. In 2013, Tom Donilon called the agreement "the centerpiece of our economic rebalancing," one that not only promised regional economic integration but could even pave the way for a US-Europe analogue, the Transatlantic Trade and Investment Partnership.[32] Kurt Campbell described the TPP as "a cardinal priority and cornerstone of the Pivot to Asia."[33] Its importance, Campbell added, "is difficult to overstate; it is the true *sine qua non* of the Pivot."[34] The agreement was, the White House said in 2015, "central to our vision of the region's future and our place in it."[35] Jeffrey Bader, the administration's top NSC official for Asia, later called the TPP "the linchpin of the Asia rebalance."[36]

It was easy to see why. The TPP promised simultaneously to serve multiple US objectives. It would boost economic growth and create jobs at home when the administration sought both. The deal would enshrine US-authored and supported rules, including in new economic areas like digital trade and intellectual property, rather than leaving such rule-making to others. It would contain rules on state-owned enterprises, an area of concern with China, that would establish a new multilateral baseline. The TPP promised to strengthen key American allies and partners, increasing their economic performance and tying them more closely to the United States and one another. Above all, it would send a broad signal of sustained American leadership and presence in Asia. Economic policy in the Pacific is foreign policy, and US regional leadership was unthinkable absent a dominant role in trade and investment. The TPP would provide pathways for it.

In the first instance, the TPP promised to boost economic growth in the United States. The US Trade Representative cited figures putting the increase in national income at more than $130 billion annually by 2030, with an increase in US exports of over $350 billion each year and higher wages for American workers.[37] By cutting 18,000 tariffs on US exports to TPP countries, the economy as a whole would benefit, even if some industries would inevitably lose out.[38] The World Bank and the US International Trade Commission, in their own analyses, each predicted modest but positive US GDP effects from the TPP.[39]

Beyond the direct economic boost, the TPP would serve as a vehicle for making economic rules that reflected American priorities, particularly in areas lacking them. The parties would, for instance, agree to ban data localization mandates and pledge to ensure the free flow of data across national borders. They adopted rules to reduce the trade-distorting effects of state-owned enterprises and enshrined high labor and environmental standards.[40]

Here there was a not-so-subtle effort to embed economic rules before others—especially China—could do so first. "TPP allows America," Obama said, "and not countries like China—to write the rules of the road in the 21st century, which is especially important in a region as dynamic as the Asia-Pacific."[41] While the TPP was negotiated, multiple countries were engaged in parallel talks on RCEP, the other pan-regional trade agreement that included China but not the United States. The sense that one set of rules would triumph—either US-written, enshrined in the TPP, or China-supported, enacted via RCEP—was palpable. In 2016, during the effort to win congressional passage of the TPP, deal supporters stressed the point. As Obama put it, "The world has changed. The rules are changing with it. The United States, not countries like China, should write them."[42]

In addition to its economic benefits, the TPP also promised to strengthen key US partners like Japan and Vietnam. The World Bank, for instance, projected that the Vietnamese economy could be as much as 10 percent larger with the TPP than without it. Japan, suffering through multiple decades of economic sluggishness, would get a boost as well. So would other countries; the World Bank estimated, for example, that the Malaysian economy would be 8 percent larger with the agreement.[43] Such effects, it was generally thought in Washington, would help the United States in its rising competition with China, by ensuring that American partners were increasingly prosperous and strong. And the TPP promised to reduce the pull of Beijing's economic gravity by diversifying trade away from China and toward parties in the agreement.

The TPP's greatest promise was also the hardest to quantify. By leading the effort to enshrine the world's biggest trade agreement, one focused on the Pacific region, the United States would signal presence, engagement, and staying power. While China's rise was felt all over the region, and as doubts about US will and capacity for global leadership endured, the TPP would represent a tangible signal of US commitment to Asia and its regional order.

## How to (Not) Sell the TPP

Over time, the strategic argument for the TPP overtook its economic rationale and the deal became "more China focused" as administration officials moved from the negotiation stage to the domestic outreach phase.[44] The pact "strengthens our strategic relationships with our partners and allies," Obama argued, "in a region that will be vital to the 21st century."[45] Secretary of Defense Ash Carter said that passing the TPP was as important to him as another aircraft carrier.[46] "If you don't do this deal," Singaporean foreign minister K. Shanmugam asked, "what are your levers of power? The choice is a very stark one: Do you want to be part of the region, or do you want to be out of the region?"[47] Japanese prime minister Shinzo Abe told a joint session of Congress that the TPP "is also about our security. . . . Long term, its strategic value is awesome."[48] US Trade Representative Michael Froman, who negotiated American membership, said that a congressional failure to pass the deal would amount to "handing the keys to the castle to China."[49]

The TPP became, by the end of the Obama administration, not only Washington's highest-profile economic initiative but the linchpin of the Pivot to Asia. It initially attracted the support of political leaders in both parties. In 2016, when the administration pressed for congressional approval, House Speaker Paul Ryan and Senate Majority Leader Mitch McConnell supported the deal, as did the US Chamber of Commerce and the National Association of Manufacturers.[50] Indiana governor Mike Pence and Senator Tim Kaine of Virginia, the vice-presidential candidates on each side in 2016, supported TPP as well.[51]

Yet the domestic politics of trade remained difficult. The White House nominated Senate Finance Committee chair Max Baucus as ambassador to China in 2013, a position he took up the following year. Baucus had up to that point led the Senate push for Trade Promotion Authority (TPA), a move widely seen as the necessary precursor to an eventual TPP agreement. His successor, Senator Ron Wyden, consumed nearly a year in deciding how to move forward with the TPA, delaying its passage. Cutler recalls that, had Capitol Hill granted the administration TPA sooner, "that would have likely enabled [the United States] to move [its] partners faster."[52] The TPA—widely seen as a proxy vote for the TPP—passed Congress in 2015, suggesting that the votes were present for approval of the trade agreement. But 2016 would turn out a very different year.

By the time the agreement was complete, time had nearly run out. By leaving the push for congressional approval to the very end of his eight-year administration, Obama sought support with few remaining levers of influence. And as 2016 was also a particularly searing presidential election year, the TPP entered squarely—and unproductively—into the debate. Ironically, as the deal's supporters stressed more heavily its national security rationale, they left a sense among skeptics that the United States would suffer, rather than benefit, economically. Opponents asked why Americans should absorb the costs of this trade agreement in exchange for some vague geopolitical benefit. Robert Lighthizer, for instance, who served as Trump's US Trade Representative, later charged supporters with believing that "if we import more from these countries and increase our trade deficits with them, they will be our friends and oppose China." This, he said, "is nonsense."[53]

As 2016 wore on, opposition to the TPP grew. Senator Elizbeth Warren, herself a presidential candidate, said, "Most of the TPP is about letting multinational corporations rig the rules—on everything from patent protection to food safety standards—all to benefit themselves"[54] Obama countered, saying that Warren's "arguments don't stand the test of fact and scrutiny," but they did resonate.[55] Despite economic models that predicted the opposite, Senator Bernie Sanders said the TPP would cost millions of jobs, lower wages for American workers, and produce a "race to the bottom."[56] Senate Minority Leader Harry Reid came out against the deal, as did House Minority Leader Nancy Pelosi. They were joined by labor unions, some Tea Party Republicans, and populist-minded conservatives.[57] Even Hillary Clinton, who as secretary of state had championed the TPP as vital to the Pivot to Asia, announced her opposition.[58]

As the 2016 presidential field winnowed to the final two candidates on each side, all four—Trump, Senator Ted Cruz, Clinton, and Sanders—opposed the TPP. Trump was, unsurprisingly, the most outspoken. The Republican candidate declared that "[t]he great American middle class is disappearing," said "the situation is about to get drastically worse if the Trans-Pacific Partnership is not stopped."[59] Pew opinion surveys showed that the percentage of Americans who had positive views of trade agreements fell from 58 percent in May 2015 to 45 percent in October 2016.[60]

As political support wavered, US national security experts and foreign leaders grew alarmed at the possibility of failure. Singapore's prime minister Lee Hsien Loong, for instance, warned in 2015, "Failing to get the TPP done will hurt the credibility and standing of the U.S., not just in Asia, but worldwide."[61] After the United States had taken such a dominant role in producing and promoting the agreement, policymakers worried that failing to pass it would signal America's inability to muster the political will necessary to lead. Michele Flournoy and Ely Ratner, two key Obama administration national security officials, wrote that, if the TPP failed in Congress, "the leadership vacuum left by the U.S. would quickly be filled by other powers, most likely China."[62]

## The End of the TPP

That is precisely what happened. On his first day in office, President Donald Trump signed an executive order pulling the United States out of the TPP, which he described as "a rape of our country."[63] The order was unnecessary; Obama, seeing plainly the opposition on Capitol Hill, never submitted it for approval. Senator John McCain called Trump's move "a troubling signal of American disengagement in the Asia-Pacific region at a time we can least afford it."[64] Other senators, including Republican Jeff Flake and Democrat Sherrod Brown, agreed, calling Trump's action a "mistake" and the "wrong decision."[65] The US Trade Representative's Cutler recalled that the US exit from the TPP "showed our trading partners the US inability to follow through with its commitments in the trade arena, opening the door for China to fill the void."[66]

Leaders in Asia were even more frustrated. Upon hearing that Trump would withdraw, Japan's prime minister Shinzo Abe said that "the TPP would be meaningless without the United States," and Singapore's foreign minister K. Shanmugam argued that, absent the trade deal, the United States would be left only with military clout in Asia, which is "not the lever you want to use."[67] It didn't matter. The Trans-Pacific Partnership was, for the United States, dead. It would not be revived.

For its other members, however, the deal was very much alive. The remaining eleven signatories convened as the "TPP-11" and sought to conclude an agreement without the United States. Two years after America's withdrawal, the parties signed the Comprehensive and Progressive Agreement for Trans-Pacific Partnership (CPTPP), which entered into force in December 2018.[68] The CPTPP market comprised nearly 500 million people with a combined GDP of $13.5 trillion.[69] Three of four top US trade partners became CPTPP members, and the parties lowered tariffs and other trade barriers for each other but not for the United States. American manufacturing and agricultural exports to CPTPP countries today face tariffs higher than if the United States were a member, and the parties harmonized standards and regulations with each other.[70] Some American desires fell by the wayside on the path to agreement; while the vast majority of the TPP text was incorporated into CPTPP, the parties suspended twenty-two TPP commitments. All had been US priorities.[71]

Since its withdrawal, partners in the region have periodically called on the United States to reconsider. Australian finance minister Mathias Cormann in 2018 observed, "We'd like to think that over time the U.S. will want to have a piece of the action. . . . Asia-Pacific is the part of the world where most of the global growth will be generated for years to come and the U.S. as a great trading economy surely will want to have the same advantageous access to those markets as we will have."[72] In 2022, Japanese prime minister Fumio Kishida encouraged Washington to join CPTPP, and New Zealand prime minister Jacinda Ardern said that the new agreement represented the best way for the United States to engage economically with Asia. Singapore prime minister Lee Hsien Loong added that his country "would dearly love to see them come back."[73]

All this fell on deaf Washington ears. Joe Biden, who as vice president supported the TPP, by 2020 had come to oppose it. Jake Sullivan, who went on to serve as Biden's national security advisor, wrote that year with Jennifer Harris (who herself would work on economic policy in the Biden White House), "Whatever one thinks of the TPP, the national security community backed it unquestioningly without probing its actual contents. U.S. trade policy has suffered too many mistakes over the years to accept pro-deal arguments at face value."[74] US trade representative Katherine Tai, in declining to endorse the TPP or its CPTPP successor, said instead that "a lot has changed in terms of our own awareness about some of the pitfalls of the trade policies that we have pursued as we have pursued them over the most recent years."[75] Increasingly, Cutler observed, the United States was entering an age where "economic security issues are trumping traditional trade issues."[76] And for the second straight presidential administration, the United States refrained from expanding market access in Asia.

## China Fills the Gap

This, and the attendant surge in America's protectionist sentiment, created an opportunity for China. Immediately following the US withdrawal, Beijing sought to assume the mantle of global economic leadership. In his Davos remarks, Xi Jinping implicitly drew a distinction with the new Trump administration. Despite presiding over a Chinese economy far more closed than America's, Xi said that leaders should "commit ourselves to growing an open global economy," embrace "global free trade and investment," and "say no to protectionism."[77]

Key to Beijing's efforts was RCEP, the trade agreement that had started in 2011 as an ASEAN initiative but grew to encompass key Pacific economies. By 2020, the deal comprised roughly 30 percent of the world's population with $26.2 trillion of global output, making it larger than either the US-Mexico-Canada Agreement (USMCA, the successor to the North American Free Trade Agreement) or the European Union.[78] That year the ten ASEAN members signed RCEP along with Australia, China, Japan, New Zealand, and South Korea, and it came into force two years later. The pact committed its members to eliminate or reduce tariffs by more than 90 percent over twenty years, and it established common rules of origin for goods produced within the region.[79] Analysts and critics were quick to point out that RCEP standards were lower than those of

CPTPP or other high-quality free-trade agreements, and that the economic benefits to members would be modest.[80] Yet the overall signal was clear. "The diplomatic messaging of RCEP," a Citi Research report said, "may be just as important as the economics—a coup for China."[81]

China was now party to RCEP. Canada, Mexico, and others were members of CPTPP, and Japan, Australia, and New Zealand were party to both. The United States belonged to neither regional mega-deal, and during the Trump administration instead imposed or threatened a raft of tariffs on partners and adversaries alike. As countries in the region pursued greater trade liberalization and the United States did not, Washington was, in the words of two experts, "going backward by standing still."[82]

The economic and strategic costs of America's absence from regional trade deals remained clear to many policymakers. As Wendy Cutler and Clete Willems wrote, "these agreements work together to encourage Asia-Pacific countries to integrate their economies and link key supply chains with one another and with China instead of the United States." As a result of CPTPP and RCEP, they added, "the United States is less competitive and less influential in the region."[83] Yet the Biden administration, when pushed to reconsider America's approach to trade in Asia, showed little willingness to budge. Tai suggested a new approach that de-emphasized market access and barriers to trade, instead attempting to bolster key supply chains and reduce dependencies on countries like China. "A lot of the assumptions that we have based our trade programs on," she said, "ha[ve] maximized efficiency without regard to the requirement for resilience."[84] Free trade was risk rather than opportunity.

## Economic Policy in Asia after the TPP

For months during the Biden administration's first year, rumors swirled that it would pursue a regional digital trade agreement in the Pacific. If a return to the TPP was off the table, and the costs of a total US absence from the Asian trade game remained steep, a digital trade pact could represent a middle course. USMCA had a digital trade chapter that had been negotiated and was agreed to by Congress (which, ironically, was essentially lifted from the TPP agreement Trump so vociferously rejected); its provisions could be adapted for a Pacific setting. The administration could also draw on CPTPP's e-commerce chapter, which reflected many US priorities, as well as on the bilateral US-Japan digital trade agreement signed in 2019.[85]

The possibility seemed unusually promising to those stung by the TPP's failure. Former World Bank president Robert Zoellick, for instance, wrote that in the absence of an agreed framework, "others are dictating the maxims of the digital economy." China, he said, "demands authoritarian controls and data local-ization, restricts transfers, discriminates, constrains technology choice, compels transfers of software, and favors national champions. Other countries, espe-cially in Asia, are adopting parts of the Chinese model."[86] David Feith, a senior China official in the Trump State Department, noted that the digital economy comprised some 10 percent of US GDP and added, "The case for expanding U.S. digital trade in the Indo-Pacific is strong because digital trade is important, and the Indo-Pacific is important."[87]

The political logic seemed impeccable: a Pacific digital trade pact would es-tablish rules in the areas most in need of them, signal America's renewed interest in regional economic leadership, and yet would not stir the political opposition that had defeated the TPP. For TPP supporters, such a deal could forge a building block for a more ambitious agenda later; for opponents, a digital deal would ex-clude the most politically sensitive areas like automobiles and agriculture.

Members of Congress, the US Chamber of Commerce, Asia policy experts, and others openly called on the administration to act.[88] Biden administration officials quietly suggested that a digital trade agreement might even become the new economic centerpiece of their forthcoming Indo-Pacific strategy.[89] Kurt Campbell, the NSC Indo-Pacific coordinator, observed that "[w]e cannot be suc-cessful without a positive trade agenda in the region. We're looking closely at what might be possible on the digital front."[90]

It was not to be. Trade Representative Tai reportedly saw the effort as incon-sistent with a "worker-centered" approach to trade—one that focused on issues like union rights and forced labor—and believed a digital agreement would be unpopular with Capitol Hill Democrats and some Republicans.[91] There would be no return to the TPP, no digital trade agreement, and no other US-led regional market access initiative.

## The Indo-Pacific Economic Framework

In September 2021, however, Beijing issued a shot across the bow. That month Beijing formally applied to join CPTPP, the regional trade pact that had replaced the TPP and had largely been authored by the United States. Skeptics dismissed the move, pointing out that Beijing was hardly likely to meet the stringent standards required for membership.[92] But China's bold move had strategic logic. As China expert Carla Freeman observed, Beijing's CPTPP bid highlighted Washington's absence from Pacific trade agreements. If it did win entry, China could shape the agreement, including by blocking Taiwan's entry and potentially even blunting any eventual US return.[93] Even if it did not soon become party, CPTPP members—including many US partners—would now have to navigate between Chinese pressure to join and their own desires to keep Beijing out.

The result was a Solomonic judgment on economic engagement with the Pacific. The Biden administration recognized that US inaction was harming the US position in Asia but also sought to avoid new trade accords. It responded with the Indo-Pacific Economic Framework for Prosperity (IPEF). The initiative aimed to create a "stronger, fairer, more resilient economy for families, workers, and businesses in the United States and in the Indo-Pacific region."[94] It would do so via four pillars: the "connected economy," focused on rules and standards for the digital economy; the "resilient economy" that aimed to create more secure supply chains; the "clean economy," focused on clean energy and decarbonization; and the "fair economy" that would seek commitments on tax, anti–money laundering, and anti-bribery measures.[95] How precisely the administration would make progress in these areas, and how it might implement any agreements, remained opaque.

Instead, IPEF was defined more by what it was *not*. Administration officials made clear that market access would not be part of the effort. Nor would it result in anything requiring congressional approval. The upshot was, as one trade expert observed, that "IPEF negotiations may deliver amazing new rules and standards to underpin resilient supply chains for a cleaner and fairer economy. But in order for American companies to take advantage of those fantastic new rules, they need market access."[96]

IPEF was better than nothing, but how much better remained to be seen. Still, the administration and partner governments made the most of it. Announcing the initiative, Biden observed that "[t]he future of the 21st century economy is going to be largely written in the Indo-Pacific—in our region," and that the member countries "are signing up to work toward an economic vision that will deliver for all peoples."[97] Secretary of Commerce Gina Raimondo called it "by any account the most significant economic agreement that the United States has ever had in this region."[98] India's finance minister described the framework as a "fantastic thought," and her government joined the talks.[99] Japanese trade minister Yasutoshi Nishimura added, "The United States clearly showed its economic re-engagement in the Indo-Pacific region. It is extremely significant."[100] Australia's trade minister observed that "[l]aunching IPEF negotiations is a significant step in the future of greater economic cooperation in the Indo-Pacific region."[101] Singapore prime minister Lee Hsien Loong added, "The IPEF is of both strategic and economic significance."[102]

The story was different behind the scenes. Senior policymakers across the Indo-Pacific insisted that they would publicly acclaim IPEF, as a way both of welcoming American economic re-engagement and signaling to China that alternatives existed. Yet they were, by and large, very dissatisfied with scope of the initiative, which they saw as a thin replacement for US membership in CPTPP. A senior Japanese official said privately that while his government was publicly trumpeting IPEF, it was no substitute for a genuine American trade policy.[103] Australian officials added their hope that IPEF would represent a steppingstone to CPTPP, and warned that they might not be able to oppose China's membership application forever.[104] Biden's Asia policy officials asked that their counterparts help make IPEF a success; even a relatively minor victory could prompt a rethinking in Washington on trade, and one day even lead back to the TPP.[105]

Even the modest IPEF accord proved too much for Washington politics. Negotiators wrapped agreed text on the four pillars ahead of the November 2023 summit of APEC leaders in San Francisco. Three of them—on supply chains, clean energy, and anti-corruption efforts—survived. The trade pillar did not, and the United States itself withdrew it, stunning its negotiating partners. Though the deal offered no US market access to trade partners—It focused on rules and trade facilitation—the White House reportedly worried about negative political implications for Democratic senators facing reelection in 2024.[106] For the time being, at least, any agreement smacking of trade—even of the modest, limited IPEF variety—seemed too much weight for US domestic politics to bear. Emily Kilcrease, an economic policy expert at the Center for a New American Security, described the defeat as "US trade policy hitting rock bottom."[107]

## A Negative Economic Agenda

In the decade-plus following the Pivot's announcement, America's positive economic agenda in Asia—opening markets, lowering barriers to trade, sealing agreements—bore virtually no fruit. Its negative, or defensive, agenda, however, gathered ever-greater support and became the focus of US economic policy in the region. Instead of lowering tariffs, the United States raised them; rather than increasing market access, Washington imposed sanctions; in place of facilitating globalized supply chains, it moved to de-risk and "friendshore" them; instead of creating new arrangements abroad, the United States established new institutions at home. The driver of nearly all this activity was China.

Two Chinese efforts, the BRI initiative, launched in 2013, and the AIIB, established in 2016, represented opening salvos in an era of heightened US-China economic competition. For years Beijing had financed ever-increasing levels of foreign infrastructure investment—by 2016, for example, China passed Japan as Southeast Asia's largest bilateral financier of infrastructure.[108] Through BRI, Beijing aimed to produce returns through overseas investment, create jobs for Chinese contractors, access natural resources held abroad, expand its export markets, and, not incidentally, expand Beijing's influence.[109]

Before diminishing in recent years, the scale and scope of BRI were astonishing. Over the course of a decade, Beijing issued some $1 trillion in loans and other funds for projects across 150 countries in Asia, Europe, Africa, and the Western Hemisphere.[110] This raised eyebrows—and worries—in Washington and friendly capitals. As economist Roland Rajah observed, "There is much geopolitical angst, particularly in the United States, about the role of BRI as a form of economic statecraft intended to enhance China's influence through state-directed investment and the creation of a more Sino-centric regional order."[111]

Indeed. INDOPACOM commander Admiral Philip Davidson called BRI "a stalking horse to advance Chinese security concerns" and Japan pointed to BRI infrastructure projects as a way of expanding PLA presence into the Indian and Pacific Oceans, as well as Africa and Europe.[112] Vice President Mike Pence in 2018 urged countries, "Do not accept foreign debt that could compromise your sovereignty. . . . The United States deals openly, fairly. We do not offer a constricting belt or a one-way road."[113] Policymakers worried that BRI would fund dual-use port projects that could one day support PLA navy operations. They also fretted that the Digital Silk Road, an element of BRI that aimed to boost telecommunications networks, cloud computing, AI capabilities, and surveillance technology, would help China collect foreign data, make technology enhancements, and export repressive surveillance tools.[114] BRI-related contracts frequently barred borrowers from pursuing collective restructuring (e.g., via the Paris Club, an informal group of official creditors who coordinate to relieve payment problems in debtor countries) or even revealing the existence of debt.[115] As a result, policymakers feared that Beijing would provide loans to governments subsequently incapable of repayment, catching them in a "debt trap."[116]

Danny Russel, the State Department's top Asia official during Obama's second term, summarized the state of affairs, writing, "We are witnessing the emergence of an integrated set of Belt and Road-related initiatives combining dual-use infrastructure, Smart Ports and Cities, and space and digital systems. These programs contribute to building a BRI ecosystem that serves to magnify Beijing's influence well beyond the economic sphere. Beijing's BRI strategy bolsters its technological, economic, political, and security interests and affords it increased rule-setting power."[117]

BRI was not the only Chinese economic initiative on Washington's radar. AIIB-supplied funding would provide capital for infrastructure throughout the region, accelerate development in countries starved for infrastructure improvements, and give China the influence it lacked in institutions like the World Bank, the Asian Development Bank, and the IMF. The Obama administration saw the AIIB as a means to water down existing standards for loans and grants and to boost China's regional influence. Publicly opposing the bank, administration officials urged countries not to join.[118]

Their efforts came to naught. Disparaging the bank, while Asia's infrastructure needs remained vast and the United States offered little in new funding alternatives, proved an unsustainable position. In a short time, Britain joined the bank, as did Australia, South Korea, Germany, France, and Italy. If Washington could not convince wealthy, allied countries to oppose AIIB, the chances of it doing so with countries in greater economic need was lower still. As former Treasury secretary Lawrence Summers observed, "We're contemplating a major institution in which the United States has no role, that the United States made substantial efforts to stop—and failed."[119] The bank went forward, and by 2021 the AIIB boasted over 100 countries as members.[120] In membership terms, it became the world's second largest development bank, disbursing most loans to co-finance projects with the World Bank or the Asian Development Bank.[121]

BRI, AIIB, and other Chinese infrastructure efforts galvanized a set of American responses. After Congress passed the BUILD Act, the Development Finance Corporation (DFC), with a $60 billion funding cap, began making loans and providing loan guarantees, insurance, and equity financing for companies investing in developing countries.[122] By mobilizing private-sector capital, the new institution aimed to compete with BRI without replicating the Chinese model. The following year, Congress passed an unprecedented seven-year authorization for the Export-Import (EXIM) Bank, and directed it to offer lower interest rates and more flexible lending terms that could compete with Chinese loans in technology sectors.[123]

In 2019, the Trump administration announced the Blue Dot Network, a joint initiative with Japan and Australia to certify infrastructure projects meeting governance and transparency standards.[124] By applying a Blue Dot seal of approval, the effort aimed to catalyze private-sector funding reassured of projects' soundness. A year later, the State Department announced its Clean Network Initiative, an effort to safeguard personal and corporate data "from aggressive intrusions by malign actors, such as the Chinese Communist Party."[125] Among its goals was to ensure that Chinese telecommunications carriers would not be connected to the US network, that Americans' data was not stored on cloud-based systems accessible to China, and that undersea cables were "not subverted for intelligence gathering by the PRC at hyper scale."[126] Upon taking office, the Biden administration launched the Build Back Better World (B3W) Initiative to "meet the enormous infrastructure needs of low- and middle-income countries."[127]

Both the Trump and Biden administrations enlisted traditional partners to compete with Beijing's infrastructure investments. In 2018, the United States, Japan, and Australia established the Trilateral Partnership for Infrastructure Investment in the Indo-Pacific to strengthen their collective efforts, and the G7 in 2022 announced a Partnership for Global Infrastructure Investments (PGII, which subsumed B3W) to counter BRI by mobilizing a total of $600 billion over five years, mostly from the private sector, for "sustainable, quality" infrastructure investment.[128]

For a number of these initiatives, aspirations outran results. A 2022 report on the Blue Dot Network, for instance, found that the program "lacks dedicated staff to vet projects, and provides nowhere for an applicant to submit a project for review."[129] The White House pledged that B3W would "collectively catalyze hundreds of billions of dollars of infrastructure investment but, a year after its announcement, its commitments totaled only $6 million.[130] The DFC's authorized cap stands at some $60 billion, but the Biden administration's fiscal year 2023 budget request totaled just $1 billion.[131] Three years after the Trilateral Partnership was established, it had initiated just one project, a $20 million undersea fiber optic cable to connect Palau.[132]

Despite much distress about the gap between US infrastructure funding and the vast sums China mobilized, Beijing appeared to have its own second thoughts. One country's debt trap is, after all, another's nonperforming loan, and by 2022, almost 60 percent of China's overseas loans were held by countries in financial distress, up from 5 percent in 2010.[133] Starting in 2021, Beijing reduced lending for large infrastructure projects by over 90 percent.[134] China emerged as the developing world's largest creditor but, after spending $1 trillion on infrastructure projects, it sought to overhaul BRI.[135]

## Huawei

The US-China infrastructure competition turned not only on which country would spend how much and where, but also on specific companies and services. Huawei, the Chinese telecommunications company that provides 5G infrastructure, emerged as a central flashpoint. Washington charged Huawei with violating sanctions on Iran and North Korea and claimed that, under Chinese law, any data passing over Huawei-built or operated systems would be subject to seizure by the government.[136] The Trump administration discerned a national security threat not only in the possible provision of Huawei 5G infrastructure in the United States but also in other countries' use of it.

Washington's response exemplified its turn toward a defensive economic policy when it came to China. In 2017, Congress moved to bar the use of Huawei equipment in some Defense Department networks, and the following year the Trump administration expanded the prohibition to other government agencies. An executive order in 2018 barred US companies from doing business with Huawei, and the Commerce Department added Huawei to the Entity List, a roster of national security threats for which Americans require licenses to do business.[137] The Federal Communications Commission in 2020 designated the company a national security threat, eliminating its access to federal broadband subsidies.[138] The Biden administration kept the raft of restrictions in place and expanded them; it stopped granting licenses to do business with Huawei in January 2023, and mulled revoking existing licenses.[139]

## Trump's Trade War

Washington's defensive economic agenda was hardly limited to infrastructure. Trump entered office blaming China for persistent US trade deficits and for stealing American jobs—"the greatest theft in the history of the world," he called it. In response, he imposed multiple rounds of tariffs on the import of Chinese goods.[140] In four separate actions, the administration imposed tariffs on a total of $370 billion in Chinese imports.[141] Between 2018 and 2020, the average US duty on Chinese products rose from 3.1 percent to 21 percent.[142]

The tariff war did not reduce the US trade deficit, which actually rose, from $568 billion in 2017 to $861 billion in 2021.[143] It also imposed costs on the US economy. Moody's Analytics estimated that the trade war cost 300,000 jobs from early 2018 through fall 2020, and the US government provided some $28 billion in federal support to farmers hurt by Chinese retaliation after tariffs took effect.[144] To win relief from the tariffs, Beijing agreed to purchase some $200 billion in American goods in 2020 and 2021. It never came close to fulfilling the commitment.[145] Nor did the protections prove just a Trump-era enthusiasm; the Biden administration retained all of the tariffs on China after taking office.[146] An analysis compared US exports to China relative to their projected levels, had they had grown at the same rate as China's imports from the world; it found American exports to China in 2022 were 23 percent lower than the trend.[147]

This period saw still more defensive and coercive economic moves. Trump in 2018 signed the Foreign Investment Risk Review Modernization Act, expanding the reach of investigations conducted by the Committee on Foreign Investment in the United States. As one legal analysis put it, " 'Modernization' is a euphemism for addressing concerns about Chinese investments."[148] In 2020, after Beijing moved to extinguish democracy in Hong Kong by rescinding its autonomous political system, the administration revoked the territory's special economic status.[149] And in 2021, Congress passed a law barring imports from Xinjiang unless businesses could prove that they were made without forced labor.[150]

## Biden Crosses a Rubicon: Export Controls

In October 2022, the Biden administration went a step further by imposing export controls on advanced semiconductors used for supercomputing. As previously elaborated, the controls aim to keep China as far behind as possible in its development of key technologies.[151] By issuing this arcane rule in a technical area of US-China economic relations, the administration took a last step in inverting the economic Pivot's original logic. In her original article, Secretary Clinton wrote, "Some in China worry that America seeks to constrain China's growth. We reject both those views. The fact is that a thriving America is good for China and a thriving China is good for America."[152] This was hardly an isolated view, and the Trump and Biden administrations affirmed it.

Yet it appeared those days were gone. Given the importance of advanced semiconductors to a modern economy, the policy's effect—if not its intent—would be to constrain Chinese growth. A year after imposing them, the Department of Commerce strengthened the restrictions and administration officials hinted at similar controls in other areas.[153] In August 2023, the administration established the first-ever US government process for reviewing—and potentially blocking—outbound investment in semiconductors, quantum information technologies, and particular artificial intelligence capabilities. The new regime applied to "countries of concern," with China foremost among them.[154] One journalist described matters well. "The White House and Congress," he wrote, "are quietly reshaping the American economic relationship with the world's second-largest economic power, enacting a strategy to limit China's technological development."[155] At the same time, efforts like the CHIPS and Science act began funneling tens of billions of dollars toward reshoring semiconductor manufacturing and funding homegrown technology development.[156] Industrial policy, now seen as vital to competing effectively with China, became popular among Democrats and Republicans alike.[157]

Administration officials insisted that the new policies focused only on national security risks and potential human rights violations, and that they would not color the entirety of US-China economic relations. Jake Sullivan in April 2023 said, "We are for de-risking and diversifying, not decoupling. . . . We are not cutting off trade."[158] Treasury Secretary Janet Yellen, who visited Beijing in July 2023, said, "We know that a decoupling of the world's two largest economies would be disastrous for both countries and destabilizing for the world. And it would be virtually impossible to undertake."[159] And in fact, for all the tariffs, export controls, licensing requirements, and investment reviews, US-China trade continued to rise during the Trump and Biden years, reaching a record high $690 billion in 2022.[160] The US trade deficit with China—the ostensible target of so much activity—reached $383 billion that year, the second-highest level ever.[161]

China's economic gravity remained undeniable. In a 2022 poll of Southeast Asian policymakers and experts, more than 75 percent believed that China was the region's most economically influential power. Just 10 percent gave that designation to the United States.[162] The numbers backed up their perception. China's total trade with the ten ASEAN nations, for instance, grew 71 percent from July

2018 to December 2022.[163] In 2022, China did more than twice as much trade with Southeast Asia than did the United States, and it was the largest trading partner of nearly every Asian country.[164]

More than a decade after the Pivot's announcement, its original economic goals seem almost quaint. The notion of Chinese political liberalization through trade and globalization was abandoned years ago. The hopes of a US-led, Pacific-wide free-trade agreement came to naught. Most of the way through the Biden administration's first term, the shift from a positive, offensive economic agenda in Asia to negative, defensive policies on China was nearly complete. Whether the United States could muster the political will necessary to combine the two remained to be seen.

# 13

# Competition and Cooperation

## Transnational Issues and the Pivot

From the outset, the Pivot's architects pursued progress on a series of transnational issues and wished to advance universal values. Much of its initial framing, and most of the activity that flowed from it, were directed at nation-states and issues related to hard security, economic relationships, and diplomatic signaling. To harness Asia's economic opportunity, hedge against China's rise, and demonstrate long-term American engagement and presence, policymakers focused on traditional issues and instruments of statecraft: summits and gatherings, military posture and exercises, trade agreements and commercial deals. Yet transnational issues and values entered into—and sometimes faded from—the set of policies to which the Pivot gave rise.

In her Pivot article, Secretary Clinton stressed that "even more than our military might or the size of our economy, our most potent asset as a nation is the power of our values—in particular, our steadfast support for democracy and human rights. This . . . is at the heart of our foreign policy, including our strategic turn to the Asia-Pacific region." The administration would urge autocratic partners to reform, she said, and its "serious concerns about human rights" in China included the detention or disappearance of public-interest lawyers, writers, artists, and others.[1] She referenced climate change in the Pacific Islands, health issues in Southeast Asia, and counterterrorism efforts in the Philippines.[2] In his speech before the Australian parliament in 2011, President Obama defined "the future we seek in the Asia-Pacific" as including security, prosperity, and "dignity for all," and he stressed the need to work with other countries on climate efforts, including clean energy.[3] The next year, National Security Advisor Tom Donilon observed that the United States sought an Asian future "where citizens increasingly have the ability to influence their governments and universal human rights are upheld."[4] He noted American efforts to support democratic transitions in the Philippines, Indonesia, and Burma, and added that US-China cooperation would be necessary to combat climate change. A year and a half later, in explaining "what rebalancing is, and what it isn't," Donilon listed "respect for universal rights and freedoms" as a core objective.[5]

As the Pivot's early proponents included transnational issues—climate, global health, nonproliferation, technology, counterterrorism, and human rights—in their agenda, they also sought new vehicles to promote their goals. Asia's regional diplomatic architecture took center stage. The Obama administration promised deeper engagement in APEC and the ASEAN Regional Forum.[6] Administration officials also created new diplomatic frameworks, including "minilateral" arrangements like the Lower Mekong Initiative, which took shape in 2009 to boost cooperation in the environment, health, education, and infrastructure between the United States and the four Lower Mekong Countries.[7]

While the specific emphasis shifted, the effort to promote key objectives across a range of transnational issues endured through three very different administrations. The emphasis on a values-based component of US policy in Asia remained as well, though the focus of that effort, and its translation from rhetoric to actual policy, veered wildly over the years. Washington continually shifted its efforts at regional architecture as well, focusing early on APEC and EAS, later reviving the Quad, and most recently developing new frameworks like AUKUS.

Tensions ran throughout the efforts. Some were endemic to American foreign policy: How far should Washington push allies like Thailand and the Philippines as they slid backward on democracy and human rights, if that meant they were less willing to work with the United States on China or terrorism? If the Pivot was a hedge against rising Chinese power, could Washington simultaneously work with Beijing in areas of shared interest, like climate change and public health? Would the raft of multilateral bodies strengthen or supplant bilateral alliances and relationships? Other dilemmas, like the role technology should play in interconnected economies, were more novel.

No single coherent strategic concept has ever answered all these questions. In the decade-plus effort to reorient US foreign policy toward Asia, the pursuit of transnational objectives and the support of values generally played second fiddle to the more tangible goals of security, prosperity, and diplomatic presence. Yet they remained ever-present, constantly moving in and out of America's agenda in the Indo-Pacific. Managing these issues was replete with adjustment and improvisation, more akin to jazz than classical music.

## Climate Change

Barack Obama entered office promising to combat climate change. "Delay is no longer an option," he announced, and "denial is no longer an acceptable response.[8] Many expected the new president to seek cap-and-trade legislation that would limit greenhouse gases and then press China and India to announce their own emissions targets.[9] In the event, no such legislation would pass, and the administration did not succeed in its early efforts to secure a treaty that would replace the Kyoto Protocol, the climate pact that exempted developing countries like China and India from emissions targets.[10] But its ambition to tackle the warming climate, and the sense that China had to be part of any potential solution, endured.

By 2014, three years after the Pivot's initial announcement, the United States and China reached an agreement to seek a legally binding commitment to limit emissions.[11] By announcing new targets, the two governments said, they hoped to "inject momentum into the global climate negotiations and inspire other countries to join in coming forward with ambitious actions," preferably by 2015.[12] They did. In December 2015, some 196 countries adopted the Paris Agreement, a legally binding treaty that sought to limit the rise in the global average temperature to two degrees Celsius above pre-industrial levels.[13] Each party to the agreement was required to submit a national climate action plan, listing the steps it would take to reduce emissions.

The administration, and indeed much of the world, saw both the United States and China as key to any climate solution. While in 2005 China's carbon dioxide emissions equaled those of the United States, a decade later its total $CO_2$ emissions were twice America's. The United States, however, stood as the world's second-largest producer of carbon dioxide per capita, with its level twice as high as those of both China and the European Union.[14] In a statement on "advancing the rebalance to Asia," the White House observed, "Asia is home to several of the world's largest greenhouse gas emitters and to many populations that are vulnerable to the impacts of climate change. . . . We will continue to strengthen our cooperation with China, including on clean energy research, development, and deployment."[15]

This new spirit of cooperation differed significantly from the previous two decades. Over those years, the United States consistently stressed the need for China—whose emissions were rising rapidly and were projected to continue—to reduce its carbon outputs. Any global effort that excluded China—as did the Kyoto Protocol—was seen by Washington as politically unsaleable and environmentally ineffective. Beijing, on the other hand, stressed its developing economy status and relatively low level of per capita emissions. It would be patently unfair, Chinese leaders said, to limit their country's economic development after Western countries were chiefly responsible for the climate problem in the first place.[16] By 2016, however, such sentiments were shifting.

The new era would not last long. Five months after taking office, President Trump announced that the United States would "cease all implementation of the Paris Agreement" and withdraw completely from the pact.[17] Citing the costs that compliance would impose on American workers, Trump charged that "China will be able to increase these emissions by a staggering number of years—13" and it would be "allowed to build hundreds of additional coal plants." India, he added, "makes its participation contingent on receiving billions and billions and billions of dollars in foreign aid from developed countries." The Paris Accord was, he said, "very unfair, at the highest level, to the United States."[18] H. R. McMaster, Trump's national security advisor, later pointed out that between 2006 and 2020, China built fifty to seventy coal-burning power plants each year. Xi Jinping, he added, "talks a good game on the environment" but by 2019 produced more carbon emissions than the United States and European Union combined.[19]

The possibility of US-China cooperation on climate change was long held up—and indeed, still is—as the paradigmatic example of how two increasingly rivalrous countries could nevertheless collaborate in areas of shared interest. Neither would benefit from a warming planet, and both stood to lose from one. Despite their competition across a range of other issues, climate change—like other transnational issues—should surely prove an exception to the rising tensions. Yet during the Trump administration, many of these very issues, including climate change, did not prove a source of bilateral cooperation, but rather created new vectors for competition.

The Biden administration took office determined to reverse that dynamic. On his first day in office, the new president rejoined the Paris Agreement.[20] In September 2021, US climate envoy John Kerry visited China for climate talks, revealing in the process a stark difference in approaches. For Kerry and the Biden administration, rising tensions in the relationship need not diminish cooperation in areas like climate. "It's not a geostrategic weapon or tool," Kerry said. "It's a global, not bilateral challenge."[21] By contrast, Foreign Minister Wang Yi warned that climate cooperation "cannot possibly be divorced" from the relationship's other components. "The U.S. side hopes," Wang said, "that climate cooperation can be an 'oasis' in China-US relations, but if that 'oasis' is surrounded by desert, it will also become desertified sooner or later."[22]

Nevertheless, after Kerry pressed Beijing to cease building coal-based power plants, China later that month made a surprise announcement. Speaking to the UN General Assembly, Xi announced that Beijing would no longer build coal-fired power projects abroad, and would instead help countries develop green and low carbon energy.[23] The new policy did not affect domestic coal-fired plants, and China continued constructing new ones at home and increasing its coal consumption.[24] Nevertheless, the announcement suggested that bilateral collaboration on shared interests could be insulated against the withering effects of rising competition. This sense grew stronger when, at the COP26 climate conference in November 2021, Kerry announced a US-China agreement to accelerate emissions reductions by sharing technology, leading a multilateral working group, and announcing new national targets by 2025.[25]

Delinking transnational issues from bilateral ones did not, however, survive tensions over Taiwan. Just months before the COP27 international climate summit, Beijing suspended bilateral climate talks in retaliation for Speaker of the House Nancy Pelosi's visit to Taiwan in August 2022. Kerry stuck to his guns. "No country," he insisted, "should withhold progress on existential transnational issues because of bilateral differences." Suspending cooperation "doesn't punish the United States—it punishes the world, particularly the developing world."[26]

Chinese leaders saw things differently. The "indispensable condition of China-US climate change cooperation," the Foreign Ministry said, was for the United States to "dispel the negative influence of Pelosi scuttling to Taiwan."[27] Beijing would not agree simply to delink issues, nor to cooperate in some areas while competing vigorously in others. The tensions that attended bilateral issues infected the spirit of collaboration on transnational ones. A few months later, Biden and Xi agreed to restart climate talks, and in November 2023 the two sides issued a joint statement pledging enhanced cooperation.[28] Still, hopes for what they might accomplish diminished. Biden administration officials continued to stress their desire to work with China on climate even as they explicitly opposed Chinese actions on virtually every other issue. The oft-invoked "mix of competition and cooperation" that should ideally characterize the US-China relationship proved easier said than done.[29]

## Global Health

If there was one transnational challenge that seemed insulated from the vicissitudes of geopolitical competition, public health represented a prime candidate. In 2009, two years before the Pivot announcement, the United States and China agreed to conduct joint health research, including on stem cells, and to cooperate on H1N1 and avian influenza prevention.[30] Generally the province of doctors, scientists, and technical officials, public health appeared a particularly promising area for US partnerships in Asia. As one expert observed in 2011, "While we are told that a critical element of the US pivot strategy is to nurture partnerships to address important common challenges, our rebalancing efforts thus far have focused almost solely on security and trade . . . other issues, like health and the environment, challenge us to promote jointly the welfare of people in the Asia-Pacific region, which still accounts for a majority of the global disease burden."[31]

To these ends, the United States and China coordinated efforts in responding to the 2014 Ebola epidemic, with Washington providing funding and personnel and Beijing sending supplies and medical workers to afflicted areas.[32] A year later, the White House pledged to work with Australia, South Korea, and Japan to combat malaria and tuberculosis in Southeast Asia, and to boost immunization and nutrition across the region.[33] These and other efforts were quiet, routine, and uncontroversial.

The COVID virus outbreak, which originated in Wuhan, China, in 2019, utterly upended the role of public health in US policy toward Asia. The United States and China, along with every country in the Indo-Pacific, shared a keen interest in containing the outbreak. None stood to benefit from the virus's spread, or from the severe human and economic costs that would attend a large-scale pandemic. Given their previous record of collaboration on similar issues, one might expect Washington and Beijing to share data on the virus's spread, to work together to determine its origin, to pursue joint research toward therapeutics and a COVID vaccine, and to identify ways to prevent the next global pandemic from emerging.

None of this happened. As China expert Bonnie Glaser observed, "Rather than seek cooperation to mitigate the COVID-19 crisis as they did in response to the global financial crisis and the Ebola outbreak, Beijing and Washington are engaged in a rancorous struggle over where and how the virus began."[34] President Trump repeatedly blamed Beijing for what he called the "China virus," saying, "It could have been stopped right where it came from, China. . . . The world is paying a very big price for what they did."[35] China's Foreign Ministry spokesman touted baseless conspiracy theories that the US Army planted the COVID virus in Wuhan.[36] What could have been an opportunity for cooperation amid rising bilateral competition turned instead into a primary vector for rivalry and a source of ever-greater tension.

Over the course of 2020 and 2021, this rivalry played out in the provision of medical aid to third countries and the development of vaccines. The United States joined its Quad counterparts to announce the supply of one billion COVID vaccine doses for Southeast Asia.[37] China coupled medical aid with requests that countries demonstrate public gratitude toward Beijing and support for its foreign policy positions.[38] For both countries, "vaccine diplomacy" became an effort to project soft power, improve their image, increase influence, and blunt that of their rival.[39]

The triumph of competition over cooperation manifested itself in multilateral venues as well. In May 2020, with the virus raging uncontrollably, the WHO held a meeting intended to coordinate a global response. Xi Jinping announced the donation of $2 billion in assistance and said that China would send medical supplies and personnel to Africa and developing countries elsewhere.[40] President Trump, who had cut off US funding to the WHO the previous month, accused the organization of an "alarming lack of independence from the People's Republic of China" and threatened to withdraw US membership.[41] His administration in July 2020 formally notified the UN that the United States would withdraw from the WHO.[42]

Biden immediately reversed the move after taking office in January 2021, but again, the sequence of events demonstrated the great difficulty of forging US-China cooperation on even the most acute transnational challenges.[43] Colin Kahl and Thomas Wright, who went on to serve as senior Biden administration officials, observed, "There is never a good time for a pandemic, but the novel coronavirus hit the world at perhaps the worst possible moment, when international cooperation had largely broken down after a tumultuous decade. . . . The US-China rivalry overshadowed nearly everything."[44]

## Counterterrorism

In the decade before the Pivot's announcement, terrorism was far and away the transnational challenge that drew the most American focus and resources. Testifying before Congress in 2003, the commander of US Pacific Command said, "Our highest USPACOM priority is sustaining and supporting the GWOT [Global War on Terror]. This includes not only operations in the Pacific, but also as a force provider to operations in Afghanistan and Iraq."[45] Within the region, many worried that Southeast Asia would emerge as the "second front" in the war on terror, after the greater Middle East.[46] US special forces deployed to the Philippines, assisting the country's military in fighting the al-Qaeda-linked Abu Sayyaf Group in Mindanao.[47] The United States helped Thailand capture a senior Jemaah Islamiyah leader responsible for deadly bombings in Bali, and the CIA operated a "black site" in Thailand.[48] The United States and Australia trained an elite Indonesian counterterrorism force, Detachment 88, that sought to disrupt Jemaah Islamiyah.[49] Washington spurred multilateral cooperation initiatives like the Container Security Initiative, the Proliferation Security Initiative, and the Regional Maritime Security Initiative in which Asian nations played key roles.[50] And the United States established key bilateral counterterrorism relationships over the course of the decade, including with Indonesia, the Philippines, Singapore, Thailand, and Australia.[51]

The Pivot to Asia represented, to a large degree, an effort to shift America's hyper-focus on terrorism to the security, economic, and transnational issues more salient in the Indo-Pacific. By acting in a more targeted way against terrorist threats, and by ending the wars in Iraq and Afghanistan, the Obama administration hoped to right-size the US response, freeing up resources and diplomatic bandwidth for other purposes. Yet if Washington hoped to be done with terrorism, terrorism was not yet done with the United States. After the withdrawal of American troops from Iraq in 2011, ISIS created history's largest-ever terrorist sanctuary across Iraq and Syria. Tens of thousands of foreign fighters descended on the region to participate in the establishment of a new caliphate, and the group began planning attacks in Europe and inspiring attacks in the United States. The terrorist threat came roaring back.

By 2014, just three years after the Pivot's announcement, American troops returned to Iraq, and they subsequently deployed to Syria as well. The United States commenced an intensive, five-year military campaign to destroy the ISIS caliphate, and forged a global coalition to defeat the terrorist group. The coalition included a number of Indo-Pacific countries, including Australia, Japan, Malaysia, New Zealand, the Philippines, Singapore, and South Korea.[52] The new effort influenced US policy across the board, including in Asia. Participating in the 2015 ASEAN and East Asia Summits, for instance, Obama attempted to rally countries to cooperate in the fight. Much of his time at the summits, he said, was spent "focused on the urgent threat of terrorism."[53] The US government reacted internally to ISIS's rise as well, including by launching a Global Engagement Center (GEC) designed, in Obama's description, to "empower voices that are countering ISIL's perversion of Islam."[54]

Not only did the United States seek Asian cooperation in the fight against ISIS in Iraq and Syria, but it also saw the spread of ISIS ideology to the region itself. In 2017, an ISIS offshoot attacked Marawi, a city on the southern Philippine island of Mindanao. US special forces deployed to the area and assisted the Philippines armed forces in their successful five-month effort to retake the city.[55] American troops did not take part in direct combat but supported their Philippine counterparts with advice and intelligence.

With the destruction of ISIS's physical caliphate in Iraq and Syria—and the enduring, indefinite presence of US troops in both countries—alongside the liberation of Marawi and the degradation of other Asia-based terrorist groups like Abu Sayyaf and Jemaah Islamiyah, the United States made a renewed effort to pivot from a counterterrorism focus to one more suited to the nation-state rivalries increasingly shaping Indo-Pacific affairs. Perhaps surprisingly, it was the Trump administration, not the Obama team, that formalized the shift. In its 2018 National Defense Strategy, the administration announced that "inter-state strategic competition, not terrorism, is now the primary concern in US national security."[56]

This time, the shift would last. Over the subsequent years, the United States would nod to the enduring terrorist threat in Asia and elsewhere and continue its counterterrorism activities, but they would not again assume a place of priority. In the 2021 AUSMIN statement, for example, Washington and Canberra pledged not only to counter extremist groups abroad, but also "the rise in Racially or Ethnically Motivated Violent Extremism."[57] The Biden administration's 2022 Indo-Pacific Strategy made just one passing reference to terrorism, and the INDOPACOM commander observed that what while "violent extremism remains an ever-present threat . . . the most comprehensive and urgent challenge to US national security interests is the increasingly provocative efforts to subvert the international system to suit . . . authoritarian preferences."[58] Even the State Department's GEC, established to counter jihadist narratives, now moved to address "state and non-state propaganda and disinformation efforts."[59]

The fall of Afghanistan to the Taliban posed new dilemmas. In March 2023, less than two years after the full withdrawal of US forces from Afghanistan, US CENTCOM commander Gen. Michael Kurilla warned that ISIS-K, the Islamic State's Afghan offshoot, had designs on attacking the West and could conduct external operations within six months.[60] Other senior defense and intelligence officials concurred in the assessment of ISIS-K's intentions and capabilities.[61] The emergence of terrorist sanctuaries has multiple times drawn the United States away from its focus on the Indo-Pacific; the Biden administration points to its "over the horizon" capability to target terrorists in Afghanistan without reintroducing US troops.[62] This claim will be tested in the coming years.

## Human Rights and Democratic Values

The degree to which the Pivot, or US policy toward Asia in general, should prioritize support for democracy and human rights remained contested. Years before its announcement, the prevailing theory in policy circles held that as China grew richer, it would follow other Asian countries, like Japan, South Korea, and Taiwan, in democratizing. Economic and information connections to the rest of the world would spark demands for liberalization, and if Chinese leaders attempted to deny such aspirations, they would inevitably constrain economic growth. Beijing, as a result, had a tangible interest in improving human rights, and the world had a values-related reason for engaging economically with China.

In his 1999 State of the Union address, President Bill Clinton summed up the long-term aspirations of this approach, stating, "It's important not to isolate China. The more we bring China into the world, the more the world will bring change and freedom to China."[63] More than a decade later, in her Pivot article, Secretary of State Hillary Clinton wrote, "We make the case to our Chinese colleagues that a deep respect for international law and a more open political system would provide China with a foundation for far greater stability and growth—and increase the confidence of China's partners. Without them, China is placing unnecessary limitations on its own development."[64]

How exactly to promote human rights and freedom in China, and where those goals stood in the pantheon of US foreign policy priorities, remained unclear after the Pivot's announcement. So too did the degree to which the United States sought domestic governance changes in countries other than China. In his speech on the rebalance before Australia's parliament, Obama observed that "certain rights are universal; among them, freedom of speech, freedom of the press, freedom of assembly, freedom of religion, and the freedom of citizens to choose their own leaders," and he promised to "speak candidly to Beijing about the importance of upholding international norms and respecting the universal human rights of the Chinese people."[65]

As Asia expert Michael Green observed, however, the president often contradicted himself. Too much emphasis on human rights smacked of George W. Bush's "freedom agenda," and advisors were divided between Wilsonian idealists and others steeped in a more *realpolitik* approach. As a result, Green noted, "The role of values in the pivot thus swung between these two competing visions—the one emphasizing universality of democratic norms and the other an uncharacteristically neorealist approach that one might associate with Nixon or George Herbert Walker Bush."[66] In time, the approach to China would settle into a pattern: Rhetorically emphasize the abstract importance of human rights there, sometimes cite or invoke particular abuses or cases, and simultaneously deal with Beijing on the remainder of the bilateral agenda.

Other countries, including friendly autocracies Washington wished to enlist in its China strategy, proved harder cases. In her initial Pivot article, for instance, Secretary Clinton wrote, "We have made it clear . . . to Vietnam that our ambition to develop a strategic partnership requires that it take steps to further protect human rights and advance political freedoms."[67] The opposite occurred. The US-Vietnam strategic partnership continued to grow, via security cooperation, trade relations, diplomatic engagement, and the relaxation of previous restrictions—all while the Communist Party of Vietnam maintained a total monopoly on political power and did not take significant steps to improve human rights.[68]

The Obama administration did take bureaucratic and funding steps to better promote values. In 2014, for example, the State Department requested a 30 percent boost in funding (to $98.6 million) for governance and democracy programs in Asia region over the 2012 level. The Department's Democracy, Human Rights, and Labor bureau sent the largest share of its regional funding to Asia, and in 2013 it created a new East Asia and Pacific office.[69] Yet the trade-off dilemmas remained acute.

Burma appeared unique in this respect. The United States adopted a tough approach to Burma after the military junta stole elections in 1990 from Aung San Suu Kyi's National League for Democracy. Over the next two decades, Washington imposed sanctions, a trade embargo, diplomatic isolation measures, and more. Free of countervailing interests, America's relationship with Burma was defined by human rights and democracy.[70] By 2011, however, stirrings of a domestic thaw became evident. The ruling junta began talks with Aung San Suu Kyi, and Washington urged it to release political prisoners and advance political freedoms.[71]

Later that year, the government released Suu Kyi from house arrest, and she promptly announced her re-entry into Burmese politics.[72] Secretary Clinton visited the country in December, making her the most senior US official to do so in over fifty years.[73] In 2014, Obama himself traveled to Myanmar—as Washington increasingly called Burma—to endorse and encourage its turn toward democracy.[74] Within two years, Suu Kyi became the de facto civilian ruler of Burma. She visited the White House and Obama announced plans to lift US sanctions on the country.[75] If there was a human rights success story in Asia, this appeared to be it.

It was, for a time. But Suu Kyi, a Nobel Peace Prize winner lauded across the globe for her commitment to freedom, publicly defended the government's alleged genocide against Burma's Rohingya population.[76] Then, in February 2021, the military seized power in a coup d'état, killing and imprisoning thousands of citizens. Aung San Suu Kyi, whose National League for Democracy had two months earlier won 83 percent of parliamentary seats, was removed from power and detained. The seizure sparked nationwide fighting that displaced more than 1.4 million people.[77] The junta was back in power and the US policy of sanctions and isolation was back in place.[78]

Pressing liberal reforms in countries lacking basic rights had an intrinsic appeal to most policymakers. Washington has long directed its foreign policy at ends broader than security, prosperity, and freedom at home; Americans have generally wished their efforts abroad to have deeper purpose. While human rights diplomacy always involves trade-offs with other interests, the United States over the years compiled a record of some success in encouraging democratization in countries ranging from Poland and Hungary to South Korea and Taiwan. Promoting representative government and the rule of law may, in addition, confer more tangible benefits. As Michael Green and Daniel Twining observed, a common political identity is a source of security cooperation among states and, as a result, more democracies in Asia should provide the United States with a greater supply of potential security partners and China with fewer. "The ideational balance of power in Asia," they conclude, "directly affects the material balance of power."[79]

The degree to which regime type affects the willingness to ally, however, remains unclear. The United States has had numerous nondemocratic allies over the decades (Portugal, Turkey, and Greece under military dictatorship; South Korea and the Philippines under autocracy; and more), while today even the commonality of Communist autocracy does not unite China and Vietnam. The United States and India have drawn closer over years as the quality of Indian democracy has deteriorated.

Yet as a general rule, the United States tends to ally, coordinate, and trade disproportionately with liberal democracies. Whether because of the self-evident appeal of shared values or the instrumental advantage they might confer, US presidents—at least since Jimmy Carter—have regularly supported the expansion of democracy and human rights in rhetoric and policy. Donald Trump entered with a different view, though like so much during his presidency, it varied widely in consistency.

Asked after taking office about the assassination of Russian political opponents, Trump fired back, saying, "There are a lot of killers. You think our country's so innocent?"[80] On his first overseas trip, to Saudi Arabia, the new president insisted, "We are not here to lecture. We are not here to tell other people how to live."[81] During his first visit to Asia, Trump did not raise the ethnic cleansing against Burma's Rohingya population, Vietnam's political crackdowns, or the Philippines' widespread extrajudicial killings.[82] H. R. McMaster observed that after his 2018 summit with Kim Jong-un, the president stopped criticizing North Korean human rights abuses and described Kim as a person "who loves his people."[83] John Bolton, who succeeded McMaster, recalled that Trump in 2019 encouraged Xi Jinping to continue building concentration camps for Uyghurs in Xinjiang.[84]

Trump's national security strategy remained nearly silent on issues like freedom and democracy, but not totally. A small portion of the document committed the administration to support individual dignity, freedom, and the rule of law. Such ideals, however, were cast as "American values," rather than rights to which all people are entitled. The strategy made several references to "individual rights," but the term "human rights" appeared just once—to warn that the United States will deny admission to human rights abusers. "We are not going to impose our values on others," the document assured readers. "The American way of life cannot be imposed upon others, nor is it the inevitable culmination of progress."[85] The administration each year proposed drastic cuts to the State Department and foreign aid, including democracy funding, which Congress promptly restored; in 2018 it unsuccessfully aimed to cut funding for the National Endowment for Democracy by two-thirds.[86]

Senior administration officials often sung from a different song sheet. Secretary of State Mike Pompeo, for example, called for the United States to join Australia, India, Japan, and South Korea, "likeminded nations" that shared "a belief in the inherent worth of human beings." Americans should, Pompeo said, "help nations protect these first things—and human rights as well."[87] Human rights remained the focus of Burma policy throughout the Trump administration, and McMaster argued that China's domestic governance generated threats to other countries. Recalling the prevailing theory that as China "became more prosperous, the Chinese government would respect the rights of its people and liberalize," he said, "I observed that the intentions, policies, and actions of the Chinese Communist Party (CCP) had rendered those assumptions demonstrably false."[88] "China is a threat to free and open societies," McMaster added, "because its policies actively promote a closed, authoritarian model as an alternative to the rules-based order."[89]

The administration's line on human rights in China grew tougher over Trump's four years in office. In 2018, for example, Mike Pence delivered an address noting the hope of previous administrations that trade with China would lead to political liberalization. "That hope," he observed, "has gone unfulfilled." Instead, "in recent years, China has taken a sharp U-turn toward control and oppression."[90] A year later, Pompeo called for excluding Chinese telecommunications companies Huawei and ZTE from US networks. "The internet of tomorrow," he said, "must have buried within it Western values and must not belong to China.[91] He subsequently called China "home to one of the worst human rights crises of our time; it is truly the stain of the century."[92]

The administration's moves went beyond rhetorical criticisms. In 2020, it imposed sanctions on Chinese officials, including a member of the Politburo, for human rights abuses against the Uyghur population.[93] Trump rescinded Hong Kong's special trade status after Beijing moved to extinguish its autonomous democratic system, and then sanctioned Chief Executive Carrie Lam and other Hong Kong officials.[94] As senators and others pointed to the dangers of China's "digital authoritarianism," the administration attempted to generate alternatives to Beijing's Digital Silk Road.[95] And it was on his last full day as secretary, Pompeo issued a declaration charging the Chinese government with genocide against the Uyghurs.[96]

By the end of Trump's term, with white-hot US-China rivalry over COVID, trade, security issues, and more, a political consensus had largely gelled: China, always autocratic, had become more so in recent years. In the period just prior to Biden's election, Republicans and Democrats had largely come to agree that Beijing and Moscow wished to contest the attractiveness of democratic government and shape a world consistent with their authoritarian model. The result was a contest not just of nations but of political systems.[97] Political leaders as different as Senators Mitt Romney and Bernie Sanders worried that alternatives to liberal democracy would gain currency. Romney, for instance, cautioned that the alternative offered by China and Russia is "autocratic, corrupt, and brutal," while Bernie Sanders called for solidarity among democracies in the face of an "authoritarian axis."[98] Jake Sullivan and Kurt Campbell, before their return to the White House under Biden, wrote that "China may ultimately present a stronger ideological challenge than the Soviet Union did, even if it does not explicitly seek to export its system. If the international order is a reflection of its most powerful states, then China's rise to superpower status will exert a pull toward autocracy."[99]

As president, Biden doubled down on this framing. "We're at an inflection point," the new president said, "between those who argue that, given all the challenges we face . . . that autocracy is the best way forward . . . and those who understand that democracy is essential—essential to meeting those challenges." He saw a "battle between the utility of democracies in the 21st century and autocracies. That's what's at stake here," he added. "We've got to prove democracy works."[100] The president convened a virtual Summit for Democracy in December 2021 and another in March 2023, and he even revived the "free world" nomenclature reminiscent of Cold War rhetoric.[101] "Our alliances were created to defend shared values," Secretary of State Antony Blinken said, observing that Beijing "is actively working to undercut the rules of the international system and the values that we and our allies share."[102] Consistent with such convictions, senior officials pledged to put human rights at the center of US foreign policy and ground it in democratic values.[103]

The democracy versus autocracy framing did not win universal adherence, even within the United States and among allied democracies. Some observers suggested that, after the Capitol riot of January 6, Trump's failure to peacefully cede power, and previous widespread protests over police brutality, America simply lacked the standing to highlight democratic transgressions abroad.[104] Chinese leaders naturally resisted the characterization as well, with Xi telling Biden, "The so-called 'democracy versus authoritarianism' narrative is not the defining feature of today's world," and insisting, "The United States has American-style democracy. China has Chinese-style democracy."[105]

The most salient criticism stemmed from the need to build multi-nation coalitions around specific issues to resist Chinese influence. As the Pivot became an open effort to balance power in the Indo-Pacific, America needed partners— for military bases, technology cooperation, trade and sanctions harmonization, and much more. How could it enlist autocratic members in such coalitions if Washington was simultaneously undermining their very political legitimacy?

The issue was hardly abstract. Two Australian experts, for example, argued, "Rallying the world's democracies should not be the organising principle of American or Australian strategy in the Indo-Pacific . . . many of the US and Australia's most important regional partners when it comes to competing with China—such as the Philippines, Singapore, Vietnam and even India—fall outside the liberal democratic club."[106] Southeast Asia, for instance, was widely seen as the most contested region in Asia; two-thirds of ASEAN members were excluded from Biden's Summit for Democracy.[107]

A few offered middle-course judgments that cut through the stark framing. "We are always, always about human rights," said Senator Jim Risch (R-Idaho), the ranking member on the Senate Foreign Relations Committee. "Having said that," he added, "not everyone agrees with our view on human rights, and you have to deal with it. It's done on a case-by-case basis, and more importantly, a transactional basis. Seldom do you change conduct by trying to publicly humiliate someone."[108] Others applauded the broad outlines. Michael Green, for example, wrote, "Defending democratic values is also essential for the multipolar influence game in the Indo-Pacific. . . . A game of geopolitical influence absent efforts to strengthen democratic governance . . . would end in failure as Beijing bribes its way across the region."[109]

In its national security strategy, the Biden administration offered a conceptual innovation: there were, it said, two different kinds of autocracies—ones with revisionist foreign policies and ones without. China and Russia represent the first sort, it said, and their behavior poses a challenge to peace and stability. By waging or preparing for wars of aggression, undermining democratic practice in other countries, and using technology for repression, China and Russia seek to remake international order "to create a world conducive to their highly personalized and repressive type of autocracy." Countries like this could expect vigorous competition from the United States. Yet many other non-democracies—unnamed, but presumably ones like Vietnam, Thailand, Singapore, and others—forswear these revisionist behaviors. With them, Washington could and would work to bolster international order.[110]

All the back and forth over the administration's democracy/autocracy construct amounted to much ado about not much. In practice, the appeal to democratic solidarity, the charge to triumph over dictatorship, and the pledge to promote human rights and democracy remained mostly rhetorical. With two exceptions—China and Burma—the emphasis on democracy had little translation into the actual policy in Asia. This was broadly true of Washington in general. For all the talk of a belated pivot to Asia and the need to arrest the regional and global decline in democracy, US assistance in 2021 fell to its lowest level in more than a decade (Figure 13.1).

Pragmatism reigned in key bilateral relationships. Secretary of Defense Lloyd Austin, for example, traveled to the Philippines to meet President Rodrigo Duterte, the architect of a counterdrug campaign that killed thousands.[111] Duterte, who previously said, "The game is killing" and "I don't care about human rights," agreed during Austin's trip to restore the Visiting Forces Agreement with the United States.[112] Blinken and his Thai counterpart signed a communiqué intended, for the first time since 1962, to lay out a comprehensive vision effort of strategic cooperation.[113] The character of Thailand's political system—a military-dominated government engaged in significant human rights abuses—proved no obstacle.[114] In multiple interactions with Indian officials, the Biden administration praised India's democracy and offered nary a criticism of Prime Minister Modi.[115] In 2022, Biden held a special US-ASEAN Summit at the White House, hosting (among others) Hun Sen, who has ruled Cambodia since 1993, and Sultan Hassanal Bolkiah of Brunei, an absolute monarch in place since 1967.[116] A strategy premised on aligning democracies versus dictatorships this

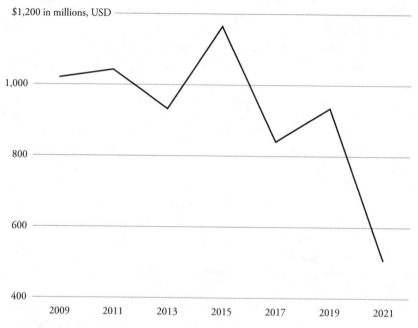

**Figure 13.1.** American democracy, human rights, and governance assistance to Asia, 2009–2021.

Source: US State Department and US Agency for International Development, *Foreign Assistance*, https://www.foreignassistance.gov/. Data for each year are based on total disbursements for democracy, human rights, and governance to the East Asia and Oceania, and South and Central Asia regions.

was not. These and other moves were aimed at solidifying partnerships and off-setting China, not at autocracy per se.

The administration embraced an overall approach to Chinese human rights essentially similar to the latter portion of the Trump term. In their first meeting with senior Chinese officials, Blinken and Sullivan raised human rights abuses and elicited a long, public rant from their counterparts.[117] The administration warned countries against adopting Chinese-sourced technology that could be used for surveillance and repression, and it encouraged Europe to align with America's stance on Beijing's domestic practices. Some of these efforts succeeded; the European Union sanctioned Chinese officials over abuses in Xinjiang and the European Parliament froze ratification of a pending EU-China investment agreement, citing human rights concerns.[118] The EU went on to impose, in coordination with the United States, its first sanctions on Chinese government officials since the Tiananmen Square massacre more than thirty years earlier.[119]

Burma represented the rare exception in which values, rather than geopolitical interest, determined US policy. The grave abuses carried out by the ruling Burmese military overrode any minor worries about damaged interests. A few regional governments worried that an overly coercive approach to Naypyidaw would push it further into Chinese hands, but such concerns found little purchase in Washington. The country's geopolitical weight simply was not that significant. Most believed that Burma, aligned with either China or the United States, would add little, and that the rollback of freedom in that country was exceptionally grave.

In his first foreign policy speech as president, Biden called on the Burmese military to relinquish power and pledged to "push back on China's attack on human rights."[120] The administration's Indo-Pacific Strategy criticizes China and North Korea for undermining human rights and promises to support democracy in Burma, but specifies no other values-related problems elsewhere in Asia.[121] The administration imposed sanctions on China over human rights abuses, especially those related to Uyghurs, and in 2022 ruled that the Burmese military was guilty of genocide against the Rohingya.[122] As noted above, in March 2023, after embracing autocrats like Egypt's Abdel Fattah el-Sisi and Saudi Arabia's Mohammed bin Salman, Biden hosted the second Summit for Democracy in Washington, DC.

The administration's pledge to place human rights at the center of its foreign policy while simultaneously forging balancing coalitions with autocracies was always bound to result in inconsistency and charges of hypocrisy. Biden's rhetoric emphasized a world split by democracies on one side and dictatorships on the other, but his policies resembled those of his predecessors. The United States has always had to balance national interests and values, deal with friendly autocrats and resist unfriendly democracies, promote human rights in some places but not others, and embed values in its foreign policy knowing full well that countervailing interests will sometimes make their pursuit impossible. For all the worry about Biden's grandiose ideological framing, his foreign policy fits squarely in the broad sweep of postwar American tradition. The United States can, and should, defend democracy and promote universal values abroad. It cannot, and will not, do that to the exclusion of everything else—even if some of its leaders' rhetoric suggests as much.

## Regional Architecture

From the beginning of the Pivot, multinational groupings of key countries emerged as a key area of focus. Policymakers typically viewed Asia's "regional architecture"—the organizations, institutions, and arrangements that structure the behavior of states—as key vehicles for pursuing transnational and other objectives. The prevailing view held that the United States should devote time and attention to regional summits and ministerials, ensure that Washington was a member of and present at various gatherings, and that it should forge new architectural elements where existing groups had gaps. As a former Australian intelligence analyst has observed, doing so provides US officials with access to a wide network of counterparts, demonstrates American engagement, prevents Chinese domination of regional institutions, and focuses busy US policymakers—including those with global responsibilities—on the Indo-Pacific.[123]

To these ends, the Obama administration early on named a first-ever US ambassador to ASEAN, acceded to the Treaty of Amity and Cooperation in Southeast Asia, and joined the East Asia Summit.[124] The State Department created a new deputy assistant secretary of state for multilateral affairs position and launched several "minilateral" groupings, including the Lower Mekong Initiative and the Asia-Pacific Clean Energy Program.[125] Clinton traveled to Rarotonga, in the Cook Islands, to become the first secretary of state to participate in the Pacific Islands Forum. Obama was the first US president to attend the East Asia Summit, and he hosted the APEC Leaders' meeting in Hawaii in November 2011.[126] The president hosted the first standalone US-ASEAN summit in 2015 and administration officials participated in other Asian "alphabet soup" gatherings, including the ARF and the ADMM-Plus.

Over the years, US participation in the various summits and ministerials would vary (Figure 13.2), depending on the press of global and domestic events, and it increasingly became a benchmark by which to measure America's regional engagement against China's. Trump tended to decline participation in key regional gatherings, skipping the US-ASEAN summit three times in a row and leaving Vietnam in 2017 before the East Asia Summit (EAS) that year kicked off. The next year, Vice President Mike Pence represented the United States at the ASEAN Summit, the APEC leaders' meeting, and the EAS. In 2019, Commerce Secretary Wilbur Ross and National Security Advisor Robert O'Brien attended the ASEAN Summit.[127] Trump never would attend the EAS during his four-year term. As earlier chapters describe, his administration seemed to favor more bilateral diplomacy and innovative groupings of likeminded countries like the Quad.

The Biden administration entered office intent on achieving a perfect attendance record at regional gatherings, or at least something close to it. Officials attended all the major meetings during their first year, and Biden virtually joined the ASEAN leaders' gathering in 2021, as well as the East Asia Summit.[128] After China that year struck a "Comprehensive Strategic Partnership" with ASEAN, the administration secured its own comprehensive partnership with ASEAN in

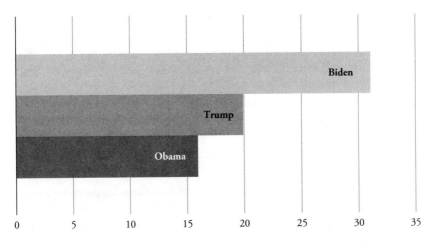

**Figure 13.2.** US senior official engagements with Indo-Pacific regional forums in the first 18 months of the Obama, Trump, and Biden administrations. All data are sourced from the United States Studies Centre.

Source: Data used to generate the chart are based on the data for the following report: Alice Nason, *Dedication or Distraction in Indo-Pacific Diplomacy*, (Sydney, Australia, United States Studies Centre, (2022), https://www.ussc.edu.au/analysis/dedication-or-distraction-in-indo-pacific-diplomacy.

2022, at the first US-ASEAN summit held in Washington.[129] In addition to Biden hosting the first-ever US-Pacific Island Country Summit, Vice President Harris participated virtually in the Pacific Islands Forum that year.[130] The United States hosted the APEC leaders' meeting in San Francisco in 2023 and the administration also named an ambassador to ASEAN, a position that went unfilled during the entirety of the Trump administration.[131]

Overall, the Biden administration compiled a record of participation in regional meetings that surpassed the Obama and Trump efforts. It sought participation both in the multilateral regional gatherings favored by the Obama administration as well as the minilateral efforts that won support under Trump. The impulse to innovate endured as well; the administration built on Trump's relaunch of the Quad and elevated it to the summit level. It also launched AUKUS and multilateral initiatives with Pacific Island nations and other countries. Yet like virtually every aspect of America's Asia policy, and characteristic of the Pivot to Asia, US-China rivalry has sharpened the competition and raised the stakes. Groupings like APEC and EAS, which include both the United States and China, were collectively hamstrung by the superpower competition, but to ignore such institutions in favor of others would cede the field to Beijing. The result has been the Biden administration's "all of the above" approach to regional architecture.

## Competition without Cooperation

In the pursuit of transnational objectives and universal values, the decade-plus after the Pivot's announcement witnessed significant change. Rising US-China competition increasingly crowded out the two countries' ability to cooperate. When bilateral cooperation became impossible, even in areas of manifestly shared interest, arranging regional and even global collaboration on issues like climate change and public health became much harder. Institutions designed in part to facilitate such cooperation grew less active.

To observe the degree of change over the years, consider the joint statement issued by Washington and Beijing in 2009. In that document, the two sides agreed to collaborate in health research, food and product safety, the Six-Party Talks on North Korea, climate change, counterterrorism, electric vehicles, wind power and bio-fuels, transnational organized crime, and more.[132] By 2015, the White House would tout joint initiatives in areas of mutual interest such as climate change, global public health, sustainable development, nonproliferation, and countering transnational organized crime, but feel the need simultaneously to warn that "we are managing the real and complex differences between us . . . with candor and resolve" in areas like cyber security, market access, and maritime security.[133]

By 2021, the fields of cooperation had shrunk dramatically and the areas to be managed with resolve expanded. In place of possible collaboration was, consistent with the overall increase in US-China rivalry, a growing sense of ideological competition. Even those rejecting Biden's "democracy versus autocracy" construct as simplistic generally acknowledged that Washington and Beijing offered two very different political models, that each saw the other as threatening to its domestic values and institutions, and that both viewed the contest of systems as intrinsic to their competition. Xi, for instance has stressed that the Chinese people "are fully confident in offering a China solution to humanity's search for better social systems," and Beijing has exported technology, employed diplomacy, and set examples in ways that strengthen autocracy.[134] When Biden and Xi met at the November 2023 APEC summit in San Francisco, the two leaders made "scant progress on the issues that have pushed the two nations to the edge of conflict," according to David Sanger and Katie Rogers of the *New York Times*.[135]

Unlike the Cold War, however, the lines are not clearly drawn. Coherent political-military-economic blocs do not exist in Asia, and most of America's closest allies—and indeed, the United States itself—are deeply dependent on productive economic ties with China. While there is an ideological component to US-China rivalry, and to US policy in the Indo-Pacific, it has not so far led to a settling out of likeminded countries on one or the other side. It will likely never do so, leaving the United States a far more differentiated and complex challenge than during the Cold War.

Another aspect of today's competition may also prove unlike the Cold War. For all their intense, existential superpower rivalry, the United States and the Soviet Union found ways to cooperate over the decades. Washington and Moscow collaborated on polio vaccines, the Non-Proliferation Treaty, manned space flight, biomedical sciences, incidents at sea, international terrorism, and in other areas.[136] Their work was episodic, often highly limited, and perennially subject to interruption or termination. But it did take place. Whether US-China competition will permit some measure of meaningful cooperation on such transnational issues seems increasingly unlikely.

# 14

# Conclusion

## The US Pivot to Asia and American Grand Strategy

It is difficult to overstate Asia's significance. It is home to 60 percent of the world's population, three of the five largest national economies, over 40 percent of global GDP, an estimated two-thirds of the world's economic growth, 41 percent of international exports and 37 percent of global imports, half of the world's active military personnel, six of the ten biggest armies, four of the ten highest defense budgets, five of the nine nuclear-weapons states, and six of the ten major carbon emitters. It is also the region in which America's chief geopolitical rival is most active. Over the 2010s and beyond, US policy sought to benefit from Asia's dynamism, respond to China's astonishing rise, end Middle East wars, and limit expenditures in Europe. This was the essence of the Pivot to Asia, and its core strategic logic was sound.[1]

### Good Ideas Falling Short

Why, then, did the Pivot not succeed as envisioned?

First, Washington persistently underestimated the China challenge. For too long, policymakers retained the belief that the proper combination of incentives and disincentives would induce Beijing to support rather than undermine international order, and that they might even prompt the development of Chinese pluralist structures and practices. While there was little evidence of any movement in these directions before Xi Jinping's ascension to political primacy, his rule dispelled any remaining doubts. As Stephen Hadley, George W. Bush's national security advisor, said more than a decade later, "We clearly misread" Xi. "He really took the country in a very different direction than Jiang Zemin or Hu Jintao."[2] Kurt Campbell and Ely Ratner observed that, rather than bowing to US preferences, "China has instead pursued its own course, belying a range of American expectations in the process."[3] Yet not until 2017, during the Trump administration, did the United States declare China a strategic competitor.[4] US policy has since scrambled to adjust to this belated realization.

Second, crises emerged in other places. From the outset, the policy was predicated on an expected peace dividend in Iraq and Afghanistan, two wars

Obama was determined to end. He announced the forthcoming withdrawal of US troops from Afghanistan in 2011, but that war would grind on, at great cost, until its end in failure a decade later.[5] Obama did follow through on his commitment to withdraw the US military from Iraq, but in neglecting to leave a residual force that could dampen instability there, the Islamic State established the world's largest terrorist sanctuary in the emergent vacuum. American troops returned to Iraq—and went to Syria as well—where they conducted a five-year, resource-intensive campaign to destroy the ISIS caliphate. They remain in both countries today. To these efforts the United States added a ruinous military intervention in Libya, which produced violent regime change and destabilized that country.

The Pivot also assumed a quiescent Europe, where major war was unthinkable, US attention and resources could remain flat or even diminish, and in which the transatlantic allies would focus on out-of-area operations rather than on continental security. Until recently, European security did not, in fact, pull the United States away from concentrating on the Indo-Pacific. Yet just as the Biden administration began to pivot in earnest, Moscow's full-scale invasion of Ukraine in 2022 upended these assumptions. US diplomats were suddenly talking to Asians about Europe rather than the other way around, American forces were deploying to Europe rather than away from it, Congress was appropriating tens of billions of dollars in aid to Ukraine, and the connection between European security and US national interests received a major new boost.

Many other events, both abroad and at home, might be added to the list of perpetual crises and difficulties. America's domestic divisions had nothing to do with China or the Indo-Pacific, but resulted in sequestration caps that shrank the US military just as leaders sought to devote more resources to Asia. The global financial crisis and its long aftermath helped fuel a backlash against trade agreements that undermined the Pivot's economic centerpiece. The siren song of Israeli-Palestinian peace redirected one secretary of state's diplomacy, while the forging of an anti-Iran coalition consumed the efforts of another. Hamas' attack on Israel and the eruption of war in the Gaza Strip prompted Washington to surge military assets to the Middle East, focus diplomatic attention there, and prepare a new, large-scale aid package for Jerusalem.

Third, the Pivot lacked a clear, commonly understood strategic articulation. Policymakers over the decade generally agreed that Asia should represent America's priority region, and that China's rise posed a historic challenge to US foreign policy. But how to translate those broad truths into specific policies and budgets remained a challenge. How to make trade-offs with other issues in other regions proved harder still. In interviews for this book, we found officials across administrations defining the Pivot differently, unable to agree on its specific objectives or identify what, precisely, constituted progress toward its ends.

Fourth, no American president put sufficient weight behind the Pivot. Focusing foreign policy on Asia yielded no domestic political benefit, and thus did not affect candidates' electoral prospects. And in the absence of a sustained presidential drive, individual government agencies were largely free to pursue their bureaucratic preferences, whether or not they accorded with the announced strategic objective. As Dwight Eisenhower stressed, "Motivation is the art of getting people to do what you want them to do because they want to do it." No president took on that task during the lost decade.

Fifth, by declaring an Asia-first foreign policy, the Obama administration attempted a grand strategic shift in the absence of forcing events or cataclysm. Yet in the history of American foreign policy, it has generally required such an upheaval—or at least the emergence of a major new threat—to turn the great ship of state. Pearl Harbor and Hitler's declaration of war on America shook the United States into full mobilization for World War II. The emergence of Stalin's Red Army on the plains of Europe, the Soviet Union's totalizing, revolutionary foreign policy, and the war in Korea pushed America to vigorously implement a strategy of containment. The 9/11 attacks made fighting terrorism the top priority of US activity. The Pivot followed no such visceral alarm.

Over more than a decade, Chinese events were never so dramatic or threatening as to become the driving factor in US policy, especially in a world of so many other priorities. The Pivot to Asia thus amounted to a test of whether a democracy like the United States could anticipate challenges to come—the rise of China, the erosion of Asia's balance of power, the economic and military vulnerability of America's Pacific allies and partners—and adjust course before it is provoked into change by crisis. Announced while the United States remained deeply engaged in the Middle East and Afghanistan, before Xi Jinping became China's paramount leader, before European countries were devising their own Indo-Pacific strategies, and before concerns over technology, supply chains, and military innovation had crystalized, the Pivot to Asia may have simply been too visionary for succeeding administrations to digest and employ.

The final reason why the United States did not pivot to Asia, however, and why it did not adequately respond to the rise of Chinese power, is the simplest of them all: It was more than successive administrations could manage. Moving military assets from Europe and the Middle East, for instance, would have entailed assuming more risk in those regions and potentially undermining US credibility there. Passing the TPP would have put members of Congress in the crosshairs of anti-trade voters at home. Sustaining the Hillary Clinton–era focus on diplomacy in the Pacific would have meant spending less time on Middle East peace or Syria ceasefires (priorities under Secretary Kerry), or Russia and Iran (areas of focus under Secretaries Tillerson and Pompeo). Ending sequestration and funding greater military resources for the Pacific would have required a bipartisan spending deal. Divesting legacy weapons systems to procure armaments better tailored for a China fight would have stirred those who support continuing existing production lines.[6] All those steps and more would have best been taken years ago. But they were hard—too hard, in the event, to get done.

## A Lost Decade

The period from roughly 2011 to 2021 thus represents a lost decade. Had the United States pivoted to Asia as intended, it would be better able to deter war with China today. It would have deeper trade relationships in the region, and countries there would be both less dependent on China and less susceptible to Beijing's coercion. America's diplomatic interactions with key countries would be stronger, and the region would have less reason to hedge against US unreliability. America's chances of prevailing in its long-term competition with China would be greater. Pivoting to Asia would by no means have eliminated the Chinese challenge. It would, however, have made it easier for the United States to manage it.

Even today, however, when policymakers and political leaders uniformly worry deeply about the China threat and see Asia as America's priority theater, the hardest things remain undone.[7] The United States has spent money to bolster its position relative to China—$50 billion for semiconductors in the CHIPS Act, increases in the defense budget, funding for the Development Finance Corporation, and so on. It is undertaking important military posture improvements in Asia, pursuing the Indo-Pacific Economic Framework, and engaging in creative, intensified regional diplomacy. All are positive steps, but even combined they are insufficient to meet the challenge. The United States remains unwilling to pursue a Pacific trade agreement, spend enough on defense, move significant military assets from Europe and the Middle East to the Indo-Pacific, shift its force structure away from legacy systems and toward weapons better suited to deter China, or pursue a strategic immigration policy to keep those with advanced technical skills in the United States. In the US political system and given the press of events elsewhere, again, these moves have so far proved just too hard.

This reality, in turn, raises the disquieting possibility that US democracy is *incapable* of doing the hardest things. We reject such fatalism. The policy recommendations that follow—indeed, many of the ideas that first animated the Pivot—are necessary to protect US vital national interests and democratic values and the world in which we wish to live. Most of them are overdue. To await the domestic political jolt supplied by some China-related calamity would be to invite the very outcome we seek to avoid.

In fact, as previously noted, the stirrings of a new pivot to Asia are detectable today. The Trump administration rightly shifted to a focus on competition with China, and the Biden administration has intensified engagement with the Indo-Pacific. Without referring explicitly to a past lost decade, policymakers have begun referring to a present "decisive decade" in the contest with China.[8] Their steps are, however, just a start. Today the United States needs a new and enveloping Pivot to Asia, one that accounts for America's enduring global role and multi-region interests, draws on lessons learned over more than a decade of effort, and is possessed by a sense of urgency. It is time to begin doing the hardest things, to take the actions left undone, and to align Washington's foreign policy agenda with its national interests and stated strategic priorities.

## Maintaining World Order

The overarching goal of US foreign policy should be to preserve the core pillars of the international order, even as specific rules and institutions change and adapt. The United States benefits from, and has a vital interest in maintaining, a global order governed by rules rather than brute power, one in which countries enjoy sovereignty, disputes are resolved peacefully, markets are open to trade, human rights are considered universal, and democracy can flourish. Since the 1940s, Washington has opposed hostile spheres of influence emerging in Eurasia precisely because they threaten the United States' desired rules-based order.

Today, China threatens to construct precisely such a hostile sphere of influence in Asia. Its military power has grown dramatically, making it more difficult for the United States to operate militarily across the region. Its economic weight has risen, permitting it to coerce countries in ways that violate their basic sovereignty. Its claims to the South China Sea run counter to long-standing maritime rules and threaten freedom of navigation, while its potential use of force against Taiwan could upend the structure of US alliances and partnerships. Its illiberal preferences crowd out the space in which democracy can thrive and promote instead the legitimacy of autocratic governance. Its current policies could lead to catastrophic war with the United States.

In this light, US policy toward China should aim to ensure that Beijing is either unwilling or unable to overturn the regional and global order. In so doing, the United States should work toward the preservation and extension of core international values that serve it and many other nations well. As we have argued throughout this book, accomplishing this goal requires a strategic pivot to Asia.

The US-China competition crosses multiple regions and domains, but rivalry and tension are most acute in the Indo-Pacific. Chinese military power is most concentrated in that region and becomes attenuated with distance from the

Western Pacific. Beijing's maritime claims, border disputes, and threats of force focus on Asia. Its economic gravity is greatest there, and countries in the Indo-Pacific are particularly vulnerable to Beijing's interference in their domestic politics.

As a result, increasing US military resources in Asia, and deepening regional security partnerships, will enhance deterrence and make China less likely to use force. An ambitious regional trade policy would reduce countries' reliance on the Chinese market and blunt Beijing's use of economic coercion. Contesting initiatives like Belt and Road would limit China's ability to convert economic involvement into geopolitical influence, particularly in subregions—like Southeast Asia—where such influence could lead to military agreements. Building new technology partnerships can ensure the free flow of information where China might otherwise restrict it, and focusing alliances on protecting democracies from external interference will enhance their independence and sovereignty. Contesting Chinese influence in international bodies will help protect universal values and key principles of international order.

A US approach to China that seeks only a pivot to Asia is incomplete, but a strategy that does not pivot to Asia will fail.

## Four Strategic Principles

As important as what to do is *how to think* about the task before the United States. We propose four principles to guide a renewed pivot to Asia.

### Articulate a Positive Vision

Defending regional and global order, including its concrete benefits for the independence and freedom of countries, permits the United States to articulate a positive vision for the Indo-Pacific. The United States is not merely competing against China, but working toward the preservation and extension of core international values that serve many nations well. US allies and partners should not be required to rupture their ties with China in order to join a unified bloc, but they should be encouraged to take part in coalitions aimed at resisting Beijing on specific issues. The accompanying message, despite Beijing's claims to the contrary, should be that Washington does not seek to suppress China's rise, but rather to establish a US-Chinese equilibrium in the long term.

The pursuit of this vision will, however, take years and involve risks. A renewed pivot to Asia involves contesting China in key areas, bolstering US power in ways that Beijing will inevitably find menacing, and collaborating with countries in ways that will leave China feeling surrounded. Diplomacy, as we propose in detail throughout this volume, can help mitigate these risks, but the United States will need to accept increased tension in the near to medium term to increase the odds for a more stable equilibrium with China over the long run.

## Endorse America's Global Role

In view of Beijing's ascendance, American policymakers should devote new diplomatic, economic, and military resources to Asia. In nearly every case, however, such additional engagement comes at the price of less attention to another area or region. Here US leaders should proceed, but carefully.

The tendency to privilege a single issue has reoccurred periodically across US foreign policy.[9] Policymakers and politicians, often backed by a vocal consensus, elevate serious, legitimate threats—communism, terrorism, now China—in a way that crowds out the attention necessary to deal with other priorities and interests. When it comes to shifting military resources, diplomatic energy, and leader-level attention from other issues to Asia, policymakers should be wary of a simple "do more" imperative.

The United States is and should remain a global power, and so a renewed pivot to Asia must account for attention and resources devoted to other regions and issues. In identifying resources that might be drawn on, policymakers should be able to demonstrate that the benefits of doing more in the Indo-Pacific outweigh the likely costs of doing less elsewhere. And when the calculation suggests that a shift in priorities is warranted, such a decision should be discussed thoroughly with allies and partners and made with as much specificity as possible—based on a particular set of policy tools or military deployments—rather than on the abstract basis that simply doing more is better.

Pivoting to Asia cannot mean the abandonment of key commitments elsewhere. Americans, after all, care not only about forestalling Chinese hegemony in Asia, but also about preventing terrorist attacks originating in the Middle East or Afghanistan, punishing and helping reverse Russian aggression in Europe, deterring Iranian malfeasance, ensuring Israel's defense, securing energy supplies and sea lanes, combating climate change and dangers to public health, and helping developing nations improve their quality of life.

America's ability to sustain focus on the long-term challenge of China depends on the lack of acute, threatening crises in Europe and the Middle East. By pulling troops completely from Iraq in 2011, for instance, the Obama administration did not redeploy them to Asia but instead ensured America's return. The same sadly may be the case in Afghanistan. Sustaining a low level of US military presence, diplomatic engagement, or funding in key non-Asia areas could aid, rather than undermine, Washington's pivot to Asia. America should tilt toward the Indo-Pacific, but not so far that it topples over.

## Calculate Trade-Offs amid Great Power Competition

Pivoting to Asia in a world of scarce resources entails trade-offs, and yet as every policy practitioner knows, setting priorities is far easier said than done. Assessed individually, every region—the Western Hemisphere, Asia, Europe, the Middle East, the Global South—has a claim to priority, and many issues have constituencies inside or outside government that argue for their importance. Making choices is harder still when the United States faces great-power competitors in both China and Russia, simultaneously and indefinitely. Both countries are globally active, and an approach that attempts to resist their influence everywhere would be unsuccessful. Even a generalized Asia-first approach represents an insufficient guide to policy and resources; after all, the Indo-Pacific is a big place.[10]

Actions by China, Russia, Iran, North Korea, or international terrorist groups that would undermine US vital national interests, contest key principles of international order, constrict the United States' freedom to act, or undermine the domestic functioning of US allies and key partners should broadly define America's national security priorities, as discussed in Chapter 2. Policymakers should thus focus most on actions in the places and on the issues where the potential damage to key US national interests is large and the potential utility to the challenger is significant. The remainder of adversaries' activities around the world that are undesirable, offensive, and even contrary to lesser interests should be relegated to a lower tier of priority. These challenges should receive a significantly smaller share of American national security resources and attention. As Steve Jobs observed, "People think focus means saying yes to the thing you've got to focus on. But that's not what it means at all. It means saying no to the hundred other good ideas that there are."[11]

Washington therefore needs a far subtler prioritization of regions and issues, and a policy process that considers the relative importance of multiple crises and opportunities rather than evaluating each on its own. This is true not only for the executive branch but also for Congress, which tends to focus on headline issues and direct funding and policy changes accordingly. The policy prescriptions in the "to-do list" below translates imperatives to set priorities and make trade-offs into a series of concrete actions.

The alternative, in this new era, would require the United States to resist undesirable Chinese (and Russian) influence wherever it exists—which is to say, every region of the world and across a wide spectrum of issues. To attempt this, even while working with allies and partners and taking every other prudent step to augment American power, ensures failure. The United States should do more but not try to do it all, everywhere.

## Pursue Unity

For all of America's many divisions, there is today—perhaps surprisingly—far more agreement than discord on the biggest foreign policy issue of all: the requirement to compete effectively with China. Broad domestic political unity is necessary to succeed in the contest, but it cannot simply be conjured by well-meaning policymakers. Pursued smartly, however, successful competition with Beijing—and the renewed pivot to Asia that is necessary for it—could bring US political leaders together rather than drive them apart. The bipartisan concern with China provides an opportunity—possibly the only major one in these gridlocked political times—to rally elected leaders around a program of American strength and renewal.

Analogies to Soviet-era containment and a Cold War II are inapt for many reasons, but in one respect Cold War history illustrates the possibilities that attend indefinite US-China competition. The imperative to confront Moscow helped spur America to a program of national greatness and international leadership. Republicans and Democrats alike wished to demonstrate democracy and capitalism's superiority over communism and central planning, to enlist more allies and friends than the Soviet bloc, and to inspire the world by showing what a free people can accomplish.[12]

To be sure, the Cold War also brought fear of Armageddon, proxy wars, covert operations, superpower crises, and national anxiety. But under its influence, the United States sharpened its edge, establishing a worldwide alliance system and aiding economic development in impoverished regions. It improved civil rights at home, built the interstate highway system, expanded research universities, and landed men on the moon.

No one should actively seek a return to the Cold War, or even a watered-down variant of it. But since America is faced with an indefinite period of competition with China—and this book makes the case that it is—its leaders should use that fact to catalyze a far grander, positive agenda of American greatness in the twenty-first century. The presence of an external threat drives Americans together. That is not a reason to pursue or hype such dangers, but if they exist nevertheless, wise policymakers will employ them to visionary and constructive ends. They may even serve as the long-awaited stimulus to a pivot, spurring the United States to do in the future the things that have proved too difficult in the past.

## The To-Do List

A genuine pivot to Asia represents a new approach to American grand strategy. The policy adjustments necessary for such a shift are legion, and too numerous to detail in this volume. Instead, we offer nine recommendations that require urgent policymaker attention. While executing them would hardly represent a fully adequate response to Chinese power, together they constitute a major step in the right direction.

## Continue to Strengthen US Alliances in the Indo-Pacific

America's regional alliances represent key comparative advantages for the United States. As this book details, recent years have seen major advances in ties with Japan, South Korea, Australia, the Philippines, and India. These critical efforts—both to support their growing strength and to solidify the ties with and among them—should continue.

## Join CPTPP and De-Risk Economic Ties with China

Following the collapse of the TPP, Washington watched as each nation in the region became ever more dependent on trade with China and more vulnerable to Beijing's geoeconomic coercion. Joining CPTPP would increase US access to lucrative Asian markets and give Washington the ability to shape rules in the region and beyond. Washington's entry would also reassure regional partners that the United States remains committed to the Indo-Pacific. More politically palatable steps toward reentry, such as pursuing a bilateral or regional digital trade deal, might help in the near term. In the meantime, the United States should identify areas of economic dependence with China that incur national security risk and pursue alternative arrangements.

## Substantially Increase the US Defense Budget and Boost US Military Assets and Power Projection in Asia

America's defense budget, with a FY2024 level of $841 billion, is in nominal terms quite sizable.[13] As a percentage of GDP, however, the 2.7 percent it represents matches 1999—the height of the post–Cold War "peace dividend"—as the lowest level since 1953.[14] In addition, given the rate of inflation, the FY2024 defense budget amounts to a small real cut compared to the previous year's figure.[15] The

United States cannot arrest the eroding balance of power in the Indo-Pacific, and meet its critical commitments elsewhere, without major increases in defense spending.

## Shift Significant Military Resources from the Middle East to Asia

For more than a decade, Washington fed the perception of US withdrawal from the Middle East without obtaining a significant resource dividend. This amounted to the worst of all worlds: deep and costly engagement in the region while fanning the fears of abandonment. Washington should invert this equation by diminishing its military presence in the region while bolstering its commitment to act. Troop levels, air bases, maritime deployments, and more should decline in the Middle East, surging only if and when necessary for significant military operations, such as the initial effort to deter other actors from joining the Israel-Hamas war in the fall of 2023.

## Shift Substantial US Air and Naval Forces from Europe to the Indo-Pacific

The ongoing degradation of Russian military power amid the war in Ukraine— and the revelation that Moscow's military might is significantly less than originally thought—is combining with European steps to increase defense budgets, acquire new capabilities, and enhance military production lines. As a result, Russia will pose no serious conventional military threat to NATO allies in Europe for the foreseeable future. This provides a historic opportunity to pivot US air and naval forces from the defense of Europe to new locations in the Indo-Pacific.

## Make European Allies Central in Washington's China Strategy

Until recently, most of Europe was reluctant to challenge the PRC, given the enormity of the Chinese market and the importance of two-way trade. Beginning in 2022, however, and following Beijing's tacit support for the Russian invasion of Ukraine, NATO allies increasingly signaled their opposition to China's destabilizing policies—and displayed greater willingness to cooperate with the United States against them. The United States should encourage the European Union to wield its significant international regulatory power to help curb China's coercive economic influence, and to set liberal economic rules, especially in technology, to which Beijing will be forced to adhere.[16] Washington should similarly work with European nations to blunt Beijing's influence in international institutions and establish a European military presence, even if modest, in the Indo-Pacific.

## Pursue Issue-Based Coalitions with Allies and Partners

The United States should encourage countries to join coalitions aimed at resisting Beijing on specific issues, such as economic coercion, theft of intellectual property, dominating international organizations and standard-setting bodies, military aggression, covert interference in other countries' domestic politics, the spread of illiberal technologies, and human rights abuses.

## Intensify Bilateral Diplomacy with China

Although no *modus vivendi* between Washington and Beijing is currently possible given their polar views on vital national interests, diplomacy remains essential. Regrettably, both nations at best will struggle for the foreseeable future to maintain the current tense state of the bilateral relationship, and to prevent it from becoming even worse. Contrary to some claims, diplomacy does not undermine US toughness, but rather represents the necessary companion of a competitive approach. An entirely confrontational approach, devoid of communication, cooperation, or compromise of any sort, would radiate systemic tension throughout Asia. If confrontation turns to conflict, the likely consequences would be catastrophic. Even as it competes vigorously, the United States should rigorously follow a One China policy and demonstrate abiding restraint on the issue, and publicly reject both Taiwan independence and regime change in China as policy objectives.

## Support the Forces of Democracy and Liberalism

The United States has an important international role to play in supporting the growth of democratic institutions where they do not exist and defending them where they are under pressure. Too rigid a delineation between free countries and autocracies could hamstring US efforts to assemble the coalitions necessary for long-term competition with China. Yet Washington should be clear about the values it represents—and wishes to see flourish—in the Indo-Pacific and beyond. America's vision of a better, freer world is a key comparative advantage in the competition with China's cramped, illiberal worldview.

## The Pacific Century

We live, it is often observed, in the Pacific century. In that region lay America's deepest national interests, its greatest geopolitical rival, its most important economic fortunes, and—in some sense—its destiny. This book has sought to illuminate the Pivot's strategic logic, analyze its successes and failures, and propose a way forward for US engagement in the region that matters most.

Here we return to the importance of leadership by the president and Congress, which a renewed Pivot to Asia requires. It will take foresight and courage by both. It requires unity and compromise by both. It means sustained effort and collaboration by both. None of these qualities is in abundance today. But no country thrives on competition, both foreign and domestic, like America. At a time of bitter domestic strife, many issues will push our political leaders apart. Amid a growing consensus about the magnitude of the stakes, renewing the Pivot to Asia should help bring them together.

US political leaders and policymakers should take seriously what they say about China and Asia, make the necessary moves before they are forced upon them, and demonstrate that a democratic America can, in fact, shift its strategic focus and policy attention to Asia, even in a world of competing priorities. Now is no time for strategic pessimism. The United States can now embark in earnest and speed on a Pivot to Asia. For the sake of its security, prosperity, and freedom, it must.

# Notes

## Chapter 1

1. Numerous former officials, across multiple administrations, will resist this definition of the Pivot. Some argue that the term "pivot" did not indicate a shift from one region to another, but rather a move from one strategy to another. Others reject the term itself and assert that "rebalance" more properly describes the approach. Still others use either of these terms as synonymous with their administration's Asia policy: doing more in Asia, by definition, then, demonstrates an American pivot or rebalance. Yet from its first description in 2011 through the present day—and in light of the obviously finite nature of many US national security resources—it is clear that the Pivot represented more than a broad "do more in Asia" mantra. It represents the attempt to do more in Asia by shifting scarce national security resources and policymaker attention from other regions of the world.
2. Hillary Clinton, "America's Pacific Century," *Foreign Policy*, October 11, 2011, https://foreignpolicy.com/2011/10/11/americas-pacific-century/.
3. Ibid.
4. Ibid.
5. In writing this book on the US Pivot to Asia, we have profited from the work of analysts and practitioners on the same subject, including: Nicholas D. Anderson and Victor D. Cha, "The Case of the Pivot to Asia: System Effects and the Origins of Strategy," *Political Science Quarterly* 132, no. 4 (Winter 2017–2018): 595–617; Richard C. Bush, "The Response of China's Neighbors to the U.S. 'Pivot' to Asia," Brookings Institution, January 31, 2012, https://www.brookings.edu/articles/the-response-of-chinas-neighbors-to-the-u-s-pivot-to-asia/; Kurt Campbell, *The Pivot: The Future of American Statecraft in Asia* (New York: Hachette Book Group, 2016); Kurt Campbell, "Explaining and Sustaining the Pivot (Rebalance) to Asia," *The Future of American Defense*, ed. Nicholas Burns and Jonathon Price (Washington, DC: Aspen Institute, 2014), 75–82; Kurt Campbell and Brian Andrews, *Explaining the US "Pivot" to Asia* (London: Chatham House, 2014); Rong Chen, "A Critical Analysis of the U.S. 'Pivot' toward the Asia-Pacific: How Realistic Is Neo-Realism?" *Connections* 12, no. 3 (2013): 39–62; Thomas Christensen, *The China Challenge: Shaping the Choices of a Rising Power* (New York: W. W. Norton, 2015); Elbridge Colby, *The Strategy of Denial: American Defense in an Age of Great Power Conflict* (New Haven, CT: Yale University Press, 2022); Zack Cooper and Adam P. Liff, "America Still Needs to Rebalance to Asia," *Foreign Affairs*, August 11, 2021, https://www.foreignaffairs.com/articles/asia/2021-08-11/america-still-needs-rebalance-asia; Zack Cooper and Adam P. Liff, *10 Years after "the Pivot": Still America's Pacific Century?* (Washington, DC: American

Enterprise Institute, 2021); Renato Cruz De Castro, "The Obama Administration's Strategic Pivot to Asia: From a Diplomatic to a Strategic Constrainment of an Emergent China?," *Korean Journal of Defense Analysis* 25, no. 3 (2013): 331–349; Janine Davidson, "The U.S. 'Pivot to Asia,'" *American Journal of Chinese Studies* 21 (June 2014): 77–82; Matteo Dian, *Japan and the US Pivot to the Asia Pacific* (London: London School of Economics, 2013); Bates Gill, *Pivotal Days: US–Asia-Pacific Alliances in the Early Stages of the Trump Administration* (London: Chatham House, June 2017); Michael J. Green, Nicholas Szechenyi, and Victor D. Cha, *Pivot 2.0* (Washington, DC: Center for Strategic and International Studies, 2015); Peter Harris and Peter Trubowitz, "The Politics of Power Projection: The Pivot to Asia, Its Failure, and the Future of American Primacy," *The Chinese Journal of International Politics* 14, no. 2 (Summer 2021): 187–217; Pasha L. Hsieh, "Revitalizing the US Pivot to Asia," *New Asian Regionalism in International Economic Law* (Cambridge: Cambridge University Press, 2021); Yogesh Joshi, "Between 'Concern' and 'Opportunity': US Pivot to Asia and Foreign Policy Debate in India," *Journal of Asian Security and International Affairs* 2, no. 3 (2015): 314–337; Kenneth G. Lieberthal, "The American Pivot to Asia," Brookings Institution, December 21, 2011, https://www.brookings. edu/articles/the-american-pivot-to-asia/; Justin Logan, *China, America, and the Pivot to Asia* (Washington DC: CATO Institute, 2013); Ahmad Rashid Malik, "The US Pivot to Asia: Recalibrating Pakistan's Vision East Asia," *Strategic Studies* 34–35 (2014): 50–69; US Library of Congress, Congressional Research Service, *Pivot to the Pacific? The Obama Administration's 'Rebalancing' Toward Asia*, by Mark E. Manyin et al., R42448, 2012, https://sgp.fas.org/crs/natsec/R42448.pdf; D. S. McDonough, "America's Pivot to the Pacific: Selective Primacy, Operational Access, and China's A2/AD Challenge," *Calgary Papers in Military and Strategic Studies* 7 (2013): 1–43; Jae-Kyung Park, "The US Pivot to Asia and Asia's Pivot to the US," *Asia Pacific Bulletin* 173 (2012); Harsh V. Pant and Yogesh Joshi, "The American 'Pivot' and the Indian Navy: It Is Hedging All the Way," *Naval War College Review* 68, no. 1 (Winter 2015): 47–69; Robert S. Ross, *The US Pivot to Asia and Implications for Australia* (Canberra: Australian National University Strategic and Defense Studies Centre, 2013); Robert S. Ross, "The Problem With the Pivot," *Foreign Affairs* 91, no. 6 (2012): 70–82; David Shambaugh, "Assessing the US 'Pivot' to Asia," *Strategic Studies Quarterly* 7, no. 2 (2013): 10–19; Douglas Stuart, *The Pivot to Asia: Can It Serve as the Foundation for American Grand Strategy in the 21st Century* (Carlisle, PA: US Army War College Press, 2016); Bjørnar Sverdrup-Thygeson et al., *"For Every Action . . .": The American Pivot to Asia and Fragmented European Responses* (Washington, DC: Brookings Institution, 2016); John C. Whitehead, Claude Barfield, and Lt. General Wallace "Chip" Gregson, Jr. (Ret.), "Understanding the US Pivot to Asia," panel event, Brookings Institution, January 31, 2012 (Panel Event), https://www.brookings. edu/wp-content/uploads/2012/04/20120131_us_asia_panel_two.pdf; Chi Wang, *Obama's Challenge to China: The Pivot to Asia* (London: Routledge, 2015); You Ji, "US Pivot to Asia and China's Strategic Dilemma and Response," *Security Outlook of the Asia Pacific Countries and Its Implications for the Defense Sector* (Tokyo: The National

Institute for Defense Studies, 2011); *Taiwan and the US Pivot to Asia: New Realities in the Region?*, ed. Shihoko Goto (Washington, DC: Wilson Center, 2013).

6. Here and throughout the book, we use the terms "pivot" and "rebalance" synonymously. Like so much else in the policy's development, the terminology remains contested. In a later chapter, we fully excavate this debate, one that existed from the Pivot's earliest days.

7. Michael Green, *By More than Providence* (New York: Columbia University Press, 2017), 19–20.

8. Throughout this book, we use the terms "Asia," "Asia-Pacific," and "Indo-Pacific" interchangeably.

# Chapter 2

1. Barack Obama, interviewed by David Remnick, "Going the Distance," *New Yorker*, January 19, 2014, https://www.newyorker.com/magazine/2014/01/27/going-the-distance-david-remnick.

2. Ibid.

3. Henry Kissinger, *American Foreign Policy: Three Essays* (New York: W. W. Norton, 1969), 51–97.

4. Shinzo Abe, "Address by Prime Minister Shinzo Abe at the Opening Session of the Sixth Tokyo International Conference on African Development" (speech, Nairobi, Kenya, August 27, 2016), Japan Ministry of Foreign Affairs, https://www.mofa.go.jp/afr/af2/page4e_000496.htm.

5. Author interview with Matthew Pottinger, November 2022.

6. White House, *Indo-Pacific Strategy of the United States*, February 2022, https://www.whitehouse.gov/wp-content/uploads/2022/02/U.S.-Indo-Pacific-Strategy.pdf.

7. Graham T. Allison and Robert Blackwill, *America's National Interests* (Cambridge: The Commission on America's National Interests, 2000).

8. Charles Evan Hughes, "The Centenary of the Monroe Doctrine" (speech, Philadelphia, PA, November 30, 1923), Hein Online, https://heinonline.org/HOL/LandingPage?handle=hein.journals/intcon10&div=5&id=&page=.

9. Hans Morgenthau, "The Primacy of the National Interest," *American Scholar* 18, no. 2 (Spring 1949): 208, https://www.jstor.org/stable/41205156.

10. "Pacificus No. III, [6 July 1793]," Founders Online, National Archives, https://founders.archives.gov/documents/Hamilton/01-15-02-0055. [Original source: *The Papers of Alexander Hamilton*, vol. 15, June 1793–January 1794, ed. Harold C. Syrett (New York: Columbia University Press, 1969), 65–69.]

11. President Trump made a mockery of all these elements of successful US foreign policy.

12. Aaron Miles, "Implications of China's Nuclear Expansion for Strategic Stability," *War on the Rocks*, July 27, 2023, https://warontherocks.com/2023/07/implications-of-chinas-nuclear-expansion-for-strategic-stability/.

13. Shannon Bugos, "Pentagon Sees Faster Chinese Nuclear Expansion," *Arms Control Today*, December 2021, https://www.armscontrol.org/act/2021-12/news/penta gon-sees-faster-chinese-nuclear-expansion; US Department of Defense, Office of the Secretary of Defense, *Military and Security Developments Involving the People's Republic of China 2022*, November 2022, https://media.defense.gov/2022/Nov/29/200 3122279/-1/-1/1/2022-MILITARY-AND-SECURITY-DEVELOPMENTS-INVOLV ING-THE-PEOPLES-REPUBLIC-OF-CHINA.PDF, 94; Hans M. Kristensen and Matt Korda, "Chinese Nuclear Forces, 2020," *Bulletin of Atomic Scientists* 76, no. 6 (2020), https://doi.org/10.1080/00963402.2020.1846432; US Department of Defense, Office of the Secretary of Defense, *Military and Security Developments Involving the People's Republic of China 2023*, October 2023, https://media.defense.gov/2023/Oct/ 19/2003323409/-1/-1/1/2023-MILITARY-AND-SECURITY-DEVELOPMENTS-INVOLVING-THE-PEOPLES-REPUBLIC-OF-CHINA.PDF.

14. Office of the Secretary of Defense, *Military and Security Developments Involving the People's Republic of China*, 2022, 92; Matt Korda and Hans Kristensen, "China Is Building a Second Nuclear Missile Silo Field," Strategic Security (Blog), Federation of American Scientists, https://fas.org/blogs/security/2021/07/china-is-building-a-sec ond-nuclear-missile-silo-field/.

15. Office of the Secretary of Defense, *Military and Security Developments Involving the People's Republic of China*, 2023, 106.

16. Demetri Sevastopulo, "China Conducted Two Hypersonic Weapons Tests This Summer," *Financial Times*, October 20, 2021, https://www.ft.com/content/c7139 a23-1271-43ae-975b-9b632330130b; Patty-Jane Geller, "China's Nuclear Expansion and Its Implications for U.S. Strategy and Security," Missile Defense (Commentary), *Heritage Foundation*, September 14, 2022, https://www.heritage.org/missile-defense/ commentary/chinas-nuclear-expansion-and-its-implications-us-strategy-and-secur ity; Brad Dress, "Pentagon: China on Pace to Almost Quadruple Nuclear Arsenal by 2035," *Hill*, November 29, 2022, https://thehill.com/policy/international/3754615-pentagon-china-on-pace-to-almost-quadruple-nuclear-arsenal-by-2035/.

17. Geller, "China's Nuclear Expansion."

18. Jon B. Alterman, "China Headaches for Iran Deal," *Center for Strategic and International Studies*, September 22, 2021, https://www.csis.org/analysis/china-headaches-iran-deal.

19. Ibid.

20. International Crisis Group, "The Iran Nuclear Issue: The View from Beijing," Asia Briefing no. 100, International Crisis Group, February 17, 2010, https://www.crisisgr oup.org/asia/north-east-asia/china/iran-nuclear-issue-view-beijing.

21. US-China Economic and Security Review Commission, *China-Iran Relations: A Limited but Enduring Strategic Partnership*, by Will Green and Taylore Roth, January 28, 2021, 19, 21, https://www.uscc.gov/sites/default/files/2021-06/China-Iran_Relations.pdf.

22. US Department of State, Michael R. Pompeo, "New Sanctions under the Iran, North Korea, and Syria Nonproliferation Act (INKSNA)," press release, February 25, 2020, https://2017-2021.state.gov/new-sanctions-under-the-iran-north-korea-and-syria-nonproliferation-act-inksna/index.html.

23. Ian Talley, "U.S. Sanctions Iran Drone Suppliers in China, 'Shadow Banking' Network," *Wall Street Journal*, March 9, 2023, https://www.wsj.com/articles/u-s-sanctions-iran-drone-suppliers-in-china-shadow-banking-network-46831875.

24. Radio Free Europe/Radio Liberty, "Iran, Russia, China Hold Joint Naval Drill amid Growing Ties," *Radio Free Europe/Radio Liberty*, January 21, 2022, https://www.rferl.org/a/iran-russia-china-exercises/31663080.html.

25. China Briefing Team, "China and Iran: Bilateral Trade Relationship and Future Outlook," *China Briefing*, August 20, 2021 .

26. "Chinese Companies Keep Exporting Nuclear and Missile Items to N. Korea," *Dong-a Ilbo*, January 27, 2023, https://www.donga.com/en/article/all/20230127/3917995/1.

27. Lindsay Maizland, "China's Modernizing Military," Backgrounder, Council on Foreign Relations, last modified February 5, 2020, https://www.cfr.org/backgrounder/chinas-modernizing-military.

28. US Defense Intelligence Agency, *China Military Power*, 2019, v, https://www.dia.mil/Portals/110/Images/News/Military_Powers_Publications/China_Military_Power_FINAL_5MB_20190103.pdf.

29. Bugos, "Pentagon Sees Faster"; US Department of Defense, Office of the Secretary of Defense, *Military and Security Developments Involving the People's Republic of China*, 2023, 106; Kristensen and Korda, "Chinese Nuclear Forces, 2020"; Paul McLeary, "Pentagon Predicts 5 Times Increase in China's Nuclear Weapons over Next 10 Years," *Politico*, November 3, 2021, https://www.politico.com/news/2021/11/03/pentagon-china-nuclear-weapons-519048; Minnie Chan, "Satellite Images of Chinese Nuclear Submarine Being Built Prompt Speculation of Vertical Launch System," *South China Morning Post*, May 14, 2022, https://www.scmp.com/news/china/military/article/3177644/satellite-images-chinese-submarine-under-construction-prompt?module=perpetual_scroll_0&pgtype=article&campaign=3177644; Geller, "China's Nuclear Expansion"; "How Are China's Land-Based Conventional Missile Forces Evolving?," China Power, Center for Strategic and International Studies, https://chinapower.csis.org/conventional-missiles/.

30. Margaret McCuaig-Johnston, *Enhancing Taiwan's Role in International Organizations* (Ottawa: Canadian Global Affairs Institute, 2021), https://www.cgai.ca/enhancing_taiwans_role_in_international_organizations; Tung Cheng-Chia and Alan H. Yang, "How China Is Remaking the UN in Its Own Image," *Diplomat*, April 9, 2020, https://thediplomat.com/2020/04/how-china-is-remaking-the-un-in-its-own-image/; Kristine Lee, "It's Not Just the WHO: How China Is Moving on the Whole U.N.," *Politico*, April 15, 2020, https://www.politico.com/news/magazine/2020/04/15/its-not-just-the-who-how-china-is-moving-on-the-whole-un-189029; Andrew Hyde, "China's Emerging Financial Influence at the UN Poses a Challenge to the U.S.," Commentary, Stimson Center, April 4, 2022, https://www.stimson.org/2022/chinas-emerging-financial-influence-at-the-un/.

31. People's Republic of China Ministry of Foreign Affairs, "Wang Yi: The U.S. Indo-Pacific Strategy Is Bound to Be a Failed Strategy," press release, May 22, 2022, https://www.fmprc.gov.cn/eng/zxxx_662805/202205/t20220523_10691136.html.

32. Wang Yi, "State Councilor and Foreign Minister Wang Yi Meets the Press" (speech, Beijing, March 7, 2022), People's Republic of China Ministry of Foreign Affairs, https://www.fmprc.gov.cn/eng/zxxx_662805/202203/t20220308_10649559.html.

33. Wang Wenbin, "Foreign Ministry Spokesperson Wang Wenbin's Regular Press Conference on May 18, 2022" (press conference, Beijing, May 18, 2022), People's Republic of China Ministry of Foreign Affairs, https://www.fmprc.gov.cn/mfa_eng/xwfw_665399/s2510_665401/2511_665403/202205/t20220518_10688532.html.

34. People's Republic of China Ministry of Foreign Affairs, "China and Japan Hold the 17th Security Dialogue," press release, February 23, 2023, https://www.fmprc.gov.cn/mfa_eng/wjbxw/202302/t20230227_11031957.html.

35. Zhao Lijian, "Foreign Ministry Spokesperson Zhao Lijian's Regular Press Conference on May 24, 2021" (press conference, Beijing, May 24, 2021), People's Republic of China Ministry of Foreign Affairs, https://www.fmprc.gov.cn/mfa_eng/xwfw_665399/s2510_665401/2511_665403/202105/t20210524_9170750.html; Jun Mai, "Don't 'Play with Fire,' China Tells US and South Korea over Taiwan Concerns," South China Morning Post, May 24, 2021, https://www.scmp.com/news/china/diplomacy/article/3134670/dont-play-fire-china-tells-us-and-south-korea-over-taiwan.

36. Wang Wenbin, "Foreign Ministry Spokesperson Wang Wenbin's Regular Press Conference on March 14, 2023" (press conference, Beijing, March 14, 2023), People's Republic of China Ministry of Foreign Affairs, https://www.fmprc.gov.cn/mfa_eng/xwfw_665399/s2510_665401/202303/t20230314_11041208.html.

37. Zhao Lijian, "Foreign Ministry Spokesperson Zhao Lijian's Regular Press Conference on September 17, 2021" (press conference, Beijing, China, September 17, 2021), People's Republic of China Ministry of Foreign Affairs, https://www.fmprc.gov.cn/mfa_eng/xwfw_665399/s2510_665401/2511_665403/202109/t20210917_9721338.html.

38. Ibid.

39. US Library of Congress, Congressional Research Service, The Senkakus (Diaoyu/Diaoyutai) Dispute: U.S. Treaty Obligations, by Mark E. Manyin, R42761, 2021, https://sgp.fas.org/crs/row/R42761.pdf.

40. Todd Hall, "More Significance than Value: Explaining Developments in the Sino-Japanese Contest over the Senkaku/Diaoyu Islands," Texas National Security Review 2, no. 4 (September 2019): 13, https://tnsr.org/2019/09/more-significance-than-value-explaining-developments-in-the-sino-japanese-contest-over-the-senkaku-diaoyu-islands/.

41. Alessio Patalano, "What Is China's Strategy in the Senkaku Islands?," War on the Rocks, September 10, 2020, https://warontherocks.com/2020/09/what-is-chinas-strategy-in-the-senkaku-islands/.

42. Ibid.

43. Troy Stangarone, "Did South Korea's Three Noes Matter? Not So Much," Diplomat, October 30, 2019, https://thediplomat.com/2019/10/did-south-koreas-three-noes-matter-not-so-much/; Matthew Ha, "China's Coercion Threatens ROK-US Alliance," Policy Brief, Foundation for Defense of Democracies, https://www.fdd.org/analysis/2020/06/01/chinas-coercion-threatens-rok-us-alliance/.

44. Josh Smith and Hyonhee Shin, "S. Korea Scrambles Jets after Chinese, Russian Warplanes Enter Air Defence Zone," *Reuters*, May 24, 2022, https://www.reuters.com/world/asia-pacific/skorea-scrambles-jets-after-chinese-russian-warplanes-enter-air-defence-zone-2022-05-24/; "Chinese Aircraft Intruded into S. Korea's Air Defense Zone More than 70 Times Last Year: Military," *Yonhap News Agency*, October 3, 2022, https://en.yna.co.kr/view/AEN20221003002400325?section=national/defense.

45. "Chinese, Russian Planes Enter South Korean Air Defense Zone," *Deutsche Welle*, November 30, 2022, https://www.dw.com/en/chinese-russian-planes-enter-south-korean-air-defense-zone/a-63939138.

46. White House, "Fact Sheet: Implementation of the Australia—United Kingdom—United States Partnership (AUKUS)," April 5, 2022, https://www.whitehouse.gov/briefing-room/statements-releases/2022/04/05/fact-sheet-implementation-of-the-australia-united-kingdom-united-states-partnership-aukus/.

47. Bonnie Girard, "China's AUKUS Response Highlights Beijing's Bunker Mentality," *Diplomat*, September 30, 2021, https://thediplomat.com/2021/10/chinas-aukus-response-highlights-beijings-bunker-mentality/; Catherine Wong, "China Hits Out at 'Highly Irresponsible' Aukus Defence Pact between US, Britain and Australia and Warns of Pacific Arms Race," *South China Morning Post*, September 16, 2021, https://www.scmp.com/news/china/diplomacy/article/3149052/china-hits-out-highly-irresponsible-aukus-defence-pact-between.

48. Jia Deng, "AUKUS: Why Beijing Didn't Go Ballistic," *Interpreter*, October 14, 2021, https://www.lowyinstitute.org/the-interpreter/aukus-why-beijing-didn-t-go-ballistic.

49. Jill Goldenziel, "China Violates the Philippines' Sovereignty While Russia Distracts the U.S.," *Forbes*, March 27, 2020, https://www.forbes.com/sites/jillgoldenziel/2022/03/27/china-violates-the-philippines-sovereignty-while-russia-distracts-the-us/?sh=432d844452fd.

50. Ibid.; Jill Goldenziel, "Here's Why China Is Afraid of an Obscure International Court," *Forbes*, July 19, 2021, https://www.forbes.com/sites/jillgoldenziel/2021/07/19/heres-why-china-is-afraid-of-an-obscure-international-court/?sh=219db7433d8c; Jill Goldenziel, "The U.S. Is Losing the Legal War against China," *Forbes*, August 3, 2021, https://www.forbes.com/sites/jillgoldenziel/2021/08/03/the-us-is-losing-the-legal-war-against-china/?sh=7bedc7226cab; Jill Goldenziel, "How the U.S. Can Fight China's Fishy Business," *Forbes*, February 8, 2022, https://www.forbes.com/sites/jillgoldenziel/2022/02/08/chinas-fishy-business-is-threatening-the-globe/?sh=2970483a6795.

51. Diana Roy, "China's Growing Influence in Latin America," Backgrounder, Council on Foreign Relations, last modified June 15, 2023, https://www.cfr.org/backgrounder/china-influence-latin-america-argentina-brazil-venezuela-security-energy-bri; Qian Zhou, "China and Ecuador Sign Free Trade Agreement," *China Briefing*, May 15, 2023, https://www.china-briefing.com/news/china-free-trade-agreement-signed-ecuador/; Fermín Koop, "Uruguay-China FTA Negotiations Raise Tensions over Mercosur's Future," *Dialogo Chino*, July 28, 2022, https://dialogochino.net/en/trade-investment/56817-uruguay-china-fta-negotiations-tensions-over-mercosur-future/.

52. Koop, "Uruguay-China FTA Negotiations"; Charles Couger, "US Military Leaders Warn China Could Militarize the Ports It Owns in Latin America," *Fox News*, September 22, 2022, https://www.foxnews.com/world/us-military-leaders-warn-china-could-militarize-ports-it-owns-latin-america; Andrew Miller, "Military Leaders Warn China Could Weaponize Ports in Latin America," *Trumpet*, October 3, 2022, https://www.thetrumpet.com/26176-military-leaders-warn-china-could-weaponize-ports-in-latin-america; Bethany Allen-Ebrahimian and Miriam Kramer, "China's Space Footprint in South America Fuels Security Concerns," *Axios*, October 4, 2022, https://www.axios.com/2022/10/04/chinas-space-footprint-south-america-security-concerns; Milton Ezrati, "China's Latin America Move," *Forbes*, November 7, 2022, https://www.forbes.com/sites/miltonezrati/2022/11/07/chinas-latin-america-move/?sh=5d364ce21d52.

53. "Full Text: China's Policy Paper on Latin America and the Caribbean," *China Daily*, November 6, 2008, http://www.chinadaily.com.cn/china/2008-11/06/content_7179488_7.htm; "Full Text of China's Policy Paper on Latin America and the Caribbean," *Xinhua*, November 24, 2016, http://en.people.cn/n3/2016/1124/c90000-9146474-8.html.

54. U.S.-China Economic and Security Review Commission, *2021 Report to Congress*, November 2021, 98, https://www.uscc.gov/annual-report/2021-annual-report-congress.

55. Li Weichao, Ministry of National Defense of the People's Republic of China, "Chinese Defense Minister Delivers Keynote Speech at Fifth Defense Forum between China, LAC Countries," press release, December 13, 2022, http://eng.mod.gov.cn/xb/News_213114/TopStories/4928315.html.

56. "中华人民共和国和古巴共和国关于深化新时代中古关系的联合声明　[Joint Statement between the People's Republic of China and the Republic of Cuba on Deepening China-Cuba Relations in the New Era]," *Ministry of Foreign Affairs of the People's Republic of China*, November 25, 2022, https://www.mfa.gov.cn/web/ziliao_674904/1179_674909/202211/t20221125_10980884.shtml; Gordon Lubold and Warren P. Strobel, "White House Says China Has Had Cuba Spy Base since at Least 2019," *Wall Street Journal*, June 11, 2023, https://www.wsj.com/articles/white-house-says-china-has-had-cuba-spy-base-since-at-least-2019-42145596.

57. U.S.-China Economic and Security Review Commission, *2021 Report to Congress*, 98.

58. UN News (@UN_News_Centre), "URGENT🚨 The UN General Assembly Votes to Suspend Russia's Membership in the UN Human Rights Council @UN_HRC In favor: 93 Abstained: 58 Against: 24," Twitter, April 7, 2022, 11:51 a.m., https://twitter.com/UN_News_Centre/status/1512095779535609862.

59. Ezrati, "China's Latin America"; Associated Press, "Honduras Establishes Ties with China after Break from Taiwan," *NPR*, March 27, 2023, https://www.npr.org/2023/03/27/1166177955/honduras-establishes-ties-with-china-after-break-from-taiwan.

60. Rob Garver, "Report: China Spends Billions of Dollars to Subsidize Favored Companies," *Voice of America*, May 24, 2022, https://www.voanews.com/a/report-china-spends-billions-of-dollars-to-subsidize-favored-companies-/6587314.html.

61. Office of the United States Trade Representative, *2021 Report to Congress on China's WTO Compliance*, February 2022, https://ustr.gov/sites/default/files/files/Press/Reports/2021USTR%20ReportCongressChinaWTO.pdf.

62. Associated Press, "China Delayed Releasing Coronavirus Info, Frustrating WHO," *PBS*, June 2, 2020, https://www.pbs.org/newshour/health/china-delayed-releasing-coronavirus-info-frustrating-who; Helen Regan and Sandi Sidhu, "WHO Team Blocked from Entering China to Study Origins of Coronavirus," *CNN*, January 6, 2021, https://www.cnn.com/2021/01/05/china/china-blocks-who-team-coronavirus-intl-hnk/index.html; Gabriel Crossley, "China Rejects WHO Plan for Study of COVID-19 Origin," *Reuters*, July 22, 2021, https://www.reuters.com/world/china/china-will-not-follow-whos-suggested-plan-2nd-phase-covid-19-origins-study-2021-07-22/; Amy Maxmen, "Scientists Struggle to Probe COVID's Origins amid Sparse Data from China," *Nature*, March 17, 2022, https://www.nature.com/articles/d41586-022-00732-0.

63. "Fentanyl Flow to the United States," *Drug Enforcement Agency Intelligence Report*, DEA-DCT-DIR-008-20 (2020).

64. *China's Role in the Fentanyl Crisis, Follow the Money: The CCP's Business Model Fueling the Fentanyl Crisis, Before the House Financial Services Committee*, 118th Cong. (2023) (statement of Vanda Felbab-Brown, Brookings Institution).

65. Ministry of Foreign Affairs of the People's Republic of China, "The Ministry of Foreign Affairs Announces Countermeasures in Response to Nancy Pelosi's Visit to Taiwan," press release, August 5, 2023, https://www.fmprc.gov.cn/eng/zxxx_662805/202208/t20220805_10735706.html.

66. Office of the Director of National Intelligence, *Annual Threat Assessment of the US Intelligence Community*, April 9, 2021, https://www.dni.gov/files/ODNI/documents/assessments/ATA-2021-Unclassified-Report.pdf.

67. US Department of Justice, Office of Public Affairs, *U.S. Charges Five Chinese Military Hackers for Cyber Espionage against U.S. Corporations and a Labor Organization for Commercial Advantage*, May 19, 2014, https://www.justice.gov/opa/pr/us-charges-five-chinese-military-hackers-cyber-espionage-against-us-corporations-and-labor.

68. "China: Events of 2021," Human Rights Watch, https://www.hrw.org/world-report/2022/country-chapters/china-and-tibet#12ffb1.

69. Lindsay Maizland, "China's Fight against Climate Change and Environmental Degradation," Backgrounder, Council on Foreign Relations, last modified May 19, 2021, https://www.cfr.org/backgrounder/china-climate-change-policies-environmental-degradation.

70. Stephan Robin, "China Facing Devastating Impacts from Climate Change," Australian Strategic Policy Institute, September 27, 2022, https://www.aspistrategist.org.au/china-facing-devastating-impacts-from-climate-change/.

71. Oriana Skylar Mastro, *Chinese Intentions in the South China Sea* (Washington, DC: Wilson Center), 338, https://fsi-live.s3.us-west-1.amazonaws.com/s3fs-public/documents/mastro_paper.pdf; Peter A. Dutton, "China Is Rewriting the Law of the Sea," Review, *Foreign Policy*, June 10, 2023, https://foreignpolicy.com/2023/06/10/china-sea-south-east-maritime-claims-law-oceans-us-disputes/.

72. Patrick Smith, "U.S. Rejects China's Claim Its Warship Illegally Entered Waters in the South China Sea," *NBC News*, March 23, 2023, https://www.nbcnews.com/news/world/china-drove-away-us-warship-illegally-entered-waters-south-china-sea-rcna76269.

73. Isaac B. Kardon, *China's Law of the Sea: The New Rules of Maritime Order* (New Haven, CT: Yale University Press, 2023), 258–262.

74. "China's Space Program: A 2021 Perspective," The State Council Information Office of the People's Republic of China, January 2022, https://www.cnsa.gov.cn/english/n6465645/n6465648/c6813088/content.html; Office of the Director of National Intelligence, *Annual Threat Assessment of the US Intelligence Community*, February 6, 2023, 8, https://www.dni.gov/files/ODNI/documents/assessments/ATA-2023-Unclassified-Report.pdf.

75. China Military Studies Institute, "In Their Own Words: Science of Military Strategy," 2020.

76. United States Defense Intelligence Agency, *2022 Challenges to Security in Space*, III, 2022, https://www.dia.mil/Portals/110/Documents/News/Military_Power_Publications/Challenges_Security_Space_2022.pdf.

77. Ashley Lin, "The Chinese Military's Skyrocketing Influence in Space," Australian Strategic Policy Institute, November 8, 2023, https://www.aspistrategist.org.au/the-chinese-militarys-skyrocketing-influence-in-space/.

78. Andrew Jones, "China Launches National-Record 41 Satellites on Single Rocket (Video)," *Space.com*, June 17, 2023, https://www.space.com/china-single-launch-record-41-satellites-video.

79. Brett Tingley, "Whew! 23-Ton Chinese Rocket Debris Falls to Earth over Pacific Ocean," *Space.com*, November 4, 2022, https://www.space.com/china-long-march-5b-rocket-falls-into-pacific-ocean; Brett Tingley, "China's Latest Giant Rocket Debris Crash Blasted by US and European Space Chiefs," *Space.com*, November 4, 2022, https://www.space.com/nasa-esa-space-chiefs-condemn-china-rocket-debris-crash.

80. Lloyd J. Austin III, "'The Decisive Decade': Remarks by Secretary of Defense Lloyd J. Austin III at the Reagan National Defense Forum (as Delivered)" (remarks, Simi Valley, CA, December 3, 2022), Department of Defense, https://www.defense.gov/News/Speeches/Speech/Article/3235391/the-decisive-decade-remarks-by-secretary-of-defense-lloyd-j-austin-iii-at-the-r/.

81. Steve Tsang, "China's Xi Visits South Africa in Just His Second Trip Abroad This Year as Domestic Woes Bubble Back Home," interviewed by Nectar Gan, *CNN*, August 21, 2023, https://www.cnn.com/2023/08/20/china/brics-summit-xi-jinping-south-africa-visit-intl-hnk/index.html?utm_campaign=wp_todays_worldview&utm_medium=email&utm_source=newsletter&wpisrc=nl_todayworld.

82. Lee Kuan Yew, quoted in Graham Allison and Robert D. Blackwill, *Lee Kuan Yew: The Grand Master's Insights on China, the United States, and the World* (Cambridge, MA: MIT Press, 2013), 2.

83. For discussions of the "engage and hedge" strategy, see John Pomfret, "The Pendulum of U.S.-China Relations Is Swinging Again," *Washington Post*, September 11, 2019,

http://washingtonpost.com/opinions/2019/09/11/pendulum-us-china-relations-is-swinging-again; Jonathan D. T. Ward, *China's Vision of Victory* (Fayetteville, NC: Atlas Publishing and Media, 2019).

84. Pharaoh clearly did not sufficiently take into account Moses's strategic and tactical assets, in this case his god, as he led the Israelites out of captivity in Egypt and into the land of Canaan. The Egyptian intelligence community's failure regarding collection, collation, evaluation, analysis, integration, and interpretation reportedly cost Pharaoh his entire army and all its equipment in the Red Sea.

85. Robert Zoellick, "Whither China? From Membership to Responsibility" (speech, New York, September 21, 2005), US Department of State Archives, https://2001-2009. state.gov/s/d/former/zoellick/rem/53682.htm. Zoellick is often misquoted. Contrary to some commentary on Zoellick's remarks, he expressed an unrealized objective regarding China's policy, not an assertion that Beijing had already become a "responsible stakeholder." For a thoughtful reflection on the history and consequences of the failed American strategy toward China, see Hal Brands, "Every President since Reagan Was Wrong about China's Destiny," *Bloomberg*, July 23, 2019, http://bloomb erg.com/opinion/articles/2019-07-23/every-president-since-reagan-was-wrong-about-china-s-destiny.

86. See Cheng Li, "Hopes and Doubts in Beijing: Resetting U.S.-Chinese Relations Won't Be Easy," *Foreign Affairs*, November 13, 2020, http://foreignaffairs.com/articles/uni ted-states/2020-11-13/hopes-and-doubts-beijing.

87. Economist, "Henry Kissinger Explains How to Avoid World War Three," Briefing, *Economist*, May 17, 2023, https://www.economist.com/briefing/2023/05/17/henry-kissinger-explains-how-to-avoid-world-war-three.

88. Rush Doshi, *The Long Game: China's Grand Strategy to Displace American Order* (New York: Oxford University Press, 2021), 6.

89. For arguments against a policy of "neo-containment," see Kurt Campbell and Jake Sullivan, "Competition without Catastrophe: How America Can Both Challenge and Coexist with China," *Foreign Affairs*, 98, no. 5 (2019): 96–110, http://foreignaffairs. com/articles/china/competition-with-china-without-catastrophe. The question does arise whether the United States should actually pursue a policy of containing China, while denying it is doing so. China seems convinced that is the current US policy, whatever Washington says.

## Chapter 3

1. George F. Kennan, "The Sources of Soviet Conduct," *Foreign Affairs* 25, no. 4 (July 1947): 575, https://www.foreignaffairs.com/russian-federation/george-kennan-sour ces-soviet-conduct.

2. John F. Kennedy, "Inaugural Address" (speech, Washington, DC, January 20, 1961), National Archives, https://www.archives.gov/milestone-documents/president-john-f-kennedys-inaugural-address.

3. Richard M. Nixon, "Remarks to the Nation Announcing Acceptance of an Invitation to Visit the People's Republic of China" (remarks, Burbank, CA, July 15, 1971), American Presidency Project, https://www.presidency.ucsb.edu/docume nts/remarks-the-nation-announcing-acceptance-invitation-visit-the-peoples-republic-china.

4. Ronald Reagan, "Address to Members of the British Parliament" (speech, London, June 8, 1982), National Archives, https://www.reaganlibrary.gov/archives/speech/address-members-british-parliament.

5. George W. Bush, "Address to a Joint Session of Congress and the American People" (speech, Washington, DC, September 20, 2001), White House Archives, https://geor gewbush-whitehouse.archives.gov/news/releases/2001/09/20010920-8.html.

6. Gwen Ifill, "Campaign 1992: Interview; Clinton Seeking Forceful Image as a Leader in Foreign Affairs," New York Times, June 28, 1992, https://www.nytimes.com/1992/06/28/us/campaign-1992-interview-clinton-seeking-forceful-image-leader-foreign-affairs.html.

7. Ibid.

8. Robert L. Suettinger, Beyond Tiananmen: The Politics of U.S.-China Relations 1989–2000 (Washington, DC: Brookings Institution Press, 2003).

9. Nicholas D. Kristof, "China Worried by Clinton's Linking of Trade to Human Rights," New York Times, October 9, 1992, https://www.nytimes.com/1992/10/09/world/china-worried-by-clinton-s-linking-of-trade-to-human-rights.html.

10. Gwen Ifill, "Clinton and the Japanese Premier Scold Each Other on Trade Issues," New York Times, April 17, 1993, https://www.nytimes.com/1993/04/17/world/clin ton-and-the-japanese-premier-scold-each-other-on-trade-issues.html.

11. Thomas W. Lippmann, "U.S. Gives China a Renewal of Favored Status in Trade," Washington Post, May 29, 1993, https://www.washingtonpost.com/archive/politics/1993/05/29/us-gives-china-renewal-of-favored-status-in-trade/60603a60-3ecb-4545-b5f5-cc3cbeae03af/.

12. Ibid.

13. Bill Clinton, "Remarks to Students and Faculty of Waseda University" (speech, Tokyo, July 7, 1993), Ministry of Foreign Affairs of Japan, https://www.mofa.go.jp/region/n-america/us/archive/1993/remarks.html.

14. Thomas L. Friedman, "The Pacific Summit; Leaders at Summit Seek Strong Pacific Community," New York Times, November 21, 1993, https://www.nytimes.com/1993/11/21/world/the-pacific-summit-leaders-at-summit-seek-strong-pacific-commun ity.html.

15. Gwen Ifill, "Clinton and Japan Chief Say Trade Talks Fail; U.S. Threatens Action," New York Times, February 12, 1994, https://www.nytimes.com/1994/02/12/world/clinton-and-japan-chief-say-trade-talks-fail-us-threatens-action.html.

16. Hobart Rowen, "Administration in Disarray on China Trade Policy," Washington Post, March 20, 1994, https://www.washingtonpost.com/archive/business/1994/03/20/administration-in-disarray-on-china-trade-policy/0cd674ae-2f26-4845-a98d-39f31c4aaffa/.

17. Mark Matthews, "President Separates China Trade from Human Rights Issues," *Baltimore Sun*, May 27, 1994, https://www.baltimoresun.com/news/bs-xpm-1994-05-27-1994147075-story.html.

18. Michael Green, "The U.S. Pivot to Asia and American Grand Strategy, Session One: Effects of the Pivot in Asia 2011–2021, and Beyond" (lecture, Washington, DC, October 10, 2021), Council on Foreign Relations.

19. US Department of Defense, *United States Security Strategy for the East Asia-Pacific Region*, February 1995, 2, https://apps.dtic.mil/sti/citations/ADA298441#:~:text=Focusing%20on%20new%20threats%20and,and%20to%20promote%20democr acy%20abroad; Green, "The U.S. Pivot to Asia and American Grand Strategy, Session One"; Joseph S. Nye, "The 'Nye Report': Six Years Later," *International Relations of the Asia-Pacific* 1, no. 1 (January 2001): 95–103, https://doi.org/10.1093/irap/1.1.95.

20. Author communication Victor Cha, April 2022.

21. Nye, "The 'Nye Report': Six Years Later," 95.

22. *United States Security Strategy for the East Asia-Pacific Region*, 5–7.

23. Joseph Nye, "The Case for Deep Engagement," *Foreign Affairs* 74, no. 4 (July–August 1995): 91, https://www.foreignaffairs.com/articles/asia/1995-07-01/case-deep-eng agement.

24. *United States Security Strategy for the East Asia-Pacific Region*, 15.

25. Nye, "The Case," 90–102.

26. Michael Mazza, "Reflections on 25 Years Ago: Risks for a Fourth Taiwan Strait Crisis," American Enterprise Institute, March 24, 2021, https://www.aei.org/articles/reflecti ons-on-25-years-ago-risks-for-a-fourth-taiwan-strait-crisis/.

27. Ash Carter, "Reflections on American Grand Strategy in Asia," Harvard Kennedy School Belfer Center, October 2018, https://www.belfercenter.org/publication/refl ections-american-grand-strategy-asia.

28. Terence K. Kelly, David C. Gompert, and Duncan Long, "Smarter Power, Stronger Partners, Volume I: Exploiting U.S. Advantages to Prevent Aggression," (Washington, DC: RAND, 2016), https://www.rand.org/content/dam/rand/pubs/research_repo rts/RR1300/RR1359/RAND_RR1359.pdf; J. Michael Cole, "The Third Taiwan Strait Crisis: The Forgotten Showdown between China and America," *National Interest*, March 10, 2017, https://nationalinterest.org/feature/the-third-taiwan-strait-crisis-the-forgotten-showdown-19742.

29. Joseph S. Nye, Jr., "Work with China, Don't Contain It," *New York Times*, January 25, 2013, https://www.nytimes.com/2013/01/26/opinion/work-with-china-dont-contain-it.html; Michael Green, *By More than Providence* (New York: Columbia University Press, 2017), 470–471.

30. Allison Mitchell, "Clinton Urges Broad Global Role for Japan," *New York Times*, April 18, 1996, https://www.nytimes.com/1996/04/18/world/clinton-urges-broad-global-role-for-japan.html.

31. Steven Mufson, "U.S.-Japan Accord Fans China's Fears," *Washington Post*, April 19, 1996, https://www.washingtonpost.com/archive/politics/1996/04/19/us-japan-acc ord-fans-chinas-fears/976920fb-3305-4c26-bb31-2371ba19c87c/.

32. US Department of Defense, *Report of the Quadrennial Defense Review*, May 1997, https://history.defense.gov/Portals/70/Documents/quadrennial/QDR1997.pdf?ver= 2014-06-25-110930-527.

33. Alastain Iain Johnston, "The Failures of the 'Failure of Engagement' with China," *The Washington Quarterly* 42, no. 2 (April 2019): 105, https://doi.org/10.1080/01636 60X.2019.1626688.

34. Seth Faison, "Analysis: U.S. Trip Is Everything Jiang Expected," *New York Times*, November 3, 1997, https://archive.nytimes.com/www.nytimes.com/library/world/ 110397us-china-assess.html.

35. "U.S. Won't Seek Condemnation of China's Human Rights Record," *Chicago Tribune*, March 14, 1998, https://www.chicagotribune.com/news/ct-xpm-1998-03-14-980 3140100-story.html; Phillip Shenon, "Annual U.N. Ritual Condemning China Loses U.S. Support," *New York Times*, March 14, 1998, https://www.nytimes.com/1998/03/ 14/world/annual-un-ritual-condemning-china-loses-us-support.html.

36. Helen Dewar and George Hager, "Tentative Accord Reached on IMF Funds, Conditions," *Washington Post*, October 13, 1998, https://www.washingtonpost.com/ archive/politics/1998/10/13/tentative-accord-reached-on-imf-funds-conditions/ 8366952b-5acc-460f-858b-9e47bf26ea59/.

37. James Bennet, "Nuclear Anxiety: The President; Clinton Calls Tests a 'Terrible Mistake' and Announces Sanctions against India," *New York Times*, May 14, 1998, https://www.nytimes.com/1998/05/14/world/nuclear-anxiety-president-clinton- calls-tests-terrible-mistake-announces.html.

38. Thomas W. Lippmann, "U.S. Lifts Sanctions on India, Pakistan," *Washington Post*, November 7, 1998, https://www.washingtonpost.com/archive/politics/1998/11/07/ us-lifts-sanctions-on-india-pakistan/3771637b-b980-40b2-b5eb-7fb8a053870d/; Raymond E. Vickery, Jr., "Looking Back: The 1998 Nuclear Wake Up Call for U.S.- India Ties," *Diplomat*, May 31, 2018, https://thediplomat.com/2018/05/looking- back-the-1998-nuclear-wake-up-call-for-us-india-ties/.

39. Ashok Sharma, "'Jaswant-Talbatt [*sic*] Talk' and India-US Strategic Engagement: A Legacy of Jaswant Singh, the Foreign Minister at the Crucial Juncture of India's International Engagement," *Times of India*, October 2, 2020, https://timesofindia.ind iatimes.com/blogs/ashoks-statecraft/jaswant-talbatt-talk-and-india-us-strategic- engagement-a-legacy-of-jaswant-singh-the-foreign-minister-at-the-crucial-junct ure-of-indias-international-engagement/; Helen Dewar, "Senate Rejects Test Ban Treaty," *Washington Post*, October 14, 1999, https://www.washingtonpost.com/wp- srv/politics/daily/oct99/senate14.htm.

40. Vickery, "Looking Back."

41. Jane Perlez, "Clinton Begins Visit to India, but First Stops in Bangladesh," *New York Times*, March 20, 2000, https://archive.nytimes.com/www.nytimes.com/library/ world/asia/032000bangladesh-prexy.html.

42. Joseph Kahn, "Trade Accord Is Reached between U.S. and Vietnam," *New York Times*, July 13, 2000, https://archive.nytimes.com/www.nytimes.com/library/world/asia/ 071300vietnam-us-trade.html.

43. The normalization of economic ties launched a major increase in economic interac- tion: According to US trade statistics, total merchandise trade between the United

States and Vietnam grew from $1.5 billion in 2001 to $77.6 billion in 2019: US Library of Congress, Congressional Research Service, *U.S.-Vietnam Economic and Trade Relations: Issues in 2020*, by Michael F. Martin, IF11107, 2020, https://sgp.fas.org/crs/row/IF11107.pdf.

44. John F. Harris and Michael Laris, "Clinton Calls for Closer U.S.-China Cooperation," *Washington Post*, June 26, 1998, https://www.washingtonpost.com/wp-srv/inatl/longterm/china/stories/xian062698.htm.

45. Andrew Glass, "Bill Clinton Apologizes to Jiang Zemin for NATO Bombing," *Politico*, May 14, 2013, https://www.politico.com/story/2013/05/this-day-in-politics-091279.

46. Bill Clinton, "Letter to Congress Advocating Granting China Permanent Normal Trade Relations," (remarks, Paul H. Nitze School of Advanced International Studies, Washington, DC, March 8, 2000), USC Annenberg, https://china.usc.edu/bill-clinton-%E2%80%9Cletter-congress-advocating-granting-china-permanent-normal-trade-relations%E2%80%9D-march-8.

47. Terry M. Neal, "Bush Vows to Push for Stronger Ties to Latin America," *Washington Post*, August 26, 2000, https://www.washingtonpost.com/archive/politics/2000/08/26/bush-vows-to-push-for-stronger-ties-to-latin-america/5a15dde4-b1f6-4961-ad93-c6d83d19e658/.

48. Ibid.

49. Luisa Angrisani, "More Latin, Less America?: Creating a Free Trade Area of the Americas," *National Interest*, no. 73 (Fall 2003): 77, https://www.jstor.org/stable/42895643.

50. White House, "Joint Statement between the United States of America and the United Mexican States," press release, September 6, 2001, https://georgewbush-whitehouse.archives.gov/news/releases/2001/09/20010906-8.html.

51. George W. Bush, "Remarks at Summit of the Americas Working Session" (speech, Quebec City, Quebec, April 21, 2001), White House Archives, https://georgewbush-whitehouse.archives.gov/news/releases/2001/04/20010423-9.html.

52. "The United States and Japan: Advancing toward a Mature Partnership," (Washington, DC: Institute for National Strategic Studies, October 11, 2000), https://armitageinternational.com/wp-content/uploads/2018/06/ArmNye-Oct-2000-Report.pdf.

53. Ibid., 1.

54. Ibid., 4–5.

55. Green, *By More than Providence*, 485.

56. "The United States and Japan," 7.

57. Author communication with Victor Cha, April 2023.

58. Green, *By More than Providence*, 485.

59. Robert D. Blackwill, "The India Imperative," *National Interest*, June 1, 2005, https://nationalinterest.org/article/the-india-imperative-578.

60. George W. Bush, "A Distinctly American Internationalism" (speech, Simi Valley, CA, November 19, 1999), *Washington Post*, https://www.washingtonpost.com/archive/business/technology/1999/11/19/text-of-remarks-prepared-for-delivery-by-texas-gov-george-w-bush-at-ronald-reagan-presidential-library-simi-valley-calif-on-november-19-1999/1e893802-88ce-40de-bcf7-a4e1b6393ad2/.

61. Elisabeth Rosenthal and David E. Sanger, "U.S. Plane in China after It Collides with Chinese Jet," *New York Times*, April 2, 2001, https://www.nytimes.com/2001/04/02/world/us-plane-in-china-after-it-collides-with-chinese-jet.html.

62. Miriam Donohoe and Patrick Smyth, "'Very Sorry' Letter from US Ends Spy Plane Stand-Off with Chinese," *Irish Times*, April 12, 2001, https://www.irishtimes.com/news/very-sorry-letter-from-us-ends-spy-plane-stand-off-with-chinese-1.300759.

63. US Department of Defense, *Quadrennial Defense Review Report*, 2001, 4, https://www.airforcemag.com/PDF/DocumentFile/Documents/2009/QDR2001_093001.pdf.

64. George W. Bush, "State of the Union Address" (speech, White House, Washington, DC, January 29, 2002), https://georgewbush-whitehouse.archives.gov/news/releases/2002/01/20020129-11.html#:~:text=In%20this%20moment%20of%20opportunity,their%20power%20to%20lift%20lives.

65. Alex Frew McMillan and Major Garrett, "U.S. Wins Support from China," *CNN*, October 19, 2001, https://www.cnn.com/2001/WORLD/asiapcf/east/10/19/bush.jiang.apec/index.html.

66. George W. Bush, "Remarks to the Diet in Tokyo" (speech, Tokyo, February 19, 2002), The American Presidency Project, https://www.presidency.ucsb.edu/documents/remarks-the-diet-tokyo-0.

67. Ibid.

68. US Department of State, *The National Security Strategy of the United States of America*, September 2002, 26, https://2009-2017.state.gov/documents/organization/63562.pdf.

69. Green, *By More than Providence*, 498.

70. Nina Silove, "The Pivot before the Pivot: U.S. Strategy to Preserve the Power Balance in Asia," *International Security* 40, no. 4 (Spring 2016): 45–88, https://doi.org/10.1162/ISEC_a_00238.

71. Defense Industry Daily staff, "U.S. & India Sign 10-Year Defense Pact," *Defense Industry Daily*, June 30, 2005, https://www.defenseindustrydaily.com/us-india-sign-10year-defense-pact-0783/.

72. Embassy of India, Washington, DC, "India-US Trade and Investment," last updated December 17, 2019, https://indianembassyusa.gov.in/pages/MzQ,#:~:text=Total%20bilateral%20trade%20(goods%20and,at%20a%20CAGR%20of%2010.6%25.

73. Steven R. Weisman, "U.S. to Broaden India's Access to Nuclear-Power Technology," *New York Times*, July 19, 2005, https://www.nytimes.com/2005/07/19/washington/us-to-broaden-indias-access-to-nuclearpower-technology.html.

74. US Library of Congress, Congressional Research Service, *U.S.-Singapore Relations*, by Ben Dolvan and Emma Chanlett-Avery, IF10228, 2023, 2, https://sgp.fas.org/crs/row/IF10228.pdf.

75. US Department of State, Office of the Spokesman, "United States-Japan Roadmap for Realignment Implementation," press release, 2006, https://2001-2009.state.gov/r/pa/prs/ps/2006/65517.htm.

76. Eric Talmadge, "U.S. Begins Rare War Games off Guam," *SeattlePi*, June 20, 2006, https://www.seattlepi.com/national/article/U-S-begins-rare-war-games-off-Guam-1206737.php.

77. Ashok Sharma, "The Malabar Exercise Bolsters Quad Group amid Growing Strategic Challenge in the Indo-Pacific," *Australian Institute of International Affairs*, September 1, 2023, https://www.internationalaffairs.org.au/australianoutlook/the-malabar-exercise-bolsters-quad-group-amid-growing-strategic-challenge-in-the-indo-pacific/#:~:text=Australia%20participated%20in%20the%20first,the%20first%20time%20since%202007.

78. Victor D. Cha, "Winning Asia: Washington's Untold Success Story," *Foreign Affairs* 86, no. 6 (November–December 2007): 98–113, https://www.foreignaffairs.com/articles/asia/2002-11-01/winning-asia; Rush Doshi, *The Long Game: China's Grand Strategy to Displace American Order* (New York: Oxford University Press, 2021).

79. "Cancellation of Bush Visit Disappoints Southeast Asia," *Dawn,* July 13, 2007, https://www.dawn.com/news/256059/cancellation-of-bush-visit-disappoints-southeast-asia.

80. Senators John McCain and Barack Obama, "The First Presidential Debate" (debate, Oxford, MS, September 26, 2008), *New York Times*, https://www.nytimes.com/elections/2008/president/debates/transcripts/first-presidential-debate.html.

# Chapter 4

1. Jeff Zeleny, "Obama Outlines His Foreign Policy Views," *New York Times*, April 23, 2007, https://www.nytimes.com/2007/04/23/us/politics/23cnd-obama.html.

2. Previous US presidents, including Taft, Hoover, Kennedy, Nixon, and George H.W. Bush, did have experience in the Pacific. In addition, John McCain, who ran against Obama in 2008, resided in Vietnam, involuntarily, for more than five years.

3. Mike Allen, "'America's First Pacific President,'" *Politico*, November 13, 2009, https://www.politico.com/story/2009/11/americas-first-pacific-president-029511.

4. Barack Obama et al., "The Democrats' First 2008 Presidential Debate" (debate, MSNBC, Oxford, MS, April 27, 2007), *New York Times*, https://www.nytimes.com/2007/04/27/us/politics/27debate_transcript.html; Barack Obama, "Full Text: Obama's Foreign Policy Speech" (speech, Washington, DC, July 16, 2008) *Guardian*, https://www.theguardian.com/world/2008/jul/16/uselections2008.barackobama.

5. Slaughter would serve in the Obama administration as the State Department director of policy planning, Blinken as deputy national security advisor and deputy secretary of state, Campbell as assistant secretary of state for East Asia and Pacific Affairs, and Steinberg as deputy secretary of state. Anne-Marie Slaughter et al., *Strategic Leadership, Framework for a 21st Century National Security Strategy*, (Washington, DC: Center for a New American Security, July 2008), 31, https://www.cnas.org/publications/reports/strategic-leadership-framework-for-a-21st-century-national-security-strategy.

6. Kurt M. Campbell, Nirav Patel, and Vikram J. Singh, *The Power of Balance: America in iAsia*, (Washington, DC: Center for a New American Security, June 2008), https://www.cnas.org/publications/reports/the-power-of-balance-america-in-iasia.

7. Authors' discussion with Tom Donilon.

8. Douglas Stuart, *The Pivot to Asia: Can It Serve as the Foundation for American Grand Strategy in the 21st Century* (Carlisle: US Army War College Press, 2016), 5–6, https://press.armywarcollege.edu/cgi/viewcontent.cgi?article=1420&context=monographs.; Jeffrey Bader, *Obama and China's Rise: An Insider's Account of America's Asia Strategy* (Washington, DC: Brookings Institution Press, 2012), 6–7.

9. Kurt Campbell, *The Pivot: The Future of American Statecraft in Asia,* (New York: Hatchette Book Group, 2016).

10. Bader, *Obama and China's Rise,* 9.

11. Ibid., 1.

12. Author interview with James Steinberg, September 2022.

13. Authors' email exchange with Danny Russel.

14. Author conversation with Mark Lippert, March 2023.

15. Author interview with Kurt Campbell, February 2023.

16. Nicholas D. Anderson and Victor D. Cha, "The Case of the Pivot to Asia: System Effects and the Origins of Strategy," *Political Science Quarterly* 132, no. 4 (2017–2018): 602, https://www.jstor.org/stable/45175868.

17. Hillary Rodham Clinton, "US-Asia Relations: Indispensable to Our Future" (speech, Asia Society, New York, February 13, 2009), US Department of State, https://2009-2017.state.gov/secretary/20092013clinton/rm/2009a/02/117333.htm.

18. Ye Yu, "Policy Coordination in the Global Financial Crisis," China-US Focus, January 16, 2021, https://www.chinausfocus.com/finance-economy/policy-coordination-in-the-global-financial-crisis.

19. Ibid.

20. Ibid.

21. The SE&D added an ampersand to the Bush administration's Strategic Economic Dialogue (SED), elevating political dialogue to the ministerial level. Bader, *Obama and China's Rise,* 22; Author communication with Jeffrey Bader, March 2023.

22. US Department of State, Bureau of Public Affairs, Office of the Spokesperson, "United States Accedes to the Treaty of Amity and Cooperation in Southeast Asia," July 22, 2009, https://2009-2017.state.gov/r/pa/prs/ps/2009/july/126294.htm#:~:text=U.S.%20Department%20of%20State&text=On%20July%2022%2C%202009%2C%20Secretary,and%20Cooperation%20in%20Southeast%20Asia; White House, Office of the Press Secretary, "Fact Sheet: Unprecedented U.S.-ASEAN Relations," February 12, 2016, https://obamawhitehouse.archives.gov/the-press-office/2016/02/12/fact-sheet-unprecedented-us-asean-relations; "The US Lower Mekong Initiative," Stimson Center, January 14, 2010, https://www.stimson.org/2010/the-us-lower-mekong-initiative/.

23. Bader, *Obama and China's Rise,* 43.

24. Helene Cooper, "China Holds Firm on Major Issues in Obama's Visit," *New York Times,* November 17, 2009, https://www.nytimes.com/2009/11/18/world/asia/18prexy.html.

25. Jonathan Weisman et al., "Obama Hits a Wall on His Visit to China," *Wall Street Journal,* November 19, 2009, https://www.wsj.com/articles/SB125857743503654225.

26. US Department of Defense, Robert Gates, *2010 Quadrennial Defense Report*, February 2010, https://history.defense.gov/Portals/70/Documents/quadrennial/QDR2010.pdf?ver=vVJYRVwNdnGb_00ixF0UfQ%3d%3d.

27. Ibid.

28. White House, *National Security Strategy*, May 2010, https://obamawhitehouse.archives.gov/sites/default/files/rss_viewer/national_security_strategy.pdf.

29. Author communication with Jeffrey Bader, March 2023.

30. Mark Landler, "Offering to Aid Talks, US Challenges China on Disputed Islands," *New York Times*, July 23, 2010, https://www.nytimes.com/2010/07/24/world/asia/24diplo.html.

31. David E. Sanger, "With Warning, Obama Presses China on Currency," *New York Times*, September 23, 2010, https://www.nytimes.com/2010/09/24/world/24prexy.html.

32. Bader, *Obama and China's Rise*, 79.

33. Zsolt Nyiri, "Americans Now Say Asia More Important than Europe," *CNN Global Public Square*, September 9, 2014.

34. Ibid.

35. Scott Wilson and Jon Cohen, "Poll: Nearly Two-Thirds of Americans Say Afghan War Isn't Worth Fighting," *Washington Post*, March 15, 2011, https://www.washingtonpost.com/world/poll-nearly-two-thirds-of-americans-say-afghan-war-isnt-worth-fighting/2011/03/14/ABRbeEW_story.html; "Afghanistan: How Troop Levels Changed over the Course of America's Longest War," *USA Facts*, September 3, 2021, https://usafacts.org/articles/afghanistan-how-troop-levels-changed-over-the-course-of-americas-longest-war/.

36. Reuters Staff, "Timeline: Invasion, Surge and Withdrawal: US Troops in Iraq," *Reuters*, October 10, 2011, https://www.reuters.com/article/us-iraq-usa-maliki-timeline/timeline-invasion-surge-and-withdrawal-u-s-troops-in-iraq-idUSTRE7991EL20111010; Niall McCarthy, "The Annual Cost of the War in Afghanistan since 2001," *Forbes*, September 12, 2019, https://www.forbes.com/sites/niallmccarthy/2019/09/12/the-annual-cost-of-the-war-in-afghanistan-since-2001-infographic/?sh=22ac4af01971.

37. Author discussions with senior Obama administration officials throughout 2023.

38. Michael J. Green and Zack Cooper, "Revitalizing the Rebalance: How to Keep US Focus on Asia," *The Washington Quarterly* 37, no. 3 (Fall 2014): 29, https://ciaotest.cc.columbia.edu/journals/twq/v37i3/f_0032947_26816.pdf.

39. Author discussions with senior Obama administration officials throughout 2023.

40. Campbell, *The Pivot*, 12.

41. Elizabeth Economy, Kurt Campbell, and Thomas Christensen, "US Strategy in Asia: Is the Pivot Working?" (lecture, New York, October 6, 2016), Council on Foreign Relations, https://www.cfr.org/event/us-strategy-asia-pivot-working.

42. Campbell, *The Pivot*, 11.

43. Author email exchange with Danny Russel.

44. Campbell, *The Pivot*.

45. Author interview with Kurt Campbell, February 2023.

46. Ali Wyne, "Tom Pickering Interviews Henry Kissinger on America's Rebalancing towards the Asia-Pacific," *Huffington Post*, December 11, 2013, https://www.huffpost.com/entry/tom-pickering-interviews-_b_4426774.

47. Haass quoted in Campbell, *The Pivot*; Richard Haass, "Which Asian Century?" *Project Syndicate*, October 28, 2013, https://www.project-syndicate.org/comment ary/richard-n—haass-on-asia-s-need-for-reconciliation-and-integration.

48. Joseph S. Nye, "Obama's Pacific Pivot," *Project Syndicate*, December 6, 2011, https://www.project-syndicate.org/commentary/obama-s-pacific-pivot-2011-12.

49. Bush administration Asia official Thomas Christensen, for example, observed that "the 'pivot' allowed Democrats to portray themselves as strong on national security, particularly as they were planning to withdraw combat troops from Iraq and, eventually, Afghanistan. . . . The United States had never left Asia and the suggestion that we had left and had suddenly returned would do diplomatic harm." From Thomas Christensen, *The China Challenge: Shaping the Choices of a Rising Power* (New York: W. W. Norton, 2015), 248.

50. Robert Kagan, "US Can't Ignore the Middle East," *Washington Post*, November 21, 2012, https://www.washingtonpost.com/opinions/robert-kagan-us-cant-ignore-the-middle-east/2012/11/20/a2b4ede0-3331-11e2-bfd5-e202b6d7b501_story.html.

51. Zachary Keck, "The Interview: Zbigniew Brzezinski," *Diplomat*, September 10, 2012, https://thediplomat.com/2012/09/the-interview-zbigniew-brzezinski/.

52. Barack Obama, "Remarks by President Obama to the Australian Parliament" (speech, Parliament House, Canberra, November 17, 2011), White House, https://obamawhi tehouse.archives.gov/the-press-office/2011/11/17/remarks-president-obama-austral ian-parliament.

53. "U.S. Navy May Station Ships in Singapore, Philippines," *Reuters*, December 16, 2011, https://www.reuters.com/article/us-usa-navy-asia-idUSTRE7BF04Y20111216/.

54. Ibid.

55. Derek Chollet, *The Long Game: How Obama Defied Washington and Redefined America's Role in the World* (New York: Public Affairs, 2016), 60.

56. Campbell, *The Pivot*, 12.

57. Thomas Christensen, *The China Challenge: Shaping the Choices of a Rising Power* (New York: W. W. Norton, 2015), 250.

58. Hillary Rodham Clinton, *Hard Choices* (New York: Simon & Schuster, 2014).

59. Barack Obama and Mitt Romney, "Transcript of Final 2012 Presidential Debate, Part 2" (debate, Boca Raton, FL, October 23, 2012), *CBS*, https://www.cbsnews.com/news/transcript-of-final-2012-presidential-debate-part-2/.

60. Barack Obama and Thaksin Shinawatra, "Remarks by President Obama and Prime Minister Shinawatra in a Joint Press Conference" (speech, Bangkok, Thailand, November 18, 2012), White House Archives, https://obamawhitehouse.archives.gov/the-press-office/2012/11/18/remarks-president-obama-and-prime-minister-shi nawatra-joint-press-confer.

61. Campbell, *The Pivot*.

62. Author interview with James Steinberg, September 2022.

63. Tom Donilon, "Remarks by Tom Donilon, National Security Advisor to the President: "The United States and the Asia-Pacific in 2013" (speech, Asia Society,

New York, March 11, 2013), White House, https://obamawhitehouse.archives.gov/the-press-office/2013/03/11/remarks-tom-donilon-national-security-advisor-president-united-states-an.

64. David Alexander, "Pentagon Urged to Stop Stalling, Start Planning Defense Cuts," *Reuters,* March 22, 2013, https://www.reuters.com/article/usa-fiscal-defense-cuts-idINDEE92L01Z20130322.

65. "Defense Outlays and Forecast in the United States from 2000 to 2032," *Statista,* June 21, 2022, https://www.statista.com/statistics/217581/outlays-for-defense-and-forecast-in-the-us-as-a-percentage-of-the-gdp/.

66. Michael Crowley, "Why Obama Is Leaving 10,000 Troops in Afghanistan," *Time,* May 27, 2014, https://time.com/119269/obama-afghanistan-iraq-troops/.

67. Amy Lieberman, "Analysis: Obama's 2014 Foreign Aid Budget Request," *Devex,* April 11, 2013, https://www.devex.com/news/analysis-obama-s-2014-foreign-aid-budget-request-80681.

68. US Congress, Senate, Committee on Foreign Relations, *Nomination of John F. Kerry to Be Secretary of State,* 113th Congress, 1st sess., 2013, https://www.govinfo.gov/content/pkg/CHRG-113shrg86451/pdf/CHRG-113shrg86451.pdf.

69. David J. Berteau et al., *Assessing the Asia-Pacific Rebalance,* (Washington, DC: Center for Strategic and International Studies, December 2014), https://csis-website-prod.s3.amazonaws.com/s3fs-public/legacy_files/files/publication/150105_Berteau_AssessingAsiaPacificRebal_Web.pdf.

70. Kevin Baron, "Pentagon Pivots within the Pivot, to Southeast Asia," *Defense One,* August 28, 2013, https://www.defenseone.com/ideas/2013/08/pentagon-pivots-within-pivot-southeast-asia/69536/.

71. Matt Spetalnick and Jeff Mason, "Obama Offers Praice, Pressure on Historic Myanmar Trip," *Reuters,* November 18, 2012, https://www.reuters.com/article/us-asia-obama-myanmar/obama-offers-praise-pressure-on-historic-myanmar-trip-idUSBRE8AI04320121119; Katie Hunt, "Territorial Row Overshadows Obama's Cambodia Visit," *CNN,* November 20, 2012, https://www.cnn.com/2012/11/20/world/asia/obama-cambodia/index.html.

72. White House, Office of the Press Secretary, "Joint Statement by Obama, Vietnamese President Sang," press release, (Washington, DC, July 25, 2013), https://www.aspeninstitute.org/wp-content/uploads/files/content/images/agent-orange/2013-7-25_Joint_Statement_by_Presidents_Obama_&_Sang_July_25_2013.pdf.

73. US Department of Defense, *Quadrennial Defense Review 2014,* 2014, https://www.acq.osd.mil/ncbdp/docs/2014_Quadrennial_Defense_Review.pdf.

74. Thomas Maresca, "Obama Visits Philippines; US Announces Defense Pact," *USA Today,* April 27, 2014, https://www.usatoday.com/story/news/world/2014/04/27/us-philippines-defense-pact/8299491/.

75. John Podesta, "Combating Climate Change: Secretary Hagel Hosts the U.S.-ASEAN Defense Forum," *White House Blog,* April 3, 2014, https://obamawhitehouse.archives.gov/blog/2014/04/03/combating-climate-change-secretary-hagel-hosts-us-asean-defense-forum; Barack Obama, "Remarks by President Obama at U.S.-ASEAN Press Conference" (remarks, Sunnylands Center, Annenberg Retreat at Sunnylands, Rancho Mirage, CA, February 16, 2016), White House, Office of the Press Secretary,

https://obamawhitehouse.archives.gov/the-press-office/2016/02/16/remarks-presid
ent-obama-us-asean-press-conference.

76. Gardiner Harris, "Vietnam Arms Embargo to Be Fully Lifted, Obama Says in Hanoi,"
    *New York Times*, May 23, 2016, https://www.nytimes.com/2016/05/24/world/asia/
    vietnam-us-arms-embargo-obama.html.

77. David Nakamura, "Obama Is in the Philippines, Looking to Strengthen US Ties in
    Southeast Asia," *Washington Post*, November 17, 2015, https://www.washingtonpost.
    com/politics/obama-is-in-the-philippines-looking-to-bolster-us-ties-in-southeast-
    asia/2015/11/17/c7530d2c-8cfb-11e5-acff-673ae92ddd2b_story.html.

78. US Department of Defense, *Sustaining US Global Leadership: Priorities for 21st
    Century Defense*, January 2012, https://www.globalsecurity.org/military/library/pol
    icy/dod/defense_guidance-201201.pdf.

79. Ibid.

80. "Leon Panetta: US to Deploy 60% of Navy Fleet to Pacific," *BBC*, June 2, 2012, https://
    www.bbc.com/news/world-us-canada-18305750.

81. Dustin Walker, "Show Me the Money: Boost the Pacific Deterrence Initiative," *War on
    the Rocks*, June 29, 2022, https://warontherocks.com/2022/06/show-me-the-money-
    boost-the-pacific-deterrence-initiative/.

82. K. Jack Riley and Scott W. Harold, "Shinzo Abe Visit Caps New Dawn in US-Japan
    Relations," RAND, April 30, 2015, https://www.rand.org/pubs/commentary/2015/
    04/shinzo-abe-visit-caps-new-dawn-in-us-japan-relations.html.

83. Choe Sang-Hun, "South Korea and U.S. Agree to Deploy Missile Defense System,"
    *New York Times*, July 7, 2016, https://www.nytimes.com/2016/07/08/world/asia/
    south-korea-and-us-agree-to-deploy-missile-defense-system.html; John Boudreu
    and Chris Blake, "U.S. Warships Make First Visit to Vietnam Base in Decades,"
    *Bloomberg*, October 3, 2016, https://www.bloomberg.com/news/articles/2016-10-
    04/u-s-warships-make-first-visit-to-vietnam-naval-base-in-21-years?in_source=
    embedded-checkout-banner; Prashanth Parameswaran, "US Gives the Philippines 2
    New Vessels amid South China Sea Tensions," *Diplomat*, November 18, 2015, https://
    thediplomat.com/2015/11/us-gives-the-philippines-2-new-vessels-amid-south-
    china-sea-tensions/; US Library of Congress, Congressional Research Service, *New
    Zealand: U.S. Security Cooperation and the U.S. Rebalancing to Asia Strategy*, by Bruce
    Vaughn, R42993 (2013), 4.

84. Thomas Donilon, "Complete Transcript: Thomas Donilon at Asia Society New York"
    (remarks, New York, March 11, 2013), Asia Society, https://asiasociety.org/new-
    york/complete-transcript-thomas-donilon-asia-society-new-york.

85. Ashton Carter, "Remarks on the Next Phase of the US Rebalance to the Asia-Pacific"
    (remarks, McCain Institute, Arizona State University, Arizona, April 6, 2015), US
    Department of Defense, https://www.defense.gov/News/Speeches/Speech/Article/
    606660/remarks-on-the-next-phase-of-the-us-rebalance-to-the-asia-pacific-mcc
    ain-instit/.

86. Barack Obama, "Remarks of President Barack Obama—State of the Union Address
    as Delivered" (remarks, Washington, DC, January 13, 2016), White House, https://

obamawhitehouse.archives.gov/the-press-office/2016/01/12/remarks-president-bar ack-obama-%E2%80%93-prepared-delivery-state-union-address.

87. Barack Obama, "President Obama: The TPP Would Let America, Not China, Lead the Way on Global Trade," *Washington Post*, May 2, 2016, https://www.washingtonp ost.com/opinions/president-obama-the-tpp-would-let-america-not-china-lead-the-way-on-global-trade/2016/05/02/680540e4-0fd0-11e6-93ae-50921721165d_st ory.html.

88. Mark Landler, "Obama Acknowledges Scars of America's Shadow War in Laos," *New York Times*, September 6, 2016, https://www.nytimes.com/2016/09/07/world/asia/ obama-laos-bombs-war.html.

89. "Trump Signs Order Withdrawing U.S. from Trans-Pacific Trade Deal," *Reuters*, January 23, 2017, https://www.reuters.com/article/us-usa-trump-executiveorders/ trump-signs-order-withdrawing-u-s-from-trans-pacific-trade-deal-idUSKBN157 2AF.

90. White House, Office of the Press Secretary, "U.S.-China Joint Statement," press release November 17, 2009, https://obamawhitehouse.archives.gov/realitycheck/the-press-office/us-china-joint-statement; James Steinberg, "Keynote Address at the Center for a New American Security" (speech, Center for a New American Security, Washington, DC, September 24, 2009), University of Southern California, https:// china.usc.edu/james-steinberg-obama-administrations-vision-us-china-relations hip-september-24-2009.

91. US Department of Defense, *Sustaining U.S. Global Leadership: Priorities for 21st Century Defense,* January 2012, 4–5, https://www.globalsecurity.org/military/libr ary/policy/dod/defense_guidance-201201.pdf.

92. Nicole Perlroth, "Cyberattack a Topic in Obama Call with New Chinese President," *New York Times*, March 14, 2013, https://archive.nytimes.com/bits.blogs.nytimes. com/2013/03/14/cyberattacks-prominent-in-obama-call-with-new-chinese-presid ent/.

93. US Congress, Senate, Committee on Foreign Relations, *Nomination of John F. Kerry to Be Secretary of State*, 113th Congress, 1st sess., 2013, https://www.govinfo.gov/cont ent/pkg/CHRG-113shrg86451/pdf/CHRG-113shrg86451.pdf.

94. Susan E. Rice, "Remarks as Prepared for Delivery by National Security Advisor Susan E. Rice" (remarks, Washington, DC, November 21, 2013), White House, https:// obamawhitehouse.archives.gov/the-press-office/2013/11/21/remarks-prepared-delivery-national-security-advisor-susan-e-rice.

95. Ely Ratner, "Defining a New Type of Major Country Relationship between the US and China," *Real Clear Defense*, January 13, 2014, https://www.realcleardefense. com/articles/2014/01/14/defining_a_new_type_of_major_country_relation-ship_between_the_us_and_china_107032.html; Paul Haenle, "What Does a New Type of Great-Power Relations Mean for the United States and China?," Carnegie Endowment for International Peace, January 15, 2014, https://carnegieendowment. org/2014/01/15/what-does-new-type-of-great-power-relations-mean-for-united-states-and-china-pub-54202.

96. Joseph Biden and Xi Jinping, "Remarks by Vice President Joe Biden and President Xi Jinping of the People's Republic of China" (remarks, Beijing, December 4, 2013), White House https://obamawhitehouse.archives.gov/the-press-office/2013/12/04/remarks-vice-president-joe-biden-and-president-xi-jinping-peoples-republ; Andrew Erickson, "Shangri-La Dialogue 2014: Links, Full Text of Speeches, and Q&A," May 31, 2014, https://www.andrewerickson.com/2014/05/shangri-la-dialogue-2014-links-full-text-of-speeches-and-qa/; Sam Roggeveen, "Hagel at Shangri-La: China's Behavior 'Destablising and Unilateral,'" *Lowy Interpreter*, May 31, 2014, https://www.lowyinstitute.org/the-interpreter/hagel-shangri-la-china-s-behaviour-destabilising-unilateral.

97. White House, *National Security Strategy*, February 2015, 24, https://obamawhitehouse.archives.gov/sites/default/files/docs/2015_national_security_strategy_2.pdf.

98. Ellen Nakashima and Steven Mufson, "U.S., China Vow Not to Engage in Economic Cyberespionage," *Washington Post,* September 25, 2015, https://www.washingtonpost.com/national/us-china-vow-not-to-engage-in-economic-cyberespionage/2015/09/25/90e74b6a-63b9-11e5-8e9e-dce8a2a2a679_story.html.

99. Julie Hirschfeld Davis and David E. Sanger, "Obama and Xi Jinping of China Agree to Steps on Cybertheft," *New York Times*, September 25, 2015, https://www.nytimes.com/2015/09/26/world/asia/xi-jinping-white-house.html.

100. Michael D. Shear, "Obama Calls on Beijing to Stop Construction in South China Sea," *New York Times*, November 18, 2015, https://www.nytimes.com/2015/11/19/world/asia/obama-apec-summit-south-china-sea-philippines.html.

101. Tom Phillips, "Barack Obama 'Deliberately Snubbed' by Chinese in Chaotic Arrival at G20," *Guardian*, September 4, 2016, https://www.theguardian.com/world/2016/sep/04/barack-obama-deliberately-snubbed-by-chinese-in-chaotic-arrival-at-g20; William Wan, "Obama's China Visit Gets off to Rocky Start, Reflecting Current Relations," *Washington Post*, September 3, 2016, https://www.washingtonpost.com/world/obamas-china-visit-gets-off-to-rocky-start/2016/09/03/a188b2c6-71df-11e6-b786-19d0cb1ed06c_story.html; Barack Obama, "Obama on China's Aggression in South China Sea," interview by Fareed Zakaria, *GPS*, September 9, 2016, video, https://edition.cnn.com/videos/tv/2016/09/02/exp-gps-obama-sot-south-china-sea.cnn.

102. Michel Green, *By More than Providence* (New York: Columbia University Press, 2019), 552.

103. Authors' conversation with intelligence community officials.

104. Sgt. Amber Robinson, "USARPAC Becomes 4-Star Headquarters during Change of Command," US Army, July 3, 2013, https://www.army.mil/article/106821/usarpac_becomes_4_star_headquarters_during_change_of_command; David Shambaugh, *Where Great Powers Meet: America and China in Southeast Asia* (New York: Oxford University Press, 2020).

105. Zachary Freyer-Biggs, "DoD Official: Asia Pivot 'Can't Happen' Due to Budget Pressures," *Defense News*, March 4, 2014, https://archive.ph/20140304150954/http://www.defensenews.com/article/20140304/DEFREG02/303040022/DoD-Official-Asia-Pivot-Can-t-Happen-.

# Chapter 5

1. Rupert Neate and Jo Tuckman, "Donald Trump: Mexican Migrants Bring 'Tremendous Infectious Disease' to US," *Guardian*, July 6, 2015, https://www.theg uardian.com/us-news/2015/jul/06/donald-trump-mexican-immigrants-tremend ous-infectious-disease.

2. Donald Trump et al., "Transcript: Republican Presidential Debate" (debate, Boulder, CO, October 28, 2015), *New York Times*, https://www.nytimes.com/2015/10/29/us/ politics/transcript-republican-presidential-debate.html.

3. Donald Trump et al., "Who Said What and What It Meant: 4th GOP Debate, Annotated" (debate, Milwaukee, WI, November 10, 2015), *Washington Post*, https:// www.washingtonpost.com/news/the-fix/wp/2015/11/10/well-be-annotating-the-gop-debate-here/.

4. Ibid.

5. Donald Trump et al., "6th Republican Debate Transcript, Annotated: Who Said What and What It Meant" (debate, North Charleston, SC, January 14, 2016), *Washington Post*, https://www.washingtonpost.com/news/the-fix/wp/2016/01/14/6th-republi can-debate-transcript-annotated-who-said-what-and-what-it-meant/.

6. Ibid.

7. Donald Trump et al., "The CBS News Republican Debate Transcript, Annotated" (debate, South Carolina, February 13, 2016), *Washington Post*, https://www.washing tonpost.com/news/the-fix/wp/2016/02/13/the-cbs-republican-debate-transcript-annotated/.

8. Satu Limaye, "Trump in Asia: A 'Rebalance' toward Trade," *NPR*, November 13, 2017, https://www.npr.org/sections/parallels/2017/11/13/563722510/trump-in-asia-a-rebalance-toward-trade.

9. Donald Trump et al., "Transcript of the New Hampshire GOP Debate, Annotated" (debate, New Hampshire, February 6, 2016), *Washington Post*, https://www.washing tonpost.com/news/the-fix/wp/2016/02/06/transcript-of-the-feb-6-gop-debate-annotated/.

10. Donald Trump et al., "The CNN-Telemundo Republican Debate Transcript, Annotated" (debate, Houston, TX, February 25, 2016), *Washington Post*, https:// www.washingtonpost.com/news/the-fix/wp/2016/02/25/the-cnntelemundo-republi can-debate-transcript-annotated/; Donald Trump et al., "Transcript of Republican Debate in Miami, Full Text" (debate, Miami, FL, March 15, 2016), *CNN*, https:// www.cnn.com/2016/03/10/politics/republican-debate-transcript-full-text; Donald Trump, "Transcript: Donald Trump Expounds on His Foreign Policy Views," interview by Maggie Haberman and David E. Sanger, *New York Times*, March 26, 2016, https://www.nytimes.com/2016/03/27/us/politics/donald-trump-transcript.html/.

11. Trump, "Transcript."

12. Nicky Woolf, Justin McCurry, and Benjamin Haas, "Trump to Withdraw from Trans-Pacific Partnership on First Day in Office," *Guardian*, November 22, 2016, https:// www.theguardian.com/us-news/2016/nov/21/donald-trump-100-days-plans-video-trans-pacific-partnership-withdraw.

13. "Japan PM Is First Foreign Leader to Meet Trump," *BBC*, November 17, 2016, https://www.bbc.com/news/world-asia-37946613.

14. Charlie Campbell, "Donald Trump Angers China with Historic Phone Call to Taiwan's President," *Time*, December 5, 2016, https://time.com/4589641/donald-trump-china-taiwan-call/.

15. Associated Press, "'One China' Principle Not Negotiable, China Tells Trump," *Los Angeles Times*, January 16, 2017, https://www.latimes.com/world/la-fg-china-trump-20170116-story.html.

16. Author interview with Matthew Pottinger, November 2022.

17. Ibid.

18. Jonah Langan-Marmur and Phillip C. Saunders, "Absent without Leave? Gauging US Commitment to the Indo-Pacific," *Diplomat*, May 6, 2020, https://thediplomat.com/2020/05/absent-without-leave-gauging-us-commitment-to-the-indo-pacific/.

19. Juliet Perry and Ravi Agrawal, "Donald Trump Tells Narendra Modi He Considers India a 'True Friend,'" *CNN*, January 25, 2017, https://www.cnn.com/2017/01/24/politics/modi-trump-conversation.

20. Ronak D. Desai, "Three Key Takeaways from Modi and Trump's First Meeting," *Forbes*, July 6, 2017, https://www.forbes.com/sites/ronakdesai/2017/07/06/three-key-takeaways-from-modi-and-trumps-first-meeting/?sh=fd2d1af11435.

21. Choe Sang-Hun, "Trump Tells South Korea That Alliance with U.S. Is 'Ironclad,'" *New York Times*, January 30, 2017, https://www.nytimes.com/2017/01/30/world/asia/trump-north-korea-south.html.

22. Adam Taylor, "What We Know So Far about Trump's Phone Calls with Foreign Leaders," *Washington Post*, February 8, 2017, https://www.washingtonpost.com/news/worldviews/wp/2017/02/02/what-we-know-so-far-about-trumps-phone-calls-with-foreign-leaders/.

23. Julie Hirschfeld Davis and Peter Baker, "In Welcoming Shinzo Abe, Trump Affirms U.S. Commitment to Defending Japan," *New York Times*, February 10, 2017, https://www.nytimes.com/2017/02/10/world/asia/trump-shinzo-abe-meeting.html; Andrew Yeo, "Did Trump and Abe Just Launch a New Chapter in U.S.-Japan Relations?," *Washington Post*, February 13, 2017, https://www.washingtonpost.com/news/monkey-cage/wp/2017/02/13/did-trump-and-abe-just-launch-a-new-chapter-in-u-s-japan-relations/.

24. Tom Phillips, "Trump Agrees to Support 'One China' Policy in Xi Jinping Call," *Guardian*, February 10, 2017, https://www.theguardian.com/world/2017/feb/10/donald-trump-agrees-support-one-china-policy-phone-call-xi-jinping.

25. David E. Sanger, "Rex Tillerson Rejects Talks with North Korea on Nuclear Program," *New York Times*, March 17, 2017, https://www.nytimes.com/2017/03/17/world/asia/rex-tillerson-north-korea-nuclear.html.

26. Simon Denyer, "In China Debut, Tillerson Appears to Hand Beijing a Diplomatic Victory," *Washington Post*, March 19, 2017, https://www.washingtonpost.com/world/in-china-debut-tillerson-offers-reassurance-receives-praise/2017/03/19/62094abc-0c66-11e7-8884-96e6a6713f4b_story.html.

27. Motoko Rich, "Rex Tillerson, in Japan, Says U.S. Needs 'Different Approach' to North Korea," *New York Times*, March 16, 2017, https://www.nytimes.com/2017/03/16/world/asia/rex-tillerson-asia-trump-us-japan.html; David E. Sanger, "Rex Tillerson Rejects Talks with North Korea on Nuclear Program."

28. Ankit Panda, "Straight from the US State Department: The 'Pivot' to Asia Is Over," *Diplomat*, March 14, 2017, https://thediplomat.com/2017/03/straight-from-the-us-state-department-the-pivot-to-asia-is-over/.

29. "Timeline: Key Dates in the U.S.-China Trade War," *Reuters*, January 15, 2020, https://www.reuters.com/article/us-usa-trade-china-timeline/timeline-key-dates-in-the-u-s-china-trade-war-idUSKBN1ZE1AA.

30. Maggie Haberman and Mark Landler, "Despite Earlier Spat, Smooth Sailing Aboard Intrepid for Trump and Turnbull," *New York Times*, May 4, 2017, https://www.nytimes.com/2017/05/04/world/australia/donald-trump-malcolm-turnbull-meeting.html.

31. Mark Landler, "Trump Hosts Prime Minister Phuc of Vietnam and Announces Trade Deals," *New York Times*, May 31, 2017, https://www.nytimes.com/2017/05/31/world/asia/vietnam-nguyen-xuan-phuc-trump.html.

32. "Trump Says U.S. Ready to Act Alone if China Won't Help with North Korea," *CBS*, April 2, 2017, https://www.cbsnews.com/news/trump-china-north-korea-us-ready-to-act-alone/.

33. David Nakamura, "At Mar-a-Lago, Trump Welcomes China's Xi in First Summit," *Washington Post*, April 7, 2017, https://www.washingtonpost.com/politics/at-mar-a-lago-trump-to-welcome-chinas-xi-for-high-stakes-inaugural-summit/2017/04/06/0235cdd0-1ac2-11e7-bcc2-7d1a0973e7b2_story.html.

34. Sophia Yan, "Trump-Xi Meeting Concluded without Gaffe, but Criticism Soon Followed," *CNBC*, April 10, 2017, https://www.cnbc.com/2017/04/10/trump-xi-meeting-concluded-without-gaffe-but-criticism-soon-followed.html; Mark Landler and Eric Schmitt, "Aircraft Carrier Wasn't Sailing to Deter North Korea, as U.S. Suggested," *New York Times*, April 18, 2017, https://www.nytimes.com/2017/04/18/world/asia/aircraft-carrier-north-korea-carl-vinson.html; David B. Larter, "Carried Away: The Inside Story of How the Carl Vinson's Canceled Port Visit Sparked a Global Crisis," *Navy Times*, April 23, 2017, https://www.navytimes.com/news/your-navy/2017/04/23/carried-away-the-inside-story-of-how-the-carl-vinson-s-canceled-port-visit-sparked-a-global-crisis/.

35. Larter, "Carried Away."

36. Ibid.

37. Christine Kim, "'Does This Guy Have Anything Better to Do?'—Trump Responds to North Korea's Latest Missile Test-Fire," *Irish Independent*, July 4, 2017, https://www.independent.ie/world-news/asia-pacific/does-this-guy-have-anything-better-to-do-trump-responds-to-north-koreas-latest-missile-test-fire-35892779.html; Ben Blanchard, "Quiet Success for China at G20 as Xi Avoids Drama and Spotlight," *Reuters*, July 10, 2017, https://www.reuters.com/article/cnews-us-g20-germany-trump-xi-idCAKBN19V1LF-OCATP.

38. Sofia Lotto Persio, "Tillerson Wants North Korea Isolated at ASEAN Meeting Despite Official Calls for Dialogue," *Newsweek*, August 3, 2017, https://www.newsweek.com/rex-tillerson-wants-north-korea-isolated-asean-meeting-despite-official-calls-645808.

39. Amy Sawitta Lefevre, "Tillerson in Thailand Presses for More Action on North Korea," *Reuters*, August 8, 2017, https://www.reuters.com/article/us-tillerson-asia-thailand/tillerson-in-thailand-presses-for-more-action-on-north-korea-idUSKBN1AO0CU.

40. Karen DeYoung and John Wagner, "Trump Threatens 'Fire and Fury' in Response to North Korean Threats," *Washington Post*, August 8, 2017, https://www.washingtonpost.com/politics/trump-tweets-news-report-citing-anonymous-sources-on-n-korea-movements/2017/08/08/47a9b9c0-7c48-11e7-83c7-5bd5460f0d7e_story.html.

41. Gerald Seib, Jay Soloman, and Carol E. Lee, "Barack Obama Warns Donald Trump on North Korea Threat," *Wall Street Journal*, November 22, 2016, https://www.wsj.com/articles/trump-faces-north-korean-challenge-1479855286.

42. Author conversation with senior Trump administration official, 2017.

43. Ali Vitali, "Trump on North Korea Feud: 'Fire and Fury' Not Tough Enough," *NBC*, August 10, 2017, https://www.nbcnews.com/politics/white-house/trump-north-korea-feud-fire-fury-not-tough-enough-n791561.

44. John Wagner, Karen DeYoung, and Jenna Johnson, "North Korea Will 'Not Get Away' with Threats to U.S. Territory, Trump Says in Latest Warnings," *Washington Post*, August 11, 2017, https://www.washingtonpost.com/news/post-politics/wp/2017/08/11/military-is-locked-and-loaded-trump-says-in-latest-warning-to-north-korea/.

45. Justin McCurry, "Donald Trump on North Korea: 'All Options Are on the Table,'" *Guardian*, August 29, 2017, https://www.theguardian.com/world/2017/aug/29/donald-trump-on-north-korea-all-options-are-on-the-table.

46. "Trump, Mattis, Mnuchin Warn North Korea of 'Overwhelming' Military Response, Halted Trade," *Fox News*, September 19, 2017, https://www.foxnews.com/politics/trump-mattis-mnuchin-warn-north-korea-of-overwhelming-military-response-halted-trade; Steve Herman, "Trump to Allow South Korea, Japan to Buy More US Military Equipment," *Voice of America*, September 5, 2017, https://www.voanews.com/a/trump-to-allow-south-korea-japan-to-buy-more-us-military-equipment/4015819.html.

47. Megan Specia, "At U.N., Trump Singles Out 'Rogue' Nations North Korea and Iran," *New York Times*, September 19, 2017, https://www.nytimes.com/2017/09/19/world/americas/united-nations-general-assembly.html.

48. Rebecca Kheel, "Allies on Edge over Trump Summit with North Korea," *Hill*, April 24, 2018, https://thehill.com/policy/defense/384519-allies-on-edge-over-trump-summit-with-north-korea/.

49. "Trump China Visit: US Leaders Strikes Warmer Tone with Xi Jinping," *BBC*, November 9, 2017, https://www.bbc.com/news/world-asia-china-41924228.

50. "Trump Signs Executive Order Targeting North Korea's Trading Partners," *Fox News*, September 22, 2017, https://www.foxnews.com/politics/trump-signs-executive-order-targeting-north-koreas-trading-partners.

51. Danielle Demetriou, "Donald Trump Says Japan Will Buy US Hardware to Shoot North Korean Missiles 'Out of the Sky,'" *Telegraph*, November 6, 2017, https://www.telegraph.co.uk/news/2017/11/06/donaldtrumpsays-japan-will-buy-us-hardware-shoot-north-korean/.

52. Kevin Liptak, "Trump Tells North Korea: 'Do Not Try Us,'" *CNN*, November 8, 2017, https://www.cnn.com/2017/11/07/politics/president-donald-trump-south-korean-address.

53. Donald Trump, "Remarks by President Trump at APEC CEO Summit" (speech, Da Nang, Vietnam, November 10, 2017), White House, https://trumpwhitehouse.archives.gov/briefings-statements/remarks-president-trump-apec-ceo-summit-da-nang-vietnam/.

54. Ceri Parker, "China's Xi Jinping Defends Globalization from the Davos Stage," World Economic Forum, January 17, 2017, https://www.weforum.org/agenda/2017/01/chinas-xi-jinping-defends-globalization-from-the-davos-stage/.

55. Xi Jinping, "Seizing the Opportunity of a Global Economy in Transition and Accelerating Development in the Asia-Pacific" (speech, APEX CEO Summit, Da Nang, Vietnam, November 10, 2017), *Xinhua*, https://www.chinadaily.com.cn/world/2017-11/11/content_34393531.htm.

56. Office of the United States Trade Representative, Executive Office of the President, *Findings of the Investigation into China's Acts, Policies, and Innovation under Section 301 of the trade Act of 1974*, March 22, 2018, https://ustr.gov/sites/default/files/Section%20301%20FINAL.PDF.

57. Prashanth Parameswaran, "US-Vietnam Defense Relations under Trump Get a Boost with First Aircraft Carrier Visit," *Diplomat*, August 9, 2019, https://thediplomat.com/2017/08/us-vietnam-defense-relations-under-trump-get-a-boost-with-first-aircraft-carrier-visit/; US State Department, US Embassy and Consulate in Vietnam, "Joint Statement: Between the United States of America and the Socialist Republic of Viet Nam," November 2017, https://vn.usembassy.gov/20171112-joint-statement-united-states-america-socialist-republic-viet-nam/.

58. Oliver Holmes, "Donald Trump Builds Relations with Authoritarian Asian Leaders," *Guardian*, May 1, 2017, https://www.theguardian.com/us-news/2017/may/01/donald-trump-rebuilds-us-relations-with-thailand-and-philippines.

59. Office of the Secretary of Defense, Historical Office, *National Security Strategy of the United States of America*, December 2017, https://history.defense.gov/Portals/70/Documents/nss/NSS2017.pdf?ver=CnFwURrw09pJ0q5EogFpwg%3d%3d.

60. Author interview with Nadia Schadlow, November 2022.

61. Ibid.

62. Ibid.

63. US Department of Defense, *Summary of the 2018 National Defense Strategy of the United States of America*, January 2018, https://dod.defense.gov/Portals/1/Documents/pubs/2018-National-Defense-Strategy-Summary.pdf.

64. Author interview with Matthew Pottinger, November 2022.

65. US Department of Defense, *Indo-Pacific Strategy Report*, June 1, 2019, https://media.defense.gov/2019/Jul/01/2002152311/-1/-1/1/DEPARTMENT-OF-DEFENSE-INDO-PACIFIC-STRATEGY-REPORT-2019.PDF.

66. Author interview with Matthew Pottinger, November 2022.

67. Ibid.

68. Donald Trump, "Read Trump's Full Speech Outlining His National Security Strategy," by Erica R. Hendry, (speech, December 18, 2017), *PBS*, https://www.pbs.org/newsh our/politics/read-trumps-full-speech-outlining-his-national-security-strategy.

69. Gregory D. Foster, "The National Defense Strategy Is No Strategy," *Defense One*, April 4, 2019, https://www.defenseone.com/ideas/2019/04/national-defense-strategy-no-strategy/156068/.

70. Kurt Campbell and Ely Ratner, "The China Reckoning: How Beijing Defied American Expectations," *Foreign Affairs* 97, no. 2 (March–April 2018): 60–70, https://www.for eignaffairs.com/articles/china/2018-02-13/china-reckoning.

71. Tarun Chhabra, "Mapping Reactions to Trump's First National Security Strategy," *Order from Chaos* (blog), Brookings Institution, January 10, 2018, https://www. brookings.edu/blog/order-from-chaos/2018/01/10/mapping-reactions-to-trumps-first-national-security-strategy/.

72. Robert Zoellick, "The China Challenge," *National Interest*, February 14, 2020, https:// nationalinterest.org/feature/china-challenge-123271.

73. US Department of Defense, *Indo-Pacific Strategy Report*.

74. US Department of State, *A Free and Open Indo-Pacific: Advancing a Shared Vision*, November 4, 2019, 4, 29, https://www.state.gov/wp-content/uploads/2019/11/Free-and-Open-Indo-Pacific-4Nov2019.pdf.

75. Mike Pompeo, "Secretary Pompeo Remarks on 'American's Indo-Pacific Economic Vision'" (speech, Indo-Pacific Business Forum, Washington, DC, July 30, 2018), US Embassy and Consulate in the Republic of Korea, https://kr.usembassy.gov/073018-secretary-pompeo-remarks-on-americas-indo-pacific-economic-vision/.

76. Mark Landler, "North Korea Asks for Direct Nuclear Talks, and Trump Agrees," *New York Times*, March 8, 2018, https://www.nytimes.com/2018/03/08/us/politics/north-korea-kim-jong-un-trump.html.

77. Ali Vitali, "President Trump Agrees to Meet with North Korea's Kim Jong Un," *NBC*, March 8, 2018, https://www.nbcnews.com/politics/white-house/south-koreans-deli ver-letter-trump-kim-jong-un-n855051.

78. Motoko Rich, "Japan Fears Being Sidelined by Trump on Trade and North Korea," *New York Times*, April 18, 2018, https://www.nytimes.com/2018/04/18/world/asia/japan-abe-trump.html.

79. Katie Rogers, "Trump Greets 3 American Detainees Freed from North Korea," *New York Times*, May 10, 2018, https://www.nytimes.com/2018/05/10/us/politics/trump-korea-detainees-pompeo.html.

80. Mark Landler, "Trump Pulls Out of North Korea Summit Meeting with Kim Jong-un," *New York Times*, May 24, 2018, https://www.nytimes.com/2018/05/24/world/asia/north-korea-trump-summit.html; Peter Baker, "Trump Announces Summit Meeting with Kim Jong-un Is Back On," *New York Times*, June 1, 2018, https://www. nytimes.com/2018/06/01/world/asia/trump-north-korea-summit-kim.html.

81. Miral Fahmy, Karishma Singh, and Kevin Krolicki "Trump and Kim's Joint Statement," *Reuters*, June 12, 2018. https://www.reuters.com/article/northkorea-usa-agreement-text/trump-and-kims-joint-statement-idINKBN1J80IW.

82. Office of the United States Trade Representative, Executive Office of the President, "Fact Sheet on U.S.-Japan Digital Trade Agreement," October 2019, https://ustr.gov/about-us/policy-offices/press-office/fact-sheets/2019/october/fact-sheet-us-japan-digital-trade-agreement.

83. Jim Tankersley, "Trump Signs Revised Korean Trade Deal," *New York Times*, September 24, 2018, https://www.nytimes.com/2018/09/24/us/politics/south-korea-trump-trade-deal.html.

84. "Trump Brags Auto Tariff Threat Forced Japan into Trade Talks," *Japan Times*, October 2, 2018, https://www.japantimes.co.jp/news/2018/10/02/business/trump-brags-auto-tariff-threat-forced-japan-trade-talks/.

85. Donald Trump, "Remarks by President Trump to the 74th Session of the United Nations General Assembly" (remarks, United Nations Headquarters, New York, September 24, 2019), White House, https://trumpwhitehouse.archives.gov/briefings-statements/remarks-president-trump-74th-session-united-nations-general-assembly/.

86. Damian Palettta et al., "Cracks Appear in Trump's Claims of China Trade Agreement," *Washington Post*, December 4, 2018, https://www.washingtonpost.com/business/economy/i-am-a-tariff-man-trump-says-as-china-talks-show-signs-of-sputtering/2018/12/04/516425e4-f7e0-11e8-8c9a-860ce2a8148f_story.html.

87. Paul McLeary, "Acting SecDef Shanahan's First Message: 'China, China, China,'" *Breaking Defense*, January 2, 2019, https://breakingdefense.com/2019/01/acting-secdef-shanahans-first-message-china-china-china/.

88. Daisuke Wakabayashi and Alan Rappepeort, "Huawei C.F.O. Is Arrested in Canada for Extradition to the U.S.," *New York Times*, December 5, 2018, https://www.nytimes.com/2018/12/05/business/huawei-cfo-arrest-canada-extradition.html?searchResultPosition=1.

89. Matthew Whitaker, "Acting Attorney General Matthew Whitaker Announces National Security Related Criminal Charges against Chinese Telecommunications Conglomerate Huawei" (remarks, Washington, DC, January 28, 2019), Office of Public Affairs, US Department of Justice, https://www.justice.gov/opa/speech/acting-attorney-general-matthew-whitaker-announces-national-security-related-criminal.

90. Laura Silver, Kat Devlin, and Christine Huang, "U.S. Views of China Turn Sharply Negative amid Trade Tensions," Pew Research Center, August 13, 2019, https://www.pewresearch.org/global/2019/08/13/u-s-views-of-china-turn-sharply-negative-amid-trade-tensions/.

91. "Timeline: Key Dates in the U.S.-China Trade War," *Reuters*.

92. Cornelia Tremann, "America Builds on Development Aid," *Interpreter*, October 23, 2018, https://www.lowyinstitute.org/the-interpreter/america-builds-development-aid.

93. Glenn Thrush, "Trump Embraces Foreign Aid to Counter China's Global Influence," *New York Times*, October 14, 2018, https://www.nytimes.com/2018/10/14/world/asia/donald-trump-foreign-aid-bill.html.

94. Ibid.

95. "Congress Finalizes FY18 Spending: Rejects 'Doctrine of Retreat,' Restores Funding for International Affairs Budget," U.S. Global Leadership Coalition, March 23, 2018,

https://www.usglc.org/the-budget/congress-finalizes-fy18-spending-rejects-doctr
ine-retreat-restores-funding-international-affairs-budget/; Alyssa Ayres, "Trump
to Cut Foreign Aid Budgets, Opening South and Central Asia's Door to Chinese
Influence," *Forbes*, May 4, 2017, https://www.forbes.com/sites/alyssaayres/2017/05/
04/trump-to-cut-foreign-aid-budgets-opening-south-and-central-asias-door-to-
chinese-influence/?sh=469b6ec85f50.

96. "Congress Finalizes FY19 Spending: Small Increase for International Affairs
Budget Holds the Line at Critical Moment for U.S. Global Leadership," U.S. Global
Leadership Coalition, February 15, 2019, https://www.usglc.org/the-budget/congr
ess-finalizes-fy19-spending-small-increase-for-international-affairs-budget-
holds-the-line-at-critical-moment-for-u-s-global-leadership/.

97. "Congress Finalizes FY21 Spending: Protects International Affairs Budget in the
Midst of Global COVID-19 Pandemic," U.S. Global Leadership Coalition, December
30, 2020, https://www.usglc.org/the-budget/congress-finalizes-fy21-spending-prote
cts-international-affairs-budget-in-the-midst-of-global-covid-19-pandemic/.

98. Carl Thayer, "ARIA: Congress Makes Its Mark on US Asia Policy," *Diplomat*, January
8, 2019, https://thediplomat.com/2019/01/aria-congress-makes-its-mark-on-us-
asia-policy/.

99. Ibid.

100. Nirmal Ghosh, "US Funding for Engagement with Asia-Pacific Modest, but a
Positive Signal," *Straits Times*, December 24, 2019, https://www.straitstimes.com/
world/united-states/us-funding-for-engagement-with-asia-pacific-modest-but-a-
positive-signal.

101. Andrew Eversden, "Pacific Deterrence Initiative Gets $2.1 Billion Boost in Final
NDAA," *Breaking Defense*, December 7, 2021, https://breakingdefense.com/2021/
12/pacific-deterrence-initiative-gets-2-1-billion-boost-in-final-ndaa/.

102. Carl Thayer, "Asia Reassurance Initiative Act: Framework for a US Indo-Pacific
Strategy?," *Diplomat*, January 7, 2020, https://thediplomat.com/2020/01/asia-reas
surance-initiative-act-framework-for-a-us-indo-pacific-strategy/.

103. US Department of Defense, *Indo-Pacific Strategy Report*, 21.

104. Gordon Lubold and Andrew Jeong, "U.S. Presses South Korea to Pay More for
Military Alliance," *Wall Street Journal*, November 15, 2019, https://www.wsj.com/
articles/u-s-presses-south-korea-to-pay-more-for-military-alliance-11573815
982?mod=article_inline.

105. Sam Nussey, "Trump Asks Japan to Hike Payments for U.S. Troops to $8
Billion: Foreign Policy," *Reuters*, November 15, 2019, https://www.reuters.com/
article/us-japan-usa/trump-asks-japan-to-hike-payments-for-u-s-troops-to-8-bill
ion-foreign-policy-idUSKBN1XQ06F.

106. Robert Burns, "Seoul Agrees to Pay More for Hosting American Troops in 2021,"
*Military Times*, March 10, 2021, https://www.militarytimes.com/news/your-milit
ary/2021/03/10/seoul-agrees-to-pay-more-for-hosting-american-troops-in-2021/.

107. "Timeline: Key Dates in the U.S.-China Trade War," *Reuters*.

108. Karishma Vaswani, "G20 Summit: Trump and Xi Agree to Restart US-China Trade
Talks," *BBC*, June 29, 2019, https://www.bbc.com/news/world-48810070.

109. Peter Baker and Michael Crowley, "Trump Steps into North Korea and Agrees with Kim Jong-un to Resume Talks," *New York Times*, June 30, 2019, https://www.nyti mes.com/2019/06/30/world/asia/trump-north-korea-dmz.html.

110. "Imran Khan: Pakistan PM Meets Trump in Bid to Mend Ties," *BBC*, July 22, 2019, https://www.bbc.com/news/world-us-canada-49032495.

111. Stuti Banerjee, "Prime Minister Modi and President Trump: Re-focusing on the Bilateral Relations," Indian Council of World Affairs, September 17, 2019, https://icwa.in/show_content.php?lang=1&level=3&ls_id=3087&lid=2363.

112. Charissa Yong and Lim Min Zhang, "PM Lee, Trump Renew Key Defence Pact on US Use of Singapore Air, Naval Bases," *Straits Times*, September 24, 2019, https://www.straitstimes.com/world/pm-lee-trump-renew-key-defence-pact-on-us-use-of-singapore-air-naval-bases.

113. Bradley Bowman, Cleo Paskal, and Maj. Liane Zivitski, "US-India Helicopter Deal Deepens Vital Partnership," *Defense News*, March 5, 2020, https://www.defensen ews.com/opinion/commentary/2020/03/05/us-india-helicopter-deal-deepens-vital-partnership/.

114. Ana Swanson and Paul Mozur, "U.S. Blacklists 28 Chinses Entities over Abuses in Xinjiang," *New York Times*, October 7, 2019, https://www.nytimes.com/2019/10/07/us/politics/us-to-blacklist-28-chinese-entities-over-abuses-in-xinjiang.html.

115. Bob Davis et al., "U.S., China Sign Deal Easing Trade Tensions," *Wall Street Journal*, January 15, 2020, https://www.wsj.com/articles/u-s-china-to-sign-deal-easing-trade-tensions-11579087018.

116. Phelim Kine, "From 'Momentous' to 'Meh'—Trump's China Trade Deal Letdown," *Politico*, January 13, 2022, https://www.politico.com/newsletters/politico-china-watcher/2022/01/13/from-momentous-to-meh-the-phase-one-trade-deal-letd own-495705.

117. Yen Nee Lee, "China's Purchases of US Goods Will Fall Way Short of 'Phase One' Trade Deal Due to the Coronavirus, Says Think Tank," *CNBC*, May 11, 2020, https://www.cnbc.com/2020/05/11/coronavirus-us-exports-to-china-to-fall-short-of-phase-one-trade-deal-says-csis.html.

118. Aaron Blake, "Before the White House and Trump Allies Blamed China for Coronavirus, Trump Vouched for China—Repeatedly," *Washington Post*, March 14, 2020, https://www.washingtonpost.com/politics/2020/03/14/before-trump-white-house-blamed-china-coronavirus-it-vouched-it/.

119. Lily Kuo, "Trump Sparks Anger by Calling Coronavirus the 'Chinese Virus,'" *Guardian*, March 17, 2020, https://www.theguardian.com/world/2020/mar/17/trump-calls-covid-19-the-chinese-virus-as-rift-with-coronavirus-beijing-escalates.

120. Katie Rogers and Apoorva Mandavilli, "Trump Administration Signals Formal Withdrawal from W.H.O.," *New York Times*, July 6, 2020, https://www.nytimes.com/2020/07/07/us/politics/coronavirus-trump-who.html.

121. David Nakamura, "With 'Kung Flu,' Trump Sparks Backlash over Racist Language—and a Rallying Cry for Supporters," *Washington Post*, June 24, 2020, https://www.washingtonpost.com/politics/with-kung-flu-trump-sparks-backlash-over-rac

ist-language—and-a-rallying-cry-for-supporters/2020/06/24/485d151e-b620-11ea-aca5-ebb63d27e1ff_story.html.

122. Author interview with Matthew Pottinger, November 2022.

123. Donald Trump, "Remarks by President Trump on Actions against China" (remarks, Rose Garden, Washington, DC, May 29, 2020), White House Archives, https://trumpwhitehouse.archives.gov/briefings-statements/remarks-president-trump-actions-china/.

124. Karishma Vaswani, "Trump Ends Preferential Economic Treatment for Hong Kong," *BBC*, July 15, 2020, https://www.bbc.com/news/world-us-canada-53412598.

125. Bobby Allyn, "Trump Signs Executive Order That Will Effectively Ban Use of TikTok in the U.S.," *NPR*, August 6, 2020, https://www.npr.org/2020/08/06/900019185/trump-signs-executive-order-that-will-effectively-ban-use-of-tiktok-in-the-u-s.

126. Bobby Allyn, "U.S. Judge Halts Trump's TikTok Ban, the 2nd Court to Fully Block the Action," *NPR*, December 7, 2020, https://www.npr.org/2020/12/07/944039053/u-s-judge-halts-trumps-tiktok-ban-the-2nd-court-to-fully-block-the-action.

127. Humeyra Pamuk and David Brunnstrom, "In Parting Shot, Trump Administration Accuses China of 'Genocide' against Uighurs," *Reuters*, January 19, 2021, https://www.reuters.com/article/us-usa-china-genocide/in-parting-shot-trump-administration-accuses-china-of-genocide-against-uighurs-idUSKBN29O25F.

128. John Hudson, "At the 11th hour, Trump Administration Declares China's Treatment of Muslims in Xinjiang 'Genocide,'" *Washington Post*, January 19, 2021, https://www.washingtonpost.com/national-security/trump-china-genocide-uighur-muslims/2021/01/19/272a9df4-5a7f-11eb-aaad-93988621dd28_story.html.

129. Deirdre Shesgreen, "'The World's on Fire' and Other Takeaways from Biden's Secretary of State Nominee Confirmation Hearing," *USA Today*, January 19, 2021, https://www.usatoday.com/story/news/politics/elections/2021/01/19/biden-nominee-antony-blinken-china-committing-genocide-uyghurs/4215835001/.

130. Author interview with Matthew Pottinger, November 2022; Pottinger observes that the effort was more successful in 2019 and 2020, including by reducing the amount of time spent by the Principals and Deputies committees on non-Asia issues and increasing the focus on China and Asia.

131. Author interview with Matthew Pottinger, November 2022.

132. Ibid.

133. Shawn Snow, "Esper Wants to Move Troops from Afghanistan to the Indo-Pacific to Confront China," *Military Times*, December 18, 2019, https://www.militarytimes.com/flashpoints/2019/12/18/esper-wants-to-move-troops-from-afghanistan-to-the-indo-pacific-to-confront-china/.

134. Helene Cooper et al., "Pentagon Eyes Africa Drawdown as First Step in Global Troop Shift," *New York Times*, December 24, 2019, https://www.nytimes.com/2019/12/24/world/africa/esper-troops-africa-china.html.

135. Idrees Ali and Phil Stewart, "U.S. Will Not Completely Withdraw Forces from Africa: Pentagon Chief," *Reuters*, January 30, 2020, https://www.reuters.com/article/us-usa-africa-military/u-s-will-not-completely-withdraw-forces-from-africa-pentagon-chief-idUSKBN1ZT2EP.

136. Phil Stewart and Idrees Ali, "France Warns Pentagon against Cutting U.S. Troops in West Africa," *Curacao Chronicle*, January 27, 2020, https://www.curacaochroni cle.com/post/world/france-warns-pentagon-against-cutting-us-troops-in-west-africa/.

137. Aaron Mehta and Joe Gould, "Esper's Africa Drawdown Snags on Capitol Hill," *Defense News*, January 16, 2020, https://www.defensenews.com/congress/2020/01/ 17/smith-thornberry-join-congressional-pushback-on-espers-africa-troop-drawd own-plan/.

138. Ali and Stewart, "U.S. Will Not Completely Withdraw Forces from Africa."

139. Robert C. O'Brien, "Why the U.S. Is Moving Troops Out of Germany," June 21, 2022, https://www.wsj.com/articles/why-the-u-s-is-moving-troops-out-of-germany-11592757552.

140. Lara Seligman, "U.S. to Pull 12,000 Troops from Germany after Trump Calls Country 'Delinquent,'" *Politico*, July 29, 2020, https://www.politico.com/news/2020/ 07/29/us-to-pull-12-000-troops-from-germany-after-trump-calls-country-delinqu ent-386136.

141. Robert Burns, "Trump Announces Major US Troop Cut in 'Delinquent' Germany," *Associated Press*, June 15, 2020, https://apnews.com/article/politics-middle-east-donald-trump-germany-military-facilities-b4ac0b046a6be385b583a816e98f2240.

142. Senator Mitt Romney (@SenatorRomney), "The Administration's plan to remove thousands of U.S. troops from Germany is a grave error. It is a slap in the face at a friend and ally when we should instead be drawing closer in our mutual com- mitment to deter Russian and Chinese aggression," Twitter, July 2020, 11:23 a.m., https://twitter.com/senatorromney/status/1288495323829149699.

143. Mitt Romney, "Romney, Colleagues Introduce Measure to Defense Bill to Limit Troop Reductions in Germany," June 29, 2020, https://www.romney.senate.gov/rom ney-colleagues-introduce-m.

144. Helene Cooper, "Biden Freezes Trump's Withdrawal of 12,000 Troops from Germany," *New York Times*, February 4, 2021, https://www.nytimes.com/2021/02/ 04/us/politics/biden-germany-troops-trump.html.

145. The data from the International Institute for Strategic Studies represent a snap- shot of total US deployments in early November of each year and do not reflect changes in rotating US personnel throughout the year. International Institute for Strategic Studies, "Chapter Three: North America," *The Military Balance* 117, no. 1 (2017): 58–60, https://www-tandfonline-com.proxy1.library.jhu.edu/doi/pdf/ 10.1080/04597222.2017.1271209?needAccess=true.; International Institute for Strategic Studies, "Chapter Three: North America," *The Military Balance* 121, no. 1 (2021): 60–62, https://www-tandfonline-com.proxy1.library.jhu.edu/doi/pdf/ 10.1080/04597222.2021.1868792?needAccess=true.

146. Eugene Kiely and Robert Farley, "Timeline of U.S. Withdrawal from Afghanistan," *FactCheck.org*, August 17, 2021, https://www.factcheck.org/2021/08/timeline-of-u-s-withdrawal-from-afghanistan/.

147. US Library of Congress, Congressional Research Service, *FY2018 Defense Appropriations Act: An Overview*, by Brendan W. McGarry and Pat Towell, IF10868,

2018, https://www.everycrsreport.com/files/2018-04-05_IF10868_49e325a5392d6 88687e79e6ef5f65841738af86e.pdf.

148. International Institute for Strategic Studies, "Chapter Three: North America," *The Military Balance* 117, no. 1 (2017); International Institute for Strategic Studies, "Chapter Three: North America," *The Military Balance,* 121, no. 1 (2021).

149. Michael O'Hanlon, "The Asia-Pacific Rebalance and Beyond," *Wall Street Journal,* May 23, 2017, https://www.wsj.com/articles/the-asia-pacific-rebalance-and-bey ond-1495559015.

150. Author interview with Matthew Pottinger, November 2022.

151. Jamie Fly, "Trump's Asia Policy and the Concept of the 'Indo-Pacific,'" *SWP,* October 2018, https://www.swp-berlin.org/publications/products/projekt_papiere/Fly_BCA S_2018_Indo-Pacific_10.pdf.

152. James Mcbride, Andrew Chatzky, and Anshu Siripurapu, "What's Next for the Trans-Pacific Partnership (TPP)?" Backgrounder, Council on Foreign Relations, last modified September 20, 2021, https://www.cfr.org/backgrounder/what-trans-pacific-partnership-tpp#chapter-title-0-6.

153. Jeanne Milot-Poulin, Rachel Sarfati, and Jonathan Paquin, "The American Strategic Pivot in the Indo-Pacific," *Network for Strategic Analysis,* October 2021, https://ras-nsa.ca/the-american-strategic-pivot-in-the-indo-pacific/.

# Chapter 6

1. Joseph Biden et al., "Full Transcript: Ninth Democratic Debate in Las Vegas" (debate, Las Vegas, NV, February 20, 2020), *NBC,* https://www.nbcnews.com/polit ics/2020-election/full-transcript-ninth-democratic-debate-las-vegas-n1139546; Joseph Biden, "Transcript: Joe Biden's DNC Speech" (speech, Democratic National Convention, Milwaukee, WI, August 21, 2020), *CNN,* https://www.cnn.com/2020/ 08/20/politics/biden-dnc-speech-transcript/index.html.

2. Deirde Shesgreen, "'The World's on Fire' and Other Takeaways from Biden's Secretary of State Nominee Confirmation Hearing," *USA Today,* January 19, 2021, https://www.usatoday.com/story/news/politics/elections/2021/01/19/biden-nomi nee-antony-blinken-china-committing-genocide-uyghurs/4215835001/.

3. Ben Blanchard, "Taiwan-Biden Ties off to Strong Start with Invite for Top Diplomat," *Reuters,* January 20, 2021, https://www.reuters.com/article/us-usa-biden-taiwan/taiwan-biden-ties-off-to-strong-start-with-invite-for-top-diplomat-idUSKBN29Q01N.

4. Justin Worland, "The Biden Administration Is Already Calling on China to Do More on Climate Change," *Time,* January 27, 2021, https://time.com/5933657/ john-kerry-china-climate-change/.

5. Senior Biden administration national security officials, private conversations with authors, 2022.

6. Kurt Campbell and Ely Ratner, "The China Reckoning: How Beijing Defied American Expectations," *Foreign Affairs* 97, no. 2 (March–April 2018): 60–70, https://www.for eignaffairs.com/articles/china/2018-02-13/china-reckoning.

7. Rush Doshi, *The Long Game: China's Grand Strategy to Displace American Order* (New York: Oxford University Press, 2021), 10.

8. Campbell and Ratner, "The China Reckoning: How Beijing Defied American Expectation."

9. Ibid.

10. White House, "Readout of President Joseph R. Biden, Jr. Call with Prime Minister Yoshihide Suga of Japan," January 27, 2021, https://www.whitehouse.gov/briefing-room/statements-releases/2021/01/27/readout-of-president-joseph-r-biden-jr-call-with-prime-minister-yoshihide-suga-of-japan/.

11. Justin McCurry, "US Takes Aim at China Territorial Claims as Biden Vows to Back Japan," *Guardian*, January 27, 2021, https://www.theguardian.com/us-news/2021/jan/28/us-takes-aim-at-china-territorial-claims-as-biden-vows-to-back-japan.

12. Joseph Biden, "Remarks by President Biden on America's Place in the World" (speech, US Department of State Headquarters, Harry S. Truman Building, Washington, DC, February 4, 2021), White House, https://www.whitehouse.gov/briefing-room/speec hes-remarks/2021/02/04/remarks-by-president-biden-on-americas-place-in-the-world/.

13. White House, *Interim National Security Strategic Guidance*, March 2021, https://www.whitehouse.gov/wp-content/uploads/2021/03/NSC-1v2.pdf.

14. White House, *National Security Strategy*, October 2022, https://www.whitehouse.gov/wp-content/uploads/2022/10/Biden-Harris-Administrations-National-Secur ity-Strategy-10.2022.pdf.

15. Richard Fontaine, "Washington's Missing China Strategy," *Foreign Affairs*, January 14, 2022, https://www.foreignaffairs.com/articles/china/2022-01-14/washingtons-miss ing-china-strategy.

16. Joe Biden et al., "Our Four Nations Are Committed to a Free, Open, Secure and Prosperous Indo-Pacific Region," *Washington Post*, March 13, 2022, https://www.was hingtonpost.com/opinions/2021/03/13/biden-modi-morrison-suga-quad-nations-indo-pacific/; Abhijnan Rej, "In 'Historic' Summit Quad Commits to Meeting Key Indo-Pacific Challenges," *Diplomat*, March 13, 2021, https://thediplomat.com/2021/03/in-historic-summit-quad-commits-to-meeting-key-indo-pacific-challenges/.

17. Kate Sullivan and Jason Hoffman, "Biden Uses Meeting with Japanese Prime Minister to Emphasize New Focus on China," *CNN*, April 16, 2021, https://www.cnn.com/2021/04/15/politics/japan-prime-minister-white-house-visit/index.html;    Paul Schemm et al., "Biden Pledges to Help India amid Worsening Crisis; U.S. to Share 60 Million Vaccine Doses with the World," *Washington Post*, April 26, 2021, https://www.washingtonpost.com/nation/2021/04/26/coronavirus-covid-live-updates-us/.

18. White House, "Carbis Bay G7 Summit Communique," June 13, 2021, https://www.whitehouse.gov/briefing-room/statements-releases/2021/06/13/carbis-bay-g7-summit-communique/; White House, "U.S.-EU Summit Statement," June 15, 2021,

https://www.whitehouse.gov/briefing-room/statements-releases/2021/06/15/u-s-eu-summit-statement/; Heads of State and Government of the 30 NATO Allies, "Brussels Summit Communiqué," June 14, 2021, https://www.nato.int/cps/en/natol ive/news_185000.htm?selectedLocale=en.

19. "Biden Meets Moon, Appoints New US Envoy for North Korea," *Al Jazeera*, May 22, 2021, https://www.aljazeera.com/news/2021/5/22/biden-meets-moon-appoi nts-us-envoy-for-north-korea.

20. Vivian Salama, "Biden Speaks with Chinese President Xi Jinping for First Time as President," *CNN*, February 11, 2021, https://www.cnn.com/2021/02/10/politics/biden-xi-call/index.html; Nahal Toosi, "China and U.S. Open Alaska Meeting with Undiplomatic War of words," *Politico*, March 18, 2021, https://www.politico.com/news/2021/03/18/china-us-alaska-meeting-undiplomatic-477118.

21. Antony Blinken, Jake Sullivan, Yang Jiechi et al., "How It Happened: Transcript of the US-China Opening Remarks in Alaska" (remarks, Anchorage, March 19, 2021), *Nikkei Asia*, https://asia.nikkei.com/Politics/International-relations/US-China-tensi ons/How-it-happened-Transcript-of-the-US-China-opening-remarks-in-Alaska.

22. William Yang, "Xi and Biden Set to Strengthen 'Guardrails' at Bali Meeting," *DW*, November 13, 2022, https://www.dw.com/en/us-and-china-strengthen-guardrails-as-xi-and-biden-meet-in-bali/a-63740823.

23. Franco Ordoñez, "Biden Wants a 'Stable, Predictable' Relationship with Russia. That's Complicated," *NPR*, May 21, 2021, https://www.npr.org/2021/05/21/999196021/biden-wants-a-stable-predictable-relationship-with-russia-thats-complicated.

24. Ibid.

25. Antony Blinken, "Secretary Antony J. Blinken at a Press Availability" (remarks, Brussels, Belgium, March 24, 2021), US Department of State, https://www.state.gov/secretary-antony-j-blinken-at-a-press-availability-3/.

26. Shawn Snow, "Esper Wants to Move Troops from Afghanistan to the Indo-Pacific to Confront China," *Military Times*, December 18, 2019, https://www.militarytimes.com/flashpoints/2019/12/18/esper-wants-to-move-troops-from-afghanistan-to-the-indo-pacific-to-confront-china/.

27. Phil Stewart, "Exclusive: North Korea Unresponsive to Behind-the-Scenes Biden Administration Outreach—U.S. Official," *Reuters*, March 13, 2021, https://www.reut ers.com/article/us-usa-northkorea/exclusive-north-korea-unresponsive-to-behind-the-scenes-biden-administration-outreach-u-s-official-idUSKBN2B50P1.

28. Madiha Afzal, "Biden Was Wrong on Afghanistan," Brookings Institution, November 9, 2021, https://www.brookings.edu/blog/order-from-chaos/2021/11/09/biden-was-wrong-on-afghanistan/.

29. Author interview with Kurt Campbell, February 2023.

30. White House, *Interim National Security Strategic Guidance*, 20.

31. Jim Garamone, "Official Talks DOD Policy Role in Chinese Pacing Threat, Integrated Deterrence," *US Department of Defense DOD News*, June 2, 2021, https://www.defe nse.gov/News/News-Stories/Article/Article/2641068/official-talks-dod-policy-role-in-chinese-pacing-threat-integrated-deterrence/; Jim Garamone, "Austin Details

Messages He Will Deliver in Indo-Pacific, Discusses Afghanistan," *US Department of Defense DOD News*, July 22, 2021, https://www.defense.gov/News/News-Stories/Arti cle/Article/2702998/austin-details-messages-he-will-deliver-in-indo-pacific-discus ses-afghanistan/.

32. Kylie Atwood, "Blinken Says the Indo-Pacific Will Shape the Trajectory of the 21st Century as Counterweight to China's Aggressive Actions," *CNN*, December 14, 2021, https://www.cnn.com/2021/12/14/politics/blinken-indo-pacific/index.html.

33. Ken Moriyasu, "Biden's Indo-Pacific Team Largest in National Security Council," *Nikkei Asia*, February 11, 2021, https://asia.nikkei.com/Politics/International-relati ons/Biden-s-Asia-policy/Biden-s-Indo-Pacific-team-largest-in-National-Security-Council.

34. James Pindell, "Obama Talked about a 'Pivot to Asia.' Biden Is Actually Doing It," *Boston Globe*, April 16, 2021, https://www.bostonglobe.com/2021/04/16/nation/obama-talked-about-pivot-asia-biden-is-actually-doing-it/.

35. Thomas Franck, "Biden Prohibits U.S. Investment in 59 Chinese Companies Allegedly Tied to Military, Surveillance," *CNBC*, June 3, 2021, https://www.cnbc.com/2021/06/03/biden-prohibits-us-investment-in-59-chinese-companies.html.

36. Trevor Hunnicutt and Michael Martina, "Biden Supply Chain 'Strike Force' to Target China on Trade," *Reuters*, June 8, 2021, https://www.reuters.com/business/biden-sup ply-chain-strike-force-target-china-trade-2021-06-08/.

37. US Congress, House, *Uyghur Forced Labor Prevention Act*, H.R. 1155, 117th Congress (2021–2022), 12/22/2022 Received in the Senate, https://www.congress.gov/bill/117th-congress/house-bill/1155/text.

38. Veerle Nouwens and Garima Mohan, "Europe Eyes the Indo-Pacific, but Now It's Time to Act," *War on the Rocks*, June 24, 2021, https://warontherocks.com/2021/06/europe-eyes-the-indo-pacific-but-now-its-time-to-act/.

39. Aamer Madhani, Jonathan Lemire, and Lorne Cook, "Biden Rallies NATO Support Ahead of Confrontation with Putin," *AP News*, June 14, 2021, https://apnews.com/article/government-and-politics-donald-trump-joe-biden-china-russia-962ddadf2 19a8ff0412d662163a33d81.

40. Joseph Biden, "Remarks by President Biden in Press Conference" (remarks, East Room, Washington, DC, March 25, 2021), White House, https://www.whitehouse.gov/briefing-room/speeches-remarks/2021/03/25/remarks-by-president-biden-in-press-conference/.

41. White House, "Summit for Democracy Summary of Proceedings," December 23, 2021, https://www.whitehouse.gov/briefing-room/statements-releases/2021/12/23/summit-for-democracy-summary-of-proceedings/.

42. John Ruwitch and Emily Feng, "Not Invited to Biden's Democracy Summit, China Launches a Propaganda Blitz," *NPR*, December 9, 2021, https://www.npr.org/2021/12/09/1062530356/china-biden-democracy-summit.

43. President of Russia, "Joint Statement of the Russian Federation and the People's Republic of China on the International Relations Entering a New Era and the Global Sustainable Development," February 4, 2022, http://en.kremlin.ru/supplement/5770.

44. "Only 3 ASEAN States at US Democracy Summit? Not Bad, Say Analysts," *Radio Free Asia*, December 7, 2021, https://www.rfa.org/english/news/myanmar/summit-120 72021193104.html.

45. White House, *Indo-Pacific Strategy of the United States*, February 2022, https://www. whitehouse.gov/wp-content/uploads/2022/02/U.S.-Indo-Pacific-Strategy.pdf.

46. *National Security Strategy*, October 2022, 8.

47. Office of the Under Secretary of Defense, *Pacific Deterrence Initiative*, May 2021, https://comptroller.defense.gov/Portals/45/Documents/defbudget/FY2022/fy2022_ Pacific_Deterrence_Initiative.pdf.

48. Jim Garamone, "Philippine President Restores Visiting Forces Agreement with U.S.," *US Department of Defense News*, July 30, 2021, https://www.defense.gov/News/ News-Stories/Article/Article/2713638/philippine-president-restores-visiting-for ces-agreement-with-us/.

49. Alastair Gale, Joyu Wang, and Laurence Norman, "U.S. Tightens Focus on China after Afghanistan Withdrawal," *Wall Street Journal*, https://www.wsj.com/articles/u-s-tightens-focus-on-china-after-afghanistan-withdrawal-11629378244.

50. Michael Martina, Dabid Brunnstrom, and Indrees Ali, "Contrary to Intent, Biden's Afghan Pullout Could Undermine Asia Shift," *Reuters*, August 19, 2021, https:// www.reuters.com/world/asia-pacific/contrary-intent-bidens-afghan-pullout-could-undermine-asia-shift-2021-08-19/.

51. Tony Czuczka, "U.S. Focus Shifting to China from Afghanistan, Blinken Says," *Bloomberg*, April 18, 2021, https://www.bloomberg.com/news/articles/2021-04-18/ afghan-pullout-fits-with-u-s-shift-to-china-focus-blinken-says.

52. Joseph Biden, "Remarks by President Biden on the Drawdown of U.S. Forces in Afghanistan" (remarks, East Room, Washington, DC, July 8, 2021), White House, https://www.whitehouse.gov/briefing-room/speeches-remarks/2021/07/08/rema rks-by-president-biden-on-the-drawdown-of-u-s-forces-in-afghanistan/.

53. Oriana Skylar Mastro, "What the U.S. Withdrawal from Afghanistan Means for Taiwan," Stanford Freeman Spogli Institute for International Studies, September 12, 2021, https://fsi.stanford.edu/news/what-us-withdrawal-afghanistan-means-taiwan.

54. Ibid.

55. "Turning from Afghanistan, the US Sets Focus on China," *France 24*, January 9, 2021, https://www.france24.com/en/live-news/20210901-turning-from-afghanis tan-the-us-sets-focus-on-china.

56. Ashley Townshend (@ashleytownshend), "Well said. The strength of US security commitments should be judged on the strength of national interests and priorities at stake. Withdrawing from Afg doesn't mean US more/less likely to back away from other commitments. In fact, US may be in better position to focus elsewhere," Twitter, August 16, 2021, 5:34 am, https://twitter.com/ashleytownshend/status/14272021 24840988672?s=20.

57. Michael J. Green, "Biden's Afghanistan Pullout Could Make the China Problem Harder," *Foreign Policy*, June 24, 2021, https://foreignpolicy.com/2021/06/24/afgh anistan-withdrawal-biden-trump-china-india-asia-pivot-us-military-geopolitics-pullout-drawdown/.

58. Peter J. Dean, "Why the Tragic Afghanistan Withdrawal Should Reassure US Allies in Asia," Atlantic Council, August 30, 2021, https://www.atlanticcouncil.org/blogs/new-atlanticist/why-the-tragic-afghanistan-withdrawal-should-reassure-us-allies-in-asia/.

59. Hamish Goodall, "Defence Minister Peter Dutton Speaks Out over Horrifying Scenes in Afghanistan," 7 News, August 17, 2021, https://7news.com.au/sunrise/on-the-show/defence-minister-peter-dutton-speaks-out-over-horrifying-scenes-in-afgh anistan-c-3700977.

60. Jung Da-min, "Afghanistan Crisis Stirs Debate over Stability of South Korea-US Alliance," Korea Times, August 17, 2021, https://www.koreatimes.co.kr/www/nation/2021/08/113_314050.html.

61. Martina, Brunnstrom, and Ali, "Contrary to Intent, Biden's Afghan Pullout Could Undermine Asia Shift."

62. Joseph R. Biden, "Remarks by President Biden Before the 76th Session of the United Nations General Assembly" (remarks, United Nations headquarters, New York, September 21, 2021), White House, https://www.whitehouse.gov/briefing-room/speeches-remarks/2021/09/21/remarks-by-president-biden-before-the-76th-sess ion-of-the-united-nations-general-assembly/.

63. Hillary Clinton, "America's Pacific Century," Foreign Policy, October 11, 2011, https://foreignpolicy.com/2011/10/11/americas-pacific-century/.

64. White House, "Joint Leaders Statement on AUKUS," September 15, 2021, https://www.whitehouse.gov/briefing-room/statements-releases/2021/09/15/joint-leaders-statement-on-aukus/; Julian Borger and Dan Sabbagh, "US, UK and Australia Forge Military Alliance to Counter China," Guardian, September 15, 2021, https://www.theguardian.com/australia-news/2021/sep/15/australia-nuclear-powered-submari nes-us-uk-security-partnership-aukus.

65. Borger and Sabbagh, "US, UK and Australia Forge Military Alliance." https://crsreports.congress.gov/product/pdf/IN/IN11949.

66. Ibid.

67. David M. Herszenhorn and Laurens Cerulus, "The Joe They Don't Know: Europe Reckons with Biden's Asia Push," Politico, September 25, 2021, https://www.politico.eu/article/us-joe-biden-eu-reckons-asia-push/.

68. Ibid.

69. Nahal Toosi, "Biden, Xi Discuss Need to Avoid Conflict amid Global Competition," Politico, September 9, 2021, https://www.politico.com/news/2021/09/09/biden-xi-conflict-competition-511036.

70. Joanna Shelton, "Look Skeptically at China's CPTPP Application," Center for Strategic and International Studies, November 18, 2021, https://www.csis.org/analysis/look-skeptically-chinas-cptpp-application.

71. Jeffrey J. Schott, "China's CPTPP Bid Puts Biden on the Spot," Peterson Institute for International Economics, September 23, 2021, https://www.piie.com/blogs/trade-and-investment-policy-watch/chinas-cptpp-bid-puts-biden-spot.

72. Richard Fontaine, "What the New China Focus Gets Wrong," Foreign Affairs, November 2, 2021, https://www.foreignaffairs.com/articles/china/2021-11-02/what-new-china-focus-gets-wrong.

73. Richard Fontaine, "The World That Putin Has Made," *Wall Street Journal*, March 11, 2022, https://www.wsj.com/articles/the-world-that-putin-has-made-11647014690.

74. Holger Hansen, "German Lawmakers Approve 100 Billion Euro Military Revamp," *Reuters*, June 3, 2022, https://www.reuters.com/world/urope/german-lawmakers-approve-100-bln-euro-military-revamp-2022-06-03/.

75. Richard Fontaine, "The Long Weekend That Changed History," *Atlantic*, March 1, 2022, https://www.theatlantic.com/international/archive/2022/03/russia-invasion-ukraine-week-decade/622957/.

76. United States Library of Congress, Congressional Research Service, *NATO: Finland and Sweden Seek Membership*, by Kristin Archick, Andrew S. Bowen, and Paul Belkin, IN11949 (2022), https://crsreports.congress.gov/product/pdf/IN/IN11949.

77. Mark Magnier, "Indo-Pacific Nations See Russian War on Neighbour as a 'Cautionary Tale,' Says US Official," *South China Morning Post*, April 6, 2022, https://www.scmp.com/news/china/article/3173182/indo-pacific-nations-see-russian-war-neighbour-cautionary-tale-says-us.

78. Richard Martin, "Sanctions against Russia—a Timeline," *S&P Global Market Intelligence*, December 21, 2022, https://www.spglobal.com/marketintelligence/en/news-insights/latest-news-headlines/sanctions-against-russia-8211-a-timeline-69602559.

79. Gilbert Rozman, "Explaining Japan's About-Face on Russia," Asan Forum, July 7, 2022, https://theasanforum.org/explaining-japans-about-face-on-russia/.

80. Gabriel Dominguez, "Kishida Outlines His Vision for a More Secure Indo-Pacific Region," *Japan Times*, June 10, 2022, https://www.japantimes.co.jp/news/2022/06/10/national/politics-diplomacy/fumio-kishida-shangri-la-speech/; Fontaine, "The World That Putin Has Made."

81. "Philippines Ready to Back US if It Gets Embroiled in War," *Associated Press*, March 10, 2022, https://apnews.com/article/russia-ukraine-putin-united-nations-general-assembly-xi-jinping-united-nations-3ac8ace02978b67a20f1fbbce695d23b.

82. US Library of Congress, Congressional Research Service, *Russia's War on Ukraine: U.S. Policy and the Role of Congress*, by Paul Belkin, Rebecca M. Nelson, and Cory Welt, IF12277, 2023, https://crsreports.congress.gov/product/pdf/IF/IF12277.

83. Asma Khalid, "How the War in Ukraine Is Challenging the Long-Sought Pivot to Asia," *NPR*, May 19, 2022, https://www.npr.org/2022/05/19/1099725081/how-the-war-in-ukraine-is-challenging-the-long-sought-pivot-to-asia.

84. Valerie Insinna, "The Upcoming Defense Strategy Dubs Russia an 'Acute Threat.' What Does That Mean?," *National Defense Strategy*, March 30, 2022, https://breakingdefense.com/2022/03/the-upcoming-defense-strategy-dubs-russia-an-acute-threat-what-does-that-mean/.

85. Elbridge Colby and Oriana Skylar Mastro, "Ukraine Is a Distraction from Taiwan," *Wall Street Journal*, February 13, 2022, https://www.wsj.com/articles/ukraine-is-a-distraction-from-taiwan-russia-china-nato-global-powers-military-invasion-jinping-biden-putin-europe-11644781247.

86. Elbridge Colby, "China, Not Russia, Still Poses the Greatest Challenge to U.S. Security," *National Interest*, July 1, 2022, https://nationalinterest.org/feature/china-not-russia-still-poses-greatest-challenge-us-security-203228.

87. Sen. Josh Hawley, "Russia-Ukraine Crisis—China Is America's Biggest Enemy, Not Moscow," *Fox News*, February 7, 2022, https://www.foxnews.com/opinion/russia-ukraine-crisis-china-america-enemy-sen-josh-hawley.

88. Matthew Kroenig, "Washington Must Prepare for War with Both Russia and China," *Foreign Policy*, February 18, 2022, https://foreignpolicy.com/2022/02/18/us-russia-china-war-nato-quadrilateral-security-dialogue/.

89. Robert Gates, "We Need a More Realistic Strategy for the Post-Cold War Era," *Washington Post*, March 3, 2022, https://www.washingtonpost.com/opinions/2022/03/03/why-ukraine-should-force-a-total-overhaul-of-our-national-security-strategy/.

90. Miya Tanaka, "FOCUS: U.S. Indo-Pacific Strategy Overshadowed as Russian Threat Looms Large," *Kyodo News*, February 25, 2022, https://english.kyodonews.net/news/2022/02/a42b2216c175-focus-us-indo-pacific-strategy-overshadowed-as-russian-threat-looms-large.html.

91. Svetlana Shkolnikova, "Congressional Support Increases for Permanent US Military Bases in the Baltics," *Stars and Stripes*, March 2, 2022, https://www.stripes.com/theaters/us/2022-03-02/congress-baltics-american-military-bases-russia-ukraine-nato-5203735.html.

92. White House, *Indo-Pacific Strategy*, 4.

93. Ibid., 5.

94. Michael E. Miller and Frances Vinall, "China Signs Security Deal with Solomon Islands, Alarming Neighbors," *Washington Post*, April 20, 2022, https://www.washingtonpost.com/world/2022/04/20/solomon-islands-china-security-agreement/.

95. Benjamin Fleton, "Solomon Islands Blocks All Naval Port Visits after U.S. Coast Guard Cutter Denied Entry," *USNI News*, August 30, 2022, https://news.usni.org/2022/08/30/solomon-islands-blocks-all-naval-port-visits-after-u-s-coast-guard-cutter-denied-entry.

96. White House, "Statement by NSC Spokesperson Adrienne Watson on Senior Administration Travel to Hawaii, Fiji, Papua New Guinea, and the Solomon Islands," April 18, 2022, https://www.whitehouse.gov/briefing-room/statements-releases/2022/04/18/statement-by-nsc-spokesperson-adrienne-watson-on-senior-administration-travel-to-hawaii-fiji-papua-new-guinea-and-the-solomon-islands/.

97. Ibid.

98. Michael E. Miller, "U.S. to Open New Embassies, Boost Aid in Pacific as China's Sway Grows," *Washington Post*, July 12, 2022, https://www.washingtonpost.com/world/2022/07/12/kamala-harris-pacific-islands-us-china/; White House, "Fact Sheet: Vice President Harris Announces Commitments to Strengthen U.S. Partnership with the Pacific Islands," July 12, 2022, https://www.whitehouse.gov/briefing-room/statements-releases/2022/07/12/fact-sheet-vice-president-harris-announces-commitments-to-strengthen-u-s-partnership-with-the-pacific-islands/.

99. Fleton, "Solomon Islands."

100. US Department of State, "U.S.-Pacific Island Country Summit," September 28–29, 2022, https://www.state.gov/u-s-pacific-islands-country-summit/.

101. Phelim Kine, "Defiance by Marshall Islands and Solomon Islands Cast Shadow over Biden's Pacific Summit," *Politico*, September 28, 2022, https://www.politico.com/news/2022/09/28/pacific-island-nations-biden-china-00059190.

102. Fumi Matsumoto, "Solomon Islands Signs U.S.-Pacific Partnership Statement in About-Face," *Nikkei Asia*, October 1, 2022, https://asia.nikkei.com/Politics/Intern ational-relations/Indo-Pacific/Solomon-Islands-signs-U.S.-Pacific-partnership-statement-in-about-face2.

103. Trevor Hunnicutt, "With China in Focus, Biden Makes $150 Million Commitment to ASEAN Leaders," *Reuters*, May 13, 2022, https://www.reuters.com/world/asia-pacific/with-china-focus-biden-plans-150-million-commitment-asean-leaders-2022-05-12/.

104. "Biden Signs $40 Billion Aid Package for Ukraine during Trip to Asia," *CNBC*, May 21, 2022, https://www.cnbc.com/2022/05/21/biden-signs-40-billion-aid-package-for-ukraine-during-trip-to-asia.html.

105. Ishaan Thahroor, "Biden Pivots to Asia as Ukraine War Rages on," *Washington Post*, May 13, 2022, https://www.washingtonpost.com/world/2022/05/13/asean-southe ast-asia-china-biden/.

106. Jim Garamone, "Austin: How the U.S. Walks, Chews Gum at the Same Time," *US Department of Defense News*, June 13, 2022, https://www.defense.gov/News/News-Stor ies/Article/Article/3061381/austin-how-the-us-walks-chews-gum-at-the-same-time/.

107. Alice Nason, "Dedication or Distraction in Indo-Pacific Diplomacy?," United States Studies Center, November 11, 2022, https://www.ussc.edu.au/analysis/dedication-or-distraction-in-indo-pacific-diplomacy.

108. Ibid.

109. Ibid.

110. Ibid.; COVID-19 border restrictions made travel to Asia especially difficult, which should be taken into account in any assessment of the Biden administration's travel to the region in its first eighteen months.

111. Peter Birgbauer, "The US Pivot to Asia Was Dead on Arrival," *Diplomat*, March 31, 2022, https://thediplomat.com/2022/03/the-us-pivot-to-asia-was-dead-on-arrival/.

112. Demetri Sevastopulo, "Fiji Joins US-Led Indo-Pacific Economic Initiative on Eve of Chinese Visit," *Financial Times*, May 26, 2022, https://www.ft.com/content/b9c26 8f3-3012-4dee-9dbc-137707965c89.

113. Trevor Hunnicutt and Sakura Murakami, "Biden Says He Would Be Willing to Use Force to Defend Taiwan against China," *Reuters*, May 23, 2022, https://www.reuters.com/world/biden-meets-japanese-emperor-start-visit-launch-regional-economic-plan-2022-05-23/.

114. Jeet Heer, "The Biden Administration's Kayfabe Cold War with China," *The Nation*, May 31, 2022, https://www.thenation.com/article/world/biden-taiwan-war-china/.

115. Ashley Townshend and James Crabtree, "US Indo-Pacific Strategy, Alliances and Security Partnerships," in *Asia-Pacific Regional Security Assessment, an IISS Strategic Dossier*, eds. Tim Huxley and Lynn Kuok (London: International Institute of Strategic Studies, June 14, 2022), 12–37, https://www.iiss.org/contentassets/57a0b e7e196445479341abe68fac940a/aprsa-2022_lr.pdf.

116. Ibid.

117. Lloyd J. Austin, "Remarks at the Shangri-La Dialogue by Secretary of Defense Lloyd J. Austin III (as Delivered)" (remarks, Singapore, June 11, 2022), US Department of Defense, https://www.defense.gov/News/Speeches/Speech/Article/3059852/rema rks-at-the-shangri-la-dialogue-by-secretary-of-defense-lloyd-j-austin-iii-a/.

118. Ibid.

119. Jim Garamone, "Austin Emphasizes Partnership as Path for Peace in Indo-Pacific," *US Department of Defense News*, June 10, 2022, https://www.defense.gov/News/News-Stories/Article/Article/3059207/austin-emphasizes-partnership-as-path-for-peace-in-indo-pacific/.

120. Demetri Sevastopulo, "US Lawmakers Push for More Money to Counter China in Indo-Pacific," *Financial Times*, June 19, 2022, https://www.ft.com/content/aade8 227-553e-45e6-8212-d08149e02d33.

121. Colin Clark, "New Info on AUKUS Sub Deal 'Shortly': NSC's Kurt Campbell," *Breaking Defense*, June 17, 2022, https://breakingdefense.com/2022/06/new-info-on-aukus-sub-deal-shortly-nscs-kurt-campbell/.

122. US Senate, Committee on Foreign Relations, *Strategic Alignment: The Imperative of Resourcing the Indo-Pacific Strategy*, February 2023, https://www.foreign.senate. gov/imo/media/doc/resourcing_the_ips_-_sfrc_democratic_staff_report_2023. pdf, 11.

123. Ibid., 11.

124. Ibid., 10.

125. Ibid., 34.

126. Ibid., 45.

127. Jude Blanchett et al., "Speaker Pelosi's Taiwan Visit: Implications for the Indo-Pacific," Center for Strategic and International Studies, August 15, 2022, https:// www.csis.org/analysis/speaker-pelosis-taiwan-visit-implications-indo-pacific.

128. Ibid.

129. Paul Haenle and Nathaniel Sher, "How Pelosi's Taiwan Visit Has Set a New Status Quo for U.S-China Tensions," Carnegie Endowment for International Peace, August 17, 2022, https://carnegieendowment.org/2022/08/17/how-pelosi-s-taiwan-visit-has-set-new-status-quo-for-u.s-china-tensions-pub-87696.

130. Ibid.

131. David Brunnstrom, "ASEAN Warns of Taiwan 'Miscalculation' as Tension Simmers at Meeting," *Reuters*, August 4, 2022, https://www.reuters.com/world/asia-pacific/ asean-concerned-over-regional-volatility-risk-miscalculations-over-taiwan-2022-08-04/; Helen Davidson, "India Accuses China of 'Militarisation of the Taiwan Strait' as Row over Navy Vessel Grows," *Guardian*, August 29, 2022, https://www. theguardian.com/world/2022/aug/29/india-accuses-china-of-militarisation-of-the-taiwan-strait-as-row-over-navy-vessel-grows.

132. Haenle and Sher, "How Pelosi's Taiwan Visit."

133. David Brunnstrom and Trevor Hunnicutt, "Biden Says U.S. Forces Would Defend Taiwan in the Event of a Chinese Invasion," *Reuters*, September 19, 2022, https:// www.reuters.com/world/biden-says-us-forces-would-defend-taiwan-event-chin ese-invasion-2022-09-18/.

134. Tim Kelly, Nobuhiro Kubo, and Yukiko Toyoda, "Analysis: Japan Rushes to Rearm with Eye on 2027—and China's Taiwan Ambitions," *Reuters*, October 18, 2022, https://www.reuters.com/world/japan-rushes-rearm-with-eye-2027-chinas-tai wan-ambitions-2022-10-18/; Yao Chung-yuan 姚中原, "Japan Taking China Threat Seriously," *Taipei Times*, January 3, 2023, https://www.taipeitimes.com/News/edi torials/archives/2023/01/03/2003791880.

135. Isabel Reynolds, "Japan's Kishida Orders Defense Spending Hike to 2% of GDP," *Bloomberg*, November 28, 2022, https://www.bloomberg.com/news/artic les/2022-11-28/japan-pm-orders-security-spending-hike-to-2-of-gdp-tbs-says#xj4y7vzkg.; "Japan Defence: China Threat Prompts Plan to Double Military Spending," *BBC*, December 16, 2022, https://www.bbc.com/news/world-asia-64001554.

136. Australian government officials, private discussions with Richard Fontaine, 2022; "Almost half of Australians support sending military to help defend Taiwan, poll suggests," *Guardian*, October 24, 2022, https://www.theguardian.com/australia-news/2022/oct/25/almost-half-of-australians-support-sending-military-to-help-defend-taiwan-poll-suggests.

137. Kathrin Jille and Demetri Sevastopulo, "US and Philippines Increase Military Ties over China Threat," *Financial Times*, September 24, 2022, https://www.ft.com/cont ent/9c295755-eadf-48a9-9818-6afa1bcbe498.

138. Sui-Lee Wee, "U.S. to Boost Military Role in the Philippines in Push to Counter China," *New York Times*, February 1, 2023, https://www.nytimes.com/2023/02/01/world/asia/philippines-united-states-military-bases.html.

139. Jim Tankersley, "Biden Sells Infrastructure Improvements as a Way to Counter China," *New York Times*, November 16, 2021, https://www.nytimes.com/2021/11/16/us/politics/biden-infrastructure-china.html.

140. Joseph Biden, "Full Transcript of Biden's State of the Union Address" (speech, Washington, DC, March 1, 2022), *New York Times*, https://www.nytimes.com/2022/03/01/us/politics/biden-sotu-transcript.html.

141. Antony J. Blinken, "The Administration's Approach to the People's Republic of China" (speech, George Washington University, Washington, DC, 2022, 26), US Department of State, https://www.state.gov/the-administrations-approach-to-the-peoples-republic-of-china/.

142. Laura Silver, Christine Huang, and Laura Clancy, "Negative Views of China Tied to Critical Views of Its Policies on Human Rights," Pew Research Center, June 29, 2022, https://www.pewresearch.org/global/2022/06/29/negative-views-of-china-tied-to-critical-views-of-its-policies-on-human-rights/.

143. Justin Badlam et al., "The CHIPS and Science Act: Here's What's in It," McKinsey & Company, October 4, 2022, https://www.mckinsey.com/industries/public-and-soc ial-sector/our-insights/the-chips-and-science-act-heres-whats-in-it.

144. White House, "Fact Sheet: CHIPS and Science Act Will Lower Costs, Create Jobs, Strengthen Supply Chains, and Counter China," August 9, 2022, https://www.whitehouse.gov/briefing-room/statements-releases/2022/08/09/

fact-sheet-chips-and-science-act-will-lower-costs-create-jobs-strengthen-supply-chains-and-counter-china/.

145. Chuck Schumer, "Majority Leader Schumer Floor Remarks on Final Senate Passage of CHIPS and Science Legislation" (remarks, Senate floor, Washington, DC, July 27, 2022), Senate Democrats, https://www.democrats.senate.gov/newsroom/press-releases/majority-leader-schumer-floor-remarks-on-final-senate-passage-of-chips-and-science-legislation.

146. US Department of Defense, "Statement by Secretary of Defense Lloyd J. Austin III on the Bipartisan Innovation Act," July 14, 2022, https://www.defense.gov/News/Releases/Release/Article/3093626/statement-by-secretary-of-defense-lloyd-j-austin-iii-on-the-bipartisan-innovati/.

147. US Department of Commerce, "Bipartisan National Security Experts Urge Congress to Pass Competitiveness Legislation to Boost Semiconductor Production and Domestic Manufacturing," March 21, 2022, https://www.commerce.gov/news/press-releases/2022/03/bipartisan-national-security-experts-urge-congress-pass-competitiveness.

148. US Senate, Todd Young, US Senator for Indiana, "Young Statement on CHIPS and Science Act Being Signed into Law," August 9, 2022, https://www.young.senate.gov/newsroom/press-releases/young-statement-on-chips-and-science-act-being-signed-into-law.

149. Demetri Sevastopulo, "US Hits China with Sweeping Tech Export Controls," *Financial Times*, October 7, 2022, https://www.ft.com/content/6825bee4-52a7-4c86-b1aa-31c100708c3e.

150. Editorial Board, "The Future Depends on Chips. Is the U.S. Ready?" *Washington Post*, December 5, 2022, https://www.washingtonpost.com/opinions/2022/12/05/future-depends-chips-is-us-ready/.

151. Stephanie Condon, "Obama: 'We Welcome China's Rise,'" *CBS*, January 20, 2011, https://www.cbsnews.com/news/obama-we-welcome-chinas-rise/.

152. Office of the President of the United States, National Security Council, *United States Strategic Approach to the People's Republic of China*, May 26, 2020, https://trumpwhitehouse.archives.gov/wp-content/uploads/2020/05/U.S.-Strategic-Approach-to-The-Peoples-Republic-of-China-Report-5.24v1.pdf.

153. Blinken, "The Administration's Approach."

154. Alan F. Estevez et al., "Special Event | A Conversation with Under Secretary of Commerce Alan F. Estevez," transcript of the event as held at the Center for a New American Security, October 27, 2022, https://www.cnas.org/events/special-event-a-conversation-with-under-secretary-of-commerce-alan-f-estevez.

155. Antony Blinken, "Remarks by National Security Advisor Jake Sullivan at the Special Competitive Studies Project Global Emerging Technologies Summit" (remarks, Washington, DC, September 16, 2022), White House, https://www.whitehouse.gov/briefing-room/speeches-remarks/2022/09/16/remarks-by-national-security-advisor-jake-sullivan-at-the-special-competitive-studies-project-global-emerging-technologies-summit/.

156. Edward Luce, "Containing China Is Biden's Explicit Goal," *Financial Times*, October 19, 2022, https://www.ft.com/content/398f0d4e-906e-479b-a9a7-e4023c298f39#comments-anchor.

157. Michelle Toh and Junko Ogura, "Japan Joins the US and Europe in Chipmaking Curbs on China," *CNN*, March 31, 2023, https://www.cnn.com/2023/03/31/tech/japan-china-chip-export-curbs-intl-hnk/index.html#:~:text=Japan%20will%20restrict%20the%20overseas,of%20key%20technology%20to%20China.

158. White House, Office of the Secretary of Defense, *National Security Strategy*, October 2022, 23, https://www.whitehouse.gov/wp-content/uploads/2022/10/Biden-Harris-Administrations-National-Security-Strategy-10.2022.pdf.

159. US Department of Defense, *2022 National Defense Strategy of the United States of America*, October 2022, 4, https://media.defense.gov/2022/Oct/27/2003103845/-1/-1/1/2022-NATIONAL-DEFENSE-STRATEGY-NPR-MDR.PDF.

160. Ibid., 7.

161. Office of the Secretary of Defense, *National Security Strategy*.

162. David Sanger, "Biden's National Security Strategy Focuses on China, Russia and Democracy at Home," *New York Times*, October 12, 2022, https://www.nytimes.com/2022/10/12/us/politics/biden-china-russia-national-security.html.

163. Office of the Secretary of Defense, *National Security Strategy*.

164. Nadia Schadlow, "Biden's National Security Strategy Is Undone by Fantasy," *Wall Street Journal*, October 23, 2022, https://www.wsj.com/articles/bidens-strategy-is-undone-by-fantasy-national-security-china-climate-change-threat-beijing-white-house-ccp-11666549038.

165. Geoff Ziezulewicz, "Why Aircraft Carriers Are No Longer a Constant in the Middle East," *Navy Times*, November 4, 2022, https://www.navytimes.com/news/your-navy/2022/11/04/why-aircraft-carriers-are-no-longer-a-constant-in-the-middle-east/; "Category Archives: Fleet Tracker," *USNI News*, 2022, https://news.usni.org/category/fleet-tracker/page/3; "U.S. Indo-Pacific Command Joint Force Conducts Dual Carrier Operations in South China Sea," *Carrier Strike Group 1 Public Affairs*, January 24, 2022, https://www.navy.mil/Press-Office/News-Stories/Article/2910170/us-indo-pacific-command-joint-force-conducts-dual-carrier-operations-in-south-c/.

166. Ashley Townshend (@ashleytownshend), "But the strategic significance of this has been missed. Australia will soon be one of the only places in the Indo-Pacific that can operate as a forward operating location for @US_STRATCOM Bomber Task Force (BTF) missions and strategic operations (w Hawaii, Guam, Diego Garcia)," Twitter, October 31, 2022, 5:43 am, https://twitter.com/ashleytownshend/status/1587017407813496832.

167. Ibid.

168. Kevin Knodell, "US Army Moving Equipment across Pacific for Training," *Stars and Stripes*, December 5, 2022, https://www.stripes.com/branches/army/2022-12-05/army-moving-equipment-pacific-training-8310071.html.

169. Rebecca Kheel and Thomas Novelly, "GOP Lawmakers Sound Alarm over Pulling F-15s from Japan, *Military Times*, October 24, 2022, https://www.military.com/

daily-news/2022/11/03/gop-lawmakers-sound-alarm-over-pulling-f-15s-japan.html.

170. Stacie L. Pettyjohn, Andrew Metrick, and Becca Wasser, "The Kadena Conundrum: Developing Resilient Indo-Pacific Posture," *War on the Rocks*, December 1, 2022, https://warontherocks.com/2022/12/the-kadena-conundrum-developing-a-resilient-indo-pacific-posture/.

171. Townshend and Crabtree, "US Indo-Pacific Strategy, Alliances and Security Partnerships," 24.

172. US Senate Committee on Armed Services, *FY23 NDAA Agreement Executive Summary,* December 2022, https://www.armed-services.senate.gov/imo/media/doc/fy23_ndaa_agreement_summary.pdf.

173. Zack Cooper and Allison Schwartz, "Five Notable Items for Asia Watchers in the National Defense Authorization Act," American Enterprise Institute, December 16, 2022, https://www.aei.org/foreign-and-defense-policy/five-notable-items-for-asia-watchers-in-the-national-defense-authorization-act/.

174. "US Likely to Bolster Military Posture in Indo-Pacific Next Year," *NHK World-Japan*, December 8, 2022, https://www3.nhk.or.jp/nhkworld/en/news/20221209_07/.

175. Ashley Townshend and James Crabtree, "The U.S. Is Losing Its Military Edge in Asia, and China Knows It," *New York Times*, June 15, 2022, https://www.nytimes.com/2022/06/15/opinion/international-world/us-military-china-asia.html.

176. Keith Bradsher, Chang Che, and Amy Chang Chien, "China Eases 'Zero Covid' Restrictions in Victory for Protesters," *New York Times*, December 7, 2022, https://www.nytimes.com/2022/12/07/world/asia/china-zero-covid-protests.html.

177. Ellen Nakashima, Shane Harris, and Jason Samenow, "U.S. Tracked China Spy Balloon from Launch on Hainan Island along Unusual Path," *Washington Post*, February 14, 2023, https://www.washingtonpost.com/national-security/2023/02/14/china-spy-balloon-path-tracking-weather/.

178. Kristen Welker, et. al., "Xi Warned Biden during Summit that Beijing Will Reunify Taiwan with China," *NBC*, December 20, 2023, https://www.nbcnews.com/news/china/xi-warned-biden-summit-beijing-will-reunify-taiwan-china-rcna130087.

179. Kathryn Watson, "Here's What's in Biden's $100 Billion Request to Congress," *CBS*, October 20, 2023, https://www.cbsnews.com/news/biden-100-billion-request-congress-ukraine-israel/.

180. Author interview with Kurt Campbell, February 2023.

## Chapter 7

1. Charles De Gaulle, "Some General Comments, Entre Nous . . . ," *Ti*, December 8, 1967, https://content.time.com/time/subscriber/article/0,33009,844233,00.html.

2. Hillary Clinton, "America's Pacific Century" (speech, Honolulu, Hawaii, November 10, 2011), US Department of State Archives, https://2009-2017.state.gov/secretary/20092013clinton/rm/2011/11/176999.htm.

3. Richard Wike et al., "America's Global Image Remains More Positive than China's," Pew Research Center, July 18, 2013, https://www.pewresearch.org/global/2013/07/18/americas-global-image-remains-more-positive-than-chinas/.

4. Ibid.

5. Personal conversation with the authors.

6. Ine Eriksen Søreide, "NATO, the EU and the Rise of East Asia" (speech, Leangkollen, Norway, April 2, 2014), Norway Ministry of Defence, https://www.regjeringen.no/en/historical-archive/solbergs-government/Ministries/fd/Speeches-and-articles/minister/taler-og-artikler-av-forsvarsminister-in/2014/nato-the-eu-and-the-rise-of-east-asia/id750385/.

7. Malcolm Rifkind, "Europe Grapples with U.S. Pivot," *Diplomat*, December 1, 2011, https://thediplomat.com/2011/12/europe-grapples-with-u-s-pivot/.

8. Tomas Valasek, "Europe and the 'Asia Pivot,'" *New York Times*, October 15, 2012, https://www.nytimes.com/2012/10/26/opinion/europe-and-the-asia-pivot.html.

9. "Population of Europe 2021," Statista, July 27, 2021, https://www.statista.com/statistics/1106711/population-of-europe/; World Bank, "Population, Total—Russian Federation," World Bank Group, https://data.worldbank.org/indicator/SP.POP.TOTL?locations=RU.

10. World Bank, "Military Expenditure (Current USD)—European Union, United Kingdom, Russian Federation," World Bank Group, https://data.worldbank.org/indicator/MS.MIL.XPND.CD?locations=EU-GB-RU.

11. World Bank, "Armed Forces Personnel, Total—European Union, Russian Federation," World Bank Group, accessed July 7, 2022, https://data.worldbank.org/indicator/MS.MIL.TOTL.P1?locations=EU-RU.

12. World Bank, "GDP (Constant 2015 US$)—European Union, Russian Federation," World Bank Group, accessed July 7, 2022, https://data.worldbank.org/indicator/NY.GDP.MKTP.KD?locations=EU-RU; World Bank, "Exports of Goods and Services (Constant 2015 US$)—European Union, Russian Federation," World Bank Group, accessed July 7, 2022, https://data.worldbank.org/indicator/NE.EXP.GNFS.KD?locations=EU-RU; World Bank, "Imports of Goods and Services (Constant 2015 US$)—European Union, Russian Federation," World Bank Group, accessed July 7, 2022, https://data.worldbank.org/indicator/NE.IMP.GNFS.KD?locations=EU-RU.

13. Rajan Menon and Daniel R. DePetris, "Europe Doesn't Need the United States Anymore," *Foreign Policy*, January 30, 2023, https://foreignpolicy.com/2023/01/30/nato-europe-eu-defense-united-states/.

14. Robert S. Norris and Hans M. Kristensen, "The British Nuclear Stockpile, 1953–2013," *Bulletin of the Atomic Scientists* 69, no. 4 (November 27, 2015): 69–75, https://www.tandfonline.com/doi/full/10.1177/0096340213493260; Center for Arms Control and Non-Proliferation, "Fact Sheet: France's Nuclear Inventory," March 27, 2020, https://armscontrolcenter.org/fact-sheet-frances-nuclear-arsenal/.

15. The International Institute for Strategic Studies found that, in the case of a Russian attack on Poland and Lithuania, these same countries would need to invest $288 billion to $357 billion. If the US abandoned its global maritime presence, NATO countries would have to invest $94 billion to $110 billion fill the gap left by Washington.

For more information, see Douglas Barrie et al., *Defending Europe: Scenario-Based Capability Requirements for NATO's European Members* (London: International Institute for Strategic Studies, 2019), https://www.iiss.org/blogs/research-paper/2019/05/defending-europe.

16. World Bank, "Military Expenditure (%of GDP)—European Union," World Bank Group, accessed July 7, 2022, https://data.worldbank.org/indicator/MS.MIL.XPND.GD.ZS?end=2011&locations=E%20U&start=1960.

17. Gallup International, "WIN/Gallup International's Global Survey Shows Three in Five Willing to Fight for Their Country," Center for Public and Political Studies, Gallup International Association, May 7, 2015, https://www.gallup-international.bg/en/33483/win-gallup-internationals-global-survey-shows-three-in-five-willing-to-fight-for-their-country/.

18. Kate Simmons, Bruce Stokes, and Jacob Poushter, "NATO Publics Blame Russia for Ukrainian Crisis, but Reluctant to Provide Military Aid," Pew Research Center, June 10, 2015, https://www.pewresearch.org/global/2015/06/10/nato-publics-blame-russia-for-ukrainian-crisis-but-reluctant-to-provide-military-aid/.

19. Gallup International, "WIN/Gallup International's Global Survey."

20. Clinton, "America's Pacific Century" (speech).

21. US Library of Congress, Congressional Research Service, *Pivot to the Pacific? The Obama Administration's 'Rebalancing' Toward Asia*, by Mark E. Manyin et al., R42448, 2012, https://sgp.fas.org/crs/natsec/R42448.pdf.

22. Cheryl Pellerin, "Obama: U.S. to Be Lead Nation for Enhanced NATO Presence in Poland," *US Department of Defense News*, July 8, 2016, https://www.defense.gov/News/News-Stories/Article/Article/831742/obama-us-to-be-lead-nation-for-enhanced-nato-presence-in-poland/.

23. Barack Obama, "Remarks by the President in Address to European Youth" (remarks, Lille, France, March 26, 2014), White House Archives, https://obamawhitehouse.archives.gov/the-press-office/2014/03/26/remarks-president-address-European-youth; US Department of Defense, *Enhancing Security and Stability in Afghanistan*, Report to Congress, June 2020, https://media.defense.gov/2020/Jul/01/2002348001/-1/-1/1/ENHANCING_SECURITY_AND_STABILITY_IN_AFGHANISTAN.PDF; Alan J. Kuperman, "Obama's Libya Debacle," *Foreign Affairs* 94, no. 2 (March–April 2015): 66–77, https://www.foreignaffairs.com/articles/libya/2019-02-18/obamas-libya-debacle.

24. Barack Obama, "Press Conference by the President" (remarks, Washington, DC, July 15, 2015), accessed July 7, 2022, White House Archives, https://obamawhitehouse.archives.gov/the-press-office/2015/07/15/press-conference-president; Uri Dadush and Michele Dunne, "American and European Responses to the Arab Spring: What's the Big Idea?" Carnegie Endowment for International Peace, September 1, 2011, https://carnegieendowment.org/2011/09/01/american-and-european-responses-to-arab-spring-what-s-big-idea-pub-45537.

25. US Department of State, Office of the Spokesperson, "The Global Coalition to Defeat ISIS," June 28, 2021, https://www.state.gov/the-global-coalition-to-defeat-isis/.

26. International Institute for Strategic Studies, "Chapter Three: North America," *Military Balance* 112, no. 1 (2012): 39–70, https://www.iiss.org/publications/the-milit

ary-balance/the-military-balance-2012/; International Institute for Strategic Studies, "Chapter Three: North America," *Military Balance* 121, no. 1 (2021): 30–65, https://www.iiss.org/publications/the-military-balance/the-military-balance-2021/.

27. International Institute for Strategic Studies, "Chapter Three: North America," *Military Balance* 115, no. 1 (2015), https://www.iiss.org/publications/the-military-balance/the-military-balance-2015/; International Institute for Strategic Studies, "Chapter Three: North America," *Military Balance* 121.

28. Department of Defense, Historical Office, *Secretary of Defense Travels*, accessed July 22, 2022, https://history.defense.gov/DOD-History/Secretary-of-Defense-Travels/; Department of State, Office of the Historian, *Travels Abroad of the Secretary of State*, accessed July 22, 2022, https://history.state.gov/departmenthistory/travels/secretary; Department of State, Office of the Historian, *Travels Abroad of the President*, accessed July 22, 2022, https://history.state.gov/departmenthistory/travels/president.

29. US Census Bureau, "Trade in Goods with European Union, Prepared," 2011 and 2020 tables, using data.census.gov, https://www.census.gov/foreign-trade/balance/c0003.html.

30. US Bureau of Economic Analysis, "Direct Investment by Country and Industry," maintained by Ryan Smith, 2020 table, using bea.gov, https://www.bea.gov/data/intl-trade-investment/direct-investment-country-and-industry.

31. US Senate Committee on Finance, "Baucus, Hatch Outline Priorities for Potential U.S.-EU Trade Agreement," press release, February 12, 2013, https://www.finance.senate.gov/chairmans-news/baucus-hatch-outline-priorities-for-potential-us-eu-trade-agreement.

32. "Quotes," Dwight D. Eisenhower Presidential Library, Museum, and Boyhood Home, National Archives, last modified January 19, 2022, https://www.eisenhowerlibrary.gov/eisenhowers/quotes.

33. Carl Bildt, "Europe's Fate Is Intimately Linked to Ukraine's Survival," *Strategist*, July 5, 2022, https://www.aspistrategist.org.au/europes-fate-is-intimately-linked-to-ukraines-survival/.

34. "Eurobarometer: Europeans Approve EU's Response to the War in Ukraine," Press Corner, European Commission, May 5, 2022, https://ec.europa.eu/commission/presscorner/detail/en/ip_22_2784.

35. "Germany—Europe—Asia: Shaping the 21st Century Together: The German Government Adopts Policy Guidelines on the Indo-Pacific Region," Foreign & European Policy, Republic of Germany Foreign Office, September 1, 2020, https://www.auswaertiges-amt.de/en/aussenpolitik/regionaleschwerpunkte/asien/german-government-policy-guidelines-indo-pacific/2380510.

36. Government of the Netherlands, *Indo-Pacific: Guidelines for Strengthening Dutch and EU Cooperation with Partners in Asia*, November 13, 2020, https://www.government.nl/documents/publications/2020/11/13/indo-pacific-guidelines.

37. United Kingdom Cabinet Office, *Global Britain in a Competitive Age: The Integrated Review of Security, Defence, Development and Foreign Policy*, July 2, 2021, https://www.gov.uk/government/publications/global-britain-in-a-competitive-age-the-int

egrated-review-of-security-defence-development-and-foreign-policy/global-brit ain-in-a-competitive-age-the-integrated-review-of-security-defence-development-and-foreign-policy.

38. European Union, External Action, "EU Strategy for Cooperation in the Indo-Pacific," press release, April 19, 2021, https://www.eeas.europa.eu/eeas/eu-strategy-cooperat ion-indo-pacific-0_en.

39. "The Indo-Pacific Region: A Priority for France," Country Files, French Republic Ministry for Europe and Foreign Affairs, https://www.diplomatie.gouv.fr/en/coun try-files/asia-and-oceania/the-indo-pacific-region-a-priority-for-france/.

40. North Atlantic Treaty Organization, "Statement by NATO Heads of State and Government—Brussels 24 March 2022," press release, March 24, 2022, https:// www.nato.int/cps/en/natohq/official_texts_193719.htm?selectedLocale=en; Jens Stoltenberg, "Pre-Summit Press Conference by NATO Secretary General Jens Stoltenberg" (speech, Madrid, Spain, June 27, 2022), North Atlantic Treaty Organization, https://www.nato.int/cps/en/natohq/opinions_197080.htm; News Wire, "NATO Plans Huge Upgrade of Rapid Reaction Force in 'Era of Strategic Competition,'" *France 24*, June 27, 2022, https://www.france24.com/en/europe/20220 627-nato-plans-huge-upgrade-of-rapid-reaction-force-in-era-of-strategic-competit ion; Associated Press, "NATO to Boost Its Rapid Reaction Force to 300,000 Troops," *CBC*, June 27, 2022, https://www.cbc.ca/news/world/nato-nrf-troops-expansion-1.6502680.

41. Stoltenberg, "Pre-Summit Press Conference."

42. Henry Ridgwell, "NATO Summit: What New Weapons Have Been Pledged to Ukraine?" *Voice of America*, June 30, 2022, https://www.voanews.com/a/nato-summit-what-new-weapons-have-been-pledged-to-ukraine-/6640386.html; Guy Chazan et al., "US and Germany to Send Main Battle Tanks to Ukraine," *Financial Times*, January 25, 2023, https://www.ft.com/content/d79c4da1-2c17-401d-9ef7-00051fe02f2a.

43. European Commission, "REPowerEU: A Plan to Rapidly Reduce Dependence on Russian Fossil Fuels and Fast Forward the Green Transition," press release, May 18, 2022, https://ec.europa.eu/commission/presscorner/detail/en/ip_22_3131; "EU Sanctions against Russia Following the Invasion of Ukraine," Priorities 2019–2024, https://ec.europa.eu/info/strategy/priorities-2019-2024/stronger-europe-world/eu-solidarity-ukraine/eu-sanctions-against-russia-following-invasion-ukraine_en.

44. European Council, *Versailles Declaration*, March 11, 2022, https://www.consilium. europa.eu/en/press/press-releases/2022/03/11/the-versailles-declaration-10-11-03-2022/; "EU Response to Russia's Invasion of Ukraine," Policies, European Council, last modified December 16, 2022, https://www.consilium.europa.eu/en/policies/ eu-response-ukraine-invasion/; "EU Solidarity with Ukraine," Policies, European Council, https://www.consilium.europa.eu/en/policies/eu-response-ukraine-invas ion/eu-solidarity-ukraine/#economic; European Parliament, "Grant EU Candidate Status to Ukraine and Moldova without Delay," press releases, June 23, 2022, https:// www.europarl.europa.eu/news/en/press-room/20220616IPR33216/grant-eu-candid ate-status-to-ukraine-and-moldova-without-delay-meps-demand.

45. Giulia Paravicini, "Angela Merkel: Europe Must Take 'Our Fate' into Own Hands," *Politico*, May 28, 2017, https://www.politico.eu/article/angela-merkel-europe-cdu-must-take-its-fate-into-its-own-hands-elections-2017/.

46. Joschka Fischer, "What the War in Ukraine Means for Europe," *Project Syndicate*, May 4, 2022, https://www.project-syndicate.org/commentary/war-in-ukraine-what-it-means-for-europe-by-joschka-fischer-2022-05.

47. Ben Hall, Henry Foy, and Felicia Schwartz, "Military Briefing: NATO Brings Back Cold War Doctrine to Counter Russian Threat," *Financial Times*, June 30, 2022, https://www.ft.com/content/357ab596-84a5-42df-9ebe-27890654a09a.

48. North Atlantic Treaty Organization, *Madrid Summit Declaration*, June 29, 2022, https://www.nato.int/cps/en/natohq/official_texts_196951.htm.

49. "Republic of Korea Opens Diplomatic Mission to NATO," NATO, November 22, 2022, https://www.nato.int/cps/en/natohq/news_209320.htm; The Asahi Shimbun, "Kishida Pledges to Strengthen Japan's Ties with NATO on Defense," *Asahi Shimbun*, February 1, 2023, https://www.asahi.com/ajw/articles/14829095.

50. Reuters, "NATO's Stoltenberg Arrives in South Korea to Deepen Alliance's Ties in Asia, Discuss China," *South China Morning Post*, January 29, 2023, https://www.scmp.com/news/asia/east-asia/article/3208359/natos-stoltenberg-arrives-south-korea-deepen-alliances-ties-asia-discuss-china.

51. North Atlantic Treaty Organization, *Vilnius Summit Communiqué*, July 11, 2023, https://www.nato.int/cps/en/natohq/official_texts_217320.htm.

52. Stu Woo and Daniel Michaels, "China Buys Friends with Ports and Roads. Now the U.S. Is Trying to Compete," *Wall Street Journal*, July 15, 2021, https://www.wsj.com/articles/china-buys-friends-with-ports-and-roads-now-the-u-s-is-trying-to-compete-11626363239.

53. Samuel Stolton, "EU Nations Breaking Rules in Bilateral Trade Deals with China," *Euractiv*, September 10, 2020, https://www.euractiv.com/section/global-europe/news/eu-nations-breaking-rules-in-bilateral-trade-deals-with-china/.

54. Joshua Kurlantzick, "China's Influence Operations Fall Flat in Central and Eastern Europe," *World Politics Review*, January 11, 2023, https://www.worldpoliticsreview.com/china-soft-power-central-eastern-europe-cee/.

55. "China Overtakes US as EU's Biggest Trading Partner," *BBC*, February 17, 2021. https://www.bbc.com/news/business-56093378#.

56. "China-EU—International Trade in Goods Statistics," Statistics Explained, Eurostat, last modified February 2022, https://ec.europa.eu/eurostat/statistics-explained/index.php?title=China-EU_-_international_trade_in_goods_statistics.

57. Suzanne Lynch et al., "The U.S. Wants Europe to Stand up to China. Europe Says: Not so Fast," *Politico*, March 8, 2023, https://www.politico.com/news/2023/03/08/us-europe-china-00086204.

58. Alice Billon-Galland and Hans Kundnani, "How Ukraine Will Change Europe's Indo-Pacific Ambitions," Expert Comment, Chatham House, April 25, 2022, https://www.chathamhouse.org/2022/04/how-ukraine-will-change-europes-indo-pacific-ambitions; Liana Fix and Thorsten Benner, "Germany's Unlearned Lessons," *Foreign Affairs*, December 15, 2022, https://www.foreignaffairs.com/china/germanys-unlearned-lessons.

59. Adam Tooze, "Germany's Economic Entanglement with China," Chartbook #168 (newsletter), Chartbook, November 6, 2022.

60. Embassy of the People's Republic of China in the Commonwealth of Australia, "Xi Jinping Holds Talks with Angela Merkel, Announcing the Establishment of China-Germany All-Round Strategic Partnership," press release, March 29, 2014, http://au.china-embassy.gov.cn/eng/zgxw_4/201403/t20140331_734874.htm.

61. Reuters, "German Dependence on China Growing 'at Tremendous Pace'—IW," *Reuters*, August 19, 2022, https://www.reuters.com/world/german-dependence-china-growing-tremendous-pace-iw-2022-08-19/; Jürgen Matthes, *Gegenseitige Abhängigkeit im Handel zwischen China, der EU und Deutschland*, IW-Report, Nr. 33, June 13, 2022, Köln, https://www.iwkoeln.de/en/studies/juergen-matthes-mutual-dependence-in-trade-between-china-the-eu-and-germany.html.

62. Norbert Röttgen, "Brauchen eine Kurskorrektur im Außenhandel," interview by Christian Sievers, *heute-journal*, ZDF, August 7, 2022, https://www.zdf.de/nachrich ten/politik/roettgen-aussenhandel-kurskorrektur-100.html.

63. Fergus Hunter and Daria Impiombato, "Olaf Scholz Is Undermining Western Unity on China," *Foreign Policy*, November 23, 2022, https://foreignpolicy.com/2022/11/23/germany-china-eu-scholz-xi-meeting-economy-trade-g-20/.

64. Melissa Eddy, "As U.S. Tries to Isolate China, German Companies Move Closer," *New York Times*, April 12, 2023, https://www.nytimes.com/2023/04/12/world/eur ope/germany-china-trade.html.

65. Bloomberg News, "China Warns Europe's Taiwan Support Is Having 'Egregious Impact,'" *Bloomberg*, October 21, 2021, https://www.bloomberg.com/news/artic les/2021-10-21/china-warns-europe-s-taiwan-support-is-having-egregious-imp act#xj4y7vzkg.

66. Zachary Basu, "As China Bullies Lithuania, EU Steps Back but Taiwan Steps In," *Axios*, January 6, 2022, https://www.axios.com/2022/01/06/china-lithuania-boycott-taiwan-investments.

67. "China Downgrades Diplomatic Ties with Lithuania over Taiwan Row," *BBC*, November 22, 2021, https://www.bbc.com/news/world-asia-china-59370521; Andrius Sytas and John O'Donnell, "China Pressures Germany's Continental to Cut Out Lithuania—Sources," *Reuters*, December 17, 2021, https://www.reuters.com/world/china/exclusive-china-asks-germanys-continental-cut-out-lithuania-sour ces-2021-12-17/.

68. "Wang Yi Meets with NATO Secretary General Jens Stoltenberg at Request via Video Link," Activities, People's Republic of China Ministry of Foreign Affairs, September 28, 2021, https://www.fmprc.gov.cn/mfa_eng/wjb_663304/wjbz_663308/activities_ 663312/202109/t20210928_9580063.html.

69. The 2017 poll included only ten EU countries. Belgium was added to the poll starting in 2020.

70. Laura Silver, Christine Huang, and Laura Clancy, "Negative Views of China Tied to Critical Views of Its Policies on Human Rights," Pew Research Center, June 29, 2022, https://www.pewresearch.org/global/2022/06/29/negative-views-of-china-tied-to-critical-views-of-its-policies-on-human-rights/.

71. William Yuen Yee, "Is the EU-China Investment Agreement Dead?," *Diplomat*, March 26, 2022, https://thediplomat.com/2022/03/is-the-eu-china-investment-agreem ent-dead/; European Commission, "Key Elements of the EU-China Comprehensive Agreement on Investment," press release, European Union, December 30, 2020, https://ec.europa.eu/commission/presscorner/detail/en/IP_20_2542.

72. Gabrielle Debinski, "What We're Watching: Russia Hits Eastern Ukraine, Finland's Election Results, UBS-Credit Suisse Probe, European Leaders Prepare for XI Meeting," *GZERO Media*, April 3, 2023, https://www.gzeromedia.com/what-were-watching-russia-hits-eastern-ukraine-finlands-election-results-ubs-credit-suisse-probe-european-leaders-prepare-for-xi-meeting.

73. George Parker, "Osborne Hails 'Golden Decade' in Sino-British Relations," *Financial Times*, September 20, 2015, https://www.ft.com/content/6d107dc4-5fae-11e5-a28b-50226830d644.

74. Elizabeth Piper, "UK PM Hopeful Sunak Takes Aim at China in Leadership Contest," *Reuters*, July 25, 2022, https://www.reuters.com/world/uk/uk-pm-hopeful-sunak-takes-aim-china-leadership-contest-2022-07-25/.

75. Ellen Milligan, "Truss Says UK Should Crack Down on Chinese Firms like TikTok," *Bloomberg*, July 25, 2022, https://www.bloomberg.com/news/articles/2022-07-25/liz-truss-says-uk-should-crack-down-on-chinese-firms-like-tiktok.

76. European Union, European Parliament, *The Situation in the Taiwan Strait*, September 15, 2022, P9_TA(2022)0331, https://www.europarl.europa.eu/doceo/document/ TA-9-2022-0331_EN.html; Reuters, "EU Lawmakers Condemn China's Live-Fire Exercises in Taiwan Strait," *Reuters*, September 15, 2022, https://www.reuters.com/ world/asia-pacific/eu-lawmakers-condemn-chinas-live-fire-exercises-taiwan-str ait-2022-09-15/; Al Jazeera, "EU Parliament Resolution Slams China's Aggression towards Taiwan," *Al Jazeera*, September 16, 2022, https://www.aljazeera.com/news/ 2022/9/16/eu-parliament-resolution-slams-chinas-aggression-toward-taiwan.

77. Barbara Moens, "Belgium Triggers Chinese Backlash with Port Security Warning," *Politico*, October 25, 2022, https://www.politico.eu/article/china-fume-accusation-belgium-ports-foreign-affairs-minister-hadja-lahbib/.

78. Henry Foy, "EU Ministers Advised to Take Tougher Line on China," *Financial Times*, October 17, 2022, https://www.ft.com/content/b83615cb-6db0-4e67-85a3-7aab1 31abeb5.

79. All quotes in this paragraph are sourced from North Atlantic Treaty Organization, *NATO 2022 Strategic Concept*, June 29, 2022, 5, https://www.nato.int/strategic-conc ept/index.html.

80. Daniel Michaels and Charlies Hutzler, "U.S., Key Allies Close Ranks against China," *Wall Street Journal*, June 30, 2022, https://www.wsj.com/articles/u-s-key-allies-close-ranks-against-china-11656591213.

81. David Pierson, Olivia Wang, and Keith Bradsher, "E.U. Leaders in China Press Xi on Russia and Trade Imbalance," *New York Times*, December 7, 2023, https://www.nyti mes.com/2023/12/07/world/asia/china-eu-xi-michel.html.

82. Agence France Presse, "In First, NATO Lays Out 'Challenges' from China," *Barron's*, June 29, 2022, https://www.barrons.com/news/nato-says-china-s-coercive-policies-challenge-our-interests-01656508507.

83. Pew Research Center, "The Berlin Pulse Survey 2022/2023," *Körber Stiftung*, July–August 2022, https://koerber-stiftung.de/en/projects/the-berlin-pulse/2022-23/.

84. European Commission, *EU-China—A Strategic Outlook*, March 2019, https://commission.europa.eu/system/files/2019-03/communication-eu-china-a-strategic-outlook.pdf.

85. Olaf Scholz, "This Is Europe" (speech, Strasbourg, France, May 9, 2023), Republic of Germany Office of the Chancellor, https://www.bundeskanzler.de/bk-en/news/addr ess-by-olaf-scholz-2189412.

86. Thorsten Benner, "Peace Through Deterrence: Why Germany and Europe Need to Invest More to Preserve the Status Quo in the Taiwan Strait," Global Public Policy Institute, March 16, 2022, https://gppi.net/2022/03/16/peace-through-deterrence.

87. Jana Puglierin and Pawel Zerka, "Keeping America Close, Russia Down, and China Far Away: How Europeans Navigate a Competitive World," Policy Brief, European Council on Foreign Relations, June 2023, https://ecfr.eu/wp-content/uploads/2023/06/Keeping-America-close-Russia-down-and-China-far-away-How-Europeans-navigate-a-competitive-world-published.pdf.

88. Sofia Brooke, "New Report to Shape EU-China Relations: Implications for Businesses," *China Briefing News*, September 29, 2021, https://www.china-briefing.com/news/eus-new-strategy-on-china-implications-for-businesses/.

89. Josep Borrell, "Speech by High-Representative/Vice-President Josep Borrell at the EP Debate on EU-China Relations" (speech, Strasbourg, France, November 22, 2022), External Action, European Union, https://www.eeas.europa.eu/eeas/china-speech-high-representativevice-president-josep-borrell-ep-debate-eu-china-relations_en.

90. Josep Borrell, "Opening Speech by High Representative/Vice-President Josep Borrell at the Brussels Indo-Pacific Forum" (speech, Brussels, Belgium, November 29, 2022), External Action, European Union, https://www.eeas.europa.eu/eeas/indo-pacific-opening-speech-high-representativevice-president-josep-borrell-brussels-indo_en.

91. Scholz, "This Is Europe."

92. Thibault Larger and Giorgio Leali, "Brussels Forges New Weapons to Shield EU Market from China," *Politico*, June 16, 2021, https://www.politico.com/news/2020/06/16/brussels-forges-new-weapons-to-shield-eu-market-from-china-325145.

93. Anu Bradford, *The Brussels Effect: How the European Union Rules the World* (New York: Oxford University Press, 2020), 153.

94. "2018 News Items—European Union Files WTO Complaint against China's Protection of Intellectual Property Rights," World Trade Organization, June 6, 2018, https://www.wto.org/english/news_e/news18_e/ds549rfc_06jun18_e.htm.

95. Andy Bounds, Richard Milne, and Kathrin Hille, "Brussels Challenges China at WTO over Block on Lithuania Imports," *Financial Times*, January 27, 2022, https://www.ft.com/content/cb036c80-5f8e-4c44-86c4-e800975a26e0; European Commission, "EU Challenges China at the WTO to Defend Its High-Tech Sector," press release, European Union, February 18, 2022, https://ec.europa.eu/commission/presscorner/detail/en/IP_22_1103.

96. "Panels Established to Review EU Complaints Regarding Chinese Trade Measures," News and Events, January 27, 2023, https://www.wto.org/english/news_e/news23_e/dsb_27jan23_e.htm.

97. "DS610: China—Measures Concerning Trade in Goods," World Trade Organization, November 3, 2023, https://www.wto.org/english/tratop_e/dispu_e/cases_e/ds610_e.htm; "EU launches probe into Chinese subsidies for electric vehicles," *Al-Jazeera*, September 14, 2023, https://www.aljazeera.com/economy/2023/9/14/eu-launches-probes-into-chinese-subsidies-for-electric-vehicles.

98. "EU Unveils Strategy to Reduce Dependency on China," *Economist Intelligence Unit*, May 18, 2021, https://www.eiu.com/n/eu-unveils-strategy-to-reduce-dependency-on-china/.

99. Ibid.

100. Henry Gao, "Will the European Union's New Anti-Coercion Instrument Work with China?" Centre for International Governance Innovation, April 22, 2022, https://www.cigionline.org/articles/will-the-european-unions-new-anti-coercion-instrument-work-with-china/; European Parliament, Members' Research Service, *Proposed Anti-Coercion Instrument*, by Marcin Szczepański, November 2022 (P.E. 729.299), https://www.europarl.europa.eu/RegData/etudes/BRIE/2022/729299/EPRS_BRI(2022)729299_EN.pdf.

101. Finbarr Bermingham, "EU Unveils 'Double Act' Plans to Cut China Dominance of Critical Supply Lines for Minerals, Clean Tech," *South China Morning Post*, March 17, 2023, https://www.scmp.com/news/china/article/3213810/eu-unveils-double-act-plans-cut-china-dominance-critical-supply-lines-minerals-clean-tech; European Commission, *Net Zero Industry Act*, COM(2023) 161, SWD(2023) 68, March 16, 2023, https://single-market-economy.ec.europa.eu/publications/net-zero-industry-act_en.

102. George Cunningham, "The EU's Strategy for Cooperation in the Indo-Pacific," *Asakawa USA*, accessed July 1, 2022, https://spfusa.org/publications/the-eus-strategy-for-cooperation-in-the-indo-pacific/#_ftn11.

103. European Union, External Action, *EU Strategy for Cooperation in the Indo-Pacific*, February 21, 2022, https://www.eeas.europa.eu/eeas/eu-indo-pacific-strategy_en.

104. France's Ministry for European and Foreign Affairs, *France's Indo-Pacific Strategy*, accessed July 1, 2022, https://au.ambafrance.org/IMG/pdf/en_indopacifique_web_cle0f44b5.pdf?13678/a892c4f93ab0687400274085650d6d72973af817; Gudrun Wacker, "Europe and the Indo-Pacific: Comparing France, Germany and the Netherlands," *Real Instituto Elcano*, March 9, 2021, https://www.realinstitutoelcano.org/en/analyses/europe-and-the-indo-pacific-comparing-france-germany-and-the-netherlands/; European Union, External Action, *EU Strategy for Cooperation in the Indo-Pacific*.

105. Billon-Galland and Kundnani, "How Ukraine Will Change Europe's Indo-Pacific Ambitions"; Ben Barry, "Posturing and Presence: The United Kingdom and France in the Indo-Pacific," *Military Balance Blog* (Blog) International Institute for Strategic Studies, June 11, 2021, https://www.iiss.org/blogs/military-balance/2021/06/france-uk-indo-pacific.

106. Liselotte Nordgaard, "Will Europe's Emerging Indo-Pacific Presence Last?" East Asia Forum, May 17, 2022, https://www.eastasiaforum.org/2022/05/17/will-europes-emerging-indo-pacific-presence-last/.

107. David Hutt, "EU Faces Uphill Task Beefing Up Defense Ties with Asia, *Deutsche Welle*, June 9, 2022, https://www.dw.com/en/eu-faces-uphill-task-beefing-up-defe nse-ties-with-asia/a-62073585; Angshuman Choudhury, "Europe in the Indo-Pacific: Germany and France Flex Their Muscles," *Diplomat*, August 19, 2022, https://thediplomat.com/2022/08/europe-in-the-indo-pacific-germany-and-fra nce-flex-their-muscles/.

108. Ingo Gerhartz, "German Air Force Takes Flight for First Indo-Pacific Deployment," interviewed by Vivienne Machi, *Defense News*, August 15, 2022, https://www.defe nsenews.com/global/europe/2022/08/15/german-air-force-takes-flight-for-first-indo-pacific-deployment/.

109. Ibid.

110. US Department of State, Office of the Spokesperson, "EU-U.S. Joint Naval Exercise," press release, March 24, 2023, https://www.state.gov/eu-u-s-joint-naval-exercise/; Lee Willett, "French Navy Chief Calls for European Navies to Increase Presence and Engagement in Key Waters," *Naval News*, May 30, 2023, https://www.navalnews. com/naval-news/2023/05/french-navy-chief-calls-for-european-navies-to-incre ase-presence-and-engagement-in-key-waters/.

111. Andrew Chuter, "Britain to Send an Aircraft Carrier to the Indo-Pacific in 2025," *Defense News*, May 18, 2023, https://www.defensenews.com/global/europe/2023/ 05/18/britain-to-send-an-aircraft-carrier-to-the-indo-pacific-in-2025/.

112. Henry Boyd, et al., *Taiwan, Cross-strait Stability and European Security: Implications and Response Options* (London: International Institute for Strategic Studies, March 2022), 36, https://www.iiss.org/globalassets/media-library---content--migration/ files/research-papers/2022/03/taiwan-cross-strait-stability.pdf.

113. Christine Lambrecht, "Policy Speech by Federal Minister of Defence on the National Security Strategy" (speech, Berlin, September 15, 2022), Republic of Germany Ministry of Defence https://www.bmvg.de/en/news/policy-speech-on-the-natio nal-security-strategy-5497180.

114. Ursula von der Leyen, "Visit of Ursula von der Leyen, President of the European Commission, to China: Press Conference" (speech, Beijing, April 6, 2023), European Commission, https://audiovisual.ec.europa.eu/en/shotlist/I-239784.

115. Emmanuel Macron (@EmmanuelMacron), "I am convinced that China has a major role to play in building peace. This is what I have come to discuss, to move forward on. With President XI Jinping, we will also talk about our businesses, the climate and biodiversity, and food security." Twitter, April 6, 2023, 3:03 am, https://twitter.com/ EmmanuelMacron/status/1643871957190885377.

116. Roger Cohen, "French Diplomacy Undercuts U.S. Efforts to Rein China In," *New York Times*, April 12, 2023, https://www.nytimes.com/2023/04/08/world/asia/ macron-xi-france-china.html.

117. Jamil Anderlini and Clea Caulcutt, "Europe Must Resist Pressure to Become 'America's Followers,' Says Macron," *Politico*, April 12, 2023, https://www.politico. eu/article/emmanuel-macron-china-america-pressure-interview/.

118. Jake Sullivan, "Remarks by National Security Advisor Jake Sullivan on the Biden-Harris Administration's National Security Strategy" (remarks, Washington, DC,

October 12, 2022), White House, https://www.whitehouse.gov/briefing-room/speeches-remarks/2022/10/13/remarks-by-national-security-advisor-jake-sullivan-on-the-biden-harris-administrations-national-security-strategy/.

119. Hal Brands, *The Twilight Struggle: What the Cold War Teaches Us about Great-Power Rivalry Today* (New Haven, CT: Yale University Press, 2022).

120. Antony Blinken, "Russia's Strategic Failure and Ukraine's Secure Future" (speech, Helsinki, Finland, June 2, 2023), Embassy of the United States in Russia, https://ru.usembassy.gov/secretary-blinken-russias-strategic-failure-and-ukraines-secure-future/.

121. Helene Cooper et al., "Troop Deaths and Injuries in Ukraine War Near 500,000, U.S. Officials Say," *New York Times*, August 18, 2023, https://www.nytimes.com/2023/08/18/us/politics/ukraine-russia-war-casualties.html; Ellen Mitchell, "Defense & National Security," *Hill*, May 2, 2023, https://nxslink.thehill.com/view/6230d9aec22ca34bdd853b71inrl1.vyx/aecd7a74; Steve Holland and Katharine Jackson, "US Believes Russians in Ukraine Have Suffered 100,000 Casualties in 5 Months," *Reuters*, May 1, 2023, https://www.reuters.com/world/europe/us-believes-russians-ukraine-have-suffered-100000-casualties-5-months-2023-05-01/; Pavel Luzin, "Russia's Military Manpower Crunch Will Worsen," Europe's Edge (Commentary), Center for European Policy Analysis, https://cepa.org/article/russias-military-manpower-crunch-will-worsen/; Ann Simons and Nancy Youssef, "Russia's Casualties in Ukraine Near 200,000," *Wall Street Journal*, February 4, 2023, https://www.wsj.com/articles/russias-casualties-in-ukraine-near-200-000-11675509981.

122. Julian E. Barnes, "Russia Has Suffered Staggeringly High Losses, U.S. Report Says," *New York Times*, December 12, 2023, https://www.nytimes.com/2023/12/12/us/politics/russia-intelligence-assessment.html.

123. Shashank Joshi, "The War in Ukraine May Be Heading for Stalemate," *Economist*, November 13, 2023, https://www.economist.com/the-world-ahead/2023/11/13/the-war-in-ukraine-may-be-heading-for-stalemate.

124. Ibid.

125. Christina Mackenzie, "Seven European Nations Have Increased Defense Budgets in One Month. Who Will Be Next?," *Breaking Defense*, March 22, 2022, https://breakingdefense.com/2022/03/seven-european-nations-have-increased-defense-budgets-in-one-month-who-will-be-next/; Richard Milne, "Sweden to Boost Defence Spending Next Year By Almost 30%," *Financial Times*, September 11, 2023, https://www.ft.com/content/d1afa268-a59b-4299-9b27-b8d716819417.

126. Imran Khalid, "US' New Security Strategy on Europe: Disconnection, Differences," *Daily Sabah*, January 14, 2023, https://www.dailysabah.com/opinion/op-ed/us-new-security-strategy-on-europe-disconnection-differences; Reuters, "NATO Allies to Spend 'At Least 2%' of GDP on Defence, Diplomats Say," *Reuters*, July 7, 2023, https://www.reuters.com/world/nato-allies-agree-spend-at-least-2-their-gdp-defence-diplomats-2023-07-07/.

127. International Institute for Strategic Studies, "Chapter Four: Europe," *Military Balance* 123, no. 1 (2023): 50–149, https://www.iiss.org/publications/the-military-balance/the-military-balance-2023/.

128. Ibid.

129. Bojan Pancevski, "When Russia Invaded Ukraine, Germany Promised to Rearm. One Year Later, It Is Having Second Thoughts," *Wall Street Journal*, March 2, 2023, https://www.wsj.com/articles/when-russia-invaded-ukraine-germany-promised-to-rearm-one-year-later-it-is-having-second-thoughts-b08d783b?mod=world_major_1_pos7; Ben Knight, "What Happened to the German Military's €100 Billion Fund?," *Deutsche Welle*, March 2, 2023, https://www.dw.com/en/what-happened-to-the-german-militarys-100-billion-fund/a-64846571.

130. Sabine Siebold, "Germany pledges to make its military 'the Backbone of Defence in Europe,'" *Reuters*, November 9, 2023, https://www.reuters.com/world/europe/germany-pledges-make-its-military-the-backbone-defence-europe-2023-11-09/.

131. Cour des Comptes, "The French Military Programming Law (LPM) 2019–2025 and the Capacities of the Armed Forces," May 11, 2022, https://www.ccomptes.fr/en/publications/french-military-programming-law-lpm-2019-2025-and-capacities-armed-forces.

132. Michele Barbero, "Can France's Big Bucks Fill the Defense Gaps?," *Foreign Policy*, June 8, 2023, https://foreignpolicy.com/2023/06/08/france-defense-budget-macron-ukraine-russia/.

133. Julie Coleman and Ryan Pickrell, "With Sweden and Finland, NATO Wouldn't Just Get Bigger. The Alliance Would Also Get a Firepower Boost," *Business Insider*, August 4, 2022, https://www.businessinsider.com/sweden-and-finland-would-give-nato-a-firepower-boost-2022-5; STT, "Gripen Is Designed to Kill Suhoi, Says the Commander of the Swedish Air Force," *YLE*, June 2, 2019, https://yle.fi/a/3-10634682.

134. Global Fire Power, "2023 Military Strength Ranking," Global Fire Power Index, https://www.globalfirepower.com/countries-listing.php.

135. Zachary Basu, "Finland and Sweden Bring Military Might to NATO," *Axios*, May 18, 2022, https://www.axios.com/2022/05/19/nato-finland-sweden-military-might.

136. Joel Hickman, "Why Finland and Sweden's Accession Is a Game-Changer for NATO," *Europe's Edge* (Blog), Center for European Policy Analysis, June 28, 2022, https://cepa.org/article/why-finland-and-swedens-accession-is-a-game-changer-for-nato/.

137. Ibid.

138. Jens Stoltenberg, "Remarks by NATO Secretary General Jens Stoltenberg with the President of the United States of America, Joe Biden at the White House" (speech, Washington, DC, June 13, 2023), North Atlantic Treaty Organization, https://www.nato.int/cps/en/natohq/opinions_215647.htm?selectedLocale=en.

# Chapter 8

1. Hillary Clinton, "America's Pacific Century," *Foreign Policy*, October 11, 2011, https://foreignpolicy.com/2011/10/11/americas-pacific-century/; Hillary Clinton, "America's Pacific Century" (speech, Honolulu, HI, November 10, 2011), United States Department of State Archives, https://2009-2017.state.gov/secretary/20092013clinton/rm/2011/11/176999.htm.

2. Clinton, "America's Pacific Century" (speech).

3. Associated Press, "Afghanistan and Iraq Wars Not Worth Fighting, Say a Third of US Veterans," *Guardian*, October 5, 2011, https://www.theguardian.com/world/2011/oct/05/afghanistan-iraq-wars-us-veterans.

4. Richard Haass, "The Irony of American Strategy," *Foreign Affairs* 92, no. 3 (May–June 2013): 64, https://www.foreignaffairs.com/articles/united-states/2013-04-03/irony-american-strategy.

5. Haviv Rettig Gur, "Saudis, Gulf States 'Unnerved by US Pivot Away from Middle East,'" *Times of Israel*, June 2, 2013, https://www.timesofisrael.com/saudis-gulf-states-unnerved-by-us-pivot-away-from-middle-east/.

6. Greg Gause, "The King and O," interviewed by Michael Crowley, *Time*, March 27, 2014, https://time.com/39872/the-king-and-o/.

7. Reem Khalifa, "At Bahrain Summit, US Says It Won't Pivot Away from the Middle East," *Times of Israel*, December 8, 2012, https://www.timesofisrael.com/at-bahrain-summit-delegates-say-us-wont-pivot-away-from-the-middle-east/.

8. Ibid.

9. William J. Clinton, "Remarks on the Israeli-Palestinian Declaration of Principles and an Exchange with Reporters" (speech, Washington, DC, September 10, 1993), American Presidency Project, University of California, Santa Barbara, https://www.presidency.ucsb.edu/documents/remarks-the-israeli-palestinian-declaration-principles-and-exchange-with-reporters.

10. George W. Bush, "President Bush Attends Saban Forum 2008" (speech, Washington, DC, December 5, 2008), White House Archives, https://georgewbush-whitehouse.archives.gov/news/releases/2008/12/20081205-8.html.

11. Barack Obama, "Press Conference by the President at the Nuclear Security Summit" (speech, Washington, DC, April 13, 2010), White House Archives, https://obamawhitehouse.archives.gov/the-press-office/press-conference-president-nuclear-security-summit.

12. Douglas Hamilton, "Israel Shocked by Obama's 'Betrayal' of Mubarak," *Reuters*, January 31, 2011, https://www.reuters.com/article/us-egypt-israel-usa/israel-shocked-by-obamas-betrayal-of-mubarak-idUSTRE70U53720110131.

13. Ben Rhodes, "A Fatal Abandonment of American Leadership," *Atlantic*, October 12, 2018, https://www.theatlantic.com/ideas/archive/2018/10/jamal-khashoggi-and-us-saudi-relationship/572905/.

14. Author's conversation with Martin Indyk.

15. Alan J. Kuperman, "Obama's Libya Debacle," *Foreign Affairs* 94, no. 2 (March–April 2015): 67, https://www.foreignaffairs.com/articles/libya/2019-02-18/obamas-libya-debacle.

16. Joseph Logan, "NATO Says Destroyed Gaddafi Compound Guard Towers," *Reuters*, May 27, 2011, https://www.reuters.com/article/uk-libya-idUKTRE74E1I420110528.

17. Macon Phillips, "President Obama: 'The Future of Syria Must Be Determined by Its People, but President Bashar Al-Assad Is Standing in Their Way,'" *White House Blog*, August 18, 2011, https://obamawhitehouse.archives.gov/blog/2011/08/18/president-obama-future-syria-must-be-determined-its-people-president-bashar-al-assad; Scott Wilson and Joby Warrick, "Assad Must Go, Obama Says," *Washington Post*,

August 18, 2011, https://www.washingtonpost.com/politics/assad-must-go-obama-says/2011/08/18/gIQAelheOJ_story.html.

18. Matt Compton, "President Obama Has Ended the War in Iraq," *White House Blog*, October 21, 2011, https://obamawhitehouse.archives.gov/blog/2011/10/21/presid ent-obama-has-ended-war-iraq.

19. Barack Obama, "Remarks by the President to the White House Press Corps" (remarks, Washington, DC, August, 20, 2012), White House Archives, https://obamawhitehouse.archives.gov/the-press-office/2012/08/20/remarks-presid ent-white-house-press-corps.

20. Derek Chollet, "Obama's Red Line, Revisited," *Politico*, July 19, 2016, https://www.politico.com/magazine/story/2016/07/obama-syria-foreign-policy-red-line-revisi ted-214059/.

21. Justin Sink, "Panetta: Obama's 'Red Line' on Syria Damaged US Credibility," *Hill*, October 7, 2014, https://thehill.com/policy/international/219984-panetta-obamas-red-line-on-syria-damaged-us-credibility/.

22. "Secret Talks Set Stage for Iran Nuclear Deal," *BBC*, November 25, 2013, https://www.bbc.com/news/world-middle-east-25086236.

23. Barak Ravid, "Netanyahu Tells Obama Iran Deal Threatens Israel's Security," *Haaretz*, July 14, 2015, https://www.haaretz.com/2015-07-14/ty-article/netanyahu-to-obama-nuke-deal-threatens-israel/0000017f-db3d-df62-a9ff-dfffa27b0000.

24. *U.S. Policy toward the Middle East after the Iranian Nuclear Agreement, before the U.S. Senate Committee on Foreign Relations*, 115th Congress, 8 (2015) (statement of Kenneth Pollack, Senior Fellow at the Brookings Institution), https://www.foreign.senate.gov/imo/media/doc/080515_Pollack_Testimony.pdf.

25. Loveday Morris and Hugh Naylor, "Arab States Fear Nuclear Deal Will Give Iran a Bigger Regional Role," *Washington Post*, July 14, 2015, https://www.washingtonp ost.com/world/middle_east/arab-states-fear-dangerous-iranian-nuclear-deal-will-shake-up-region/2015/07/14/96d68ff3-7fce-4bf5-9170-6bcc9dfe46aa_story.html.

26. Jeffrey Goldberg, "The Obama Doctrine," *Atlantic*, April 2016, https://www.theatlan tic.com/magazine/archive/2016/04/the-obama-doctrine/471525/.

27. Barack Obama, "The Obama Doctrine," interviewed by Jeffrey Goldberg, *Atlantic*, April 2016, http://theatlantic.com/magazine/archive/2016/04/the-obama-doctrine/471525.

28. Ibid.

29. Darren Samuelsohn, "Obama's Slippery Foreign Oil Promise," *Politico*, October 14, 2012, https://www.politico.com/story/2012/10/obamas-slippery-foreign-oil-promi ses-082377.

30. Steve Hargreaves, "Romney: Energy Independence by 2020," *CNN Money*, August 23, 2012, https://money.cnn.com/2012/08/23/news/economy/romney-energy/index.html.

31. "Oil and Petroleum Products Explained," Oil and Petroleum Products, US Energy Information Administration, last modified November 2, 2022, https://www.eia.gov/energyexplained/oil-and-petroleum-products/imports-and-exports.php.

32. Ibid.

33. Ibid.

34. Matt Egan, "The United States Is Producing More Oil Than Any Country in History," *CNN*, December 19, 2023, https://www.cnn.com/2023/12/19/business/us-product ion-oil-reserves-crude/index.html; "Weekly U.S. Field Production of Crude Oil," *Petroleum and Other Liquids, United States Energy Information Administration*, accessed December 20, 2023, https://www.eia.gov/dnav/pet/hist/LeafHandler. ashx?f=W&n=PET&s=WCRFPUS2.

35. Common Dreams Staff, "Obama Administration Quietly Selling Arms to Bahrain Despite Continuing Human Rights Abuses," *Common Dreams*, January 31, 2012, https://www.commondreams.org/news/2012/01/31/obama-administration-quietly-selling-arms-bahrain-despite-continuing-human-rights.

36. Michael Crowley, "'We Caved,'" *Politico* 3, no. 2 (January–February 2016), https://www.politico.com/magazine/story/2016/01/we-caved-obama-foreign-policy-leg acy-213495/.

37. Ibid.

38. Ben Hubbard, "Despite Displeasure with U.S., Saudis Face Long Dependency," *New York Times*, May 11, 2015, https://www.nytimes.com/2015/05/12/world/mid dleeast/persian-gulf-allies-confront-crisis-of-confidence-in-us.html; Jeff Abramson, "Obama Acts on Arms Exports," *Arms Control Today*, January–February 2017, https://www.armscontrol.org/act/2017-01/news/obama-acts-arms-exports.

39. Seth J. Frantzman, "America's Good Intentions in Syria Have Led to This Dismal Outcome," *National Review*, October 8, 2019, https://www.nationalreview.com/2019/ 10/us-withdrawal-syria-how-good-intentions-led-to-dismal-outcome/.

40. Jeremy Diamond and Elise Labott, "Trump Told Turkey's Erdogan in Dec. 14 Call about Syria, 'It's All Yours. We Are Done,'" *CNN*, December 24, 2018, https://www. cnn.com/2018/12/23/politics/donald-trump-erdogan-turkey/index.html.

41. Liz Sly, "The Hasty U.S. Pullback from Syria Is a Searing Moment in America's Withdrawal from the Middle East," *Washington Post*, October 16, 2019, https://www. washingtonpost.com/world/middle_east/the-hasty-us-pullback-from-syria-is-a-searing-moment-in-americas-withdrawal-from-the-middle-east/2019/10/16/82c0f f3c-ef5a-11e9-bb7e-d2026ee0c199_story.html.

42. Tara Law, "Iran Shot Down a $176 Million U.S. Drone. Here's What to Know about the RQ-4 Global Hawk," *Time*, June 21, 2019, https://time.com/5611222/rq-4-global-hawk-iran-shot-down/.

43. Michael D. Shear et al., "Strikes on Iran Approved by Trump, Then Abruptly Pulled Back," *New York Times*, June 20, 2019, https://www.nytimes.com/2019/06/20/world/ middleeast/iran-us-drone.html.

44. Peter Baker, Eric Schmitt, and Michael Crowley, "An Abrupt Move That Stunned Aides: Inside Trump's Aborted Attack on Iran," *New York Times*, September 21, 2019, https://www.nytimes.com/2019/09/21/us/politics/trump-iran-decision.html.

45. US Library of Congress, Congressional Research Service, *Attacks on Saudi Oil Facilities: Effects and Responses*, by Heather L. Greenley, Christopher M. Blanchard, and Michael Ratner, IN11173, 2019, https://crsreports.congress.gov/product/pdf/ IN/IN11173.

46. Donald J. Trump (@realDonaldTrump), "Saudi Arabia oil supply was attacked. There is reason to believe that we know the culprit, are locked and loaded depending on verification, but are waiting to hear from the Kingdom as to who they believe was the cause of this attack, and under what terms we would proceed!" Twitter, September 15, 2019, 6:50 pm, https://twitter.com/realDonaldTrump/status/1173368423381962752.

47. Donald J. Trump (@realDonaldTrump), "I have just instructed the Secretary of the Treasury to substantially increase Sanctions on the country of Iran!" Twitter, September 18, 2019, 8:53 am, https://twitter.com/realDonaldTrump/status/1174 305447513186304?lang=en.

48. US Library of Congress, *Attacks on Saudi Oil Facilities: Effects and Responses.*

49. Trita Parsi and Khalid Aljabri, "How China Became a Peacemaker in the Middle East," *Foreign Affairs*, March 15, 2023, https://www.foreignaffairs.com/china-bec ame-peacemaker-middle-east.

50. Daniel L. Byman, "Trump's Reckless Middle East Policy Has Brought the US to the Brink of War," Brookings Institution, January 6, 2020, https://www.brookings.edu/ blog/order-from-chaos/2020/01/06/trumps-reckless-middle-east-policy-has-brou ght-the-us-to-the-brink-of-war/.

51. Donald Trump (@realDonaldTrump), "The United States has spent EIGHT TRILLION DOLLARS fighting and policing in the Middle East. Thousands of our Great Soldiers have died or been badly wounded. Millions of people have died on the other side. GOING INTO THE MIDDLE EAST IS THE WORST DECISION EVER MADE . . . ," Twitter, October 9, 2019, 8:14 am, https://twitter.com/realDonaldTr ump/status/1181905659568283648.

52. Joseph Biden, "The November Democratic Debate" (remarks, Atlanta, GA, November 20, 2019), *Washington Post*, https://www.washingtonpost.com/politics/2019/11/21/ transcript-november-democratic-debate/.

53. Peter Baker and Susan Glasser, *The Divider: Trump in the White House* (New York: Knopf Doubleday, 2022), 424.

54. Michael Singh, "The Middle East in a Multipolar Era," *Foreign Affairs*, December 7, 2022, https://www.foreignaffairs.com/middle-east/middle-east-multipolar-era.

55. Mohamed Abdelaziz, "In New Poll, Most Egyptians Split on Relations with Foreign Powers, Pessimistic about Domestic Economy," Policy Analysis, Fikra Forum, Washington Institute for Near East Policy, September 9, 2022, https://www.washingt oninstitute.org/policy-analysis/new-poll-most-egyptians-split-relations-foreign-powers-pessimistic-about-domestic.

56. Madiha Afzal, Bruce Riedel, and Natan Sachs, *The United States, China, and the "New Non-Aligned" Countries*, Policy Brief, Brookings Institution, February 2023, https:// www.brookings.edu/wp-content/uploads/2023/02/FP_20230213_china_regional_s trategy.pdf.

57. Marc Lynch, "Does the Decline of U.S. Power Matter For the Middle East," *Washington Post*, March 19, 2019, https://www.washingtonpost.com/politics/2019/03/19/does-decline-us-power-matter-middle-east/.

58. "Qatar Plans to Invest $35 Billion in US over 5 Years," *Real Deal*, September 28, 2015,      https://therealdeal.com/new-york/2015/09/28/qatar-plans-35b-in-u-s-inv

estment-over-next-five-years/; "Qatar Plans to Invest $35 Billion in US over 5 Years," *Fashion Network*, September 28, 2015, https://in.fashionnetwork.com/news/Qatar-plans-to-invest-35-billion-in-us-over-5-years,652609.html; Jonathan Saul, Marwa Rashad, and Davide Barbuscia, "EXCLUSIVE: Qatar Targets $10 Billion of Investments in U.S. Ports—Sources," *Reuters*, December 21, 2021, https://www.reuters.com/markets/europe/exclusive-qatar-targets-10-billion-investments-us-ports-sources-2021-12-21/; "Qatar Lauded for Its Role in Afghanistan Evacuations," *Al Jazeera*, August 30, 2021, https://www.aljazeera.com/news/2021/8/30/qatar-emerges-as-key-player-in-afghanistan-after-us-pullout; Adam Taylor, "As Trump Tries to End 'Endless Wars,' America's Biggest Mideast Base Is Getting Bigger," *Washington Post*, August 21, 2019, https://www.washingtonpost.com/world/as-trump-tries-to-end-endless-wars-americas-biggest-mideast-base-is-getting-bigger/2019/08/20/47ac5854-bab4-11e9-8e83-4e6687e99814_story.html.

59. Amos Yadlin (@YadlinAmos), "A pre-Ukrain [*sic*] FA piece with Assaf orion: "Absent Without Leaving" . . . The US has not left the ME nor is it leaving. More than its physical military footprint, its reputational footprint is dimming, reflecting in the regional players' behaviors." Twitter, February 18, 2022, 1:08 pm, https://twitter.com/YadlinAmos/status/1494780896796418052.

60. Karen Elliott House, "Saudi Arabia Turns toward China," *Wall Street Journal*, November 9, 2021, https://www.wsj.com/articles/saudi-arabia-china-crown-prince-mohammed-bin-salman-energy-prices-climate-xi-biden-iran-11636493333.

61. Phil Mattingly, Allie Malloy, Tamara Qiblawi, and Celine Alkhaldi, "MBS Hits Back at Biden after the President Confronts Saudi Prince about Khashoggi," *CNN*, July 17, 2022, https://www.cnn.com/2022/07/16/middleeast/biden-mbs-khashoggi-abu-akleh-intl/index.html.

62. Frank Gardner, "Qatar Crisis: Saudi Arabia and Allies Restore Diplomatic Ties with Emirate," *BBC*, January 5, 2021, https://www.bbc.com/news/world-middle-east-55538792.

63. Associated Press, "Qatar and Saudi Arabia Officially End Three-Year Feud at GCC Summit," *Euronews*, May 1, 2021, https://www.euronews.com/2021/01/05/qatar-and-saudi-arabia-officially-end-three-year-feud-at-gcc-summit.

64. Vivian Salama, "'An Open Secret': Saudi Arabia and Israel Get Cozy," *NBC*, November 15, 2017, https://www.nbcnews.com/news/mideast/open-secret-saudi-arabia-israel-get-cozy-n821136.

65. Dennis Ross, "The Abraham Accords and the Changing Shape of the Middle East," *Caravan*, *Hoover Institution*, June 21, 2022, https://www.hoover.org/research/abraham-accords-and-changing-shape-middle-east.

66. Barak Ravid, "Scoop: Israel OKs Red Sea Islands Deal, Paving Way for Saudi Normalization Steps," *Axios,* July 14, 2022, https://www.axios.com/2022/07/14/saudi-israel-normalization-red-sea-deal.

67. Times of Israel Staff, "Report: Saudi Arabia to Okay All Overflights from Israel, and Direct Travel for Hajj," *Times of Israel,* July 14, 2022, https://www.timesofisrael.com/report-saudi-arabia-may-ok-overflight-from-israel-allow-direct-travel-for-hajj/.

68. Ryan Bohl, "Will the Saudi Crown Prince Risk the Monarchy's Mystique for Israeli Normalization?," *Stratfor Worldview*, July 25, 2022, https://worldview.stratfor.com/article/will-saudi-crown-prince-risk-monarchy-s-mystique-israeli-normalization?mc_cid=a4496ee8fb&mc_eid=b9e464c520; Haaretz, "Israel, Saudi Arabia Reportedly in Talks over Increasing Military and Intelligence Ties," *Haaretz*, February 18, 2023, https://www.haaretz.com/israel-news/2023-02-18/ty-article/israel-saudi-arabia-reportedly-in-talks-over-increasing-military-and-intelligence-ties/00000186-6536-de14-a387-7fbe8df80000.

69. Agnes Helou, Hamas Attack Might Freeze Saudi-Israeli Normalization, but Won't Likely Kill It: Analysts," *Breaking Defense*, October 12, 2023, https://breakingdefense.com/2023/10/hamas-attack-might-freeze-saudi-israeli-normalization-but-wont-likely-kill-it-analysts/.

70. Natasha Turak, "Saudi Foreign Minister Says the Kingdom's Hands Are 'Stretched Out' to Iran," *CNBC*, May 24, 2022, https://www.cnbc.com/2022/05/24/saudi-arabia-says-the-kingdoms-hands-are-outstretched-to-iran.html.

71. Stephen Kalin et al., "Saudi Arabia, Iran Restore Relations in Deal Brokered by China," *Wall Street Journal*, March 10, 2023, https://www.wsj.com/articles/saudi-arabia-iran-restore-relations-in-deal-brokered-by-china-406393a1.

72. Ishaan Tharoor, "Assad in Saudi Arabia Reflects the Middle East's New Normal," *Today's World View* (newsletter), *Washington Post*, May 22, 2023, https://www.washingtonpost.com/world/2023/05/22/assad-saudi-arabia-reflects-middle-easts-new-normal/.

73. Lin Noueihed, "Middle East Pursues Peace on Its Own Terms," *Bloomberg*, May 10, 2023, https://www.bloomberg.com/news/newsletters/2023-05-10/middle-east-pursues-peace-on-its-own-terms.

74. Karen Elliott House, "Opinion: Behind China's Mideastern Diplomacy," *Wall Street Journal*, March 12, 2023, https://www.wsj.com/articles/behind-chinas-mideastern-diplomacy-iran-saudi-arabia-mbs-jinping-israel-oil-vacuum-biden-talks-weapons-78bc1617?mod=djemMER_h.

75. Ibid.

76. Author's conversation with senior Saudi government officials, February 2023.

77. Gordon Lubold, Nancy A. Youssef, and Michael R. Gordon, "U.S. Military to Withdraw Hundreds of Troops, Aircraft, Antimissile Batteries from Middle East," *Wall Street Journal*, June 18, 2021, https://www.wsj.com/articles/u-s-military-to-withdraw-hundreds-of-troops-aircraft-antimissile-batteries-from-middle-east-11624045575.

78. Associated Press, "U.S. Pulls Missile Defenses in Saudi Arabia Amid Yemen Attacks," *Politico*, September 11, 2021, https://www.politico.com/news/2021/09/11/missile-defense-saudi-arabia-511320.

79. David S. Cloud, "U.S. Sends Patriot Missiles to Saudi Arabia, Fulfilling Urgent Request," *Wall Street Journal*, March 21, 2022, https://www.wsj.com/articles/u-s-sends-patriot-missiles-to-saudi-arabia-filling-an-urgent-request-11647822871.

80. Kong Defang, "China, Saudi Arabia Form Comprehensive Strategic Partnership," *People's Daily*, January 20, 2016, http://en.people.cn/n3/2016/0120/c98389-9006770.html.

81. Middle East Eye and Agencies, "China's Saudi Drone Factory Compensates for US Ban," *Middle East Eye,* March 30, 2017, https://www.middleeasteye.net/fr/news/china-build-factory-saudi-arabia-fill-drone-shortage-1200657135.

82. Ibid.

83. Fareed Zakaria, "The Rise of the Persian Gulf Is Reshaping the World," *Washington Post,* June 16, 2023, https://www.washingtonpost.com/opinions/2023/06/16/saudi-arabia-gulf-reshaping-world/.

84. Michelle Nichols, "Saudi Arabia Defends Letter Backing China's Xinjiang Policy," *Reuters,* July 18, 2019, https://www.reuters.com/article/us-china-rights-saudi-idUSKCN1UD36J; Evan Freidin, "Saudi Arabia and China: A Blossoming Friendship," *Interpreter,* May 10, 2022, https://www.lowyinstitute.org/the-interpreter/saudi-arabia-china-blossoming-friendship; Rayhan Asat, "China's Transnational Repression Gets Saudi Backing," *Foreign Policy,* April 14, 2022, https://foreignpolicy.com/2022/04/14/saudi-uyghur-refugees-china/.

85. Wang Wenbin, "Foreign Ministry Spokesperson Wang Wenbin's Regular Press Conference on August 15, 2022," (press conference, August 15, 2022) *People's Republic of China Ministry of Foreign Affairs,* https://www.fmprc.gov.cn/mfa_eng/xwfw_665399/s2510_665401/202208/t20220815_10743533.html; Ali Shihabi, "Saudis Roll Out Red Carpet for Xi Jinping as Gulf Looks Past US," interviewed by Ben Bartenstein and Sylvia Westall, *Bloomberg,* December 6, 2022, https://www.bloomberg.com/news/articles/2022-12-06/xi-s-riyadh-trip-showcases-deeper-china-mideast-ties-and-sinking-us-relations.

86. Fahad Abuljadayel and Abeer Abu Omar, "Saudi Arabia Says $50 Billion Investments Agreed with China," *Bloomberg,* December 11, 2022, https://www.bloomberg.com/news/articles/2022-12-11/saudi-arabia-says-50-billion-investments-agreed-at-china-summit; Kawala Xie, "Is the US Row with Saudi Arabia Driving Riyadh into the Arms of China?," *South China Morning Post,* December 8, 2022, https://www.scmp.com/news/china/diplomacy/article/3202115/us-row-saudi-arabia-driving-riyadh-arms-china.

87. Saudi Press Agency, "Joint Statement at the Conclusion of the Saudi-Chinese Summit," December 9, 2022, https://www.spa.gov.sa/2407997; Nadeen Ebrahim, "Saudi Arabia and China Will Align on Everything from Security to Oil, but Agree Not to Interfere on Domestic Issues," *CNN,* December 9, 2022, https://edition.cnn.com/2022/12/09/middleeast/china-xi-jinping-saudi-arabia-policy-intl/index.html.

88. Stephen Kalin and Summer Said, "Saudi Arabia Strengthens Relations with China amid Strained U.S. Ties," *Wall Street Journal,* March 29, 2023, https://www.wsj.com/articles/saudi-arabia-strengthens-relations-with-china-amid-strained-u-s-ties-c5819114.

89. Ruby Lian, Josephine Mason, and Rania El Gamal, "Saudi Arabia, Russia Sign Oil Pact, May Limit Output in Future," *Reuters,* September 5, 2016, https://www.reuters.com/article/us-g20-china-saudi-russia-oil/saudi-arabia-russia-sign-oil-pact-may-limit-output-in-future-idUSKCN11B0UF.

90. Stanley Reed, "Russia and Others Join OPEC in Rare, Coordinated Push to Cut Oil Output," *New York Times,* December 10, 2016, https://www.nytimes.com/2016/12/10/business/russia-opec-saudi-arabia-cut-oil-output.html.

91. Patrick Wintour, "Saudi King's Visit to Russia Heralds Shift in Global Power Structures," *Guardian*, October 5, 2017, https://www.theguardian.com/world/2017/oct/05/saudi-russia-visit-putin-oil-middle-east.

92. Chyrine Mezher, "Russia, KSA Strengthen Military Ties in Signal to Washington; UAVs, Helos Potentially on Table," *Breaking Defense*, September 1, 2021, https://breakingdefense.com/2021/09/russia-ksa-strengthen-military-ties-in-signal-to-washington-uavs-helos-potentially-on-table/; Mark N. Katz, "Saudi Arabia Is Trying to Make America Jealous with Its Budding Russia Ties," MENA Source, Atlantic Council, August 27, 2021, https://www.atlanticcouncil.org/blogs/menasource/saudi-arabia-is-trying-to-make-america-jealous-with-its-budding-russia-ties/.

93. Cathrin Shaer, "Why the US Can't Get the Middle East to Support It on Ukraine," *Deutsche Welle*, June 15, 2022, https://www.dw.com/en/why-usa-no-middle-east-support-ukraine/a-62131430.

94. "The Blow-Up with Saudi Arabia Reveals a New American Strategic Weakness," *Economist*, October 19, 2022, https://www.economist.com/united-states/2022/10/19/the-blow-up-with-saudi-arabia-reveals-a-new-american-strategic-weakness.

95. Jack Farchy, Annmarie Hordern, and Ben Bartenstein, "Saudi Arabia Snubs Biden and Aids Putin with Oil Output Cut," *Bloomberg*, October 5, 2022, https://www.bloomberg.com/news/articles/2022-10-05/saudi-arabia-enrages-biden-and-aids-putin-with-oil-output-cut?sref=0Xh9npns; Karen E. Young, "How Saudi Arabia Sees the World," *Foreign Affairs*, November 1, 2022, https://www.foreignaffairs.com/saudi-arabia/how-saudi-arabia-sees-world.

96. Bill Law, "How 2022 Saw a Tectonic Shift in Power between Gulf States and the West," *Middle East Eye*, December 21, 2022, https://www.middleeasteye.net/opinion/gulf-west-tectonic-shift-power-how.

97. Alex Longley, "What Next for Oil after Surprise OPEC+ Cuts? Try $100 a Barrel," *Bloomberg*, April 3, 2023, https://www.bloomberg.com/news/articles/2023-04-03/what-next-for-oil-after-surprise-opec-cuts-try-100-a-barrel.

98. Adam Taylor, "The Saudi-U.S. Relationship Was Always a Marriage of Convenience," *Washington Post*, October 14, 2022, https://www.washingtonpost.com/world/2022/10/14/saudi-united-states-relationship-history-oil/.

99. Vivian Nereim and Ivan Nechepurenko, "Putin Makes Rare Visit to Mideast," *New York Times*, December 6, 2023, https://www.nytimes.com/2023/12/06/world/europe/putin-saudi-arabia-visit.html; Aziz El Yaakoubi and Vladimir Soldatkin, "Russia's Putin, Saudi Crown Prince Discuss Further OPEC+ Cooperation in Whirlwind Visit," *Reuters*, December 6, 2023, https://www.reuters.com/world/middle-east/putin-talk-oil-uae-saudi-meet-crown-prince-mohammed-bin-salman-2023-12-06/.

100. "UK Arms Sales to Saudi Arabia," Stop Arming Saudi Arabia, Campaign Against Arms Trade, last modified May 27, 2022, https://caat.org.uk/homepage/stop-arming-saudi-arabia/uk-arms-to-saudi-arabia/.

101. Stockholm International Peace Research Institute, "USA and France Dramatically Increase Major Arms Exports; Saudi Arabia Is Largest Arms Importer, Says SIPRI," press release, March 9, 2020, https://www.sipri.org/media/press-release/2020/

usa-and-france-dramatically-increase-major-arms-exports-saudi-arabia-largest-arms-importer-says.

102. "Israel Vows to 'Act Freely' against Iran's Nuclear Programme," *Middle East Monitor*, February 6, 2022, https://www.middleeastmonitor.com/20220206-israel-vows-to-act-freely-against-irans-nuclear-programme/.

103. Yair Lapid, "A Billion Dollar a Year Prize for Breaking Their Commitments? PM Lapid on the Bad Iranian Nuclear Deal" (speech, Jerusalem, August 24, 2022), State of Israel Ministry of Foreign Affairs, https://www.gov.il/en/departments/news/pm-lapid-holds-briefing-for-foreign-correspondents-24-aug-2022.

104. Jonathan Lis, "Iran Nuke Deal 'Based on Lies,' Mossad Chief Says," *Haaretz*, August 25, 2022, https://www.haaretz.com/israel-news/2022-08-25/ty-article/.premium/mossad-chief-leaving-nuclear-watchdog-cases-open-against-iran-is-fraud/00000 182-d5da-d9c0-a3d3-fdda26e50000.

105. Dalia Dassa Kaye, Alireza Nader, and Parisa Roshan, *Israel and Iran: A Dangerous Rivalry* (Santa Monica, CA: RAND, 2011), https://www.rand.org/pubs/monogra phs/MG1143.html; Amir Bohbot and Walla!, "Israel Makes Dramatic Upgrades to Military Plans to Attack Iran," *Jerusalem Post*, June 8, 2022, https://www.jpost.com/arab-israeli-conflict/article-708875.

106. Emanuel Fabian, "Gantz, Kohavi Visit Major IDF Drill in Cyprus, Hail 'Strategic Alliance' between Nations," *Times of Israel*, May 31, 2022, https://www.timesofisrael.com/liveblog_entry/gantz-kohavi-visit-major-idf-drill-in-cyprus-hail-strategic-alliance-between-nations/.

107. David Makovsky, "A New Regional Role for Israel, as Washington Shows Signs of Stepping Back," Policy Analysis, Washington Institute for Near East Policy, March 28, 2022, https://www.washingtoninstitute.org/policy-analysis/new-regional-role-israel-washington-shows-signs-stepping-back.

108. Dave Lawler and Barak Ravid, "Israel Hopes U.S. Will Mend Ties with Saudi Arabia, Ambassador Says," *Axios*, April 14, 2022, https://www.axios.com/2022/04/14/isr ael-us-improve-saudi-relations-herzog; Sam Dagher and Fiona MacDonald, "Israel Steps Up Talks with Saudi Arabia over Ties to Combat Iran," *Bloomberg*, February 17, 2023, https://www.bloomberg.com/news/articles/2023-02-17/israel-steps-up-talks-with-saudi-arabia-over-ties-to-combat-iran.

109. Barak Ravid, "U.S. Officials Angry: Israel Doesn't Back Stance on Russia," *Haaretz*, April 13, 2014, https://www.haaretz.com/2014-04-13/ty-article/.premium/u-s-angry-at-israel-for-silence-on-ukraine/0000017f-e15c-d9aa-afff-f95c6f4d0000.

110. Ora Coren, "After Shunning Europe, Russia Turning to Israel for Fruit Imports," *Haaretz*, August 13, 2014, https://www.haaretz.com/israel-news/business/2014-08-13/ty-article/russia-turning-to-israel-for-fruit-imports/0000017f-e60d-dea7-adff-f7ffcfde0000; World Bank, "Israel Product Exports to Russian Federation 2014," World Integrated Trade Solutions, World Bank, https://wits.worldbank.org/CountryProfile/en/Country/ISR/Year/2014/TradeFlow/Export/Partner/RUS/Product/all-groups.

111. Maria Tsvetkova, "Israel, Russia to Coordinate Military Action on Syria: Netanyahu," *Reuters*, September 21, 2015, https://www.reuters.com/article/cnews-us-mideast-crisis-russia-israel-idCAKCN0RL10K20150921.

112. Herb Keinon, "Analysis: The Message in the Netanyahu-Putin Meeting," *Jerusalem Post*, July 11, 2018, https://www.jpost.com/Israel-News/Analysis-The-message-in-the-Netanyahu-Putin-meeting-562248.

113. Reuters Staff, "Israel to Russia: We Sat Out Western Sanctions, So Help Us in Mideast," *Reuters*, May 3, 2018, https://www.reuters.com/article/us-mideast-crisis-syria-israel-russia/israel-to-russia-we-sat-out-western-sanctions-so-help-us-in-mideast-idUSKBN1I41AB; Judah Ari Gross, "Liberman to Russian Media: Israel 'Did Not Join' Western Action against Moscow," *Times of Israel*, May 3, 2018, https://www.timesofisrael.com/liberman-to-russian-media-israel-did-not-join-western-action-against-moscow/.

114. Jacob Magid, "Despite US Request Israel Refrains from Co-Sponsoring UNSC Resolution against Russia," *Times of Israel*, February 26, 2022, https://www.timesofisrael.com/despite-us-request-israel-refrains-from-backing-unsc-resolution-against-russia/.

115. Anton Troianovski, "Putin Offers Muted Response to Attack on Israel. That Speaks Volumes," *New York Times*, October 10, 2023, https://www.nytimes.com/2023/10/10/world/europe/israel-hamas-russia-putin.html.

116. Reuters, "Hamas Delegation Visits Moscow, Discusses Release of Hostages in Gaza—Agencies," *Reuters*, October 26, 2023, https://www.reuters.com/world/hamas-delegation-is-visiting-moscow-russian-foreign-ministry-2023-10-26/; Ellie Cook, "Hamas Says Russia 'Our Closest Friend'," *Newsweek*, October 29, 2023, https://www.newsweek.com/hamas-russia-israel-gaza-strip-hostages-1838886.

117. Reuters, "Israel Summons Russian Ambassador to Protest at Moscow's Hosting of Hamas," *Reuters*, October 29, 2023, https://www.reuters.com/world/israel-summons-russian-ambassador-protest-moscows-hosting-hamas-2023-10-29/.

118. Tzvi Joffre, "Israel Has No Right To Defend Itself, Says Russia at UN," *Jerusalem Post*, November 2, 2023, https://www.jpost.com/breaking-news/article-771270.

119. Sam Dagher, Henry Meyer, and Ethan Bronner, "Israel's Fight with Iran Proxies in Syria Poisons Russia Ties," *Bloomberg*, November 3, 2023, https://www.bloomberg.com/news/articles/2023-11-03/israel-russia-ties-worsen-as-it-fights-iran-proxies-in-syria-amid-war-with-hamas.

120. Ali Bagheri Kani, "Iran Nuclear Negotiator: Talks Must Address Removal of Sanctions," *Financial Times*, November 28, 2021, https://www.ft.com/content/ecd4d7c1-f166-4263-a31c-93bcebccfd47.

121. Laurence Norman, "Iran Demands Legal Pledge That U.S. Won't Quit Nuclear Deal Again," *Wall Street Journal*, January 17, 2022, https://www.wsj.com/articles/iran-demands-legal-pledge-that-u-s-wont-quit-nuclear-deal-again-11642429074.

122. Seth G. Jones, *War by Proxy: Iran's Growing Footprint in the Middle East*, (Washington, DC: Center for International and Strategic Studies, 2019), https://www.csis.org/war-by-proxy.

123. Ibid., Chapter 5; International Institute for Strategic Studies, "Chapter Seven: Middle East and North Africa," *Military Balance* 123, no. 1 (2023): 324–328, https://www.iiss.org/publications/the-military-balance/the-military-balance-2023/.

124. April Brady, "Russia Completes S-300 Delivery to Iran," *Arms Control Association*, December 2016, https://www.armscontrol.org/act/2016-11/news-briefs/russia-completes-s-300-delivery-iran; Ardavan Khoshnood, "Iran-Russia Ties: Never Better but Maybe Not Forever?," *Middle East Institute*, February 12, 2020, https://www.mei.edu/publications/iran-russia-ties-never-better-maybe-not-forever.

125. Nima Khorrami, "Putin's Visit to the Islamic Republic: Bringing Iran Closer to Russia While Building Long-Term Leverage over Tehran," Middle East Institute, August 1, 2022, https://mei.edu/publications/putins-visit-islamic-republic-bring ing-iran-closer-russia-while-building-long-term.

126. Anton Troianovski and Farnaz Fassihi, "Putin Finds a New Ally in Iran, a Fellow Outcast," *New York Times*, July 19, 2022, https://www.nytimes.com/2022/07/19/world/europe/putin-ayatollah-erdogan-summit.html.

127. David Ignatius, "Beware the Emerging Alliance between Russia and Iran," *Washington Post*, August 24, 2022, https://www.washingtonpost.com/opinions/2022/08/24/russia-iran-drones-sanctions/; Associated Press, Aamer Madhani, Edith M. Lederer, and Colleen Long, "US: Russia Looking to Iran to Supply More Drones, Missiles," *Associated Press*, December 7, 2022, https://apnews.com/arti cle/russia-ukraine-iran-government-united-states-034b4e4ae2e9a4cb0ec0922ca c82dc54; Paul Iddon, "How Iran's Acquisition of Russian Military Hardware Could Impact the Middle East," *Forbes*, February 22, 2023, https://www.forbes.com/sites/pauliddon/2023/02/22/how-irans-acquisition-of-russian-military-hardware-could-impact-the-middle-east/?sh=29a34c5f232e.

128. William Burns, "Transcript: CIA Director William Burns on 'Face the Nation,' Feb. 26, 2023," interviewed by Margaret Brennan, *CBS*, February 26, 2023, https://www.cbsnews.com/news/william-burns-cia-director-face-the-nation-transcript-02-26-2023/.

129. Benoit Faucon, "China Buys More Iranian and Venezuelan Oil, in a Test for Biden," *Wall Street Journal*, March 19, 2021, https://www.wsj.com/articles/china-buys-more-iranian-and-venezuelan-oil-in-a-test-for-biden-11616146203?mod=hp_lead_pos7; "China 'Sharply' Increases Oil Imports from Iran, Challenging US Sanctions," *Iran International*, March 19, 2021, https://old.iranintl.com/en/iran-in-brief/china-sharply-increases-oil-imports-iran-challenging-us-sanctions?_gl=1*1nni1se*_ga*NTcxNjk3MTM0LjE2NTg4NjU5MzI.

130. Radio Free Europe/Radio Liberty, "Iran, Russia, China Hold Joint Naval Drill amid Growing Ties" updated January 21, 2022, https://www.rferl.org/a/iran-russia-china-exercises/31663080.html.

131. Scott W. Harold and Alireza Nader, *China and Iran: Economic, Political, and Military Relations* (Santa Monica, CA: RAND, 2012), https://www.rand.org/pubs/occasional _papers/OP351.html; Farzin Nadimi, "Iran and China Are Strengthening Their Military Ties," *Washington Institute for Near East Policy*, November 22, 2016, https://www.washingtoninstitute.org/policy-analysis/iran-and-china-are-strengthening-their-military-ties.

132. Harold and Nader, *China and Iran: Economic, Political, and Military Relations*; China Briefing Team, "China and Iran: Bilateral Trade Relationship and Future

Outlook," *China Briefing*, August 20, 2021, https://www.china-briefing.com/news/china-and-iran-bilateral-trade-relationship-and-future-outlook/; "China Remains Iran's Largest Trade Partner for Ten Consecutive Years," *Financial Tribune*, February 18, 2023, https://financialtribune.com/articles/domestic-economy/117145/china-remains-irans-largest-trade-partner-for-ten-consecutive-years; Silk Road Briefing, "China Increases BRI Investments into Iran by 150%," *Silk Road Briefing*, May 29, 2023, https://www.silkroadbriefing.com/news/2023/05/29/china-increases-bri-investments-into-iran-by-150/.

133. Bryan Clark and Michael Doran, "Why Russia and China Build Up Iran," *Wall Street Journal*, January 27, 2022, https://www.wsj.com/articles/why-russia-and-china-build-up-iran-biden-administration-foreign-relations-nuclear-negotiations-11643317565.

134. Al Jazeera, "Syrian War: All You Need to Know about the Astana Talks," *Al Jazeera*, October 30, 2017, https://www.aljazeera.com/news/2017/10/30/syrian-war-all-you-need-to-know-about-the-astana-talks.

135. Radio Free Europe/Radio Liberty, "Turkey, Iran Back Qatar in Dispute with Other Arab States," *Radio Free Europe/Radio Liberty*, June 8, 2017, https://www.rferl.org/a/turkey-iran-back-qatar-dispute-saudi-arabia-other-arab-states/28535012.html.

136. Reuters Staff, "Erdogan Says Turkey Values Iranian Stability, Praises Rouhani," *Reuters*, January 3, 2018, https://www.reuters.com/article/us-iran-rallies-turkey-idUSKBN1ES0MC; Reuters Staff, "Turkey Told U.S. It Opposes Sanctions on Iran: Foreign Minister," *Reuters*, July 24, 2018, https://www.reuters.com/article/us-oil-iran-turkey-idUSKBN1KE27J; Aykan Erdemir, "Turkey's Elite Unsure Whether Soleimani Was Hero or War Criminal," *Jerusalem Post*, January 20, 2020, https://www.jpost.com/opinion/turkeys-elite-unsure-whether-soleimani-was-hero-or-war-criminal-614751.

137. Troianovski and Fassihi, "Putin Finds a New Ally."

138. Steven A. Cook, "Why Turkey Is Resetting Relations with Saudi Arabia," Council on Foreign Relations, May 4, 2022, https://www.cfr.org/in-brief/why-turkey-resetting-relations-saudi-arabia.

139. Ahmed al-Masri, "Turkish-Saudi Relations: A Burgeoning Relationship," *Anadolu Agency*, September 30, 2016, https://www.aa.com.tr/en/economy/turkish-saudi-relations-a-burgeoning-relationship/656010; Reuters Staff, "Saudi Arabia, Turkey to Set up 'Strategic Cooperation Council'—Saudi FM," *Reuters*, December 29, 2015, https://www.reuters.com/article/uk-saudi-turkey/saudi-arabia-turkey-to-set-up-strategic-cooperation-council-saudi-fm-idUKKBN0UC1GX20151229.

140. Cook, "Why Turkey Is Resetting Relations with Saudi Arabia"; Safak Timur and Ben Hubbard, "Turkey Transfers Khashoggi Murder Trial to Saudi Arabia," *New York Times*, April 7, 2022, https://www.nytimes.com/2022/04/07/world/middleeast/khashoggi-murder-trial-turkey-saudi-arabia.html.

141. Kareem Fahim and Zeynep Karatas, "Turkey's Erdogan Hosts Saudi Crown Prince, Ending Rift over Khashoggi Murder," *Washington Post*, June 22, 2022, https://www.washingtonpost.com/world/2022/06/22/turkey-saudi-mbs-khashoggi/.

142. Ibid.

143. WAM, AFP, "UAE Announces $10 Billion Turkey Investment Fund," *Khaleej Times*, November 25, 2021, https://www.khaleejtimes.com/uae/uae-announces-10-billion-fund-for-investments-in-turkey.

144. Ragip Soylu, "UAE-Turkey: Emirati Foreign Minister Calls Turkish Counterpart for First Time in Five Years," *Middle East Eye*, April 23, 2021, https://www.middleeasteye.net/news/uae-turkey-foreign-minister-call-first-five-years; Natasha Turak, "Erdogan's Celebrity Welcome in the UAE Affirms a Sea-Change in Relations, Lifeline for Turkey's Economy," *CNBC*, February 15, 2022, https://www.cnbc.com/2022/02/15/erdogans-uae-visit-affirms-shift-in-relations-help-for-turkeys-economy.html; Ragip Soylu, "Turkey and UAE Launch Free Trade Deal Talks," *Middle East Eye*, February 14, 2022, https://www.middleeasteye.net/news/turkey-uae-free-trade-deal-talks-launched.

145. Arab News, "Turkey Orders Muslim Brotherhood TV Channels to Stop Criticizing Egypt: Reports," *Arab News*, March 19, 2021, https://www.arabnews.com/node/1828181/media.

146. Ibrahim Kalin, "Turkey Says Better Ties with Cairo Could Boost Libya Peace Efforts," interviewed by Dominic Evans and Orhan Coskun, *Reuters*, April 26, 2021, https://www.reuters.com/world/middle-east/turkey-says-better-ties-with-cairo-could-boost-libya-peace-efforts-2021-04-26/.

147. Barak Ravid, "Israel and Turkey Officially Announce Rapprochement Deal, Ending Diplomatic Crisis," *Haaretz*, June 27, 2016, https://www.haaretz.com/israel-news/2016-06-27/ty-article/israel-and-turkey-officially-announce-rapprochement-deal/0000017f-e18e-d804-ad7f-f1fed9d00000.

148. Tal Schneider, Agencies, and TOI Staff, "Hosting Herzog In Landmark Visit, Erdogan Lauds 'Turning Point' in Relations," *Times of Israel*, March 9, 2022, https://www.timesofisrael.com/herzog-meets-erdogan-in-landmark-visit-as-israel-and-turkey-attempt-detente/.

149. "Hosting Herzog in Landmark Visit, Erdogan Lauds 'Turning Point' in Relations," *Deutsche Welle*, May 25, 2022, https://www.dw.com/en/turkey-israel-agree-to-strengthen-ties-in-historic-talks/a-61931977.

150. Lazar Berman, "Israel, Turkey Sign Updated Aviation Agreement as Bilateral Ties Continue to Improve," *Times of Israel*, July 7, 2022, https://www.timesofisrael.com/israel-turkey-sign-updated-aviation-agreement-as-bilateral-ties-continue-to-improve/; Brenda Shaffer, "Washington Wins as Turkey and Israel Restore Normal Ties," *TURKEYSource* (blog), Atlantic Council, August 23, 2022, https://www.atlanticcouncil.org/blogs/turkeysource/washington-wins-as-turkey-and-israel-restore-normal-ties/; James Mackenzie and Ece Toksabay, "Turkey, Israel to Re-Appoint Ambassadors after Four-Year Chill," *Reuters*, August 17, 2022, https://www.reuters.com/world/middle-east/israel-says-restore-full-diplomatic-relations-with-turkey-2022-08-17/; Asli Aydintasbas, "Why Is Erdogan Suddenly Making Nice to His Enemies?" *Washington Post*, August 26, 2022, https://www.washingtonpost.com/opinions/2022/08/26/erdogan-turkey-diplomacy-mideast-syria-assad/; Jonathan Lis, "Israel Announces First Ambassador to Turkey in Four Years amid Warming Ties," *Haaretz*, September 19, 2022, https://www.haaretz.com/israel-news/

2022-09-19/ty-article/.premium/israel-announces-first-ambassador-to-turkey-in-four-years/00000183-5661-d4ae-a3e7-7f695ba00000.

151. Burak Ünveren, "Israel-Hamas War Strains Ties with Turkey," *DW*, November 4, 2023, https://www.dw.com/en/israel-hamas-war-strains-ties-with-turkey/a-67302382.

152. "Israel Bringing Diplomats Home from Turkey After Warning Its Citizens to Leave," *Times of Israel*, October 19, 2023, https://www.timesofisrael.com/israel-bringing-diplomats-home-from-turkey-after-warning-citizens-to-leave/.

153. Güney Yildiz, "Turkish-Russian Adversarial Collaboration in Syria, Libya, and Nagorno-Karabakh," *Stiftung Wissenschaft und Politik Comment*, no. 22 (March 2021), https://www.swp-berlin.org/10.18449/2021C22/; "Turkey-Syria Offensive: Russia Vows to Prevent Clashes with Assad Forces," *BBC*, October 15, 2019, https://www.bbc.com/news/world-middle-east-50058859.

154. Amin Saikal, "Strategic Shifts in the Middle East after the US Withdrawal from Afghanistan," *Strategist*, October 14, 2021, https://www.aspistrategist.org.au/strategic-shifts-in-the-middle-east-after-the-us-withdrawal-from-afghanistan/.

155. Patricia Cohen, "Turkey Is Strengthening Its Energy Ties with Russia," *New York Times*, December 12, 2022, https://www.nytimes.com/2022/12/09/business/turkey-erdogan-energy-russia.html; Valerie Hopkins, Safak Timur, and Stanley Reed, "Putin Offers to Make Turkey a Gas Hub to Preserve E.U. Energy Hold," *New York Times*, October 13, 2022, https://www.nytimes.com/2022/10/13/world/europe/putin-russia-turkey-gas-eu-energy.html?searchResultPosition=2.

156. Kuzzat Altay, "Why Erdogan Has Abandoned the Uyghurs," *Foreign Policy*, March 2, 2021, https://foreignpolicy.com/2021/03/02/why-erdogan-has-abandoned-the-uyghurs/.

157. Arie Egozi, "Turkey Is Cozying Up to China after F-35 Expulsion, Israelis Warn," *Breaking Defense*, July 26, 2019, https://breakingdefense.com/2019/07/turkey-is-cozying-up-to-china-after-f-35-expulsion-israelis-warn/; Lina Wang, "Will Turkey Join the Shanghai Cooperation Organization Instead of the EU?," *Diplomat*, November 24, 2016, https://thediplomat.com/2016/11/will-turkey-join-the-shanghai-cooperation-organization-instead-of-the-eu/.

158. "Türkiye-People's Republic of China Economic and Trade Relations," People's Republic of China Ministry of Foreign Affairs, https://www.mfa.gov.tr/turkey_s-commercial-and-economic-relations-with-china.en.mfa; Middle East Eye Correspondent, "Turkey and China Keep Relations on Track Despite Uighur Dispute," *Middle East Eye*, February 5, 2022, https://www.middleeasteye.net/news/turkey-china-uighur-relations-track-despite-dispute.

159. Iain MacGillivray, "Burgeoning Ties between Beijing and Ankara Create an Existential Problem for the West," *Strategist*, August 18, 2022, https://www.aspistrategist.org.au/burgeoning-ties-between-beijing-and-ankara-create-an-existential-problem-for-the-west/.

160. Private conversation with the authors.

161. Geoff Ziezulewicz, "Why Aircraft Carriers Are No Longer a Constant in the Middle East," *Navy Times*, November 4, 2022, https://www.navytimes.com/news/

your-navy/2022/11/04/why-aircraft-carriers-are-no-longer-a-constant-in-the-middle-east/.

162. Luis Martinez, "US Moves Carrier to Middle East Following Attacks on US Forces," *ABC*, October 22, 2023, https://abcnews.go.com/International/us-moves-carrier-middle-east-attacks-us-forces/story?id=104201064#:~:text=In%20a%20major%20change%2C%20the,Hezbollah%20from%20broadening%20the%20conflict.

163. Ibid. In 2014, there were also twelve F-16Cs in Jordan as part of Operation Inherent Resolve.

164. US Bureau of Economic Analysis, "Direct Investment by Country and Industry," maintained by Ryan Smith, 2020 table, using bea.gov, https://www.bea.gov/data/intl-trade-investment/direct-investment-country-and-industry.

165. US Department of State, Agency for International Development, *FY 2013—FY 2020 Congressional Budget Justifications*, https://www.usaid.gov/results-and-data/budget-spending/congressional-budget-justification.

166. Peter Baker and Julie Hirschfeld Davis, "U.S. Finalizes Deal to Give Israel $38 Billion in Military Aid," *New York Times*, September 13, 2016, https://www.nytimes.com/2016/09/14/world/middleeast/israel-benjamin-netanyahu-military-aid.html.

167. US Department of State, *FY 2013—FY 2020 Congressional Budget Justifications*.

168. Ibid.

169. Beacon Research, "U.S. National Survey of Defense Attitudes on Behalf of the Ronald Reagan Foundation Final Topline Results," Ronald Reagan Foundation, 2022, https://www.reaganfoundation.org/media/358081/reagan-foundation-november-2021-survey-topline-results.pdf.

170. Ibid.

171. Terri Moon Cronk, "Biden Announces Full U.S. Troop Withdrawal from Afghanistan by Sept. 11," *US Department of Defense News*, April 14, 2021, https://www.defense.gov/News/News-Stories/Article/Article/2573268/biden-announces-full-us-troop-withdrawal-from-afghanistan-by-sept-11/; Lubold, Youssef, and Gordon, "U.S. Military to Withdraw Hundreds of Troops, Aircraft, Antimissile Batteries from Middle East"; Nicolas Pelham, "MBS: Despot in the Desert," *Economist*, July 28, 2022, https://www.economist.com/1843/2022/07/28/mbs-despot-in-the-desert.

172. Natasha Bertrand and Lara Seligman, "Biden Deprioritizes the Middle East," *Politico*, February 22, 2021, https://www.politico.com/news/2021/02/22/biden-middle-east-foreign-policy-470589.

173. James Phillips and John Venable, "Biden's Middle East Trip Should Be Judged by Its Long-Term Security Results," Commentary, Heritage Foundation, August 1, 2022, https://www.heritage.org/middle-east/commentary/bidens-middle-east-trip-should-be-judged-its-long-term-security-results.

174. Joseph Biden, "Remarks by President Biden and Prime Minister Yair Lapid of the State of Israel" (remarks, Jerusalem, July 14, 2022), Briefing Room, White House, https://www.whitehouse.gov/briefing-room/statements-releases/2022/07/14/remarks-by-president-biden-and-prime-minister-yair-lapid-of-the-state-of-israel/.

175. Joseph Biden, "Remarks by President Biden at the GCC + 3 Summit Meeting" (speech, Jeddah, Saudi Arabia, July 16, 2022), Briefing Room, White House, https://

www.whitehouse.gov/briefing-room/speeches-remarks/2022/07/16/remarks-by-president-biden-at-the-gcc-3-summit-meeting/.

176. Walter Russell Mead, "A Feckless American Foreign Policy's Legacy," *Wall Street Journal*, July 18, 2022, https://www.wsj.com/articles/a-feckless-foreign-policys-leg acy-cold-war-biden-saudi-arabia-middle-east-rules-based-order-hard-power-afgh anistan-11658174386?mod=MorningEditorialReport&mod=djemMER_h.

177. Dennis Ross and James F. Jeffrey, "The True Promise of Joe Biden's Middle East Trip," *National Interest*, July 27, 2022, https://nationalinterest.org/blog/middle-east-watch/true-promise-joe-biden's-middle-east-trip-203856.

178. Olivia Rockerman, "US Inflation Quickens to 9.1%, Amping Up Fed Pressure to Go Big," *Bloomberg*, July 13, 2022, https://www.bloomberg.com/news/articles/2022-07-13/us-inflation-accelerates-to-9-1-once-again-exceeding-forecasts#xj4y7vzkg.

179. Alexander Ward and Jonathan Lemire, "'Even if It Hurts': Biden's Middle East Trip Could Bring Short-Term Pain for Long-Term Gain," *Politico*, July 12, 2022, https://www.politico.com/news/2022/07/12/biden-middle-east-trip-00045256.

180. David E. Sanger and Peter Baker, "As Biden Reaches Out to Mideast Dictators, His Eyes Are on China and Russia," *New York Times*, July 16, 2022, https://www.nytimes.com/2022/07/16/world/middleeast/biden-saudi-arabia-china-russia.html.

181. The Carter Doctrine was a US policy in the Middle East, announced by President Jimmy Carter in his 1980 State of the Union Address, which pledged to employ any means necessary, including military force, to prevent an outside power—namely, the Soviet Union—from gaining control in the Persian Gulf. In his 1980 State of the Union Address, President Carter said, "Let our position be absolutely clear: An attempt by any outside force to gain control of the Persian Gulf region will be regarded as an assault on the vital interests of the United States of America, and such an assault will be repelled by any means necessary, including military force." Jimmy Carter, "State of the Union Address" (speech, Washington, DC, January 23, 1980), Jimmy Carter Presidential Library, https://www.jimmycarterlibrary.gov/assets/documents/speeches/su80jec.phtml; Biden, "Remarks by President Biden at the GCC + 3 Summit Meeting."

182. Grant Smith, Justin Sink, and Salma El Wardany, "Biden Expects More Saudi Oil after Trip to Kingdom," *Bloomberg*, July 15, 2022, https://www.bloomberg.com/news/artic les/2022-07-15/white-house-expects-more-saudi-oil-after-biden-met-with-king.

183. Biden, "Remarks by President Biden at the GCC + 3 Summit Meeting."

184. White House, "Fact Sheet: The United States Strengthens Cooperation with Middle East Partners to Address 21st Century Challenges," July 16, 2022, https://www.whi tehouse.gov/briefing-room/statements-releases/2022/07/16/fact-sheet-the-united-states-strengthens-cooperation-with-middle-east-partners-to-address-21st-cent ury-challenges/.

185. White House, *The Jerusalem U.S.-Israel Strategic Partnership Joint Declaration*, July 14, 2022, https://www.whitehouse.gov/briefing-room/statements-releases/2022/07/14/the-jerusalem-u-s-israel-strategic-partnership-joint-declaration/.

186. Patsy Widakuswara, "Biden Ends Tour to Reassert US Influence in Middle East," *Voice of America*, July 16, 2022, https://www.voanews.com/a/biden-ends-tour-to-reassert-us-influence-in-middle-east/6661635.html.

187. White House, "Fact Sheet: The United States Strengthens Cooperation with Middle East Partners to Address 21st Century Challenges."

188. Ibid.; Matthew Lee, "US Approves Massive Arms Sale to Saudi, UAE to Counter Iran," *Military.com*, August 3, 2022, https://www.military.com/daily-news/2022/08/03/us-approves-massive-arms-sale-saudi-uae-counter-iran.html; Tommy Steiner, "The China Factor: US Strategic Turning Point in the Middle East—Opinion," *Jerusalem Post*, July 29, 2022, https://www.jpost.com/opinion/article-713372.

189. White House "Statement from Press Secretary Karine Jean-Pierre on President Biden's Travel to Israel and Jordan," press release, October 16, 2023, https://www.whitehouse.gov/briefing-room/statements-releases/2023/10/16/statement-from-press-secretary-karine-jean-pierre-on-president-bidens-travel-to-israel-and-jordan/; US Department of State, "Secretary Blinken's Travel to Israel, Jordan, Qatar, Bahrain, Saudi Arabia, the United Arab Emirates, and Egypt," press release, October 12, 2023, https://www.state.gov/secretary-blinkens-travel-to-israel-jordan-qatar-saudi-arabia-the-united-arab-emirates-and-egypt/; US Department of State, "Secretary Blinken's Travel to Tel Aviv, Amman, Ramallah, Baghdad, Ankara, Tokyo, Seoul, and New Delhi," press release, November 1, 2023, https://www.state.gov/secretary-blinkens-travel-to-tel-aviv-amman-ramallah-baghdad-ankara-tokyo-seoul-and-new-delhi.

190. Eric Schmitt and Helene Cooper, "U.S. Missiles Strike Targets in Yemen Linked to the Houthi Militia," *New York Times*, January 11, 2024, https://www.nytimes.com/2024/01/11/us/politics/us-houthi-missile-strikes.html.

191. Stockholm International Peace Research Institute, "SIPRI Military Expenditure Database," https://milex.sipri.org/sipri.

192. All data presented in this paragraph are sourced from International Institute for Strategic Studies, "Chapter Seven: Middle East and North Africa," *Military Balance* 123, no. 1 (2023): 324–328.

193. Yun Li, "Saudi Oil Production Cut by 50% after Drones Attack Crude Facilities," *CNBC*, September 14, 2019, https://www.cnbc.com/2019/09/14/saudi-arabia-is-shutting-down-half-of-its-oil-production-after-drone-attack-wsj-says.html.

194. Abdel Aziz Aluwaisheg, "Houthis' Organic Links with IRGC and Hezbollah Revealed," *Arab News*, November 1, 2022, https://www.arabnews.com/node/2191941.

195. Ido Levy, "How Iran Fuels Hamas Terrorism," *Washington Institute for Near East Policy*, June 1, 2021, https://www.washingtoninstitute.org/policy-analysis/how-iran-fuels-hamas-terrorism.

196. Elbridge Colby, *Strategy of Denial* (New Haven, CT: Yale University Press, 2021), 35.

197. Edward Wong, "Citing Iranian Threat, U.S. Sends Carrier Group and Bombers to Persian Gulf," *New York Times*, May 5, 2019, https://www.nytimes.com/2019/05/05/world/middleeast/us-iran-military-threat-.html.

198. C. Todd Lopez, "U.S., Partners Find Success in Mission to Defeat ISIS," *US Department of Defense News*, January 12, 2023, https://www.defense.gov/News/News-Stories/Article/Article/3266973/us-partners-find-success-in-mission-to-defeat-isis/.

199. US Library of Congress, Congressional Research Service, *United States Central Command*, by Nathan J. Lucas and Brendan W. McGarry, IF11428, last modified December 16, 2022, https://crsreports.congress.gov/product/pdf/IF/IF11428.

200. Ibid.

201. Information in these last three paragraphs can be found in International Institute for Strategic Studies, "Chapter Seven: Middle East and North Africa," 123.

202. Brett McGurk, "Remarks at Atlantic Council on Biden Doctrine for the Middle East" (speech, Washington, DC, February 14, 2023), Atlantic Council, https://www.atlanticcouncil.org/commentary/transcript/brett-mcgurk-sets-out-the-biden-doctrine-for-the-middle-east/.

203. Bruce Hoffman and Jacob Ware, "Israel's 9/11? How Hamas Terrorist Attacks Will Change the Middle East," *War on the Rocks*, October 10, 2023, https://warontherocks.com/2023/10/israels-9-11-how-hamas-terrorist-attacks-will-change-the-middle-east/.

204. Ishan Tharoor, "Welcome to the New, 'New' Middle East," *Today's World View* (Newsletter) *Washington Post*, October 16, 2023, https://www.washingtonpost.com/world/2023/10/16/new-new-middle-east-israel-region-saudi-relations-fututre/.

205. Bryant Harris and Noah Robertson, "Biden Asks Congress for Israel, Ukraine Aid in Giant Defense Package," *Defense News*, October 19, 2023, https://www.defensenews.com/congress/2023/10/20/biden-asks-congress-for-israel-ukraine-aid-in-giant-defense-package/; and Jeremy Bowen, "Joe Biden's Search for a Middle East Solution Just Got Harder," *BBC*, October 18, 2023, https://www.bbc.com/news/world-middle-east-67148622; and Vivian Nereim, Alissa J. Rubin, and Euan Ward, "U.S. Response to Israel-Hamas War Draws Fury in Middle East," *New York Times*, October 17, 2023, https://www.nytimes.com/2023/10/17/world/middleeast/biden-israel-gaza-anger.html.

206. Nereim, Rubin, and Ward, "U.S. Response to Israel-Hamas War Draws Fury in Middle East."

207. Didi Tang, "Israel-Hamas War Upends China's Ambitions in the Middle East But May Serve Beijing in the End," *Associated Press*, October 15, 2023, https://apnews.com/article/china-israel-hamas-mideast-war-arab-countries-33d78c0ad6f7cb116d87417ff81ed727; and Steven Erlanger, "New Global Divisions on View as Biden Goes to Israel and Putin to China," *New York Times*, October 18, 2023, https://www.nytimes.com/2023/10/18/world/europe/biden-israel-putin-china.html

208. Agnes Helou, "Hamas Attack Might Freeze Saudi-Israeli Normalization, but Won't Likely Kill It: Analysts," *Breaking Defense*, October 12, 2023, https://breakingdefense.com/2023/10/hamas-attack-might-freeze-saudi-israeli-normalization-but-wont-likely-kill-it-analysts/.

209. Henry Foy, "Rush by West to Back Israel Erodes Developing Countries' Support for Ukraine," *Financial Times*, October 18, 2023, https://www.ft.com/content/e0b43918-7eaf-4a11-baaf-d6d7fb61a8a5.

210. Aaron McLean, "America Cannot Ignore the Middle East," Foundation for the Defense of Democracies, October 13, 2023, https://www.fdd.org/analysis/2023/10/13/america-cannot-ignore-the-middle-east/.

211. Gordon Lubold, Nancy A. Youssef, and Michael R. Gordon, "War in the Middle East Challenges Biden's Defense Strategy," *Wall Street Journal*, October 17, 2023, https://www.wsj.com/politics/national-security/war-in-the-middle-east-challenges-bidens-defense-strategy-534808f5.

212. Natasha Bertrand and Oren Liebermann, "US Marine Rapid Response Force Moving toward Israel as Pentagon Strengthens Military Posture in Region," *CNN*, October 16, 2023, https://www.cnn.com/2023/10/16/politics/us-marines-pentagon-israel/index.html; US Department of Defense, "Statement from Secretary Lloyd J. Austin III on U.S. Force Posture Changes in the Middle East," press release, October 8, 2023, https://www.defense.gov/News/Releases/Release/Article/3551716/statement-from-secretary-lloyd-j-austin-iii-on-us-force-posture-changes-in-the/; Idrees Ali and Phil Stewart, "U.S. Sending Additional Air Defense Systems to Middle East, Pentagon Says," *Reuters*, October 21, 2023, https://www.reuters.com/world/middle-east/us-sending-additional-air-defense-systems-middle-east-pentagon-2023-10-22/.

213. Jennifer Kavanagh and Frederic Wehrey, "Washington's Looming Middle Eastern Quagmire," *Foreign Affairs*, November 24, 2023, https://www.foreignaffairs.com/united-states/washingtons-looming-middle-eastern-quagmire; Chris Kobel, "Can the U.S. Military Avoid Another Middle East War?," *National Interest*, December 21, 2023, https://nationalinterest.org/feature/can-us-military-avoid-another-middle-east-war-208033.

214. "Only America Can Save Israel and Gaza from Greater Catastrophe," *Economist*, October 19, 2023, https://www.economist.com/leaders/2023/10/19/the-stakes-could-hardly-be-higher-in-the-israel-gaza-conflict.

# Chapter 9

1. Clarita Carlos, "Philippines Balances Security and Trade in US-China Contest," interviewed by Financial Times, *Financial Times*, September 27, 2022, https://www.ft.com/content/b63e6e30-5dea-40a2-bcb8-9b9f1bea400e.

2. "China Wraps Anti-Japan Propaganda Campaign," *Associated Press*, August 16, 2014, https://apnews.com/article/42d21642e3c24a9791fb5ef7e937daa6.

3. "Unfavorable Views of China Reach Historic Highs in Many Countries," Pew Research Center, Washington, DC, October 6, 2020, https://www.pewresearch.org/global/2020/10/06/unfavorable-views-of-china-reach-historic-highs-in-many-countries/.

4. "How Global Public Opinion of China Has Shifted in the Xi Era," Pew Research Center, Washington, DC, September 28, 2022, https://www.pewresearch.org/global/2022/09/28/how-global-public-opinion-of-china-has-shifted-in-the-xi-era/.

5. "Article 9 and the U.S.-Japan Security Treaty," Asia for Educators, Columbia University, http://afe.easia.columbia.edu/special/japan_1950_usjapan.htm; Jeffrey W. Hornung, "Japanese Public Needs to Know SDF to Appreciate It," *Stars and*

*Stripes*, February 18, 2021, https://www.stripes.com/opinion/japanese-public-needs-to-know-sdf-to-appreciate-it-1.662632.

6. Shingo Yoshida, "Nuclear Deterrence: Mixed Messages for Japan," *Diplomat*, October 17, 2019, https://thediplomat.com/2019/10/nuclear-deterrence-mixed-messages-for-japan/.

7. Japan Ministry of Foreign Affairs, "Japan-U.S. Foreign Ministerial Meeting (Summary)," press release November 11, 2011, https://warp.ndl.go.jp/info:ndljp/pid/11525605/www.mofa.go.jp/region/n-america/us/fmm1111.html; Japan Ministry of Foreign Affairs, "Japan-U.S. Summit Meeting (Summary)," press release, November 18, 2011, https://warp.ndl.go.jp/info:ndljp/pid/11525605/www.mofa.go.jp/region/n-america/us/meeting1111.html.

8. Koichiro Gemba, "Speech by Foreign Minister Koichiro Gemba at the Japan National Press Club Japan's Prosperity Depends on its Ties to the Asia-Pacific" (speech, Tokyo, December 14, 2011), Ministry of Foreign Affairs, https://warp.ndl.go.jp/info:ndljp/pid/11525605/www.mofa.go.jp/announce/fm/gemba/speech_111214.html.

9. Noriyuki Shikata, "Trade, Security On Agenda For Obama, Japan's Noda," interviewed by Jackie Northman, Morning Edition, *NPR*, April 30, 2012, https://www.npr.org/transcripts/151663842.

10. Michael Green, *Line of Advantage: Japan's Grand Strategy in the Era of Abe Shinzō* (New York: Columbia University Press, 2022).

11. Isabel Reynolds, "Japan Defense Budget to Increase for First Time in 11 Years," *Bloomberg*, January 30, 2013, https://www.bloomberg.com/news/articles/2013-01-29/japan-s-defense-spending-to-increase-for-first-time-in-11-years.

12. Takahashi Kosuke, "Japanese Defense Ministry Requests Largest Ever Budget for Fiscal Year 2023," *Diplomat*, August 31, 2022, https://thediplomat.com/2022/08/japanese-defense-ministry-requests-largest-ever-budget-for-fiscal-year-2023/ ; for year by year reports on Japan's defense budget, see "Defense Budget," Japan Ministry of Defense, https://www.mod.go.jp/en/d_act/d_budget/index.html.

13. "Reinventing the Indo-Pacific," *Economist*, January 4, 2023, https://www.economist.com/asia/2023/01/04/reinventing-the-indo-pacific.

14. Ibid.

15. Tyler Roney, "China Blasts Japan's Defense White Paper," *Diplomat*, July 12, 2013, https://thediplomat.com/2013/07/china-blasts-japans-defense-white-paper/.

16. Yuka Hayashi, "Japan Raises Alarm over Defense," *Wall Street Journal*, July 9, 2013, https://www.wsj.com/articles/SB10001424127887323823004578594703681295448.

17. David Sacks, "Shinzo Abe Transformed Japan's Relationship with Taiwan to Counter Threats from China," *Asia Unbound* (Blog), Council on Foreign Relations, July 13, 2022, https://www.cfr.org/blog/shinzo-abe-transformed-japans-relationship-taiwan-counter-threats-china.

18. Michael Green, "Line of Advantage: Japan's Grand Strategy in the Era of Shinzo Abe," interviewed by H. Andrew Schwartz, Asia Chessboard Podcast, Center for Strategic and International Studies, May 28, 2022, https://www.csis.org/analysis/line-advantage-japans-grand-strategy-era-shinzo-abe.

19. David Berteau, Michael J. Green, and Zack Cooper, *Assessing the Asia-Pacific Rebalance* (Washington, DC: Center for Strategic and International Studies, 2014), 19, https://csis-website-prod.s3.amazonaws.com/s3fs-public/legacy_files/files/publ ication/150105_Berteau_AssessingAsiaPacificRebal_Web.pdf.

20. Shinzo Abe, "Toward an Alliance of Hope" (speech, Washington, DC, April 29, 2015), Kantei Archives, https://japan.kantei.go.jp/97_abe/statement/201504/uscongr ess.html.

21. Shinzo Abe, "Remarks by Prime Minister Shinzo Abe at a Symposium hosted by Sasakawa Peace Foundation USA" (remarks, Washington, DC, April 29, 2015), Kantei Archives, https://japan.kantei.go.jp/97_abe/statement/201504/1210942_9918.html.

22. Stockholm International Peace Research Institute, "SIPRI Arms Transfers Database," https://www.sipri.org/databases/armstransfers; US Department of State, Bureau of Political-Military Affairs, "Fact Sheet: U.S. Security Cooperation with Japan," January 20, 2021, https://www.state.gov/u-s-security-cooperation-with-japan/; David Vergun, "U.S.-Japan Alliance Increasingly Strengthened since End of WWII," *US Department of Defense News*, August 14, 2020, https://www.defense.gov/News/Feature-Stories/ Story/Article/2306658/us-japan-alliance-increasingly-strengthened-since-end-of- wwii/.

23. US Department of State, "Fact Sheet: U.S. Security Cooperation with Japan."

24. Rumi Aoyama, "Japan Walks on a Tightrope with Its China Policy," East Asia Policy Forum, May 20, 2021, https://www.eastasiaforum.org/2021/05/20/japan-walks-on- a-tightrope-with-its-china-policy/; Antoine Roth and Andrea A. Fischetti, "Japan's Growing Reliance on the Chinese Market," *Tokyo Review*, February 1, 2021, https:// www.tokyoreview.net/2021/02/japans-growing-reliance-on-the-chinese-market/.

25. World Bank, "Japan Trade Balance, Exports and Imports by Country and Region 2010," World Integrated Trade Solutions, World Bank, https://wits.worldbank.org/ CountryProfile/en/Country/JPN/Year/2010/TradeFlow/EXPIMP.

26. Nikkei Staff Writers, "China Passes US as Top Japanese Export Buyer, Topping 20%," *Nikkei Asia*, January 22, 2021, https://asia.nikkei.com/Economy/Trade/China-pas ses-US-as-top-Japanese-export-buyer-topping-20; Aoyama, "Japan Walks on a Tightrope"; World Bank, "Japan Trade Balance."

27. Nikkei Staff Writers, "China Passes US."

28. "Japanese Foreign Trade in Figures," Santander, last updated January 2024, July 2023, https://santandertrade.com/en/portal/analyse-markets/japan/foreign-trade-in- figures.

29. Shin Kawashima, "How China, Japan's Hot Trade and Economic Relationship Is Being Tested by Cold Politics," interviewed by Ji Siqi, *South China Morning Post*, August 18, 2022, https://www.scmp.com/economy/china-economy/article/3189234/ how-china-japans-hot-trade-and-economic-relationship-being.

30. Rieko Miki, "Japan Ruling Parties Call China 'Challenge' in Defense Strategy," *Nikkei Asia*, December 13, 2022, https://asia.nikkei.com/Politics/Japan-ruling-parties- call-China-challenge-in-defense-strategy; "Japan's 2022 National Security Strategy, National Defense Strategy," *USNI News*, December 20, 2022, https://news.usni.org/ 2022/12/20/japans-2022-national-security-strategy-national-defense-strategy.

31. Mike Yeo, "Japan Seeks to Increase Defense Spending to 2% of GDP," *Defense News*, December 1, 2022, https://www.defensenews.com/global/asia-pacific/2022/12/01/japan-seeks-to-increase-defense-spending-to-2-of-gdp/.

32. Takahashi Kosuke, "Japan Approves 26.3% Increase in Defense Spending for Fiscal Year 2023," *Diplomat*, December 24, 2022, https://thediplomat.com/2022/12/japan-approves-26-3-increase-in-defense-spending-for-fiscal-year-2023/; Felix K. Chang, "Japan's Bigger Defense Budget: Getting to Effective Deterrence," Analysis, Foreign Policy Research Institute, January 31, 2023, https://www.fpri.org/article/2023/01/japans-bigger-defense-budget-getting-to-effective-deterrence/.

33. Mike Yeo, "New Japanese Strategy to Up Defense Spending, Counterstrike Purchases," *Defense News*, December 20, 2022, https://www.defensenews.com/global/asia-pacific/2022/12/20/new-japanese-strategy-to-up-defense-spending-counterstrike-purchases/; Walter Russell Mead, "Global Tensions Spur a Sea Change in Japan," *Wall Street Journal*, November 28, 2022, https://www.wsj.com/articles/global-tensions-spur-a-sea-change-in-japan-national-security-defense-invasion-weapons-spending-asia-china-missiles-11669673013; Wall Street Journal Editorial Board, "The Sleeping Japanese Giant Awakes," *Wall Street Journal*, December 16, 2022, https://www.wsj.com/articles/the-sleeping-japanese-giant-awakes-tokyo-defense-strategy-fumio-kishida-11671227810.

34. Mead, "Global Tensions Spur."

35. White House, "Statement by National Security Advisor Jake Sullivan on Japan's Historic National Security Strategy," press release, December 16, 2022, https://www.whitehouse.gov/briefing-room/statements-releases/2022/12/16/statement-by-national-security-advisor-jake-sullivan-on-japans-historic-national-security-strategy/.

36. Felicia Schwartz, Kana Inagaki, and Demetri Sevastopulo, "US and Japan Agree to Expand Security Alliance into Space," *Financial Times*, January 11, 2023, https://www.ft.com/content/27a8e51c-be10-4ed9-8a00-64e7c61cf5fd; Antony Blinken, "Secretary Antony J. Blinken, Secretary of Defense Lloyd J. Austin III, Japanese Foreign Minister Hayashi Yoshimasa, and Japanese Defense Minister Hamada Yasukazu at a Joint Press Availability" (speech, Washington, DC, January 11, 2023), US Department of State, https://www.state.gov/secretary-antony-j-blinken-secretary-of-defense-lloyd-j-austin-iii-japanese-foreign-minister-hayashi-yoshimasa-and-japanese-defense-minister-hamada-yasukazu-at-a-joint-press-availability/.

37. "Chronology of U.S.-North Korean Nuclear and Missile Diplomacy," Fact Sheets & Briefs, Arms Control Association, last modified April 2022, https://www.armscontrol.org/factsheets/dprkchron#2011.

38. CNN Wire Staff, "North Korea Threatens 'a Sea of Fire' upon South Korea," *CNN*, November 25, 2011, https://www.cnn.com/2011/11/24/world/asia/north-korea-sea-of-fire; Associated Press, "N. Korea Threatens South with 'Sea of Fire'" *CBS*, November 24, 2011, https://www.cbsnews.com/news/n-korea-threatens-south-with-sea-of-fire/; Choe Sang-Hun, "North Korea Warns South on Maritime Drills," *New York Times*, November 24, 2011, https://www.nytimes.com/2011/11/25/world/asia/north-korea-threatens-south-korea-with-a-sea-of-fire.html.

39. Lee Myung-bak, "Remarks by President Obama and President Lee of the Republic of Korea in a Joint Press Conference" (remarks, Washington, DC, October 13, 2011), White House Archives, https://obamawhitehouse.archives.gov/the-press-office/2011/10/13/remarks-president-obama-and-president-lee-republic-korea-joint-press-con.

40. Park Geun-hye, "Remarks by President Obama and President Park of South Korea in a Joint Press Conference" (speech, Washington, DC, May 7, 2013), White House Archives, https://obamawhitehouse.archives.gov/the-press-office/2013/05/07/remarks-president-obama-and-president-park-south-korea-joint-press-confe.

41. Ji-Young Lee, *The Geopolitics of South Korea–China Relations: Implications for U.S. Policy in the Indo-Pacific* (Santa Monica, CA: RAND, 2020), https://www.rand.org/pubs/perspectives/PEA524-1.html.

42. Voice of America News, "South Korea's Park in Beijing for Summit with Xi," *Voice of America*, June 27, 2013, https://www.voanews.com/a/skoreas-park-in-beijing-for-summit-with-xi/1690147.html.

43. Jaeho Hwang, "The ROK's China Policy under Park Geun-hye: A New Model of ROK-PRC Relations," (working paper, Brookings Institution, Washington, DC, August, 14, 2014), https://www.brookings.edu/research/the-roks-china-policy-under-park-geun-hye-a-new-model-of-rok-prc-relations/.

44. Berteau et al., "Assessing the Asia-Pacific Rebalance," 24.

45. Shannon Tiezzi, "It's Official: China, South Korea Sign Free Trade Agreement," *Diplomat*, June 2, 2015, https://thediplomat.com/2015/06/its-official-china-south-korea-sign-free-trade-agreement/.

46. Lee, *The Geopolitics of South Korea–China Relations*.

47. Ibid.

48. Ibid.; U.S.-China Economic and Security Review Commission, *China's Response to U.S.-South Korean Missile Defense System Deployment and Its Implications*, by Ethan Meick and Nargiza Salidjanova, July 26, 2017, 4, https://www.uscc.gov/research/chinas-response-us-south-korean-missile-defense-system-deployment-and-its-implications.

49. Lee, *The Geopolitics of South Korea–China Relations*; U.S.-China Economic and Security Review Commission, *China's Response to U.S.-South Korean Missile Defense System Deployment and Its Implications*, 7; Song Jung-a, "Seoul Missile Move Sparks Fears for Pop Culture Exports to China," *Financial Times*, August 8, 2016, https://www.ft.com/content/2fea068e-5d48-11e6-bb77-a121aa8abd95; Amy Qin and Choe Sang-Hun, "South Korean Missile Defense Deal Appears to Sour China's Taste for K-Pop," *New York Times*, August 7, 2016, https://www.nytimes.com/2016/08/08/world/asia/china-korea-thaad.html?_r=0; Patrick Frater, "China Reportedly Bans Korean TV Content, Talent," *Variety*, August 4, 2016, https://variety.com/2016/biz/asia/china-confirms-ban-on-korean-content-talent-1201830391/; Amy Qin, "3 Performances by Sumi Jo, Korean Soprano, Canceled in China," *New York Times*, January 23, 2017, https://www.nytimes.com/2017/01/23/world/asia/sumi-jo-soprano-maria-callas.html; Echo Huang and Josh Horwitz, "Online Videogames Are the Latest Casualty of China's War against Korean Businesses,"

*Quartz*, March 8, 2017, https://qz.com/928459/online-video-games-are-the-latest-casualty-of-chinas-retaliation-against-korean-businesses-for-the-thaad-antimiss ile-defense-system/.

50. Kim Tong-Hyung and the Associated Press, "China, South Korea Clash over THAAD Anti-Missile System," *Defense News*, August 10, 2022, https://www.defensenews. com/global/asia-pacific/2022/08/10/china-south-korea-clash-over-thaad-anti-missile-system/; Christine Kim and Ben Blanchard, "China, South Korea Agree to Mend Ties after THAAD Standoff," *Reuters*, October 30, 2017, https://www.reuters. com/article/us-northkorea-missiles/china-south-korea-agree-to-mend-ties-after-thaad-standoff-idUSKBN1D003G; Troy Stangarone, "Did South Korea's Three Noes Matter? Not So Much," *Diplomat*, October 30, 2019, https://thediplomat.com/2019/ 10/did-south-koreas-three-noes-matter-not-so-much/.

51. Stangarone, "Did South Korea's Three Noes Matter."

52. Pew Research Center, "Unfavorable Views of China."

53. James Pomfret, "Opinion of China in Advanced Economies Sours 'Precipitously' under Xi—Pew," *Reuters*, September 29, 2022, https://www.reuters.com/world/ china/opinion-china-advanced-economies-sours-precipitously-under-xi-pew-2022-09-29/.

54. Edith M. Lederer, "US, Allies Clash with Russia, China over NKorea Missiles," *Associated Press*, November 4, 2022, https://apnews.com/article/europe-china-united-states-nations-south-korea-5d44df2e419d816c3c9b295fd1d8553d; Edith M. Lederer, "US, Allies Clash with Russia, China over North Korea Tests," *Associated Press*, November 21, 2022, https://apnews.com/article/europe-china-united-states-nati ons-linda-thomas-greenfield-f93525d7eed426d5cf5dea72e97af217.; Jon Herskovitz, Sangmi Cha, and Jenny Leonard, "North Korea Fires Suspected ICBM after Warning US on Exercises," *Bloomberg*, November 17, 2022, https://www.bloomberg.com/news/ articles/2022-11-18/north-korea-fires-suspected-ballistic-missile-toward-east-coast.

55. Lee, *The Geopolitics of South Korea–China Relations: Implications for U.S. Policy in the Indo-Pacific.*

56. World Bank, "Korea, Rep. Imports from China in US$ Thousand 2001–2020," World Integrated Trade Solutions, World Bank, https://wits.worldbank.org/CountryProfile/ en/Country/KOR/StartYear/2001/EndYear/2020/TradeFlow/Import/Partner/CHN/ Indicator/MPRT-TRD-VL#; World Bank, "Korea, Rep. Exports to China in US$ Thousand 2001–2020," World Integrated Trade Solution, World Bank, https://wits. worldbank.org/CountryProfile/en/Country/KOR/StartYear/2001/EndYear/2020/ TradeFlow/Export/Partner/CHN/Indicator/XPRT-TRD-VL.

57. US Library of Congress, Congressional Research Service, *U.S.-South Korea Relations*, by Mark E. Manyin et al., R41481, 2016, https://www.hsdl.org/?view&did=796340.

58. US Department of State, Office of the Spokesperson, "Joint Statement of the 2012 United States–Republic of Korea Foreign and Defense Ministers' Meeting," June 14, 2012, https://2009-2017.state.gov/r/pa/prs/ps/2012/06/192333.htm.

59. US Library of Congress, *U.S.-South Korea Relations*.

60. Ibid.

61. Ibid.

62. Prashanth Parameswaran, "US, Japan, South Korea Conduct Joint Missile Drill," *Diplomat*, June 30, 2016, https://thediplomat.com/2016/06/us-japan-south-korea-conduct-joint-missile-drill/.

63. Moon Jae-in, "Opening Remarks by President Moon Jae-in at Joint Press Conference Following Korea-U.S. Summit" (remarks, Seoul, South Korea, June 30, 2019), Japan Ministry of Foreign Affairs, https://www.mofa.go.kr/eng/brd/m_5674/view.do?seq=319902&srchFr=&srchTo=&srchWord=&srchTp=&multi_itm_seq=0&itm_seq_1=0&itm_seq_2=0&company_cd=&company_nm.

64. Thompson Chau, "Taiwan Vows to Safeguard Interests amid U.S.-Led 'Chip 4' Talks," *Nikkei Asia*, October 5, 2022, https://asia.nikkei.com/Business/Tech/Semiconductors/Taiwan-vows-to-safeguard-interests-amid-U.S.-led-Chip-4-talks; Alan Patterson, "In a Switch, South Korea Joining Chip 4 Talks," *EE Times*, September 30, 2022, https://www.eetimes.com/in-a-switch-south-korea-joining-chip-4-talks/; Kotaro Hosokawa and Taisei Hoyama, "U.S. Chip Alliance against China Tests South Korea's Loyalty," *Nikkei Asia*, September 24, 2022, https://asia.nikkei.com/Business/Tech/Semiconductors/U.S.-chip-alliance-against-China-tests-South-Korea-s-loyalty.

65. Stockholm International Peace Research Institute, "SIPRI Arms Transfers Database"; Elizabeth Shim, "South Korea a Top Buyer of U.S. Weapons, Annual Report Says," *United Press International*, December 16, 2019, https://www.upi.com/Top_News/World-News/2019/12/16/South-Korea-a-top-buyer-of-US-weapons-annual-report-says/4681576512463/.

66. Shim, "South Korea a Top Buyer"; Stockholm International Peace Research Institute, "Importer/Exporter TIV Tables," https://armstrade.sipri.org/armstrade/page/values.php.

67. Simon Denyer and Min Joo Kim, "In South Korea, Military Cost Dispute and Trump's Moves in Syria Fuel Doubts over U.S. Commitment," *Washington Post*, November 4, 2019, https://www.washingtonpost.com/world/asia_pacific/in-south-korea-military-cost-dispute-and-trumps-moves-in-syria-fuel-doubts-over-us-commitment/2019/11/01/7048b030-fa30-11e9-9534-e0dbcc9f5683_story.html.

68. Chun In-bum, "Nervous South Koreans Seek Ways to Counter North's Nuclear Threat," interviewed by Christian Davies, *Financial Times*, May 10, 2022, https://www.ft.com/content/b0cf218f-d893-40aa-9994-0d3ce8e4adc5.

69. J. James Kim, Kang Chungku, and Ham Geon Hee, *South Korean Public Opinion on ROK-U.S. Bilateral Ties* (Seoul: Asan Institute for Policy Studies, 2022), 29, http://en.asaninst.org/contents/south-korean-public-opinion-on-rok-u-s-bilateral-ties/.

70. Choe Sang-hun, "In a First, South Korea Declares Nuclear Weapons a Policy Option," *New York Times*, January 12, 2023, https://www.nytimes.com/2023/01/12/world/asia/south-korea-nuclear-weapons.html.

71. Christian Davies, "South Korea's Ruling Party Leader Hints at Need for Nuclear Weapons," *Financial Times*, February 20, 2023, https://www.ft.com/content/ef4d3f20-72db-4e0e-82b6-eb36ecfc4c84.

72. White House, *Washington Declaration*, April 26, 2023, https://www.whitehouse.gov/briefing-room/statements-releases/2023/04/26/washington-declaration-2/.

73. Ibid.

74. Ibid.

75. Robert E. Kelly, "South Korea's Nuclear Anxieties Haven't Gone Away," *Foreign Policy*, June 9, 2023, https://foreignpolicy.com/2023/06/09/south-korea-nuclear-weapons-north-korea-washington-declaration/.

76. Republic of Korea, *Strategy for a Free, Peaceful, and Prosperous Indo-Pacific Region*, December 28, 2022, 14, 37, https://www.mofa.go.kr/eng/brd/m_5676/view.do?seq=322133.

77. Ibid., 29.

78. Ibid., 13, 31.

79. Office of the President of the Republic of Korea, *National Security Strategy*, June 8, 2023, 52, https://www.mofa.go.kr/eng/brd/m_25772/view.do?seq=16&page=1.

80. Timothy W. Martin, "U.S. Antimissile System in South Korea, a Source of Chinese Anger, Cleared for Full Deployment," *Wall Street Journal*, June 21, 2023, https://www.wsj.com/articles/u-s-antimissile-system-in-south-korea-a-source-of-chinese-anger-cleared-for-full-deployment-8141b4dc.

81. Julia Gillard, "Remarks by President Obama and Prime Minister Gillard of Australia in Joint Press Conference" (speech, Canberra, November 16, 2011), White House Archives, https://obamawhitehouse.archives.gov/the-press-office/2011/11/16/remarks-president-obama-and-prime-minister-gillard-australia-joint-press.

82. Kevin Rudd, "Beyond the Pivot," *Foreign Affairs* 92, no. 2 (March–April 2013): 9–10, https://www.foreignaffairs.com/articles/china/2013-02-11/beyond-pivot.

83. Sam Roggeveen, "What the New Defence White Paper Will Say about China," *Interpreter*, September 23, 2013, https://www.lowyinstitute.org/the-interpreter/what-new-defence-white-paper-will-say-about-china.

84. Australia Department of Defence, *Defence White Paper 2013*, 2013, https://www.files.ethz.ch/isn/172498/Australia%20defense%20WP_2013_web.pdf.

85. Mark Kenny, "Gillard Scores Coup with China Agreement," *Sydney Morning Herald*, April 10, 2013, https://www.smh.com.au/politics/federal/gillard-scores-coup-with-china-agreement-20130409-2hjin.html.

86. Reuters, "Australia Ready to Join China-Led Bank, Seeks Clarity on Governance," *Reuters*, March 4, 2015, https://www.reuters.com/article/us-asia-aiib/australia-ready-to-join-china-led-bank-seeks-clarity-on-governance-idUSKBN0ML08120150325; Jane Perlez, "China Creates a World Bank of Its Own, and the US Balks," *New York Times*, December 4, 2015, https://www.nytimes.com/2015/12/05/business/international/china-creates-an-asian-bank-as-the-us-stands-aloof.html.

87. Helen Davidson, "Malcolm Turnbull Defends Northern Territory's Sale of Port to Chinese Firm," *Guardian*, November 20, 2015, https://www.theguardian.com/australia-news/2015/nov/20/malcolm-turnbull-defends-northern-territorys-sale-of-port-to-chinese-firm.

88. "China-Australia Free Trade Agreement (ChAFTA)," Free Trade Agreements, Australian Trade and Investment Commission, https://www.austrade.gov.au/australian/export/free-trade-agreements/chafta.

89. Gareth Hutchins, "South China Sea: Marise Payne Says Julie Bishop Right to Warn Beijing," *Guardian*, July 15, 2016, https://www.theguardian.com/world/2016/jul/15/south-china-sea-marise-payne-says-julie-bishop-right-to-warn-beijing.

90. Bill Birtles, "South China Sea: China Warns Australia Must 'Cautiously Behave' in Row over Contested Waterway," *ABC*, August 1, 2016, https://www.abc.net.au/news/2016-08-01/china-turns-defeat-into-victory-in-south-china-sea/7676260?nw=0&r=HtmlFragment.

91. ABC, "Sam Dastyari Resignation: How We Got Here," *ABC*, December 11, 2017, https://www.abc.net.au/news/2017-12-12/sam-dastyari-resignation-how-did-we-get-here/9249380.

92. Clive Hamilton, *Silent Invasion* (Victoria: Hardie Grant Books, 2018).

93. The Strait Times, "Australia Toughens Foreign Investment Rules amid China Concerns," *Strait Times*, February 1, 2018, https://www.straitstimes.com/asia/australianz/australia-toughens-foreign-investment-rules-amid-china-concerns.

94. Cassell Bryan-Low et al., "Hobbling Huawei: Inside the U.S. War on China's Tech Giant," *Reuters*, May 21, 2019, https://www.reuters.com/investigates/special-report/huawei-usa-campaign/; Jade Gailberger, "Huawei Australia Says Ban Is a 'Slap in the Face' to China," *AU*, September 10, 2020, https://www.news.com.au/technology/online/internet/huawei-australia-says-ban-is-a-slap-in-the-face-to-china/news-story/4d6ba569b153c0e068a5be515e9da36f.

95. Zoya Sheftalovich and Ryan Heath, "Australia Offers Europe a Warning on a Trade Deal with China," *Politico*, January 8, 2021, https://www.politico.eu/article/australia-europe-china-trade-deal-warning/.

96. Colin Packham, "Australia Says World Needs to Know Origins of COVID-19," *Reuters*, September 25, 2020, https://www.reuters.com/article/us-health-coronavirus-australia-china/australia-says-world-needs-to-know-origins-of-covid-19-idUSKCN26H00T.

97. Natasha Kassam, "Great Expectations: The Unraveling of the Australia-China Relationship," Brookings Institution, July 20, 2020, https://www.brookings.edu/articles/great-expectations-the-unraveling-of-the-australia-china-relationship/; Sheftalovich and Heath, "Australia Offers Europe a Warning."

98. Helen Davidson, "'Chewing Gum Stuck on the Sole of Our Shoes': The China-Australia War of Words—Timeline," *Guardian*, April 29, 2020, https://www.theguardian.com/world/2020/apr/29/chewing-gum-stuck-on-the-sole-of-our-shoes-the-china-australia-war-of-words-timeline.

99. Kristy Needham, "Beijing Wanted to 'Break' Australia -U.S. Indo-Pacific Adviser," *Reuters*, November 30, 2021, https://www.reuters.com/world/china/beijing-wanted-break-australia-us-indo-pacific-adviser-2021-12-01/.

100. Australia Bureau of Statistics, "Exports to China in Australia decreased to 14179976.35 AUD THO in July from 16342996.17 AUD THO in June of 2022," Trading Economics, https://tradingeconomics.com/australia/exports-to-china.

101. World Bank, "Australia Import Partner Share by Country in Percentage 2010–2020," World Integrated Trade Solution, World Bank, https://wits.worldbank.org/CountryProfile/en/Country/AUS/StartYear/2010/EndYear/2020/TradeFlow/Import/Partner/BY-COUNTRY/Indicator/MPRT-PRTNR-SHR; World Bank, "Australia

Export Partner Share by Country in Percentage 2010–2020," World Integrated Trade Solution, World Bank, https://wits.worldbank.org/CountryProfile/en/Country/AUS/StartYear/2010/EndYear/2020/TradeFlow/Export/Partner/BY-COUNTRY/Indicator/XPRT-PRTNR-SHR.

102. "How China's Trade Restrictions Are Affecting the Australian Economy," *BT*, November 26, 2020, https://www.bt.com.au/personal/smsf/manage-your-smsf/investment-insights/australia-china-relations.html.

103. David Uren, "Despite the Risks, Australian Exports to China Are Booming Again," *Strategist*, August 22, 2023, https://www.aspistrategist.org.au/despite-the-risks-australian-exports-to-china-are-booming-again/.

104. Gavin Fernando, "'Cold War': Chinese Government Issues Warning to Australia after Trade War Threats with US," *NZ Herald*, May 25, 2020, https://www.nzherald.co.nz/business/cold-war-chinese-government-issues-warning-to-australia-after-trade-war-threats-with-us/KBWZQFFFOHSZEYDQ4STDSAN6NE/.

105. Wang Jiamei, "Australia's Economy Cannot Withstand 'Cold War' with China," *Global Times*, June 10, 2020, https://www.globaltimes.cn/content/1191226.shtml.

106. Weizhen Tan, "Australian Official Urges International Students to Consider Studying in the Country as China Claims Racism," *CNBC*, June 12, 2020, https://www.cnbc.com/2020/06/12/australia-tensions-with-china-amid-racism-warning-to-students.html; Jason Fang and Alan Weedon, "Chinese Australians Caught in the Crossfire from Beijing's Australian Travel Warning," *ABC*, June 7, 2020, https://www.abc.net.au/news/2020-06-07/china-travel-warning-australia-racism-coronavirus-covid-19/12330618.

107. BBC, "Chinese Investment in Australia Plummets 61%," *BBC*, March 1, 2021, https://www.bbc.com/news/business-56234776.

108. Pew Research Center, "Unfavorable Views of China."

109. Zoya Sheftalovich and Stuart Lau, "How Xi Jinping Lost Australia," *Politico*, September 27, 2021, https://www.politico.eu/article/how-china-xi-jinping-lost-australia-trade-diplomacy/.

110. Australia Department of the Prime Minister and Cabinet, *Strong and Secure: A Strategy of Australia's National Security*, 2013, 22, https://www.files.ethz.ch/isn/167267/Australia%20A%20Strategy%20for%20National%20Securit.pdf.

111. Katharine Murphy, "Australia Embraces Missile and Naval Ties as It Cements US Defence Pact," *Guardian*, August 12, 2014, https://www.theguardian.com/world/2014/aug/12/australia-embraces-missile-naval-ties-us-defence-pact; BBC, "Australia to Buy 58 New F-35 Fighter Jets," *BBC*, April 23, 2014, https://www.bbc.com/news/business-27122188.

112. Stockholm International Peace Research Institute, "SIPRI Arms Transfers Database."

113. White House, Office of the Press Secretary, "Fact Sheet: United States–Australia Cooperation: Deepening Our Strategic Partnership," January 19, 2016, https://obamawhitehouse.archives.gov/the-press-office/2016/01/19/fact-sheet-united-states---australia-cooperation-deepening-our-strategic.

114. Tobias Feakin, Liam Nevill, and Zoe Hawkins, *The Australia–US Cyber Security Dialogue* (Barton: Australian Strategic Policy Institute, 2017), https://www.aspi.org.au/report/australia-us-cyber-security-dialogue.

115. Australia Department of Defence, *2016 Defence White Paper*, 2016, https://www. defence.gov.au/sites/default/files/2021-08/2016-Defence-White-Paper.pdf.

116. "Talisman Sabre 21," Exercises, Australia Department of Defence, https://www. defence.gov.au/exercises/talisman-sabre-21.; Colin Packham, "Australia, United States Begin Their Biggest Joint Military Exercise," *Reuters*, June 29, 2017, https:// www.reuters.com/article/us-australia-usa-military-idUSKBN19K0ID; Australian Aviation, "Exercise Talisman Sabre Formally Launched on USS Ronald Reagan," *Australian Aviation*, July 8, 2019, https://australianaviation.com.au/2019/07/exerc ise-talisman-sabre-formally-launched-on-uss-ronald-reagan/.

117. US Department of State, Bureau of Political-Military Affairs, "Fact Sheet: U.S. Security Cooperation with Australia," September 14, 2021, https://www.state.gov/ u-s-security-cooperation-with-australia/.

118. Angus Grigg, Lesley Robinson, and Meghna Bali, "US Air Force to Deploy Nuclear-Capable B-52 Bombers to Australia as Tensions with China Grow," *ABC*, October 30, 2022, https://www.abc.net.au/news/2022-10-31/china-tensions-taiwan-us-milit ary-deploy-bombers-to-australia/101585380;

119. Rod McGuirk, "US Pledges to Help Australia Manufacture Guided Missiles by 2025," *Associated Press*, July 29, 2023, https://apnews.com/article/australia-aus tin-blinken-5d9f0e53b637b4923b4715362ed93d9a; Jeff Seldin, "US, Australian Defense Cooperation Going Big," *Voice of America*, July 29, 2023, https://www.voan ews.com/a/us-australian-defense-cooperation-going-big/7203145.html.

120. Seldin, "US, Australian Defense Cooperation."

121. Richard Marles, "Australia-US Joint Press Conference Following the Australia-US Ministerial Consultations (AUSMIN)" (speech, Brisbane, July 29, 2023), US Department of Defense, https://www.defense.gov/News/Transcripts/Transcript/ Article/3476106/australia-us-joint-press-conference-following-the-australia-us-ministerial-cons/.

122. Tanvi Madan, "The Rise, Fall and Rebirth of the Quad," *War on the Rocks*, November 16, 2017, https://warontherocks.com/2017/11/rise-fall-rebirth-quad/.

123. Scott Morrison, "Launch of the 2020 Defence Strategy Update" (speech, Australia, June 30, 2020), Commonwealth of Australia Department of Defence, https://defe nce.gov.au/ADC/Publications/AJDSS/volume2-number2/prime-minister-address-launch-2020-defence-strategic-update.asp.

124. White House, "Joint Leaders Statement on AUKUS," September 15, 2021, https:// www.whitehouse.gov/briefing-room/statements-releases/2021/09/15/joint-lead ers-statement-on-aukus/.

125. Rohan Thomson/Bloomberg News, "Australia to Buy U.S. Nuclear-Powered Submarines in Naval Expansion," *Wall Street Journal*, March 15, 2023, https://www. wsj.com/articles/australia-to-buy-u-s-nuclear-powered-submarines-in-naval-expansion-1bd94418.

126. Patrick Triglavcanin, "AUKUS Binds Britain to Australia and a Free and Open Indo-Pacific," *Strategist*, March 14, 2023, https://www.aspistrategist.org.au/aukus-binds-britain-to-australia-and-a-free-and-open-indo-pacific/.

127. Commonwealth of Australia Department of Foreign Affairs and Trade, "Launch of the Indo-Pacific Economic Framework for Prosperity (IPEF)—Joint Statement,"

May 23, 2022, https://www.dfat.gov.au/news/media-release/launch-indo-pacific-economic-framework-prosperity-ipef-joint-statement; White House, "Statement by Australia, Japan, New Zealand, the United Kingdom, and the United States on the Establishment of the Partners in the Blue Pacific (PBP)," June 24, 2022, https://www.whitehouse.gov/briefing-room/statements-releases/2022/06/24/statement-by-australia-japan-new-zealand-the-united-kingdom-and-the-united-states-on-the-establishment-of-the-partners-in-the-blue-pacific-pbp/.

128. Pew Research Center, "How Global Public Opinion"; Lowy Institute, "In Your Own View, Is China More of an Economic Partner or More of a Security Threat to Australia?," Lowey Institute Poll, 2023, https://poll.lowyinstitute.org/charts/china-economic-partner-or-security-threat.

129. "China's Approach to Foreign Policy Gets Largely Negative Reviews in 24-Country Survey," Pew Research Center, Washington, DC, July 27, 2023, https://www.pewresearch.org/global/2023/07/27/chinas-approach-to-foreign-policy-gets-largely-negative-reviews-in-24-country-survey/.

130. Ben Westcott, "Australia PM Albanese Touts 'Strong Relationship' in Xi Meeting," *Bloomberg*, November 5, 2023, https://www.bloomberg.com/news/articles/2023-11-05/australia-s-pm-albanese-to-meet-with-xi-jinping-in-beijing#xj4y7vzkg.

131. Damian Crave, "Why China and Australia Are Reconciling. Sort Of," *New York Times*, November 2, 2023, https://www.nytimes.com/2023/11/03/world/australia/china-xi-albanese-relations.html; Nic Fildes, "Australia Seeks Reset with Xi Jinping While Balancing Ties with US," *Financial Times*, November 2, 2023, https://www.ft.com/content/3fd85427-a3ab-4960-80d7-4497e2d7c5f7.

132. James Curran, "Why China and Australia Are Reconciling. Sort Of," interviewed by Damian Crave, *New York Times*, November 2, 2023, https://www.nytimes.com/2023/11/03/world/australia/china-xi-albanese-relations.html.

133. Sukh Deo Muni, "Obama Administration's Pivot to Asia-Pacific and India's Role" (working paper, Institute of South Asian Studies, National University of Singapore, 2012), 8, https://www.files.ethz.ch/isn/152376/ISAS_Working_Paper_159_-_Obama%27s_Administrations_31082012100801.pdf.

134. Authors' correspondence with strategists in the region.

135. Anisha Dutta, "India Was Wary of US for 5 decades, Overcame Assumptions after Much Efforts: Jaishankar," *Indian Express*, September 22, 2022, https://indianexpress.com/article/india/india-was-wary-of-us-for-5-decades-overcame-assumptions-after-much-efforts-jaishankar-8165271/.

136. Livemint, "'Indo-Pacific Is New Strategic Concept': What Jaishankar Said on India's Maritime Interest," *Livemint*, September 4, 2022, https://www.livemint.com/news/india/indopacific-is-new-strategic-concept-what-jaishankar-said-on-india-s-maritime-interest-11662287968663.html.

137. Sutirtho Patranobis, "China Cements Its Place as Pakistan's Largest Supplier of Major Arms: Report," *Hindustan Times*, April 26, 2022, https://www.hindustantimes.com/world-news/china-cements-its-place-as-pakistan-s-largest-supplier-of-major-arms-report-101650973184494.html; Richard Fisher and John Dori, "The Strategic Implications of China's Nuclear Aid to Pakistan," Executive Memorandum no. 532, Heritage Foundation, June 16, 1998, https://www.heritage.org/asia/report/

the-strategic-implications-chinas-nuclear-aid-pakistan; Sumit Ganguly, "Think Again: India's Rise," *Foreign Policy*, July 5, 2012, https://foreignpolicy.com/2012/07/05/think-again-indias-rise/.

138. Geeta Mohan, "China Blocked India's Bid for Membership at UN Security Council, NSG: S Jaishankar," *India Today*, January 28, 2021, https://www.indiatoday.in/india/story/china-blocked-india-s-bid-for-membership-at-un-security-council-nsg-s-jaishankar-1763679-2021-01-28.

139. Arun Kumar, "India Welcomes US 'Asia Pivot,'" *Two Circles*, February 6, 2013, http://twocircles.net/2013feb06/india_welcomes_us_asia_pivot.html; Nirupama Rao, "America's 'Asian Pivot': The View from India" (speech, Providence, RI, February 5, 2013), Watson Institute, Brown University, https://watson.brown.edu/southasia/news/2013/honorable-nirupama-rao-america-s-asian-pivot-view-india-full-text-available.

140. C. Raja Mohan, "India: Between 'Strategic Autonomy' and 'Geopolitical Opportunity,'" *Asia Policy*, no. 15 (January 2013): 21, 24, https://www.researchgate.net/publication/265839666_India_Between_Strategic_Autonomy_and_Geopolitical_Opportunity.

141. Reuters, "Wen Says World Big Enough for India, China Growth," *Reuters*, December 15, 2020, https://www.reuters.com/article/india-china/wrapup-6-wen-says-world-big-enough-for-india-china-growth-idUKL3E6NF0OW20101215; Global Times, "Peaceful Negotiation 'Only Way Out' of China-India Border Clash: Chinese FM," *Global Times*, March 7, 2021, https://www.globaltimes.cn/page/202103/1217562.shtml.

142. "India, China to Restore Defence Co-Operation," *India Today*, April 13, 2011, https://www.indiatoday.in/world/neighbours/story/india-china-to-restore-defence-co-operation-132122-2011-04-13.

143. "China Wants to Deepen Strategic Cooperation with India: Hu Jintao," *Economic Times*, March 30, 2012, https://economictimes.indiatimes.com/news/politics-and-nation/china-wants-to-deepen-strategic-cooperation-with-india-hu-jintao/articleshow/12469429.cms.

144. Consulate General of the People's Republic of China in Perth, "Premier Li Keqiang Addresses Indian Council of World Affairs Stressing to Seize New Opportunities in China-India Strategic Cooperation," May 22, 2013, http://perth.china-consulate.gov.cn/eng/zgyw/201308/t20130822_200510.htm.

145. "India Says China Agrees Retreat to de facto Border in Faceoff Deal," *Reuters*, May 6, 2013, https://www.reuters.com/article/us-india-china-idUSBRE9440B220130506; Vijaita Singh, "Chinese Troops Said to Be 2 km Inside LAC, Build-Up on the Rise," *Indian Express*, September 23, 2014, https://indianexpress.com/article/india/india-others/chinese-troops-said-to-be-2-km-inside-lac-build-up-on-the-rise/.

146. Joel Wuthnow, Satu Limaye, and Nilanthi Samaranayake, "Doklam One Year Later: China's Long Game in the Himalayas," *War on the Rocks*, June 7, 2018, https://warontherocks.com/2018/06/doklam-one-year-later-chinas-long-game-in-the-himalayas/.

147. Ankit Panda, "A Skirmish in the Galwan Valley: India and China's Deadliest Clash in More than 50 Years," *Diplomat*, June 17, 2020, https://thediplomat.com/2020/06/

a-skirmish-in-galwan-valley-india-and-chinas-deadliest-clash-in-more-than-50-years/.

148. Pew Research Center, "How Global Public Opinion."

149. Sandeep Unnithan, "Enemy Number One," *India Today,* August 17, 2020, https://www.indiatoday.in/magazine/nation/story/20200817-enemy-number-one-1708698-2020-08-08.

150. Sonnet Frisbie and Scott Moskowitz, "India in Between: Modi's Delicate Dance of Diplomatic Moderation Offers Risks and Rewards," *Morning Consult,* January 13, 2023, https://pro.morningconsult.com/analysis/india-diplomatic-moderation-offers-risks-and-rewards.

151. India Department of Commerce, Trade, https://tradestat.commerce.gov.in/eidb/default.asp.

152. Chris Ogden, "The Double-Edged Sword: Reviewing India–China Relations," *India Quarterly* 78, no. 2 (March 2022), https://doi.org/10.1177/09749284221089530.

153. Biswajit Dhar and Chalapati Rao, "India's Economic Dependence on China," *India Forum,* July 23, 2020, https://www.theindiaforum.in/article/india-s-dependence-china.

154. US Library of Congress, Congressional Research Service, *India-U.S. Relations,* by K. Alan Kronstadt et al., R46845, 2021, https://crsreports.congress.gov/product/pdf/R/R46845; "India Refuses to Support China's Belt and Road Project at SCO Meet," *Hindustan Times,* November, 30, 2020, https://www.hindustantimes.com/india-news/india-doesn-t-join-sco-members-in-endorsing-china-s-belt-and-road-project/story-CBH22ODWVImRFpwkkhehWI.html; Sutirtho Patranobis, "India Refuses to Endorse China's Belt and Road Initiative in SCO Summit Statement," *Hindustan Times,* June 10, 2018, https://www.hindustantimes.com/india-news/india-refuses-to-endorse-china-s-belt-and-road-initiative-in-sco-summit-statement/story-sk9cC8d1zD3Zwje6Rnh0uI.html; "PM Modi, Xi Jinping to Meet on Sunday, May Discuss China-Pakistan Corridor," *Times of India,* September 2, 2016, https://timesofindia.indiatimes.com/india/pm-modi-xi-jinping-to-meet-on-sunday-may-discuss-china-pakistan-corridor/articleshow/53982854.cms.

155. Shivshankar Menon, "How China Got Sri Lanka to Cough Up a Port," interviewed by Maria Abi-Habib, *New York Times,* June 25, 2018, https://www.nytimes.com/2018/06/25/world/asia/china-sri-lanka-port.html; Umesh Moramudali, "The Hambantota Port Deal: Myth and Reality," *Diplomat,* January 1, 2020, https://thediplomat.com/2020/01/the-hambantota-port-deal-myths-and-realities/.

156. Ashok Malik, "India Takes Its Tussle with China to the High Seas," interviewed by Amy Kazmin, *Financial Times,* October 27, 2020, https://www.ft.com/content/bbe548c4-b437-4965-a651-592d0e969890.

157. Congressional Research Service, *India-U.S. Relations.*

158. Ibid., 9.

159. Ibid., 6.

160. Sandeep Unnithan, "In a Graphic: India-US—Brothers in Arms," *India Today,* September 23, 2021, https://www.indiatoday.in/india-today-insight/story/india-us-brothers-in-arms-1856465-2021-09-23; Steve Holland and Aftab Ahmed, "After

Raucous Welcome in India, Trump Clinches $3 Billion Military Equipment Sale," *Reuters*, February 25, 2020, https://www.reuters.com/article/us-india-usa-trump/after-raucous-welcome-in-india-trump-clinches-3-billion-military-equipment-sale-idUSKCN20J0J5; Rajat Pandit, "India Lining Up Defense Deals Worth $10 Billion with US amid Trade Row," *Times of India*, June 24, 2019, https://timesofindia.indiatimes.com/india/india-lining-up-defence-deals-worth-10-billion-with-us-amid-trade-row/articleshow/69919916.cms.

161. "Reinventing the Indo-Pacific."

162. Brahma Chellaney, "The US–India Partnership Is Too Important to Lose," *Strategist*, October 12, 2022, https://www.aspistrategist.org.au/the-us-india-partnership-is-too-important-to-lose/.

163. White House, "Fact Sheet: United States and India Elevate Strategic Partnership with the Initiative on Critical and Emerging Technology (ICET)," January 31, 2023, https://www.whitehouse.gov/briefing-room/statements-releases/2023/01/31/fact-sheet-united-states-and-india-elevate-strategic-partnership-with-the-initiative-on-critical-and-emerging-technology-icet/.

164. Ibid.

165. White House, "Joint Statement from the United States and India," June 22, 2023, https://www.whitehouse.gov/briefing-room/statements-releases/2023/06/22/joint-statement-from-the-united-states-and-india/.

166. Ibid.; Manjari Chatterjee Miller, "What Did Prime Minister Modi's State Visit Achieve?," *Asia Unbound* (Blog), Council on Foreign Relations, https://www.cfr.org/blog/asia-unbound; Mayank Pandey, "India to Buy 31 Predator Drones from US for $3.5 Bn; All You Need to Know," *Business Standard*, June 20, 2023, https://www.business-standard.com/india-news/india-to-buy-31-predator-drones-from-us-for-3-5-bn-all-you-need-to-know-123062000324_1.html.

167. Miller, "What Did Prime Minister Modi's State Visit Achieve."

168. Office of the United States Trade Representative, Press Office, "United States Announces Major Resolution on Key Trade Issues with India," June 22, 2023, https://ustr.gov/about-us/policy-offices/press-office/press-releases/2023/june/united-states-announces-major-resolution-key-trade-issues-india.

169. White House, "Joint Statement from the United States and India."

170. United States Department of Defense, "Joint Statement on the Fifth Annual India-U.S. 2+2 Ministerial Dialogue," November 10, 2023, https://www.defense.gov/News/Releases/Release/Article/3586228/joint-statement-on-the-fifth-annual-india-us-22-ministerial-dialogue/.

171. "Overview," ASEAN-China Economic Relation, Association of Southeast Asian Nations, https://asean.org/our-communities/economic-community/integration-with-global-economy/asean-china-economic-relation/.

172. Stewart Patterson, "To Ease ASEAN's Import Dependency, Strengthen Intra-ASEAN Trade," Hinrich Foundation, February 22, 2022, https://www.hinrichfoundation.com/research/article/ftas/aseans-import-dependency-intra-asean-trade/.

173. Jason Douglas, "China Increases Trade in Asia as U.S. Pushes toward Decoupling," *Wall Street Journal*, December 28, 2022, https://www.wsj.com/articles/china-increases-trade-in-asia-as-u-s-pushes-toward-decoupling-11672231684.

174. ASEAN, "Trade in Goods (IMTS), Annually, HS 2-digit up to 8-Digit (AHTN), in US\$," ASEANStatsDataPortal, ASEAN, https://data.aseanstats.org/trade-annually.

175. Tom Allard, "Indonesia Fears US Forces Could Create 'Vicious Circle of Tension,'" *Sydney Morning Herald,* November 17, 2011, https://www.smh.com.au/world/indonesia-fears-us-forces-could-create-vicious-circle-of-tension-20111117-1nk0e.html.

176. Staff Writers, "Southeast Asia Caught between US and China," *Space War,* November 17, 2011, https://www.spacewar.com/reports/Southeast_Asia_caught_between_US_and_China_999.html.

177. Ibid.

178. Ibid.

179. Albert F. del Rosario, "An Independent and Principled Philippine Foreign Policy for Economic Growth" (speech, Manila, October 24, 2013), Republic of the Philippines Department of Foreign Affairs, https://dfa.gov.ph/authentication-functions/78-newsroom/dfa-releases/1110-an-independent-and-principled-philippine-foreign-policy-for-economic-growth; Berteau et al., "Assessing the Asia-Pacific Rebalance," 19.

180. Tomotaka Shoji and Hideo Tomikawa, "Southeast Asia: Duterte Takes Office, South China Sea in Flux," in *East Asian Strategic Review 2017*, ed. Shinji Hyodo (Tokyo: National Institute of Defense Studies, 2017), http://www.nids.mod.go.jp/english/publication/east-asian/pdf/2017/east-asian_e2017_05.pdf; Rodrigo Duterte, "Speech of President Rodrigo Roa Duterte during the Philippines-China Trade and Investment Forum" (speech, Beijing, October 20, 2016), Republic of the Philippines Office of the President, https://ops.gov.ph/oct-20-2016-speech-of-president-rodrigo-roa-duterte-during-the-philippines-china-trade-and-investment-forum/; Andreo Calonzo and Cecilia Yap, "China Visit Helps Duterte Reap Funding Deals Worth \$24 Billion," *Bloomberg,* October 21, 2016, https://www.bloomberg.com/news/articles/2016-10-21/china-visit-helps-duterte-reap-funding-deals-worth-24-billion; Bienvenido S. Oplas Jr., "The Meager Truth of China's Aid to the Philippines," *Asia Times,* December 5, 2018, https://asiatimes.com/2018/12/the-meager-truth-of-chinas-aid-to-the-philippines/; Kyodo, "Duterte Pushes China-Backed Trade Pact on ASEAN's 50th Anniversary," *South China Morning Post,* August 8, 2017, https://www.scmp.com/news/asia/diplomacy/article/2105971/duterte-pushes-china-backed-trade-pact-aseans-50th-anniversary.

181. BBC, "Duterte in China: Xi Lauds 'Milestone' Duterte Visit," *BBC,* October 20, 2016, https://www.bbc.com/news/world-asia-37700409.

182. Duterte, "Speech of President Rodrigo Roa Duterte during the Philippines-China Trade and Investment Forum."

183. Ibid.

184. Reuters, "Philippines, U.S. Hold Biggest Military Exercises in Seven Years," *Reuters,* March 28, 2022, https://www.reuters.com/world/philippines-us-hold-biggest-military-exercises-seven-years-2022-03-28/.

185. Manuel Mogato, "Duterte Says He Wants U.S. Special Forces Out of Southern Philippines," *Reuters,* September 12, 2016, https://www.reuters.com/article/us-philippines-usa-duterte/duterte-says-he-wants-u-s-special-forces-out-of-southern-philippines-idUSKCN11I10J.

186. Reuters, "US Joins Battle as Philippines Takes Losses in Besieged City," *CNBC*, June 10, 2017, https://www.cnbc.com/2017/06/10/u-s-special-forces-helping-philippi nes-troops-in-battle-against-militants-allied-to-islamic-state.html.

187. Nick Aspinwall, "Duterte Terminates U.S. Defense Pact, Pleasing Trump but Few Others," *Foreign Policy*, February 14, 2020, https://foreignpolicy.com/2020/02/ 14/vfa-philippines-china-duterte-terminates-us-defense-pact-trump/.; Raissa Robles, "Philippines' Visiting Forces Agreement with US in Full Force after Duterte 'Retracts' Termination Letter," *South China Morning Post*, July 30, 2021, https://www.scmp.com/week-asia/politics/article/3143126/philippines-visiting-forces-agreement-us-full-force-after.

188. Jim Gomez, "Philippines Notifies US of Intent to End Major Security Pact," *Military Times*, February 11, 2020, https://www.militarytimes.com/news/your-milit ary/2020/02/11/philippines-notifies-us-of-intent-to-end-major-security-pact/ ; Teodoro Locsin Jr., "Speech to the Senate" (speech, Manila, February 6, 2020), Rappler, https://www.rappler.com/nation/251198-full-text-locsin-speech-impact-assessment-visiting-forces-agreement-termination/; Mico A. Galang, "A Decade of Philippines-Japan Strategic Partnership," *Diplomat*, April 26, 2019, https://thed iplomat.com/2019/04/a-decade-of-philippines-japan-strategic-partnership/; Jaime Laude, "Philippines Reaffirms Partnership with Japan," *Philippine Star*, April 21, 2019, https://www.philstar.com/headlines/2019/04/21/1911200/philippines-reaffi rms-partnership-japan.

189. Gregory B. Poling, "The Transformation of the U.S.-Philippines Alliance," Center for Strategic and International Studies, February 2, 2023, https://www.csis.org/analy sis/transformation-us-philippines-alliance.

190. Ferdinand R. Marcos Jr., "State of the Nation Address of His Excellency Ferdinand R. Marcos Jr. President of the Philippines to the Congress of the Philippines" (speech, Manila, Philippines, July 25, 2022), Office of the President of the Republic of the Philippines, https://pbbm.com.ph/speeches/state-of-the-nation-address-of-his-excellency-ferdinand-r-marcos-jr-president-of-the-philippines-to-the-congr ess-of-the-philippines/.

191. Kathrin Jille and Demetri Sevastopulo, "US and Philippines Increase Military Ties over China Threat," *Financial Times*, September 24, 2022, https://www.ft.com/cont ent/9c295755-eadf-48a9-9818-6afa1bcbe498.

192. Bloomberg News, "Philippines to Speed Up US Defense Pact for Troops, Bases," *Bloomberg*, November 7, 2022, https://www.bloomberg.com/news/articles/2022-11-08/philippines-to-speed-up-us-defense-pact-for-troops-facilities; Philip Heijmans, "Biden Gets Key Break as Southeast Asia Bolsters Militaries," *Bloomberg*, November 9, 2022, https://www.bloomberg.com/news/articles/2022-11-09/biden-gets-rare-break-as-southeast-asia-bolsters-its-militaries; Maria Siow, "South China Sea: As US Eyes a Subic Bay Return, Was Chinese 'Coercion' of Philippines the Reason?," *South China Morning Post*, December 4, 2022, https://www.scmp.com/week-asia/politics/ article/3201826/south-china-sea-us-eyes-subic-bay-return-was-chinese-coercion-philippines-reason.

193. Andreo Calonzo and Ditas B. Lopez, "US to Gain Military Access in North Philippines Near Taiwan," *Bloomberg*, March 21, 2023, https://www.bloomberg.

com/news/articles/2023-03-22/us-to-gain-military-access-in-northern-philippi
nes-marcos-says.

194. Bloomberg News, "Philippines to Speed Up."

195. Philip Heijmans and Andreo Calonzo, "US, Philippines Follow Taiwan Drills with
Biggest Exercises," *Bloomberg*, April 10, 2023, https://www.bloomberg.com/news/
articles/2023-04-10/us-philippines-follow-taiwan-drills-with-biggest-exercises-
yet#xj4y7vzkg.

196. White House, "Joint Statement on the Fifth Annual India-U.S. 2+2 Ministerial
Dialogue," May 1, 2023, https://www.whitehouse.gov/briefing-room/statements-
releases/2023/05/01/joint-statement-of-the-leaders-of-the-united-states-and-the-
philippines/.

197. Maria Siow, "Philippines-China Relations: As Manila Cancels Billions in Chinese
Rail Funding, Are South China Sea Tensions to Blame?," *South China Morning Post*,
November 11, 2023, https://www.scmp.com/week-asia/politics/article/3241067/
philippines-china-relations-manila-cancels-billions-chinese-rail-funding-are-
south-china-sea; Cliff Harvey Venzon, "Philippines Drops China Railway Deals,
Seeks Other Funders," *Bloomberg*, October 27, 2023, https://www.bloomberg.com/
news/articles/2023-10-27/philippines-drops-china-railway-deals-seeks-other-
funders; Ryo Nakamura and Ken Moriyasu, "Philippines' Marcos to Visit U.S. Indo-
Pacific Command in Hawaii," *Nikkei Asia*, November 5, 2023, https://asia.nikkei.
com/Politics/International-relations/Indo-Pacific/Philippines-Marcos-to-visit-
U.S.-Indo-Pacific-Command-in-Hawaii; Ryo Nakamura and Ramon Royandoyan,
"U.S. Advises Philippines on Warship Repair on China-Claimed Atoll," *Nikkei
Asia*, November 21, 2023, https://asia.nikkei.com/Politics/International-relations/
South-China-Sea/U.S.-advises-Philippines-on-warship-repair-on-China-claimed-
atoll; Rebecca Ratcliffe, "Why the Rusting Wreck of a Second World War Ship is So
Important to China," *Guardian*, October 29, 2023, https://www.theguardian.com/
world/2023/oct/30/sierra-madre-phillippines-ship-china-blockade.

198. United States Department of State, "U.S. Support for the Philippines in the South
China Sea," press release, December 10, 2023, https://www.state.gov/u-s-support-
for-the-philippines-in-the-south-china-sea-7/.

199. Lee Jones and Shahar Hameiri, "Malaysia and the BRI," in *Debunking the Myth of
"Debt-Trap Diplomacy"* (London: Chatham House, 2020), https://www.chath
amhouse.org/2020/08/debunking-myth-debt-trap-diplomacy/5-malaysia-and-
bri; Malay Mail, "Malaysia, China Ink Eight MoUs, Agreements in Various Fields,"
*Malay Mail*, November 23, 2015, https://www.malaymail.com/news/malaysia/
2015/11/23/malaysia-china-ink-eight-mous-agreements-in-various-fields/1010
397; The Star, "Najib Reiterates Benefits of China's One Belt One Road Initiative,"
*Star*, May 16, 2017, https://www.thestar.com.my/news/nation/2017/05/16/najib-rei
terates-benefits-of-china-one-belt-one-road.

200. Yantoultra Ngui, "China Elevates Malaysia Ties, Aims to Triple Trade by 2017,"
*Reuters*, October 4, 2017, https://www.reuters.com/article/us-malaysia-china/
china-elevates-malaysia-ties-aims-to-triple-trade-by-2017-idUSBRE9930402
0131004; Ngeow Chow Bing, "Malaysia-China Defence Relations: Disruptions
amid Political Changes and Geopolitical Tensions," *ISEAS Perspective* 57 (2021),

https://www.iseas.edu.sg/articles-commentaries/iseas-perspective/2021-57-malay
sia-china-defence-relations-disruptions-amid-political-changes-and-geopoliti
cal-tensions-by-ngeow-chow-bing/; Federation of Malaysia Ministry of Foreign
Affairs, "Joint Press Statement," https://www.kln.gov.my/web/guest/home?p_p_
id=101&p_p_state=maximized&_101_struts_action=%2Fasset_publisher%2Fv
iew_content&_101_type=content&_101_viewMode=view&_101_urlTitle=joint-
press-statement; Prashanth Parameswaran, "China, Malaysia to Hold First Ever
Joint Live-Troop Exercises," *Diplomat*, August 31, 2015, https://thediplomat.com/
2015/08/china-malaysia-to-hold-first-ever-joint-live-troop-exercise/.

201. Reuters Staff, "Najib Asks West to Stop 'Lecturing' as Malaysia Embraces China,"
*Reuters*, November 2, 2016, https://www.reuters.com/article/us-china-malay
sia/najib-asks-west-to-stop-lecturing-as-malaysia-embraces-china-idUSKB
N12X0CH; "Malaysia, China Sign 14 MOUs Worth RM143.6b," *Malaysiakini*,
November 1, 2016, https://www.malaysiakini.com/news/361327; "Malaysian,
Chinese Companies Make History with Signing of 14 Agreements Worth RM144b,"
*Malaymail*, November 1, 2016, https://www.malaymail.com/news/malaysia/2016/
11/01/malaysian-chinese-companies-make-history-with-signing-of-14-agreeme
nts-wort/1240749; "M'sian, Chinese Firms Sign Agreements Worth RM144bil,"
*Star*, November 1, 2016, https://www.thestar.com.my/business/business-news/
2016/11/01/malaysian-and-chinese-firms-sign-14-agreements-worth-rm144bil/.

202. Hannah Beech and Austin Ramzy, "Malaysia's Ex-Leader, Najib Razak, Is Charged
in Corruption Inquiry," *New York Times*, July 3, 2018, https://www.nytimes.com/
2018/07/03/world/asia/najib-razak-arrested-malaysia.html.

203. Ngeow Chow Bing, "Have Friendly Malaysia-China Relations Gone Awry?,"
Carnegie Endowment for International Peace, July 16, 2021, https://carnegieen
dowment.org/2021/07/16/have-friendly-malaysia-china-relations-gone-awry-
pub-84981; Jennifer Fei, *Bridging Regions, Strengthening Ties: The East Coast Rail
Line (ECRL) in Malaysia*, Case Study, Leadership Academy Development, https://
fsi.stanford.edu/publication/bridging-regions-strengthening-ties-east-coast-rail-
line-ecrl-malaysia.

204. Mahathir bin Mohamed, "Former Malaysian PM Mahathir Mohamad on the Rise
of China," interviewed by Jamil Anderlini, *Financial Times*, May 26, 2017, https://
www.ft.com/content/b4affab0-4076-11e7-82b6-896b95f30f58?segmentid=acee4
131-99c2-09d3-a635-873e61754ec6.

205. Bing, "Have Friendly Malaysia-China"; Tashny Sukamaran, "How Will Malaysia and
China's Maritime Consultation Mechanism Affect the South China Sea Dispute?,"
*South China Morning Post*, September 22, 2019, https://www.scmp.com/week-asia/
explained/article/3029732/how-will-malaysia-and-chinas-maritime-consultation-
mechanism; Collins Chong Yew Keat, "Malaysia's China Pivot May Make It Richer—
But Also More Vulnerable," *South China Morning Post*, September 18, 2022, https://
www.scmp.com/comment/letters/article/3191706/malaysias-china-pivot-may-
make-it-richer-also-more-vulnerable; Herman Tiu Laurel, "Mahathir's Clarion
Call: Pivot to China," *Philippine News Agency*, September 5, 2022, https://www.pna.
gov.ph/opinion/pieces/538-mahathirs-clarion-call-pivot-to-china.

206. "Malaysia's Anwar Says 'Not Tilting to China, but Is Geographically Closer' than US, ahead of Xi-Biden Summit at Apec," *South China Morning Post*, November 15, 2023, https://www.scmp.com/news/asia/southeast-asia/article/3241613/anwar-says-malaysia-not-tilting-china-it-geographically-closer-us-ahead-xi-biden-sum mit-apec.

207. Muhammad Zulfikar Rakhmat and M. Habib Pashya, "Indonesia's Delicate Dance between China and the US," *Diplomat*, July 20, 2021, https://thediplomat.com/2021/07/indonesias-delicate-dance-between-china-and-the-us/; World Bank, "Indonesia Export Partner Share by Country in Percentage 2011–2020," World Integrated Trade Solution, World Bank, https://wits.worldbank.org/CountryProfile/en/Coun try/IDN/StartYear/2011/EndYear/2020/TradeFlow/Export/Partner/BY-COUN TRY/Indicator/XPRT-PRTNR-SHR; World Bank, "Indonesia Import Partner Share by Country in Percentage 2011–2020," World Integrated Trade Solution, World Bank, https://wits.worldbank.org/CountryProfile/en/Country/IDN/StartY ear/2011/EndYear/2020/TradeFlow/Import/Partner/BY-COUNTRY/Indicator/ MPRT-PRTNR-SHR.

208. Bridget Welsh, "Jokowi 2.0: Indonesia Amid US-China Competition," interviewed by Mercy A. Kuo, *Diplomat*, November 12, 2019, https://thediplomat.com/2019/11/jokowi-2-0-indonesia-amid-us-china-competition/; Dewi Fortuna Anwar, "Indonesia-China Relations," *Southeast Asian Affairs* (2019): 156, https://www.jstor. org/stable/26939692; John McBeth, "China's Belt and Road Staggers and Stalls in Indonesia," *Asia Times*, July 29, 2022, https://asiatimes.com/2022/07/chinas-belt-and-road-staggers-and-stalls-in-indonesia/; Risha Rahman, "Billions on Offer for Belt and Road," *Jakarta Post*, March 20, 2019, https://www.thejakartapost.com/news/2019/03/20/billions-offer-belt-and-road.html; "Indonesia to Propose Projects Worth US$91 Billion for China's Belt and Road," *Straits Times*, March 20, 2019, https://www.straitstimes.com/asia/se-asia/indonesia-to-propose-projects-worth-us91-bilion-for-chinas-belt-and-road.

209. Daniel Peterson, Greg Barton, Shahram Akbarzadeh, and Joshua Roose, "Indonesia and China: Geostrategic Implications for the ADF," *Forge*, https://theforge.defence. gov.au/publications/indonesia-and-china-geostrategic-implications-adf.

210. World Bank, "Indonesia Export Partner Share by Country in Percentage 2011–2020"; World Bank, "Indonesia Import Partner Share by Country in Percentage 2011–2020."

211. Ken Moriyasu, "U.S. and Indonesia Upgrade Ties with Eye on Critical Minerals Pact," *Nikkei Asia*, November 13, 2023.

212. US Department of State, Bureau of Political-Military Affairs, "U.S. Security Cooperation with Indonesia," fact sheet, March 31, 2021, https://www.state.gov/u-s-security-cooperation-with-indonesia/.

213. World Bank, "Exports of Goods and Services (% of GDP)—Thailand," World Bank Data, World Bank, https://data.worldbank.org/indicator/NE.EXP.GNFS.ZS?locati ons=TH.

214. World Bank, "Thailand Export Partner Share by Country in Percentage 2011–2020," World Integrated Trade Solution, World Bank, https://wits.worldbank.org/Country

Profile/en/Country/THA/StartYear/2011/EndYear/2020/TradeFlow/Export/Part
ner/BY-COUNTRY/Indicator/XPRT-PRTNR-SHR.

215. World Bank, "Thailand Import Partner Share by Country in Percentage 2011–2020,"
World Integrated Trade Solution, World Bank, https://wits.worldbank.org/Country
Profile/en/Country/THA/StartYear/2011/EndYear/2020/TradeFlow/Import/Part
ner/BY-COUNTRY/Indicator/MPRT-PRTNR-SHR.

216. Charlie Campbell, "'It Will Be Catastrophic.' Asia's Tourism-Dependent Economies
Are Being Hit Hard by the Coronavirus," *Time*, February 13, 2020, https://time.com/
5783505/thailand-asia-tourism-covid-19-china-coronavirus/.

217. Prashanth Parameswaran, "Thailand Turns to China," *Diplomat*, December 20, 2014,
https://thediplomat.com/2014/12/thailand-turns-to-china/; Shawn W. Crispin,
"China Losing, US Gaining Crucial Ground in Thailand," *Asia Times*, June 9, 2022,
https://asiatimes.com/2022/06/china-losing-us-gaining-crucial-ground-in-thail
and/; Amy Sawitta Lefevre, "Thailand Boost Military Ties with China amid US Spat,"
*Reuters*, February 6, 2015, https://www.reuters.com/article/us-thailand-china/thail
and-boosts-military-ties-with-china-amid-u-s-spat-idUSKBN0LA0LD20150206.

218. Lefevre, "Thailand Boost Military."

219. Prashanth Parameswaran, "China-Thailand Submarine Deal in the Headlines
with Keel-Laying Ceremony," *Diplomat*, September 23, 2019, https://thediplomat.
com/2019/09/china-thailand-submarine-deal-in-the-headlines-with-keel-laying-
ceremony/; Prashanth Parameswaran, "Thailand to Buy Battle Tanks from China,"
*Diplomat*, May 18, 2016, https://thediplomat.com/2016/05/thailand-to-buy-battle-
tanks-from-china/.

220. Prashanth Parameswaran, "China-Thailand Military Ties in the Headlines with New
Shipbuilding Pact," *Diplomat*, September 13, 2019, https://thediplomat.com/2019/
09/china-thailand-military-ties-in-the-headlines-with-new-shipbuilding-pact/.

221. Patpicha Tanakasempipat and Jutarat Skulpichetrat "China, Thailand, Joint
Airforce Exercise Highlights Warming Ties," *Reuters*, November 24, 2015, https://
www.reuters.com/article/uk-china-thailand-military/china-thailand-joint-air-
force-exercise-highlights-warming-ties-idUKKBN0TD0CB20151124; Prashanth
Parameswaran, "What's in China's Military Exercises with Malaysia and Thailand,"
*Diplomat*, October 17, 2018, https://thediplomat.com/2018/10/whats-in-chinas-
military-exercise-with-malaysia-and-thailand/.

222. Prashanth Parameswaran, "What's with the New China-Thailand Military Facility?,"
*Diplomat*, November 17, 2017, https://thediplomat.com/2017/11/whats-with-the-
new-china-thailand-military-facility/.

223. Zhao Ziwen, "China and Thailand Launch Air Combat Drills as Beijing Shores Up
Military Ties in Southeast Asia," *South China Morning Post*, July 10, 2023, https://
www.scmp.com/news/china/military/article/3227189/china-and-thailand-launch-
air-combat-drills-beijing-shores-military-ties-southeast-asia#.

224. Ibid.

225. "People's Republic of China," Foreign Policy, Republic of Singapore Ministry of
Foreign Affairs, https://www.mfa.gov.sg/SINGAPORES-FOREIGN-POLICY/
Countries-and-Regions/Northeast-Asia/Peoples-Republic-of-China.

226. World Bank, "Singapore Trade Balance, Exports and Imports by Country and Region 2014," World Integrated Trade Solution, World Bank, https://wits.worldb ank.org/CountryProfile/en/Country/SGP/Year/2014/TradeFlow/EXPIMP.

227. World Bank, "Singapore Exports to China in US$ Thousand 2011–2020," World Integrated Trade Solution, World Bank, https://wits.worldbank.org/CountryProf ile/en/Country/SGP/StartYear/2011/EndYear/2020/TradeFlow/Export/Partner/ CHN/Indicator/XPRT-TRD-VL#; World Bank, "Singapore Imports from China in US$ Thousand 2011–2020," World Integrated Trade Solution, World Bank, https:// wits.worldbank.org/CountryProfile/en/Country/SGP/StartYear/2011/EndYear/ 2020/TradeFlow/Import/Partner/CHN/Indicator/MPRT-TRD-VL.

228. Republic of Singapore Ministry of Foreign Affairs, "People's Republic of China"; Republic of Singapore Ministry of Foreign Affairs, "MFA Press Statement: State Visit to Singapore by His Excellency Xi Jinping, President of the People's Republic of China, 6 to 7 November 2015," press release, November 7, 2015, https://www. mfa.gov.sg/Newsroom/Press-Statements-Transcripts-and-Photos/2015/11/ MFA-Press-Statement-State-Visit-to-Singapore-by-His-Excellency-Xi-Jinping_ 20151107; "China and Singapore Held the First Round of Follow-up Negotiations on FTA Upgrade," China FTA Network, People's Republic of China Ministry of Commerce, last modified April 9, 2021, http://fta.mofcom.gov.cn/enarticle/enrele ase/202104/44818_1.html; Lim Yan Liang, "Singapore, China Look to New Areas of Cooperation," *Strait Times*, September 21, 2017, https://www.straitstimes.com/asia/ east-asia/singapore-china-look-to-new-areas-of-cooperation.

229. Bureau of Political-Military Affairs, "U.S. Security Cooperation with Indonesia"; Singapore Ministry of Defense, "Singapore and the US Renew Memorandum of Understanding," press release, September 24, 2019, https://www.mindef.gov.sg/ web/portal/mindef/news-and-events/latest-releases/article-detail/2019/Septem ber/24sep19_nr; Charissa Yong and Lim Min Zhang, "PM Lee, Trump Renew Key Defence Pact on US Use of Singapore Air, Naval Bases," *Straits Times*, September 24, 2019, https://www.straitstimes.com/world/pm-lee-trump-renew-key-defence- pact-on-us-use-of-singapore-air-naval-bases.

230. Singapore Ministry of Defense, "Singapore and the US Renew Memorandum of Understanding."

231. "Singapore," Defense Security Cooperation Agency, https://www.dsca.mil/tags/ singapore?page=0.

232. US Library of Congress, Congressional Research Service, *U.S.–Singapore Relations*, by Ben Dolven and Emma Chanlett-Avery, IF10228, last modified July 25, 2022, https://crsreports.congress.gov/product/pdf/IF/IF10228.

233. Sourced from a private email exchange with the authors.

234. K. Shanmugam, "Transcript of Sydney Morning Herald's Interview with Mr K Shanmugam, Minister for Home Affairs and Minister for Law, on 15 September 2022 interview by *Sydney Morning Herald*, Republic of Singapore Ministry of Home Affairs, September 15, 2022, https://www.mha.gov.sg/mediaroom/speeches/transcr ipt-of-sydney-morning-herald-interview-with-mr-k-shanmugam-on-15-septem ber-2022/.

235. World Bank, "Vietnam Import Partner Share by Country in Percentage 2011–2020," World Integrated Trade Solution, World Bank, https://wits.worldbank.org/Country Profile/en/Country/VNM/StartYear/2011/EndYear/2020/TradeFlow/Import/Part ner/BY-COUNTRY/Indicator/MPRT-PRTNR-SHR.

236. World Bank, "Vietnam Capital Goods Imports from China in US$ Thousand 2011– 2020," World Integrated Trade Solution, World Bank, https://wits.worldbank.org/ CountryProfile/en/Country/VNM/StartYear/2011/EndYear/2020/TradeFlow/Imp ort/Indicator/MPRT-TRD-VL/Partner/CHN/Product/UNCTAD-SoP4#.

237. Gardiner Harris, "Vietnam Arms Embargo to Be Fully Lifted, Obama Says in Hanoi," *New York Times*, May 23, 2016, https://www.nytimes.com/2016/05/24/world/asia/ vietnam-us-arms-embargo-obama.html; "Obama Lifts US Embargo on Lethal Arms Sales to Vietnam," *BBC*, May 23, 2016, https://www.bbc.com/news/world- asia-36356695; Bloomberg, "United States Warships Make First Visit to Vietnam Base in Decades," *South China Morning Post*, October 4, 2016, https://www.scmp. com/news/asia/southeast-asia/article/2024978/united-states-warships-make-first- visit-vietnam-base.

238. Agencies, "US Aircraft Carrier Arrives in Vietnam for Historic Visit as China Ties Are Put to the Test," *South China Morning Post*, March 5, 2018, https://www.scmp. com/news/asia/southeast-asia/article/2135725/us-aircraft-carrier-arrives-viet nam-historic-visit-china; James Pearsona and Robert Birsel, "U.S. Says Completes Second Aircraft Carrier Visit to Vietnam," *Reuters*, March 10, 2020, https://www. reuters.com/article/us-vietnam-usa/u-s-says-completes-second-aircraft-carrier- visit-to-vietnam-idUSKBN20Y0F3.

239. Agencies, "US Aircraft Carrier Arrives."

240. Derek Grossman and Christopher Sharman, "How to Read Vietnam's Latest Defense White Paper: A Message to Great Powers," *War on the Rocks*, December 31, 2019, https://warontherocks.com/2019/12/how-to-read-vietnams-latest-defense-white- paper-a-message-to-great-powers/.

241. Sui Lee-Wee, "Vietnam and U.S. Forge Deeper Ties as Worries Rise about China," *New York Times*, September 8, 2023, https://www.nytimes.com/2023/09/08/world/ asia/biden-vietnam-china.html; Mercedes Ruehl et al., "Vietnam and US Upgrade Relations in Move to Counter China," *Financial Times*, September 10, 2023, https://www.ft.com/content/19b2f8f4-830a-469d-b633-226e2bb1a9d1;      White House, "Joint Leaders' Statement: Elevating United States-Vietnam Relations to a Comprehensive Strategic Partnership," press release, September 11, 2023, https:// www.whitehouse.gov/briefing-room/statements-releases/2023/09/11/joint-lead ers-statement-elevating-united-states-vietnam-relations-to-a-comprehensive- strategic-partnership/.

242. World Bank, "Cambodia Import Partner Share by Country in Percentage 2011– 2020," World Integrated Trade Solution, World Bank, https://wits.worldbank.org/ CountryProfile/en/Country/KHM/StartYear/2011/EndYear/2020/TradeFlow/Imp ort/Partner/BY-COUNTRY/Indicator/MPRT-PRTNR-SHR.

243. World Bank, "Cambodia Imports by Country in US$ Thousand 2011–2020," World Integrated Trade Solution, World Bank, https://wits.worldbank.org/CountryProf

ile/en/Country/KHM/StartYear/2011/EndYear/2020/TradeFlow/Import/Partner/BY-COUNTRY/Indicator/MPRT-TRD-VL.

244. Tomoya Onishi, "In Cambodia, Even Debt-Free Roads Lead to More Chinese Influence," *Nikkei Asia*, April 29, 2019, https://asia.nikkei.com/Spotlight/Belt-and-Road/In-Cambodia-even-debt-free-roads-lead-to-more-Chinese-influence; Callum Burkitt, "Countering Cambodia's Economic Reliance on China," La Trobe University, February 14, 2022, https://www.latrobe.edu.au/news/announcements/2022/countering-cambodias-economic-reliance-on-china.

245. Kearrin Sims, "Laos Set Its Own Debt Trap," East Asia Forum, October 31, 2020, https://www.eastasiaforum.org/2020/10/31/laos-set-its-own-debt-trap/; US Library of Congress, Congressional Research Service, *Laos*, by Ben Dolven and Thomas Lun, IF10236, last updated October 17, 2022, https://crsreports.congress.gov/product/pdf/IF/IF10236.

246. US Library of Congress, *Laos*.

247. World Bank, "LAO PDR Export Partner Share by Country in Percentage 2011–2020," World Integrated Trade Solution, World Bank, https://wits.worldbank.org/CountryProfile/en/Country/LAO/StartYear/2011/EndYear/2020/TradeFlow/Export/Partner/BY-COUNTRY/Indicator/XPRT-PRTNR-SHR.

248. Ernest Z. Bower, "China Reveals Its Hand on ASEAN in Phnom Penh," *Center for Strategic and International Studies*, July 20, 2012, https://www.csis.org/analysis/china-reveals-its-hand-asean-phnom-penh.

249. Jacob Lew, et al., *China's Belt and Road: Implications for the United States*, Task Force Report No. 81, Council on Foreign Relations, updated March 2021, https://www.cfr.org/task-force-report/chinas-belt-and-road-implications-for-the-united-states; Manuel Mogato, Michael Martina, and Ben Blanchard, "ASEAN Deadlocked on South China Sea, Cambodia Blocks Statement," *Reuters*, July 25, 2016, https://www.reuters.com/article/us-southchinasea-ruling-asean/asean-deadlocked-on-south-china-sea-cambodia-blocks-statement-idUSKCN105 0F6; Prashanth Parameswaran, "Cambodia: A New South China Sea Mediator between China and ASEAN?," *Diplomat*, July 28, 2015, https://thediplomat.com/2015/07/cambodia-a-new-south-china-sea-mediator-between-china-and-asean/.

250. Prashanth Parameswaran, "China Just Gave Cambodia's Military a Boost," *Diplomat*, May 27, 2015, https://thediplomat.com/2015/05/china-just-gave-cambodias-military-a-boost/; Joanne Stocker, "Cambodia to Spend $40 Million More on Chinese Military Equipment," *Defense Post*, July 29, 2019, https://www.thedefensepost.com/2019/07/29/cambodia-china-weapons-spending/; AFP, "China Pledges $100 Million to Modernize Cambodia's Military," *Defense Post*, June 19, 2018, https://www.thedefensepost.com/2018/06/19/china-pledges-100-million-cambodia-military/; U.S.-China Economic Security Review Commission, *2022 Annual Report to Congress*, 2, November 2022, https://www.uscc.gov/annual-report/2022-annual-report-congress; Jack Detsch, "U.S. Looks to Check Chinese Advances at Cambodian Naval Base," *Foreign Policy*, December 5, 2022, https://foreignpolicy.com/2022/12/05/us-china-cambodia-ream-naval-base/.

251. Demetri Sevastopulo, "Chinese Base in Cambodia Nears Completion in Challenge to US Naval Power," *Financial Times*, July 24, 2023, https://www.ft.com/content/cec4bbb9-8e92-4fc1-85fb-ded826a735c5.

252. Catherine Putz, "Which Countries Are for or against China's Xinjiang Policies?," *Diplomat*, July 15, 2019, https://thediplomat.com/2019/07/which-countries-are-for-or-against-chinas-xinjiang-policies/.

253. Catherine Putz, "2020 Edition: Which Countries Are for or against China's Xinjiang Policies, "*Diplomat*, October, 9, 2020, https://thediplomat.com/2020/10/2020-edition-which-countries-are-for-or-against-chinas-xinjiang-policies/; Dave Lawler, "The 53 Countries Supporting China's Crackdown on Hong Kong," *Axios*, July 2, 2020, https://www.axios.com/2020/07/02/countries-supporting-china-hong-kong-law; Eleanor Albert, "Which Countries Support the New Hong Kong National Security Law?," *Diplomat*, July 6, 2020, https://thediplomat.com/2020/07/which-countries-support-the-new-hong-kong-national-security-law/.

254. Lee Hsien Loong, "Remarks by President Trump and Prime Minister Lee of Singapore in Joint Statements" (speech, Washington, DC, October 23, 2017), White House Archives, https://trumpwhitehouse.archives.gov/briefings-statements/remarks-president-trump-prime-minister-lee-singapore-joint-statements/.

255. W. P. S. Sidhu, "The US's Challenge: Pivot or Pirouette?," *Live Mint*, November 25, 2012, https://www.livemint.com/Opinion/vaoNKY3umT7U1V1uGGXLnN/The-USs-challenge-pivot-or-pirouette.html.

256. William Choong, "US Pivot to Asia Must Come with Reassurances," *Straits Times*, April 24, 2013.

257. Conversation with the authors.

258. Stuart Grudgings, "As Obama's Asia 'Pivot' Falters, China Steps into the Gap," *Star*, October 6, 2013, https://www.thestar.com.my/news/world/2013/10/06/as-obamas-asia-pivot-falters-china-steps-into-the-gap.

259. Ellen Nakashima and Christian Shepherd, "Rattled by China, U.S. and Allies Are Beefing Up Defenses in the Pacific," *Washington Post*, February 22, 2023, https://www.washingtonpost.com/national-security/2023/02/20/china-taiwan-invasion-deterrence/.

260. In this chapter we use separate sources to assess each branch of the US Military assigned to the Pacific. We do not use the International Institute for Strategic Studies *Military Balance* in this chapter, as the *Military Balance* does not split deployments by military branch. The number of US troops assigned to the Pacific in general (which we use in this chapter) is significantly higher than the number of US troops deployed to specific countries in the Indo-Pacific in early November of each year (which we use in Chapter 5, "Turning on China: The Pivot during the Trump Administration"), because a very large percentage of US troops assigned to the Pacific are either based in the US or are aboard ships, rather than deployed to specific countries in the Indo-Pacific. Scott Smith, "US to Counter China Uncertainty with Combined Pacific Fleet," interviewed by Ken Moriyasu, *Nikkei Asia*, June 14, 2016, https://asia.nikkei.com/Politics/US-to-counter-China-uncertainty-with-combined-Pacific-Fleet.

261. "About Us," United States Pacific Fleet, https://www.cpf.navy.mil/About-Us/.

262. As US naval vessels and aircraft rarely stay permanently deployed to one place—due to varying costs—we are forced to estimate and use Department of Defense sources.

263. "U.S. 7th Fleet Forces," United States 7th Fleet, October 2011, accessed September 7, 2022, http://www.c7f.navy.mil/forces.htm, archived at https://web.archive.org/web/20111018082134/http://www.c7f.navy.mil/forces.htm.

264. "The United States Seventh Fleet Fact Sheet," About Us, United States 7th Fleet, https://www.c7f.navy.mil/About-Us/Facts-Sheet/.

265. Correspondence between the authors and US Navy Captain Christa N. Almonte.

266. Private conversation with the authors.

267. This count includes active-duty personnel permanently assigned to Australia, British Indian Ocean Territory, Guam, Japan, the Philippines, Singapore, South Korea, and Thailand. This data does not include personnel on temporary duty or deployed in support of contingency operations. US Department of Defense, "DoD Personnel, Workforce Reports & Publications," Defense Manpower Data Center, https://dwp.dmdc.osd.mil/dwp/app/dod-data-reports/workforce-reports.

268. "DAF Personnel," 2021 USAF & USSF Almanac: Personnel, Air & Space Forces Magazine, June 30, 2021, https://www.airandspaceforces.com/article/2021-usaf-ussf-almanac-people/; "The Air Force in Facts and Figures," Air Force Magazine 95, no. 5 (May 2012): 42, https://www.airandspaceforces.com/PDF/MagazineArchive/Magazine%20Documents/2012/May%202012/0512facts_figs.pdf.

269. "The Air Force in Facts and Figures."

270. Demetri Sevastopulo, "Republicans Slam Pentagon Plan to Pull Permanent F-15 Force from Okinawa," Financial Times, November 1, 2022, https://www.ft.com/content/eef5faaf-cb2c-4d63-ba47-d3a772fc30eb.

271. US Department of Defense, Summary of the 2018 National Defense Strategy, 2018, 3, https://dod.defense.gov/Portals/1/Documents/pubs/2018-National-Defense-Strategy-Summary.pdf.

272. Jason Sherman, "Davidson: China on Track to Unseat US as Dominant Military in the Pacific as Soon as 2026," Inside Defense, March 5, 2021, https://insidedefense.com/daily-news/davidson-china-track-unseat-us-dominant-military-pacific-soon-2026; Adela Suliman, "China Could Invade Taiwan in the Next 6 years, Assume Global Leadership Role, U.S. Admiral Warns," NBC, March 10, 2021, https://www.nbcnews.com/news/world/china-could-invade-taiwan-next-6-years-assume-global-leadership-n1260386.

273. Michael Green et al., "Case Studies of Maritime Coercion," in Countering Coercion in Maritime Asia: The Theory and Practice of Gray Zone Deterrence (Washington, DC: Center for Strategic and International Studies, 2017), http://www.jstor.org/stable/resrep23165.7.

274. Ibid.; James B. Steinberg, "What Went Wrong? U.S.-China Relations from Tiananmen to Trump," The Strategist 3, no. 1 (Winter 2019/2020): 119-133, https://tnsr.org/2020/01/what-went-wrong-u-s-china-relations-from-tiananmen-to-trump/.

275. Steinberg, "What Went Wrong."

276. Michael Sobolik, "America Has a Credibility Problem in Southeast Asia," American Foreign Policy Council, October 27, 2021, https://www.afpc.org/publications/articles/america-has-a-credibility-problem-in-southeast-asia; "China Island Tracker,"

Asia Maritime Transparency Initiative, Center for Strategic and International Studies, https://amti.csis.org/island-tracker/china/.

277. Sobolik, "America Has a Credibility Problem."

278. Michael Green, Kathleen Hicks, and Mark Cancian, *Asia-Pacific Rebalance 2025* (Washington, DC: Center for Strategic and International Studies, 2016), vii, https://csis-website-prod.s3.amazonaws.com/s3fs-public/legacy_files/files/publication/160119_Green_AsiaPacificRebalance2025_Web_0.pdf.

279. Associated Press, "China Is Challenging 'Dominance' of US in South China Sea, Diplomat Says," *NBC*, February 19, 2018, https://www.nbcnews.com/news/world/china-challenging-dominance-u-s-south-china-sea-diplomat-says-n849296.

280. Australia Department of Defence, *Australia Defence Strategic Update*, 3, July 1, 2020, https://www.defence.gov.au/about/strategic-planning/2020-defence-strategic-update.

281. Michael Memoli, "Hillary Clinton Once Called TPP the 'Gold Standard.' Here's Why, and What She Says about the Trade Deal Now," *Los Angeles Times*, September 26, 2016, https://www.latimes.com/politics/la-na-pol-trade-tpp-20160926-snap-story.html.

282. CBS and Associated Press, "Biden Supports Trade Deal Despite Opposition from Unions," *CBS*, October 7, 2015, https://www.cbsnews.com/news/biden-supports-trade-deal-despite-opposition-from-unions/.

283. Peter Baker, "Trump Abandons Trans-Pacific Partnership, Obama's Signature Trade Deal," *New York Times*, January 23, 2017, https://www.nytimes.com/2017/01/23/us/politics/tpp-trump-trade-nafta.html.

284. Timothy Heath, "Strategic Consequences of U.S. Withdrawal from TPP," *The Cipher Brief* (blog), RAND, March 27, 2017, https://www.rand.org/blog/2017/03/strategic-consequences-of-us-withdrawal-from-tpp.html.

285. Lowy Institute, *Asia Power Index 2023 Edition*, Lowy Institute, https://power.lowyinstitute.org.

## Chapter 10

1. Harold Brown, speaking on February 21, 1979, 1982, 96th Cong., 1st sess., *Congressional Record* 126, pt. 3: 2832.

2. White House, "Joint U.S.-China Statement," October 29, 1997, https://1997-2001.state.gov/regions/eap/971029_usc_jtstmt.html.

3. George W. Bush, "President Bush and President Hu of People's Republic of China Participate in Arrival Ceremony" (speech, Washington, DC, April 20, 2006), White House Archives, https://georgewbush-whitehouse.archives.gov/news/releases/2006/04/20060420.html.

4. Barack Obama and Xi Jinping, "Remarks in Joint Press Conference" (joint press conference, Washington, DC, September 25, 2015), White House Archives, http://obamawhitehouse.archives.gov/the-press-office/2015/09/25/remarks-president-obama-and-president-xi-peoples-republic-china-joint.

5. Barack Obama, "The Obama Doctrine," interviewed by Jeffrey Goldberg, *Atlantic*, April 2016, http://theatlantic.com/magazine/archive/2016/04/the-obama-doctrine/471525.

6. Zhong Sheng, "Goals of US 'Return-to-Asia' Strategy Questioned," *People's Daily*, October 18, 2011, http://www.china.org.cn/opinion/2011-10/19/content_23666853.htm.

7. "US Asia-Pacific Strategy Brings Steep Price," *Global Times*, November 20, 2011, https://www.globaltimes.cn/content/684596.shtml.

8. Reuters Staff, "PLA Researcher Says U.S. Aims to Encircle China," *Reuters*, November 28, 2011, https://www.reuters.com/article/us-china-usa-pla/pla-researcher-says-u-s-aims-to-encircle-china-idUSTRE7AR07Q20111128.

9. Shen Dingli, "China's Fury Building over Obama's New Asia Policy," interviewed by Barbara Demick, *Los Angeles Times*, November 21, 2022, https://www.latimes.com/archives/blogs/world-now/story/2011-11-21/chinas-fury-building-over-obamas-new-asia-policy.

10. Ibid.

11. Wu Xinbo, "Not Backing Down: China Responds to the US Rebalance to Asia," *Global Asia* 7, no. 4 (December 2012), https://globalasia.org/v7no4/cover/not-backing-down-china-responds-to-the-us-rebalance-to-asia_wu-xinbo.

12. Cui Tiankai, "Ambassador Cui Tiankai's Interview with the Foreign Policy," interview by Foreign Policy, *Foreign Policy*, November 6, 2014, http://us.china-embassy.gov.cn/eng/sgzc/201411/t20141107_4900884.htm.

13. Hillary Rodham Clinton, *Hard Choices* (New York and London: Simon & Schuster Paperbacks, 2014), 71.

14. China Information Office of the State Council, *China's Military Strategy*, May 2015, http://english.www.gov.cn/archive/white_paper/2015/05/27/content_281475115610833.htm.

15. People's Republic of China Ministry of Foreign Affairs, Office of the Spokesperson, Foreign Ministry Spokesperson Lu Kang's Regular Press Conference on July 12, 2016, http://np.china-embassy.gov.cn/eng/fyrth/201607/t20160713_1594384.htm.

16. Zhao Tong, "'Wolf Warrior' Diplomats Reveal China's Ambitions," interviewed by Kathrin Hille, *Financial Times*, May 11, 2020, https://www.ft.com/content/7d500105-4349-4721-b4f5-179de6a58f08.

17. While this source was previously available on *Global Times*, it is no longer publicly accessible. https://opinion.huanqiu.com/article/45XGeOAeYR0.

18. Ye Zicheng, *Inside China's Grand Strategy: The Perspective from the People's Republic* (Lexington: University of Kentucky Press, 2011), 74.

19. Robert D. Blackwill and Ashley J. Tellis, *Revising US Grand Strategy toward China* (New York: Council on Foreign Relations, 2015), 14, https://www.cfr.org/report/revising-us-grand-strategy-toward-china.

20. Robert D. Blackwill and Philip Zelikow, *The United States, China, and Taiwan: A Strategy to Prevent War* (New York: Council on Foreign Relations, 2021), 8, https://www.cfr.org/report/united-states-china-and-taiwan-strategy-prevent-war.

21. Robert D. Blackwill, *Implementing Grand Strategy toward China* (New York: Council on Foreign Relations, 2020), 13, https://www.cfr.org/report/implementing-grand-strategy-toward-china.

22. Michael Dahm, "China's Desert Storm Education," *Proceedings*, 147, no. 3/1 (March 2021), https://www.usni.org/magazines/proceedings/2021/march/chinas-desert-storm-education.

23. Liu Zhen, "China-US Rivalry: How the Gulf War Sparked Beijing's Military Revolution," *South China Morning Post*, January 18, 2021, https://www.scmp.com/news/china/military/article/3118083/china-us-rivalry-how-gulf-war-sparked-beijings-military.

24. People's Republic of China Ministry of Foreign Affairs, Information Office of the State Council, *China's National Defense in 2010*, March 2011, https://www.fmprc.gov.cn/mfa_eng/wjb_663304/zzjg_663340/jks_665232/kjfywj_665252/201104/t20110402_599668.html.

25. US Department of Defense, Office of the Secretary of Defense, *2011 Annual Report to Congress: Military and Security Developments Involving the People's Republic of China*, 2011, https://dod.defense.gov/Portals/1/Documents/pubs/2011_CMPR_Final.pdf.

26. US Department of Defense, Office of the Secretary of Defense, *2020 Annual Report to Congress: Military and Security Developments Involving the People's Republic of China*, 2020, https://media.defense.gov/2020/Sep/01/2002488689/-1/-1/1/2020-DOD-CHINA-MILITARY-POWER-REPORT-FINAL.PDF.

27. US Congress, Senate, Committee on Armed Services, *Department of Defense Authorization for Appropriations for Fiscal Year 2011,* 111th Cong., 2nd sess., 2010, S. Hrg. 111–701, Pt. 1, https://www.govinfo.gov/content/pkg/CHRG-111shrg62155/html/CHRG-111shrg62155.htm.

28. Committee on Armed Services, *Department of Defense Authorization for Appropriations for Fiscal Year 2011*.

29. International Institute for Strategic Studies, "Chapter 6: Asia," *Military Balance* 112, no. 1 (2012), https://www.iiss.org/publications/the-military-balance/the-military-balance-2012/.

30. Ashley J. Tellis, "China's Military Challenge," in *Strategic Asia 2012–13*, ed. Ashley J. Tellis and Travis Tanner (Seattle: The National Bureau of Asian Research, 2012), 14, https://www.nbr.org/publication/strategic-asia-2012-13-chinas-military-challenge/.

31. Thomas G. Mahnken et al., "Asia in the Balance: Transforming US Military Strategy in Asia," American Enterprise Institute, June 2012, https://www.aei.org/wp-content/uploads/2012/05/-asia-in-the-balance-transforming-us-military-strategy-in-asia_134736206767.pdf?x91208.

32. Ibid.

33. United States Department of Defense, *Military and Security Developments Involving the People's Republic of China*, II, October 2023.

34. Ibid, 173.

35. Lindsay Maizland, "China's Modernizing Military," Backgrounder, Council on Foreign Relations, last modified February 5, 2020, https://www.cfr.org/backgrounder/chinas-modernizing-military.

36. Roger Cliff, "A New U.S. Strategy for the Indo-Pacific," *National Bureau of Asia Research*, no. 86 (June 16, 2020), https://www.nbr.org/publication/a-new-u-s-strat egy-for-the-indo-pacific/.

37. Ken Moriyasu, "China's Stealth Fighter Inventory Set to Eclipse America's F-22s," *Nikkei Asia*, February 15, 2023, https://asia.nikkei.com/Politics/Defense/China-s-stea lth-fighter-inventory-set-to-eclipse-America-s-F-22s; Michael R. Gordon, "The U.S. Is Not Yet Ready for the Era of 'Great Power' Conflict," *Wall Street Journal*, March 6, 2023, https://www.wsj.com/articles/u-s-military-china-taiwan-russia-great-power-conflict-481f7756; Luisa Gyhn, "China Military Watch," *Strategist*, June 7, 2023, https://www.aspistrategist.org.au/china-military-watch-13/.

38. Gyhn, "China Military Watch"; Maizland, "China's Modernizing Military"; David Lague and Benjamin Kang Lim, "Ruling the Waves: The China Challenge," *Reuters*, April 30, 2019, https://www.reuters.com/investigates/special-report/china-army-navy/#article-ruling-the-waves.

39. Felix K. Chang, "Sustaining the Chinese Navy's Operations at Sea: Bigger Fists, Growing Legs," Asia Program, Foreign Policy Research Institute, May 3, 2023, https://www.fpri.org/article/2023/05/sustaining-the-chinese-navys-operations-at-sea-bigger-fists-growing-legs/; Associated Press, "China Launches Its First Home-Built Aircraft Carrier," *Guardian*, April 26, 2017, https://www.theguardian.com/world/2017/apr/26/china-launches-second-aircraft-carrier-that-is-first-built-at-home; Mike Yeo, "China Launches Third Aircraft Carrier," *Defense News*, June 17, 2022, https://www.defensenews.com/naval/2022/06/17/china-launches-third-aircr aft-carrier/; Eric Heginbotham et al., *The U.S.-China Military Scorecard: Forces, Geography, and the Evolving Balance of Power, 1996–2017* (Santa Monica, CA: RAND, 2015), https://www.rand.org/pubs/research_reports/RR392.html; Maizland, "China's Modernizing Military."

40. US Library of Congress, Congressional Research Service, *China Naval Modernization: Implications for U.S. Navy Capabilities*, by Ronald O'Rourke, RL33153, 2022, https://sgp.fas.org/crs/row/RL33153.pdf. The relative totals provide only a rough comparison. US ships are on average far larger than Chinese, and so America's total naval tonnage is more than twice China's. See Michael E. O'Hanlon, "Does the Pentagon Report on China's Military Correctly Judge the Threat?," Brookings Institution, December 2, 2022, https://www.brookings.edu/blog/order-from-chaos/2022/12/02/does-the-pentagon-report-on-chinas-military-correctly-judge-the-threat/. By the same token, however, the total number of PLA Navy vessels does not include patrol craft that carry anti-ship cruise missiles. See Congressional Research Service, *China Naval Modernization*, 7.

41. Alastair Gale, "The Era of Total U.S. Submarine Dominance Over China Is Ending," *Wall Street Journal*, November 20, 2023, https://www.wsj.com/world/china/us-submarine-dominance-shift-china-8db10a0d.

42. David Roza, "Worried about China's Air Force? Here's Everything You Need to Know," *Task and Purpose*, December 16, 2022, https://taskandpurpose.com/news/china-peoples-liberation-army-air-force/; John Xie, "Will China Surpass the US in Military Air Superiority," *Voice of America*, October 13, 2021, https://www.voanews.com/a/when-will-china-surpass-the-us-in-military-air-superiority-/6270069.html.

43. Maizland, "China's Modernizing Military"; Heginbotham et al., *The U.S.-China Military Scorecard.*

44. Hans Binnendijk and David C. Gompert, "Towards Nuclear Stewardship with China," *Survival* 65, no. 1 (February 2, 2023): 13, https://doi.org/10.1080/00396 338.2023.2172846.

45. Patty-Jane Geller, "China's Nuclear Expansion and Its Implications for U.S. Strategy and Security," Missile Defense (Commentary), Heritage Foundation, September 14, 2022, https://www.heritage.org/missile-defense/commentary/chinas-nuclear-expansion-and-its-implications-us-strategy-and-security; Paul McLeary, "Pentagon Predicts 5 Times Increase in China's Nuclear Weapons over Next 10 Years," *Politico*, November 3, 2021, https://www.politico.com/news/2021/11/03/pentagon-china-nuclear-weapons-519048; Minnie Chan, "Satellite Images of Chinese Nuclear Submarine Being Built Prompt Speculation of Vertical Launch System," *South China Morning Post*, May 14, 2022, https://www.scmp.com/news/china/military/article/ 3177644/satellite-images-chinese-submarine-under-construction-prompt?module= perpetual_scroll_0&pgtype=article&campaign=3177644; Geller, "China's Nuclear Expansion"; Minnie Chan, "Upgrades for China's Nuclear Triad as Xi Jinping Pushes for Stronger Strategic Deterrence," *South China Morning Post*, October 29, 2022, https://www.scmp.com/news/china/military/article/3197705/upgrades-chinas-nucl ear-triad-xi-jinping-pushes-stronger-strategic-deterrence-analysts.

46. Office of the Secretary of Defense, *Military and Security Developments*, November 2022, 65 & 94.

47. Ellie Kaufman and Barbara Starr, "US Military Nuclear Chief Sounds the Alarm about Pace of China's Nuclear Weapons Program," *CNN*, November 4, 2022, https:// www.cnn.com/2022/11/04/politics/us-china-nuclear-weapons-warning/index.html.

48. Erik Seedhouse, "The Growing Chinese Space Threat," *Space News*, February 21, 2023, https://spacenews.com/the-growing-chinese-space-threat/; US Department of Defense, *Military and Security Developments Involving the People's Republic of China*, 2022, https://media.defense.gov/2022/Nov/29/2003122279/-1/-1/1/2022-MILITARY-AND-SECURITY-DEVELOPMENTS-INVOLVING-THE-PEOPLES-REPUBLIC-OF-CHINA.PDF.

49. US Department of Defense, Office of the Secretary of Defense, *Annual Report to Congress: Military and Security Developments Involving the People's Republic of China 2011*, 2011, https://dod.defense.gov/Portals/1/Documents/pubs/2011_CMPR_Fi nal.pdf.

50. Office of the Secretary of Defense, *Military and Security Developments*, November 2022, 87–89.

51. Ibid.

52. Ibid.

53. Ibid.

54. Office of the Director of National Intelligence, *Annual Threat Assessment of the US Intelligence Community*, February 6, 2023, 8, https://www.dni.gov/files/ODNI/ documents/assessments/ATA-2023-Unclassified-Report.pdf.

55. Frank Kendall, "Six Questions with US Air Force Secretary Frank Kendall," interviewed by Rachel S. Cohen, *Air Force Times*, September 20, 2021, https://www.

airforcetimes.com/news/your-air-force/2021/09/20/six-questions-with-us-air-force-secretary-frank-kendall/.

56. Graham Allison and Jonah Glick-Unterman, "The 21st Century's Great Military Rivalry," *National Defense University Press*, September 30, 2022, https://ndupress.ndu.edu/Media/News/News-Article-View/Article/3174507/the-21st-centurys-great-military-rivalry/.

57. Mike Ives and Zixu Wang, "Mostly Bluster: Why China Went Easy on Taiwan's Economy," *New York Times*, August 12, 2022, https://www.nytimes.com/2022/08/12/business/china-taiwan-economy.html; Christina Wilkie, "China Ratchets Up Military and Economic Pressure on Taiwan as Pelosi Begins Her Visit," *CNBC*, August 2, 2022, https://www.cnbc.com/2022/08/02/china-ratchets-up-military-and-economic-pressure-on-taiwan-as-pelosi-begins-her-visit-.html.

58. "Countries that Recognize Taiwan 2022," World Population Review, https://worldpopulationreview.com/country-rankings/countries-that-recognize-taiwan.

59. Burkina Faso: People's Republic of China National Development and Reform Commission, Department of International Cooperation, "The Chinese Government and the Government of Burkina Faso Signed the Belt and Road Initiative Cooperation Document," last updated November 30, 2021, https://en.ndrc.gov.cn/news/pressreleases/202111/t20211130_1306258.html; Africanews with Reuters, "Burkina Faso Strengthens Developmental Ties with China," *Africanews*, June 1, 2019, https://www.africanews.com/2019/01/06/burkina-faso-strengthens-developmental-ties-with-china/; Dominican Republic: Evan Ellis, "Chinese Engagement in the Dominican Republic: An Update," *Global Americans*, May 7, 2021, https://theglobalamericans.org/2021/05/chinese-engagement-in-the-dominican-republic-an-update/; Panama: Christopher Cairns, "China's Investment Setbacks in Panama," *Diplomat*, February 26, 2022, https://thediplomat.com/2022/02/chinas-investment-setbacks-in-panama/; Nicaragua: Silk Road Briefing, "Nicaragua Joins China's Belt and Road Initiative," *Silk Road Briefing*, January 16, 2022, https://www.silkroadbriefing.com/news/2022/01/16/nicaragua-joins-chinas-belt-and-road-initiative/; El Salvador: Nelson Renteria, "UPDATE 1-China Signs on for 'Gigantic' Investment in El Salvador Infrastructure," *Reuters*, December 3, 2019, https://www.reuters.com/article/el-salvador-china/update-1-china-signs-on-for-gigantic-investment-in-el-salvador-infrastructure-idUSL1N28E00J; Gambia: "China-Gambia Ties Enter New Stage, Ambassador Says," China-African Relations, Forum on China-African Cooperation, August 19, 2021, http://www.focac.org/eng/zfgx_4/zzjw/202108/t20210818_9153867.htm; Solomon Islands: Zongyuan Zoe Liu, "What the China-Solomon Islands Pact Means for the U.S. and South Pacific," Council on Foreign Relations, May 4, 2022, https://www.cfr.org/in-brief/china-solomon-islands-security-pact-us-south-pacific; São Tomé and Príncipe: "São Tomé Signs a Five-Year Co-operation Agreement with China," São Tomé and Príncipe, *Economist Intelligence*, May 2, 2017, http://country.eiu.com/article.aspx?articleid=1235375707&Country=São%20Tomé%20and%20Pr%C3%ADncipe&topic=Economy&subtopic=Forecast&subsubtopic=Economic+growth&u=1&pid=1985626782&oid=1985626782&uid=1; Kiribati: People's Republic of China Ministry of Foreign Affairs, Kiribati President and Foreign

Minister, "Taneti Maamau Meets with Wang Yi," May 27, 2022, https://www.fmprc. gov.cn/eng/zxxx_662805/202205/t20220527_10693845.html.

60. Lindsay Maizland, "Why China-Taiwan Relations Are So Tense," Backgrounder, Council on Foreign Relations, last modified August 3, 2022, https://www.cfr.org/ backgrounder/china-taiwan-relations-tension-us-policy-biden#chapter-title-0-1; Chris Buckley and Amy Chang Chien, "China's Military, 'Chasing the Dream,' Probes Taiwan's Defenses," *New York Times*, August 11, 2023, https://www.nytimes.com/ 2023/08/11/world/asia/china-taiwan-military.html.

61. China Power Team, "Tracking the Fourth Taiwan Strait Crisis," China Power, Center for Strategic and International Studies, last modified August 30, 2022, https://chinapo wer.csis.org/tracking-the-fourth-taiwan-strait-crisis/.

62. Department of State, "Telephonic Briefing with U.S. Assistant Secretary of State for the Bureau of East Asian and Pacific Affairs Daniel J. Kritenbrink," press release, August 17, 2022, https://www.state.gov/telephonic-briefing-with-u-s-assistant-se cretary-of-state-for-the-bureau-of-east-asian-and-pacific-affairs-daniel-j-krit enbrink/.

63. Wei Fenghe, "Speech at the 18th Shangri-La Dialogue by Gen. Wei Fenghe, State Councilor and Minister of National Defense, PRC" (speech, Singapore, June 2, 2019), People's Republic of China Ministry of Defense, http://eng.mod.gov.cn/xb/Leaders hip/WeiFenghe/4842884.html.

64. Bloomberg News, "China Sends Most Bombers Toward Taiwan in at Least Two Years," *Bloomberg*, December 13, 2022, https://www.bloomberg.com/news/articles/ 2022-12-13/china-sends-most-bombers-toward-taiwan-in-at-least-two-years.

65. Ibid.

66. Lawrence Chung, "PLA Sends Record 71 Warplanes Near Taiwan after US Increases Military Aid," *South China Morning Post*, December 26, 2022, https://www.scmp. com/news/china/military/article/3204580/pla-sends-record-71-warplanes-near-tai wan-after-us-increases-military-aid.

67. Orange Wang, "China's Military 'Testing Ability to Control Sea and Air around Taiwan,'" *South China Morning Post*, April 10, 2023, https://www.scmp.com/news/ china/diplomacy/article/3216376/china-sets-military-drills-after-taiwan-lea der-tsai-ing-wens-us-trip.

68. Chris Buckley, Amy Chang Chien, and Lam Yik Fei, "China Brandishes Military Options in Exercises around Taiwan," *New York Times*, April 10, 2023, https://www. nytimes.com/2023/04/10/world/asia/china-military-exercises-taiwan.html.

69. Kathrin Hille and Demetri Sevastopulo, "How China's Military Is Slowly Squeezing Taiwan," *Financial Times*, July 24, 2023, https://www.ft.com/content/f7922fdb-01bf- 4ffd-9c5c-79f15468aa71.

70. Ben Blanchard and Michael Martina, "Taiwan Reports First Major Chinese Military Activity after Election," *Reuters*, January 17, 2024, https://www.reuters.com/world/ asia-pacific/taiwan-reports-first-major-post-election-chinese-military-activity- 2024-01-17/; Kathrin Hille, "China Launches Military Manoeuvres Around Taiwan in Wake of Election," *Financial Times*, January 17, 2024, https://www.ft.com/content/ 872c0ceb-9dc8-4451-9a36-b58b880b9742.

71. Hope Yen, "Despite Readiness Plans, China Has Doubts on Ability to Invade Taiwan, CIA Chief Says," *Los Angeles Times*, February 27, 2023, https://www.latimes.com/world-nation/story/2023-02-27/china-doubts-ability-invade-taiwan-cia-burns-says.

72. Chao Chun-shan, "Xi Jinping Warns Off US as He Piles Political and Military Pressure on Taiwan," interviewed by Kathrin Hille, *Financial Times*, October 16, 2022, https://www.ft.com/content/faa1664f-0961-4718-9b72-f0b763db6ae1.

73. Chang Wu-ueh, "Xi's Looming Third Term in China Raises Threat of War over Taiwan," interviewed by Lily Kuo, *Washington Post*, October 12, 2022, https://www.washingtonpost.com/world/2022/10/12/china-taiwan-war-xi-jinping/.

74. US Department of State "A Conversation on the Evolution and Importance of Technology, Diplomacy, and National Security with 66th Secretary of State Condoleezza Rice," press release, October 17, 2022, https://www.state.gov/secretary-antony-j-blinken-at-a-conversation-on-the-evolution-and-importance-of-technology-diplomacy-and-national-security-with-66th-secretary-of-state-condoleezza-rice/.

75. Rupert Wingfield-Hayes, "William Lai: Taiwan Just Chose a President China Loathes. What Now?," *BBC*, January 13, 2024, https://www.bbc.com/news/world-asia-67920530; "Who Is Taiwan's President-Elect Lai Ching-te?," Explainer, *Al Jazeera*, January 14, 2024, https://www.aljazeera.com/news/2024/1/14/who-is-taiwans-president-elect-lai-ching-te.

76. Kyle Mizokami, "The U.S. Military 'Failed Miserably' in a Fake Battle over Taiwan," *Popular Mechanics*, August 2, 2021, https://www.popularmechanics.com/military/a37158827/us-military-failed-miserably-in-taiwan-invasion-wargame/; Dario Leone, "Pentagon War Games Reveal That the US Would Lose Any War Fought in the Pacific with China," *Aviation Geek Club*, May 18, 2020, https://theaviationgeekclub.com/pentagon-war-games-reveal-that-us-would-lose-any-war-fought-in-the-pacific-with-china/; Richard Berstein and RealClearInvestigations, "The Scary War Game over Taiwan That the U.S. Loses Again and Again," *RealClearInvestigations*, August 17, 2020, https://www.realclearinvestigations.com/articles/2020/08/17/the_scary_war_game_over_taiwan_that_the_us_loses_again_and_again_124836.html.

77. Justin Katz and Valerie Insinna, "'A Bloody Mess' with 'Terrible Loss of Life': How a China-US Conflict over Taiwan Could Play Out," *Breaking Defense*, August 11, 2022, https://breakingdefense.com/2022/08/a-bloody-mess-with-terrible-loss-of-life-how-a-china-us-conflict-over-taiwan-could-play-out/.

78. Susan M. Gordon, Michael G. Mullen, and David Sacks, *U.S.-Taiwan Relations in a New Era*, Independent Task Force Report No. 81, Council on Foreign Relations, June 5, 2023, https://www.cfr.org/task-force-report/us-taiwan-relations-in-a-new-era.

79. Ankit Panda, "It's Official: Xi Jinping Breaks His Non-Militarization Pledge in the Spratlys," *Diplomat*, December 16, 2016, https://thediplomat.com/2016/12/its-official-xi-jinping-breaks-his-non-militarization-pledge-in-the-spratlys/.

80. Karl Thomas, "China Is Capable of Blockading Taiwan, U.S. Navy Commander Says," interviewed by the *Wall Street Journal* in Niharika Mandhana, "China Is Capable of

Blockading Taiwan, U.S. Navy Commander Says," *Wall Street Journal*, September 20, 2022, https://www.wsj.com/articles/china-is-capable-of-blockading-taiwan-u-s-navy-commander-says-11663585457.

81. Gregory Poling, "The Conventional Wisdom on China's Island Bases Is Dangerously Wrong," *War on the Rocks*, January 10, 2020, https://warontherocks.com/2020/01/the-conventional-wisdom-on-chinas-island-bases-is-dangerously-wrong/; "Air Power in the South China Sea," Asia Maritime Transparency Initiative, Center for Strategic and International Studies, July 19, 2015, https://amti.csis.org/airstr ips-scs/; "Territorial Disputes in the South China Sea," Center for Preventative Action, Council on Foreign Relations, last modified May 4, 2022, https://www.cfr. org/global-conflict-tracker/conflict/territorial-disputes-south-china-sea; "China Island Tracker," Asia Maritime Transparency Initiative, Center for Strategic and International Studies, https://amti.csis.org/island-tracker/china/; Stephen Chen, "Chinese Scientists Develop Long-Distance Underwater Communication in South China Sea," *South China Morning Post*, September 17, 2022, https://www.scmp.com/news/china/science/article/3192719/chinese-scientists-develop-long-distance-und erwater.

82. Poling, "The Conventional Wisdom"; "Air Power in"; "Territorial Disputes"; "China Island Tracker; Gregory Poling, "Beijing's Upper Hand in the South China Sea," *Foreign Affairs*, August 18, 2022, https://www.foreignaffairs.com/china/beij ing-upper-hand-south-china-sea.

83. *Advance Policy Questions for Admiral Philip Davidson, USN Expected Nominee for Commander, U.S. Pacific Command, before the Senate Armed Services Committee*, 115th Cong. 18 (2018) (Philip Davidson, Admiral in the US Navy).

84. Skandha Gunasekara and Mujib Mashal, "Chinese Military Ship Docks in Sri Lanka Despite India's Concerns," *New York Times*, August 16, 2022, https://www.nytimes.com/2022/08/16/world/asia/sri-lanka-chinese-ship-india.html; C. Uday Bhaskar, "China-India Row over Yuan Wang 5 'Spy Ship' Is Sending Ripples through the Indian Ocean," *South China Morning Post*, August 24, 2022, https://www.scmp.com/comment/opinion/article/3189850/china-india-row-over-yuan-wang-5-spy-ship-sending-ripples-through; Nick Danby, "China's 'Spy Ship' Visit to Sri Lanka Symbolises Looming Sino-Indian Maritime Competition," *Strategist*, September 28, 2022, https://www.aspistrategist.org.au/chinas-spy-ship-visit-to-sri-lanka-symbolises-looming-sino-indian-maritime-competition/; Christopher Colley, "A Future Chinese Indian Ocean Fleet?," *War on the Rocks*, April 2, 2021, https://warontherocks.com/2021/04/a-future-chinese-indian-ocean-fleet/; Gregory B. Poling, "Kyaukpyu: Connecting China to the Indian Ocean," *Center for Strategic and International Studies*, April 2, 2018, https://www.csis.org/analysis/kyaukpyu-connect ing-china-indian-ocean; Angela Stanzel, "China Trends #2—China's String of Ports in the Indian Ocean," *Institut Montaigne*, June 25, 2019, https://www.institutmontai gne.org/en/analysis/china-trends-2-chinas-string-ports-indian-ocean.

85. U.S.-China Economic Security Review Commission, *2022 Annual Report to Congress*, 16, November 2022, https://www.uscc.gov/annual-report/2022-annual-report-congress.

86. Rajeswari Pillai Rajagopalan, "India Feels the Squeeze in Indian Ocean with Chinese Projects in Neighborhood," interviewed by Anjana Pasricha, *Voice of America*, September 16, 2021, https://www.voanews.com/a/india-feels-the-squeeze-in-indian-ocean-with-chinese-projects-in-neighborhood-/6230845.html.

87. Zongyuan Zoe Liu, "What the China-Solomon Islands Pact Means for the U.S. and South Pacific," Council on Foreign Relations, May 4, 2022, https://www.cfr.org/in-brief/china-solomon-islands-security-pact-us-south-pacific; Michael E. Miller and Matthew Abbott, "China Hoped Fiji Would Be a Template for the Pacific. Its Plan Backfired," *Washington Post*, August 21, 2023, https://www.washingtonpost.com/world/interactive/2023/china-fiji-police-mou-pacific-islands/.

88. Patricia M. Kim, "Does the China-Solomon Islands Security Pact Portend a More Interventionist Beijing?," Brookings Institution, May 6, 2022, https://www.brookings.edu/blog/order-from-chaos/2022/05/06/does-the-china-solomon-islands-security-pact-portend-a-more-interventionist-beijing/.

89. Andrew Tillet, "Albanese Opens Borders in Landmark 'Climate Refuge' Deal with Tuvalu," *Australian Financial Review*, November 10, 2023, https://www.afr.com/politics/federal/albanese-opens-borders-in-landmark-climate-refuge-deal-with-tuvalu-20231110-p5ej0i?utm_source=dailybrief&utm_medium=email&utm_campaign=DailyBrief2023Nov13&utm_term=DailyNewsBrief.

90. Keith Bradsher, "Amid Tension, China Blocks Vital Exports to Japan," *New York Times*, September 22, 2010, https://www.nytimes.com/2010/09/23/business/global/23rare.html.

91. Andrew Higgins, "In Philippines, Banana Growers Feel Effect of South China Sea Dispute," *Washington Post*, June 10, 2012, https://www.washingtonpost.com/world/asia_pacific/in-philippines-banana-growers-feel-effect-of-south-china-sea-dispute/2012/06/10/gJQA47WVTV_story.html.

92. Sanjeev Miglani and Neha Dasgupta, "Exclusive: China Warns India of 'Reverse Sanctions' if Huawei Is Blocked—Sources," *Reuters*, August 6, 2019, https://www.reuters.com/article/us-huawei-india-exclusive/exclusive-china-warns-india-of-reverse-sanctions-if-huawei-is-blocked-sources-idUSKCN1UW1FF.

93. Daniel Hurst, "China Warns Australia and Japan over 'Confrontational' New Defence Pact," *Guardian*, November 18, 2020, https://www.theguardian.com/australia-news/2020/nov/18/china-warns-australia-and-japan-over-confrontational-new-defence-pact.

94. Bonnie Glaser, "Time for Collective Pushback against China's Economic Coercion," Global Forecast 2021 essay series, Center for Strategic and International Studies, January 13, 2021, https://www.csis.org/analysis/time-collective-pushback-against-chinas-economic-coercion.

95. Victoria Kim, "When China and U.S. Spar, It's South Korea That Gets Punched," *Los Angeles Times*, November 19, 2020, https://www.latimes.com/world-nation/story/2020-11-19/south-korea-china-beijing-economy-thaad-missile-interceptor; Andrew Higgins, "In an Uneven Fight with China, a Tiny Country's Brand Becomes Toxic," *New York Times*, February 21, 2022, https://www.nytimes.com/2022/02/21/world/europe/china-lithuania-taiwan-trade.html.

96. Higgins, "In an Uneven Fight with China"; Emily Rauhala, "Canada Arrested Huawei's Meng for the United States. As China Retaliates, It's on Its Own," *Washington Post*, May 8, 2019, https://www.washingtonpost.com/world/the_ameri cas/canada-helped-the-us-arrest-meng-wanzhou-as-it-gets-punished-by-china-its-on-its-own/2019/05/07/c8152fbe-6d18-11e9-bbe7-1c798fb80536_story.html.

97. Yaroslav Trofimov, Drew Hinshaw, and Kate O'Keeffe, "How China Is Taking over International Organizations, One Vote at a Time," *Wall Street Journal*, September 29, 2020, https://www.wsj.com/articles/how-china-is-taking-over-international-organizations-one-vote-at-a-time-11601397208; Andrew Hyde, "China's Emerging Financial Influence at the UN Poses a Challenge to the U.S.," *Stimson*, April 4, 2022, https://www.stimson.org/2022/chinas-emerging-financial-influence-at-the-un/.

98. Higgins, "In an Uneven Fight with China"; Elisabeth Braw, "China Takes Lithuania as an Economic Hostage," *Wall Street Journal*, January 6, 2022, https://www.wsj.com/articles/china-takes-lithuania-as-economic-hostage-taiwan-global-supply-chain-trade-goods-beijing-11641506297.

99. U.S.-China Economic Security Review Commission, *2022 Annual Report to Congress*, 2, November 2022, https://www.uscc.gov/annual-report/2022-annual-report-congress.

100. China Power Team, "Will the Dual Circulation Strategy Enable China to Compete in a Post-Pandemic World?," China Power, Center for Strategic and International Studies, https://chinapower.csis.org/china-covid-dual-circulation-economic-strategy/.

101. Thomas J. Christensen, *The China Challenge: Shaping the Choices of a Rising Power* (New York: W. W. Norton, 2015), 91.

102. "Veto List," UN Security Council Meetings & Outcomes Tables, United Nations Library, https://research.un.org/en/docs/sc/quick.

103. Reuters Staff, "China, Russia Block U.N. Council Concern about Myanmar Violence," *Reuters*, March 17, 2017, https://www.reuters.com/article/us-myanmar-rohingya-un/china-russia-block-u-n-council-concern-about-myanmar-violence-idUSKBN16O2J6; "Myanmar Coup: China Blocks UN Condemnation as Protest Grows," *BBC*, February 23, 2021, https://www.bbc.com/news/world-asia-55913947.

104. "Veto List," UN Security Council Meetings & Outcomes Tables, United Nations Library, https://research.un.org/en/docs/sc/quick.; Luv Puri, "Political Expediency Rules Terror Listing in UNSC," *Tribune* (India), September 3, 2022, https://www.tribu neindia.com/news/comment/political-expediency-rules-terror-listing-in-unsc-427 980; "China Obstructs Discussion on Coronavirus in UNSC, Blocks Draft Seeking 'Full Transparency,'" *Statesman*, March 27, 2020, https://www.thestatesman.com/world/china-obstructs-discussion-coronavirus-unsc-blocks-draft-seeking-full-transpare ncy-1502870418.html; OpIndia Staff, "China Refuses to Allow Discussion on Wuhan Coronavirus in UNSC, Blocks Draft That Called for 'Full Transparency' over the Outbreak," *OpIndia*, March 25, 2020, https://www.opindia.com/2020/03/china-unsc-un-security-council-block-discussion-draft-coronavirus-covid-19-transparency/.

105. David Wainer, "China Blocks U.S. Call for UN Security Council Hong Kong Meeting," *Bloomberg*, May 27, 2020, https://www.bloomberg.com/news/articles/2020-05-28/china-blocks-u-s-call-for-un-security-council-hong-kong-meeting; Robert Delaney, "China Says It Blocked US, UK Move for Formal Discussion of

Hong Kong National Security Law at UN," *South China Morning Post*, May 29, 2020, https://www.scmp.com/news/world/united-states-canada/article/3086776/us-brit ain-plan-raise-hong-kong-national-security; Alina Rizvi, "Uighur Crisis Highlights Flawed Structure of UN Security Council," *Jurist*, July 10, 2020, https://www.jurist. org/commentary/2020/07/alina-rizvi-unsc-reform-uighurs/; Reuters Staff, "U.S., Germany Slam China at U.N. Security Council over Xinjiang: Diplomats," *Reuters*, July 2, 2019, https://www.reuters.com/article/us-china-usa-rights/us-germany-slam-china-at-un-security-council-over-xinjiang-diplomats-idUSKCN1TX2YZ; Ethan Lederer, "Diplomats: UN Fails to Approve Call to End Tigray Violence," *Associated Press*, March 6, 2021, https://apnews.com/article/russia-violence-india-humanitarian-assistance-ethiopia-f93a9a6bc7c0845a37cf7e3e3757e1e7.

106. Associated Press, "UN Security Council Rejects China-Backed Russian Humanitarian Resolution on Ukraine," *South China Morning Post*, March 24, 2022, https://www.scmp.com/news/china/diplomacy/article/3171653/un-security-coun cil-rejects-china-backed-russian-humanitarian; Edith M. Lederer and Jennifer Peltz, "UN Council Defeats Russia Humanitarian Resolution on Ukraine," *U.S. News and World Report*, March 23, 2022, https://www.usnews.com/news/us/articles/ 2022-03-23/un-taking-up-3-resolutions-on-ukraine-humanitarian-crisis; United Nations Security Council, 9002nd mtg., UN Doc. S/PV.9002 (March 23, 2022), available from https://undocs.org/en/S/PV.9002.

107. Linda Thomas-Greenfield, "Remarks by Ambassador Linda Thomas-Greenfield at a UN Security Council Briefing on the DPRK's Ballistic Missile Launches" (remarks, New York, October 5, 2022), United States Mission to the United Nations, https:// usun.usmission.gov/remarks-by-ambassador-linda-thomas-greenfield-at-a-un-security-council-briefing-on-the-dprks-ballistic-missile-launches/.

108. Margaret McCuaig-Johnston, *Enhancing Taiwan's Role in International Organizations* (Ottawa: Canadian Global Affairs Institute, 2021), https://www.cgai. ca/enhancing_taiwans_role_in_international_organizations; Tung Cheng-Chia and Alan H. Yang, "How China Is Remaking the UN in Its Own Image," *Diplomat*, April 9, 2020, https://thediplomat.com/2020/04/how-china-is-remaking-the-un-in-its-own-image/; Kristine Lee, "It's Not Just the WHO: How China Is Moving on the Whole U.N.," *Politico*, April 15, 2020, https://www.politico.com/news/magaz ine/2020/04/15/its-not-just-the-who-how-china-is-moving-on-the-whole-un-189 029; Hyde, "China's Emerging Financial Influence at the UN Poses a Challenge to the U.S."

109. Phelim Kine, "China Launches New Bid for Internet Dominance," *Politico*, July 21, 2022, https://www.politico.com/newsletters/politico-china-watcher/2022/07/21/ china-launches-new-bid-for-internet-dominance-00047037.

110. Ted Piccone, *China's Long Game on Human Rights at the United Nations* (Washington, DC: Brookings Institution, 2018), https://www.brookings.edu/wp-content/uploads/2018/09/FP_20181009_china_human_rights.pdf.

111. Matthew Impelli, "China Votes with Russia at U.N. after Kremlin Issues Threat," *Newsweek*, April 7, 2022, https://www.newsweek.com/china-votes-russia-un-human-rights-couincl-1696080; Sam Boone, "China's Influence on Interpol—Progress and

Pushback," *China Studies Review* 5, no. 1 (2019), https://saiscsr.org/2019/10/30/csr-2019-chinas-influence-on-interpol-progress-and-pushback/; "View Red Notices," Red Notices, Interpol, https://www.interpol.int/en/How-we-work/Notices/Red-Noti ces/View-Red-Notices.

112. Courtney J. Fung and Shing-hon Lam, "Mixed Report Card: China's Influence at the United Nations," Analyses, Lowy Institute, December 18, 2022, https:// www.lowyinstitute.org/publications/mixed-report-card-china-s-influence-uni ted-nations#heading-7008; Yuan Yang and Henry Foy, "'Under Tremendous Pressure': The Battle behind the UN Report on China's Xinjiang Abuses," *Financial Times*, September 13, 2022, https://www.ft.com/content/0d69e178-8f56-4153-84b2-7ca2d4fa80a4?desktop=true&segmentId=7c8f09b9-9b61-4fbb-9430-9208a 9e233c8#myft:notification:daily-email:content.

113. Blackwill and Tellis, *Revising US Grand Strategy*, 16.

114. China Power Team, "What Are the Key Strengths of the China-Russia Relationship?," China Power, Center for Strategic and International Studies, last modified August 23, 2022, https://chinapower.csis.org/china-russia-relations hip-strengths-benefit/; Presidential Executive Office of the Russian Federation, President of Russia, "Joint Statement of the Russian Federation and the People's Republic of China on the International Relations Entering a New Era and the Global Sustainable Development," February 4, 2022, http://en.kremlin.ru/supplem ent/5770.

115. Lingling Wei and Marcus Walker, "Xi Jinping Doubles Down on His Putin Bet. 'I Have a Similar Personality to Yours,'" *Wall Street Journal*, December 14, 2022, https:// www.wsj.com/articles/xi-jinping-putin-china-russia-relations-11671030896.

116. People's Republic of China Ministry of Foreign Affairs, "Xi Jinping Holds Talks with Russian President Vladimir Putin," October 18, 2023, https://www.fmprc.gov.cn/ mfa_eng/zxxx_662805/202310/t20231018_11163382.html.

117. Authors' conversation with Shivshankar Menon.

118. Graham Allison, "China and Russia: A Strategic Alliance in the Making," *National Interest*, December 14, 2018, https://nationalinterest.org/feature/china-and-russia-strategic-alliance-making-38727.

119. "China's Position on Russia's Invasion of Ukraine," Research, U.S.-China Economic and Security Review Commission, last modified August 17, 2022, https://www.uscc. gov/research/chinas-position-russias-invasion-ukraine.

120. Xiao Zibang, "Russia Overtakes Saudi Arabia as China's Top Oil Supplier," *Bloomberg*, June 20, 2022, https://www.bloomberg.com/news/articles/2022-06-20/ china-buys-7-5-billion-of-russian-energy-with-oil-at-record.

121. US Library of Congress, Congressional Research Service, *China's Economic and Trade Ties with Russia*, by Karen M. Sutter and Michael D. Sutherland, IF12120, 2022, 1, https://crsreports.congress.gov/product/pdf/IF/IF12120.; Mrugank Bhusari and Maia Nikoladze, "Russia and China: Partners in Dedollarization," Atlantic Council, February 18, 2022, https://www.atlanticcouncil.org/blogs/econographics/russia-and-china-partners-in-dedollarization/.

122. U.S.-China Economic and Security Review Commission, *China-Russia Military-to-Military Relations: Moving toward a Higher Level of Cooperation*, by Ethan Meick, March 20, 2017, https://www.uscc.gov/research/china-russia-military-military-relations-moving-toward-higher-level-cooperation; Richard Weitz, *Assessing Chinese-Russian Military Exercises: Past Progress and Future Trends* (Washington, DC: Center for Strategic and International Studies, 2021), https://www.csis.org/analysis/assessing-chinese-russian-military-exercises-past-progress-and-future-trends; Guo Yuandan and Liu Xuanzun, "For 1st Time China Sends Ground, Naval, Air Forces to Join Russian Vostok Drills," *Global Times*, August 25, 2022, https://www.globaltimes.cn/page/202208/1273883.shtml.

123. U.S.-China Economic and Security Review Commission, *China-Russia Military-to-Military Relations*.

124. Thomas Newdick, "Russian, Chinese Bombers Land at Each Other's Airfields after Joint Patrols," *War Zone*, November 30, 2022, https://www.thedrive.com/the-war-zone/russian-chinese-bombers-land-at-each-others-airfields-after-joint-patrols.

125. Ann M. Simmons, "Russia, China to Hold Joint Naval Drills as Moscow and Belarus Vow to Cement Ties," *Wall Street Journal*, December 19, 2022, https://www.wsj.com/articles/russia-and-china-to-hold-joint-naval-drills-11671457894?mod=itp_wsj&mod=djemITP_h.

126. Darlene Superville, "China, Russia, Iran Hold Joint Naval Drills in Gulf Of Oman," *Associated Press*, March 15, 2023, https://apnews.com/article/china-russia-iran-naval-drills-oman-gulf-9f515b3246e4cbe0d98a35e8399dc177.

127. Richard Weitz, "Assessing Chinese-Russian Military Exercises: Past Progress and Future Trends," Center for Strategic & International Studies, July 9, 2021, https://www.csis.org/analysis/assessing-chinese-russian-military-exercises-past-progress-and-future-trends; Graham Allison, "China and Russia: A Strategic Alliance in the Making," *National Interest*, December 14, 2018, https://nationalinterest.org/feature/china-and-russia-strategic-alliance-making-38727.

128. US Library of Congress, Congressional Research Service, *Russian Arms Sales and Defense Industry*, by Andrew S. Bowen, R46937, 2021, https://crsreports.congress.gov/product/pdf/R/R46937; Al Jazzera Staff, "Infographic: Which Countries Buy the Most Russian Weapons?," *Al Jazeera*, March 9, 2022, https://www.aljazeera.com/news/2022/3/9/infographic-which-countries-buy-the-most-russian-weapons; Franz-Stefan Gady, "US Sanctions China over Purchase of S-400 Air Defense Systems, Su-35 Fighter Jets from Russia," *Diplomat*, September 21, 2018, https://thediplomat.com/2018/09/us-sanctions-china-over-purchase-of-s-400-air-defense-system-su-35-fighter-jets-from-russia/.

129. Dmitry Stefanovich, "Russia to Help China Develop an Early Warning System," *Diplomat*, October 25, 2019, https://thediplomat.com/2019/10/russia-to-help-china-develop-an-early-warning-system/.

130. Keith Bradsher, "In Global Slowdown, China Holds Sway over Countries' Fates," *New York Times*, October 6, 2022, https://www.nytimes.com/2022/10/06/business/china-debt-economy-global-slowdown.html.

131. Brahma Chellaney, "Kenya Revelations Shine a Light on China's Predatory Lending Practices," *Strategist*, November 24, 2022, https://www.aspistrategist.org.au/kenya-revelations-shine-a-light-on-chinas-predatory-lending-practices/;    Kai    Wang, "China: Is It Burdening Poor Countries with Unsustainable Debt," *BBC*, January 6, 2022, https://www.bbc.com/news/59585507; Lu Xu, "China, World's Biggest Creditor, Delays Debt Repayments for 77 Nations," *Voice of America*, June 10, 2020, https://www.voanews.com/a/east-asia-pacific_voa-news-china_china-worlds-biggest-creditor-delays-debt-repayments-77-nations/6190886.html.

132. Michael Robbins, "Public Views of the U.S.-China Competition in MENA," *Arab Barometer*, July 2022, https://www.arabbarometer.org/wp-content/uploads/ABVII_US-China_Report-EN-1.pdf; Ilan Berman, "In the War for Global Opinion, China Is Winning | Opinion," *Newsweek,* September 20, 2022, https://www.newsweek.com/war-global-opinion-china-winning-opinion-1744007.

133. Berman, "In the War for Global Opinion."

134. Charles W. Dunne, "China's Belt and Road Initiative and US Middle East Policy," Arab Center Washington DC, January 31, 2021, https://arabcenterdc.org/resource/chinas-belt-and-road-initiative-and-us-middle-east-policy/.

135. "Trade Route Revival," *China Business Law Journal*, August 9, 2022, https://law.asia/china-ambitious-investment-strategies/; Christoph Nedopil, *China Belt and Road Initiative (BRI) Investment Report* (Shanghai: FISF Fudan University, 2022) https://greenfdc.org/wp-content/uploads/2022/02/Nedopil-2022_BRI-Investment-Report-2021.pdf.

136. Ali Noureddine, "China's Silent Expansion in the Middle East and North Africa," *Fanack*, October 3, 2022, https://fanack.com/politics-en/chinas-silent-expansion-in-the-middle-east-and-north-africa~241378/; Nedopil, *China Belt and Road Initiative (BRI) Investment Report*.

137. Nadeem Ahmed Moonakal, "The Impact and Implications of China's Growing Influence in the Middle East," *Diplomat*, July 9, 2022, https://thediplomat.com/2022/07/the-impact-and-implications-of-chinas-growing-influence-in-the-middle-east/.

138. Ibid.

139. 习近平 [Xi Jinping], "习近平在网信工作座谈会上的讲话全文发表" [The Full Text of Xi Jinping's Speech at the Forum on Cybersecurity and Informatization Work]; Dale Aluf, "China's Tech Outreach in the Middle East and North Africa," *Diplomat*, November 17, 2022, https://thediplomat.com/2022/11/chinas-tech-outreach-in-the-middle-east-and-north-africa/.

140. Camille Lons, et al., "China's Great Game in the Middle East," European Council on Foreign Relations, October 21, 2019, https://ecfr.eu/publication/china_great_game_middle_east/; "Saudi Arabia—China Bilateral Trade," Observatory of Economic Complexity, https://oec.world/en/profile/bilateral-country/sau/partner/chn.

141. Andrea Ratiu, "Full Throttle in Neutral: China's New Security Architecture for the Middle East," Atlantic Council, February 17, 2023, https://www.atlanticcouncil.org/in-depth-research-reports/issue-brief/full-throttle-in-neutral-chinas-new-

security-architecture-for-the-middle-east/; "Saudi Arabia—China Bilateral Trade," Observatory of Economic Complexity, https://oec.world/en/profile/bilateral-country/sau/partner/chn.

142. Una Galani, "Middle East Pivot to Asia Is Strategic This Time," *Reuters*, March 13, 2023, https://www.reuters.com/breakingviews/middle-east-pivot-asia-is-strategic-this-time-2023-03-14/.

143. Kawala Xie, "Is US-Saudi Row Giving China a Chance to Expand Its Role in the Middle East?," *South China Morning Post*, October 30, 2022, https://www.scmp.com/news/china/diplomacy/article/3197706/us-saudi-row-giving-china-cha nce-expand-its-role-middle-east.; Summer Said and Stephen Kalin, "Saudi Arabia Considers Accepting Yuan Instead of Dollars for Chinese Oil Sales," *Wall Street Journal*, March 15, 2022, https://www.wsj.com/articles/saudi-arabia-considers-ac-cepting-yuan-instead-of-dollars-for-chinese-oil-sales-11647351541.

144. Fares Braziat, "The Middle East between US and China," *Jordan News*, October 30, 2022, https://www.jordannews.jo/Section-36/Opinion/The-Middle-East-betw een-US-and-China-23866.

145. Ricky Ben-David, "Israel Inaugurates Chinese-Run Haifa Port Terminal, in Likely Boost for Economy," *Times of Israel*, September 2, 2021, https://www.timesofisr ael.com/israel-inaugurates-new-haifa-port-terminal-in-expected-boost-for-economy/.

146. John Hudson, Ellen Nakashima, and Liz Sly, "Buildup Resumed at Suspected Chinese Military Site in UAE, Leak Says," *Washington Post*, April 27, 2023, https://www.was hingtonpost.com/national-security/2023/04/26/chinese-military-base-uae/.

147. Jack Lau, "China, UAE Set for Joint Air Force Training in Military First, as Beijing Forges Closer Middle East Ties," *South China Morning Post*, July 31, 2023, https://www.scmp.com/news/china/military/article/3229485/china-uae-set-joint-air-force-training-military-first-beijing-forges-closer-middle-east-ties#.

148. Ratiu, "Full Throttle in Neutral."

149. Farnaz Fassihi and Steven Lee Myers, "Defying U.S., China and Iran Near Trade and Military Partnership," *New York Times*, September 24, 2021, https://www.nytimes.com/2020/07/11/world/asia/china-iran-trade-military-deal.html.

150. Reuters, "Iran, China and Russia Hold Naval Drills in North Indian Ocean," *CNN*, January 21, 2022, https://www.cnn.com/2022/01/21/world/iran-china-russia-naval-drills-intl/index.html.

151. Seima Oki, "China Increasing Arms Exports to Middle East and Eastern Europe," *Asia News Network*, May 5, 2022, https://asianews.network/china-increasing-arms-exports-to-middle-east-and-eastern-europe/.

152. Ratiu, "Full Throttle in Neutral."

153. Ibid.

154. Vivian Nereim, "China to Cooperate with Gulf Nations on Nuclear Energy and Space, Xi Says," *New York Times*, December 9, 2022, https://www.nytimes.com/2022/12/09/world/middleeast/china-saudi-arabia-gulf-summit.html.

155. Ben Bartenstein and Sylvia Westall, "Saudis Roll Out Red Carpet for Xi Jinping as Gulf Looks Past US," *Bloomberg*, December 7, 2022, https://news.yahoo.com/

xi-expected-riyadh-middle-east-120311036.html; Global Times, "Xi's Attendance of First China-Arab States Summit to Become Milestone for China-Arab Relations: Chinese FM," *Global Times*, December 7, 2022, https://www.globaltimes.cn/page/202212/1281350.shtml.

156. People's Republic of China Ministry of Foreign Affairs, Press and Media Service, Mao Ning, "Foreign Ministry Spokesperson Mao Ning's Regular Press Conference on December 7, 2022," (press conference, December 7, 2022), People's Republic of China Ministry of Foreign Affairs, https://www.fmprc.gov.cn/mfa_eng/xwfw_665399/s2510_665401/202212/t20221207_10986586.html.

157. James T. Areddy and Charles Hutzler, "China's Model of a New Diplomacy Scores a Win with Iran-Saudi Deal," *Wall Street Journal*, last modified March 10, 2023, https://www.wsj.com/articles/iran-saudi-deal-scores-a-win-for-chinas-model-of-a-new-diplomacy-bacba072.

158. Didi Tang, "Israel-Hamas War Upends China's Ambitions in the Middle East But May Serve Beijing in the End," *Associated Press*, October 15, 2023, https://apnews.com/article/china-israel-hamas-mideast-war-arab-countries-33d78c0ad6f7cb116d87417ff81ed727.

159. Zhao Ziwen, "Chinese Foreign Minister Wang Yi Backs Efforts to Give Palestinians Their 'Legitimate National Rights' in Call with Egyptian Counterpart," *South China Morning Post*, October 17, 2023, https://www.scmp.com/news/china/diplomacy/article/3238262/chinese-foreign-minister-wang-yi-backs-efforts-give-palestinians-their-legitimate-national-rights.

160. Permanent Mission of the People's Republic of China to the UN, "Explanation of Vote by Ambassador Zhang Jun on the UN Security Council Draft Resolution Regarding the Palestinian-Israeli Situation," October 25, 2023, http://un.china-mission.gov.cn/eng/hyyfy/202310/t20231026_11168489.htm.

161. People's Republic of China Ministry of Foreign Affairs, "Wang Yi Holds Talks with the Delegation of Arab-Islamic Foreign Ministers," November 20, 2023, https://www.fmprc.gov.cn/eng/wjb_663304/wjbz_663308/activities_663312/202311/t20231120_11183697.html.

162. Michael M. Phillips, "China Seeks First Military Base on Africa's Atlantic Coast, U.S. Intelligence Finds," *Wall Street Journal*, December 5, 2021, https://www.wsj.com/articles/china-seeks-first-military-base-on-africas-atlantic-coast-u-s-intelligence-finds-11638726327.

163. Jevans Nyabiage, "As African Countries Pivot, China Seizes Chance to Become a Major Military Player," *South China Morning Post*, September 20, 2022, https://www.scmp.com/news/china/diplomacy/article/3193036/african-countries-pivot-china-seizes-chance-become-major; Jevans Nyabiage, "China Boosts Tariff-Free Access for African Countries," *South China Morning Post*, September 5, 2022, https://www.scmp.com/news/china/diplomacy/article/3191298/china-boosts-tariff-free-access-african-countries?module=inline&pgtype=article.

164. Jevans Nyabiage, "China's Growing Influence in Africa Extends to Arms Sales, Report Says," *South China Morning Post*, https://www.scmp.com/news/china/diplomacy/article/3206160/chinas-growing-influence-africa-extends-arms-sales-report-says.

165. Jevans Nyabiage, "China Arms Sales Cement Its Economic and Security Ties in Africa: Study," *South China Morning Post*, March 14, 2023, https://www.scmp.com/news/china/diplomacy/article/3213458/china-arms-sales-cement-its-economic-and-security-ties-africa-study; Amin Mohseni-Cheraghlou and Naomi Aladekoba, *China in Sub-Saharan Africa: Reaching Far beyond Natural Resources* (Washington, DC: Atlantic Council, March 2023), Issue Brief, Geoeconomics Center, https://www.atlanticcouncil.org/wp-content/uploads/2023/03/China-in-Sub-Saharan-Africa-Reaching-far-beyond-natural-resources.pdf.

166. Thomas P. Sheehy, "10 Things to Know about the U.S.-China Rivalry in Africa," United States Institute of Peace, December 12, 2022, https://www.usip.org/publications/2022/12/10-things-know-about-us-china-rivalry-africa; Antony Sguazzin, "China to Focus on Trade to Deepen Africa Ties, EIU Says," *Bloomberg*, August 3, 2022, https://www.bloomberg.com/news/articles/2022-08-03/china-to-deepen-africa-ties-over-next-decade-with-focus-on-trade?sref=RGkt8hNg.

167. Jack Lau, "China Welcomes Dozens of African States to Security Conference as It Seeks Greater Role in Continent," *South China Morning Post*, August 29, 2023, https://www.scmp.com/news/china/diplomacy/article/3232607/china-welcomes-dozens-african-states-security-conference-it-seeks-greater-role-continent.

168. Jevans Nyabiage, "China 'Winning Lion's Share' of Construction Projects in Africa, Study Finds," *South China Morning Post*, August 13, 2023, https://www.scmp.com/news/china/diplomacy/article/3230790/china-winning-lions-share-construction-projects-africa-study-finds.

169. Ibid.

170. Sheehy, "10 Things to Know"; Sguazzin, "China to Focus on Trade to Deepen Africa Ties, EIU Says."

171. Eleanor Albert, "China in Africa," Backgrounder, Council on Foreign Relations, last modified July 12, 2017, https://www.cfr.org/backgrounder/china-africa.

172. Six African countries (Algeria, Djibouti, Gambia, Mauritania, Niger, and Somalia) supported China's actions in Hong Kong, but did not defend China's human rights abuses in Xinjiang. Catherine Putz, "2020 Edition: Which Countries Are for or against China's Xinjiang Policies?," *Diplomat*, October 9, 2020, https://thediplomat.com/2020/10/2020-edition-which-countries-are-for-or-against-chinas-xinjiang-policies/; Shannon Tiezzi, "Which Countries Support China on Hong Kong's National Security Law?," *Diplomat*, October 9, 2020, https://thediplomat.com/2020/10/which-countries-support-china-on-hong-kongs-national-security-law/.

173. Ana Monteiro and Tom Hancock, "China to Waive Some Africa Loans, Offer $10 Billion in IMF Funds," *Bloomberg*, August 23, 2022, https://www.bloomberg.com/news/articles/2022-08-23/china-to-waive-some-africa-loans-offer-10-billion-in-imf-funds.

174. United Nations Office of the High Commissioner for Human Rights, "Human Rights Council Adopts 21 Texts and Rejects One Draft Decision, Extends Mandates on Older Persons, Right to Development, Arbitrary Detention, Mercenaries, Slavery, Indigenous Peoples, Safe Drinking Water and Sanitation," news release, October 6,

2022, https://www.ohchr.org/en/news/2022/10/human-rights-council-adopts-21-texts-and-rejects-one-draft-decision-extends-mandates.

175. Abraham White and Leo Holtz, "Figure of the Week: African Countries' Votes on the UN Resolution Condemning Russia's Invasion of Ukraine," Brookings Institution, March 9, 2022, https://www.brookings.edu/blog/africa-in-focus/2022/03/09/fig ure-of-the-week-african-countries-votes-on-the-un-resolution-condemning-russ ias-invasion-of-ukraine/.

176. General Assembly Resolution ES-11/6, *Principles of the Charter of the United Nations Underlying a Comprehensive, Just and Lasting Peace in Ukraine: Resolution / Adopted by the General Assembly*, A/RES/ES-11/2 (February 23, 2023), available from https:// digitallibrary.un.org/record/4003921?ln=en.

177. Bethany Allen-Ebrahimian, "In Tanzania, Beijing Is Running a Training School for Authoritarianism," *Axios*, August 21, 2023, https://www.axios.com/2023/08/21/ chinese-communist-party-training-school-africa.

178. Todd Wasmund, "Advisors in Africa Provide Commanders Access to Partners" (speech, Washington, DC, October 10, 2022), US Army, https://www.army.mil/arti cle/261288/advisors_in_africa_provide_commanders_access_to_partners; Jevans Nyabiage, "It May Not Say So, but US Sees Africa as a Growing Military Competition with China and Russia," *South China Morning Post*, October 15, 2022, https://www. scmp.com/news/china/diplomacy/article/3196070/it-may-not-say-so-us-sees-afr ica-growing-military-competition.

179. Zhang Hongming, "China's Presence in Africa Is at Heart Political," interviewed by Thierry Pairault, *Diplomat*, August 11, 2021, https://thediplomat.com/2021/08/chi nas-presence-in-africa-is-at-heart-political/.

180. Diana Roy, "China's Growing Influence in Latin America," Backgrounder, Council on Foreign Relations, last modified April 12, 2022, https://www.cfr.org/backgroun der/china-influence-latin-america-argentina-brazil-venezuela-security-energy-bri; Michael Stott, "US Reluctance on Trade Deals Sends Latin America Towards China," *Financial Times*, May 23, 2023, https://www.ft.com/content/19ff62c3-5c75-4ba7-8f73-75a7a902aa90.

181. Ibid; Lucy Stevenson-Yang and Henry Tugendhat, "China's Engagement in Latin America: Views from the Region," United States Institute for Peace, August 8, 2022, https://www.usip.org/publications/2022/08/chinas-engagement-latin-america-views-region; Roy, "China's Growing Influence."

182. Julio Armando Guzmán, "China's Latin American Power Play," *Foreign Affairs*, January 16, 2023, https://www.foreignaffairs.com/central-america-caribbean/chi nas-latin-american-power-play.

183. Ibid; Fermín Koop, "Uruguay-China FTA negotiations raise tensions over Mercosur's future," *Dialogo Chino*, July 28, 2022, https://dialogochino.net/en/trade-investment/56817-uruguay-china-fta-negotiations-tensions-over-mercosur-future/ ; Rich Brown, "The Quiet Official behind China's Policy in Latin America," *Americas Quarterly*, August 28, 2023, https://www.americasquarterly.org/article/the-quiet-official-behind-chinas-policy-in-latin-america/.

184. Roy, "China's Growing Influence"; Guzmán, "China's Latin American Power Play"; Stott, "US Reluctance on Trade."

185. Milton Ezrati, "China's Latin America Move," *Forbes*, November 7, 2022, https://www.forbes.com/sites/miltonezrati/2022/11/07/chinas-latin-america-move/?sh=5d364ce21d52.

186. Laura Richardson, "Looking South: A Conversation with GEN Laura Richardson on Security Challenges in Latin America" (remarks, Washington, DC, August 4, 2023) Center for Strategic and International Studies, https://www.csis.org/analysis/looking-south-conversation-gen-laura-richardson-security-challenges-latin-america.

187. Ismael Lopez, "Central America Parliament Expels Taiwan, Makes China Permanent Observer," *Reuters*, August 22, 2023, https://www.reuters.com/world/americas/central-america-parliament-expels-taiwan-makes-china-permanent-observer-2023-08-22/.

188. Roy, "China's Growing Influence."

189. Karoun Demirjian and Edward Wong, "China Has Had a Spy Base in Cuba for Years, U.S. Official Says," *New York Times*, June 10, 2023, https://www.nytimes.com/2023/06/10/us/politics/china-spy-base-cuba.html; Warren P. Strobel et al., "Beijing Plans a New Training Facility in Cuba, Raising Prospect of Chinese Troops on America's Doorstep," *Wall Street Journal*, June 20, 2023, https://www.wsj.com/articles/beijing-plans-a-new-training-facility-in-cuba-raising-prospect-of-chinese-troops-on-americas-doorstep-e17fd5d1.

190. Charles Couger, "US Military Leaders Warn China Could Militarize the Ports It Owns in Latin America," *Fox News*, September 22, 2022, https://www.foxnews.com/world/us-military-leaders-warn-china-could-militarize-ports-it-owns-latin-america; Andrew Miller, "Military Leaders Warn China Could Weaponize Ports in Latin America," *Trumpet*, October 3, 2022, https://www.thetrumpet.com/26176-military-leaders-warn-china-could-weaponize-ports-in-latin-america.

191. Demirjian and Wong, "China Has Had a Spy Base"; Strobel, Lubold, Salama, and Gordon, "Beijing Plans a New Training Facility"; Roy, "China's Growing Influence"; Bethany Allen-Ebrahimian and Miriam Kramer, "China's Space Footprint in South America Fuels Security Concerns," *Axios*, October 4, 2022, https://www.axios.com/2022/10/04/chinas-space-footprint-south-america-security-concerns.

192. Cate Cadell and Marcelo Perez del Carpio, "A Growing Global Footprint for China's Space Program Worries Pentagon," *Washington Post*, November 21, 2023, https://www.washingtonpost.com/world/interactive/2023/china-space-program-south-america-defense/.

193. Margaret Besheer, "At UN: 39 Countries Condemn China's Abuses of Uighurs," *Voice of America*, October 6, 2020, https://www.voanews.com/a/east-asia-pacific_voanews-china_un-39-countries-condemn-chinas-abuses-uighurs/6196815.html.

194. Antigua and Barbuda supported China's actions in Hong Kong, but did not defend China's human rights abuses in Xinjiang. Putz, "2020 Edition: Which Countries Are for or against China's Xinjiang Policies?"; Shannon Tiezzi, "Which Countries Support China on Hong Kong's National Security Law?," *Diplomat*, October 9,

2020, https://thediplomat.com/2020/10/which-countries-support-china-on-hong-kongs-national-security-law/.

195. Office of the High Commissioner for Human Rights, "Human Rights Council Adopts 21 Texts and Rejects One Draft Decision."

196. General Assembly resolution ES-11/2, *Humanitarian Consequences of the Aggression against Ukraine*, A/RES/ES-11/2 (March 24, 2022), available from undocs.org/en/A/RES/ES-11/2.

197. People's Republic of China Ministry of Foreign Affairs, "China's Position on the Political Settlement of the Ukraine Crisis," February 24, 2023, https://www.fmprc.gov.cn/mfa_eng/zxxx_662805/202302/t20230224_11030713.html.

198. Tom O'Connor, "Xi Jinping Is Outplaying Biden in Europe's Ukraine Diplomacy," *Newsweek*, May 2, 2023, https://www.newsweek.com/xi-jinping-outplaying-biden-europes-ukraine-diplomacy-1797465.

199. "The World According to Xi," *Economist*, March 23, 2023, https://www.economist.com/leaders/2023/03/23/the-world-according-to-xi.

200. The Commission on the Theft of American Intellectual Property, *Update to the IP Commission Report* (Seattle: The National Bureau of Asian Research, 2017), https://www.nbr.org/wp-content/uploads/pdfs/publications/IP_Commission_Report_Update.pdf; Megan Gates, "An Unfair Advantage: Confronting Organized Intellectual Property Theft," *Security Management*, July 1, 2020, https://www.asisonline.org/security-management-magazine/articles/2020/07/an-unfair-advantage-confronting-organized-intellectual-property-theft/.

201. Nicole Sganga, "Chinese Hackers Took Trillions in Intellectual Property from about 30 Multinational Companies," *CBS*, May 4, 2022, https://www.cbsnews.com/news/chinese-hackers-took-trillions-in-intellectual-property-from-about-30-multinational-companies/.

202. Eric Rosenbaum, "1 in 5 Corporations Say China Has Stolen Their IP within the Last Year: CNBC CFO Survey," *CNBC*, March 1, 2019, https://www.cnbc.com/2019/02/28/1-in-5-companies-say-china-stole-their-ip-within-the-last-year-cnbc.html.

203. Agence France-Presse, "FBI Has 1,000 Investigations into Chinese Intellectual Property Theft, Director Christopher Wray Says, Calling China the Most Severe Counter-Intelligence Threat to US," *South China Morning Post*, July 24, 2019, https://www.scmp.com/news/china/article/3019829/fbi-has-1000-probes-chinese-intellectual-property-theft-director.

204. Yudhijit Bhattacharjee, "The Daring Ruse That Exposed China's Campaign to Steal American Secrets," *New York Times*, March 7, 2023, https://www.nytimes.com/2023/03/07/magazine/china-spying-intellectual-property.html.

205. Derek Scissors, "The Rising Risk of China's Intellectual-Property Theft," American Enterprise Institute, July 16, 2021, https://www.aei.org/articles/the-rising-risk-of-chinas-intellectual-property-theft/; Editorial Board, "America Is Struggling to Counter China's Intellectual Property Theft," *Financial Times*, April 18, 2022, https://www.ft.com/content/1d13ab71-bffd-4d63-a0bf-9e9bdfc33c39.

206. U.S.-China Economic and Security Review Commission, *How Chinese Companies Facilitate Technology Transfer from the United States*, by Sean O'Connor, May 6, 2019,

https://www.uscc.gov/research/how-chinese-companies-facilitate-technology-transfer-united-states.

207. Ellen Barry and Gina Kolata, "China's Lavish Funds Lured U.S. Scientists. What Did It Get in Return?," *New York Times*, February 7, 2020, https://www.nytimes.com/2020/02/06/us/chinas-lavish-funds-lured-us-scientists-what-did-it-get-in-return.html; "The China Threat," What We Investigate, Federal Bureau of Investigation, https://www.fbi.gov/investigate/counterintelligence/the-china-threat/chinese-talent-plans.

208. Lingling Wei and Bob Davis, "How China Systematically Pries Technology from U.S. Companies," *Wall Street Journal*, September 26, 2018, https://www.wsj.com/articles/how-china-systematically-pries-technology-from-u-s-companies-1537972066.

209. Keith Bradsher, "How China Obtains American Trade Secrets," *New York Times*, January 15, 2020, https://www.nytimes.com/2020/01/15/business/china-technology-transfer.html.

210. Scissors, "The Rising Risk of China's Intellectual-Property Theft."

211. Chun Han Wong and Dan Strumpf, "China Spy Law Adds to Chilling Effect of Detentions," *Wall Street Journal*, April 27, 2023, https://www.wsj.com/articles/chinas-expanded-spy-law-adds-to-chilling-effect-of-detentions-ce8cea1a?mod=article_inline.

212. Kate O'Keefe, "New Chinese Law Raises Risks for American Firms in China, U.S. Officials Say," *Wall Street Journal*, June 30, 2023, https://www.wsj.com/articles/new-chinese-law-raises-risks-for-american-firms-in-china-u-s-officials-say-cf62c1a0.

213. Ellen Nakashima, "Chinese Breach Data of 4 Million Federal Workers," *Washington Post*, June 4, 2015, https://www.washingtonpost.com/world/national-security/chinese-hackers-breach-federal-governments-personnel-office/2015/06/04/889c0e52-0af7-11e5-95fd-d580f1c5d44e_story.html; "Chinese Military Hackers Charged in Equifax Breach," News, Federal Bureau of Investigation, February 10, 2020, https://www.fbi.gov/news/stories/chinese-hackers-charged-in-equifax-breach-021020.

214. Ellen Nakashima and Aaron Schaffer, "Chinese Hackers Compromise Dozens of Government Agencies, Defense Contractors," *Washington Post*, April 21, 2021, https://www.washingtonpost.com/national-security/chinese-hackers-compromise-defense-contractors-agencies/2021/04/20/10772f9e-a207-11eb-a7ee-949c574a09ac_story.html; GuidePoint Security, "Chinese Hackers Targeting Critical US Infrastructure and Businesses," *GuidePoint Security*, July 27, 2021, https://www.guidepointsecurity.com/blog/chinese-hackers-targeting-critical-us-infrastructure-and-businesses/.

215. US Department of Justice, Office of Public Affairs, "U.S. Charges Five Chinese Military Hackers for Cyber Espionage against U.S. Corporations and a Labor Organization for Commercial Advantage," press release, May 19, 2014, https://www.justice.gov/opa/pr/us-charges-five-chinese-military-hackers-cyber-espionage-against-us-corporations-and-labor; Department of Homeland Security, Cybersecurity and Infrastructure Security Agency, "People's Republic of China State-Sponsored Cyber Actors Exploit Network Providers and Devices," last modified June 10, 2022, https://www.cisa.gov/uscert/ncas/alerts/aa22-158a.

216. Kate Conger and Sheera Frenkel, "Thousands of Microsoft Customers May Have Been Victims of Hack Tied to China," *New York Times*, March 6, 2021, https://www.nytimes.com/2021/03/06/technology/microsoft-hack-china.html; Callum Hoare,

"Google Disclosed 'Cyber Attack' by China in 2009 was 'Highly Sophisticated' Hack on Data," *Express*, December 16, 2020, https://www.express.co.uk/news/world/1373272/google-gmail-youtube-down-hack-cyber-attack-china-operation-aurora-security-breach-spt; Jose Pagliery, "China Hacked the FDIC—and US Officials Covered It Up, Report Says," *CNN*, July 13, 2016, https://money.cnn.com/2016/07/13/technology/china-fdic-hack/; Roslyn Layton, "Hackers Are Targeting U.S. Banks, and Hardware May Give Them an Open Door," *Forbes*, March 17, 2021, https://www.forbes.com/sites/roslynlayton/2021/03/17/hackers-are-targeting-us-banks-and-hardware-may-give-them-an-open-door/?sh=4a06ff7914dc.

217. Arik Hesseldahl, "Chinese Hackers Stole Info on 4.5 Million U.S. Hospital Patients," *CNBC*, August 18, 2014, https://www.cnbc.com/2014/08/18/chinese-hackers-stole-info-on-45-million-us-hospital-patients.html; Joseph Marks and Aaron Schaffer, "Chinese Hackers Breached Six State Governments, Researchers Say," *Washington Post*, March 8, 2022, https://www.washingtonpost.com/politics/2022/03/08/chinese-hackers-breached-six-state-governments-researchers-say/.

218. Nicole Sganga, "Chinese Hackers Took Trillions in Intellectual Property from about 30 Multinational Companies," *CBS*, May 4, 2022, https://www.cbsnews.com/news/chinese-hackers-took-trillions-in-intellectual-property-from-about-30-multinational-companies/.

219. U.S.-China Economic Security Review Commission, *2022 Annual Report to Congress*, 14.

220. Julian E. Barnes, "Hacking of Government Email Was Traditional Espionage, Official Says," *New York Times*, July 20, 2023, https://www.nytimes.com/2023/07/11/us/politics/china-hack-us-government-microsoft.html; Ellen Nakashima, Joseph Menn, and Shane Harris, "Chinese Hackers Breach Email of Commerce Secretary Raimondo and State Department Officials," *Washington Post*, July 14, 2023, https://www.washingtonpost.com/national-security/2023/07/12/microsoft-hack-china/?utm_source=alert&utm_medium=email&utm_campaign=wp_news_alert_revere&location=alert.

221. David E. Sanger and Julian E. Barnes, "U.S. Hunts Chinese Malware That Could Disrupt American Military Operations," *New York Times*, July 29, 2023, https://www.nytimes.com/2023/07/29/us/politics/china-malware-us-military-bases-taiwan.html.

222. Laura Kelly and Brad Dress, "Why the Discovery of a Chinese Balloon in US Skies Is Such a Big Deal," *Hill*, February 3, 2023, https://thehill.com/policy/defense/3843240-why-the-discovery-of-a-chinese-balloon-in-us-skies-is-such-a-big-deal/.

223. Sophia Ankel, "A Suspected Chinese Spy Balloon Was Seen Operating Near a US Nuclear Base Housing 150 Minuteman ICBMs," *Business Insider*, February 3, 2023, https://www.businessinsider.com/chinese-spy-balloon-us-nuclear-base-minuteman-surveillance-montana-2023-2.

224. Nirmal Ghosh, "White House Must Navigate Anti-China Hysteria, Stabilise Relations with Beijing," *Straits Times*, February 10, 2023, https://www.straitstimes.com/world/united-states/white-house-must-contain-anti-china-hysteria-stabilise-relations-with-beijing.

225. Christopher Wray, "China Stealing Technology Secrets—from AI to Computing and Biology, 'Five Eyes' Intelligence Leaders Warn," interviewed by Scott Pelly, *60 Minutes*, CBS, https://www.cbsnews.com/news/china-stealing-technology-secrets-five-eyes-intelligence-leaders-warn-60-minutes-transcript/.

226. Michael Burgess, "China Stealing Technology Secrets—from AI to Computing and Biology, 'Five Eyes' Intelligence Leaders Warn," interviewed by Scott Pelly, *60 Minutes*, CBS, https://www.cbsnews.com/news/china-stealing-technology-secrets-five-eyes-intelligence-leaders-warn-60-minutes-transcript/.

227. Edward Wong, et al., "Chinese Spy Agency Rising to Challenge the C.I.A.," *New York Times*, December 27, 2023, https://www.nytimes.com/2023/12/27/us/politics/china-cia-spy-mss.html.

228. Ibid.

229. Office of the Director of National Intelligence, *Annual Threat Assessment of the US Intelligence Community*, April 9, 2021, 8, https://www.dni.gov/files/ODNI/documents/assessments/ATA-2021-Unclassified-Report.pdf.

230. Joshua Kurlantzick, "China's Growing Attempts to Influence U.S. Politics," Asia Program, Council on Foreign Relations, October 31, 2022, https://www.cfr.org/article/chinas-growing-attempts-influence-us-politics; Phelim Kine, "China's Ambassador Soars from White House Outcast to CCP Powerbroker," *Politico*, November 3, 2022, https://www.politico.com/newsletters/politico-china-watcher/2022/11/03/chinas-ambassador-soars-from-white-house-outcast-to-ccp-powerbroker-00064791.

231. Muyi Xiao, Paul Mozur, and Gray Beltran, "Buying Influence: How China Manipulates Facebook and Twitter," *New York Times*, December 20, 2021, https://www.nytimes.com/interactive/2021/12/20/technology/china-facebook-twitter-influence-manipulation.html; Steven Lee Myers, "Meta Removes Chinese Effort to Influence U.S. Elections," *New York Times*, September 27, 2022, https://www.nytimes.com/2022/09/27/technology/meta-chinese-influence-us-elections.html; Jon Bateman, "Limiting Chinese Influence Operations," in *U.S.-China Technological "Decoupling": A Strategy and Policy Framework* (Washington, DC: Carnegie Endowment for International Peace Publishing Department, 2022), https://carnegieendowment.org/2022/04/25/limiting-chinese-influence-operations-pub-86923.

232. According to a January 2020 Center for International Policy report, the following think tanks receive Chinese funding: Center for Strategic and International Studies, Inter-American Dialogue, and World Resources Institute. According to a February 2020 study by *Bloomberg*, almost 115 American universities received nearly $1B in Chinese funding between 2013 and 2020. The universities with the highest amount of Chinese funding were Harvard University, University of Southern California, University of Pennsylvania, Stanford University, and New York University. Janet Lorin and Brandon Kochkodin, "Harvard Leads U.S. Colleges That Received $1 Billion from China," *Bloomberg*, February 6, 2020, https://www.bloomberg.com/news/articles/2020-02-06/harvard-leads-u-s-colleges-that-received-1-billion-from-china; Ben Freeman, *Foreign Funding of Think Tanks in America* (Washington, DC: Center for International Policy, 2020), https://static.wixstatic.com/ugd/

3ba8a1_4f06e99f35d4485b801f8dbfe33b6a3f.pdf; Koh Gui Qing and John Shiffman, "Beijing's Covert Radio Network Airs China-Friendly News across Washington, and the World," *Reuters*, November 2, 2015, https://www.reuters.com/investigates/special-report/china-radio/; Lachlan Markay, "DOJ Brands Chinese-Owned U.S. Newspaper a Foreign Agent," *Axios*, August 25, 2021, https://www.axios.com/2021/08/25/doj-chinese-owned-sing-tao-newspaper-foreign-agent; Cathy He, "'Beijing Is Doubling Down': Report Warns China's Media Influence Efforts in US Are 'Very High,'" *Epoch Times,* September 9, 2022, https://www.theepochtimes.com/beijing-is-doubling-down-report-warns-chinas-media-influence-efforts-in-us-are-very-high_4718771.html.

233. Although 104 of the Confucius Institutes closed (as of June 2022), at least 28 have replaced the program with a similar one and at least 58 still maintain close ties with their Confucius Institute partner. Lee Edwards, "Confucius Institutes: China's Trojan Horse," Heritage Foundation, May 27, 2021, https://www.heritage.org/home land-security/commentary/confucius-institutes-chinas-trojan-horse; "How Many Confucius Institutes Are in the United States?," National Association of Scholars, last modified June 21, 2022, https://www.nas.org/blogs/article/how_many_con fucius_institutes_are_in_the_united_states; Lin Yang, "Controversial Confucius Institutes Returning to U.S. Schools under New Name," *Voice of America*, June 27, 2022, https://www.voanews.com/a/controversial-confucius-institutes-returning-to-u-s-schools-under-new-name/6635906.html.

234. Michael Martina and Ted Hesson, "FBI Director 'Very Concerned' by Chinese 'Police Stations' in U.S.," *Reuters*, November 17, 2022, https://www.reuters.com/world/us/fbi-director-very-concerned-by-chinese-police-stations-us-2022-11-17/.

235. Office of the President, Office of the United States Trade Representative, *2021 Report to Congress on China's WTO Compliance*, February 2022, https://ustr.gov/sites/defa ult/files/files/Press/Reports/2021USTR%20ReportCongressChinaWTO.pdf.

236. Rob Garver, "Report: China Spends Billions of Dollars to Subsidize Favored Companies," *Voice of America*, May 24, 2022, https://www.voanews.com/a/report-china-spends-billions-of-dollars-to-subsidize-favored-companies-/6587314.html.

237. Ibid.

238. Steven Lee Myers, Agnes Chang, Derek Watkins, and Claire Fu, "How China Targets the Global Fish Supply," *New York Times*, September 26, 2022, https://www.nytimes.com/interactive/2022/09/26/world/asia/china-fishing-south-america.html.

239. Thomas L. Friedman, "How China Lost America," *New York Times*, November 1, 2022, https://www.nytimes.com/2022/11/01/opinion/china-united-states-trade-economy.html.

240. Lindsay Maizland, "China's Fight against Climate Change and Environmental Degradation," Backgrounder, Council on Foreign Relations, last modified May 19, 2021, https://www.cfr.org/backgrounder/china-climate-change-policies-environmen tal-degradation; Edward White, "Pressure Remains on Xi Jinping to Kick China's Coal Habit," *Financial Times*, November 7, 2022, https://www.ft.com/content/6cf54ab7-2172-4157-96b6-41a097e86925.

241. Maizland, "China's Fight against Climate Change."
242. White, "Pressure Remains on Xi."
243. Stephan Robin, "China Facing Devastating Impacts from Climate Change," Australian Strategic Policy Institute, September 27, 2022, https://www.aspistrateg ist.org.au/china-facing-devastating-impacts-from-climate-change/.
244. Maizland, "China's Fight against Climate Change."
245. Yanzhong Huang, *The COVID-19 Pandemic and China's Global Health Leadership* (New York: Council on Foreign Relations, 2022), https://www.cfr.org/report/covid-19-pandemic-and-chinas-global-health-leadership.
246. Associated Press, "China Delayed Releasing Coronavirus Info, Frustrating WHO," *PBS*, June 2, 2020, https://www.pbs.org/newshour/health/china-delayed-releasing-coronavirus-info-frustrating-who.
247. Helen Regan and Sandi Sidhu, "WHO Team Blocked from Entering China to Study Origins of Coronavirus," *CNN*, January 6, 2021, https://www.cnn.com/2021/01/05/china/china-blocks-who-team-coronavirus-intl-hnk/index.html; Gabriel Crossley, "China Rejects WHO Plan for Study of COVID-19 Origin," *Reuters*, July 22, 2021, https://www.reuters.com/world/china/china-will-not-follow-whos-suggested-plan-2nd-phase-covid-19-origins-study-2021-07-22/; Amy Maxmen, "Scientists Struggle to Probe COVID's Origins Amid Sparse Data from China," *Nature*, March 17, 2022, https://www.nature.com/articles/d41586-022-00732-0.
248. "China: Events of 2021," Human Rights Watch, https://www.hrw.org/world-report/2022/country-chapters/china-and-tibet#12ffb1.
249. "Xi Jinping Builds a 21st-Century Police State," *Economist*, September 14, 2023, https://www.economist.com/china/2023/09/14/xi-jinping-builds-a-21st-century-police-state.
250. Isabelle Qian et al., "Four Takeaways from a Times Investigation into China's Expanding Surveillance State," *New York Times*, July 26, 2022, https://www.nytimes.com/2022/06/21/world/asia/china-surveillance-investigation.html.
251. Vivian Wang, "China to Its People: Spies Are Everywhere, Help Us Catch Them," *New York Times*, September 2, 2023, https://www.nytimes.com/2023/09/02/world/asia/china-spies-campaign.html.
252. Qian, et al., "Four Takeaways."
253. Human Rights Watch and Mills Legal Clinic, *Break Their Lineage, Break Their Roots: China's Crimes against Humanity Targeting Uyghurs and Other Turkic Muslims* (New York: Human Rights Watch, 2021), 24, https://www.hrw.org/report/2021/04/19/break-their-lineage-break-their-roots/chinas-crimes-against-humanity-targeting#_ftn3.
254. Ibid; Lindsay Maizland, "China's Repression of Uyghurs in Xinjiang," Backgrounder, Council on Foreign Relations, last modified March 1, 2021, https://www.cfr.org/backgrounder/chinas-repression-uyghurs-xinjiang.
255. Ibid.; United Nations, Office of the High Commissioner for Human Rights, *OHCHR Assessment of Human Rights Concerns in the Xinjiang Uyghur Autonomous Region, People's Republic of China*, August 31, 2022, https://www.ohchr.org/sites/default/files/documents/countries/2022-08-31/22-08-31-final-assesment.pdf.

256. Office of the High Commissioner for Human Rights, *OHCHR Assessment of Human Rights Concerns in the Xinjiang Uyghur Autonomous Region, People's Republic of China.*

257. "Beijing Sends a New Flood of Han Migrants to Lhasa: Tibetans Risk Disappearing," *PIME Asia News*, January 27, 2015, https://www.asianews.it/news-en/Beijing-sends-a-new-flood-of-Han-migrants-to-Lhasa:-Tibetans-risk-disappearing-33294.html; Hannah Ellis-Petersen, "Tibet and China Clash over Next Reincarnation of the Dalai Lama," *Guardian*, July 31, 2021, https://www.theguardian.com/world/2021/jul/31/tibet-and-china-clash-over-next-reincarnation-of-the-dalai-lama.

258. Ellis-Petersen, "Tibet and China Clash."

259. Kenji Kawase, "China's Boarding Schools Strip Tibetan Children of Language: Study," *Nikkei Asia,* December 9, 2021, https://asia.nikkei.com/Politics/China-s-boarding-schools-strip-Tibetan-children-of-language-study; United Nations Office of the High Commissioner for Human Rights, Media Center, "China: UN Experts Alarmed by Separation of 1 Million Tibetan Children from Families and Forced Assimilation at Residential Schools," press release, February 6, 2023, https://www.ohchr.org/en/press-releases/2023/02/china-un-experts-alarmed-separation-1-million-tibetan-children-families-and.

260. Sangyal Kunchok, "Chinese Officials Restrict What Tibetan Children Are Taught about the Dalai Lama," *Radio Free Asia*, November 11, 2021, https://www.rfa.org/english/news/tibet/taught-11302021155455.html.

261. "China: Tibetan Monks Harshly Sentenced," *Human Rights Watch*, July 6, 2021, https://www.hrw.org/news/2021/07/06/china-tibetan-monks-harshly-sentenced; Nolan Peterson, "The Refugees Who Risk Frostbite to Escape Communism," *Newsweek*, December 29, 2015, https://www.newsweek.com/refugees-risking-frostbite-escape-communism-409785.

262. Pak Yiu, "Hong Kong's Independent Media Fight to Survive," *Nikkei Asia*, February 9, 2022, https://asia.nikkei.com/Spotlight/The-Big-Story/Hong-Kong-s-independent-media-fight-to-survive.

263. U.S.-China Economic Security Review Commission, *2022 Annual Report to Congress*, 19.

264. Samuel Bickett, "The Dangers of a Song in Hong Kong," China Watcher (newsletter), *Politico*, June 29, 2023, https://www.politico.eu/newsletter/china-watcher/the-dangers-of-a-song-in-hong-kong/.

265. Christina Lu, "China's Checkbook Diplomacy Has Bounced," *Foreign Policy*, February 21, 2023, https://foreignpolicy.com/2023/02/21/china-debt-diplomacy-belt-and-road-initiative-economy-infrastructure-development/?utm_source=PostUp&utm_medium=email&utm_campaign=Editors+Picks+OC&utm_term=70512&tpcc=Editors+Picks+OC.

266. Susan Shirk, *Overreach: How China Derailed Its Peaceful Rise* (New York: Oxford University Press, 2023), 13.

267. World Bank, "GDP Growth (Annual %)—China," World Bank Group, accessed August 29, 2022, https://data.worldbank.org/indicator/NY.GDP.MKTP.KD.ZG?locations=CN.

268. Ibid.; Bloomberg News, "China's Growth Prospects Weaken as Economists Cut 2023 Forecasts," *Bloomberg*, August 28, 2022, https://www.bloomberg.com/news/articles/2022-08-28/china-s-growth-prospects-weaken-as-economists-cut-2023-forecasts.

269. Jason Douglas, "China's Economic Growth Fell to Near-Historic Lows as Covid Took a Bite," *Wall Street Journal*, January 17, 2023, https://www.wsj.com/articles/chinas-economic-growth-fell-to-near-historic-lows-as-covid-took-a-bite-11673921199.

270. "China Debt Problem," Reuters Graphics, *Reuters*, http://fingfx.thomsonreuters.com/gfx/rngs/CHINA-DEBT-HOUSEHOLD/010030H712Q/index.html; Michael Pettis, "The Only Five Paths China's Economy Can Follow," Carnegie Endowment for International Peace, April 27, 2022, https://carnegieendowment.org/chinafinancialmarkets/87007; Michael Pettis, "How China Trapped Itself," *Foreign Affairs*, October 5, 2022, https://www.foreignaffairs.com/china/how-china-trapped-itself; Logan Wright, "China's Slow-Motion Financial Crisis Is Unfolding as Expected," Center for Strategic and International Studies, September 21, 2022, https://www.csis.org/analysis/chinas-slow-motion-financial-crisis-unfolding-expected.

271. Stella Yifan Xie and Jason Douglas, "China's Fading Recovery Reveals Deeper Economic Struggles," *Wall Street Journal*, May 30, 2023, https://www.wsj.com/articles/chinas-fading-recovery-reveals-deeper-economic-struggles-31f4097b.

272. Ruchir Sharma, "China's Rise Is Reversing," *Financial Times*, November 19, 2023, https://www.ft.com/content/c10bd71b-e418-48d7-ad89-74c5783c51a2.

273. Laura He, "Chinese State-Owned Companies Are in Trouble. That Could Hurt the Global Recovery," *CNN*, December 11, 2020, https://www.cnn.com/2020/12/09/economy/china-debt-defaults-state-companies-intl-hnk/index.html; Ivan Eland, "China's Internal Weakness," *Inside Sources*, December 20, 2021, https://insidesources.com/chinas-internal-weakness/.

274. Eland, "China's Internal Weakness."

275. "China Is Having a Hard Time Wooing Foreign Investors Back," *Bloomberg*, November 7, 2023, https://www.bloomberg.com/news/articles/2023-11-08/china-is-having-a-hard-time-wooing-foreign-investors-back#xj4y7vzkg.

276. Jonathan Tepperman, "China's Dangerous Decline," *Foreign Affairs*, December 19, 2022, https://www.foreignaffairs.com/china/chinas-dangerous-decline; Zongyuan Zoe Liu, "China's Village Bank Collapses Could Cause Dangerous Contagion," *Foreign Policy*, July 27, 2022, https://foreignpolicy.com/2022/07/27/china-village-banks-economic-growth-dangerous-contagion/; Bloomberg News, "China Arrests Hundreds in Nation's Biggest-Ever Bank Fraud Probe," *Bloomberg*, August 29, 2022, https://www.bloomberg.com/news/articles/2022-08-30/china-makes-sweeping-arrests-in-bank-scam-pay-more-victims.

277. Tepperman, "China's Dangerous Decline"; Bloomberg News, "China Youth Jobless Rate Hits Record 20%in July on Covid Woes," *Bloomberg*, August 14, 2022, https://www.bloomberg.com/news/articles/2022-08-15/china-youth-jobless-rate-hits-record-20-in-july-on-covid-woes.

278. Zen Soo, "China's Economy Grows 4.9% in Q3, Beating Expectations but Slowing from Previous Quarter," *Washington Post*, October 18, 2023, https://www.washingtonpost.com/business/2023/10/17/china-gdp-economy-growth-decline/4431b

804-6d5c-11ee-b01a-f593caa04363_story.html; Nathaniel Taplin, "China Stabilizes, in the Shadow of Country Garden and Evergrande," *Wall Street Journal*, October 18, 2023, https://www.wsj.com/economy/housing/china-stabilizes-in-the-shadow-of-country-garden-and-evergrande-7574010a; Ishaan Tharoor, "Xi's Moment of Dominance Can't Hide His Weakness," *Today's World View* (newsletter), *Washington Post*, October 17, 2022, https://www.washingtonpost.com/world/2022/10/17/china-xi-weakness-power-party-congress/.

279. Keith Bradsher and Joy Dong, "Xi Jinping Is Asserting Tighter Control of Finance in China," *New York Times*, December 5, 2023, https://www.nytimes.com/2023/12/05/business/china-finance-xi-jinping.html.

280. "From Hypersonic Missiles to Undersea Drones, the PLA Is Making Leaps," *Economist*, November 6, 2023, https://www.economist.com/special-report/2023/11/06/from-hypersonic-missiles-to-undersea-drones-the-pla-is-making-leaps.

281. Abhishek Vishnoi, Amy Bainbridge, and Eliyahu Kamisher, "China Is Fast Losing Its Place as Must-Have in Global Portfolios," *Bloomberg*, January 10, 2024, https://www.bloomberg.com/news/articles/2024-01-11/china-is-fast-losing-its-place-as-must-have-in-global-portfolios.

282. George F. Will, "Why China Will Become Ever More Dangerous as Its Baby Bust Worsens," *Washington Post*, August 19, 2022, https://www.washingtonpost.com/opinions/2022/08/19/dangerous-china-demographic-decline/; Howard W. French, "A Shrinking China Can't Overtake America," *Foreign Policy*, July 29, 2022, https://foreignpolicy.com/2022/07/29/china-population-decline-demographics-ecomomic-growth/; Hal Brands, "The Dangers of China's Decline," *Foreign Policy*, April 14, 2022, https://foreignpolicy.com/2022/04/14/china-decline-dangers/; Andrew S. Erickson and Gabriel B. Collins, "A Dangerous Decade of Chinese Power Is Here," *Foreign Policy*, October 18, 2021, https://foreignpolicy.com/2021/10/18/china-danger-military-missile-taiwan/.

283. 2022 United Nations, DESA, Population Division. Licensed under Creative Commons license CC BY 3.0 IGO. *World Population Prospects 2022*. http://population.un.org/wpp.

284. Sebastian Mallaby, "Demographics Are Destiny," in "What Just Happened: Storm Clouds Loom for China's Economy," *Washington Post*, August 18, 2023, https://www.washingtonpost.com/opinions/2023/08/18/china-economy-deflation-debt-analysis/.

285. Alexandra Stevenson and Zixu Wang, "China's Population Falls, Heralding a Demographic Crisis," *New York Times*, January 17, 2023, https://www.nytimes.com/2023/01/16/business/china-birth-rate.html.

286. Special Correspondant, "China's Protests Electrify the Global Diaspora," *Foreign Policy*, December 12, 2022, https://foreignpolicy.com/2022/12/12/china-zero-covid-protests-overseas-students-diaspora/; Chang Che and Amy Chang Chien, "Protest in Xinjiang against Lockdown after Fire Kills 10," *New York Times*, November 25, 2022, https://www.nytimes.com/2022/11/25/world/asia/china-fire.html; Vivian Wang, "A Protest? A Vigil? In Beijing, Anxious Crowds Are Unsure How Far to Go," *New York Times*, November 28, 2022, https://www.nytimes.com/2022/11/28/world/asia/china-protests-covid-beijing.html.

287. Minxin Pei, "Xi Jinping's Covid Crisis Is Really an Opportunity," *New York Times*, December 14, 2022, https://www.nytimes.com/2022/12/14/opinion/china-covid-protest-democracy-xi.html.

288. Tom Mitchell, Thomas Hale, Sun Yu, and Edward White, "The Humbling of Xi Jinping," *Financial Times*, December 2, 2022, https://www.ft.com/content/71bf8 a5d-3816-450b-bbfb-ec320b0dba0d.

289. Helen Davidson, "Eight in 10 People in China Caught Covid since Early December, Say Officials," *Guardian*, January 23, 2023, https://www.theguardian.com/world/2023/jan/23/80-of-people-in-china-caught-covid-since-early-december-say-offici als; CNN's Beijing Bureau, "China Says 80% of Population Have Had Covid-19, as Millions Travel for Lunar New Year," *CNN*, January 22, 2023, https://www.cnn.com/2023/01/22/china/china-covid-80-lunar-new-year-intl-hnk/index.html; Primrose Riordan, "China Celebrates Lunar New Year as Covid Infections Hit 80%," *Financial Times*, January 22, 2023, https://www.ft.com/content/50de38e2-b2ae-41ab-b9ab-8d07d009d8a8; Reuters, "China Says COVID Outbreak Has Infected 80% of Population," *Reuters*, January 21, 2023, https://www.reuters.com/world/china/china-says-covid-outbreak-has-infected-80-population-2023-01-21/.

290. "China COVID Deaths Probably Running above 5,000 per Day—UK Research Firm Airfinity," *Reuters*, December 22, 2022, https://www.reuters.com/world/china/china-covid-deaths-probably-running-above-5000-per-day-uk-research-firm-2022-12-22/.

291. Liu Zhen, "US Report Finds Big Weaknesses in China's Defence Industry Base," *South China Morning Post*, February 19, 2022, https://www.scmp.com/news/china/military/article/3167693/us-report-finds-big-weaknesses-chinas-defence-industry-base; Steve Sacks, "China's Military Has a Hidden Weakness," *Diplomat*, April 20, 2021, https://thediplomat.com/2021/04/chinas-military-has-a-hidden-weakness/.

292. Alastair Gale, "China's Military Is Catching Up to the U.S. Is It Ready for Battle?," *Wall Street Journal*, October 20, 2022), https://www.wsj.com/articles/china-milit ary-us-taiwan-xi-11666268994.

293. Kathrin Hille and Edward White, "'Absolute Loyalty': Xi Jinping Turns Anti-Corruption Focus to China's Military," *Financial Times*, July 30, 2023, https://www.ft.com/content/279a90a3-c550-40a2-9484-8a6eebca628b.

294. Ibid.; Kathrin Hille, "China Ousts Top Generals from Nuclear Rocket Force," *Financial Times*, July 31, 2023, https://www.ft.com/content/0375c760-7902-4a41-b8f4-1b41026a38fd.; Chris Buckley, "Xi Rebuilt the Military to His Liking. Now a Shake-Up Threatens Its Image," *New York Times*, August 7, 2023, https://www.nyti mes.com/2023/08/07/world/asia/china-nuclear-military-xi.html.

295. Christian Shepherd, "What China's New Defense Minister Tells Us about Xi's Military Purge," *Washington Post*, December 30, 2023, https://www.washingtonp ost.com/world/2023/12/30/china-defense-minister-xi-military/; Liu Zen, "China Removes 9 PLA Generals from Top Legislature in Sign of Wider Purge," *South China Morning Post*, December 30, 2023, https://www.scmp.com/news/china/politics/arti cle/3246738/china-removes-nine-pla-generals-top-legislature-sign-wider-purge; James Palmer, "China Closed 2023 with a Military Purge," *Foreign Policy*, January

2, 2024, https://foreignpolicy.com/2024/01/02/china-military-purge-pla-rocket-force-ccp/.

296. Christopher K. Johnson, "Abrupt Dismissals Point to Xi Jinping's Quiet Shake-up of China's Military," interviewed by Chris Buckley, *New York Times*, January 3, 2024, https://www.nytimes.com/2024/01/03/world/asia/xi-jinping-military-purge.html.

297. Peter Martin and Jennifer Jacobs, "US Intelligence Shows Flawed China Missiles Led Xi to Purge Army," *Bloomberg*, January 6, 2024, https://www.bloomberg.com/news/articles/2024-01-06/us-intelligence-shows-flawed-china-missiles-led-xi-jinping-to-purge-military.

298. "China v America: How Xi Jinping Plans to Narrow the Military Gap," *Economist*, May 8, 2023, https://www.economist.com/china/2023/05/08/china-v-america-how-xi-jinping-plans-to-narrow-the-military-gap.

299. Ray Weichieh Wang, "China's Wolf Warrior Diplomacy Is Fading," *Diplomat*, July 27, 2022, https://thediplomat.com/2022/07/chinas-wolf-warrior-diplomacy-is-fading/; Joshua Kurlantzick, "Why China's Global Image Is Getting Worse," Council on Foreign Relations, January 24, 2022, https://www.cfr.org/in-brief/why-chinas-global-image-getting-worse.

300. Bloomberg News, "China's Fragile Economy Is Being Hammered by Driest Riverbeds since 1865," *Bloomberg*, August 23, 2022, https://www.bloomberg.com/news/articles/2022-08-23/worst-drought-in-decades-threatens-china-s-economic-recovery; Bloomberg News, "Next China: Who's Got the Power?," *Bloomberg*, August 26, 2022, https://www.bloomberg.com/news/newsletters/2022-08-26/power-crisis-sichuan-three-gorges-minions-property-crisis?cmpid=BBD082622_CN&utm_medium=email&utm_source=newsletter&utm_term=220826&utm_campaign=china; Adam Tooze, "Chartbook #145: China on the Tightrope," *Chartbook*, August 23, 2022, https://adamtooze.substack.com/p/chartbook-145-china-on-the-tightrope; "China's Environmental Abuses—United States Department of State," US Department of State, December 18, 2020, https://2017-2021.state.gov/chinas-environmental-abuses/index.html; Harlan Ullman, "China's Strengths Shouldn't Blind Us to Its Weaknesses," Atlantic Council, April 6, 2021, https://www.atlanticcouncil.org/blogs/new-atlanticist/chinas-strengths-shouldnt-blind-us-to-its-weaknesses/.

301. Simone McCarthy, "China's Belt and Road Is Facing Challenges. But Can the US Counter It?," *CNN*, August 22, 2022, https://www.cnn.com/2022/08/22/china/china-belt-and-road-us-infrastructure-overseas-development-intl-hnk-mic/index.html; Adnan Aamir, Marwaan Macan-Markar, Shaun Turton, Cissy Zhou, and Grace Li, "Road to Nowhere: China's Belt and Road Initiative at Tipping Point," *Nikkei Asia*, August 10, 2022, https://asia.nikkei.com/Spotlight/The-Big-Story/Road-to-nowhere-China-s-Belt-and-Road-Initiative-at-tipping-point; Abhishek Mishra, "China's BRI Continues to Remain Popular amongst Africans Despite Intense Backlash," Observer Research Foundation, October 9, 2021, https://www.orfonline.org/expert-speak/chinas-bri-continues-to-remain-popular-amongst-africans-despite-intense-backlash/.

302. "What China Gets Wrong," *Economist*, April 16, 2022, https://www.economist.com/leaders/2022/04/16/what-china-gets-wrong; "What Is at Stake in Ukraine,"

*Economist*, April 16, 2022, https://www.economist.com/leaders/2022/04/16/what-is-at-stake-in-ukraine.

303. Brands, "The Dangers of China's Decline"; Tepperman, "China's Dangerous Decline"; Bret Stephens, "China's Decline Became Undeniable This Week. Now What?," *New York Times*, January 17, 2023, https://www.nytimes.com/2023/01/17/opinion/china-population-decline.html.

304. For sources that argue China has peaked, see the three articles above and Hal Brands and Michael Beckley, "China Is a Declining Power—and That's the Problem," *Foreign Policy*, September 24, 2021, https://foreignpolicy.com/2021/09/24/china-great-power-united-states/; Yi Fuxian, "The Chinese Century Is Already Over," *Project Syndicate*, https://www.project-syndicate.org/commentary/china-population-decline-will-mean-economic-geopolitical-decline-by-yi-fuxian-2023-02?barrier=accesspaylog; William A. Galston, "Is China Past Its Peak?," *Wall Street Journal*, August 15, 2023, https://www.wsj.com/articles/china-past-peak-demographic-bomb-aging-youth-unemployment-grad-recession-taiwan-34fda75f; Gordon C. Chang, "China Has Peaked," *Newsweek*, July 31, 2023, https://www.newsweek.com/communist-china-has-peaked-opinion-1816247; Hal Brands and Michael Beckley, *Danger Zone: The Coming Conflict with China* (London: W. W. Norton, 2022); Maximilian Mayer and Emilian Kavalski, "Have We Reached Peak China?," *Politico*, October 21, 2021, https://www.politico.eu/article/have-we-reached-peak-china/. For sources that argue it is too early to conclude whether China has reached the height of its power, see Oriana Skylar Mastro and Derek Scissors, "China Hasn't Reached the Peak of Its Power," *Foreign Affairs*, August 22, 2022, https://www.foreignaffairs.com/china/china-hasnt-reached-peak-its-power; Shawn Donnan, Viktoria Dendrinou, Alessandra Migliaccio, and Philip Aldrick, "The US, Allies See Opportunity and Risk in China's Slowing Economy," *Bloomberg*, August 31, 2023, https://www.bloomberg.com/news/features/2023-08-31/how-china-s-economic-slowdown-will-impact-its-rise-to-top-economy; Bethany Allen-Ebrahimian, "China's Post-Reform Era has Arrived—and Its Future Is Unclear," *Axios*, August 29, 2023, https://www.axios.com/2023/08/29/chinas-post-reform-era; Henry M. Paulson Jr., "A Deep Crisis in China Would Pose a Choice for Two Leading Powers," *Washington Post*, August 21, 2023, https://www.washingtonpost.com/opinions/2023/08/21/paulson-china-economy-xi-jinping-test/; Ian Bremmer, "Has China's Power Peaked?," *GZERO*, June 7, 2023, https://www.gzeromedia.com/by-ian-bremmer/has-chinas-power-peaked. For discussions on the topic, see Jonathan Eyal, "The Emerging Debate in America: How to Deal with a China in Decline," *Straits Times*, September 5, 2023, https://www.straitstimes.com/opinion/the-emerging-debate-in-america-how-to-deal-with-a-china-in-decline; "Is Chinese Power about to Peak," *Economist*, May 11, 2023, https://www.economist.com/leaders/2023/05/11/is-chinese-power-about-to-peak; Joseph S. Nye, Jr., "Peak China?," *Project Syndicate*, January 3, 2023, https://www.project-syndicate.org/commentary/peak-china-debate-calls-for-careful-assessment-by-joseph-s-nye-2023-01; Amy Hawkins, "Have We Reached Peak China? How the Booming Middle Class Hit a Brick Wall," *Guardian*, September 10, 2023, https://www.theguardian.com/world/2023/sep/11/have-we-reached-peak-china-how-the-booming-middle-class-hit-a-brick-wall.

305. Robert Gates, "The Dysfunctional Superpower," *Foreign Affairs*, September 29, 2023, https://www.foreignaffairs.com/united-states/robert-gates-america-china-russia-dysfunctional-superpower.

306. Lee Kwan Yew, *Lee Kwan Yew* (Cambridge: Belfer Center for Science and International Affairs, 2013), interviewed by Robert Blackwill and Graham Allison, 42.

# Chapter 11

1. Hillary Clinton, "America's Pacific Century," *Foreign Policy*, October 11, 2011, https://foreignpolicy.com/2011/10/11/americas-pacific-century/.

2. Ibid.

3. Tom Donilon, "Remarks by National Security Advisor Tom Donilon," (speech, Center for Strategic and International Studies, Washington, DC, November 15, 2012), White House, https://obamawhitehouse.archives.gov/the-press-office/2012/11/15/remarks-national-security-advisor-tom-donilon-prepared-delivery.

4. US Department of Defense, Office of the Secretary of Defense, *Annual Report to Congress: Military and Security Developments Involving the People's Republic of China 2011*, 2011, https://dod.defense.gov/Portals/1/Documents/pubs/2011_CMP R_Final.pdf, 28–29.

5. Author interview with Robert O. Work, February 2023.

6. John J. Mearsheimer, "The Gathering Storm: China's Challenge to US Power in Asia," *The Chinese Journal of International Politics* 3, no. 4 (Winter 2010): 381–396, https://doi.org/10.1093/cjip/poq016.

7. Author interview with Robert O. Work, February 2023.

8. Michael Green, *By More than Providence* (New York: Columbia University Press, 2017).

9. Hal Brands, "U.S. Needs to Deny, Not Dominate, China in the Indo-Pacific," *Bloomberg*, January 31, 2021, https://www.bloomberg.com/opinion/articles/2021-02-01/u-s-needs-to-deny-not-dominate-china-in-the-indo-pacific.

10. US Congress, Senate, Committee on armed Services, *Alternative Approaches to Defense Strategy and Force Structure*, 114th Cong., 1st sess., 2015, https://www.govi nfo.gov/content/pkg/CHRG-114shrg99538/html/CHRG-114shrg99538.htm.

11. Barry D. Watts, "The Maturing Revolution in Military Affairs," (Washington, DC: Center for Strategic and Budgetary Assessments, 2011), https://csbaonline.org/uploads/documents/2011.06.02-Maturing-Revolution-In-Military-Affairs1.pdf.

12. F. Brinley Bruton, "U.S. Bombed Iraq, Syria, Pakistan, Afghanistan, Libya, Yemen, Somalia in 2016," *NBC*, January 9, 2017, https://www.nbcnews.com/news/world/u-s-bombed-iraq-syria-pakistan-afghanistan-libya-yemen-somalia-n704636.

13. John T. Bennett and Jeremy Herb, "Obama Takes 2012 Risk by Ending Pentagon's Two-War Strategy," *Hill*, January 5, 2012, https://thehill.com/policy/defense/102 005-obama-takes-2012-risk-by-ending-pentagons-two-war-strategy/.

14. Robert A. Crisostomo, "Strategic Guam: Past, Present and Future," (Strategy research project, United States Army War College, 2013), https://apps.dtic.mil/sti/pdfs/ADA589132.pdf.

15. 1st Lt. Colin Kennard, "U.S. Marines Reach 2,500 in Darwin for First Time," US Indo-Pacific Command, July 26, 2019, https://www.pacom.mil/Media/News/News-Article-View/Article/1918439/us-marines-reach-2500-in-darwin-for-first-time/.

16. White House, Office of the Press Secretary, "Prime Minister Gillard and President Obama Announce Force Posture Initiatives," November 16, 2011, https://obamawhitehouse.archives.gov/the-press-office/2011/11/16/prime-minister-gillard-and-president-obama-announce-force-posture-init-0.

17. Franz-Stefan Gady, "US Navy Littoral Combat Ship Arrives in Singapore for Rotational Deployment," *Diplomat,* July 9, 2019, https://thediplomat.com/2019/07/us-navy-littoral-combat-ship-arrives-in-singapore-for-rotational-deployment/.

18. "US Ship Force Levels 1886–present," Naval History and Heritage Command, https://www.history.navy.mil/research/histories/ship-histories/us-ship-force-levels.html; Carlo Munoz, "Navy to Review 313-Ship Plan, VCNO Says, *Breaking Defense,* January 11, 2012, https://breakingdefense.com/2012/01/navy-could-scrap-313-ship-plan-in-new-force-structure-review-vc/.

19. US Library of Congress, Congressional Research Service, *Pivot to the Pacific? The Obama Administration's "Rebalancing" toward Asia,* by Mark E. Manyin, Stephen Dagget, and Ben Dolven, R42448, 2012, https://sgp.fas.org/crs/natsec/R42448.pdf.

20. US Department of Defense, *Sustaining U.S. Global Leadership: Priorities for 21st Century Defense,* January 2012, https://www.globalsecurity.org/military/library/policy/dod/defense_guidance-201201.pdf.

21. Congressional Research Service, *Pivot to the Pacific?.*

22. "Philippines Agrees to 10-Year Pact Allowing US Military Presence," *Guardian,* April 27, 2014, https://www.theguardian.com/world/2014/apr/27/philippines-us-military-presence-china-dispute; Rob Wittman, "Funding the Indo-Pacific Pivot," *War on the Rocks,* September 2, 2022, https://warontherocks.com/2022/09/funding-the-indo-pacific-pivot/.

23. US Department of State, Bureau of Political-Military Affairs, "U.S. Security Cooperation with India Fact Sheet," fact sheet, January 20, 2021, https://www.state.gov/u-s-security-cooperation-with-india/.

24. James Pearsona and Robert Birsel, "U.S. Says Completes Second Aircraft Carrier Visit to Vietnam," *Reuters,* March 10, 2020, https://www.reuters.com/article/us-vietnam-usa/u-s-says-completes-second-aircraft-carrier-visit-to-vietnam-idUSKBN20Y0F3.

25. Ashley Townshend and James Crabtree, "US Indo-Pacific Strategy, Alliances and Security Partnerships," in *Asia-Pacific Regional Security Assessment, an IISS Strategic Dossier,* eds. Tim Huxley and Lynn Kuok, June 14, 2022, https://www.iiss.org/contentassets/57a0be7e196445479341abe68fac940a/aprsa-2022_lr.pdf, 24.

26. Kathrin Jille and Demetri Sevastopulo, "US and Philippines Increase Military Ties over China Threat," *Financial Times,* September 24, 2022, https://www.ft.com/content/9c295755-eadf-48a9-9818-6afa1bcbe498.

27. Jim Garamone, "U.S.-Philippine Alliance Strengthens as It Enters New Phase," *US Department of Defense News*, February 2, 2023, https://www.defense.gov/News/News-Stories/Article/Article/3286055/us-philippine-alliance-strengthens-as-it-enters-new-phase/.

28. Townshend and Crabtree, "US Indo-Pacific Strategy."

29. Charles Edel, "The United States, Britain, and Australia Announce the Path Forward for AUKUS," Center for Strategic and International Studies, critical questions, March 16, 2023, https://www.csis.org/analysis/united-states-britain-and-australia-announce-path-forward-aukus.

30. Jim Garamone, "U.S. and Japanese Leaders Chart Path to Strengthen 'Cornerstone' Alliance," *US Department of Defense News*, January 11, 2023, https://www.defense.gov/News/News-Stories/Article/Article/3265569/us-and-japanese-leaders-chart-path-to-strengthen-cornerstone-alliance/; Jasmin Alsaied, "How to Make the Indo-Pacific Partnership for Maritime Domain Awareness Work," *Diplomat*, October 11, 2022, https://thediplomat.com/2022/10/how-to-make-the-indo-pacific-partnership-for-maritime-domain-awareness-work/.

31. Helene Cooper et al., "Pentagon Eyes Africa Drawdown as First Step in Global Troop Shift," *New York Times*, December 24, 2019, https://www.nytimes.com/2019/12/24/world/africa/esper-troops-africa-china.html.

32. Robert C. O'Brien, "Why the U.S. Is Moving Troops Out of Germany," *Wall Street Journal*, June 21, 2020, https://www.wsj.com/articles/why-the-u-s-is-moving-troops-out-of-germany-11592757552.

33. Gordan Lubold, Nancy A. Youssef, and Michael R. Gordon, "U.S. Military to Withdraw Hundreds of Troops, Aircraft, Antimissile Batteries from Middle East," *Wall Street Journal*, June 18, 2021, https://www.wsj.com/articles/u-s-military-to-withdraw-hundreds-of-troops-aircraft-antimissile-batteries-from-middle-east-11624045575.

34. Jon Gambrell, "US Pulls Missile Defenses in Saudi Arabia Amid Yemen Attacks," *Associated Press*, September 11, 2021, https://apnews.com/article/iran-asia-afghanistan-dubai-middle-east-b6aaf30d689d0a8e45901e51f0457381.

35. Jim Garamone, "Biden Announces Changes in U.S. Force Posture in Europe," *US Department of Defense News*, June 29, 2022, https://www.defense.gov/News/News-Stories/Article/Article/3078087/biden-announces-changes-in-us-force-posture-in-europe/.

36. Oriana Skylar Mastro, "Deterrence in the Indo-Pacific," in "Minilateral Deterrence in the Indo-Pacific: Roundtable Deterrence in the Indo-Pacific," *Asia Policy* 17, no. 4 (October 2022), https://www.nbr.org/publication/minilateral-deterrence-in-the-indo-pacific/.

37. Chris Dougherty, "Don't Trust the Process: Moving from Words to Actions on the Indo-Pacific Posture," *War on the Rocks*, February 23, 2022, https://warontherocks.com/2022/02/dont-trust-the-process-moving-from-words-to-actions-on-the-indo-pacific-posture/.

38. Author interview with Stacie Pettyjohn, February 2023.

39. Michael Green et al., *Asia-Pacific Rebalance 2025: Capabilities, Presence, and Partnerships* (Washington, DC: Center for Strategic and International Studies, January 19, 2016), https://www.csis.org/analysis/asia-pacific-rebalance-2025.

40. Ibid.

41. Ibid.

42. US Department of Defense, *Summary of the 2018 National Defense Strategy, of the United States of America*, 2018, https://dod.defense.gov/Portals/1/Documents/pubs/2018-National-Defense-Strategy-Summary.pdf.

43. Ibid.

44. Ibid.

45. Ashley Townshend and Brendan Thomas-Noone, *Averting Crisis: American Strategy, Military Spending and Collective Defence in the Indo-Pacific*, (Sydney: United States Studies Centre, August 19, 2019), https://united-states-studies-centre.s3.amazonaws.com/uploads/32c/cd3/8dd/32ccd38ddb0ead934d743d487bd6080c01dc950a/Averting-crisis-American-strategy-military-spending-and-collective-defence-in-the-Indo-Pacific.pdf.

46. Eric Sayers, "Assessing America's Indo-Pacific Budget Shortfall," *War on the Rocks*, November 15, 2018, https://warontherocks.com/2018/11/assessing-americas-indo-pacific-budget-shortfall/.

47. Randy Schriver and Eric Sayers, "The Case for a Pacific Deterrence Initiative," *War on the Rocks*, March 10, 2020, https://warontherocks.com/2020/03/the-case-for-a-pacific-deterrence-initiative/.

48. Bruce Klingner, "Rebalancing to the Pacific: Asia Pivot or Divot?," Heritage Foundation, October 7, 2014, https://www.heritage.org/military-strength-topical-essays/2015-essays/rebalancing-the-pacific-asia-pivot-or-divot.

49. Sayers, "Assessing America's Indo-Pacific Budget Shortfall."

50. US Department of State, *Congressional Budget Justification: Department of State, Foreign Operations, and Related Programs FY2021*, 2020, 99, https://www.state.gov/wp-content/uploads/2020/02/FY-2021-CBJ-Final-508compliant.pdf.

51. Ibid., 131.

52. Sayers, "Assessing America's Indo-Pacific Budget Shortfall."

53. US Department of State, *Congressional Budget Justification FY2021*, 128.

54. Wittman, "Funding the Indo-Pacific Pivot."

55. Ibid.

56. Ibid.

57. Ibid.

58. Outside analysts, including one of this volume's authors, called for such a move as early as 2017. See Richard Fontaine, "Reassuring Asia of America's Commitment to the Region," *Wall Street Journal*, March 8, 2017, https://www.wsj.com/articles/reassuring-asia-of-americas-commitment-to-the-region-1488994821.

59. Dustin Walker, "Show Me the Money: Boost the Pacific Deterrence Initiative," *War on the Rocks*, June 29, 2022, https://warontherocks.com/2022/06/show-me-the-money-boost-the-pacific-deterrence-initiative/.

60. *U.S. Indo-Pacific Command before the Senate Armed Services Committee on U.S. Indo-Pacific Command Posture, before the Committee on Armed Services,* (March 9, 2021) (Admiral Philip S. Davidson, U.S. Navy Commander) https://www.armed-services.senate.gov/imo/media/doc/Davidson_03-09-21.pdf.

61. Walker, "Show Me the Money."

62. Ibid.

63. US Senate Committee on Armed Services, *Summary of the Fiscal Year 2023 National Defense Authorization Act,* December 2022, 9, https://www.armed-services.senate.gov/imo/media/doc/fy23_ndaa_agreement_summary.pdf.

64. Stacie Pettyjohn and Hannah Dennis, *Precision and Posture,* (Washington, DC: Center for a New American Security, 2022), 15–16, https://s3.us-east-1.amazonaws.com/files.cnas.org/documents/Budget2022_Final.pdf?mtime=20221116160642&focal=none.

65. "Headquarters, United States Indo-Pacific Command," US Indo-Pacific Command, https://www.pacom.mil/About-USINDOPACOM/; Pettyjohn and Dennis, *Precision and Posture,* 14.

66. Author interview with Robert O. Work, February 2023.

67. US Department of Defense, *Quadrennial Defense Review Report,* February 2010, https://dod.defense.gov/Portals/1/features/defenseReviews/QDR/QDR_as_of_29JAN10_1600.pdf.

68. Author interview with Robert O. Work, February 2023.

69. White House, Office of the Press Secretary, "U.S.–China Joint Statement," January 19, 2011, https://obamawhitehouse.archives.gov/the-press-office/2011/01/19/us-china-joint-statement.

70. US Department of Defense, *Air-Sea Battle: Service Collaboration to Address Anti-Access & Area Denial Challenges,* May 2013, https://dod.defense.gov/Portals/1/Documents/pubs/ASB-ConceptImplementation-Summary-May-2013.pdf.

71. Ibid.

72. Sam LaGrone, "Pentagon Drops Air Sea Battle Name, Concept Lives On," *USNI News,* January 20, 2015, https://news.usni.org/2015/01/20/pentagon-drops-air-sea-battle-name-concept-lives.

73. US Library of Congress, Congressional Research Service, *Renewed Great Power Competition: Implications for Defense,* by Ronald O'Rourke, R43838, 2022, https://crsreports.congress.gov/product/pdf/R/R43838/87.

74. Author interview with Robert O. Work, February 2023.

75. "Out of the Shadows: The Pentagon's Strategic Capabilities Office," *Aviation Week Network,* November 22, 2016, https://aviationweek.com/defense-space/out-shadows-pentagons-strategic-capabilities-office; Jon Harper, "Secretive Pentagon Office Developing Next-Generation Swarming Drones," *National Defense,* September 8, 2016, https://www.nationaldefensemagazine.org/articles/2016/9/8/secretive-pentagon-office-developing-next-generation-swarming-drones.

76. Steve Hirsch, "Work at CSIS: Idea That DOD Ignored Space a 'Crock,'" *Air and Space Forces Magazine,* September 10, 2018, https://www.airandspaceforces.com/Idea-That-DOD-Ignored-Space-a-Crock-Work-Tells-Meeting/.

77. Author interview with Robert O. Work, February 2023.

78. US Department of Defense, *Memorandum for Deputy Secretary of Defense: The Defense Innovation Initiative*, November 15, 2014, https://defenseinnovationmark etplace.dtic.mil/wp-content/uploads/2018/04/DefenseInnovationInitiative.pdf.

79. Ibid.

80. Kathleen H. Hicks et al., *Assessing the Third Offset Strategy* (Washington, DC: Center for Strategic and International Strategies, 2017), https://csis-website-prod.s3.amazon aws.com/s3fs-public/publication/170302_Ellman_ThirdOffsetStrategySumm ary_Web.pdf; Ashton Carter, "Remarks on 'The Path to an Innovative Future for Defense'" (CSIS Third Offset Strategy Conference)" (speech, Washington, DC, October 28, 2016), US Department of Defense, https://www.defense.gov/News/ Speeches/Speech/Article/990315/remarks-on-the-path-to-an-innovative-future- for-defense-csis-third-offset-strat/.

81. Carter, "Remarks."

82. Gian Gentile et al., *A History of the Third Offset, 2014–2018* (Santa Monica, CA: RAND, 2021), 53, https://www.rand.org/pubs/research_reports/RRA454-1.html.

83. Author interview with Stacie Pettyjohn, February 2023.

84. Ibid.

85. Courtney Albon, "Defense Innovation Unit highlights 2021 technology transition efforts," *C4ISRNET*, January 26, 2022, https://www.c4isrnet.com/battlefield- tech/2022/01/26/defense-innovation-unit-highlights-2021-technology-transit ion-efforts/.

86. Author interview with Robert O. Work, February 2023.

87. Paul Scharre, *Four Battlegrounds: Power in the Age of Artificial Intelligence* (New York: W.W. Norton, 2023), 36–37.

88. Ibid., 37.

89. Zachary Basu, "Where 100,000 U.S. Troops Are Stationed in Europe," *Axios,* March 22, 2022, https://www.axios.com/2022/03/23/where-100000-us-troops-are-statio ned-europe.

90. Robert C. O'Brien, "The Navy's Hidden Crisis: It's Too Small—and Getting Smaller," Pacific Council on International Policy, September 21, 2015, https://www.pacific council.org/newsroom/navys-hidden-crisis-its-too-small-and-getting-smaller; US Library of Congress, Congressional Research Service, *China Naval Modernization: Implications for U.S. Navy Capabilities*, by Ronald O'Rourke, RL33153, 2022, https://crsreports.congress.gov/product/pdf/RL/RL33153; US Library of Congress, Congressional Research Service, *Navy Force Structure and Shipbuilding Plans*, by Ronald O'Rourke, RL32665, 2022, https://sgp.fas.org/crs/weapons/RL32665.pdf.

91. Geoff Ziezulewicz, "Why Aircraft Carriers Are No Longer a Constant in the Middle East," *Navy Times*, November 4, 2022, https://www.navytimes.com/news/your-navy/ 2022/11/04/why-aircraft-carriers-are-no-longer-a-constant-in-the-middle-east/.

92. Mike Watson, "Germany Shirks Its Defense Pledge, Imperiling the Asia 'Pivot,'" *Wall Street Journal*, December 15, 2022, https://www.wsj.com/articles/germany-shi rks-its-defense-pledge-imperiling-the-asia-pivot-military-budget-spending-japan- china-russia-beijing-11671123354?mod=Searchresults_pos1&page=1.

93. US Department of Defense, "Biden Administration Announces Additional Security Assistance for Ukraine," press release, February 3, 2023, https://www.defense.gov/ News/Releases/Release/Article/3287992/biden-administration-announces-add itional-security-assistance-for-ukraine/.

94. C. Todd Lopez, "U.S. Commitment to Indo-Pacific Region Not Limited by Security Assistance to Ukraine," *US Department of Defense News*, May 19, 2022, https://www. defense.gov/News/News-Stories/Article/Article/3037989/us-commitment-to-indo-pacific-region-not-limited-by-security-assistance-to-ukra/; David Vergun, "Hicks Says U.S. Strengthening Indo-Pacific Alliances," *US Department of Defense News*, December 9, 2022, https://www.defense.gov/News/News-Stories/Article/Arti cle/3242146/hicks-says-us-strengthening-indo-pacific-alliances/.

95. US Department of Defense, *2022 National Defense Strategy of the United States of America*, October 2022, 4, https://media.defense.gov/2022/Oct/27/2003103845/-1/ -1/1/2022-NATIONAL-DEFENSE-STRATEGY-NPR-MDR.PDF.

96. Kevin Liptak and Brad Lendon, "Biden Again Says US Forces Would Defend Taiwan against Chinese Aggression," *CNN*, September 19, 2022, https://www.cnn. com/2022/09/19/asia/biden-us-troops-defend-taiwan-intl-hnk/index.html.

97. "'Ukraine Today Could Be East Asia Tomorrow': Japan PM Warns," *France 24*, October 6, 2022, https://www.france24.com/en/live-news/20220610-ukraine-today-could-be-east-asia-tomorrow-japan-pm-warns.

98. "Japan Defence: China Threat Prompts Plan to Double Military Spending," *BBC*, December 16, 2022, https://www.bbc.com/news/world-asia-64001554; Michelle Ye Hee Lee and Ellen Nakashima, "Japan Moves to Shed Pacifist Ways with Major Defense Buildup," *Washington Post*, December 12, 2022, https://www.washingtonp ost.com/world/2022/12/12/japan-tomahawk-missiles-ukraine-war/.

99. Michelle Ye Hee Lee and Min Joo Kim, "South Koreans Wonder: Will the U.S. Still Protect Us from North Korea?," *Washington Post*, February 7, 2023, https://www. washingtonpost.com/world/2023/02/07/south-north-korea-nuclear-weapons-security/.

100. Samson Ellis and Cindy Wang, "Taiwan Plans 14% Boost in Defense Spending to Counter China," *Bloomberg*, August 25, 2022, https://www.bloomberg.com/ news/articles/2022-08-25/taiwan-plans-14-boost-in-defense-spending-to-coun ter-china; Eric Cheung, "Taiwan Extends Mandatory Military Service Period to Counter China Threat," *CNN*, December 27, 2022, https://www.cnn.com/2022/12/ 27/asia/taiwan-military-conscription-intl-hnk/index.html.

101. Alessio Patalano, "Why Is a British Carrier Strike Group Heading to the Indo-Pacific?," *War on the Rocks*, August 11, 2021, https://warontherocks.com/2021/08/ why-is-a-british-carrier-strike-group-heading-to-the-indo-pacific/.

102. Sébastian Seibt, "France Wades into the South China Sea with a Nuclear Attack Submarine," *France 24*, December 2, 2021, https://www.france24.com/en/fra nce/20210212-france-wades-into-the-south-china-sea-with-a-nuclear-attack-submarine; The French Republic, *France's Indo-Pacific Strategy*, 2022, https:// www.diplomatie.gouv.fr/IMG/pdf/en_dcp_a4_indopacifique_022022_v1-4_we b_cle878143.pdf.

103. North Atlantic Treaty Organization, *NATO 2022 Strategic Concept*, June 29, 2022, https://www.nato.int/nato_static_fl2014/assets/pdf/2022/6/pdf/290622-strategic-concept.pdf.

104. North Atlantic Treaty Organization, "NATO Leaders Meet with Key Partners to Address Global Challenges, Indo-Pacific Partners Participate in a NATO Summit for the First Time," press release, June 29, 2022, https://www.nato.int/cps/en/nat ohq/news_197287.htm.

105. Author interview with Stacie Pettyjohn, February 2023.

106. Anthony Capaccio, "Pentagon Warns China on Asia-Pacific: US Will Keep War-Fighting Edge," *Bloomberg,* December 3, 2022, https://www.bloomberg.com/news/articles/2022-12-03/pentagon-warns-china-on-asia-pacific-us-will-keep-war-fighting-edge.

# Chapter 12

1. Jean-Claude Trichet, "The Growing Importance of the Asia-Pacific region" (speech, Frankfurt, Germany, February 25, 2008), European Central Bank, https://www.ecb.europa.eu/press/key/date/2008/html/sp080225.en.html.

2. US Library of Congress, Congressional Research Service, *Pivot to the Pacific? The Obama Administration's "Rebalancing" Toward Asia* by Mark E. Manyin, Stephen Daggett, and Ben Dolven, R42448, 2012, https://sgp.fas.org/crs/natsec/R42448.pdf.

3. *Asia 2050: Realizing the Asian Century*, ed. Harinder S. Kohli, Ashok Sharma, and Anil Sood (New Delhi: SAGE Publications India, 2011), https://doi.org/10.4135/9781446270349; Jonathan Woetzl and Jeongmin Seong, "We've Entered the Asian Century and There Is No Turning Back," World Economic Forum, October 11, 2019, https://www.weforum.org/agenda/2019/10/has-world-entered-asian-century-what-does-it-mean/.

4. Author email with Robert Zoellick, March 2023.

5. Iori Kawate, "China's Trade with World Surges Ninefold after 20 Years in WTO," *Nikkei Asia*, November 7, 2021, https://asia.nikkei.com/Economy/China-s-trade-with-world-surges-ninefold-after-20-years-in-WTO.

6. Ibid.; Bloomberg News, "China Eclipses U.S. as Biggest Trading Nation Measured in Goods," *Bloomberg*, February 10, 2013, https://www.bloomberg.com/news/articles/2013-02-09/chinapasses-u-s-to-become-the-world-s-biggest-trading-nation#.

7. The World Bank, 2021, GDP (Current US$)—China, https://data.worldbank.org/indicator/NY.GDP.MKTP.CD?locations=CN.

8. Hillary Clinton, "America's Pacific Century," *Foreign Policy*, October 11, 2011, https://foreignpolicy.com/2011/10/11/americas-pacific-century/.

9. US Department of Labor, US Bureau of Labor Statistics, "Unemployment Rate Falls to 8.6 Percent in November 2011," December 5, 2011, https://www.bls.gov/opub/ted/2011/ted_20111205.htm.

10. Barack Obama, "Remarks by President Obama to the Australian Parliament" (remarks, Parliament House, Canberra, November 17, 2011), White House, https://obamawhitehouse.archives.gov/the-press-office/2011/11/17/remarks-president-obama-australian-parliament.

11. Clinton, "America's Pacific Century."

12. Author interview with Wendy Cutler, April 2023.

13. Robert Zoellick, "Whither China: From Membership to Responsibility?" (speech, New York, September 21, 2005), US Department of State, https://2001-2009.state.gov/s/d/former/zoellick/rem/53682.htm.

14. Obama, "Remarks by President Obama to the Australian Parliament."

15. Author interview with Wendy Cutler, April 2023.

16. Author interview with Robert Zoellick, March 2023.

17. Robert Kahn, "China and the United States: A G2 within the G20," Council on Foreign Relations Global Economics Monthly, April 2016, https://www.cfr.org/sites/default/files/pdf/2016/04/GEM%20April%202016.pdf.

18. Kawai Masahiro and Ganeshan Wignaraja, "A Closer Look at East Asia's Free Trade Agreements," World Trade Organization, https://www.wto.org/english/res_e/publications_e/wtr11_forum_e/wtr11_10may11_e.htm.

19. Kawai Masahiro and Ganeshan Wignaraja, "Introduction," in Asia's Free Trade Agreements: How Is Business Responding?, ed. Kawai Masahiro and Ganeshan Wignaraja (Cheshire, UK: Asian Development Bank and the ADB Institute with Edward Elgar Publishing, 2011), 8, 27, https://www.adb.org/sites/default/files/publication/159340/adbi-asia-free-trade-agreements.pdf.

20. European Commission, "Association of Southeast Asian Nations (ASEAN) EU Trade Relations with the Association of Southeast Asian Nations. Facts, Figures and Latest Developments," European Union, https://policy.trade.ec.europa.eu/eu-trade-relationships-country-and-region/countries-and-regions/association-south-east-asian-nations-asean_en.

21. Murry Hiebert, "ASEAN and Partners Launch Regional Comprehensive Economic Partnership," Center for Strategic and International Studies, December 7, 2012, https://www.csis.org/analysis/asean-and-partners-launch-regional-comprehensive-economic-partnership.

22. Roland Rajah and Alyssa Leng, "Chart of the Week: Global Trade through a US-China Lens," Interpreter, December 18, 2019, https://www.lowyinstitute.org/the-interpreter/chart-week-global-trade-through-us-china-lens; Matt Schrader, "China Is Weaponizing Globalization," Foreign Policy, June 5, 2020, https://foreignpolicy.com/2020/06/05/china-globalization-weaponizing-trade-communist-party/.

23. Mark A. Green, "China Is the Top Trading Partner to More than 120 Countries," Stubborn Things (blog), Wilson Center, January 17, 2023, https://www.wilsoncenter.org/blog-post/china-top-trading-partner-more-120-countries.

24. David Barboza, "China Passes Japan as Second-Largest Economy," New York Times, August 15, 2010, https://www.nytimes.com/2010/08/16/business/global/16yuan.html.

25. In 2008, during the Great Recession, a majority of Americans perceived trade as a threat rather than an opportunity, the only time that has occurred in Gallup polling.

See Jeffrey M. Jones, "U.S. Views of Foreign Trade Nearly Back to Pre-Trump Levels," Gallup, March 10, 2022, https://news.gallup.com/poll/390614/views-foreign-trade-nearly-back-pre-trump-levels.aspx. By 2016, a POLITICO-Harvard survey found that two-thirds of independents and 54 percent of Democrats believed trade deals had cost US jobs. Two-thirds of Republicans thought free trade lowered wages. Half of independents and 38 percent of Democrats believed the same. See Doug Palmer, "POLITICO-Harvard Poll: Americans Say 'TPP Who?,'" *Politico*, September 23, 2016, https://www.politico.com/story/2016/09/americans-say-tpp-who-228598.

26. Jungkun Seo, "Security Ties or Electoral Connections? The US Congress and the Korea–US Free Trade Agreement, 2007–2011," *International Relations of the Asia-Pacific* 15, no. 2 (May 2015): 217–243, https://doi.org/10.1093/irap/lcu024.

27. Edwin Feulner, "S. Korea-US Alliance Hinges on US Election: Experts," *Korea Times*, September 28, 2008, https://www.koreatimes.co.kr/www/news/nation/2008/09/205_31804.html.

28. US Library of Congress, Congressional Research Service, *The U.S.-South Korea Free Trade Agreement (KORUS FTA): Provisions and Implementation*, by Brock R. Williams, et al., RL34330, 2014, 4, https://crsreports.congress.gov/product/pdf/RL/RL34330/47.

29. 임정요, "Trump Vows to Renegotiate FTA with Korea," *Korea Herald*, July 23, 2016, https://www.koreaherald.com/view.php?ud=20160722000518.

30. James McBride, Andrew Chatzky, and Anshu Siripurapu, "What's Next for the Trans-Pacific Partnership (TPP)?," Backgrounder, Council on Foreign Relations, last modified September 20, 2021, https://www.cfr.org/backgrounder/what-trans-pacific-partnership-tpp.

31. Clinton, "America's Pacific Century."

32. Tom Donilon, "The United States and the Asia-Pacific in 2013" (speech, New York, March 11, 2013), Asia Society, https://asiasociety.org/new-york/complete-transcript-thomas-donilon-asia-society-new-york.

33. Kurt Campbell, *The Pivot: The Future of American Statecraft in Asia* (New York: Hachette Book Group, 2016), 266–271.

34. Ibid.

35. White House, Office of the Press Secretary, "Fact Sheet: Advancing the Rebalance to Asia and the Pacific," November 16, 2015, https://obamawhitehouse.archives.gov/the-press-office/2015/11/16/fact-sheet-advancing-rebalance-asia-and-pacific.

36. Jeffrey A. Bader and David Dollar, "Why the TPP is the Linchpin of the Asia Rebalance," *Order from Chaos* (blog), Brookings Institution, July 28, 2015, https://www.brookings.edu/blog/order-from-chaos/2015/07/28/why-the-tpp-is-the-linchpin-of-the-asia-rebalance/.

37. Executive Office of the President, Office of the United States Trade Representative, "Previous Findings on the Economic Impact of TPP," 2016, https://ustr.gov/about/TPP/Previous-Findings-Economic-Impact-TPP.

38. Wendy Cutler and Clete Willems, *Reimagining the TPP: Revisions That Could Facilitate U.S. Reentry*, (Washington, DC: Asia Society Policy Institute, December 12, 2022), https://asiasociety.org/policy-institute/reimaginingTPP.

39. Max Ehrenfreund, "How the TPP Became the Most Divisive Policy in the Democratic Party," *Washington Post*, July 26, 2016, https://www.washingtonpost.com/news/wonk/wp/2016/07/26/how-the-tpp-became-the-most-divisive-policy-in-the-democratic-party/.

40. Cutler and Willems, *Reimagining the TPP*.

41. White House, Office of the Press Secretary, US Mission Geneva, "Statement by the President on the Signing of the Trans-Pacific Partnership," press release, February 4, 2016, https://geneva.usmission.gov/2016/02/04/statement-by-president-obama-on-the-signing-of-the-trans-pacific-partnership/.

42. Barack Obama, "President Obama: The TPP Would Let America, Not China, Lead the Way on Global Trade," *Washington Post*, May 2, 2016, https://www.washingtonpost.com/opinions/president-obama-the-tpp-would-let-america-not-china-lead-the-way-on-global-trade/2016/05/02/680540e4-0fd0-11e6-93ae-50921721165d_story.html.

43. "World Bank Says Japan, Vietnam to Gain Significantly," *Nikkei Asia*, January 8, 2016, https://asia.nikkei.com/Economy/World-Bank-says-Japan-Vietnam-to-gain-significantly; Ehrenfreund, "How the TPP Became the Most Divisive Policy."

44. Author interview with Wendy Cutler, April 2023.

45. White House, Office of the Press Secretary, "Statement by President Obama on the Trans-Pacific Partnership," press release, October 5, 2015, https://obamawhitehouse.archives.gov/the-press-office/2015/10/05/statement-president-trans-pacific-partnership.

46. Prashanth Parameswaran, "TPP as Important as Another Aircraft Carrier: US Defense Secretary," *Diplomat*, April 8, 2015, https://thediplomat.com/2015/04/tpp-as-important-as-another-aircraft-carrier-us-defense-secretary/.

47. Jonathon Soble, "Failure of Obama's Trans-Pacific Trade Deal Could Hurt U.S. Influence in Asia," *New York Times*, June 16, 2015, https://www.nytimes.com/2015/06/17/world/asia/obama-trans-pacific-partnership-asia.html.

48. Ibid.

49. Michael Froman, "Killing TPP Would Hand China 'Keys to the Castle': U.S. Trade Representative," interviewed by Mitra Taj, *Reuters*, July 29, 2016, https://www.reuters.com/article/us-usa-trade/killing-tpp-would-hand-china-keys-to-the-castle-u-s-trade-representative-idUSKCN1090QZ.

50. Andrew Glass, "Trump Scuttles Trans-Pacific Trade Pact, Jan. 23, 2017," *Politico*, January 23, 2019, https://www.politico.com/story/2019/01/23/trans-pacific-trade-pact-2017-1116638.

51. Ehrenfreund, "How the TPP Became the Most Divisive Policy."

52. Author interview with Wendy Cutler, April 2023.

53. Robert Lighthizer, "Just Say No to Rejoining TPP," *American Compass*, March 30, 2022, https://americancompass.org/just-say-no-to-rejoining-tpp/.

54. Elizabeth Warren, "Senator Warren Urges Congress to Reject TPP Agreement" (remarks, Senate floor, Washington, DC, February 2, 2016), https://www.warren.senate.gov/newsroom/press-releases/senator-warren-urges-congress-to-reject-tpp-agreement.

55. "The Trans-Pacific Partnership Trade Deal: Opposition," Ballotpedia, 2017, https://ballotpedia.org/The_Trans-Pacific_Partnership_trade_deal:_Opposition.

56. Bernie Sanders, "Sanders Statement on Trans-Pacific Partnership," January 23, 2017, https://www.sanders.senate.gov/press-releases/sanders-statement-on-trans-pacific-partnership/.

57. "The Trans-Pacific Partnership Trade Deal: Opposition," Ballotpedia.

58. Ehrenfreund, "How the TPP Became the Most Divisive Policy."

59. Donald Trump, "Disappearing Middle Class Needs Better Deal on Trade," *USA Today*, March 14, 2016, https://www.usatoday.com/story/opinion/2016/03/14/donald-trump-tpp-trade-american-manufacturing-jobs-workers-column/81728584/.

60. Wendy Cutler, "America Must Return to the Trans-Pacific Partnership," *Foreign Affairs*, September 10, 2021, https://www.foreignaffairs.com/united-states/america-must-return-trans-pacific-partnership.

61. Timothy R. Heath, "Strategic Consequences of U.S. Withdrawal from TPP," *TheRANDblog*, (blog), RAND, March 27, 2017, https://www.rand.org/blog/2017/03/strategic-consequences-of-us-withdrawal-from-tpp.html.

62. Michèle Flournoy and Ely Ratner, "A Trade Deal with a Bonus for National Security," *Wall Street Journal*, March 8, 2015, https://www.wsj.com/articles/michele-flournoy-and-ely-ratner-a-trade-deal-with-a-bonus-for-national-security-1425854510.

63. Glass, "Trump Scuttles Trans-Pacific Trade Pact."

64. Ibid.

65. "Senator Calls U.S. Departure From Trans-Pacific Pact a Mistake," *Bloomberg Law*, September 19, 2017, https://news.bloomberglaw.com/international-trade/senator-calls-us-departure-from-trans-pacific-pact-a-mistake; Feliks Garcia, "President Donald Trump Scraps TPP Trade Deal by Executive Order," *Independent*, January 23, 2017, https://www.independent.co.uk/news/world/americas/donald-trump-tpp-scraps-trade-deal-executive-order-signs-us-president-white-house-day-one-a7542211.html.

66. Author interview with Wendy Cutler, April 2023.

67. Jonathon Soble, "Failure of Obama's Trans-Pacific Trade Deal Could Hurt U.S. Influence in Asia," *New York Times*, June 16, 2015, https://www.nytimes.com/2015/06/17/world/asia/obama-trans-pacific-partnership-asia.html.

68. McBride, Chatzky, and Siripurapu, "What's Next for the Trans-Pacific Partnership (TPP)?."

69. Alexander Chipman Koty, "The UK Starts Talks to Join CPTPP, Seeking Access to ASEAN," *ASEAN Briefing*, August 27, 2021, https://www.aseanbriefing.com/news/the-uk-starts-talks-to-join-cptpp-seeking-access-to-asean/.

70. Cutler and Willems, *Reimagining the TPP*.

71. US Library of Congress, Congressional Research Services, *CPTPP: Overview and Issues for Congress*, by Cathleen D. Cimino-Isaacs, IF2078, 2022, https://crsreports.congress.gov/product/pdf/IF/IF12078.

72. Silvia Amaro, "Australia Is Hopeful That the US Will Join TPP, Finance Minister Says," *CNBC*, January 24, 2018, https://www.cnbc.com/2018/01/24/trade-australia-hopes-the-us-will-join-tpp-finance-minister-says.html.

73. Cutler and Willems, *Reimagining the TPP*.

74. Jennifer Harris and Jake Sullivan, "America Needs a New Economic Philosophy. Foreign Policy Experts Can Help," *Foreign Policy*, February 7, 2020, https://foreignpol icy.com/2020/02/07/america-needs-a-new-economic-philosophy-foreign-policy-experts-can-help/.

75. US Congress, Senate, Committee on Finance, *Nomination of Katherine C. Tai to Be United States Trade Representative, with the rank of Ambassador Extraordinary and Plenipotentiary, Executive Office of the President*, 17th Cong., 1st Sess., February 25, 2021, 38, https://www.finance.senate.gov/imo/media/doc/47345.pdf.

76. Author interview with Wendy Cutler, April 2023.

77. Xi Jinping, "Jointly Shoulder Responsibility of Our Times, Promote Global Growth" (speech, World Economic Forum Annual Meeting, Davos, Switzerland, January 17, 2017), The State Council Information Office, The People's Republic of China, http://www.china.org.cn/node_7247529/content_40569136.htm.

78. Yen Nee Lee, "'A Coup for China': Analysts React to the World's Largest Trade Deal That Excludes the U.S.," *CNBC*, November 15, 2020, https://www.cnbc.com/2020/11/16/rcep-15-asia-pacific-countries-including-china-sign-worlds-largest-trade-deal.html.

79. US Library of Congress, Congressional Research Service, *Regional Comprehensive Economic Partnership (RCEP)*, by Cathleen D. Cimino-Isaacs, Ben Dolven, and Michael D. Sutherland, IF11891, 2022, https://crsreports.congress.gov/product/pdf/IF/IF11891.

80. Lee, "'A Coup for China.'"

81. Ibid.

82. Clete Willems and Niels Graham, "TTC, IPEF, and the Road to an Indo-Pacific Trade Deal: A New Model," Frankfurt Forum with Atlantic Council's Geoeconomics Center and Atlantik-Brücke, September 27, 2022, 4, https://www.atlanticcouncil.org/wp-content/uploads/2022/09/TTC_IPEF_and_the_Road_to_an_Indo-Pacific_Tr ade_Deal___-.pdf.

83. Cutler and Willems, *Reimagining the TPP*, 5.

84. Committee on Finance, *Nomination of Katherine C. Tai*.

85. Eric Emerson and Chris Forsgren, "The US Appears Poised to Pursue a Digital Trade Agreement in Asia—What Does that Mean?," *Steptoe*, October 15, 2021, https://www.steptoeglobaltradeblog.com/2021/10/the-us-appears-poised-to-pursue-a-digital-trade-agreement-in-asia-what-does-that-mean/.

86. Robert B. Zoellick, "If America Doesn't Set the Digital Trade Agenda, China Will," *Wall Street Journal*, February 1, 2022, https://www.wsj.com/articles/if-the-u-s-doe snt-set-the-digital-trade-agenda-china-will-economy-cloud-computing-globalizat ion-data-11643755347

87. *The Strategic Importance of a U.S. Digital Trade Agreement in the Indo-Pacific, before the U.S. House Foreign Affairs Committee Subcommittee on Asia, the Pacific, Central Asia, and Nonproliferation* (January 19, 2022) (David Feith), https://www.cnas.org/publications/congressional-testimony/the-strategic-importance-of-a-u-s-digital-trade-agreement-in-the-indo-pacific.

88. Chris Coons, "Sen. Coons, Colleagues Call on Administration to Use New Indo-Pacific Economic Framework to Set Global Standards on Digital Trade," press release, December 17, 2021, https://www.coons.senate.gov/news/press-releases/sen-coons-colleagues-call-on-administration-to-use-new-indo-pacific-economic-framework-to-set-global-standards-on-digital-trade.

89. Claude Barfield, "A US-Led Indo-Pacific Digital Trade Deal? Part I," American Enterprise Institute, January 24, 2022, https://www.aei.org/technology-and-innovation/a-us-led-indo-pacific-digital-trade-deal-part-i/.

90. Bob Davis, "U.S.-Asia Digital Pact Held Up by Squabble among Biden Officials," *Wall Street Journal*, July 20, 2021, https://www.wsj.com/articles/u-s-asia-digital-pact-held-up-by-squabble-among-biden-officials-11626781120.

91. Ibid.

92. Joanna Shelton, "Look Skeptically at China's CPTPP Application," Center for Strategic and International Studies, November 18, 2021, https://www.csis.org/analysis/look-skeptically-chinas-cptpp-application.

93. Carla Freeman, "How Will China's Bid to Join a Trans-Pacific Trade Pact Affect Regional Stability?," United States Institute of Peace, October 7, 2021, https://www.usip.org/publications/2021/10/how-will-chinas-bid-join-trans-pacific-trade-pact-affect-regional-stability.

94. White House, "Fact Sheet: In Asia, President Biden and a Dozen Indo-Pacific Partners Launch the Indo-Pacific Economic Framework for Prosperity," May 23, 2022, https://www.whitehouse.gov/briefing-room/statements-releases/2022/05/23/fact-sheet-in-asia-president-biden-and-a-dozen-indo-pacific-partners-launch-the-indo-pacific-economic-framework-for-prosperity/.

95. Ibid.

96. Chad P. Brown and Barbara Weisel, "What Is the Indo-Pacific Economic Framework and Will It Work?," excerpts of the Trade Talks Podcast, Peterson Institute for International Economics, December 12, 2022, https://www.piie.com/blogs/realtime-economics/what-indo-pacific-economic-framework-and-will-it-work.

97. Joseph Biden, "Remarks by President Biden at Indo-Pacific Economic Framework for Prosperity Launch Event" (speech, Izumi Garden Gallery, Tokyo, May 23, 2022), White House, https://www.whitehouse.gov/briefing-room/speeches-remarks/2022/05/23/remarks-by-president-biden-at-indo-pacific-economic-framework-for-prosperity-launch-event/.

98. Greg Earl, "Economic Diplomacy: New Supply Chains to Jakarta and Beyond," *Interpreter*, June 27, 2022, https://www.lowyinstitute.org/the-interpreter/economic-diplomacy-new-supply-chains-jakarta-and-beyond.

99. "US Proposes Pick-and-Choose Indo-Pacific Economic Framework," *Hindustan Times*, May 13, 2022, https://www.hindustantimes.com/india-news/usproposes-pick-and-choose-indo-pacific-economic-framework-101652379717072.html.

100. Takaki Tominaga, "Focus: U.S., Japan Commitment Vital to Indo-Pacific Framework's Success," *Kyodo News*, September 13, 2022, https://english.kyodonews.net/news/2022/09/ca82138541ee-focus-us-japan-commitment-vital-to-indo-pacific-frameworks-success.html.

101. Government of Australia, Minister for Trade and Tourism, Special Minister of State, Senator the Hon Don Farrell, "Indo-Pacific Economic Framework—Negotiations Have Commenced," press release, September 12, 2022, https://www.trademinister.gov.au/minister/don-farrell/media-release/indo-pacific-economic-framework-negotiations-have-commenced.

102. Prime Minister's Office Singapore, "Intervention by PM Lee Hsien Loong at the Virtual Launch of the Indo-Pacific Economic Framework," May 23, 2022, https://www.pmo.gov.sg/Newsroom/Intervention-by-PM-Lee-Hsien-Loong-at-the-Virtual-Launch-of-the-Indo-Pacific-Economic-Framework#:~:text=Singapore%20welcomes%20the%20IPEF.,both%20strategic%20and%20economic%20significance.

103. Author conversation with senior Japanese official, May 2022.

104. Author conversation with Australian officials, December 2022.

105. Author conversation with senior administration official, March 2023.

106. "America's Crumbling Trade Initiative in Asia," *Economist*, November 23, 2023, https://www.economist.com/asia/2023/11/23/americas-crumbling-trade-initiative-in-asia; Wendy Cutler, "U.S. Made the Most of APEC Given What It Had to Work with," *Nikkei Asia*, November 27, 2023, https://asia.nikkei.com/Opinion/U.S.-made-the-most-of-APEC-given-what-it-had-to-work-with.

107. Emily Kilcrease, "CNAS Responds: APEC Summit," Center for a New American Security, November 15, 2023, https://www.cnas.org/press/press-note/cnas-responds-apec-summit.

108. Roland Rajah, "Mobilizing the Indo-Pacific Infrastructure Response to China's Belt and Road Initiative in Southeast Asia," Brookings Institution, April 2020, https://www.brookings.edu/wp-content/uploads/2020/04/FP_20200429_mobilize_compete_rajah.pdf.

109. Lingling Wei, "China Reins In Its Belt and Road Program, $1 Trillion Later," *Wall Street Journal*, September 26, 2022, https://www.wsj.com/articles/china-belt-road-debt-11663961638.

110. Ibid.

111. Rajah, "Mobilizing the Indo-Pacific Infrastructure Response."

112. Daniel R. Russel and Blake H. Berger, "Weaponizing the Belt and Road Initiative," Asia Policy Institute, September 2020, https://asiasociety.org/sites/default/files/2020-09/Weaponizing%20the%20Belt%20and%20Road%20Initiative_0.pdf.

113. Mike Pence, "Remarks by Vice President Pence at the 2018 APEC CEO Summit | Port Moresby, Papua New Guinea" (remarks, Pacific Explorer Marquee Theatre, Port Moresby, Papua New Guinea, November 16, 2018), White House, https://trumpwhitehouse.archives.gov/briefings-statements/remarks-vice-president-pence-2018-apec-ceo-summit-port-moresby-papua-new-guinea/.

114. Jacob J. Lew et al., *China's Belt and Road: Implications for the United States*, Independent Task Force Report No. 79, Council on Foreign Relations, March 2021, https://www.cfr.org/report/chinas-belt-and-road-implications-for-the-united-states/.

115. Anna Gelpern, et al., *How China Lends: A Rare Look into 100 Debt Contracts with Foreign Governments*, (Peterson Institute for International Economics, Kiel Institute

for the World Economy, Center for Global Development, and AidData at William & Mary, 2021), 2, https://docs.aiddata.org/ad4/pdfs/How_China_Lends__A_Rare_Look_into_100_Debt_Contracts_with_Foreign_Governments.pdf.

116. John Hurley, Scott Morris, and Gailyn Portelance, "Examining the Debt Implications of the Belt and Road Initiative from a Policy Perspective," Center for Global Development, March 4, 2018, https://www.cgdev.org/publication/examining-debt-implications-belt-and-road-initiative-a-policy-perspective; Deborah Brautigam and Meg Rithmire, "The Chinese 'Debt Trap' Is a Myth," *Atlantic*, February 6, 2021, https://www.theatlantic.com/international/archive/2021/02/china-debt-trap-diplomacy/617953/.

117. Russel and Berger, "Weaponizing the Belt and Road Initiative."

118. Matthias Sobolewski and Jason Lange, "U.S. Urged Allies to Think Twice before Joining China-Led Bank," *Reuters*, March 16, 2015, https://www.reuters.com/article/us-europe-asia-bank/u-s-urges-allies-to-think-twice-before-joining-china-led-bank-idUSKBN0MD0B320150317.

119. Jim Zarroli, "New Asian Development Bank Seen as Sign of China's Growing Influence," *NPR*, April 16, 2015, https://www.npr.org/2015/04/16/400178364/finance-officials-to-discuss-asian-development-bank-at-spring-meetings.

120. *2021 AIIB Annual Report and Financials*, (Beijing, China: Asian Infrastructure Investment Bank, 2021), https://www.aiib.org/en/news-events/annual-report/2021/home/index.html.

121. Kai Yin Allison Haga, "The Asian Infrastructure Investment Bank: A Qualified Success for Beijing's Economic Statecraft," *Journal of Current Chinese Affairs* 50, no. 3 (2021): 391–421, https://doi.org/10.1177/18681026211046967; Author interview with Bob Zoellick, March 2023.

122. Roland Rajah, "Mobilizing the Indo-Pacific Infrastructure Response to China's Belt and Road Initiative in Southeast Asia," Brookings Institution, April 2020, https://www.brookings.edu/wp-content/uploads/2020/04/FP_20200429_mobilize_compete_rajah.pdf.

123. Lew et al., "China's Belt and Road: Implications for the United States," 85.

124. "China's 'Belt and Road' Strategy Has a New Competitor—Enter America's 'Blue Dot Network,'" *Australia Broadcasting Company*, November 5, 2019, https://www.abc.net.au/news/2019-11-06/us-introduces-blue-dot-network-as-answer-to-belt-and-road/11675226.

125. "The Clean Network," US Department of State, https://2017-2021.state.gov/the-clean-network/index.html.

126. Ibid.

127. White House, "Fact Sheet: President Biden and G7 Leaders Launch Build Back Better World (B3W) Partnership," June 12, 2021, https://www.whitehouse.gov/briefing-room/statements-releases/2021/06/12/fact-sheet-president-biden-and-g7-leaders-launch-build-back-better-world-b3w-partnership/.

128. Australian Government, Export Finance Australia, "Australia, US and Japan Announce Trilateral Partnership," press release, https://www.exportfinance.gov.au/newsroom/australia-us-and-japan-announce-trilateral-partnership/; US Mission

Italy, "G7 Launches Plan to Boost Global Infrastructure Investment," July 9, 2022, https://it.usembassy.gov/g7-launches-plan-to-boost-global-infrastructure-inv estment/.

129. Lew et al., "China's Belt and Road: Implications for the United States," 85.

130. Charles Kenny and Scott Morris, "American Shouldn't Copy China's Belt and Road Initiative," *Foreign Affairs*, June 22, 2022, https://www.foreignaffairs.com/articles/ united-states/2022-06-22/america-shouldnt-copy-chinas-belt-and-road-initiative.

131. US International Development Finance Corporation, *Congressional Budget Justification: Fiscal Year 2023*, https://www.dfc.gov/sites/default/files/media/docume nts/DFC%20FY23%20CBJ%20_%202022-04-05%20FINAL_Branded_R.pdf.

132. Haley Channer, "Revitalizing the Trilateral Partnership," Reconnecting Asia, *Center for Strategic and International Studies*, May 26, 2021, https://reconasia.csis.org/revit alizing-the-trilateral-partnership/.

133. Wei, "China Reins In Its Belt and Road Program."

134. Elizabeth Losos, "Is This the West's Answer to China's Belt and Road Initiative?," Duke Nicholas Institute for Energy, Environment, & Sustainability, August 23, 2022, https://nicholasinstitute.duke.edu/articles/wests-answer-chinas-belt-and-road-ini tiative.

135. Tom Hancock, "China Has a Debt Problem—Other People's Debt," *Bloomberg*, October 1, 2022, https://www.bloomberg.com/news/newsletters/2022-10-01/ china-has-a-debt-problem-other-people-s-debt-new-economy-saturday; Wei, "China Reins In Its Belt and Road Program."

136. Karen Freifeld, "U.S. Accuses Huawei of Stealing Trade Secrets, Assisting Iran," *Reuters*, February 13, 2020, https://www.reuters.com/article/us-usa-huawei-tech- indictment/u-s-accuses-huawei-of-stealing-trade-secrets-assisting-iran-idUSKB N2072KG; Arjun Kharpal, "Huawei Says It Would Never Hand Data to China's Government. Experts Say It Wouldn't Have a Choice," *CNBC*, March 4, 2019, https:// www.cnbc.com/2019/03/05/huawei-would-have-to-give-data-to-china-governm ent-if-asked-experts.html.

137. Noah Berman, Lindsay Maizland, and Andrew Chatzky, "Is China's Huawei a Threat to U.S. National Security?," Backgrounder, Council on Foreign Relations, last modi- fied February 8, 2023, https://www.cfr.org/backgrounder/chinas-huawei-threat-us- national-security#chapter-title-0-6.

138. David McCabe, "F.C.C. Designates Huawei and ZTE as National Security Threats," *New York Times*, June 30, 2020, https://www.nytimes.com/2020/06/30/technology/ fcc-huawei-zte-national-security.html.

139. "U.S. Stops Granting Export Licenses for China's Huawei, Sources Say," *CNBC*, January 30, 2023, https://www.cnbc.com/2023/01/31/us-stops-granting-export- licenses-for-chinas-huawei-sources-say.html; Ian Talley and Asa Fitch, "Huawei Export Licenses Could Be Revoked by U.S.," *Wall Street Journal*, February 28, 2023, https://www.wsj.com/articles/huawei-export-licenses-could-be-revoked-by-u-s- 567c998d.

140. "Trump Accuses China of 'Raping' US with Unfair Trade Policy," *BBC*, May 2, 2016, https://www.bbc.com/news/election-us-2016-36185012.

141. Doug Palmer, "Biden Considers Tiny China Tariff Relief Package," *Politico*, July 5, 2022, https://www.politico.com/newsletters/weekly-trade/2022/07/05/biden-considers-tiny-china-tariff-relief-package-00043952.

142. Bob David and Linling Wei, "Who Won the U.S.-China Trade War?," *Wall Street Journal*, May 20, 2022, https://www.wsj.com/articles/who-won-the-u-s-china-trade-war-11653059611; Chad P. Brown, "US-China Trade War Tariffs: An Up-to-Date Chart," Peterson Institute for International Economics, last updated April 22, 2022, https://www.piie.com/research/piie-charts/us-china-trade-war-tariffs-date-chart.

143. Bureau of Economic Analysis, US Department of Commerce, "2017 Trade Gap Is $568.4 Billion," March 7, 2018, https://www.bea.gov/news/blog/2018-03-07/2017-trade-gap-5684-billion; Bureau of Economic Analysis, US Department of Commerce, "2021 Trade Gap Is $861.4 Billion," March 8, 2022, https://www.bea.gov/news/blog/2022-03-08/2021-trade-gap-8614-billion.

144. Katie Lobosco, "Breaking Down the Costs of Trump's Trade War with China," *CNN*, January 14, 2020, https://www.cnn.com/2020/01/14/politics/cost-of-china-tariff-trade-war/index.html.

145. Chad P. Bown, "US-China Phase One Tracker: China's Purchases of US Goods," Peterson Institute for International Economics, July 19, 2022, https://www.piie.com/research/piie-charts/us-china-phase-one-tracker-chinas-purchases-us-goods.

146. Katie Lobosco, "Why Biden Is Keeping Trump's China Tariffs in Place," *CNN*, January 26, 2022, https://www.cnn.com/2022/01/26/politics/china-tariffs-biden-policy/index.html.

147. Chad P. Bown and Yilin Wang, "Five Years into the Trade War, China Continues Its Slow Decoupling from US Exports," March 16, 2023, *Realtime Economics* (blog), Peterson Institute for International Economics, https://www.piie.com/blogs/realtime-economics/five-years-trade-war-china-continues-its-slow-decoupling-us-exports.

148. Farhad Jalinous, et al., "CFIUS Reform Becomes Law: What FIRRMA Means for Industry," White & Case, August 13, 2018, https://www.whitecase.com/insight-alert/cfius-reform-becomes-law-what-firrma-means-industry.

149. Zoey Zhang, "US Revokes Hong Kong's Special Status: What Are the Implications?," *China Briefing*, July 16, 2020, https://www.china-briefing.com/news/us-revokes-hong-kongs-special-status-implications-trade-business/.

150. Amar Madhani, "U.S. Imposes Sanctions on China over Human Rights Abuses of Uighurs," *PBS*, December 16, 2021, https://www.pbs.org/newshour/world/u-s-imposes-sanctions-on-china-over-human-rights-abuses-of-uighurs.

151. Jake Sullivan, "Remarks by National Security Advisor Jake Sullivan at the Special Competitive Studies Project Global Emerging Technologies Summit" (remarks, September 16, 2022), White House, https://www.whitehouse.gov/briefing-room/speeches-remarks/2022/09/16/remarks-by-national-security-advisor-jake-sullivan-at-the-special-competitive-studies-project-global-emerging-technologies-summit/.

152. Clinton, "America's Pacific Century."

153. Shiva Aminian, et al., "Commerce Imposes Significant New Controls on Advanced Semiconductors," *Akin Export Controls and Economic Sanctions Practice Group*,

October 24, 2023, https://www.akingump.com/en/insights/alerts/commerce-impo ses-significant-new-controls-on-advanced-semiconductors; Evelyn Cheng, "U.S. Export Controls need to 'Change Constantly' Even if it's Tough for Businesses, Secretary Raimondo Says," *CNBC*, December 5, 2023, https://www.cnbc.com/ 2023/12/05/commerce-sec-raimondo-us-export-controls-need-to-change-constan tly.html.

154. White House, *Executive Order on Addressing United States Investments in Certain National Security Technologies and Products in Countries of Concern*, August 9, 2023, https://www.whitehouse.gov/briefing-room/presidential-actions/2023/08/ 09/executive-order-on-addressing-united-states-investments-in-certain-national-security-technologies-and-products-in-countries-of-concern/.

155. Gavin Bade, "'A Sea Change': Biden Reverses Decades of Chinese Trade Policy," *Politico*, December 26, 2022, https://www.politico.com/news/2022/12/26/china-trade-tech-00072232.

156. White House, "Fact Sheet: CHIPS and Science Act Will Lower Costs, Create Jobs, Strengthen Supply Chains, and Counter China," August 9, 2022, https://www.whi tehouse.gov/briefing-room/statements-releases/2022/08/09/fact-sheet-chips-and-science-act-will-lower-costs-create-jobs-strengthen-supply-chains-and-counter-china/.

157. Jeanne Whalen, "To Counter China, Some Republicans Are Abandoning Free-Market Orthodoxy," *Washington Post*, August 26, 2020, https://www.washingtonp ost.com/business/2020/08/26/republicans-favor-industrial-policy/.

158. Jake Sullivan, "Remarks by National Security Advisor Jake Sullivan on Renewing American Economic Leadership at the Brookings Institution" (remarks, Brookings Institution, April 27, 2023), White House, https://www.whitehouse.gov/brief ing-room/speeches-remarks/2023/04/27/remarks-by-national-security-advisor-jake-sullivan-on-renewing-american-economic-leadership-at-the-brookings-inst itution/.

159. Janet Yellen, "Remarks by Secretary of the Treasury Janet L. Yellen at Press Conference in Beijing, the People's Republic of China" (remarks, Beijing, July 8, 2023), US Department of the Treasury, https://home.treasury.gov/news/press-relea ses/jy1603.

160. Monica Miller, "US-China Trade Hits Record High despite Rising Tensions," *BBC*, February 8, 2023, https://www.bbc.com/news/business-64563855.

161. Ana Swanson, "America's Trade Deficit Surged in 2022, Nearing $1 Trillion," *New York Times*, February 7, 2023, https://www.nytimes.com/2023/02/07/business/ economy/us-trade-deficit.html.

162. "In Charts: The US and China's Economic Footprints in Asia," *Economist Intelligence*, May 24, 2022, http://country.eiu.com/article.aspx?articleid=802132863&Country= China&topic=Politics&subtopic=Forecast&subsubtopic=International+relations.

163. Jeremy Ney, "United States Entity List: Limits on American Exports," Harvard Kennedy Center, Belfer Center for Science and International Affairs, February 2021, https://www.belfercenter.org/publication/united-states-entity-list-limits-ameri can-exports.

164. "Lowy Institute Asia Power Index 2023 Edition: Trade with Region: Total Value of Trade with Index Countries, Current Dollars (2020)," Lowy Institute, 2023, https://power.lowyinstitute.org/data/economic-relationships/regional-trade-relati ons/trade-with-region/; "Lowy Institute Asia Power Index 2023 Edition: Primary Trade Partner, Number of Index Countries in Which State Is the Primary Regional Trading Partner (2020)," Lowy Institute, 2023, https://power.lowyinstitute.org/data/ economic-relationships/regional-trade-relations/primary-trade-partner/.

# Chapter 13

1. Hillary Clinton, "America's Pacific Century," *Foreign Policy*, October 11, 2011, https://foreignpolicy.com/2011/10/11/americas-pacific-century/.
2. Clinton, "America's Pacific Century."
3. Barack Obama, "Remarks by President Obama to the Australian Parliament" (remarks, Parliament House, Canberra, Australia, November 17, 2011), White House, https://obamawhitehouse.archives.gov/the-press-office/2011/11/17/rema rks-president-obama-australian-parliament.
4. Tom Donilon, "Remarks by National Security Advisor Tom Donilon—As Prepared for Delivery" (remarks, Center for Strategic and International Studies, November 15, 2012), White House, https://obamawhitehouse.archives.gov/the-press-office/ 2012/11/15/remarks-national-security-advisor-tom-donilon-prepared-delivery.
5. Tom Donilon, "Complete Transcript: Thomas Donilon at Asia Society New York" (remarks, Asia Society, New York, March 11, 2013), https://asiasociety.org/new-york/complete-transcript-thomas-donilon-asia-society-new-york.
6. Hillary Clinton, "America's Engagement in the Asia-Pacific" (speech, Kahala Hotel, Honolulu, Hawaii, October 28, 2010), US Department of State, https://2009-2017. state.gov/secretary/20092013clinton/rm/2010/10/150141.htm.
7. US Department of State, Bureau of East Asian and Pacific Affairs, "Lower Mekong Initiative," February 21, 2019, https://www.state.gov/lower-mekong-initiative/.
8. Jackson Ewing, "How U.S.-China Cooperation Spurred Global Momentum on Climate Change," *Asia Society*, July 25, 2016, https://asiasociety.org/blog/asia/how-us-china-cooperation-spurred-global-momentum-climate-change.
9. Suzanne Goldenberg and Jonathan Watts, "US Aims for Bilateral Climate Change Deals with China and India," *Guardian*, October 14, 2009, https://www.theguard ian.com/environment/2009/oct/14/obama-india-china-climate-change.
10. Samuel Thernstrom, "The Quiet Death of the Kyoto Protocol," *The American*, November 5, 2009, https://web.archive.org/web/20101026234940/http://american. com/archive/2009/november/the-quiet-yet-historic-death-of-the-kyoto-protoco/.
11. White House, Office of the Press Secretary, "U.S.-China Joint Announcement on Climate Change," November 11, 2014, https://obamawhitehouse.archives.gov/the-press-office/2014/11/11/us-china-joint-announcement-climate-change.
12. "U.S.-China Joint Announcement on Climate Change."

13. "Paris Agreement," December 12, 2015, United Nations Treaty Series Online, registration no. I-54113, https://treaties.un.org/pages/AdvanceSearch.aspx?tab=UNTS&clang=_en.

14. PBL Netherlands Environmental Assessment Agency, "Trends in Global CO2 Emissions: 2015 Report," November 25, 2015, https://www.pbl.nl/en/publications/trends-in-global-co2-emissions-2015-report.

15. White House, Office of the Press Secretary, "Fact Sheet: Advancing the Rebalance to Asia and the Pacific," November 16, 2015, https://obamawhitehouse.archives.gov/the-press-office/2015/11/16/fact-sheet-advancing-rebalance-asia-and-pacific.

16. Jackson Ewing, "How U.S.-China Cooperation Spurred Global Momentum on Climate Change," *Asia Society*, July 25, 2016, https://asiasociety.org/blog/asia/how-us-china-cooperation-spurred-global-momentum-climate-change.

17. Donald Trump, "Statement by President Trump on the Paris Climate Accord" (statement, Rose Garden, Washington, DC, June 1, 2017 https://trumpwhitehouse.archives.gov/briefings-statements/statement-president-trump-paris-climate-accord/; "President Trump Announces Withdrawal from Paris Agreement," *Sabin Center for Climate Change*, https://climate.law.columbia.edu/content/president-trump-announces-withdrawal-paris-agreement-0.

18. Donald Trump, "Statement by President Trump on the Paris Climate Accord."

19. H. R. McMaster, *Battlegrounds: The Fight to Defend the Free World* (New York: Harper, 2020), 418.

20. Antony Blinken, US Department of State, "The United States Officially Rejoins the Paris Agreement," February 19, 2021, https://www.state.gov/the-united-states-officially-rejoins-the-paris-agreement/#.

21. Chris Buckley and Lisa Friedman, "Climate Change Is 'Not a Geostrategic Weapon,' Kerry Tells Chinese Leaders," *New York Times*, September 1, 2021, https://www.nytimes.com/2021/09/02/world/asia/climate-china-us-kerry.html.

22. Ibid.

23. Amy Gunia, "Why China's Promise to Stop Funding Coal Plants around the World Is a Really Big Deal," *Time*, September 22, 2021, https://time.com/6100439/china-stop-funding-coal-plants/.

24. Keith Brasher and Clifford Krauss, "China Is Burning More Coal, a Growing Climate Challenge," *New York Times*, November 10, 2022, https://www.nytimes.com/2022/11/03/business/energy-environment/china-coal-natural-gas.html.

25. Ari Shapiro, Ashley Brown, Noah Caldwell, et al., "U.S. and China Announce Surprise Climate Agreement at COP26 Summit," *NPR*, November 11, 2021, https://www.npr.org/2021/11/11/1054648598/u-s-and-china-announce-surprise-climate-agreement-at-cop26-summit.

26. Valerie Volcovici, "U.S.-China Diplomatic Breakdown Clouds Outlook for Global Climate Progress," *Reuters*, August 6, 2022, https://www.reuters.com/business/environment/un-warns-no-way-tackle-climate-change-without-us-china-cooperation-2022-08-05/.

27. Eduardo Baptista, "U.S. Must Dispel Pelosi's 'Negative Influence' before Climate Talks: China," *Reuters*, August 31, 2022, https://www.nasdaq.com/articles/u.s.-must-dispel-pelosis-negative-influence-before-climate-talks:-china.

28. Jim Tankersley and Lisa Friedman, "U.S. and China Restart Climate Talks," *New York Times,* November 14, 2022, https://www.nytimes.com/2022/11/14/business/china-us-climate-change.html; US Department of State, "Sunnylands Statement on Enhancing Cooperation to Address the Climate Crisis," November 14, 2023, https://www.state.gov/sunnylands-statement-on-enhancing-cooperation-to-address-the-climate-crisis/.

29. Michael Crowley, "Burns Calls for a Mix of Competition and Cooperation with China," *New York Times,* October 20, 2021, https://www.nytimes.com/2021/10/20/us/politics/burns-china.html.

30. White House, Office of the Press Secretary, "U.S.-China Joint Statement," November 17, 2009, https://obamawhitehouse.archives.gov/realitycheck/the-press-office/us-china-joint-statement.

31. Yanzhong Huang, "Presidential Inbox: Integrating Global Health into the Pivot Strategy," Blog, Council on Foreign Relations, January 25, 2013, https://www.cfr.org/blog/presidential-inbox-integrating-global-health-pivot-strategy.

32. Michael Schuman and David O. Shullman, "Cooperation with China: Challenges and Opportunities," Atlantic Council, July 28, 2022, https://www.atlanticcouncil.org/in-depth-research-reports/report/cooperation-with-china-challenges-and-opportunities/.

33. White House, Office of the Press Secretary, "Fact Sheet: Advancing the Rebalance to Asia and the Pacific," November 16, 2015, https://obamawhitehouse.archives.gov/the-press-office/2015/11/16/fact-sheet-advancing-rebalance-asia-and-pacific.

34. Bonnie S. Glaser, "US-China Competition," Lowy Institute, 2020, https://interactives.lowyinstitute.org/features/covid19/issues/us-china/.

35. Dan Mangan, "Trump Blames China for Coronavirus Pandemic: 'The World Is Paying a Very Big Price for What They Did,'" *CNBC,* March 19, 2020, https://www.cnbc.com/2020/03/19/coronavirus-outbreak-trump-blames-china-for-virus-again.html.

36. Thomas J. Christensen, "A Modern Tragedy? COVID-19 and US-China Relations," *Brookings Institution,* May 2020, https://www.brookings.edu/research/a-modern-tragedy-covid-19-and-us-china-relations/.

37. White House, "Fact Sheet: Quad Summit," March 12, 2021, https://www.whitehouse.gov/briefing-room/statements-releases/2021/03/12/fact-sheet-quad-summit/.

38. China Power Team, "Is China's Covid-19 Diplomacy Succeeding," Center for Strategic and International Studies, updated March 17, 2022, https://chinapower.csis.org/china-covid-medical-vaccine-diplomacy/.

39. Seow Ting Lee, "Vaccine Diplomacy: Nation Branding and China's COVID-19 Soft Power Play," *Place Branding and Public Diplomacy* 19, no. 1 (2023): 64–78, https://www.ncbi.nlm.nih.gov/pmc/articles/PMC8259554/.

40. Andrew Jacobs, Michael D. Shear, and Edward Wong, "U.S.-China Feud over Coronavirus Erupts at World Health Assembly," *New York Times,* May 18, 2020, https://www.nytimes.com/2020/05/18/health/coronavirus-who-china-trump.html.

41. Donald Trump, @realDonaldTrump, "This is the letter sent to Dr. Tedros of the World Health Organization. It is self-explanatory!," Twitter, May 18, 2020, 10:55 pm, https://twitter.com/realDonaldTrump/status/1262577580718395393.

42. Katie Rogers and Apoorva Mandavilli, "Trump Administration Signals Formal Withdrawal from W.H.O.," *New York Times*, July 7, 2020, https://www.nytimes.com/2020/07/07/us/politics/coronavirus-trump-who.html.

43. Karen Weintraub, "Biden Administration Renewed Support for World Health Organization Is 'Good News for America and the World,' Scientists Say," *USA Today*, January 22, 2021, https://www.usatoday.com/story/news/health/2021/01/22/scientists-applaud-biden-decision-rejoin-world-health-organization/4243377001/.

44. Colin Kahl and Thomas Wright, *Aftershocks: Pandemic Politics and the End of the Old International Order* (New York: St. Martin's, 2021).

45. US Congress, House of Representatives, Subcommittee on Asia and the Pacific, *US Security Policy in Asia and the Pacific: Restructuring America's Forward Deployment*, 108th Cong., 1st sess., 2003.

46. US Embassy and Consulates in Indonesia, "Fact Sheet: Unprecedented U.S.-ASEAN Relations," February 12, 2016, https://id.usembassy.gov/our-relationship/policy-history/embassy-fact-sheets/fact-sheet-unprecedented-u-s-asean-relations/.

47. Simone Orendain, "US Scales Back Counter-terrorism Help in S. Philippines," *Voice of America*, July 10, 2014, https://www.voanews.com/a/us-troops-scale-back-counter-terrorism-help-in-southern-philippines/1954615.html.

48. Maria Ressa, Atika Shubert, and Amy Chew, "Asia's Most Wanted in U.S. Hands," *CNN*, August 15, 2003, http://www.cnn.com/2003/WORLD/asiapcf/southeast/08/15/hambali.capture/; Carol Rosenberg and Julian E. Barnes, "Gina Haspel Observed Waterboarding at C.I.A. Black Site, Psychologist Testifies," *New York Times*, June 3, 2022, https://www.nytimes.com/2022/06/03/us/politics/cia-gina-haspel-black-site.html.

49. US Library of Congress, Congressional Research Service, *Terrorism in Southeast Asia*, R44501, 2017, https://www.everycrsreport.com/files/20170505_R44501_355e3437898708ad42305150ba1a54c2ebe32c54.pdf.

50. Senia Febrica, "An Assessment of the United States Counter-Terrorism Cooperation in Southeast Asia," American Studies Center, Universitas Indonesia, October 12, 2020, https://mesbar.org/an-assessment-of-the-united-states-counter-terrorism-cooperation-in-southeast-asia/.

51. White House, *National Strategy for Counterterrorism*, June 2011, https://obamawhitehouse.archives.gov/sites/default/files/counterterrorism_strategy.pdf.

52. US Department of State, *Members—The Global Coalition to Defeat ISIS*, https://www.state.gov/the-global-coalition-to-defeat-isis-partners/#eap.

53. Mary Alice Salinas, "Obama's Message on Terror: 'We Do Not Succumb to Fear,'" *Voice of America*, November 22, 2015, https://www.voanews.com/a/obama-message-on-terror/3068761.html.

54. Barack Obama, "Remarks by the President on the Administration's Approach to Counterterrorism" (remarks, MacDill Air Force Base, Tampa, FL), White House, Office of the Press Secretary, December 6, 2016, https://obamawhitehouse.archives.gov/the-press-office/2016/12/06/remarks-president-administrations-approach-counterterrorism.

55. Inspectors General of the Department of Defense, Department of State, and U.S. Agency for International Development, *Operation Pacific Eagle-Philippines*, April 1, 2020–June 30, 2020, https://media.defense.gov/2020/Aug/11/2002474708/-1/-1/1/LEAD%20INSPECTOR%20GENERAL%20FOR%20OPERATION%20PACIFIC%20EAGLE-PHILIPPINES%20APRIL%201,%202020%20-%20JUNE%2030,%202020.PDF; Jim Garamone, "Austin Visit to Philippine Base Highlights Benefits of U.S-Philippine Alliance, *US Department of Defense DOD News*, February 1, 2023, https://www.defense.gov/News/News-Stories/Article/Article/3284587/austin-visit-to-philippine-base-highlights-benefits-of-us-philippine-alliance/.

56. US Department of Defense, *Summary of the 2018 National Defense Strategy of the United States of America*, 2018, https://dod.defense.gov/Portals/1/Documents/pubs/2018-National-Defense-Strategy-Summary.pdf, 1.

57. US Embassy and Consulates in Australia, US Embassy in Canberra, "Joint Statement on Australia-U.S. Ministerial Consultations (AUSMIN) 2021," September 17, 2021, https://au.usembassy.gov/joint-statement-on-australia-u-s-ministerial-consultations-ausmin-2021/.

58. White House, *Indo-Pacific Strategy of the United States*, February 2022, https://www.whitehouse.gov/wp-content/uploads/2022/02/U.S.-Indo-Pacific-Strategy.pdf; Admiral John C. Aquilino, "Hearing to Receive Testimony on the Posture of United States Indo-Pacific Command and the United States Forces Korea," transcript of testimony as given before the Senate Armed Services Committee, United States Senate, in Washington, DC, March 10, 2022, https://www.armed-services.senate.gov/imo/media/doc/INDOPACOM%20Statement%20(ADM%20Aquilino)%20_SASC2.PDF.

59. US Department of State, Global Engagement Center, "Mission & Vision," https://www.state.gov/bureaus-offices/under-secretary-for-public-diplomacy-and-public-affairs/global-engagement-center/.

60. Jeff Seldin, "US General: Islamic State Afghan Affiliate Closer to Attacking Western Targets," *Voice of America*, March 16, 2023, https://www.voanews.com/a/us-general-islamic-state-afghan-affiliate-closer-to-attacking-western-targets/7008633.html.

61. Ibid.

62. Joseph Biden, "Remarks by President Biden on the End of the War in Afghanistan" (remarks, State Dining Room, Washington, DC, August 31, 2021), White House, https://www.whitehouse.gov/briefing-room/speeches-remarks/2021/08/31/remarks-by-president-biden-on-the-end-of-the-war-in-afghanistan/.

63. US Library of Congress, Congressional Research Service, *Human Rights in China and U.S. Policy: Issues for the 117th Congress*, by Thomas Lum and Michael A. Weber, R46750, 2021, https://crsreports.congress.gov/product/pdf/R/R46750.

64. Clinton, "America's Pacific Century."

65. Obama, "Remarks by President Obama to the Australian Parliament."

66. Michael Green, *By More than Providence* (New York: Columbia University Press, 2017).

67. Clinton, "America's Pacific Century."

68. US Library of Congress, Congressional Research Service, *U.S.-Vietnam Relations,* by Mark E. Manyin and Liana Wong, IF10209 (2022), 1, https://crsreports.congress.gov/product/pdf/IF/IF10209/14.

69. US Congress, Majority Staff, *Re-Balancing the Rebalance: Resourcing U.S. Diplomatic Strategy in the Asia-Pacific Region,* report prepared for the use of the Committee on Foreign Relations United States Senate, 113th Cong., 2d sess., April 17, 2014, Committee Print 113–24, 21, https://www.foreign.senate.gov/imo/media/doc/872 692.pdf.

70. Derek Mitchell, "American Leadership in the Asia Pacific, Part 3: Promoting Democracy, Human Rights, and the Rule of Law," transcript of testimony as prepared to be given before the Senate Foreign Relations Subcommittee on East Asia, the Pacific, and International Cybersecurity Policy, Washington, DC, July 12, 2017, https://www.foreign.senate.gov/imo/media/doc/071217_Mitchell_Testimony.pdf.

71. Clinton, "America's Pacific Century."

72. Joshua Kurlantzick, "Hillary Clinton to Myanmar," Blog, Council on Foreign Relations, November 18, 2011, https://www.cfr.org/blog/hillary-clinton-myanmar.

73. Jason Burke, "Hillary Clinton Begins Burma Visit," *Guardian,* November 30, 2011, https://www.theguardian.com/world/2011/nov/30/hillary-clinton-burma-visit-ref orm-hopes.

74. Joshua Kurlantzick, "Obama's Visit to Myanmar: A Mixed Result," Blog, Council on Foreign Relations, November 18, 2014, https://www.cfr.org/blog/obamas-visit-myan mar-mixed-result.

75. Grace Aranow, "President Obama and Aung San Suu Kyi Celebrate Progress in Burma," *White House Blog,* September 15, 2016, https://obamawhitehouse.archives. gov/blog/2016/09/15/president-obama-and-daw-aung-san-suu-kyi-celebrate-burm ese-progress.

76. Marlise Simons and Hannah Beech, "Aung San Suu Kyi Defends Myanmar against Rohingya Genocide Accusations," *New York Times,* December 11, 2019, https://www. nytimes.com/2019/12/11/world/asia/aung-san-suu-kyi-rohingya-myanmar-genoc ide-hague.html.

77. Richard C. Paddock, "Myanmar's Coup and Its Aftermath, Explained," *New York Times,* December 9, 2022, https://www.nytimes.com/article/myanmar-news-prote sts-coup.html.

78. Daphne Psaledakis and Simon Lewis, "U.S. and Allies Mark Anniversary of Myanmar Coup with More Sanctions," *Reuters,* January 31, 2023, https://www.reuters.com/ world/asia-pacific/us-canada-australia-impose-new-sanctions-myanmar-2023-01-31/.

79. Michael Green and Daniel Twining, "Democracy and American Grand Strategy in Asia: The Realist Principles behind an Enduring Idealism," *Contemporary Southeast Asia* 30, no. 1 (2008): 1–28, http://www.jstor.org/stable/41220489.

80. Sophie Tatum, "Trump Defends Putin: 'You Think Our Country's So Innocent?,'" *CNN,* February 6, 2017, https://www.cnn.com/2017/02/04/politics/donald-trump-vladimir-putin/index.html.

81. Abby Phillip and David Nakamura, "Autocrats Hear a Clear Message during Trump Trip: U.S. Will Not 'Lecture' on Human Rights," *Washington Post*, May 22, 2017, https://www.washingtonpost.com/politics/autocrats-hear-a-clear-message-during-trump-trip-us-will-not-lecture-on-human-rights/2017/05/22/1c7328b4-3f0c-11e7-8c25-44d09ff5a4a8_story.html.

82. David Nakamura and Emily Rauhala, "From Burma to the Philippines, Trump Largely Ignores Human Rights on Asia Trip," *Washington Post*, November 13, 2017, https://www.washingtonpost.com/politics/from-burma-to-the-philippines-trump-largely-ignores-human-rights-on-asia-trip/2017/11/13/27ba576a-c896-11e7-8321-481fd63f174d_story.html.

83. H. R. McMaster, *Battlegrounds: The Fight to Defend the Free World* (New York: Harper, 2020).

84. Aaron Blake, "Bolton Says Trump Didn't Just Ignore Human Rights but Encouraged China's Concentration Camps," *Washington Post*, June 17, 2020, https://www.washingtonpost.com/politics/2020/06/17/bolton-says-trump-didnt-just-ignore-human-rights-encouraged-chinas-concentration-camps/.

85. Richard Fontaine, "The Enduring Relevance of Reagan's Westminster Speech" (speech, Ronald Reagan Institute, November 9, 2018), Ronald Reagan Presidential Foundation & Institute, https://www.reaganfoundation.org/media/355164/fontaine_westminster.pdf; White House, National Security Strategy of the United States of America, December 2017, https://trumpwhitehouse.archives.gov/wp-content/uploads/2017/12/NSS-Final-12-18-2017-0905.pdf.

86. Carlos Ballesteros, "Trump State Department Accused of Abandoning Global Democracy in New Budget," *Newsweek*, March 5, 2018, https://www.newsweek.com/state-department-democracy-promotion-funding-rex-tillerson-830858.

87. Michael R. Pompeo, "A Foreign Policy from the Founding" (speech, Claremont Institute 40th Anniversary Gala, Beverly Wilshire Hotel, Beverly Hills, CA, May 11, 2019), US Department of State, https://2017-2021.state.gov/a-foreign-policy-from-the-founding/index.html.

88. McMaster, *Battlegrounds*.

89. Ibid.

90. Mike Pence, "Remarks by Vice President Pence on the Administration's Policy towards China" (remarks, Hudson Institute, Washington, DC, October 4, 2018), White House, https://trumpwhitehouse.archives.gov/briefings-statements/remarks-vice-president-pence-administrations-policy-toward-china/.

91. Pompeo, "A Foreign Policy from the Founding,"

92. David Brunnstrom and Lesley Wroughton, "Pompeo Calls China's Treatment of Uighurs 'Stain of the Century,'" *Reuters*, July 18, 2019, https://www.reuters.com/article/us-usa-religion-china/pompeo-calls-chinas-treatment-of-uighurs-stain-of-the-century-idUSKCN1UD20P.

93. Pranshu Verma and Edward Wong, "U.S. Imposes Sanctions on Chinese Officials over Mass Detention of Muslims," *New York Times*, July 9, 2020, https://www.nytimes.com/2020/07/09/world/asia/trump-china-sanctions-uighurs.html.

94. White House, *The President's Executive Order on Hong Kong Normalization*, July 14, 2020, https://trumpwhitehouse.archives.gov/presidential-actions/preside nts-executive-order-hong-kong-normalization/; US Department of the Treasury, "Treasury Sanctions Individuals for Undermining Hong Kong's Autonomy," August 7, 2020, https://home.treasury.gov/news/press-releases/sm1088.

95. US Congress, Democratic Staff, *The New Big Brother: China and Digital Authoritarianism*, a minority staff report prepared for the use of the Committee on Foreign Relations, United States Senate, 116th Cong., 2nd sess., July 21, 2020, Committee Print, 115–147, https://www.govinfo.gov/content/pkg/CPRT-116SP RT42356/pdf/CPRT-116SPRT42356.pdf.

96. Austin Ramzy, "China's Oppression of Muslims in Xinjiang, Explained," *New York Times*, July 27, 2021, https://www.nytimes.com/2021/01/20/world/asia/china-genocide-uighurs-explained.html.

97. Fontaine, "The Enduring Relevance of Reagan's Westminster Speech."

98. Mitt Romney, "Mitt Romney: The President Shapes the Public Character of the Nation. Trump's Character Falls Short," *Washington Post*, January 1, 2019, https:// www.washingtonpost.com/opinions/mitt-romney-the-president-shapes-the-pub lic-character-of-the-nation-trumps-character-falls-short/2019/01/01/37a3c8c2-0d1a-11e9-8938-5898adc28fa2_story.html; Bernie Sanders, "A New Authoritarian Axis Demands an International Progressive Front," *Guardian*, September 13, 2018, https://www.theguardian.com/commentisfree/ng-interactive/2018/sep/13/bernie-sanders-international-progressive-front.

99. Kurt M. Campbell and Jake Sullivan, "Competition without Catastrophe: How America Can Both Challenge and Coexist with China," *Foreign Affairs* 98, no. 5 (September–October 2019): 96–110, https://www.foreignaffairs.com/articles/ china/competition-with-china-without-catastrophe.

100. Nicole Gaouette, "Biden Says US Faces Battle to 'Prove Democracy Works,'" March 26, 2021, *CNN*, https://www.cnn.com/2021/03/25/politics/biden-autocracies-ver sus-democracies/index.html.

101. Jacqueline Feldscher, "'Battle between Democracy and Autocracy' Leads Biden's First State of the Union," *Defense One*, March 1, 2022, https://www.defenseone. com/policy/2022/03/battle-between-democracy-and-autocracy-leads-bidens-first-state-union/362643/.

102. Antony J. Blinken, "Reaffirming and Reimagining America's Alliances—Speech by Secretary Blinken at NATO Headquarters" (speech, NATO headquarters Agora, Brussels, Belgium, March 24, 2021), US Department of State, https://ru.usemba ssy.gov/reaffirming-and-reimagining-americas-alliances-speech-by-secretary-blin ken-at-nato-headquarters/.

103. US Department of State, Antony Blinken, "Putting Human Rights at the Center of U.S. Foreign Policy," February 24, 2021, https://www.state.gov/putting-human-rig hts-at-the-center-of-u-s-foreign-policy/; US Department of State, Antony Blinken, "Election of the United States to the UN Human Rights Council (HRC)," October 14, 2021, https://www.state.gov/election-of-the-united-states-to-the-un-human-rights-council-hrc/.

104. Rachel Oswald, "Jan. 6 Riot Weakened Congress' Soft Power Abroad, Experts Say," *Roll Call*, February 9, 2021, https://rollcall.com/2021/02/09/jan-6-riot-weakened-congress-soft-power-abroad-experts-say/.

105. Nandita Bose, Michael Martina, and Heather Timmons, "Xi to Biden: Knock off the Democracy vs. Autocracy Talk," *Reuters*, November 14, 2022, https://www.reuters.com/world/asia-pacific/xi-biden-knock-off-democracy-vs-autocracy-talk-2022-11-14/.

106. Ashley Townshend and Susannah Patton, "Australia Should Steer the US off a Values-Based Indo-Pacific Strategy," *Interpreter*, June 11, 2021, https://www.lowyinstitute.org/the-interpreter/australia-should-steer-us-values-based-indo-pacific-strategy.

107. Kelly A. Grieco, "Reality Check #11: America's Indo-Pacific Strategy Requires Tough Choices," Atlantic Council, April 6, 2022, https://www.atlanticcouncil.org/content-series/reality-check/reality-check-11-americas-indo-pacific-strategy-requires-tough-choices/.

108. Yaroslav Trofimov, "Can the U.S. Lead a Human-Rights Alliance against China?," *Wall Street Journal*, May 21, 2021, https://www.wsj.com/articles/can-the-u-s-lead-a-human-rights-alliance-against-china-11621610176.

109. Michael Green, "An Alliance of Democracies Is Essential," *Interpreter*, June 16, 2021, https://www.lowyinstitute.org/the-interpreter/alliance-democracies-essential.

110. White House, *National Security Strategy*, October 2022, https://www.whitehouse.gov/wp-content/uploads/2022/10/Biden-Harris-Administrations-National-Security-Strategy-10.2022.pdf.

111. Karen Lema, John Geddie, and Mark Heinrich, "Philippines' Duterte Says He Takes Full Responsibility for Drugs War," *Reuters*, October 21, 2021, https://www.reuters.com/world/asia-pacific/philippines-duterte-says-he-takes-full-responsibility-drugs-war-2021-10-21/.

112. Franco Luna, "'I don't care about human rights,' Duterte Says, Urging Cops to 'Shoot First,'" *Philstar Global*, December 3, 2020, https://www.philstar.com/headlines/2020/12/03/2061268/i-dont-care-about-human-rights-duterte-says-urging-cops-shoot-first; Jim Garamone, "Philippine President Restores Visiting Forces Agreement with U.S.," *US Department of Defense News*, July 30, 2021, https://www.defense.gov/News/News-Stories/Article/Article/2713638/philippine-president-restores-visiting-forces-agreement-with-us/#.

113. US Department of State, Office of the Spokesperson, "United States-Thailand Communiqué on Strategic Alliance and Partnership," July 10, 2022, https://www.state.gov/united-states-thailand-communique-on-strategic-alliance-and-partnership/; Murray Hiebert, "The United States Makes Up Critical Terrain in Thailand," Center for Strategic and International Studies, September 2, 2022, https://www.csis.org/analysis/united-states-makes-critical-terrain-thailand.

114. Freedom House, "Freedom in the World: Thailand," 2022, https://freedomhouse.org/country/thailand/freedom-world/2022; US Department of State, *2022 Country Reports on Human Rights Practices: Thailand*, 2022, https://www.state.gov/reports/2022-country-reports-on-human-rights-practices/thailand/.

115. Debasish Roy Chowdhury, "How Long Will Joe Biden Pretend Narendra Modi's India Is a Democratic Ally?," *Time*, February 15, 2021, https://time.com/5939510/joe-biden-india-democracy/.

116. John Sifton, "How Does Inviting Autocrats to the White House Make Asia More Free?," *Diplomat*, April 22, 2022, https://thediplomat.com/2022/04/how-does-inviting-autocrats-to-the-white-house-make-asia-more-free/.

117. Nahal Toosi, "China and U.S. Open Alaska Meeting with Undiplomatic War of Words," *Politico*, March 18, 2021, https://www.politico.com/news/2021/03/18/china-us-alaska-meeting-undiplomatic-477118.

118. Trofimov, "Can the U.S. Lead a Human-Rights Alliance against China?"

119. Ibid.

120. Joseph Biden, "Remarks by President Biden on America's Place in the World" (remarks, US Department of State Headquarters, Harry S. Truman Building, Washington, DC), February 4, 2021, https://www.whitehouse.gov/briefing-room/speeches-remarks/2021/02/04/remarks-by-president-biden-on-americas-place-in-the-world/.

121. *Indo-Pacific Strategy of the United States*, February 2022.

122. Associated Press, "Biden Administration Imposes Sanctions against China over Abuse of Uyghurs," *NBC*, December 16, 2021, https://www.nbcnews.com/politics/national-security/biden-administration-imposes-sanctions-against-china-over-abuse-uyghurs-n1286100; Humeyra Pamuk and Simon Lewis, "Biden Administration Rules Myanmar Army Committed Genocide against Rohingya," *Reuters*, March 20, 2022, https://www.reuters.com/world/asia-pacific/exclusive-biden-administration-rules-myanmar-army-committed-genocide-against-2022-03-20/.

123. Susannah Patton, *A Seat at the Table: The Role of Regional Multilateral Institutions in US Indo-Pacific Strategy*, (Sydney: United States Studies Centre, December 3, 2021), 2, https://apo.org.au/node/315410.

124. US Department of State, Bureau of Public Affairs, Office of the Spokesman, "United States Accedes to the Treaty of Amity and Cooperation in Southeast Asia," https://2009-2017.state.gov/r/pa/prs/ps/2009/july/126294.htm; interview with Ann Marie Murphey, The United States Joins East Asia Summit: Implications for Regional Cooperation, National Bureau of Asian Research, November 17, 2011, https://www.nbr.org/publication/u-s-joins-east-asia-summit-implications-for-regional-cooperation/.

125. US Congress, Majority Staff, *Re-Balancing the Rebalance: Resourcing U.S. Diplomatic Strategy in the Asia-Pacific Region*; Clinton, "America's Pacific Century."

126. Hillary Rodham Clinton, "Remarks at the Pacific Islands Forum Post-Forum Dialogue" (remarks, Cook Islands National Auditorium, Rarotonga, Cook Islands, August 31, 2012), US Department of State, https://2009-2017.state.gov/secretary/2009 2013clinton/rm/2012/08/197266.htm; White House, Office of the Press Secretary, "Fact Sheet: East Asia Summit," https://obamawhitehouse.archives.gov/the-press-office/2011/11/19/fact-sheet-east-asia-summit#; Clinton, "American's Pacific Century."

127. Josh Rogin, "Trump's Latest Summit No-Shows Are His Final Insult to America's Asian Allies," *Washington Post*, November 17, 2020, https://www.washingtonpost.

com/opinions/2020/11/17/trump-asean-east-asia-summit-no-shows-insult-asian-allies/.

128. White House, "Readout of President Biden's Participation in the East Asia Summit," press release, October 27, 2021, https://www.whitehouse.gov/briefing-room/sta tements-releases/2021/10/27/readout-of-president-bidens-participation-in-the-east-asia-summit/.

129. *Indo-Pacific Strategy of the United States*, February 2022; White House, "ASEAN-U.S. Special Summit 2022, Joint Vision Statement," May 13, 2022, https://www.whi tehouse.gov/briefing-room/statements-releases/2022/05/13/asean-u-s-special-summit-2022-joint-vision-statement/.

130. White House, "Fact Sheet: Roadmap for a 21st-Century U.S.-Pacific Island Partnership," September 29, 2022, https://www.whitehouse.gov/briefing-room/sta tements-releases/2022/09/29/fact-sheet-roadmap-for-a-21st-century-u-s-pacific-island-partnership/.

131. White House, "Fact Sheet: Vice President Harris Announces Commitments to Strengthen U.S. Partnership with the Pacific Islands," July 12, 2022, https://www.whi tehouse.gov/briefing-room/statements-releases/2022/07/12/fact-sheet-vice-presid ent-harris-announces-commitments-to-strengthen-u-s-partnership-with-the-paci fic-islands/. Sebastian Strangio, "The US Fills ASEAN Ambassadorial Posting after 5-Year Vacancy," *Diplomat*, September 21, 2022, https://thediplomat.com/2022/09/ the-us-fills-asean-ambassadorial-posting-after-5-year-vacancy/.

132. White House, Office of the Press Secretary, "U.S.-China Joint Statement," November 17, 2009, https://obamawhitehouse.archives.gov/realitycheck/the-press-office/us-china-joint-statement.

133. White House, Office of the Press Secretary, "Fact Sheet: Advancing the Rebalance to Asia and the Pacific," November 16, 2015, https://obamawhitehouse.archi ves.gov/the-press-office/2015/11/16/fact-sheet-advancing-rebalance-asia-and-pacific.

134. Jessica Chen Weiss, "A World Safe for Autocracy?: China's Rise and the Future of Global Politics," *Foreign Affairs* 98, no. 4 (July–August 2019): 92–102, https://www.foreignaffairs.com/articles/china/2019-06-11/world-safe-autocracy.

135. "APEC Summit: Biden-Xi Talks Lead to Little but a Promise to Keep Talking," *New York Times*, November 16, 2023, https://nytimes.com/live/2023/11/15/world/ biden-xi-apec-summit.

136. William Potter and Sarah Bidgood, "The Good Old Days of the Cold War: U.S.-Soviet Cooperation on Nonproliferation," *War on the Rocks*, August 7, 2018, https:// warontherocks.com/2018/08/the-good-old-days-of-the-cold-war-u-s-soviet-cooperation-on-nonproliferation/; Roald Sagdeev and Susan Eisenhower, "United States-Soviet Space Cooperation during the Cold War," NASA, https://www.nasa.gov/50th/50th_magazine/coldWarCoOp.html; Naval History and Heritage Command, "Conflict and Cooperation: The U.S. and Soviet Navies in the Cold War," Colloquium on Contemporary History, No. 10, June 12, 1996, https://www.history.navy.mil/research/library/online-reading-room/title-list-alphabetically/c/conflict-coop-us-soviet-navies-cold-war.html.

# Chapter 14

1. "Population Trends," United Nations Population Fund, accessed August 3, 2023, https://asiapacific.unfpa.org/en/populationtrends; "The Top 10 Largest Economies in the World in 2023," *Forbes India*, July 25, 2023, https://www.forbesindia.com/arti cle/explainers/top-10-largest-economies-in-the-world/86159/1; World Bank, "GDP (Current US$)—World, South Asia, East Asia & Pacific, India," World Bank, https://data.worldbank.org/indicator/NY.GDP.MKTP.CD?locations=1W-8S-Z4-IN; Thomas Helbling, Shanaka J. Peiris, and Krishna Srinivasan, "Asia Poised to Drive Global Economic Growth, Boosted by China's Reopening," *IMF Blog* (blog), International Monetary Fund, May 1, 2023, https://www.imf.org/en/Blogs/Articles/2023/05/01/asia-poised-to-drive-global-economic-growth-boosted-by-chinas-reopening; United Nations, Economic and Social Commission for Asia and the Pacific, *Trade in Goods Outlook in Asia and the Pacific 2021/2022* (Bangkok: United Nations, 2021), https://hdl.handle.net/20.500.12870/4050; International Institute for Strategic Studies, "Chapter Three: North America," *The Military Balance* 123 (2023): 34–99, https://doi-org.proxy1.library.jhu.edu/10.4324/9781003400226; "Which Countries Are the World's Biggest Carbon Polluters?," *Climate Trade*, May 17, 2012, https://climatetrade.com/which-countries-are-the-worlds-biggest-carbon-polluters/.
2. Stephen Hadley, "Intel Community 'Clearly 'Misread' China's Xi Jinping, Fmr. National Security Adviser Says," interview by Chuck Todd, *Meet the Press*, NBC, February 22, 2023, video, 4:09, https://www.nbcnews.com/meet-the-press/video/intel-commun ity-clearly-misread-china-s-xi-jinping-fmr-national-security-adviser-says-16383 9045666.
3. Kurt M. Campbell and Ely Ratner, "The China Reckoning: How Beijing Defied American Expectations," *Foreign Affairs* 97, no. 2 (March–April 2018): 60–70, https://www.foreignaffairs.com/articles/china/2018-02-13/china-reckoning.
4. Demetri Sevastopulo, "Trump labels China a strategic 'competitor,'" *Financial Times*, December 18, 2017, https://www.ft.com/content/215cf8fa-e3cb-11e7-8b99-0191e 45377ec.
5. Mark Landler and Helene Cooper, "Obama Will Speed Pullout from War in Afghanistan," *New York Times*, June 22, 2011, https://www.nytimes.com/2011/06/23/world/asia/23prexy.html.
6. For examples of this phenomenon, see (among other sources) Eric Lipton, "Faced with Evolving Threats, U.S. Navy Struggles to Change," *New York Times*, September 4, 2023, https://www.nytimes.com/2023/09/04/us/politics/us-navy-ships.html.
7. Vance Serchuk, "Bipartisan Support for Taking On China Goes Only so Far," *Washington Post*, June 29, 2021, https://www.washingtonpost.com/opinions/2021/06/29/bipartisan-support-taking-china-goes-only-so-far/.
8. Jake Sullivan, "The Administration's Approach to the People's Republic of China" (speech, George Washington University, Washington, DC, May 26, 2022), US Department of State, https://www.state.gov/the-administrations-approach-to-the-peoples-republic-of-china/.

9. This and subsequent paragraphs draw on Richard Fontaine, "What the New China Focus Gets Wrong: Competition Requires Balance," *Foreign Affairs*, November 2, 2021, https://www.foreignaffairs.com/articles/china/2021-11-02/ what-new-china-focus-gets-wrong.

10. This draws on Richard Fontaine, "Taking on China and Russia: To Compete, the United States Will Have to Pick Its Battles," *Foreign Affairs*, November 18, 2022, https://www.foreignaffairs.com/united-states/taking-china-and-russia.

11. Marcel Scwantes, "Steve Job's Advice on the Only 4 Times You Should Say No Is Brilliant," *Inc.*, January 31, 2018, https://www.inc.com/marcel-schwantes/first-90-days-steve-jobs-advice-on-the-only-4-times-you-should-say-no.html.

12. This and subsequent paragraphs draw on Richard Fontaine, "In an Era of Divided Government, China Can Unite," *National Interest*, December 14, 2018, https://natio nalinterest.org/feature/era-divided-government-china-can-unite-38707.

13. US Department of Defense, "Department of Defense Releases the President's Fiscal Year 2024 Defense Budget," press release, March 13, 2023, https://www.defense.gov/ News/Releases/Release/Article/3326875/department-of-defense-releases-the-pre sidents-fiscal-year-2024-defense-budget/.

14. US Department of Defense, Defense Media Activity, *Defense Spending as a % of Gross Domestic Product (GDP)*, image, .29 MB, https://www.defense.gov/Multimedia/Pho tos/igphoto/2002099941/.

15. Brad Dress and Ellen Mitchell, "Biden's Defense Budget Concentrates on Rising Threats from China, Russia," *Hill*, March 9, 2023, https://thehill.com/policy/defe nse/3892532-bidens-defense-budget-concentrates-on-rising-threats-from-china-russia/.

16. Thibault Larger and Giorgio Leali, "Brussels Forges New Weapons to Shield EU Market from China," *Politico*, June 16, 2021, https://www.politico.com/news/2020/ 06/16/brussels-forges-new-weapons-to-shield-eu-market-from-china-325145.

# Index